A Volume in:
Language, Literacy,
and Learning

Reconceptualizing Literacy in the
New Age of Multiculturalism
and Pluralism

RECONCEPTUALIZING LITERACY IN THE NEW AGE OF MULTICULTURALISM AND PLURALISM

Edited by

Patricia Ruggiano Schmidt
Le Moyne College

Peter B. Mosenthal
Syracuse University

INFORMATION AGE
PUBLISHING

80 Mason Street
Greenwich, Connecticut 06830

CONTENTS

BIOGRAPHICAL INFORMATION

Kathryn H. Au is a professor in the College of Education at the University of Hawai'i at Mānoa. Au's research in the area of the school literacy development of students of diverse cultural and linguistic backgrounds has earned her national recognition. She received the first National Scholar Award presented by the National Association for Asian and Pacific American Education, the Distinguished Scholar Award presented by the American Educational Research Association Standing Committee on the Role and Status of Minorities, and the Oscar S. Causey Award for outstanding contributions to reading research presented by the National Reading Conference. She is a fellow of the National Conference on Research in Language and Literacy and has been elected to the Reading Hall of Fame. She serves on the board of directors of the International Reading Association and has been president of the National Reading Conference.

L. Pauahi Bogac earned a Bachelor of Arts degree in Hawaiian Studies from the University of Hawai'i at Mānoa and successfully completed the College of Education Preservice Teacher Education Program as a member of the Ka Lama O Ke Kaiāulu Cohort. During her studies, Pauahi worked in both Hawaiian language immersion and English language immersion classrooms. On completion of her Master's degree in education, Pauahi plans to study for her doctoral degree. Her research interests include the politics of Native Hawaiian self-determination and the development of curriculum for Hawaiian language immersion schools. Pauahi is a Hawaiian language immersion teacher at Waiau Elementary School on O'ahu.

Ward Cockrum is an Associate Professor at Northern Arizona University. He is a teacher educator working with undergraduate and graduate students in reading and language arts methods courses. He has eleven years of teaching experience in Arizona pubic schools. He is currently researching the impact of distance education on nontraditional student populations.

Karen Damphousse has taught middle school language arts for ten years and contributed to this chapter while on leave from University-Liggett School and living in Luxembourg. She completed her Master's degree at Oakland University in Reading and Language Arts in December 1997. Ms Damphousse is committed to highlighting quality literature and multiple genres for writing within the context of thematic units through which the study of self and of culture emerge as a natural and inevitable part of the curriculum. She has presented her work on the Book Club program at regional and national conferences such as the National Council of Teachers of English.

Jennifer C. Danridge is a doctoral student in the Educational Psychology program at Michigan State University. Currently, she is a MSU/Spencer Research Training Grant (RTG) Fellow. She has recently published articles in *The Reading Teacher* and *The National Reading Conference Yearbook*. Her research interests center on urban education, literacy, and development of educational resiliency in culturally-diverse students.

Barbara J. Diamond is a professor at the College of Education at Eastern Michigan University where she teaches courses in reading/language arts instruction in urban settings and multicultural literacy. In addition, she is a Faculty Associate with the Comer Schools and Family Initiative, a program partnership between Eastern Michigan University and the Detroit Public Schools. She has conducted research on literacy development of African American students in urban settings, supported by the Spencer Foundation. The multicultural literacy research project was awarded the Christa McAuliffe Award for Excellence in Applied Research by the American Association for State Colleges and Universities. The project also became part of the U.S. Department of Education's National Diffusion Network. She has co-authored *Multicultural Literacy: Mirroring the Reality of the Classroom* with Margart Moore (Longman), which chronicles her research. Barbara has also published several articles and book chapters, most recently, *Literature-Based Instruction: Reshaping the Curriculum* (Raphael & Au, Editors, 1998) and *Literature for Diversity in a Democratic Society* in *Early Literacy Instruction for the Millennium* (Hammond & Raphael, Editors, 1999). Barbara has worked on state and national committees that focus on language arts and multicultural issues, including Chair of the Multicultural Issues Committee, National Reading Conference, and member of the federally funded Michigan English Language Arts Framework (MELAF) Standards Project.

Patricia A. Edwards is a Professor of Language and Literacy and a Senior Researcher at the National Center for the Improvement of Early Reading Achievement at Michigan State University. She is also the author of two nationally acclaimed family literacy programs—Parents as Partners in Reading: A Family Literacy Training Program and Talking Your Way to Literacy: A Program to Help Nonreading Parents Prepare Their Children for Reading. She is also the co-author of a recent Heinemann book titled *A Path to Follow: Learning to Listen to Parents* (Edwards, Pleasants, & Franklin, 1999). She is currently on the Board of Directors of the International Reading Association. Professor Edwards is widely published and a recognized national authority on family literacy and role of parents in the learning-to-read-and-write process.

Jill Fitzgerald is a professor of Literacy Studies at the University of North Carolina at Chapel Hill. She recently took a yearlong reassignment from her university job to be a full-time first-grade teacher. Her current primary research interests center on literacy issues for English-language learners. In 1998, her article "English-as-a-Second-Language Learners' Cognitive Reading Processes: A Review of Research in the United States" won the American Educational Research Association's Outstanding Review of Research Award. She may be contacted at the School of Education, Peabody Hall CB 3500, University of North Carolina at Chapel Hill, Chapel Hill, NC 27599-3500. E-mail: jfitzger@email.unc.edu.

Susan Florio-Ruane is a Professor of Teacher Education at Michigan State University and Senior Researcher in the Center for the Improvement of Early Reading Achievement (CIERA). Dr. Florio-Ruane has written numerous articles and chapters on the ethnographic study of classroom discourse, teacher/researcher collaboration in ethnographic research, and teachers' learning about literacy and culture. Her forthcoming book is titled, *In Good Company: Autobiography, Conversation, and Culture in Teacher Education* (Erlbaum). Dr. Florio-Ruane is a former President of the Council on Anthropology and Education and Associate Editor of the *Anthropology and Education Quarterly.*

Dr. Georgia Earnest García is Associate Professor and Associate Head of the Department of Curriculum and Instruction at the University of Illinois at Urbana-Champaign. She also holds a zero-time appointment in the Department of Educational Policy Studies and is a faculty affiliate with the Latina/Latinos Studies Program. A former Title VII Bilingual Education Fellow, she obtained he Ph.D. from the University of Illinois in 1988. Prior to obtaining her Ph.D., she taught at a variety of levels (elementary, junior high school, high school, college) and in a variety of settings (Peace Corps, U.S. public schools, migrant education, community college). She currently teaches courses in literacy, bilingual education/ESL instruction, sociolinguistics, and multicultural education. Dr. García was named a College of Education Distinguished Scholar in 1997, and awarded the Faculty Award for Excellence in Graduate Teaching, Advising, and Research by the Council of Graduate Students in Education in 1993. She was a Fellow in the Bureau of Educational Research from 1993–1996.

Claude Goldenberg is Associate Dean of the College of Education and Principal Investigator for the Center for Research on Education, Diversity and Excellence at California State University, Long Beach. His areas of interest include Spanish speaking children's literacy development, early literacy instruction, home school connections to support academic achievement, and processes of school change and improvement.

Carl A. Grant is Hoefs-Bascom Professor of Teacher Education the Department of Curriculum and Instruction at the University of Wisconsin-Madison. In 1997, he received the Distinguished Achievement Award from the School of Education at the University of Wisconsin. He has written more than 125 articles, and written or edited 20 books of monographs on multicultural education and teacher education, including *Multicultural Research: A Reflective Engagement with Race, Class, Gender and Sexual Orientation, Making Choices For Multicultural Education* with Christine E. Sleeter, and the *Dictionary of Multicultural Education* with Gloria Ladson-Billings.

A former classroom teacher and administrator, Grant has been a Fulbright in England, researching and studying multicultural education. Since 1993 he has served as president of the National Association of Multicultural Education.

Dawnene Hammerberg is in the Department of Curriculum and Instruction at the University of Wisconsin-Madison, where she has taught both undergraduate and graduate level courses in reading and language arts. She is also a reading and language arts resource teacher for the Madison Metropolitan School District, where she works with students and teachers of all ages in reading, writing, and the English language arts. She is currently a Ph.D. candidate at the University of Wisconsin-Madison in the area of literacy education, with special interests in the historical functions and designs of literacy in relation to electronic communication technologies. Previously, Dawnene was the Reading and Language Arts Coordinator for the Mount Horeb Area School District (Mount Horeb, Wisconsin), as well as a classroom teacher at the elementary level.

Kathy Hasenstab, a veteran primary grade teacher, has been a Title VII Project Director in the Los Angeles Unified School District and currently serves as Project Advisor in The Literacy Network. Her areas of interest include early literacy instruction, oral English language development and instruction, bilingual and alternative programs for English language learners, and professional development programs for teachers.

Kathy Highfield, a third-grade teacher in the Holly Area Schools, received her M.A. in Literacy Instruction from Michigan State University. She has over ten years of teaching experience, as well as serving as a tutor from grades Kindergarten to 12 in a range of subjects, including French. She has worked as an Instructional Facilitator supporting professional development efforts within Holly Area Schools. She is currently working on her doctoral degree at Oakland University, in the Department of Reading and Language Arts. She has engaged in teacher research examining students' written and oral response within her Book Club instructional program and has coauthored articles and chapters describing the potential of teacher research and the outcomes of her studies that have appeared in the Teacher Research Journal, and in an edited volume on literature-based instruction (Raphael & Au, 1998, Christopher Gordon Publishers). Ms. Highfield is co-author of Book Club: A Literature-Based Curriculum (Small Planet Publishing, Inc.)

Diane M. Hoffman is currently as Assistant Professor of anthropology and comparative education in the Department of Leadership and Foundations at the Curry School of Education, University of Virginia. She received her Ph.D. in education and anthropology from Stamford University. Her research focuses on the implications of differing cultural psychologies of self and identity on education, with primary emphasis on East Asia. She has published in the areas of minority experience and cultural adaptation, multiculturalism, identity and self, and early education in the United States, Japan, and South Korea.

Margaret C. Laughlin is an Assistant Professor of Literacy/Biliteracy in the Center for Collaborative Education and Professional Studies at California State University, Monterey Bay, where she teaches courses in Literacy/Biliteracy for the teacher preparation and Master of Arts in Education programs. Before entering higher education, she worked with immigrant and migrant populations as a bilingual teacher for over 17 years and consulted extensively in schools with linguistically and culturally diverse populations. She was awarded a Title VII Fellowship to complete her doctoral studies at the University of San Francisco, and her research on Euro American bilingual teachers is being published in an edited book, *Transformative Approaches to Multicultural Education: A Critical Approach* (Allyn & Bacon). Her work in critical pedagogy and participatory research has been presented at conferences nationally.

Yvonne K. Lefcourt is a graduate of the University of Hawai'i at Mānoa College of Education Ka Lama O Ke Kaiāulu Preservice Teacher Education Cohort. Currently, she is studying for her Master's degree in education and is looking forward to graduating in May 2000. Her future plans include earning her doctoral degree in education and working as a teacher educator and curriculum researcher. Her research interests include indigenous research and education with an emphasis on issues of equity in education;

the implementation of an effective curriculum for diverse classrooms; and the recruitment and retention of Native Hawaiians to higher education. Yvonne is a teacher at Kapunahala Elementary School on Oʻahu.

Margaret J. Maaka is an associate professor in the College of Education at the University of Hawaiʻi at Mānoa. Maaka has over twenty-seven years of teaching experience across all levels of the curriculum from kindergarten to graduate school. She taught for many years in New Zealand elementary and secondary schools and has an expert knowledge of that country's literacy curriculum. For her dedication to teaching excellence, the New Zealand Department of Education recognized Maaka early in her career as a role model for new teachers. She also holds three teaching excellence awards from the University of Hawaiʻi. Her research interests are language, learning, and teaching; issues of power and equity in education, especially relating to indigenous peoples; and the school success of students of diverse cultural and linguistic backgrounds.

David Marcelletti is a veteran upper grade teacher at Felton Elementary School in the Lennox School District, the original research site for the work reported in this chapter. He currently serves as a consultant to the Getting Results/School Change project and is a collaborating teacher-researcher at the Center for Research on Education, Diversity and Excellence at California State University, Long Beach. His areas of interest include reading and writing instruction for upper grade English language learners, school change and leadership, and instructional technology.

Herbert Martin, Jr. is an Associate Professor in the Center for the Collaborative Education and Professional Studies Center at California State University Monterey Bay. He works in the Liberal Studies Institute as the cross-cultural competence specialist and is the Chairperson for the Culture and Equity University Learning Requirement Committee. He has published articles in print and electronic media, and has also received several small funded grants. He is a nationally recognized scholar in cross-cultural Rites of Passage and recently published two articles in *Crossroads: The Quest for Contemporary Rites of Passage*. He has a chapter in press in *Integrating Service Learning and Multicultural Education* (edited by Carolyn O'Grady), which is scheduled for publication in Winter 2000.

Gwendolyn T. McMillon is a doctoral candidate in the Curriculum, Teacher Education, and Social Policy program at Michigan State University. She is a second-year recipient of the MSU/Spencer Research Training Grant Fellowship. Her research focuses upon the incongruencies of children's literacy experiences inside and outside of schools; and helping urban at-risk learners become border crossers by connecting faith communities and public schools.

Peter Mosenthal is a professor at Syracuse University in the Reading and Language Arts Center. He also is president of Performance by Design, Inc. At Syracuse University, he teaches statistics, educational tests and measurement, and writing for professional publication in education and the social sciences. As president of Performance by Design, he works with rural and urban schools (with funding from New York State's VESID program and with support from OCM BOCES) to enhance students' achievement on state standards assessments in the areas of literacy, social studies, and math. For the past 15 years, he served as a consultant to Educational Testing Service's Adult Literacy Learning and Assessment Group. He is co-editor of the *Handbook of Reading Research* (Vols. 1–3) and recently has assumed the editorship of Information Age's *Language, Literacy, and Learning* Series. For this year (i.e., 2001), he is serving as President of the National Reading Conference. His primary area of interest includes developing a K-12 literacy curriculum for rural and urban schools districts that integrates assessment, instruction and management and that significantly enhances students' literacy achievement through the use of knowledge modeling.

Gisela O'Brien, a recipient of a Title VII fellowship, is a doctoral candidate in the School of Education at the University of Southern California. An experienced elementary school teacher, she has served as a Title VII Project Advisor in the Los Angeles Unified School District for the past 9 years and currently serves as a Project Advisor for The Literacy Network. Her areas of interest are early literacy, reading comprehension, bilingual and alternative programs for English language learners, oral English language development and instruction, and professional development programs for teachers.

Jyotsna Pattnaik is an associate professor in elementary and early childhood education at Central Missouri State University, Missouri. She is a native of India and has taught in public schools and higher education in India. Her area of expertise is multicultural education, cross-cultural research, early childhood education, and teacher education.

Heather M. Pleasants is a recent graduate of the Ph.D. Program in Educational Psychology at Michigan State University and a 1998-99 Spencer Dissertation Fellow. Presently, she is an assistant professor in the Department of Educational and School Psychology at Indiana State University. She is the co-author of a book titled, *A Path to Follow: Learning to Listen to Parents* (Edwards, Pleasants, & Franklin, 1999, Heinemann). She has co-authored several book chapters as well as articles in *The Reading Teacher* and *The National Reading Conference Yearbook*. Her research interests focus on home-school connections, and the role of African American parents in charter schools.

Taffy E. Raphael is a Professor in the Reading and Language Arts Department of Oakland University, Rochester, Michigan and Senior Researcher in the Center for the Improvement of Early Reading Achievement (CIERA). Dr. Raphael has worked extensively in teacher education, and was recognized with the Outstanding Teacher Educator in Reading Award from the International Reading Association, May 1997. Dr. Raphael's research interests have focused on issues related to instruction, including strategies used in reading and writing, teacher and student talk in literacy instruction settings, and teacher inquiry about their own practice. She has authored and co-edited several books on the Book Club Program, including *The Book Club Connection: Literacy Learning and Classroom Talk* (Teachers College Press, 1997). Dr. Raphael has been an active member of several professional organizations and is the 1999-2000President of the National Reading Conference.

Jon Reyhner is Associate Professor of Education at Northern Arizona University (NAU). Before coming to NAU in 1995, he taught Native American Studies and Education classes for seven years at Montana State University-Billings and was a teacher and school administrator in reservation schools for 14 years in Arizona, New Mexico, and Montana. He co-edited *Revitalizing Indigenous Languages* (Northern Arizona University, 1999), edited *Teaching Indigenous Languages* (Northern Arizona University, 1997), *Teaching American Indian Studies* (University of Oklahoma, 1992), and co-wrote *A History of Indian Education* (Eastern Montana College, 1989). He is currently researching the history of American Indian education and how best to teach American Indian languages.

Randy F. Rush received his Ph.D. from the Ohio State University in Columbus. He is an assistant professor of Secondary Reading at Eastern Michigan University. His research interests are young adult literature for African Americans and science fiction and fantasy literature.

Tina Saldivar, a recipient of a Title VII fellowship, is a doctoral candidate in the School of Education at the University of Southern California. An experienced elementary school teacher, she has served as a Title VII Project Advisor in the Los Angeles Unified School District and currently directs The Literacy Network. Her areas of interest are bilingual and alternative programs for English language learners, Spanish speaking children's literacy development, home school connections to support academic achievement, and parent leadership and education.

William M. Saunders is a Research Associate and Study Director at the Center for Research on Education, Diversity and Excellence at California State University, Long Beach. His areas of interest are K-12 language arts curriculum, instruction and assessment; bilingual and alternative programs for English language learners; and school change.

Patricia Ruggiano Schmidt, a reading teacher for twenty-five years, earned the M.Ed. from University of Massachusetts and Ed.D. from the Reading and Language Arts Center, Syracuse University. Her dissertation entitled, *Cultural Conflict and Struggle: Literacy Learning in Kindergarten Program*, a classroom ethnography, earned recognition in 1994, from the International Reading Association and was published by Peter Lang in 1998. Additionally, Dr. Schmidt, an Associate Professor in the Education Department of Le Moyne College, Syracuse, NY, has authored numerous journal articles related to multicultural literacy. In 1996, she was honored with the Le Moyne College *Matteo Ricci Award* for service and achievement related to campus diversity. Recently, Dr. Schmidt's research, teaching, and service have revolved around her model known as the ABC's of Cultural Understanding and Communication. The model is used in teacher education programs, nationally and internationally, to develop home/school communication and culturally sensitive pedagogy. In 2000, Dr. Schmidt received the *Minerva Award* presented to an Alumna or Alumnus of Potsdam College for outstanding professional achievement.

Christine E. Sleeter is a Professor in the Center for Collaborative Education and Professional Studies at California State University, Monterey Bay, where she coordinates the Master of Arts in Education program. She consults nationally in multicultural education and multicultural teacher education. Dr. Sleeter has received several awards for her work including the National Association for Multicultural Education Research Award, and the AERA Committee on the Role and Status of Minorities in Education Distinguished Scholar Award. She has published numerous books and articles in multicultural education; her most recent books include *Multicultural Education as Social Activism* (SUNY Press), *Multicultural Education, Critical Pedagogy, and the Politics of Difference*, with Peter McLaren (SUNY Press), and *Making Choices for Multicultural Education*, with Carl A. Grant (Merrill). In addition, she edits the book series titled, *The Social Context of Education* for SUNY Press.

Henry T. Trueba, Ph.D. is a distinguished educational anthropologists whose ethnographic studies reveal the cultural conflicts and struggles that people of minority status suffer in the United States. His countless books and articles are published by the most competitive and prestigious journals and presses. Additionally, Dr. Trueba's scholarly research is world renowned and lauded for its significant findings and implications related to power issues and social justice. As a result numerous awards honor his work. In 1986, he received the American Educational Research Association Distinguished Scholarship Award for Research on Linguistic Minorities. In 1995, he was recognized for his contributions to educational anthropology with The George and Louise Spindler Award. In 1999, the University of Pennsylvania, Center for Urban Ethnography presented him with The Ethnographic Forum Award.

Arlette Ingram Willis, received her Ph.D. from the Ohio State University. She is currently an associate professor at the University of Illinois at Urbana-Champaign, in the Department of Curriculum and Instruction, the division of Language and Literacy. Her research interests include the history of reading research in the United States, socio-historical foundations of literacy, pre-service teacher education in English and Language Arts, and teaching/learning multicultural literature for grades 6–12. Among her publications are *Teaching and Using Multicultural Literature in Grades 9–12: Moving Beyond the Canon, Multiple and Intersecting Identities in Qualitative Research* (with Betty Merchant), and numerous articles that have appeared in *Reading Research Quarterly, Language Arts,* and *Harvard Educational Review.*

Hong Xu is an Assistant Professor of Language and Literacy at Texas Tech University. She teaches graduate and undergraduate literacy courses. She earned her B.A. in English and Education from East China Normal University in Shanghai, People's Republic of China, her M.Ed., in TESL and Ed.D. in Literacy from the University of Nevada, Las Vegas. She has taught English as a foreign language in the People's Republic of China, and English as a Second Language in the United States. Her research interests include multiculturalism and literacy instruction, school and home contexts for ESL, and bilingual children's early literacy development, and teacher education.

PREFACE

Literacy in a broader Freirean sense brings a distinct commitment to social justice, commitment to defend human dignity and respect for cultural and linguistic varieties associated with different nations, cultures and life styles. The quintessence of multicultural literacy is embedded in the notion of emancipation from oppression, particularly oppression for the sake of profit, cultural hegemony and the myopic advocacy of ethnocentric values. Therefore, the opposite, liberation from ethnocentrism, appreciation of cultural diversity and respect for differences implies a new knowledge and a free access to this knowledge. The ability to link historically our present (albeit oppressive it may be) to a brighter future in which a new social order may permit us to be who we are, is the roots and foundation of genuine democracy and cultural pluralism. We are not talking only about the cognitive skills required to decipher new linguistic and cultural symbols, We are talking about a profound commitment to a social order in which the powerful and rich have the same rights as the poor, and in which mainstream middle and upper classes live by the same rules as the working class, recent immigrants, and disenfranchised people. The nature of multicultural literacy is an integral part of democracy, and democracy without multicultural literacy cannot exist.

This book offers a array of essays with challenging ideas and provoking new analyses of power asymmetries, multiple epistemologies and vital concerns for the education of a different America, the America of new immigrants, people of color with other cultures, languages and values. The new American that many want to ignore and is becoming the only America. This book also forces us to reflect on the educational challenges we must face, especially in teacher education and the preparation of intellectual leaders. None of the major agenda items associated with a new era of social justice can be either comprehended or accomplished without a profound understanding of multicultural literacy, and of its relationship to ethnic, racial, cultural and linguistic diversity. While in previous decades we used frequently a rhetoric of multiculturalism (at a safe distance), today we are living multiculturalism and practicing ethnic, cultural and racial diversity in our daily lives as we seek a marriage partner, a business associate, a friend, a church. Most of all, we must live multiculturalism as we go school and see children's faces. There is no way to escape the reality of ethnic, racial and linguistic diversity as it comes entangled with many other cultural and class differences between and within each group we encounter. Suddenly, an abrupt awakening for many mainstream educators, what was peculiar of some areas in the Southwest, has become common scenario in most metropolis and large cities.

The present volume brings us face to face with issues and challenges we can no longer sweep under the rug. This outstanding volume lays down a solid general conceptual foundation that permits us to link our theoretical past with the post-modern era. It also provides a clear context for the discussion of contrasting notions of monocultural literacy and the relationship of literacy and power. The volume goes on to deal with the relationship of literacy and culture (actually to specific cultures, especially African American). At this point the discourse turns to strategies for incorporating minority perspectives into the literacy curriculum and including the home cultures of disenfranchised peoples. The last section of the book offers help on the practical issues of teacher education for student populations often ignored, and linkages between schools and homes in order to empower the disenfranchised and isolated.

In contrast with other books (for example, on critical theory, on race and ethnicity), this volume does not focus primarily on the abstract theories of multicultural literacy, or on the nature of ethnic conflict in school and hegemonic structures. It is a volume that combines important practical approaches to meet serious daily challenges facing our schools. Therefore, it is a volume that teachers will understand and use for their planning discussions and the formulation of curriculum reform efforts in the teaching of reading and writing. While this volume is theoretically strong, it is also eminently practical and relevant both for professors and practitioners in schools.

I strongly recommend this volume to all teachers and teacher educators, administrators and to social scientists (sociolinguists, anthropologists and psychologists) interested in diversity. It is a volume that experts in ethnic studies will also find refreshing and provoking. Finally, critical theorists and scholars working in post-modern issues, will find in this book important practical applications of their theories on social, economic and educational phenomena. Many readers will find in this books the other side of the theoretical coin often forgotten and lost in esoteric discourse.

—Henry T. Trueba, Ph.D.

FOREWORD

Eighteen of us walked into our first embryology class. The microscopes were set up six to a table, three tables in all. We each assumed a seat next to our own respective microscope. The professor explained that the purpose of today's lecture was on "observing through the looking glass." The professor went on, "Each of you has been given a chick embryo on your slide. Each embryo is at exactly the same stage in development. Your job is to describe what you see. Feel free to draw or use words to show what you are observing."

Each of us worked diligently for nearly one hour. At that point, the professor asked for a representative from each of the three tables to share their observations with the class. Each student presented an entirely different view of what they had seen.

The professor then asked the students who hadn't presented their descriptions to write a short essay on which of the three descriptions was correct. As one might have expected, students at each table identified the description of their table representative as being correct, the other descriptions from the other tables as wrong.

As our discussions began to turn into arguments, the professor stepped in to point out the source of confusion. What he had done was to change the magnification of each of the microscopes. Students at one table had viewed the embryo under 30× magnification. Students at the second table had viewed it under a 200× magnification. And students at table three (where I sat) had viewed it under at 500× magnification. Although we were looking at the same phenomenon (i.e., the "chick embryo"), we saw something different, depending upon which table we were sitting at and how our looking glass was set.

In subsequent classes, the professor had us change tables. In the process, we saw the world of the chick embryo under other levels of magnification. But we also did more. We learned that, in observing and defining, there are different looking glasses and, with each, different takes on reality.

While each looking glass has a calibration that yields understanding, each view yields a different impression and experience. It is by understanding the range of ways of observing and knowing that we come to understand the broader picture. It is as Ed Young (1992) so cleverly described in his book, *Seven Blind Mice*:

> 'Ah,' said [the] Mouse. 'Now I see.
> The Something is
> > as sturdy as a pillar,
> > supple as a snake,
> > wide as a cliff,
> > sharp as a speak,
> > breezy as a fan,
> > stringy as a rope,
> > but altogether the Something is... an 'elephant!'...
>
> The Mouse Moral:
> Knowing in part may make a fine tale, but wisdom comes from seeing the whole. (n.p.)

As the proverbial elephant tale would remind us, there is the saying that "believing is seeing." As humans, we like to take the easy way out: We see what we believe. What we believe, we assume is "what ought to be." Since there are no other possibilities, we then make the final assumption that our "what ought to be" (or "what should be") is, in essence, "what is." This approach to understanding represents what traditionally has been called "monism"—that is, the belief that there is but one correct looking glass for understanding the world.

For over a century, monism has been the dominant view for defining and understanding reading and literacy. Even to this day, governmental agencies still charge elite panels of researchers to cull the research in an effort to find the "best theory of reading," the "best practices of literacy instruction." Never considered are the questions: "Best for whom?" and "Best according to whose looking glass?"

The purpose of this book is to argue that education, based on a monistic view of the world, not only fails to acknowledge the world of many looking glasses, it is wrong on grounds of inhumanity. By subscribing to monism, schools privilege a few and disenfranchise many. Monism empowers one table of embryologists and their looking glass but minimizes (even disempowers) embryologists at the other tables.

This book makes the case that, instead of monism, there are many ways of understanding the world; in short, the world is replete with possible ways for seeing, experiencing, interpreting, and believing. Associated with these possible ways are different looking glasses, each with their own internally consistent calibration. To understand the world at large, we need to be able to understand this world as seen through these different looking glasses. If we don't change tables and look at the world differently, we delude ourselves into believing that the view at our table is the world view—when, in fact, it is little more than the tip of a trunk, the wisp of tail, the lobe of an ear, the curve of the tusk.

This book, at one level, joins an entire cadre of books that challenges monism by promoting the view of multiculturalism and pluralism. Among these books are Hollins and Oliver's (1999) *Finding Pathways to Success: Teaching Culturally Diverse Populations;* Banks' (1996) *Multicultural Education, Transformative Knowledge, and Action;* Derman-Sparks and the ABC Task Force (1989), *Anti-bias Curriculum: Tools for Empowering Young Children;* Dilg's (1999) *Race and Culture in the Classroom: Teaching and Learning Through Multicultural Education;* Garcia's (1999) *Student Cultural Diversity: Understanding the Meeting the Challenge;* Gay's (1994), *At the Essence of Learning: Multicultural Education;* Golnick and Chinn's (1990) *Multicultural Education in a Pluralistic Society* (3rd ed.); Harris' (1997) *Using Multiethnic Literature in the K-8 Classroom;* Trueba, Jacobs, and Kirton's (1990) *Cultural Conflict and Adaptation: The Case of the Hmong Children in American Society;* Howard's (1999) *We Can't Teach What We Don't Know: White Teachers, Multicultural Schools;* Nieto's (2000) *Affirming Diversity: The Sociopolitical Context of Multicultural Education* (3rd ed.); Pang and Cheng's (1998) *Struggling to be Heard: The Unmet Needs of Asian Pacific American Children;* and Sleeter's (1996) *Multicultural Education as Social Activism.*

These books all represent important contributions as they illustrate poignantly the shortcomings of monism in the broader educational enterprise. However, what has been missing is a book that challenges monism through the specific looking glass of literacy education *per se* as recounted by an extremely diverse group of noted scholars.

The book begins with two chapters that present broad theoretical frameworks for reconceptualizing literacy from the looking glass lens of multiculturalism and pluralism. In Chapter 1 ("Frameworks for Understanding Multicultural Literacies"), Georgia Earnest Garcia and Arlette Ingram Willis explore some of the major theoretical and applied characteristics of a multicultural perspective as related to literacy. To help literacy educators, researchers, and policymakers understand how culture can inform literacy practices, research, and policies, the authors present a review of cultural definitions and caveats, drawn primarily from the fields of educational anthropology, sociolinguistics, and critical theory. Next, they examine how multicultural instructional and curricula approaches can be extended to multicultural literacy practices. They proceed to review the contributions of critical theory, critical literacy, and multiple literacies to broadening notions of multicultural literacies. The authors end the chapter by arguing why social justice and an emancipatory paradigm should be integral features of multicultural literacies and how their inclusion needs to impact the literacy field.

In Chapter 2 ("Multicultural Belief: A Global or Domain-Specific Construct? An Analysis of Four Case Studies"), Jyotsna Pattnaik examines four highly effective, early childhood practitioners' beliefs and practices about diversity using Banks' (1994) four hierarchical levels (i.e., contribution, additive, transformative, and social action). Pattnaik's findings suggest that there is a lack of recognition (or inclusion) of different domains of diversity in her participants' formal definition of multicultural education, as well as in their practices. All her participants included race in their formal definition of multicultural education. On the other hand, her participants' classroom practices tended to be consistent with their beliefs regarding a particular domain of diversity. The study raises several important questions for teacher education programs, including: (a) How do (and how should) universities and preservice preparation be planned so students understand the historical, philosophical, moral, and political bases of multicultural education in general and the rationale for including many domains of diversity in particular?, (b) How do (and how should) teacher educators and teacher education departments' beliefs and practices affect their students' monocultural (or domain-specific) beliefs of diversity?, (c) How do (and how should) teachers reconceptualize and implement the construct "teacher effectiveness" so that multicultural effectiveness becomes an integral part of identifying teachers and preservice teachers' effectiveness?, and (d) What role should national/state accreditation/certification agencies play to institute a comprehensive concept of multicultural education?

To transform literacy from a monistic, monocultural approach to a pluralistic, multicultural approach, educators must first recognize that there must be a shift so that power is redistributed from the few to the many and, among the many, shared equitably. In the process, literacy content and practices need to be designed in ways that validate differences rather than the reality and experiences of a few. Such power issues are addressed in the next three chapters.

In Chapter 3 ("Monocultural Literacy: The Power of Print, Pedagogy, and Epistemological Blindness"), Dawnene D. Hammerberg and Carl Grant examine several prominent notions of literacy from a historical perspective for the purpose of showing how limited current monocultural assumptions are in current literacy practices. In the first section of their paper, the authors critically examine the notion that literacy is necessary and powerful. In short, they argue that power and necessity presently attached to literacy is an effect of historical tensions and cultural dominations rather than an effect of progressive development of humankind. Next, the authors examine the sorting and classifying mechanisms present in current understandings of how children learn to be print literate. In the final section of their paper, the authors question how it is possible that teachers can accept educational theories and practices that maintain educational inequities through a kind of expert-mediated oppression that is often promoted under the guise of "best practices." The authors conclude by arguing that not until practitioners, researchers, and policymakers understand how tied current literacy instruction is to an "unyielding history of oppression and exclusion that continues today" will literacy practices ever become truly "best practices."

In Chapter 4 ("Liberating Literacy"), Margaret C. Laughlin, Herbert Martin, Jr., and Christen E. Sleeter continue to examine the notion of what counts as literacy, how literacy is defined, and how particular definitions of literacy are coded into standards for curricula and student testing. While recognizing the importance of definitions of literacy that address decoding and comprehension, the authors argue the need to liberate literacy from its narrow skills definition. In proposing to extend literacy's definition, they argue the need to embrace a more emancipatory definition, that is, one that includes thinking critically about and participating in the very transformation of society and how people think of and interact toward one another in that society. They begin by considering the limits of the current instrumental approach to literacy and the current ideology that pervades school literacy curricula. They next present alternative ways of approaching literacy that critically examine "the what" makes children "literate" in terms of different types of knowledge. Here they discuss a project that connects literacy with community knowledge, drawing on work done in Mexico. They also examine a "New West" focus for reshaping knowledge, arguing that for a more pluralistically-centered curriculum.

In Chapter 5 ("Taking Ownership of Literacy: Who Has the Power?"), Patricia A. Edwards, Jennifer Danridge, Gwendolyn T. McMillon, and Heather M. Pleasants further note the need to for teachers to rethink their conceptions of literacy for culturally-diverse students. They argue that, within the contexts of school, literacy is sociopolitical in nature and reflects the unequal power structures and relationships in society. Thus, culturally-diverse children and their families often feel disempowered by teachers, which can ultimately alienate these children from the process of schooling. Using personal narratives, the authors present four short stories that illuminate the power struggles that can surface between teachers and African American students and their families. Further, the authors offer practical instructional strategies for mainstream teachers that connect schools to the multiple contexts in which African American children (and other children from culturally-diverse backgrounds) reside—including in the community, home, and the church.

While the first five chapters make reference to "culture" in general ways, the next five chapters address cultures as different looking glasses for understanding the world; as cultures change, so change the very nature of the looking glasses.

In Chapter 6 ("An African-Centered Perspective on Literacy: Promises and Possibilities"), Barbra J. Diamond returns to the use of case study to illuminate an African-centered approach to literacy learning. In her study, Diamond describes how literacy comes to be defined within the context of a first/second grade classroom in an African-centered school, and how teachers used literacy instruction to construct meaning in students' lives. The author found that literacy instruction became liberating when students read and wrote about the world that they experienced and the connection between their lives, their roots and traditions, and the lives of others in the wider world. Literacy instruction had an implicit dimension in students' lives because, through this instruction, students were guided by a set of principles, rituals, and protocols that reinforced the values of their specific community and broader culture. Literacy instruction also had an explicit dimension in students' lives because it equipped them to engage fully in literature and texts that included African and African American characters, traditions, and culture. The authors conclude by discussing the ways for enhancing African American students' literacy learning and achievement in urban settings.

In Chapter 7 ("Reading, Language, Culture, and Ethnic Minority Students"), John Reyhner and Ward Cockrum address the question of what makes for an effective reading program. Rather than focusing simply on qualities of instruction that lead to improved achievement scores, the authors argue the need to consider personality, cultural background, motivation, and skills of individual teachers and students who, together, can create effective reading programs. Throughout much of this chapter, the authors examine current trends in reading and the impact that these trends have on the methods, materials, and means of motivation that teachers use to turn students (with a special emphasis) into effective readers. The authors conclude their chapter with a discussion of what would constitute effective instruction for ethnic minority students.

In Chapter 8 ("Best Practice(s)? The Cultural Discourse of Developmentalism in American Early Education: A Cross-Cultural Comparison"), Diane M. Hoffman further examines the question of what constitutes best literacy practices for students of diverse cultural and ethnic backgrounds. According to Hoffman, although best practice has become central to early childhood education and literacy learning in recent years, concerns have emerged over the ways in which underlying ideas of developmental appropriateness that are inherent in best practice fail to address issues of cultural diversity and difference. In her chapter, Hoffman explores the notion of best practice as contextualized within culturally grounded discourses of developmental appropriateness, child-centeredness, and individualism. Comparing assumptions regarding children's selves and adult-child relations that underlie best practice in the United States with evidence from Japanese early education and Reggio Emilia schools in Italy, the author points to alternative views of self, cognition, emotion, and adult-child relations that can serve as a source of critical self-reflection, as well as a means for improving literacy practice among U.S. early childhood educators.

In Chapter 9 ("African American Young-Adult Science Fiction and Fantasy Literature: Realism for the 21st Century"), Randy F. Rush argues that science fiction and fantasy literature, written by and for African Americans, lacks recognition in the African American literature canon. This same lack of recognition is reflected in young adult literature written for the African American young adult. Although the number of works reflective of these genres are few in comparison to other genres, there are sufficient number to introduce to young adults. To bring this "sufficient number to light," Rush identifies key African American authors and their works of science fiction, fantasy, as well as nonfiction. By understanding these works, the reader is provided unique insights into the Black experience, whether it has an American, Caribbean, or African flavor. Through this understanding, readers gain in four ways by: (a) developing empathy for others; (b) understanding Black culture; (c) understanding the effects of racism; and (e) understanding human reactions to racism. For Black readers in particular, reading the books that Rush identifies should enable them to affirm their history and cultural traditions and become proactive in shaping their futures as well as their daily lives.

In Chapter 10 ("Rocks in the Brook: A Teacher Educator's Reflections"), Arlette Ingram Willis writes a personal narrative about her teaching experiences as an African American teaching largely white students in a predominantly white university. She states that she saw this as an opportunity for "introspection and a chance to learn more about my teaching and myself." In her chapter, Willis describes how she learns to accommodate the dual roles of teacher and researcher as she reflects on the process of teaching preservice literacy courses that address issues of race, class, gender, and power in the English/Language Arts Classrooms. She describes how she attempts to help her undergraduate students understand their social responsibilities that move beyond the confines of their past, present, and future into a global community. She concludes her chapters by recounting guiding principles that, while important to her, apply to all who wish to understand their life narratives in the context of reaching out to others while broadening their own perspective of who they are and who they might become.

In Chapter 11 ("English Language Learners' Reading: New Age Issues"), Jill Fitzgerald moves beyond the pluralism of multiculturalism and ethnicity per se and examines speakers whose native language is not English. Consequently, in this chapter, the author examines numerous controversial cultural issues about United States English language learners' English reading and reading instruction. Among the questions that the author addresses in this chapter are the following: Is a special theory necessary to explain English language learners' processes? Are English language learners' reading processes different at different developmental stages? Must native language reading precede learning to reading English? Must English orality precede English literacy? Are special reading instruction methods necessary for English language learners? After exploring answers to these questions,

the author discusses the implications for how teachers might best accommodate second-language learners acquisition of literacy skills.

In Chapter 12 ("Home-School Collaboration: Successful Models in the
Hispanic Community"), Flora V. Rodriguez-Brown draws upon her experience working with Hispanic parents during the past ten years to describe
Hispanic parents' aspirations for increased parental involvement in their
children's education. The author presents two parent-involvement models
that delineate successful practices to involve parents in their children's
education. One model is a family literacy program, "Project FLAME," that
directly teaches parents how to share literacy with their children at home.
The other is a "Funds of Knowledge" teacher/researcher collaboration in
which parents allow teacher-researchers to learn about their culture, home
life, and knowledge through home visits. These visits serve to inform and,
through reflection, transform the way teachers regard their students'
home life. Suggestions are provided as to how teacher-researchers can use
their newly acquired knowledge to make the curriculum and their teaching more relevant to the children in the community in which they teach.

In Chapter 13 ("Getting the Most out of Professional Development in
Culturally Diverse Schools"), William M. Saunders, Gisela O'Brien, David
Marcelletti, Kathy Hasenstab, and Claude Goldenberg begin by noting that
culturally-diverse schools are being encouraged to establish ongoing,
school-based professional development settings within and around the
school day. Improving professional development programs for teachers in
such schools is central to reforming and improving low-income, urban
schools that serve large numbers of language and cultural minority children. As the authors note, such schools often have less experienced staffs
and more new teachers with little, if any, preservice training. In the
absence of concrete descriptions of how to make such school settings work,
the authors describe elements of four specific school characteristics that
can make a substantial contribution to improved teaching and learning.
These include: (a) teacher work groups; (b) grade level or department
meetings; (c) the academic achievement leadership team; and (d) faculty-
wide settings and training workshops. The authors begin their chapter by
providing background information on the projects in which these settings
have been studied and a set of core principles for effective, school-based
professional development. The authors then devote a section to each setting, including a general description of what it is. In each section, the
authors provide specific guidelines for achieving success in that setting.

In the last section of the book, the authors turn to the issue of teacher
education. Although this topic is touched upon in many of the earlier
chapters, this issue is the primary focus in the remaining chapters. In short,
the last four chapters address the challenge of how to best promote pluralism and multiculturalism through a variety of innovative means.

In Chapter 14 ("Preservice Teachers Connect Multicultural Knowledge
and Perspectives with Literacy Instruction for Minority Students"), Hong

Xu begins by noting that little research has documented how preservice teachers apply a knowledge base gained from a professional course on multicultural education to working with students of diverse cultural and linguistic backgrounds. To address this problem, the author explores how preservice teachers connect multicultural knowledge and perspectives with literacy instruction for minority students when they are placed in a minority school for field experiences. Using Schmidt's ABC's Model as an instructional means for promoting multicultural knowledge, Xu provided preservice teachers with opportunities to learn about themselves and their students, as well as examine and challenge their own belief systems about students of other culture. Xu shows how the use of the ABC model, along with teaching case studies, can provide students representing diverse backgrounds with a context for translating multicultural knowledge into literacy instruction for themselves and the students whom they will teach some day.

In Chapter 15 ("'Raccoon? Wass Dat?': Hawaiian Preservice Teachers Reconceptualize Culture, Literacy, and Schooling"), Margaret J. Maaka, Kathryn Hl. Au, Yvonne K. Lefcourt, and L. Pauahi Bogac present a study in which they examine ways to raise the level of school literacy achievement of Hawaiian children and others from underrepresented groups by improving teacher education. The authors examine two preservice teachers' views of their own cultural identity; how their experiences as students shape their beliefs about culture, literacy, and schooling; and how their views of their cultural identity and their experiences as students inform their development as teachers. The findings underscore two critical areas of need. First, they suggest the need for the development of school curricula that acknowledge and respect the culture and life experiences of Hawaiian children. Second, they suggest the need for programmatic efforts that increase the number of well-prepared teachers of Hawaiian ancestry to serve as role models and developers of culturally responsive curricula. The authors conclude by arguing that, for an education system to be truly meaningful, powerful, and culturally sustaining, Hawaiians must take active roles in the development of educational theories, curricula, and practices.

In Chapter 16 ("Understanding Culture in Our Lives and Work: Teachers' Literature Study in the Book Club Program"), Taffy E. Raphael, Karen Damphousse, Kathy Highfield, and Susan Florio-Ruane focus on helping teachers come to understand themselves as cultural beings (i.e., as members of one or more cultural groups), to understand literacy as cultural practice; and to extend these understandings to their curriculum development and instructional practices. In addition, they describe the use of book clubs to promote three types of learning; that is, learning about literature and literacy; learning about instruction; and learning about self and others. As the authors note, this learning is situated within and is inseparable from the social context of the peer-led book conversations and the nature and content of autobiographies that students share with one another. By means of this experience, participants learn a powerful lesson about literacy and literacy education. In short, literacy is not merely "reading, writing, listening, and speaking." Nor is it simply a repertoire of skills and strategies for decoding and encoding. Rather, literacy is viewed as situated, meaningful, text-based interaction with others. As such, literacy teaches about humanity reflected in and seen through the perspective of our own and others' stories.

In Chapter 17 ("The Power to Empower: Creating Home/School Relationships with the ABC's of Cultural Understanding and Communication"), Patricia Ruggiano Schmidt talks about the divide that separates students and families from minority backgrounds from fully participating in classrooms and schools at all educational levels. To close this divide, Schmidt has devised an instructional model known as the ABC's of Cultural Understanding and Communication. This model is based on the sociocultural perspective and the premise, "Know thyself and understand others." Through the use of this model that promotes intense study of human similarities and differences, multiple perspectives emerge, and teachers begin to use their power to empower. In the process, teachers gain a better understanding of diversity and successfully connect home and school for literacy learning. As a further result, teachers' classrooms and schools evolve into communities of sharing and learning. In light of the importance of her work, Schmidt explains the background and the literature related to her ABC's Model. She next reports personal responses to the models. She then describes adaptations of the model and discusses further implications of the model for teacher education programs.

As Ayn Rand once observed, "We have freedom *of* choice but *not from* choice." As the chapters of this book suggest, the better able we are at understanding all possible choices and why they are important in different ways to different people, the wiser we are. Not only are we more tolerant, we are better at accommodating the view of our looking glass with those of others. By sharing of our looking glasses, we come to more fully understand our world at large. And in the process, the more we share in being part of a greater community of humanity.

Peter B. Mosenthal, Syracuse University
Patricia Ruggiano Schmidt, Le Moyne College

REFERENCES

Banks, J.A. (1996). *Multicultural education, transformative knowledge, and action.* New York: Teachers College Press.

Derman-Sparks, L., & the ABC Task Force. (1989). *Anti-bias curriculum: Tools for empowering young children.* Washington, DC: National Association for the Education of Young Children.

Dilg, M.A. (1999). *Race and culture in the classroom: Teaching and learning through multicultural education.* New York: Teachers College Press.

Garcia, E. (1999). *Student cultural diversity: Understanding the meeting the challenge.* Boston: Houghton Mifflin.

Gay, G. (1994). *At the essence of learning: Multicultural education.* West Lafayette, IN: Kappa Delta Pi.

Golnick, D.M., & Chinn, P.C. (1990). *Multicultural education in a pluralistic society* (3rd ed.). Columbus, OH: Merrill.

Harris, V. (Ed.). (1997). *Using multiethnic literature in the K-8 classroom.* Norwood, MA: Christopher Gordon.

Hollins, E.R., & Oliver, E.I. (Eds.). (1999). *Finding pathways to success: Teaching culturally diverse populations.* Mahwah, NJ: Erlbaum.

Howard, G.R. (1999). *We can't teach what we don't know: White teachers, multicultural schools.* New York: Teacher's College Press.

Nieto, S. (2000). *Affirming diversity: The sociopolitical context of multicultural education* (3rd ed.). New York: Longman.

Pang, V.O., & Cheng, L.L. (Eds.). (1998). *Struggling to be heard: The unmet needs of Asian Pacific American children.* Albany: SUNY Press.

Sleeter, C. (1996). *Multicultural education as social activism.* Albany: SUNY Press.

Trueba, H.T., Jacobs, L., & Kirton, E. (1990). *Cultural conflict and adaptation: The case of Hmong children in American society.* New York: Falmer Press.

Young, E. (1992). *Seven blind mice.* New York: Philomel Books.

PART I

THEORETICAL FRAMEWORK

CHAPTER 1

FRAMEWORKS FOR UNDERSTANDING MULTICULTURAL LITERACIES

Georgia Earnest García and Arlette Ingram Willis

Abstract: This chapter explores some of the major theoretical and applied characteristics of a multicultural perspective as related to literacy. To help literacy educators, researchers, and policymakers understand how culture can inform literacy practices, research, and policies, we present a review of cultural definitions and caveats, drawn primarily from the fields of educational anthropology, sociolinguistics, and critical theory. Next, we examine how multicultural instructional and curricula approaches may be extended to multicultural literacy practices. Then, we review the contributions of critical theory, critical literacy, and multiple- or multiliteracies to our understanding of multicultural literacies. We end the chapter by explaining why social justice and an emancipatory paradigm should be integral features of multicultural literacies and how their inclusion needs to impact the literacy field.

INTRODUCTION

If we could shrink the Earth's population to a village of precisely 100 with all the existing human nations remaining the same, it would look like this: there would be 57 Asians, 21 Europeans, 14 people of Western Hemisphere origin (North and South America), and 8 Africans; 70 of the 100 would be non-white, 30 would be white; 70 of the 100 would be unable to read; 50 would suffer from malnutrition; 80 would live in substandard housing; 70 of the 100 would be non-Christians, 30 would be Christians; only one would have a university education; half of the entire world's wealth would be in the hands of only 6 people and all 6 would be citizens of the United States....We are, in fact, a diverse world community. We owe it to generations to come to understand and value that diversity in order to achieve social peace. (Fox, 1999, n. p.)

Given the extensive human diversity in the world and in the United States, multicultural issues, once historically tied to ethnic and cultural studies, have become major governmental and educational concerns. Geneva Gay[1] (1994) has observed that "the increasing ethnic diversity of the United States population makes multicultural education for all students an imperative, particularly if education is to fulfill its basic function of being personally meaningful, socially relevant, culturally accurate, and pedagogically sound" (n. p.).

When applied to literacy, multiculturalism often is translated into something known as "multicultural literacy or literacies." What these terms actually mean is unclear. Gay (1994) has warned that the underlying assumptions and goals inherent in conceptualizations of multicultural literacy represent "varying levels of understanding." Sometimes omitted from these conceptualizations are the value that multiculturalists place on cultural diversity and the recognition that "the specific content, structures, and practices employed in achieving multicultural education will differ depending on the setting" (Gay, p. 2).

In our call for papers for a thematic issue on multicultural literacy (Willis, García, & Harris, 1998), we defined multicultural literacy(ies) as an emphasis on "the manner in which elements of difference—race or ethnicity, gender, class, language, sexual preference—create dynamic tensions that influence literacy access, acquisition, instruction, performance, or assessment" (García, Willis, & Harris, 1998, p. 183).[2] Yet, a content analysis of articles published in the *Journal of Literacy Research* between 1992–1996 revealed that only 18 articles out of 116 (or 16%) specifically dealt with issues of difference from a multicultural perspective. Although the term multicultural literacy recently has been used in the titles of numerous conference presentations and text,[3] a multicultural perspective still does not seem to have seriously influenced the literacy research canon, literacy policy reports, or even literacy instruction. On the other hand, as illustrated by this volume, some progress has been made.

The study of multicultural literacy draws upon an extensive philosophical and ideological foundation within the field of multiculturalism. For example, definitions of multiculturalism reflect varying philosophical, ideological, and educational purposes and goals (Giroux & McLaren, 1989). Reviewing all of these definitions is beyond the scope of this chapter. Instead, we have chosen to explore some of the major theoretical and applied characteristics of a multicultural perspective as related to literacy. We have used the term "multicultural literacies" in our title and discussion to better reflect the different modes, functions, and forms of literacy inherent in multicultural views.

We have organized this chapter so that we first lay the groundwork for understanding the cultural features and implications of multicultural literacies by reviewing cultural definitions and caveats, drawing from the fields of cultural anthropology, sociolinguistics, and critical theory. Next, we discuss the link between multicultural education and literacy and how the instructional and curricula approaches identified by Christine Sleeter and Carl Grant (1987), as well as James Banks (1997a), can be extended to examine multicultural literacy practices. Then, we briefly examine the contributions of three overlapping and interrelated areas—critical theory, critical literacy, and multiple or multiliteracies—to our understanding of multicultural literacies. We end the chapter by explaining why social justice and an emancipatory paradigm should be integral features of multicultural literacies and how their inclusion needs to impact the literacy field.

A RICH UNDERSTANDING OF CULTURE

According to Rosalinda Barrera (1992), educational researchers generally have demonstrated a "cultural gap" or a "void in [their] knowledge bases about culture as it relates to literacy and literature" (p. 227). In particular, they tend to see literacy as a universal construct that is not influenced by culture. Table 1 depicts Barrera's (1992) theoretical framework. It highlights the different ways in which an enhanced understanding of culture can add to our understanding of multicultural literacies.

To help literacy educators, researchers, and policymakers become aware of the complex and ever-evolving nature of culture, and how a complex understanding of culture can inform literacy practices, research, and policies, we present a review of cultural definitions and caveats (see García, 1997).

Table 1.   Barrera's Theoretical Framework

Knowledge Dimension	Focal Idea
Cultural	Making meaning is culturally mediated.
	Human meaning is cultural meaning.
Cross-cultural	Literacy and literature are cultural phenomena.
	Practices in literacy and literature differ across cultures.
Multicultural	Cultures involve relations of power.
	Literacy teaching is culturally mediated.

Source: Barrera (1992, p. 232).

Cultural Definitions and Implications

Emic and Etic Concerns

Ward Goodenough (1981) has explained that the term culture was derived from the nineteenth century use of the German term "Kulture." "Kulture" reflected the "customs, beliefs, and arts" of the better educated classes of Europe. Societies were judged and ranked according to how close their customs, beliefs, and arts approximated those of educated Europeans. Then, in the late 1800s and early 1900s, many anthropologists adopted Tylor's (1903, p. 1) definition of culture as "that complex whole which includes knowledge, belief, art, morals, law, custom, and any other capabilities and habits acquired by man as a member of society" (as cited in Goodenough, p. 48). Culture now was not genetically determined but acquired socially (Trueba, Jacobs, & Kirton, 1990). Although anthropologists began to view each society as having its own unique culture, many of them still focused on the exotic and described cultural characteristics of another population from an "etic" or outsider perspective. Few of them took into account their own cultural biases.

In 1964, Frake warned that anthropologists needed to go beyond merely describing cultural behavior, as reflected in Tylor's definition, to interpreting cultural appropriateness by specifying "the conditions under which it is culturally appropriate to anticipate that he [the observed], or persons occupying his role, will render an equivalent performance" (as cited in Trueba et al., 1990, p. 112). Goodenough's (1981) work broadened the concept of culture to include norms that guided the behavior and thinking of members of the same culture. Goodenough conceded that it might not be possible to predict a specific individual's behavior within a culture, but he argued that it should be possible to predict the "standards" or norms that guided the individual's behavior and thinking. According to Goodenough (1963, p. 259),

> Culture, then, consists of standards for deciding what is, standards for deciding what can be, standards for deciding how one feels about it, standards for deciding what to do about it, and standards for deciding how to go about doing it. (as cited in Goodenough, 1981, p. 62)

The emphases on cultural appropriateness and norms eventually led to the advancement of the "insider's" perspective or the "emic" perspective—what George and Louise Spindler (1987) have called "the view of and the knowledge of the native" (p. 70). The Spindlers have explained that, as ethnographers (researchers who are interested in cultural descriptions and interpretations), they begin with the "emic position ... and work our way to the etic, interpretive position" (p. 70). They warn that it is the "interpretive product ... that usually gets us into trouble with the natives when they read it" (p. 70).

The distinction between an emic perspective and an etic perspective (including the Spindlers' warning about the latter) seems particularly important for a discussion of multicultural literacy frameworks. An emic approach requires a respect for cultural relativity, or the understanding that all cultures develop ways to satisfy humans' basic needs that are appropriate to their respective settings. An emic approach should help us to offset cultural bias when we attempt to identify and characterize literacy practices different from our own. However, it means that we not only have to rely on individuals with expert knowledge about individual cultures but also become experts ourselves. Eleanor Lynch's (1992) suggestions for how educators can better prepare themselves to work with children and adults from diverse cultural backgrounds seem applicable to literacy researchers and practitioners. According to Lynch, educators should heighten their cultural self-awareness, learn about other cultures by reading and studying, rely on knowledgeable individuals from the respective cultures to serve as guides or mediators, actively participate in the culture, and learn the language of the culture.

In arriving at the cross-cultural interpretation, or etic perspective, we need to carefully, and continuously, assess how our own behavior, norms, and beliefs are shaped by our own cultural identities. We need to acknowledge the cultural standards that guide how we view, define, and respond to literacy and literacy research. Without this type of self-reflection, the interpretation or characterization of other peoples' literacy practices will come dangerously close to the nineteenth century practice of ranking and judging cultures.

Educational researchers have shown how appropriate uses of the emic and etic approaches can lead to the identification of literacy and pedagogical practices within cultural groups in our own society that conflict with those of larger society. For example, Susan Philips (1972) reported that Native American children on the Warm Springs Reservation in Oregon were reluctant to participate in whole class activities, where the teacher called on individual children, because these activities contradicted the types of participant structures to which the children were accustomed outside of school. Concha Delgado-Gaitán's (1990) ethnographic account of a Mexican American community has revealed similar findings. She reported that, in contrast to their Anglo (non-Hispanic White) teacher's emphasis on individualism and competitiveness, the Mexican American children preferred to work together, reflecting how they carried out tasks at home and in their community. Sarah Michaels (1981) described how several African American first graders used a storytelling style that their Anglo teachers did not know how to interpret, interrupting the children inappropriately, and essentially silencing them. When audio-recordings of the Anglo and African American children's stories were played anonymously (and with the dialect features removed) to groups of Anglo and African American professionals (see Cazden, 1988), the Anglos ranked the

African American children's stories below those of the Anglo children, whereas, the African Americans ranked the African American children's stories much higher than those of the Anglo children. They considered the African American children's stories to be more complex and sophisticated.

Motivational Goals, Power, and Survival

In the 1980s, Roy D'Andrade (1984) focused on understanding cultures as systems or functions of meaning. He proposed four functions of meaning: (1) the representational (representing knowledge and beliefs about the world); (2) the constructive (creating cultural entities, allowing for adaptation, variation, and change); (3) the directive (explaining how socialization results in our responding to needs and obligations); and (4) the evocative (the creation of certain feelings). By viewing culture in this way, he could account for Tylor (1901), Frake (1964), and Goodenough's (1984) definitions, acknowledge that culture is both learned and transmitted, and propose that culture affected individuals' motivational goals and sense of satisfaction or anxiety. D'Andrade has argued that "through the process of socialization, individuals come to find achieving culturally prescribed goals and following cultural directives to be motivationally satisfying and to find not achieving such goals or following such directives to be anxiety producing" (p. 98).

The anxiety that is produced when an individual's cultural identity is not respected by larger society is poignantly illustrated in Juan Flores's account of a childhood of exclusion:

> As brown-skinned choir boys in grade school, we sang a fan-fair of Texican songs…yet, no matter how I or my Chicano compadres tried to harmonize our feelings with words like these, something remained uncomfortable for us. Despite our own authentic, cultural contributions that sprang from names like Zavala, Hinojosa, and Gonzalez, we were not the authenticated and valued hosts whose White ancestries endorsed "historic inclusion." (http://www.wmc.edu/pub/researcher/issueXI-2/flores.html)

Flores's experience illustrates Gay's (1994) observation that "deeply ingrained cultural socialization becomes problematic in education when the schooling process operates on one cultural model to the exclusion of all others, or when culturally different children are expected to set aside all their cultural habits as a condition of succeeding in school" (p. 5).

Critical theorists, such as Henry Giroux (1988), Paulo Freire and Donaldo Macedo (1987), also have talked about culture and cultural processes in terms of goals and goal fulfillment. However, they have focused on how ideological and historic misconceptions of race, class, and gender have resulted in unequal power relationships, and the influences that such relationships have had on social groups and individuals' goal definitions. Giroux's definition of culture takes into account the different cultural interpretations that can occur in the same society due to the differential experiences of individual social groups. For him, culture is "the distinctive ways in which a social group lives out and makes sense of its 'given' circumstances and conditions of life" (p. 132). Similarly, Brian Bullivant (1993) has defined culture as how a social group survives and adapts to its environment. According to Bullivant, culture involves the shared beliefs, symbols, and interpretations that help the culture to make sense of the world around them.

Definitions of culture related to motivational goals, power, and survival certainly have implications for the literacy field. They help us to understand why we become anxious when our own understandings and assumptions are challenged. For example, why is it that we become nervous when we are asked to report findings that do not fit the paradigm in which we have been trained? Why are some findings privileged over others? Why are some researchers' voices heard more than others? To what extent does the privileging of paradigms, methods, and researchers' voices reflect the unequal power relationships within society? To what extent does this privileging silence the voices of insiders or minority researchers? Given the privileging of some voices and findings, how is research used to make instructional and assessment changes that benefit *all* children?

Communication and Discourse

Although anthropologists historically have been fascinated with the link between culture and language, it has been the work of Dell Hymes and subsequent sociolinguists that inextricably linked language and culture. Part of the controversy about the language and culture relationship is due to the fact that there are universal features of language that cut across cultures. However, research in the field of ethnography of communication has demonstrated that patterns of communicative behavior (both verbal and nonverbal) comprise a key element of culture, at the same time that they are affected by the cultural context and relate to other elements of culture (such as belief systems, values, etc.) (Saville-Troike, 1989). As James Wertsch (1987, pp. 20–21) has explained, "culture either determines or at least it facilitates a conscious, collective choice of communicative strategies" (as cited in Trueba et al., 1990, p. 126).

Communicative competence is a key construct for understanding cultural differences in communication strategies. According to Muriel Saville-Troike (1989), communicative competence refers to what a cultural participant needs to know both linguistically and in terms of roles and norms to communicate appropriately with other cultural members:

> Communicative competence extends to both knowledge and expectation of who may or may not speak in certain settings, when to speak and when to remain silent, whom one may speak to, how one may talk to persons of different statuses and roles, what appropriate nonverbal behaviors are in various

contexts, what the routines for turn-taking are in conversation, how to ask for and give information, how to request, how to offer or decline assistance or cooperation, how to give commands, how to enforce discipline, and the like—in short, everything involving the use of language and other communicative dimensions in particular social settings. (p. 21)

A number of researchers in the US have documented cultural differences in communicative practices of specific linguistic and racial/ethnic groups that conflict with the communicative practices rewarded and expected by teachers (see García, Pearson, & Jiménez, 1994). Both Georgia García (1998) and Robert Jiménez and his colleagues (Jiménez, García, & Pearson, 1995, 1996) have illustrated how successful Hispanic bilingual readers effectively used cross-linguistic transfer strategies unique to their bilingual status (e.g., cognates, code-mixing, code-switching, and translating) to improve their reading comprehension. Lisa Delpit (1996), Michele Foster (1989), Carol Lee (1995), and Geneva Smitherman (1994), among others, have demonstrated that there are culturally specific African American communication features that can be used to nurture and promote the literacy understanding and achievement of African American students.

Cultural differences in communicative strategies and competencies have major implications for how we convey information, assess children's progress, and implement instruction. If a cultural communicative practice, such as questioning strategies (see Heath, 1982), conflicts with a mainstream practice typically accepted and rewarded by schools and larger society, then we are confronted with a dilemma. Several questions arise: Do we work to change the minority cultural group's practice, violating what is considered to be communicatively competent within that culture, and possibly provoking resistance, an identity crisis, or high anxiety? Do we work to change mainstream society's practice, a particularly difficult task given the practice's widespread acceptance and presence? Or, do we work to bridge the differences by helping students from the culture become aware of the mainstream practice, make teachers aware of the conflict, and work with both groups to bridge the differences (see García, 1992)?

James Gee (1990) has discussed the link among language, culture, and thought in terms of discourses. He has defined discourses as instantiations of specific roles by identifiable groups of people in terms of how they behave, interact, value, think, believe, speak, read, and write. Discourses reflect ideologies, tend to be tacit or taken for granted, and generally imply "what counts as a 'normal' person and the 'right' ways to think, feel, and behave" (p. xx). In a sense, discourses reflect our membership or identification with a range of cultural subgroups because we all employ a number of discourses.

Recently, a colleague questioned whether multiple discourses that students have to read in school (mathematics, science, history, English) could be called "multicultural discourses." Even though the respective fields rep-

resent different types of discourse, from our viewpoint, they are not instantiations of different ideologies. Although each field involves different
metacognitive knowledge, overall, they reflect the mainstream ideology
that currently dominates U.S. schooling. They are not multicultural. In
contrast, language brokering—a term that is used to describe when bilingual children serve as mediators between their limited- or non-English
speaking parents and school personnel who are monolingual English
speakers—is a type of multicultural discourse (Tse, 1996). Language brokering involves skills, values, and ideology that typically are not reflected
within the dominant, monolingual, Anglo society. According to Tse, children who are language brokers are bilinguals who have not had any formal
translating or interpretation training. Their role as a translator or inter-
preter is one that has been conveyed to them due to their developing bilingualism, bicultural presence in their home culture and the culture of
dominant society, and the dominant society's general disdain for other languages. Children who are language brokers in the US not only translate or
interpret what is being said, but also make educational decisions and serve
as socializing agents (McQuillan & Tse, 1995; Tse, 1996). For example,
McQuillan and Tse (1995) found that when Cambodian, Chinese, Korean,
Vietnamese, and Mexican-American children translated, they modified
what they reported according to their cultural understanding of dominant
society and their own cultural backgrounds, often helping to facilitate
interactions among the various participants. This type of discourse is
unique to bilingual children from language minority backgrounds and
tends to occur in societies where monolingualism is privileged to the point
that school, government, and business officials do not provide trained
adult interpreters or translators.

Knowledge Acquisition

When literacy researchers or educators think about knowledge acquisition, they often refer to schema theory. Johann Friedrich Herbart (1777–
1841), commonly referred to as the father of the scientific study of education, first identified "apperception" as the process of adding new ideas to
the ideas already known, or the precursor of what is known today as
schema theory. Sir Frederick Bartlett's (1932) experiment—in which he
tested how well English-speaking students comprehended a myth about
dying told by Native Americans in Western Canada—was an excellent
example of cultural schemata.

Since Barlett's experiment, a number of researchers (Droop & Verhoeven, 1998; García, 1991; Kintsch & Greene, 1978; Lipson, 1983) have
reported that adults and students (as young as third grade and from
diverse linguistic and cultural groups, often within the same country) interpret and recall passages according to their own cultural interpretation—
reading material that is culturally familiar quicker than material that is not
familiar, remembering more of the important ideas, and adding (or elabo-

rating) information not in the passage based on their cultural interpretation, as well as distorting information in the passage that does not fit their
interpretation.

In some of the early experiments, researchers (Anderson, Reynolds,
Schallert, & Goetz, 1977) showed that people's interpretation of ambiguous passages frequently is affected by the social context, the type of classroom (music versus physical education) or group of people with whom
they completed the experiment. Margaret Steffensen and her colleagues
(Steffensen, Joag-Dev, & Anderson, 1979) also found that people generally
are not aware of the fact that they have misinterpreted, elaborated, or distorted the original passage.

Although cultural schemata experiments clearly show the role of culture
in knowledge acquisition, researchers in this line of work have not investigated how these cultural interpretations are created. Researchers (Moll,
1990; Wertsch, 1985) who hold sociocultural and sociohistorical perspectives of learning, in which children are viewed as constructing meaning
through social interactions in specific contexts, have attempted to explain
the social and cultural construction of knowledge. According to Vera John-
Steiner and her colleagues (John-Steiner, Panofsky, & Smith, 1994),
researchers from these perspectives emphasize the social interrelatedness
of knowledge and action, subject and object, and individual and social context. They focus on the roles that institutions, history, and cultures play in
mental functioning (Wertsch, 1985). A theoretical cornerstone of this perspective is Vygotsky's contention that children acquire linguistic and cognitive skills "first in relations between people as an interpsychological
category, afterwards within the child as an intrapsychological category" (in
Valsiner, 1987, p. 67, as cited in John-Steiner et al., p. 9). John-Steiner and
her colleagues have noted that a major and defining influence on children's development is the sociocultural context in which they acquire their
linguistic and cognitive skills.

Roland Tharp and Ronald Gallimore's (1988) work on activity settings is
particularly useful in understanding how sociocultural contexts can affect
knowledge acquisition. According to Tharp and Gallimore, how and why
children acquire knowledge are influenced by the five W's: *who*, or the activity participants; *what*, or how the activity is defined and executed; *when*, or the
appropriate timing of the activity; *where*, the setting or context of the activity;
and *why*, or the child's motivation for successfully pursuing the activity.

Henry Trueba, Lila Jacobs, and Elizabeth Kirton (1990), in their book
on Hmong children's adaptation in U.S. society, have explained each of
the five W's in terms of the academic performance of diverse groups in the
United States and international settings. For example, *who* (the activity participants) affects children's knowledge acquisition in terms of the social
roles that they learn to play and the type of knowledge that comes with
those roles. *What* (the activity) is based on the action that needs to occur
and how it is to be performed. They have explained that the

Actual patterns of behavior learned in one setting are built on daily cultural experiences and understanding. This understanding is in turn taken into the intra-mental plane to permit the child to structure cognitively that knowledge and experience so they may be applied to a future setting. (p. 121)

When refers to the timing of events in different cultures. Trueba et al. have pointed out that the timing of key cultural events, and the cultural rituals that accompany them, may vary considerably from one culture to another. Such differences can adversely affect children's motivation to learn or participate in such events when there are major variations between the home culture and societal culture.

Where, or the cultural context through which children acquire certain types of knowledge, clearly impacts its appropriateness. When children acquire knowledge within their primary social community, this affects their identity. Children crossing cultural boundaries have to learn to become adept at "cultural code-switching" to survive (p. 123). *Why* relates to motivation. If the activity is not culturally appropriate, or if there is not "a strong cultural value associated with the effort" then the acquisition and structuring of new knowledge on the intrapsychological and interpsychological planes will not occur (p. 123).

In terms of literacy, a socially mediated view of knowledge has major implications for how children view what counts as literacy, their motivation to participate in literacy practices, and their overall attitudes toward literacy. Gee (1990) has explained that "literacy has no effects—indeed, no meaning—apart from particular cultural contexts in which it is used, and it has different effects in different contexts" (p. 60). Arlette Willis's (in press) account of her African American child's response to a required writing assignment on the Civil War illustrates how a socially mediated view of knowledge can affect children's literacy acquisition, participation, and motivation. She describes how her son questioned what he should write about in response to his teacher's assignment to pretend that he was alive during the time of a Civil War novel, *Across Five Aprils* (1964), and write a letter to someone who was alive during the same time period. Willis explains that neither the novel nor the teacher dealt with issues of race and slavery, relegating them both to historical footnotes. Her son's question and comment poignantly illustrate the quandary that the assignment posed for him: "Mom, if I were alive during this time, wouldn't I have been a slave?....If I were a slave, I probably wouldn't even have known how to write a letter to anyone." Although her son courageously decided to pretend that he was a slave, as Willis explains,

This wasn't where he wanted to be, singled out in a class, using the 'R'word, race, to describe the experiences of those most like him in the past.... Mentioning African Americans and slavery meant making visible that he was African American, a fact that was most often ignored [in his classroom].

Willis questions the teacher's purpose in assigning the novel and the essay. Clearly, the teacher was not taking into account the message that the two sent in terms of whose participation and identity were important in the classroom. Her son's experience demonstrates how a hegemonic view of literacy can prevail, silencing and marginalizing students whose knowledge of the context is quite different.

Cultural Caveats

There are several important cultural caveats of importance to literacy researchers and educators that were not covered in the definitions. *First,* culture is not static, but ever changing and *dynamic* (see Hernandez, 1989). Culture is influenced by the individuals who share and transmit it, at the same time that it is affected by their interactions and participation within and outside their cultural groups. *Second,* culture is *continuous* (see Hernandez, 1989). Its influence on our lives is not finite. The invisible, and taken-for-granted nature of culture, often makes it difficult for us to recognize its ongoing influence on our own lives. *Third,* individuals within a society are affected by the macro culture (dominant culture) as well as the micro culture(s) or individual cultural groups to which they belong (see Banks, 1997b; Hernandez, 1989). How the macro culture affects micro cultures will *vary* according to the individual group's level of acculturation (contact with the macro culture) and level and type of assimilation (integration within the macro culture).

Fourth, individuals also will *vary* in how they participate and identify with the macro and micro cultures according to their cultural identity and the inhibiting and promoting environmental factors (health care, neighborhoods, schools) that affect them (see García Coll et al., 1996). Factors that can differentially affect members of the same cultural group include gender, racial features (including skin color), occupation, education, discrimination, racism, oppression, socioeconomic class, social stratification, segregation—residential (neighborhood), economic, social, or psychological—and age (García Coll et al., 1996). Other potential areas of variation include geographic locale, English fluency, bilingual status, religious affiliation, immigration pattern and generation, birth order, cultural identity and level of acculturation (Rumbaut, 1995).

Fifth, differences between and within "panethnic" categories, such as Latina/Latinos or Hispanics, Asians or Asian Americans, Native Americans, and African Americans are very important to acknowledge. For example, Cuban Americans, Puerto Ricans, and Mexican Americans tend to have different economic and educational backgrounds, levels of acculturation, political concerns and philosophies, employment opportunities, immigration histories, and patterns of entrance into U.S. society (Rumbaut, 1995; Smart & Smart, 1995; Vega, 1990). It is somewhat ironic that Asian groups

(Japanese, Chinese—Taiwanese and the People's Republic of China, Korean—North and South, Filipinos, Vietnamese, Cambodian, and Hmong), who have had historical confrontations (such as wars and armed hostilities), and who do not all speak the same language, are often lumped together.

To avoid overgeneralizing or stereotyping, it always is best to specify the actual group for which the research has been reported. If research has not been done with a specific group, then we need to state this and question whether the findings can be generalized to the specific group, the pan-ethnic group, or to the overall population. For example, both the First Grade Studies from the 1960s and the more recent tome, *Preventing reading difficulties in young children* (Snow, Griffin, & Burns, 1998) gave the impression that their findings were relevant for all US children. However, the First Grade Studies neglected to fund and investigate the reading of children from diverse lingustic and racial/ethnic backgrounds (Willis & Harris, 1997), while the authors of the reading difficulties tome did not point out the limited amount of research that specifically has focused on low-performing children from diverse backgrounds (see García et al., 1994) but instead generalized from a certain set of mainstream findings.

INSTRUCTIONAL APPROACHES THAT LINK MULTICULTURAL EDUCATION AND LITERACY

When literacy experts deal with multicultural education, they tend to focus on multicultural literature, or what Hilda Hernandez (1989) has called the content or curricula aspects of multicultural education: that is, "what is read, written, studied, or assessed" (García et al., 1998, p. 183). Few literacy experts deal with the process or cultural aspects of multicultural education: How instruction is implemented or organized, the values that underlie it, the languages used, the attitudes involved in teacher-student interactions, and the messages that are sent to students about their participation and perspectives (see Hernandez, 1989). Literacy experts also sometimes forget that multicultural education is "a philosophy, a methodology for educational reform" that includes ideology as well as content and process (Gay, 1994, n. p.).

In a historical review of how American schools have dealt with issues of difference during the twentieth century, Sleeter and Grant (1987) defined five instructional approaches to multicultural education: *teaching the exceptional and culturally different, the human relations approach, the single studies approach, the multicultural education approach,* and *the education that is multicultural and reconstructionist approach.* To some extent, the literacy field's orientation toward multicultural literacies reflects some of these approaches, or if not the approaches themselves, the general public's attitudes toward them.

The first approach, *Teaching the Exceptional and Culturally Different*, was very popular during the1960s and tended to reflect the War on Poverty. This approach focuses on providing additional instructional help to children who are ethnically, racially, linguistically, economically, mentally, or physically different from the general population of supposedly successful school children. Its goal is not to change schools, but to change children. Although children may improve their reading, none of these programs really tackle the reasons for why these children are in need of such services. The general instructional approach is one of fitting the children into the status quo or general educational environment as soon as possible. The conceptual lumping together of children from diverse classes and racial/ ethnic and linguistic backgrounds with children who qualify for special education, reveals the deficit attitude that often characterizes this approach. An historical example of this approach was a reading program for "culturally deprived children" (Bereiter & Engleman, 1966), which not only was oriented toward teaching low-income children how to speak in complete sentences, but which also incorporated moral lessons into the instruction. For example, in the following transcript children are taught to speak in complete sentences in a lesson that later teaches them that weapons can hurt people:

Teacher: [Presents picture of rifle] This is a_____.

Child B: Gun.

Teacher: Good. It is a gun.

Let's all say it. This is a gun. This is a gun. Again. This is a gun.

…

Teacher: [Presents pictures of knife, cannon, pistol]. This is a weapon. This is a weapon. This is a weapon. These are weapons. Say it with me … These are weapons. Let's hear that last one again. Make it buzz. These are weaponzzz. (pp. 106–107)

The second approach is the *Human Relations Approach*. As Sleeter and Grant (1987) have explained, the goal of this approach is to increase tolerance and create a sense of unity and acceptance. Although a focus of the approach is on reducing prejudice and stereotypes, the approach does not lead to changes within the status quo. In literacy, this approach is most readily seen in the use of books, discussion, and writing to improve human understanding. For example, teachers would use books such as *People* (Spier, 1980) that emphasize how humans from different parts of the world are similar and different. They would have students talk and write about how they are similar or different from other students. Both *Teaching the Exceptional and Culturally Different and Human Relations Approaches* are considered assimilationist because major changes in the educational process do not occur.

The *Single Group Studies Approach* refers to an emphasis on a particular group of people not typically emphasized in the curriculum. The roots for this approach are in the aftermath of the Civil Rights movement in the 1960s, with the development of ethnic studies courses (Banks, 1994). In terms of literacy, this approach is best illustrated in multicultural literature, where books about specific ethnic/racial/linguistic groups or from viewpoints not frequently heard (e.g., feminist) are emphasized. For teachers to implement this approach well, they need to be knowledgeable about the books, the groups discussed or perspectives presented, and know how to help students to grapple with difficult social, economic, and political issues covered in the books.

In its ideal form, this approach is nonassimilationist. However, when teachers only use multicultural literature during a specific time period, such as Black History Month, or when difficult social and political issues are skirted, then the status of multicultural literature, and its impact on the curriculum, is marginalized. Banks's (1997a) guidelines for the integration of curriculum with ethnic content illustrate some of the limited ways in which teachers use multicultural literature: for example, some of them use multicultural literature to implement the contributions approach, with a focus on foods, folk music, *fiestas* or holidays, and heroes.

To a certain extent, the *Multicultural Education Approach* encompasses each of the previous three approaches, but its goals are quite different. It involves a major change in the status quo so that schools strive to reflect equality and cultural pluralism. A literacy approach that reflects this approach would include the infusion of multicultural literacy into the curriculum, or what Banks (1997a) has called the *Transformation Approach*, where the structure of the curriculum is changed to enable "students to view concepts, issues, events, and themes from several ethnic perspectives and points of view" (p. 237). It also would involve changes in assessment, instruction, school organization and policy that would make sure that all students, regardless of race/ethnicity, language, class, or perspective, are given the opportunity to participate in high level thinking and provided with the literacy support and instruction to do so. Because it often is difficult for Anglo teachers by themselves to open up their instruction to focus on other points of view and to take a critical look at current practices, implementation of this approach almost always requires the extensive hiring of cultural insiders.

Current and complete examples of this instructional approach in the field of literacy are not easy to find. However, researchers who have identified successful teachers of African American (Ladson-Billings, 1994) and Latina/o students (Jiménez & Gersten, 1999) show us the possibilities. The Cultural Funds of Knowledge approach, developed by Luís Moll, Norma González, and their colleagues (Moll & González, 1994)—where teachers are taught to be ethnographers, investigate the funds of knowledge in their low-income Latina/o students' homes, and then work to incorporate this information into their curriculum—is an example. By getting the teachers to view their students and homes from an "emic" perspective, they were able to get the teachers to debunk myths about their working-class students' capabilities. The KEEP program (Au & Jordan, 1981), which was developed over a period of years in Hawaii—with its focus on a cultural speech event (talk story), inclusion of culturally relevant text, and emphasis on forms of authority that more closely paralleled the Hawaiian community—is another example.

The last approach is the *Education that is Multicultural and Social Reconstructionist.* This approach goes beyond the multicultural approach to get students to actually analyze and think about their own life circumstances and those of others in terms of social justice, accountability, and opportunity. According to Sleeter and Grant (1987), in its ideal form, this approach involves four components: Democratic participation of students, teachers, and administrators; participants' analysis of their own life circumstances; participants' acquisition of social action skills to enable them to actualize the first two components; and the coalition of disenfranchised groups to work together. In terms of this approach's implementation in the literacy field, one of the closest examples was that of Paulo Freire's (1970) use of critical literacy to empower the oppressed.

The late Freire (1970), who based his philosophy and pedagogy of literacy on his work with adults in remote areas of Brazil, wrote that literacy is "a strategy of liberation [that] teaches people to read not only the word but also the world" (p. 141). Over the last 30 years, Freire reworked and refined his definitions and purposes of literacy, resulting in the following restatement:

> Reading the world always precedes reading the word, and reading the word implies continually reading the world … reading the world is not preceded merely by reading the world, but by a certain form of writing and rewriting it, that is, of transforming it by means of conscious, practical work. (Freire & Macedo, 1987, p. 35)

While Freire was working to bring literacy to oppressed people in Brazil, there also were social and cultural movements within the United States that supported the expansion of definitions and purposes of literacy as social and cultural constructs as they pushed forward political agendas. One example is the work of Septima Clark with Myles Horton's Highlander Folk School of New Market, Tennessee. Clark and others taught African Americans to read and write in what has become known as citizenship classes (Barnett, 1994; Clark, 1986). Another example comes from the work of the Freedom Riders, Civil Rights Activists whose voting rights and literacy campaigns envisioned literacy as a means of fighting oppression.

CRITICAL THEORY AND CRITICAL LITERACY

Since the late 1960s, there has been a growing expansion of the definitions and purposes of literacy to include the influences of historical, social, cultural, and economic contexts. Much of this research has grown out of the work of critical theorists. The foundation of critical theory is drawn from a host of intellectual stars, and just as an attempt to name every star in the universe is difficult, listing all of the philosophers and social, cultural, and educational theorists who embrace critical theory is beyond the scope of this chapter.

Critical theorists draw from the work of the first generation Frankfurt School scholars, most particularly Max Horkheimer, who is credited with coining the term. According to Mark Poster (1989), Horkheimer's version of critical theory "attempts to promote the project of emancipation by furthering what it understands as the theoretical effort of the critique of domination begun by the Enlightenment and continued by Karl Marx" (p. 1). Later, a "critique of culture" was employed to account for "ideological hegemony of capitalism and the cultural supremacy of mass society" (Poster, 1989, p. 2). Modern day critical theorists have expanded notions of critical theory to include multiple forms of domination under which people are oppressed. This argument especially is true in the United States where oppressive conditions experienced by people of color, women, the poor, and those who do not speak English present a challenge for views of critical theory that highlight only capitalism.

Educational theorists, such as Banks, Gay, Giroux, Peter McLaren, Sleeter, Grant, Thomas Popkewitz, and Ira Shor, use critical theory to critique contemporary American society. In addition, these thinkers have developed their own theories to address centuries of oppression, the need for reform, and visions of possibility in American education. A number of critical theorists and educators, such as Clark, Friere, Delgado-Gaitán, González, Myles Horton, Macedo, Moll, and Sonia Nieto, have moved beyond theory to social action, or "walked the walk" and not just "talked the talk."

Although there are various definitions of critical literacy (Shor, 1999), within the framework of multicultural literacies, critical literacy generally refers to sociocultural and political views of literacy that are informed by critical theory. Shor, one of this country's foremost authorities on critical literacy, recently wrote a thoughtful article entitled "What is critical literacy?" (1999). In his article, he reviewed the use of the term, ranging from Burke's (1984) notion of "an attitude towards history" to his and Freire's (1987) "dream of a new society against the power now in power" to Gloria Anzaldúa's (1990) "multicultural resistance invented on the borders of crossing." Shor noted how his own definitions of critical literacy have developed. For example, he has moved beyond the following definition:

> Habits of thought, reading, writing, and speaking which go beneath surface meaning, first impressions, dominant myths, official pronouncements, traditional cliches, received wisdom, and mere opinions, to understand the deep meaning, root causes, social context, ideology, and personal consequences of any action, event, object, process, organization, experience, text, subject matter, policy, mass media, or discourse. (Shor, 1992, p. 129)

In a more modern day version, Shor states that critical literacy is a reflective and reflexive social practice that can be used to study other social practices, including language use and education. Although Shor's (1999) discussion of critical literacy has acknowledged the relationship between power and knowledge, his focus has tended to be on how individuals can and should use critical literacy to question the "social construction of self" and "the subjective positions from which we make sense of the world and act on it" (n. p.).

Shor (1999) also has linked culture and critical literacy by pointing out how our own socialization can affect our interpretations and views of the world. He recounted how teachers can use language and instruction to disenfranchise and disempower children. In a personal example, he noted that one of his teachers had asked third-grade children from a working class Jewish community in New York whether their fathers went to work in suits and ties. He explained that "the teacher's question that morning invited me to be ashamed of my family and our clothes, which like our thick urban accents and bad table manners, marked us as socially inferior, despite the white skin which gave us some decisive privileges" (n. p.).

Giroux has defined literacy as critical literacy. Citing the work of social theorist Antonio Gramsci, Giroux (1997) noted that "literacy is both a concept and a social practice that must be linked historically to configurations of knowledge and power, on the one hand, and the political struggle over language and experience on the other" (pp. 1–2). He also observed that literacy is neither a skill nor knowledge, but is "an emerging act of consciousness and resistance" (Giroux, 1995, p. 367). Giroux situated his definition of literacy within what he refers to as a "politics of difference" (p. 367) and argued that

> Literacy is a discursive practice in which difference becomes crucial to understanding not simply how to read, write, or develop aural skills, but also how to recognize that the identities of 'others' matter as part of the progressive set of politics and practices aimed at the reconstruction of a democratic public life. (p. 368)

Finally, Giroux called for literacy practices that would dismantle definitions and purposes of literacy that support and maintain inequalities in literacy education.

Getting students to view their worlds from a critical literacy perspective is not easy. Willis and Julia Johnson (1999) found that high school students

who read Ernest Gaines's (1997) book *A Lesson about Dying* and who participated in instruction on the death penalty, framed by critical literacy and
social justice, heightened their responses but didn't really change them. It
was difficult for most students to acknowledge that difference—race, gender, and class—mattered in most death penalty cases, where the prosecu-
tors differed considerably from the people accused of first degree murder
and who were sentenced to death. Although the process may be slow, Willis
and Johnston recommend that this type of informed literacy is what is
needed to get students to move toward issues of social justice.

MULTIPLE- OR MULTILITERACIES

A number of literacy researchers (Courts, 1997; Gee, 1999; The New London Group, 1996) have argued that our view of literacy needs to extend
beyond traditional language-based approaches to encompass the range of
communication modes in which meaning currently is conveyed and constructed (e.g., music, television, movies, video, internet, oral story telling,
rapping, sign language, cultural brokering, etc.). The New London Group,
a coalition of educational researchers from English-speaking countries,
have provided examples of the different modes of meaning that characterize their approach, ranging from the multimodal (e.g., electronic multime-
dia texts), which encompasses how all of the modes interact, to spatial (e.g.,
geographic and architectonic meanings), audio (e.g., music, sound effects),
linguistic (e.g., vocabulary and metaphor, information structure); visual
(e.g., colors, perspective, foregrounding), and gestural (e.g., behavior,
bodily physicality, sensuality). By moving beyond literacy pedagogy that currently is "restricted to formalized, monolingual, monocultural, ... forms of
language" (p. 61), the New London Group has contended that the literacy
field can better negotiate the linguistic and cultural differences that characterize our society, with the goal of reducing disparities, as well as reflect
changing technologies that present new ways of interacting and conveying
meaning. They have pointed out that analyzing mass media for its linguistic
meaning does not take into account how the media uses visual, audio, and
gestural effects to influence the consumer or reader. To just analyze the linguistic meanings would result in a very limited reading of the script. Patrick
Courts has talked about developing a critical pedagogy that "invites careful
examination and assessment of everyone's articulations" (p. 135) through a
variety of media that are central to students' lives.

The New London Group (1996) has termed their literacy approach,
multiliteracies. Courts (1997) has used the term multicultural literacies.
Gee (1999), an original member of the New London Group, has characterized a recent merging of perspectives from different disciplines as the New
Literacy Studies. Gee explains that the New Literacy Studies views literacy
in terms of the sociocultural and political contexts in which it occurs. As

such, it is impossible to extricate literacy practices from their sociocultural settings. Because literacy practices in sociocultural settings are characterized by the combination of written and oral practices with values, behavior, beliefs, norms, identity, and "nonverbal symbols, sites, tools, objects, and technologies" (p. 356), it is multiple.

What all three approaches have in common are sociocultural views of literacy that reflect Freire's contention that literacy should involve "reading the world." For example, Courts' (1997) approach emphasizes the need to get all students to critically reflect on the past, the present, and the future. He especially is interested in getting students to "recover that knowledge which we choose not to know" (p. 135). The New London Group has designed a multiliteracies pedagogical approach—involving situated practice, overt instruction, critical framing, and transformed practice—that they hope will provide all students, especially those who are marginalized, with the language they need for "work, power, and community," and "the critical engagement necessary for them to design their social futures and achieve success through fulfilling employment" (p. 60). In a critique of the National Academy of Sciences report on reading (Snow, Burns, & Griffin, 1998), Gee (1999) has explained that literacy and literacy learning cannot be divorced from the cultural and social forces that shape them, especially the forces of racism and poverty. He argues that what we need to do is study how

> People from childhood to adulthood, learn to leverage new school-based (and other public sphere) social languages—in speech, writing, and action—to participate in, and eventually critque and transform specific sociocultural practices. (p. 371)

Elizabeth Noll's (1998) ethnographic case studies of two American Indian youths illustrate why it is important to expand our definitions of literacy to include "multiple literacy activities" (p. 210). When the youths' literacy practices only were viewed from what they officially were assigned to do in school, a very limited perspective emerged. This perspective, clearly based on the teachers' instruction and assessments, did not take into account the racism and prejudice that the students felt in school and actually talked about in their school writing. It also did not take into account the Indian parent association's distrust of the word "literacy."

On the other hand, when the youth's engagements with nonassigned literacy activities in and out of school were documented, and when the definition of literacy was expanded to include how the two youths made sense of their worlds through demonstrations and explanations of music, dance, and art, then a more complete view of their literacies became apparent. This view of their literacy development reflected the multiple cultures in which they were engaged: American Indian culture, mainstream popular culture, and school culture. As Noll has explained, by expanding the definition of literacy beyond reading and writing, it was possible to see how the youths "'read the word and the world' (Freire & Macedo, 1987) in a variety of contexts" (p. 211). It also was possible to identify what school personnel needed to be doing to recognize the youth's perspectives and competencies.

CONCLUDING REMARKS: THE NEED FOR SOCIAL JUSTICE AND AN EMANCIPATORY PARADIGM

The current state of affairs, with a wide range of definitions characterizing multicultural literacies, is problematic. The lack of an agreed upon definition requires each proponent or opponent to redefine the field within her/his individual orientation, often leading to misunderstandings and a general watering down of the potential power and reform behind the concept of multicultural literacies. As we saw in our review of multicultural educational practices, attempts to address issues of difference often have resulted in simplistic curricula responses or adaptations, or what Daniel Wiel (1998) has called discrete and cosmetic multiculturalism. A decade ago, literacy educators, at all levels, were considered "enlightened" to include readings written by authors of color on their reading lists. Today, to only do this in the name of multicultural literacies is a form of new "canonical tokenism" (Flores, n. p.). We agree with Wiel's argument that

> In a pluralistic society, education should affirm and encourage the quest for self-examination through social transformation by creating relevant problem-solving activities that allow students to confront in their reasoning the challenges the diversity of everyday life offer. (pp. 11–12)

In fact, we would argue that there are two areas that were not emphasized strongly enough in our earlier discussion of multicultural literacies: social justice and the emancipatory paradigm.

A Commitment to Social Justice

Banks (1997b) has warned that the "challenge to multicultural education, in both theory and practice, is how to increase equity for a participating victimized group without further limiting the opportunities of another" (p. 7). Yet, opponents of multicultural education and multicultural literacies view the fields as anti-White, anti-male, anti-heterosexual, anti-English, and anti-American (Ravitch, 1990; Schlesinger, 1991), mistakenly replacing patriotism with a form of racism. They fail to acknowledge that a goal of multicultural education and multicultural literacies is not to exclude groups, but to expand our definitions of education and literacy so that those groups whose voices and interests have not been heard can inform our definitions of education, literacy, and pedagogy. However, to develop a more inclusive and socially just society, we have to acknowledge society's role and the school's role in the persistent failure of ethnically and linguistically diverse students. We agree with Freire's (1985) contention that:

> To think of education independent from the power that constitutes it, divorced from the concrete world where it is forged, leads us either to reduce it to a world of abstract values and ideals (which the pedagogue constructs inside his consciousness without even understanding the conditioning that makes him think this way), or to convert it to a repertoire of behavioral techniques.... (p. 140)

Key to this examination of education and literacies in terms of power and the status quo, is the importance of self-examination and reflection, two tasks that are particularly difficult for those in power. Although we like the emic/etic distinctions that we reviewed at the beginning of our discussion of cultural definitions, we think that it is important to point out that addressing culture in a binary fashion is merely a starting point for reflection. The insider/outsider positions do not take into account how a society's hegemonic forces blind the majority from creating a more inclusive, socially just, and democratic society. The following account, which was posted on the listserv for the American Indian Literacy Association, clearly documents how some members of society lack sensitivity to racially offensive terms as well as the powerful majority's response when its authority is challenged:

> 0/18/2000—Pinellas County School, Florida
>
> The American Indian Movement of Florida learned last month that a teacher at TYRONE ELEMENTARY SCHOOL in Saint Petersburg was teaching her students that the word "Squaw" is an appropriate term to describe American Indian women. A letter was sent to Mrs. Jacobs and Tyrone Elementary School explaining that the word is racially demeaning and derogatory as well as [a] sexually demeaning term for American Indian women both in its usage and its origins in Mohawk in which it refers to female genitalia.
>
> Included with the letter was a copy of the Oyate teaching guide and its "Teaching Respect for American Indians" as a guide. A request was made that the teacher refrain from using the word "squaw" in the future and teach the 5th grade class that the word is offensive....

On January 5, 2000, Mrs. Jacobs responded informing Florida AIM of the following:

1. She will continue to teach the word squaw as an appropriate term for American Indians because she will not be censored in America.

2. She believes Florida AIM is simply being politically correct as the word has been used for two centuries and further it appears in award winning books.

3. Because of the request to stop using the word she will no longer donate to any American Indian charity because if Indian people are offended by the use of the word squaw they don't deserve her money.

One reason why we think that an emphasis on social justice has not occurred in the literacy field is because systemic policies in society, the schools, and our profession have helped to maintain the status quo. In part, this is due to lack of leadership within the literacy field. However, it also is due to the majority's unwillingness to acknowledge and act based on what is known about the connections among race/ethnicity, language, culture, and literacy.

Implementing an Emancipatory Paradigm

A number of us have lamented the limited focus on issues of difference in the literacy field from the very groups' perspectives being studied (Au, 2000; García, 2000; García et al., 1994; Willis & Harris, 1997, 2000). Individuals and groups, often well-intended, like the New London Group (1996), describe what needs to be done within a diverse society, while they leave the research conducted by people of color to parenthetical notes, thus unwittingly committing the same "sin of omission" they accuse the field at large of perpetuating. Issues related to biliteracy or second-language literacy, and the researchers who investigate these topics, also are ignored or marginalized.

If research by people of color, like-minded Anglos, and committed folks of all hues is not published or acknowledged, then it is difficult to judge the trustworthiness of research by Anglos among people of color. Henry Louis Gates, Jr. (1993) eloquently has explained the important role that maintaining, transmitting, and highlighting cultural knowledge has played in African American history:

Telling our own stories—interpreting the nature of our world to ourselves, asking and answering epistemological and ontological questions in our own voices and on our own terms—has as much as any single factor been responsible for the survival of African Americans and their culture (p. 17).

A similar problem occurs when monolingual researchers discuss and investigate the literacy processes and practices of bilingual and second-language learners of English. García (1998, 2000) has pointed out that a monolingual perspective often results in a deficit view of these learners' language and literacy capabilities.

To alleviate the current situation, we strongly recommend that literacy researchers, policymakers, and educators embrace an emancipatory paradigm (see Mertens, 1999), where multiple realities and the political, social, economic, linguisitic, and cultural elements of difference that shape such realities are recognized, especially those that result in oppression. Some might say "multiple realities," isn't that a key term for the interpretive/constructive paradigm? Perhaps, but as Donna Mertens has observed, although interpretive/constructive researchers changed the rules for conducting research (in contrast to positivistic or post-positivistic researchers), they "still consist of a relatively small group of powerful experts doing work on a larger number of relatively powerless research subjects" (p. 15). Whereas, the emancipatory paradigm:

> Directly addresses the politics in research by confronting social oppression at whatever level it occurs [subject or participant, policy-maker, reseacher]…. go[ing] beyond the issue of the powerful sharing power with the powerless and relinquish[ing] control of the research to the marginalized groups. (p. 15)

Most importantly, the emancipatory paradigm is transformative; the results are to be used to remedy or rectify oppression, or "empowering to those without power" (Mertens, p. 20).

When we review the various frameworks and theories that we have discussed in this chapter, it becomes clear to us that our definition of multicultural literacies involves more than the definition we originally gave, "an emphasis on the manner in which elements of difference—race or ethnicity, gender, class, language, sexual preference—create dynamic tensions that influence literacy access, acquisition, instruction, performance, or assessment." Our definition of multicultural literacies reflects a complex understanding of culture; a strong commitment to diversity; an understanding of how language and literacy practices are socially mediated and ideologically constructed; a recognition of the multiple forms of literacies; and an enlightened examination of the social, political, and economic contexts that shape language and literacy practices, policies, and research. Most importantly, our definition involves a strong commitment to social justice, the emancipatory paradigm, and a transformative mission that will positively affect individuals and cultural and linguistic groups whose voices often are marginalized, leading to an improved society as a whole.[4] Clearly, this new definition will not only have instructional but also research and policy implications that we hope will be illustrated in the subsequent chapters in this book.

NOTES

1.   Throughout the chapter, we have initially introduced authors in the text by using their first and last names. We have purposely done this so that female *and* male authors are acknowledged and credited for their work.

2.   We did not include exceptionality, a topic that frequently is included in definitions of multicultural education, because reading disability not only is a topic of considerable attention in the literacy field but also one that has received consider-

able funding and attention through the establishment of the Office of Special Education Programs at the federal level.

   3.   A review of *amazon.con* in September 1999 revealed 70 texts that included multicultural literacy as a key word.

   4.   To improve society as a whole certainly requires an examination of critical race theory, which while implied, really was not covered in this chapter. We leave this topic to future work.

REFERENCES

Anderson, R.C., & Pichert, J.W. (1978). Recall of previously unrecalled information following a shift in perspective. *Journal of Verbal Learning, 17*, 1–12.

Anderson, R.C., Reynolds, R.E., Schallert, D.L., & Goetz, E.T. (1977). Frameworks for comprehending discourse. *American Educational Research Journal, 14*(4), 433–440.

Au, K.H. (2000). A multicultural perspective on policies for improving literacy achievement: Equity and excellence. In M. Kamil, P. Rosenthal, P.D. Pearson, & R. Barr (Eds.), *Handbook of reading research* (vol. 3, pp. 835–851). Mahwah, NJ: Lawrence Erlbaum.

Au, K.H., & Jordan, C. (1981). Teaching reading to Hawaiian children: Finding a culturally appropriate solution. In H.T. Trueba, G.P. Guthrie, & K.H. Au (Eds.), *Culture in the bilingual classroom: Studies in classroom ethnography* (pp. 139–152). Rowley, MA: Newbury House.

Banks, J.A. (1994). *Multiethnic education: Theory and practice* (3rd ed.). Boston: Allyn & Bacon.

Banks, J.A. (1997a). Approaches to multicultural curriculum reform. In J.A. Banks & C.M. Banks (Eds.), *Multicultural education: Issues and perspectives* (3rd ed., pp. 229–250). Boston: Allyn & Bacon.

Banks, J.A. (1997b). Multicultural education: Characteristics and goals. In J.A. Banks & C.M. Banks (Eds.), *Multicultural education: Issues and perspectives* (3rd ed., pp. 3–31). Boston: Allyn & Bacon.

Barnett, B. (1993). Invisible Southern Black women leaders in the Civil Rights Movement: The triple constraints of gender, race, and class. *Gender and Society, 7*(2), 162–182.

Barrera. R. (1992). The cultural gap in literature-based literacy instruction. *Education and Urban Society, 24*, 227–243.

Bartlett, F.C. (1932). *Remembering: A study in experimental and social psychology.* Cambridge: Cambridge University Press.

Bereiter, C., & Engelmann, S. (1966). *Teaching disadvantaged children in the preschool.* Englewood Cliffs, NJ: Prentice-Hall.

Brown, C. (Ed.). (1990). *Septima Clark and the Civil Rights Movement: Ready from within.* Trenton, NJ: African World Press.

Bullivant, B. (1993). Culture: Its nature and meaning for educators. In J.A. Banks & C.M. Banks (Eds.), *Multicultural education: Issues and perspectives* (2nd ed., pp. 29–47). Boston: Allyn and Bacon.

Cazden, C.B. (1988). *Classroom discourse: The language of teaching and learning.* Portsmouth, NH: Heinemann Educational Books, Inc.

Courts, P.L. (1997). *Multicultural literacies: Dialect, discourse, and diversity.* New York: Peter Lang.

D'Andrade, R.G. (1984). Cultural meaning systems. In R.A. Shweder & R.A. Leine (Eds.), *Culture theory* (pp. 88–119). Cambridge: Cambridge University Press.

Delgado-Gaitán, C. (1990). *Literacy for empowerment: The role of parents in children's education.* London: Falmer Press.

Delpit, L. (1996). *Other people's children: Cultural conflict in the classroom.* New York: New Press.

Droop, M., & Verhoeven, L. (1998). Background knowledge, linguistic complexity, and second-language reading comprehension. *Journal of Literacy Research, 30*(2), 251–271.

Flores, J. *Authentic multiculturalism and nontraditional students: Voices from the "contact zone."* http://www.wmc.edu/pub/researcher/issueXI-2/flores.html.

Foster, M. (1989). "It's cookin' now": A performance analysis of the speech events of a Black teacher in an urban community college. *Language and Society, 18,* 1–29.

Fox, L. (1999). Executive Director, Bank America Foundation, presentation at the CASE Conference.

Freire, P. (1970). *Pedagogy of the oppressed.* New York: Continuum.

Freire, P. (1985). *The politics of education: Culture, power, and liberation.* South Hadley, MA: Bergin & Garvey.

Freire, P., & Macedo, D. (1987). *Literacy: Reading the word and the world.* Westport, CT: Bergin & Garvey.

Gaines, E.(1997). *A lesson before dying.* New York: Knopf.

García, G.E. (1991). Factors influencing the English reading test performance of Spanish-speaking Hispanic children. *Reading Research Quarterly, 26*(4), 371–392.

García, G.E. (1992). Ethnography and classroom communication: Taking an "emic" perspective. *Topics in Language Disorders, 12*(3), 54–66.

García, G.E. (1997). *Cultural definitions and issues.* Urbana: University of Illinois, Culturally and Linguistically Appropriate Services, Early Childhood Research Institute.

García, G.E. (1998). Mexican-American bilingual students' metacognitive reading strategies: What's transferred, unique, problematic? *National Reading Conference Yearbook, 47,* 253–263.

García, G.E. (2000). Bilingual children's reading. In M. Kamil, P. Rosenthal, P.D., Pearson, & R. Barr (Eds.), *Handbook of reading research* (vol.3, pp. 813–834). Mahwah, NJ: Lawrence Erlbaum.

García, G.E., Pearson, P.D., & Jiménez, R.T. (1994). *The at-risk situation: A synthesis of reading research* (Special Report). Champaign, IL: Center for the Study of Reading, University of Illinois.

García, G.E., Willis, A.I., & Harris, V.J. (1998). Introduction: Appropriating and creating space for difference in literacy research. *Journal of Literacy Research, 30*(2), 181–186.

García Coll, C. , Lamberty, G., Jenkins, R., McAdoo, H.P., Crnic, K., Waskik, B.H., & García, H.V. (1996). An integrative model for the study of developmental competencies in minority children. *Child Development, 67,* 1891–1914.

Gates, H.L. (1993). *Loose canons: Notes on the culture wars.* New York: Oxford University Press.

Gay, G. (1994). *A synthesis of scholarship in multicultural education.* Urban Monograph Series. Oakbrook, IL: North Central Regional Educational Library. (Online: http://www.shss.montclair.edu/english/classes/stuehler/engl105/leogay.html).

Gee, J. (1990). *Social linguistics and literacies: Ideology in discourse.* London: The Falmer Press.

Gee, J.P. (1999). Critical issues: Reading and the New Literacy Studies: Reframing the National Academy of Sciences report on reading. *Journal of Literacy Research,* (333), 355–374.

Giroux, H. (1987). Introduction. In P. Freire & D. Macedo (Eds.). *Literacy: Reading the word and the world* (pp. 1 -27). Westport, CT: Bergin & Garvey.

Giroux, H. (1993). Literacy and the politics of difference. In C. Lankshear & P. McLaren (Eds.), *Critical literacy: Politics, praxis, and the postmodern* (pp. 367–377). Albany: State University of New York Press.

Giroux, H. (1988). *Teachers as intellectuals: Toward a critical pedagogy of learning.* South Hadley, MA: Bergin & Garvey.

Giroux, H., & McLaren, P. (1989). Introduction: Schooling, cultural politics, and the struggle for democracy. In H. Giroux & P. McLaren (Eds.). *Critical pedagogy, the state, and cultural struggle* (pp. xi-xxxv). Albany: State University of New York Press.

Goodenough, W.H. (1981). *Culture, language, and society.* Menlo Park, CA: The Benjamin/Cummings Publishing Co., New York: Merrill.

Heath, S.B. (1982). Questioning at home and at school: A comparative study. In G. Spindler (Ed.), *Doing the ethnography of schooling: Educational anthropology in action* (pp. 102–131). New York: Holt, Rinehart, & Winston.

Hernandez, H. (1989). *Multicultural education: A teacher's guide to content and process.* New York: Merrill.

Jiménez, R.T., García, G.E., & Pearson, P.D. (1995). Three children, two languages, and strategic reading: Case studies in bilingual/monolingual reading. *American Educational Research Journal, 32,* 31–61.

Jiménez, R. T., García, G.E., & Pearson, P.D. (1996). The reading strategies of bilingual Latina/o students who are successful English readers: Opportunities and obstacles. *Reading Research Quarterly, 31*(1), 90–112.

Jiménez, R.T., & Gersten, R. (1999). Lessons and dilemmas in the literacy instruction of two Latina/o teachers. *American Educational Research Journal, 36*(2), 265–301.

John-Steiner, V., Panofsky, C.P., & Smith, L.W. (1994). Introduction. In V. John-Steiner, C.P. Panofsky, & L.W. Smith (Eds.), *Sociocultural approaches to language and literacy. An Interactionist perspective* (pp. 1–33). New York: Cambridge University Press.

Kintsch, W., & Greene, E. (1978). The role of culture-specific schemata in the comprehension and recall of stories. *Discourse Processes, 1,* 1–13.

Ladson-Billings, G. (1994). *The dreamkeepers: Successful teachers of African American children.* San Francisco: Jossey-Bass.

Ladson-Billings, G. (1995). Multicultural teacher education: Research , practice, and policy. In J. Banks & C. Banks (Eds.), *Handbook on the research in multicultural education.* New York: Macmillian.

Lee, C. (1995). A culturally based cognitive apprenticeship: Teaching African American students skills in literary interpretation. *Reading Research Quarterly, 30*(4), 608–630.

Lipson, M.Y. (1983). The influence of religious affiliation on children's memory for text information. *Reading Research Quarterly, 18*, 448–457.

Lynch, E.W. (1992). Developing cross-cultural competence. In E.W. Lynch & M. J. Hanson (Eds.). *Developing cross-cultural competence: A guide for working with young children and their families* (pp. 35–59). Baltimore, MD: Paul H. Brookes.

McQuillan, J., & Tse, L. (1995). Child language brokering in linguistic minority communities: Effects on cultural interaction, cognition, and literacy. *Language and Education, 9*(3), 195–215.

Michaels, S. (1981). Sharing time: Children's narrative styles and differential access to literacy. *Language in Society, 10*, 423–442.

Mertens, D.M. (1998). *Research methods in education and psychology: Integrating diversity with quantitative and qualitative approaches.* Thousand Oaks, CA: Sage Publications, Inc.

Moll, L.C. (1990). *Vygotsky and education: Instructional implications and applications of sociohistorical psychology.* Cambridge: Cambridge University Press.

Moll, L.C., & González, N. (1994). Critical issues: Lessons from research with language-minority children. *Journal of Reading Behavior: A Journal of Literacy, 26*(4), 439–456.

Noll, E. (1998). Experiencing literacy in and out of school: Case studies of two American Indian youths. *Journal of Literacy Research, 30*(2), 205–232.

Philips, S.U. (1972). Participant structures and communicative competence: Warm Springs children in community and classroom. In C.B. Cazden, V.P. John, & D. Hymes (Eds.), *Functions of language in the classroom* (pp. 370–394). New York: Teachers College Press.

Poster, M. (1989). *Critical theory and poststructuralism: In search of a context.* Ithaca, NY: Cornell University Press.

Ravitch, D. (1990). Multiculturalism: E pluribus plures. *The American Scholar, 54*, 337–354.

Rumbaut, R.G. (1995). The crucible within: Ethnic identity, self-esteem, and segmented assimilation among children of immigrants. *International Migration Review, 28*(4), 748–794.

Saville-Troike, M. (1989). *The ethnography of communication: An introduction.* New York: Basil Blackwell.

Schlesinger, A. (1991). *The disuniting of America: Reflections on a multicultural society.* New York: W. W. Norton Co.

Shor, I. (1992). *Empowering education: Critical teaching for social change.* Chicago: University of Chicago Press.

Shor, I. (1999). What is critical literacy? *Journal for Pedagogy, Pluralism & Practice, 1*(4). http://www.lesley.edu/journals/jppp/4/shor.html. (Originally published as "Introduction" to *Critical Literacy in Action*, edited by Ira Shor & Caroline Pari, Heinemann Press, 1999).

Sleeter, C.E., & Grant, C.A.(1987). An analysis of multicultural education in the United States. *Harvard Educational Review, 57*, 421–444.

Smart, J.F., & Smart, D.W. (1995). Acculturative stress: The experience of the Hispanic immigrant. *The Counseling Psychologist, 23*(1), 25–42.

Smitherman, G. (1994). "The blacker the berry, the sweeter the juice": African American student writers. In A. Dyson & C. Genishi (Eds.), *The Need for story: Cultural diversity in classroom and community.* Urbana, IL: National Council of Teachers of English.

Snow, C.E., Burns, M.S., & Griffin, P. (Eds.). (1998). *Preventing reading difficulties in young children.* Washington, DC: National Academy Press.

Spier , P. (1980). *People.* New York: Doubleday.

Spindler, G., & Spindler, L. (1992). Cultural process and ethnography: An anthropological perspective. In M.D. LeCompte, W.L. Millroy, & J. Preissle (Eds.), *The handbook of qualitative research in education* (pp. 53–92). San Diego, CA: Academic Press.

Steffensen, M.S., Joag-Dev, C., & Anderson, R.C. (1979). A cross-cultural perspective on reading comprehension. *Reading Research Quarterly, 15*(1), 10–29.

Tharp, R.G., & Gallimore, R. (1988). *Rousing minds to life: Teaching, learning, and schooling in social context.* Cambridge: Cambridge University Press.

The New London Group. (1996). A pedagogy of multiliteracies: Designing social futures. *Harvard Educational Review, 66*(1), 60–92.

Trueba, H.T., Jacobs, L., Kirton, E. (1990). *Cultural conflict and adaptation: The case of Hmong children in American society.* New York: The Falmer Press.

Tse, L. (1996). Language brokering in linguistic minority communities: The case of Chinese- and Vietnamese-American students. *The Bilingual Research Journal, 20*(3 & 4), 485–498.

Vega, W.A. (1990). Hispanic families in the 1980s: A decade of research. *Journal of Marriage and the Family, 52,* 1015–1024.

Wertsch, J.V. (Ed.). (1985). *Culture, communication, and cognition: Vygotskian perspectives.* Cambridge: Cambridge University Press.

Weil, D. (1998). *Towards a critical multicultural literacy: Theory and practice for education for liberation.* New York: Peter Lang.

Willis, A. I., García, G.E., & Harris, V.J. (Eds.). (1997). *Multicultural Issues in Literacy Research and Practice, Journal of Literacy Research, 30*(2).

Willis, A. I. (in press). Dissin' and disremembering: Motivation and culturally and linguistically diverse students' literacy learning. *Reading and Writing Quarterly.*

Willis, A., & Johnson, J. (1999, November). *Reader response and social action.* Paper presentation at the annual conference of the National Reading Conference, Orlando, FL.

Willis, A., & Harris, V. (2000). Political acts: Literacy learning and teaching. *Reading Research Quarterly, 35*(1), 72–88.

CHAPTER 2

MULTICULTURAL BELIEF: A GLOBAL OR DOMAIN-SPECIFIC CONSTRUCT?

An Analysis of Four Case Studies

Jyotsna Pattnaik

Abstract: The multicultural beliefs of teachers/preservice teachers have been generally studied with the assumption that multucultural belief is a global construct. Therefore, one either believes in all domains of diversity (such as race/ethnicity, social class, gender, exceptionalities, etc.) or does not believe in any kind of diversity. Because of its approach to conduct a domain-spedific analysis of participants' multicultural beliefs, this ethnographic study is unique in its scope.

The study was conducted with four highly effective early childhood practitioners in western Pennsylvania. Drawing on various qualitative research designs (such as ethnography, case study, narrative research), the study examined participants' beliefs/practices about various domains of diversity, as well as the levels of complexity in which these beliefs were held and practices were exhibited toward a particular domain (or domains) of diversity according to Banks' (1994) four hierarchal levels (contribution, additive, transformative, and social action). The findings suggest that there was lack of recognition or inclusion of different domains of diversity in participants' formal definition of multicultural education and in their practices. Only one participant exhibited a maximum of three domains of diversity (race/ethnicity, social class, gender) both in her beliefs/practices. Race/ethnicity appeared in the formal definition of multicultural education by all the participants. Participants' classroom practices were consistent with their beliefs regarding a particular domain(s) of diversity. The study raises some important questions for teacher education programs: (a) How do we plan our inservice and preservice preparation so that students understand the historical, philosophical, moral, and political bases of multicultural education in general and the rationale for including many domains of diversity in particular?; (b) How do teacher educators' and teacher education departments' beliefs and practices affect their students' monocultural or domain-specific beliefs of diiversity?; (c) How do we reconceptualize and implement the construct, "teacher effectiveness," so that multicultural effectiveness becomes an integral part of identifying teachers' and preservice teachers' effectiveness?; and (d) What role could national/state accreditation/certification agencies play to institute a comprehensive concept of multicultural education?

INTRODUCTION

What makes multicultural education unique (at least ideologically) from analogous postmodern attempts of "curriculum reform" is its promise to include many disenfranchised groups (e.g., racial/ethnic minorities, the poor, the females, the gay/lesbians, people with disabilities, to name but a few) into the sociopolitical arena of American schools and society. Yet, this broader inclusion (of many referent groups) is ignored by teachers (Marshall, 1994), battled over by scholars (Bossard, 1994), and overlooked by researchers (Grant, 1994). Invariably, race/ethnicity (mostly with a tourist approach) predominate the discourse and practices of multicultural education in public schools and college classrooms. Rarely one encounters lessons or unit ideas on gender, social class, sexual orientation, and exceptionalities. If beliefs influence teachers' knowledge and practices (Pajares, 1993), then one wonders if teachers' preference for some domains of diversity over others is a function of their belief system which does not assign equal importance to many domains of human diversity. Studies on teachers' beliefs about diversity mostly focus on monocultural versus multicultural beliefs. This particular qualitative study examines four highly effective (through nominations from different sources) early childhood practitioners' beliefs about and practices of various domains of diversity, as well as the levels of complexity (Banks', 1994 levels of multicultural curriculum reform) in which these beliefs were held and practices were exhibited.

Defining Multicultural Education

Multiculturalism has been defined from many different standpoints. For the purpose of this paper, the discussion will be limited to the issue of inclusion of various groups in multicultural discourse and practices. Perhaps, no other dissonance has divided the multicultural community as seriously as the debate over the qualifications of referent groups for inclusion within the discipline of multicultural education (Pope, 1995). This debate originates from two conflicting viewpoints over the issue of "centrality" in multicultural education. Some scholars (Banks, 1992; Grant, 1998; Nieto, 1992) argue for an expanded scope because of their belief that issues involving many domains of diversity are equally important in the discourse of pluralism, whereas others perceive race and ethnicity as the central domain of multicultural discourse and the rest are peripheral. In fact, Gay (1983, 1998) argues that inclusion of other forms of diversity diverts the attention from "white racism" and the plight of ethnic minorities. Scholars who defend an exclusive definition of multiculturalism (inclusion of only ethnic and racial minorities) also identify the impossibility and hollowness of an inclusive agenda where no issue can be addressed deeply (Marshall, 1994). On the other hand, advocates of different groups present their arguments to merit their inclusion within the multicultural discourse. For example, drawing similarities between racial/ethnic minorities and the sexual minority population, Pope (1995) writes,

> ...the identity formation tasks racial and ethnic minorities must accomplish are the same for sexual minorities ... and finally that gay and lesbian oppression as well as the results of that oppression by the majority culture are very real, with real effects on real people's lives, development, and careers. (p. 301)

Various emancipatory movements, such as feminism, ethnic studies, afrocentrism, gay/lesbian rights movement, and biracial/multiracial movement, have emerged at various points in the postmodern era. What combines these philosophies under the banner of postmodern scholarship is their struggle to give voice to one or the other historically marginalized group. What makes multicultural education common, yet distinct, from other postmodern movements is its scope and complexity. It not only includes and analyzes issues involving race, ethnicity, gender, exceptionalities, and sexual orientation as individual issues, but also draws our attention to the overlapping spaces where these issues operate simultaneously (e.g., the intersection of race, gender, and social class). Musil (1996) highlights multiculturalism's complexity and comprehensiveness that acknowledge people's multiple, simultaneous, and intersecting identities as compared to singular identities professed by other liberatory movements. Musil writes:

> ...more often than not, in the early decades, those identities were studied as if you had to pick only one ... black studies was typically about only men. Women's studies was typically only about white women. Gay and lesbian studies had no practicing Christian or Jews. And none of the three paid much attention to those in their group who were old, working-class, or disabled. (p. 227)

Thompson and Tyagi (1993) rightly term multicultural education as an expansive and inclusive scholarship advocating the need for an interdisciplinary approach that embraces perspectives of many different groups. In fact, multiculturalism's essence lies in its egalitarian attitude of addressing every group's problems with equal importance "without grading, comparing, or making them as better or worse than one another and without denying the very distinct and complementary or even contradictory perspectives that each group brings with it" (Pedersen, 1991, p. 4). Unfortunately, present perceptions and practices of multicultural education by preservice/classroom teachers and teacher educators are mostly limited to race and ethnicity (Marshall, 1994). Gender-related instruction is reported to be absent in teacher education programs (Mader & King, 1995), as are issues related to social class (Singer, 1996). Instruction related to children with exceptional needs for regular preservice teachers is very limited (Fender & Fiedler, 1990) and discussions on sexual orientation in college classrooms is still a taboo issue (Britzman, 1995). The lack of broader inclusion also permeates the field of empirical research. From his review of empirical research, Grant (1994) concludes that very few studies in the field focus on race, class, and gender simultaneously.

Circularity in Teachers' Beliefs, Knowledge, and Practices

The study acknowledges the current exhortation to include teacher belief as a valuable psychological construct in teacher education programs and as a legitimate field of inquiry (Pajares, 1993). Findings from a growing volume of research on teachers' belief unequivocally reject the naive notion of knowledge as an uncontaminated and self-contained domain (Vavrus & Ozcan, 1996). In fact, empirical research suggests that teachers' beliefs serve as important indicators of teacher knowledge, teacher decision making, and teacher behavior (Bennett, 1997).

Belief systems seem to rely more on affective and subjective evaluations than knowledge systems (Abelson, 1979; Nespor, 1987) and individual beliefs have a strong root in the process of enculturation and social construction (Pajares, 1993). When situated in the context of multicultural belief, it is not surprising then to understand why some people tend to hold a monocultural belief or why those who hold multicultural beliefs do not assign equal importance to various forms of diversity. People who emphasize monocultural beliefs do not perceive the affective significance of diversity either for themselves or for the society. In the same vein, teachers' beliefs about diversity tend to assign higher affective value for some domain of diversity over others. In other words, in a ladder of hierarchy, some forms of diversity seem to receive lower or higher value than the others. Because of the strong familial/societal influence on individual beliefs, the forms of diversity that receive higher attention (or inattention) may have been nurtured (or ignored) through the influence of family and community.

What makes the role of belief quintessentially significant as well as alarming is its undeniable and pervasive influence on classroom practices (Zembylas, 1998). The findings of the last two decades of carefully conducted research (both quantitative and qualitative) highlight the inseparable connection between teachers' belief and their behavior in the classroom (Pajares, 1993). In fact, the belief-behavior connection operates in a circular fashion. Nespor (1987) writes, "Beliefs influence perceptions that influence behaviors that are consistent with and that reinforce, the original beliefs" (p. 317). Explaining belief-praxis interrelationship, Siegel (1985) maintains that the intensity with which a belief is held will determine the occurrence of the actual behavior. Therefore, when a teacher holds strong beliefs toward a particular domain(s) of diversity, there is a greater possibility that his/her classroom practice will include that particular domain(s) of diversity.

Levels of Complexity in Multicultural Beliefs and Practices

Banks' (1994) approaches to "curriculum reform" served as a guide post to categorize the complexity in participants' multicultural beliefs and practices. Banks' model incorporates four levels which are hierarchically placed: *Level 1: The contributions approach* (focuses on heroes, holidays, and discrete cultural elements); *Level 2: The additive approach* (content, concepts, themes, and perspectives are added to the curriculum without changing its structure; *Level 3: The transformative approach* (the structure of curriculum is transformed to foster multicultural perspectives among students); and *Level 4: The social action approach* (involves students making decisions and actions on important social issues).

In the recent years, multicultural education has faced severe criticisms, especially from its adherents for its inability to deal with broader societal issues (Giroux, 1995). Multicultural education for example, has become a study of "others" not about self (challenging one's own world views, taken-for-granted privileges, self's passivity to take action against biased practices), learning the glamorous, exotic aspects of ethnic cultures (heroes/holidays) and not reflecting and analyzing the messy, hidden, and unjust historical as well as existing macropolitics that marginalize minority groups. The cultural tourism approach to pluralism, in fact, serves as a perfect scapegoat for teacher education faculty to avoid the tensions and conflicts that are inevitable from the discussions on much deeper issues of pluralism that threaten cultural, economic, and political parity among different groups (Newfield & Gordon, 1996). Gollnick (1992), and Vavrus and Ozcan (1996) point out that, in most multicultural courses in colleges and universities, there is a failure in the content to provide a critical or systematic framework to understand issues of gender, class, and ethnicity both as societal and institutional practices. At best, the approach used by teacher educators is limited to "human relations" approach (Messner, 1994) or Banks' (1994) "additive/contribution" approach (Vavrus & Ozcan, 1996). In summary, there is a growing consensus within the multi-cultural community to detour multicultural education from its much traveled route of uncritical stand and to explore its "social transformative power" (Jackson & Solis, 1995, p. 3).

As a researcher standing on a particular theoretical platform, it is important that I clarify my position within the context of this particular study. My own minority status crosses the borders of many domains of diversity such as race/ethnicity, gender, language, and religion. I am a nonwhite, non-Christian woman of international origin whose first language is not English. My passion for a comprehensive definition of multicultural education comes from my own multiple identities, as well as my critical engagement with issues related to many marginalized groups. The present in which I position myself also comes from my constant shifting of status, between the majority (the privileged) and the minority (the marginalized) within the contexts of two different countries. This particular positionality endows me with a very unique yet uncommon opportunity to understand the issues of privilege versus marginality from both locations (being within and outside the boundary). By virtue of my multiple identities and positionalities, I see the connecting strands that result from marginalizations across groups and the need to address the issue of marginalization while keeping in mind the unique historical and contemporary realities of different groups.

THE PRESENT INVESTIGATION

As a topic of study, teachers' multicultural beliefs are presently drawing greater attention among researchers (Gormley, 1995). However, no research attempt has been made to clarify multicultural belief as a "global or domain-specific construct." A review of literature revealed that researchers examining participants' definition of multicultural education analyzed their data on the basis of complexities of participants' beliefs (human relation versus critical multiculturalism approach) or stages of their practices on Banks' (1994) four hierarchical stages. Interestingly, the literature review conducted by the researchers included references to a broader definition of multicultural education (race/class/gender/exceptionalities, etc.). Those studies which included more than one domain of diversity in their tools of inquiry did not conduct separate analysis for those different domains, suggesting a global nature of the construct (one either believes in all domains of diversity or does not believe in any domain of diversity). From his review of research, Grant (1994) writes, "Most of the studies focused on race/ethnicity, some focused on race and class, and a few on race and language. However, very few focused on race, class and gender"

(p. 14). Because of its focus to conduct a domain-specific analysis of participants' multicultural beliefs and practices, this particular study is unique in its approach.

The following question guided the present investigation: How do participants define multicultural education (on Banks', 1994, four levels of multicultural curriculum reform) with regard to different domains of diversity such as race/ethnicity, social class, gender, physical abilities, language, sexual orientation, and religion? As I collected data through interviews, participant observations, and document analysis, I also examined the consistency between participants' beliefs (as revealed through interviews and informal discussions) and their classroom practices. Participants' personal and professional life stories also encouraged me to explore the role of contextual factors such as life experiences, professional contexts, and training play on participants' beliefs regarding different domains of diversity.

METHODOLOGICAL APPROACH

A qualitative framework (Lincoln & Guba, 1985) with emphasis on phenomenology, ethnography, and narrative studies served as the methodological landscapes for the study. A phenomenological approach of interviewing the participants was approached to explore "the way people experience their world, what it is like for them, how to best understand them" (Tesch, 1990, p. 68). The ethnographic data collection procedures, such as participant observation and document analysis, were adopted to corroborate participants' beliefs with their practices. The study also borrowed heavily from the tradition of "narrative studies" (Ayers, 1992; Connelly & Clandinin, 1994) and Lawrence-Lightfoot's (1983) work on "portraiture as a method of inquiry" that allowed participants to perceive and construct self through the intersection of personal experiences with time and space, as well as through available discourse of the context. This particular study was part of a larger project which focused many aspects of participants' early childhood philosophies/practices. Multicultural education was explored in isolation as well as in connection with other aspects of the participants' pedagogical philosophies/practices to perceive the "gestalt" that characterizes one's personal/professional self and guides one's practices.

Participants

This particular qualitative study was conducted with four "highly effective" early childhood practitioners from western Pennsylvania. Effective teachers were selected with the assumption that they would be able to reflect on issues involving self, school, and society (Zeichner & Liston,

1987). Nominations from various sources (early childhood professors in the area, the Pennsylvania Association for the Education of Young Children, Academic Alliance in Early Childhood Education, building administrators) served as the basis for identifying "effective teachers" for the study. In the final phase, the researcher selected four practitioners based on professional experiences (preservice teacher/beginning teacher/experienced teacher), reviews of resume (to garner professional success/involvement), the variation in setting (rural/urban), and diversity in racial background.

Data Source

The following data sources were included in the study: (a) discourse that was formal and informal, direct and indirect (metaphors/pictorial representations, questions on images of an ideal early childhood curriculum/content/pedagogy, parent-home connections, assessment, school policies); (b) field notes (lesson teaching, classroom interaction, classroom environment; (c) document analysis (dialogue journal writings, contact logs, lesson plans, pictorial representations, philosophy statements of student teachers, curriculum vitae, recommendation letters, evidences of involvement in professional organizations, and the researcher's journal entries).

Data Analysis and Interpretation

Data collection, data analysis, and literature review proceeded simultaneously for each individual participant. The process of analysis was "a layered one in that, each time data were analyzed, the texts that were generated as a consequence of that analysis became a new source of data" (Alverman, Commeyars, Young, Randall, & Hinson, 1997, p. 78) for further inquiry or for further readings. For example, data analysis of the first phase, preliminary interview with participants, provided directions for the second phase, classroom observation and document analysis, which, in turn, led to further discussions with participants for clarifications/rationale and to the exit interview. A combination of inductive (layered nature of the data) and deductive (matching the data to Banks', 1994, model) procedures were approached for data gathering and analysis.

The data analysis included two major aspect: *analysis of individual portraits* and *cross-case analysis*. During the analysis of individual portraits, I subjected the data gathered from various sources (described before) to a qualitative content analysis (Simpson & Nist, 1997). The qualitative content analysis proceeded through four stages. In the first stage, reviewing and coding of questionnaire responses, transcriptions of the interview/informal discussions, field notes, documents, observation checklists were completed. In the second phase, categories for different domains of diversity were defined and so were the properties and dimensions for each category. In the third phase, the categories were solidified through rereading and discussion with the participants if needed. In the last phase, a descriptive commentary was written for each category based on the data collected from various sources. The data analysis for each individual participant's beliefs and practices was approached from both *scope* (domains of diversity) as well as *complexity* or levels of understanding (on Banks' 1994, model of curriculum reform). The analysis resulted in individual portraits (of multicultural beliefs/practices).

The process of cross-case analysis was conducted keeping in mind the purposes of the study. Major categories emerged consequently through a "constant comparison" method of comparing the individual case studies (Bogdan & Biklen, 1994).

PORTRAITS OF FOUR TEACHERS

Each portrait revealed many unaccounted moments, unexpressed thoughts, and unarticulated practices in participants' lives which remained tacit yet assigned meaning to their identity as a teacher. To search, describe, and interpret these tacit, hermeneutically organized experiences, and to locate their deep-seated roots, my narrative adopted indirect pathways (besides formal/informal discourses, and classroom observation), such as inscribing meaning to interpretive activities (images, pictures, metaphors, and career graphs), digging childhood memories, describing family events, and many more.

CASE STUDY 1: MELISSA BALDWIN (STUDENT TEACHER)

Schooling is a power game adults play at the expense of children's lives.
—Melissa Baldwin

Melissa Baldwin was student teaching in a second grade classroom of a remote rural school in western Pennsylvania. The school building housed only first and second grade classrooms. The school was part of a quiet residential low-income white community with a handful of minority families. The virtual monoracial composition of the student population was in sharp contrast to Melissa's own childhood experiences. She grew up in a big, progressive suburb outside of Washington, DC. Starting from high school through her college years, Melissa has spent her spare time in summer camps for children, in day-care centers, in community improvement centers, and in tutoring programs. Her reasons for choosing teaching as a career ("You touch lives, flesh and blood. Everything you do, you see its impact on kids right there. What could be more rewarding than that?")

reflects her strong conviction to reach all children through teaching. "Shadows on the wall, Noises down the hall, Life does not frighten me at all," this passage from Maya Angelou's poem (1993) in picture book format, *Life Does Not Frighten Me At All,* (posted in the back of her desk) is Melissa's favorite reminder to herself and her students not to let their own voices be subdued by the voices of authority. From my data analysis I gathered that social class and race/ethnicity aspects of diversity predominated her discussions and practices.

Race/Ethnicity and Social Class

Melissa's discussion on these two domains of diversity included both individual as well as intersecting aspects (poor children of minority backgrounds). Because of the reflective and enlightened nature of her discussions on school policies and practices that marginalize low-income and minority children/families and her constant struggle to change children's and teachers' attitudes toward diversity, I interpreted her beliefs and practices of diversity with regard to social class and race at Banks' transformative and social action levels. She stated, "Most of the efforts on multicultural education focus on acceptance of diversity which is not enough. Not just that children accept differences, but look at them as enriching experiences, as something valuable and necessary for life. So celebrate it as something special." As the president of the student chapter of the National Association of Education of the Young Children, Melissa has been involved with discussions of race related issues in her university. Her concern for diversity issues was evident in her letter to the provost of her university to open up more avenues for students to organize/participate in race related discussions and action in the campus.

Politics of Tracking

Melissa was concerned about the politics of grouping children into different reading groups. During her student teaching experience, she realized that intelligence and achievement are not often the criteria for placement in lower groups. Many times children are put into lower groups because of their family backgrounds, or they are perceived as behavior problems by the teachers and administrators. Invariably, children who are in the low ability groups are children who are from low-income or minority backgrounds or have some problems (as perceived by the teachers) in the family. To clarify her position, she continued,

> It is a very small district. The teachers are not very respectful of students' rights. There is a lack of regard for children's privacy and our teachers' lunch room is a gossip center. They know about every student's family background and the family problems of each one. Every time a child or a family member

does something that offends the teacher, you hear about it in the teachers' room. Things like that always happen with the children in lower groups. I have found that these children are very intelligent. Part of the reason why these children are misbehaving is that they are bored.

Giving a concrete example, she talked about a child named Don. "None of the teachers like Don. They say he is such a bad seed, a bad kid," Melissa confided. Even if he gets all A's Don remains in the middle group. The middle group remains in Melissa's classroom. In that way, Don stays with his own classroom teacher and does not become a burden to any other teacher. She was also skeptical of the accuracy of the criteria and the materials used to group children. The tracking in her school is determined by two criteria: (1) the child's chapter test scores in the reading series, and (2) the comments from the teacher of the last year. Referring to the chapter test she said, "It is just one test. Unfortunately this is the first thing the teachers look at and they do not realize how limited it is. It is just one number. It does not tell anything about the child."

Politics of Retention

"If Public Law 142 guarantees provision of services for children who are in need of assistance, where does the question of retention come from?" Melissa wondered aloud. She reminded me, "Did you hear during math class today, one boy (an African-American child) was shouting, 'We learned it last year, we did this last year.' He was retained last year. So he gets bored learning the same material and starts talking in the class." There were many of them in her class who were retained. She said, "I can see it causes a lot of distraction already now in the second grade. They have gotten a sense of their destiny, and where they are going to be. Every time their next grade teacher opens up their file, the first thing he/she is going to see is that they were retained in first grade."

Politics of Standardized and Readiness Tests

Melissa stated, "It is public education. We ought to accept everybody to be inclusive. It is time for schools to be ready for children at whatever level they have come in. Moreover, all these standardized tests are very one-dimensional and judging children with one test will be a big mistake. What kind of readiness test can really tell the truth about a child?" For Melissa, all these tests serve the administrators' and the teachers' interest, not the needs and interests of children. To further clarify her viewpoints she commented, "Admitting the so-called academically ready students will free the administrators from making extra accommodations for the 'not so ready' children and, of course, it is less work for teachers." Melissa had introduced a variety of assessment strategies such as peer evaluation, portfolios, checklists, student journals, individual and group presentations, and context related spelling instructions in her teaching.

Image of an Ideal Classroom

Melissa's image of an ideal classroom is a laboratory. According to her, a laboratory is a place where environmental features (space, tools, seating arrangement) and children's emotional needs (trust, freedom, enjoyment) are appropriately catered to create a conducive setting for experimentation, discovery/prediction, and open exploration for *all* children. She believed that a laboratory approach promotes a learning to learn mentality in children so that they could become lifelong learners. Here children are not tracked or retained. Teachers carry high expectations for all children irrespective of social class, race, and gender. Children who were tracked into low or medium ability reading and math groups appeared to be engaged in Melissa's lessons. Her second graders' "Undersea Antarctica Project" was awarded by Carnegie Science Center. For their dinosaur project, children wrote to different museums in the United States and Canada for information. She had designed many cooperating learning activities (peer evaluation, proofreading activities, group projects) to provide children a sense of success and to bridge the gap between the differently tracked children in her classroom. Her lesson activities incorporated the issues of diversity. For example, her lesson activity on fractions included discussion on the issue of equality and fairness in distribution. Whatever units she taught, she made sure that her literature library included books from other cultures to go with the unit.

Home-school Connection

Melissa's strong conviction on the issue came from her experiences during her student teaching in a school district where educational decisions were in the hands of administrators and teachers. Students and parents had no say. Most of the parents in her school were from low-income backgrounds. She commented, "Parents are just there to fill out the paper work. They are so out of touch with their children's classroom. Children need to have some power to be a part of the classroom rules and in the choice of their own learning experiences." She had seen the abuse of autonomy in the hands of some teachers. She questioned, "Why do my cooperating teacher and some other teachers in the building put only comments about negative behavior in children's folders? That is what my cooperating teacher shares with the parents. I have been making copies of journals, work samples, and many other things to put in children's folders."

In her own teaching, she made attempts to open the process of communication between the parents and herself. Throughout her dinosaur unit, Melissa sent letters to parents requesting various materials and explaining the activities they were doing for the unit. At the end of the unit, she designed a "prehistoric party" for parents where children performed the role of dinosaur experts to share their knowledge about dinosaurs with the parents. She was thrilled with the high percentage of parent attendance.

Conclusion

In a traditional rural school, Melissa was instrumental in bringing many positive changes in her mentoring teachers' attitudes toward multiculturalism, developmentally appropriate practices, whole language approach, authentic assessment, and parental involvement. In the teacher lounge, she had freely discussed the ills of tracking, retention, standardized tests as the sole method of assessment, and students' and families' rights to privacy. Her unconditional trust of her knowledge base/ideological viewpoints and her defiance and non-conforming attitude allowed her to move beyond the approved myths of public schooling.

CASE STUDY 2: MICHAEL TOWNSEND (BEGINNING TEACHER)

Believe me! It will not take that much time for black children to understand the power dynamics in U. S. society ... Before these children hear their mother's lullaby, they hear the guns and police sirens.
—Michael Townsend

Michael Townsend was a 26-year-old African American male teaching in a predominantly black school in Pittsburgh. The school served children from four different neighborhoods. Children who attended the school were usually from the least-privileged population of the city. Michael revealed that more than 90% of the children were on some type of public assistance and received free or reduced lunches. The school was surrounded by housing projects, dilapidated buildings, unkempt streets, and shabby sidewalks bearing the living testimonies of neglect and apathy of the government and flight and silence of the affluent. Michael's school was a leader in the urban reform movement of the city and had instituted many innovative projects.

Michael realized the importance of strong leadership for his community. Voicing his reasons for choosing a teaching career, Michael stated, "The need for me in the profession preceded my need for it.... That is why I stick to it. I have accepted the responsibility and challenge of educating poor black children...." Michael confided that love and caring is very important for poor black children who carry bruised and wounded self-images and a thirst for adult acceptance.

Race/ethnicity and Social Class

Michael's discourse and practice of multicultural education focused on two domains of multiculturalism, the issues of race/ethnicity and social class especially as it relates to African Americans. His understanding of the issue of race was at Bank's transformative and social action levels. According to him, inclusion of many different domains of diversity in multiculturalism had diluted the discussion of racism and the plight of poor blacks in American society.

Disempowerment of Black Culture

Michael discussed many issues surrounding children in low-income black communities. He explained the ways African-American children are disempowered in school. Michael discussed three forms of power: language is power, knowledge is power, and choice is power. According to Michael, schools disempower minority children by denying them access to their group's language and culture. He believed that by not validating minority children's culture, history, and heritage and by forcing them to accept the mainstream culture, schools limit minority children's power to participate in social discourse within and outside the classroom. While criticizing the power dynamics in American society, Michael also discussed the responsibility of minority youth to make informed choices, to stay away from the ills of the society that surround them, "I want them to be able to discriminate what they truly want, what is meaningful for their lives as opposed to what is given to them by society."

The Cultural Biases in Standardized Tests

Michael viewed standardized tests as implicit strategies to diempower young black children. Rationalizing black children's low scores on standardized tests, Michael stated, "The individualism, the spirit of competition, the all day seat-work, does not reflect components of African American culture. African American culture values kinship, cooperation, and communality." He also discussed the cultural biases in standardized tests, both from the point of view of language and contexts. Michael recalled a test item, "What is the thing to do if you lose a ball that belongs to one of your friends?" According to the test designer, the best answer is to buy him a new ball. The worse answer is to apologize for losing the ball. But, Michael emphasized, "Some of the choices a child can easily eliminate. This item penalizes the child for realizing that he cannot afford to replace the ball. In this way the test is biased against poor children."

Culturally Responsive Pedagogy

Michael defined culturally responsive pedagogy as, "Understanding, respecting and valuing the culture of the individual and using those characteristics and information to reach them." He continued, "There is no excuse for teachers to go through the years of schooling and not spend the time to get to know and study the students they will be teaching." Michael's understanding of his children was expressed in his discourse and practices. For example, Michael described the behavior of some children who have been involved in some kinds of aggressive play during the recess time. He stated:

> ...rather than punishing them for their actions or taking away their free play, I spend time playing with them. I try to show them a safer more appropriate way of using their physical energy, to usefully channel the aggression they have inside them.

Michael's image, "teacher is a sculptor," expressed symbolically his belief in understanding children. Michael equated the sculptor's medium with children's potentiality, such as interests, intelligence, creativity, and imagination. He said, "As a sculptor-teacher, my craftsmanship, involves listening to the child carefully to understand what the child wants. An important tool of a sculptor-teacher is a culturally relevant curriculum which includes appropriate resource materials, support systems, and teaching strategies. Michael also believed that it was necessary to validate a child as an individual besides his membership in the group, so he conducted a family study with his kindergarten students. They talked about the structure of their families, number of family members, their occupations, family hobbies and outings, favorite foods, and variations in their skin colors and hair textures.

Understanding the Out-of-School Curriculum

Discussing the drugs, the drive-by shootings, and police brutality surrounding the lives of children in his classroom, Michael stated, "They do not get many opportunities to talk about the things that bother them.... It is like suppressing anxiety.... That is one of the reasons why I am a big supporter of recess—giving students an opportunity to just kind of go wild, to just let it out. I call it 'controlled chaos." During the creative writing time, Michael encouraged children to express their feelings and concerns. (Children wrote a shooting scenario they had witnessed, or an older brother's death from taking an overdose of illegal drug, or an uncle who recently returned from jail with signs of brutal police beatings.) With a cautionary note Michael later added, "Some teachers use a student's background as an excuse for the student not to learn. In fact, some people use it as an excuse not to teach because they think that children coming from certain backgrounds cannot learn." Michael feels that teachers need to change their expectations. He emphasized, "The background may be rough and dark, but the future does not have to be."

Classroom as a Workshop

His practice was consistent with his image, "the classroom as a workshop." Lack of financial resources did not deter his determination to include relevant materials in his classroom for children to manipulate. Most of the materials such as old computer keyboards, used kitchen accessories, measuring cups, cardboard, and recycled materials were collected by Michael. In his classroom workshop, children were exposed to work-related experiences, visited various community places and interviewed workers. He believed that it was important for his children to see the African American work force and learn the significant contributions made by African Americans to U.S. society.

Conclusion

Embedded in insight, action, and vision, this particular biography portrayed an African-American teacher's unconditional trust in the power of education to rescue poor black children from the marginality of their lives. While recognizing the marginality in black children's lives, Michael was determined to transform that imposed marginality to what hooks (1990) perceived as a self-chosen "site of resistance, a location of radical openness and possibilities" (p. 22) through a pedagogy of empowerment. Empowered with the critical knowledge, language, and informed choices, he hoped his students would be able to fight the realities of "white privilege and power" and overcome all that are impediments to success.

CASE STUDY 3: DONNA FOSTER (EXPERIENCED TEACHER)

Mainstreaming prepares children for their adult life and the real world. They will be prepared to understand/accept/appreciate diversity in people around them.
—Donna Foster

Donna Foster has taught for 15 years in a rural elementary school in western Pennsylvania. At the time of the study, the school had a student population of 393 and as was typical in rural towns of Pennsylvania, white middle class children predominated. The culturally diverse student population of the school constituted around 30% of the total population and most of these students were children of students or faculty from the local university and from a subsidized housing complex close to the school. The school was a pioneer in instituting mainstreaming in its building and Donna was the first teacher who volunteered to experiment with the idea in her classroom. Donna's metaphor, "curriculum as a puzzle piece," included special need students (along with parents, grandparents, community). Donna's mastery of the three D's, determination, devotion, and diligence (her criteria for success), was evident in her winning of the Best Teacher Award from the district for her success with mainstreaming.

Race/Ethnicity

Donna's formal definition of diversity included only ethnic/cultural diversity and was at the additive level of Banks' (1994) model. She perceived diversity as separate from the central curriculum. She stated, "Whenever the festival time comes, the mothers come and talk about the festivals and bring some special food." During the time of this study, she invited a Jewish parent for the festival Hanukkah. Minority parents cooked ethnic food for children. Donna shared honestly her lack of expertise and knowledge in multicultural education. Donna completed her bachelors 15 years ago and later took graduate level courses. However, the university did not emphasize multicultural education in its teacher preparation programs. According to her, the multicultural ideas practiced in her classrooms came from teacher resource books, workshop sessions, and fellow teachers in the building. She shared her desire to know more about multicultural education.

Physical Abilities

Donna did not include physical disability in her definition of multicultural education. However, her practices and discussions of the issue was at Banks' (1994) social action level where regular education children in her classroom supported their special education peers in every possible way. Her pictorial representation "curriculum as a puzzle piece," included special education children as an integral piece of that puzzle. Without any training in special education, she took the risk of volunteering for mainstreaming in her classroom. She involved herself with training programs, conferences, workshops, panel discussions related to mainstreaming. She also visited programs in other districts. However, according to Donna, most of her learning came from life-skill children themselves. She confided, "They have taught me so much. Everyone's disabilities are different and they need different attention. The boy with cerebral-palsy who walks clumsily and trips and falls every second will take different attention than the one who cannot walk at all."

Going Beyond What Is Expected

To the question, "Please describe one of the most memorable moments of your teaching life," Donna provided an anecdote that included her success in helping Nathan, a spina bifida child, who was paralyzed from the waist down and was confined to a wheel chair with braces around his legs and upper body, to walk with crutches. Donna sought help from the nurse and the physical education teacher and learned how to lift Nathan from his chair and put him on the floor without hurting her own back. The most memorable day of her life, for Donna, was the day when Nathan walked

down the hall with his crutches to receive the award as the child who had
worked hard that year to achieve.

Building an Emotional Culture Through Mainstreaming

Donna voiced her strong belief about the positive aspects of mainstreaming and the need for regular education children to learn and support their life-skill peers. Building an emotional culture through
mainstreaming was her goal of teaching. She was amazed from her experiences with mainstreaming how empathetic young children could become.
Every year Donna gets at least one life-skill child. During the time of my
observation, Donna had a life-skill child in her class who appeared normal
but she did not speak. The regular education children developed a loving
relationship with her. If she was painting something and a strand of hair
fell in her eyes, somebody would gently brush it back. If she was confused
about crayon colors, they helped her select particular colors. Donna also
set boundaries between independence and dependence so that emotional
attachment did not turn to "pity." With the permission and support of parents, Donna allowed some of the life-skill children to talk to other children
about their disabilities with a belief that it would facilitate connections
among children.

Classroom as a Stage Where All Mixed In

Life-skill children in Donna's class participated in all kinds of activities,
such as field trips, talent shows, and other extracurricular activities. They
dressed up in costumes and did all kinds of dramatization along with the
other children. "On stage, you really cannot pick out the life-skill students
from the regular education students. They are all mixed in," Donna
remarked. She suggested that an ideal classroom is one where special education children should be an integral and meaningful part of all classroom
activities. For Donna, mainstreaming has contributed to the development of
social selves in the children in her classroom. She stated, "Mainstreaming prepares children for their adult life and the real world. They will be prepared to
understand, accept, and appreciate diversity in people around them."

Conclusion

Donna's practices with regard to exceptionalities portray her success in
constructing professional territory to harbor, nurture, and enact her vision
regarding the benefits of mainstreaming for all children. Lack of prior
training or support from peers, or even early failures did not deter her
from participating in it. Donna's strong emotional and academic involvement with the issue matched Banks' (1994) characteristics of the "social
action" level where regular education children in her kindergarten classroom were involved in supporting their life-skill peers.

CASE STUDY 4: BETTY WEBER (EXPERIENCED TEACHER)

The promises and prospects of an anti-bias curriculum are hidden in teachers,
the real curriculum planners.
—Betty Weber

The elementary school where Betty Weber taught the second grade was located in a rural university town in western Pennsylvania. The great majority of the students in the school were white. Betty's involvement in multicultural issues was revealed in her writings and national presentations. During her session at the annual meeting of the National Association of Education for Young Children, Betty, and copresenters from her school, candidly articulated the need for multicultural education even in classrooms where teachers perceive little diversity. She emphasized that it is impossible to find a setting where there is no diversity of any kind. The data analysis of this case study revealed three domains of diversity, race/ethnicity, gender, and social class, and I interpreted her beliefs and practices related to these three domains at Banks' (1994) transformative and social action levels.

Social Class

Equal Opportunity for All: A Symbolic Vision
"Two hands holding a seedling," was Betty's representation of an ideal early childhood curriculum. The two hands literally and figuratively expressed Betty's nurturing and caring approach to early education. These hands could very well be the responsible and determined hands of a teacher that hold a young child as tenderly as a fragile seedling, sensitive to its vulnerability to social, emotional, and environmental insecurities and odds. The hands also represented a nurturing environment or a firm foundation, one that very well could elicit possibilities still dormant within the child. Moreover, implicit in this metaphor was Betty's vision for the future, a hope, a longing to see the seedling become strong, healthy, and secure in its own way. According to her, these symbolic hands of the teacher are very important with regard to the issues of equity for all children, especially children from poverty who have been denied an equal access to life's opportunities.

Teachers' Treatment of Poor Children
As a child, Betty had witnessed how some teachers implicitly or explicitly perpetuated the myth that poverty is the fault of an individual. Betty described, "I can remember some of my teachers being very unfair to these children. I remember them saying very unkind, cruel things to these children in front of the class...." She confided, "I could see how differently they treated some children who probably needed a lot more help than I

did." In her teaching she made sure to rule out the naive, archaic arguments regarding social class and attempts to make children realize that poverty is not a fault or choice of an individual, rather, it is a circumstantial burden imposed on an individual. To convey her message, she selected literature books to engage children in this discussion.

Gender

Perpetuation of Gender Stereotypes by Schools and Society

Betty critically examined how gender relations are constructed socially. She cited one example of how parents' differential expectations do not allow girls to harbor interests toward disciplines traditionally defined for boys. The local university advertised a science program for girls through local schools. The program was a public program, but it was up to the individual parents to follow through and take their children to campus. To her regret, many parents did not take advantage of it. The school also did little to publicize or endorse the program. Betty also traced her own tracking into the teaching profession, in spite of her interest in the field of science, because of a lack of other career options for women in her rural community.

Betty offered an incident from her own sixth grade experience. She explained "I scored higher than all those smart boys. The superintendent said in front of the class, 'You boys better work hard. You cannot let a girl beat you.' I was embarrassed...." In fact, according to Betty, the superintendent reminded the boys of their superior place, now in school and later in society, a place defined for white males within a social order of patriarchal hegemony. In their presentation at the annual conference of the National Association for the Education of Young Children, Betty and her colleagues countered the myth that the monopolization of white males in occupations laden with power is purely the result of their superior intellects and extraordinary efforts. They argued that these privileges are granted to them because of the prevailing male domination in society's infrastructure.

Changing Children's Gender-role Stereotypes Through Reflective and Deliberate Strategies

On one occasion, Betty reflected that she was more comfortable with boys than girls because of her experience of raising two sons. She continued, "Because I have two sons, I feel more comfortable with boys. Sometimes I feel I give boys more attention. That's why I said I have to constantly work on it ... I ask myself, 'Am I talking to the girls as much as I pay attention to boys who are more verbal and assertive?'" After Betty read the research findings that teachers tend to call on boys more than girls during the instructional time, she requested colleagues to evaluate her behavior during teaching.

From her experiences, she had realized how children at an early age are tracked into the stereotypical gender-based interests. She herself was not a big fan of sports but most of the boys in her class were. She stated, "I learned to be accepting of that interest … I look at it to see what I can learn from it and, how I can grow from this. It also expands my own horizon, broadens my interest." Because of Betty's efforts, the entire class was engaged in the discussion of sports events during the morning news time. She had one boy in her class who liked poetry and was very artistic. "I always commend him for his interest in that area," Betty offered. Her hands-on, exploratory approach of teaching science units attracted quite a few girls who showed an interest in environmental objects/animals/plants, and processes. She also discussed the future possibilities of those interests in terms of pursuing a career.

Race/Ethnicity

Textuality and Curriculum

Corrigan (1987) defined textuality as "(1) what is taught, (2) how it is taught, (3) its social meaning" (p. 28). Betty's article on Native Americans published in *Young Children* truly captured her own conviction that a group's culture cannot be represented in the curriculum through a process of displacement, disjunction, and fragmentation. A continuity between historical and contemporary aspects in a culture need to be maintained, questions of injustices, omissions, and misinterpretations of historical and cultural facts need to be addressed, and the meaningfulness and impact of that knowledge on children need to be evaluated. She said that Dorris' (1991) article, "Why I Am Not Thankful for Thanksgiving," was an eye-opener for her to think more critically about debatable issues.

Enacting an Anti-bias Curriculum

Derman-Sparks and ABC Task Force' (1989) *Anti-bias Curriculum* is Betty's multicultural bible. She has adopted and adapted many activities from it. Her "family studies project" was adapted from this book in which children collected information about their family histories. One African American child's family revealed that the child's grandmother had applied to work on the ship *Titanic*, but was denied employment because of her skin color. Children discussed the unfairness in a practice which denied people equal opportunity. During my observation, her second graders read *Follow the Drinking Gourd*, a story about the underground railroad, slavery, and racism prior to the Civil War. The class discussed slavery, its origin, problems, and consequences and racism in the present U.S. society against black people. Because many of her children were interested in sports, Betty used Golenbock's (1990), *Teammates*, to engage them in a critical discussion on the issue of racism in sports and about Jackie Robinson, the first player from the Negro League to play major league baseball.

Resistance and Reflection: Pathways for Professional Development

Betty was the first teacher in her school district to resist the stereotypical approach of studying native American culture. She described, "There should be some dignity in representing a culture. In the name of cultural studies, they were doing things that seemed to misrepresent Native Americans, although they did not perceive it that way ... It was more of a lack of critical consciousness than anything else." Betty stated, "I could not participate. I had to talk to the parents about the reasons why it was not okay. The parents did see my point ... " Instead of doing Native American units Betty taught a theme on "harvesting celebrations" that focused on different cultures. Later, Betty, in collaboration with two colleagues, received a grant from the school district to purchase appropriate resources on teaching of Native American culture.

Conclusion

Amidst the negative manifestations of public schooling—testing bias, curriculum bias, hidden curriculum—this biography entailed the story of a teacher who instituted her own ideological context for practice. Slowly, Betty brought colleagues, parents, and children under the banner of her ideological tradition. The children enjoyed her class, colleagues collaborated, and parents consented. As a researcher/co-biographer, I imagine this portrait as an ideological artifact, which may leave a shadow behind for others to follow or may entice others with the intention of preparing ground for critical discourse on the nature and politics of schooling in America.

CROSS-CASE ANALYSIS, DISCUSSION, AND IMPLICATION

Based on the themes that emerged from the cross-case analysis, this section simultaneously provides criticisms of current practices and possibilities for the future.

Lack of Recognition or Inclusion of Different Domains of Diversity

The analysis revealed that there was a lack of recognition or inclusion of different domains of diversity in participants' formal definition of multicultural education and in their practices. Only one participant, Betty, in this study attributed equal emphasis to a maximum of three domains of diversity (race, social class, and gender) in beliefs and classroom practices. Melissa, a student teacher included race/social/class/gender/physical abilities/religion in her formal definition of multicultural education. However, social class and race/ethnicity aspects of diversity dominated her discourse/practices. As a student teacher she may not have had the freedom, opportunities, time, or expertise to translate her beliefs to practice. Interestingly, race/ethnicity aspects of diversity appeared in the formal definition of multicultural education of all the participants. However, in the case of Donna, an experienced teacher, and Malcolm, a beginning teacher, the definition of multicultural education was limited to this aspect only.

This particular finding suggests that colleges/universities need to design policy and pedagogical interventions in preservice/inservice programs that foster a true understanding of multicultural education. The historical as well as the contemporary realities of marginality and the future possibilities for many disenfranchised groups should be included in these discussions. Empirical inquiry on students' own definition of multicultural education and their reasons for exclusion or inclusion of certain referent groups needs to be conducted for successful planning and implementation of intervention strategies or course procedures. Marshall's (1994) concerns regarding impossibility and hollowness of inclusion of many domains of diversity in teacher preparation may be addressed by a planned distribution of the domains of diversity (accompanied with assessment of competence) into different courses/field teaching. The goal of multicultural education is to foster a balanced and positive attitude toward many domains of diversity, not a skewed perspective.

Connection Between Higher Levels of Understanding and the Preferred Domain(s) of Diversity

The data analysis revealed that participants have their preferred domain(s) of diversity. Commitment toward diversity in physical abilities was evident in beliefs and practices of one participant, Donna (experienced teacher). Commitment toward social class was evident in beliefs and practices of three participants, Michael, beginning teacher, Melissa, student teacher, and Betty, experienced teacher. Sensitivity toward gender issues was reflected only in Betty's practices.

Interestingly, whenever participants hold strong belief toward a particular domain(s) of diversity, their discourse and practices were at higher levels of Banks' (1994) model and vice versa. For example, Donna's, an experienced teacher, beliefs/practices for exceptionality was at social action level whereas race/ethnicity and social class were at Banks' additive level. As a teacher who volunteered for full inclusion in her classroom, Donna strongly felt that regular education children need to take responsibilities for their life-skill peers emotionally, socially, and academically. In her classroom, special education students took part in all activities with regular education students. Michael's understanding and practices of race and social class as it relates to African Americans were at Banks' transformative and social action level. For example, to root children (all black) in their ethnic heritage, Michael's literature selection drew primarily from African American culture; to expose children to an African American work force, he purposefully selected an all black-worker McDonald's for a field trip; to encourage African American parents' involvement in schools, he designed many activities for parent involvement in his curriculum.

This particular finding bears two important implications. First, it reiterates Abelson's (1979) and Nespor's (1987) suggestion that belief systems rely more on affective and subjective evaluation. The affective and subjective evaluation toward a particular belief are rooted in the process of enculturation and social construction (Pajares, 1993). For the participants in this study, the life and academic experiences fostered preferences for particular domain(s) of diversity. Therefore, the study strengthened the thesis that teacher education students do not come as blank states on which teacher educators can write the knowledge base of the field (Britzman, 1991). Engaging students to assess, challenge and change their prior beliefs toward diversity in general and various domains of diversity in particular should be an integral part of inservice/preservice preparation. It is important to note that because of the acquired nature of beliefs, it has been possible, though time consuming and difficult, for some programs/teacher educators to change students' perceptions toward issues involving women (McCall, 1994), homosexuals (Wallick, 1995), poor (Allen, 1993), and the disabled (Reber, Marshek, Glor-Scheib, & Noll, 1996) through cross-cultural discussions and exposure.

Secondly, the evidence of strong association between belief and practices, as revealed by participants in this study, is very important to the field of teaching. It suggests that the multicultural practices in public school classrooms will be significantly altered if the multicultural training could foster a strong commitment toward diversity among teachers. However, the commitment of teacher education departments toward multicultural education is very important in this context (Gollnick, 1992; Thompson & Tyagi, 1993). In the absence of a broader definition of diversity in curriculum and the trivializations that characterize multicultural curriculum transaction in college classrooms, one wonders if Ghosh and Tarrow's (1993) insinuation, "medium is the message" (p. 81) partly explains preservice/inservice teachers' skewed perceptions of multiculturalism. Therefore, multicultural training for teacher educators that focus on critical multiculturalism as well as rationale for inclusion of different referent groups in multicultural practices is warranted. Case studies of teachers/teacher educators who have successfully incorporated many domains of diversity in their curriculum should be included in multicultural training of teachers/ teacher educators.

Role of Background Factors in Fostering Domain-specific Multicultural Beliefs

The influence of background factors on participants' beliefs and practices was reflected in the individual case studies. Yet, background factors such as contexts, experiences, and training (as they impact multicultural beliefs) could be best described in intersection, not in isolation from each other. Moreover, this overlapping of background factors functioned in an idiographic manner, therefore, it was difficult to draw generalizations across cases. For example, Donna's experiences in mainstreaming classrooms may have influenced her sensitivity toward the issue. Participants who did not focus on this aspect were found to be in schools where mainstreaming was not yet introduced. With regard to social class, Michael's and Melissa's teaching experiences in low-income urban and rural schools respectively and Michael's life experiences as a poor black child were found to have contributed to their sensitivities to the issue. Betty's sensitivity to the issue stems from her own schooling experiences where she observed the blatant differential treatment of her peers from poverty backgrounds in the hands of her teachers and school administrators.

However, there were times when contextual evidences failed to provide sufficient reasons for participants' domain-specific multicultural beliefs/ practices. For example, Michael's single-minded focus on race/ethnicity, for the most part, grew out of his life and teaching experiences. On the other hand, a middle class white background and an all-white rural school teaching experience failed to provide any explanation regarding Betty's multifocused interest in social class, gender, and race/ethnicity. Her multicultural training, readings, and professional involvement with the issue was found to have influenced her beliefs and practices. Although three out of four participants were females in this study, only one participant reflected on gender issues and exposed her students to nongender specific roles. It was also difficult to garner whether contextual factors had reinforced, supplemented or instituted participants' beliefs/practices or vice versa. Further exploration in this matter is required.

This particular finding suggests that contextual factors and life experiences do influence one's beliefs and practices (Pajares, 1993). However, it also suggests the possibility of creating desired contexts to foster new learning. Teacher education courses can very well become sites for creating such contexts through providing authentic multicultural experiences and engaging students in critical multicultural issues. Cross-cultural learning strategies such as Schmidt's (1998) ABC's of cultural understanding and communication through autobiography, biography, and cultural analysis, will be helpful in creating desired contexts. In this particular strategy, teachers/preservice teachers interview a person from a particular marginalized group, across gender, racial/ethnic, sexual orientation, social class, religion, or language borders, and compare their own lives with that of their interviewee's. Such a model will help students who are predominantly white, middle class, protestant, English-speaking, and heterosexuals to learn and accept those who live outside these fixed societal boundaries. Moreover, the recruitment/retention of students and faculties from many referent multicultural groups may create contexts for students to challenge their own biases through available alternative role models and perspectives.

Redefining the Construct, "Teacher Effectiveness"

The study suggests "demystifying" the present conception of "teacher effectiveness." Teachers' personal qualities, subject matter expertise, general pedagogical excellence have dominated the conception of and research on teacher effectiveness, but not their multicultural effectiveness. Most of the participants in this study were nominated as effective by their peers, administrators, and educational organizations. However, the findings of this study reflect that in most part, participants' multicultural expertise in dealing with various domains of diversity were not considered as criteria for effectiveness by the nominators. In the same vein, the national/state accreditation/certification agencies have not emphasized many domains of diversity in their accreditation requirements of teacher education programs. This researcher suggests that critical pedagogy (Giroux, 1989) and culturally appropriate pedagogy (Ladson-Billings, 1995) should serve as important criteria to assess effectiveness of teachers, teacher educators and that of teacher education departments.

Future Research Implications

Future research may explore what role the teacher education curriculum plays instituting or reinforcing students' preferential beliefs about one or the other domains of diversity. Experimental and longitudinal studies need to be conducted to gather information on the systematic training of many domains of diversity and how the training influences students' attitude toward and practices of different domains of diversity.

CONCLUSION

It is concluded that for the participants in this study, multicultural belief was not a global construct that permeated all domains of diversity. It operated both at the level of acknowledgment of various domains of diversity, or lack of it, and levels of complexity. Moreover, teachers who are perceived as effective by others may or may not be multiculturally effective in many domains of diversity. Race/ethnicity seems to dominate the present perception of diversity. The historical connection of multicultural education with the earlier intercultural/ethnic studies movement should not be overlooked. However, as an "educational concept which is continually evolving" (Borland, 1994, p. 3), multicultural education needs to become more inclusive rather than exclusive. Defending multicultural education on the grounds of demographic changes shortchanges its ideological telos, its promise to address the issue of social equity and societal marginalizations faced by women, gay/lesbians, and many others.

REFERENCES

Abelson, R. (1979). Differences between belief systems and knowledge systems. *Cognitive Science, 3*, 355–366.

Allen, K.W. (1993). *Cultural diversity and collaboration: Educating teachers for the future.* (ERIC Document Reproduction Service No. ED 365 640)

Alverman, D.E., Commeyras, M., Young, J.P., Randall, S., & Hinson, D. (1997). Interpreting gendered discursive practices in classroom talk about texts: easy to think about, difficult to do. *Journal of Literacy Research, 29*(1), 73–104.

Angelou, M. (1993). *Life does not frighten me at all.* New York: Stewart Tabori & Chang.

Ayers, W. (1992). *The good preschool teacher: Six teachers reflect on their lives.* New York: Teachers College Press.

Banks, J.A (1994). *An introduction to multicultural education.* Boston: Allyn & Bacon.

Banks, J.A. (1992). African-American Scholarship and the evolution of multicultural education. *Journal of Negro Education, 61*(3), 273–286.

Bennett, C.I. (1997). How can teacher perspectives affect teacher decision making? In D.M. Byrd & D.J. McIntyre (Eds.), *Research on the education of our nations' teachers: Teacher Education Year Book* (pp. 75–91). Thousand Oaks, CA: Corwin.

Bogdan, R.C., & Biklen, S.K. (1994). *Qualitative research for education: An introduction to theory and method.* Boston: Allyn & Bacon.

Borland, B. (1994). *How two school faculties look at multicultural education.* (ERIC Document Reproduction Service NO. ED 390721)

Bossard, C.A. (1994). Why do we avoid class in the SIG? Why do we fail to integrate two or more topics across race, class, and gender in our papers? *Critical Examination of Race, Class, and Gender in Education, 9*(1), 3–7.

Britzman, D.P. (1991). *Practice makes practice: A critical study of learning to teach.* Albany: State University of New York Press.

Britzman, D.P. (1995). Is there a queer pedagogy? Or, stop reading straight. *Educational Theory, 45*(2), 151–165.

Connelly, F.M., & Clandinin, D.J. (1994). Telling teaching stories. *Teacher Education Quarterly, 21*(1), 145–58.

Corrigan, P. (1987). In/forming schooling. In D.D. Livingstone (Ed.), *Critical pedagogy and cultural power* (pp. 17–40). South Hadley, MA: Bergin and Gravey.

Derman-Sparks, L., & ABC Task Force. (1989). *Anti-bias curriculum: Tools for empowering young children.* Washington, DC: National Association for the Education of Young Children.

Dorris, M. (1991). Why I am not thankful for Thanksgiving. In B. Bigelow, B. Miner, & B. Peterson (Eds.), *Rethinking Columbus* (pp. 12–13). Milwaukee, WI: Rethinking schools.

Fender, M.J., & Fiedler, C, (1990). Preservice preparation of regular educators: A national survey of curricular content in introductory exceptional children and youth courses. *Teacher Education and Special Education, 13*(3–4), 203–09.

Gay, G. (1998). *Asking touch questions: Who should be included in multicultural education? Which group(s) should we focus on? What united position can we take?* P. Larke (Chair). Interactive symposium conducted at the 1998 annual meeting of American Educational Research Association, San Diego, CA.

Gay, G. (1983). Multiethnic education: Historical development and future prospects. *Phi Delta Kappan, 64*(8), 560–563.

Ghosh, R., & Tarrow, N. (1993). Multiculturalism and teacher educators: Views from Canada and the U.S.A. *Comparative Education, 29*(1), 81–92.

Giroux, H.A. (1995). The politics of insurgent multiculturalism in the era of the Los Angeles uprising. In B. Kanpal & P. McLaren (Eds.), *Critical multiculturalism: Uncommon voices in a common struggle* (107–124). Westport, CT: Bergin & Garvey.

Giroux, H.A. (1989). Educational reform and teacher empowerment. Educational reform and teacher empowerment. In H. Holtz, I. Marcus, J. Dougherty, & J. Michaels (Eds.), *Education and the American dream: Conservatives, liberals and the radicals debate the future of education* (pp. 162–173). Granby, MA: Bergin & Garvey.

Golenbock, P. (1990). *Teammates.* New York: Harcourt Brace Jovanovich.

Gollnick, D.M. (1992). Understanding the dynamics of race, class, and gender. In M.E. Dilworth (Ed.), *Diversity in teacher education* (pp. 63–78.). San Francisco, CA: Jossey-Bass.

Gormley, K.(1995). *Expert and novice teachers' beliefs about culturally responsive pedagogy.* (ERIC Document Reproduction Service No. ED 384 599).

Grant, C.A. (1998). *Asking touch questions: Who should be included in multicultural education? Which group(s) should we focus on? What united position can we take?* P. Larke (Chair). Interactive symposium conducted at the 1998 annual meeting of American Educational Research Association, San Diego, CA.

Grant, C.A. (1994). Best practices in teacher preparation for urban schools: Lessons from the multicultural teacher education literature. *Action in Teacher Education, 16*(3), 1–18.

hooks, b. (1990). *Yearning: Race, gender, and cultural politics.* Boston: South End Press.

Jackson, S., & Solis, J. (1995). Introduction: Resisting zones of comfort in multiculturalism. In S. Jackson & J. Solis (Eds.), *Beyond comfort zones in multiculturalism: Confronting the politics of privilege* (pp. 1–14). Westport, CT: Bergin & Garvey.

Ladson-Billings, G. (1995). Toward a theory of culturally relevant pedagogy. *American Educational Research Journal, 32*(3), 465–491.

Lawrence-Lightfoot, S. (1983). *The good high school: Portraits of character and culture.* New York: Basic Books.

Lincoln, Y., & Guba, E. (1985). *Naturalistic inquiry.* Beverly Hills, CA: Sage.

Mader, C.E., & King, C.M. (1995). *Awareness of gender within teacher education programs.* (ERIC Document Reproduction Service No. ED 385503)

Marshall, P.L. (1994). Four misconceptions about multicultural education that impede understanding. *Action in Teacher Education, 16*(3), 19–27.

McCall, A.L. (1994). Rejoicing and despairing: Dealing with feminist pedagogy in teacher education. *Teaching Education, 6*(2), 59–69.

Messner, K.A. (1994). *Multicultural infusion in teacher education: Teacher educator voices.* (ERIC Document Reproduction Service No. ED 380 444)

Musil, C.M. (1996). The maturing of diversity initiative in American campuses. *American Behavioral Scientist, 40*(2), 222–232.

Nieto, S. (1992). *Affirming diversity: The sociopolitical context of multicultural education.* New York: Longman.

Nespor, J. (1987). The role of beliefs in the practice of teaching. *Journal of Curriculum Studies, 19,* 317–328.

Newfield, C., & Gordon, A.F. (1996). Multiculturalism's unfinished business. In A.F. Gordon & C. Newfield (Eds.), *Mapping multiculturalism* (pp. 76–115). Minneapolis: University of Minnesota Press.

Pajares, M.F. (1993). Teachers' beliefs and educational research: Cleaning up a messy construct. *Review of Educational Research, 62*(3), 307–332.

Pedersen, P. (1991). Introduction to the special issue on multiculturalism as a fourth force in counseling. *Journal of Counseling & Development, 70*(1), 4.

Pope, M. (1995). The "salad bowl" is big enough for us all: An argument for the inclusion of lesbian and gay men in any definition of multiculturalism. *Journal of Counseling and Development, 73*(3), 301–304.

Reber, C.K., Marshak, L.E., Glor-Scheib, S., & Noll, M.B. (1995). *Attitudes of preservice teachers toward students with disabilities: Do practicum experiences make a difference?* (ERIC Document Reproduction Service No. ED 390825).

Schmidt, P. (1998). The ABC's Model: Teachers' connect home and school. In T. Sharahan & F. Rodriguez (Eds.), *47th Yearbook of the National Reading Conference* (pp. 94–208). Chicago: National Reading Conference.

Siegel, I. (1985). A conceptual analysis of beliefs. In I. Siegel (Ed.), *Parental belief system: The psychological consequences for children.* Hillsdale, NJ: Erlbaum.

Simpson, M.L, & Nist, S.L. (1997). Perspectives on learning history: A case study. *Journal of Literacy Research, 29*(3), 363–396.

Singer, A. (1996). *"Star Teachers" and "Dreamkeepers": Can Teacher Educators Prepare Successful Urban Educators?* (ERIC Document Reproduction Service No. ED395898)

Tesch, R. (1990). *Qualitative research: Analysis types and software tools.* New York: The Falmer Press.

Thompson, W.B., & Tyagi, S. (1993). The politics of inclusion: Reskilling the academy. In B.W. Thompson & S. Tyagi (Eds.), *Beyond a dream deferred* (pp. 83–99). Minneapolis: University of Minnesota Press.

Vavrus, M., & Ozcan, M. (1996). *Preservice teacher acquisition of a critical multicultural and global perspective: A reform with ideological tensions.* (ERIC Document Reproduction Service No. ED 393 826)

Wallick, M.M. (1995). Influence of a freshman-year panel presentation on medical students' attitudes toward homosexuality. *Academic Medicine, 70*(9), 839–841.

Zeichner, K.M., & Liston, D.P. (1987). Teaching student teachers to reflect. *Harvard Educational Review, 57*(1), 23–43.

Zembylas, M. (1998). *Epistemological and affective dimensions of elementary science teachers' work.* (ERIC Document Reproduction Service No. ED 419676)

PART II

POWER ISSUES

CHAPTER 3

MONOCULTURAL LITERACY

The Power of Print, Pedagogy, and Epistemological Blindness

Dawnene D. Hammerberg and Carl Grant

INTRODUCTION

This chapter examines contemporary notions of literacy from a historical perspective for the purpose of disrupting the monocultural assumptions present in contemporary literacy education. These assumptions include, but are not limited to: (a) assumptions about the power and necessity of print literacy; (b) assumptions about literacy learning as developmental and progressive; and (c) assumptions about the teaching of literacy as dependent upon expert mediated knowledge. These interrelated assumptions about teaching, learning and literacy have emerged through a history of power relations and mass dominations, as they now work in limited and limiting ways to fix children in a system where massive inequalities are already institutionalized. The first section investigates the contemporary notion that literacy is necessary and powerful. The power and necessity presently attached to literacy is viewed as an effect of historical tensions and cultural dominations, not as an effect of the progressive development of humankind. This contextualizes the divide between literacy and illiteracy as only relational to reading and writing (print literacy), as the assumption involving the primacy and power of print is called into question. The second section examines the sorting and classifying mechanisms present in contemporary understandings of how children learn to be print literate.

The assumption that literacy learning is developmental and natural becomes harmful when those students who are "behind" are thought to have a "deficit" that can be "fixed." This assumption is disrupted through a brief history of literacy education in the United States, which shows that literacy learning is influenced by the dominant culture, not by natural development. The third section considers how it is possible that teachers can accept educational theories and practices as given, even though these theories and practices clearly represent the dominant culture (as opposed to multicultures). These theories and practices clearly maintain educational inequities through a kind of expert mediated oppression that is disguised as "best practice." This section looks at the ways in which expert mediated knowledges, in the forms of pedagogies and practices, uncritically maintain existing power structures and monoculturalisms. Uncritically maintaining the existing order of things as given, teachers have been operating on a conception of literacy which might be beneficial to those with a particular kind of (mono)cultural capital, but which has not been serving those typically seen as "on the margins." In the end, the point of this chapter is to think about literacy differently—perhaps outside of the monocultural assumptions specified here—so that we may awaken in ourselves an understanding of how tied contemporary literacy instruction is to an unyielding history of oppression and exclusion that continues today. This is a first step, then, toward reconceptualizing literacy in multicultural and pluralistic terms.

THE LITERACY/ILLITERACY DIVIDE: THE DOMINANCE AND POWER OF PRINT

There is a contemporary assumption that literacy, specifically in the form of reading and writing, is necessary and powerful. Print literacy is seen as necessary for democracy and emancipation, as well as for science and modernity. Surely, it is true that to compete in this world, indeed to upset the power structures that exist, one needs to be literate, meaning mostly to read and write. The basic thrust of this assumption is reflected especially well in any document published by or for the United Nations Educational, Scientific and Cultural Organization (UNESCO). It informs individuals that all they have to do is become literate, and then they have a chance at success in their worlds. This, of course, is a myth—a dangling carrot. Undoubtedly, learning how to read and write is indispensable in today's world of print, and yet, the rewards of prestige and power are not dependent upon print literacy alone. Learning how to read and write, by itself, is no guarantee for achieving success or one's dreams. It has been well established historically that there are no direct casual links between literacy and power, literacy and development, literacy and equal opportunity, literacy and tolerance, literacy and success, literacy and whatever (see e.g., Gee, 1991, 1996; Graff, 1979, 1987, 1995; Street, 1984; Tyner, 1998).

While it appears that literacy is necessary and even powerful in the present, this understanding of literacy has its history, and the power associated with print is not an automatic given. For example, in primary oral cultures, which Ong (1982) defines as "cultures with no knowledge at all of writing" (p. 1), literacy has no power, since there is no knowledge whatsoever of "it," or of what it can do. Instead, value and power are attached in these cultures to accustomed oral traditions, just as value and power are attached in the dominant cultures of our time to accustomed literate traditions.

It may be difficult to understand, from a literate standpoint in the present, how the "invention" of the alphabet had little to no consequence to the cultures of the time. And yet, as Whitaker (1996) points out:

> It is an obvious but sometimes neglected point that, in the eighth century, when the alphabet was invented and used for the first time to write Greek, it had neither a long tradition of written literature nor any of the associations of a dominant culture attaching to it—as it almost always did when it was used in later periods of history to write other languages. To put it crudely: the first Greek who learned the alphabet had nothing to read. (p. 216)

Print literacy, in other words, has not always been a necessary form of communication, and in fact, has been seen as a hindrance to truly communicative communication. Plato's Socrates, for example, criticized writing because it interfered with established habits of communication, destroying memory rather than enhancing it, and fragmenting social relationships (see Langham, 1994; Gee, 1991, pp. 26–31). "In the *Phaedrus*," writes Langham (1994), "Plato has Socrates deliver what may be the earliest protest in Western history against the dehumanizing effects of 'modern' technology." In Socrates' story of writing's beginning in Egypt, King Thamus is concerned that "external" and "alien" marks (writing) will "produce forgetfulness," concluding that "it's not a recipe for memory, but for reminding, that you have discovered" (see Langham, 1994).

Beyond the earliest objections to print literacy, important power struggles against reading and writing occurred throughout history. Tensions between "literate" ways of being and "oral" ways of being, as if the two can be separated, divided whole countries and groups of people, as the winners of the wars turned out to authenticate print. For example, Myers (1996) explains that Medieval France "became split between Southern France (*le Pays du Droit Écruit*), which acknowledged the written laws of Roman law, and Northern France (*le Pays du Droit Coutumier*), which acknowledged oral societies and local uses" (p. 30). In addition, Myers goes on to say that similar tensions existed during the Norman invasion (1066–1307) when the "Normans wanted to eliminate the use of local, oral authentication of ownership of property in the England of the Middle Ages because those methods allowed the local, native Anglo-Saxons of England to control their own property through personal relations (oaths of witness) and other methods of local authentication" (p. 30; see also Clanchy, 1979; Street, 1984). Despite growing reliance on print, writing was often viewed as secondary to oral communications throughout history. For example, during the late 1200s in Europe, writing was not considered "trustworthy" when compared to face-to-face oral communications in courts and in daily business interactions. Continuing through the Reformation (1600s), in Europe and in the colonies of North America, oral connections linked people and businesses more so than print literacy (see Myers, 1996; Street, 1984; Clanchy, 1979).

These tensions, however, did not occur because of some "natural" divide between literacy and orality. In fact, how print literacy was used and valued depended upon the already established rules of oral traditions. In other words, understandings of appropriate oral communication methods and topics were already invested with enough relevance that these practices were able to shape understandings of the "appropriate" methods and topics for reading and writing. For example, when written records slowly became more customary during the late 1700s in the United States, it was due to "an increasing amount of travel [which] helped to shift social practices from face-to-face interactions with acquaintances to interactions with strangers" (Myers, 1996, p. 32). However, these written interactions were based on the preservation of oral agreements. Tensions between accepted communications techniques occur when the rules governing how one "should" communicate in one local space come in conflict with how one "should" communicate in another local space. As writing and print gained leverage in the 1700s, the tensions between various communication techniques were less apparent as print penetrated people's lives indirectly through an understanding that oral sermons and speeches were written down, and through a general acceptance that writing and print were effective ways to conduct business (see Myers, 1996, p. 33, 39). In other words, the circumstances of cultures which accept versions of print literacy are such that various social needs are obviously fulfilled through writing and print, not that the technologies of writing and print enter the culture on vacant grounds. Particular acts of reading and writing, therefore, become viewed as "necessary" in particular social circumstances and discourses of what is worthwhile. This is not a matter of the "essence" of literacy being better than the "essence" of orality, but rather a matter of history and power over the movements that name and essentialize that which is "better."

The divide between "orality" and "literacy" is a recent phenomenon, a discourse that's worthwhile only in the context of reading and writing (print literacy). In fact, "orality" is a relatively recent term devised and used by anthropologists, sociologists, and psychologists over the past thirty years as a parallel to "literacy" (see Ong, 1982, p. 5; Thomas, 1992, p. 6). It is meant for purposes of analysis and comparison in light of the overwhelming influence of writing and print. The term has been useful and positive in the work of Ong and others who mean to dispel the misconception that strictly oral cultures are severely limited in cultural growth and refinement. Yet the term "orality" can also serve to separate two forms of cultural production which are deeply interwoven.

When it is presumed that there has been a natural and progressive development in communication techniques from the oral to the written to the printed and now to the electronic, "differences" between orality and print literacy (including presumed levels of intelligence, wealth, health and well-being) manifest themselves in terms defined on "literate" grounds which are already presumed to be superior. On this terrain, where writing and print are viewed as necessary for fields of thought such as science, philosophy, and history, where "literacy" is equated with "civilization" and "progress," it is easy to (mis)understand writing, print, and electronic communications as the tools which have brought about levels of knowledge that are "higher" or "better" than the wisdom (often viewed as folksy) available in primary oral cultures or the oral cultures of "the street." However, it should be remembered that the separation of "literacy" from "orality" only occurs on a terrain where print literacy is already overwhelmingly dominant. On this terrain, "literacy" can be outlined on the rooftops and garden penthouses of a civilized skyline, or electrified in the gated communities of technological advancements, or perpetuated in the ivory towers of scholarship and intellectual racism, while the contours of "primary orality" can barely be glimpsed from a "literate" perspective and most often must be imagined, which makes them look identical to the contours of "illiteracy."

Pattanayak (1991) depicts the contours represented in particular discourses surrounding "literacy" and its "opposite" by writing: "Illiteracy is grouped with poverty, malnutrition, lack of education, and health care, while literacy is often equated with growth of productivity, child care, and the advance of civilization" (p. 105). However, this conception of literacy/ illiteracy is not without its history, and is completely tied with relations of power. If we were to imagine the terrains of "primary orality," we would have to imagine a land where illiteracy is not a problem, not an issue by any means. "Orality," when it is truly "primary," has no visions of literacy or illiteracy, since the centuries of intellectual "growth" associated with the techniques of writing are not at all significant to cultures with no knowledge whatsoever of writing. "The introduction of writing," writes Hoyles (1977), "made illiterates inevitable" (p. 23). However, in our imaginations, we have to wonder how "inevitable" the "illiterates" could have possibly been in cultures that had been operating for centuries without writing. These cultures lived in what we might term "illiterate" environments, but they didn't know these were faulty and inferior environments, because they weren't. There was nothing to be inferior to.

The point here is that the power of print literacy, in diametric opposition to the weaknesses associated with illiteracy or oral literacy, is a power consummated through dominating control and authority. At the expense of other ways of being, other ways of knowing, print literacy has gained a foothold to the extent that it appears to be indispensable. More than that, it appears to be the key to emancipation from the very same power structures which made print literacy an aspect of the dominant culture in the first place. Yet, as we have shown, if literacy is seen as a necessity today, or if it is equated with power in the present, this is only because it has been shaped that way through a history that has placed particular versions of literacy into dominant stations. We are at a time now where literacy is seen as a mechanism of power, a way to be powerful, but this misplaced understanding of literacy is not only a myth, but is also based on a monocultural and oppressive history. Since literacy is never by itself outside of society and history, it is also not automatically equal to power all by itself outside of societal functions and rationales. Instead, cultural and historical relationships of power shape the conventions and meanings of literacy, even if the meaning of literacy looks like power itself.

THE LEARNING: DEVELOPMENTAL DEFICITS AND A HISTORY OF PEDAGOGICAL POWER

Still, we are at a time now where literacy is seen as a mechanism of power, a way to be powerful, and it is up to teachers to teach and students to learn the literacy of the day. To become literate today means to progress through a continuum of literate behaviors as defined (in part) by educational research and as captured in the grade level standards created by school districts and states. While technicalities may vary over how these literate behaviors need to be taught (phonics versus whole language, for example), the underlying assumption of a progression from less literate to more literate remains. Aspects of literacy instruction today include reading, writing, speaking, listening, media, technology, inquiry and research, but no matter which aspect students are learning, the assumption is that the learning is part of a developmental and procedural process. Part of learning to be literate today also includes the evaluation practices meant to classify and label students according to their progress. For example, the "best" reading teachers today listen to their students read while taking "running records" of their reading performances. The purpose is to find out the students' instructional reading levels as well as the types of reading errors the students are making, so that guided reading groups can be formed around focused instruction and appropriate materials. After performing by reading out loud, students can be fairly easily placed on a continuum that informs teachers where the students are and where they need to go in terms of their literacy development. In general, then, the overall epistemology (varieties, grounds, and validity) of contemporary literacy instruction is based on an assumption that there are particular skills and strategies that students must learn first before they are able to build on that knowledge and move on.

Presently, there are a number of frameworks built upon this assumption of developmental learning. While differences abound between any two models, it's interesting to note how different frameworks for understanding the nature of reading acquisition begin to look similar when compared in developmental terms. Two models of reading acquisition, Jeanne Chall's (1983) *Stages of Reading Development* and the Australian First Steps reading model (Education Department of Western Australia, 1994), serve as examples of a kind of pedagogical belief system that buys into an epistemology of developmental learning. Chall's *Stages of Reading Development* depicts how students are thought to progress through phases of cognitive development on their way to becoming better readers. Students begin at a "Prereading" or "Pseudo-reading" level where the "[c]hild 'pretends' to read, retells [a] story when looking at pages of a book previously read to him/her; names letters of [the] alphabet; recognizes some signs; prints own name; [and] plays with books, pencils, and paper" (p. 85). This stage parallels Phases 1 and 2 of the Australian First Steps reading model, where the child "role plays" reading (Phase 1) or engages in "experimental reading" (Phase 2). Here, the child "displays reading-like behavior" such as holding the book in the right direction (p. 21), and learns about the sounds of oral language, that thoughts can be divided into words which can be divided into sounds (phonemic awareness). Much of the learning that takes place at this level occurs orally/aurally when the student hears stories, rhymes, and the patterns of language. Appropriate materials for this level could include anything by Dr. Seuss for its rhyming alliteration, something like *King Bidgood's in the Bathtub* by Audrey Wood (1985) for the same reasons, or stories with strong language structures such as the books by Kevin Henkes or Maira Kalman. The point here is to fill children's ears with sounds, their eyes with concepts, and their heads with story structure. Chall's next stage of reading development, "Initial Reading and Decoding," requires more "[d]irect instruction in letter-sound relations (phonics) and practice in their use" (p. 85). Here, the child becomes "tied to the print" as they learn words that are high frequency and/or phonetically regular. This parallels the Australian model's "Early Reading Phase," in that the new reader "relies heavily on beginning letters and sounding-out for word identification (graphophonic strategies)" (p. 38). Students are invited to really focus on the text on the page, perhaps by using their finger to point at the words, as pattern books or picture-dependent books with increasingly new vocabulary are repeatedly read to encourage students to "have-a-go" at decoding what's in front of them. After a reader gains the necessary decoding skills for determining the meaning of unfamiliar words, they are ready to become more fluent in Chall's stage of "Confirmation and Fluency" or in the Australian model's phase of "Transitional Reading." During this phase of reading development, students are "becoming efficient" in their word identification strategies in the Australian model (p. 47), or able to consolidate "the basic decoding elements, sight vocabulary, and meaning context" in Chall's framework (p. 86). This leads to a stage that Chall calls "Reading for Learning the New" and the Australian model labels "Independent Reading," during which students use reading "to learn new ideas, to gain new knowledge ... generally from one viewpoint" in Chall's framework (p. 86), or students "[c]ritically respond to and reflect on text meanings and provide different levels of interpretation and points of view" in the Australian model (p. 63). Chall's stages continue through a stage called "Multiple Viewpoints" where students read "widely from a broad range of complex materials ... with a variety of viewpoints" (p. 87) and a stage called "Construction and Reconstruction" in college and beyond where "[r]eading is used for one's own needs and purposes" (p. 87). This parallels the Australian model's last phase of "Advanced Reading" where the reader "critically reflects on and responds to text, providing different levels of interpretation and adopting alternative viewpoints" (p. 72). Note that in both models, "multiple" or "alternative" viewpoints don't occur until much later in the developmental continuum.

It is important to recognize that these two models have a number of significant differences. Indeed, any two models are different, thus the need for multiple models: a way to explain things differently, or to add and expand upon previous thought. These two particular models are different in their general approaches to making and interpreting meaning: for example, there are differences in where and when meaning-making at the whole text level is thought to occur; there are differences in the extent to which meaning is controlled through vocabulary and content; there are differences in the extent to which varieties of perspectives are valued as forms of interactive interpretation. These two models are also different in major teaching philosophies: for example, there are differences in the extent to which various skills either are taught directly or learned "naturally" through experience. Yet, no matter what the differences, these two models are similar in their assumption that learning to read is developmental. They are also similar in that each model (any model, for that matter) sorts, classifies, and evaluates students according to the developmental continuum. The point is that, no matter what the differences—no matter what the reading wars—literacy acquisition is believed to follow a continuum of growth, progressive and developmental.

The same developmental assumption (sometimes referred to as scope and sequence) is present in state and national performance standards, as well as in local school district reading outcomes. In addition, while we have been focusing on reading acquisition thus far, the same argument can be made for the frameworks which speak to writing development, spelling development, oral language development, and development in inquiry or research. In all aspects of literacy instruction, there is a presumed developmental progression in the skills and strategies that students must learn first in order to build on that knowledge and move on.

This way of thinking about literacy learning, however, is based on a particular system of reasoning about how students are "supposed" to learn to be literate, and this system of reasoning has its history. It's important to note that if students are presumed to "develop" through these stages, it has less to do with the "nature" of literacy acquisition and more to do with a history of educational thought and knowledge about what a student needs to do in order to be seen as "literate." The ways in which students learn how to "be literate" vary greatly over time: for example, students living at the end of the 1800s practiced a kind of recitation literacy by loosening and wagging their tongues in unison (Myers, 1996, pp. 64–65; Rice, 1893, pp. 176–177), whereas students living at the end of the 1900s might engage in small group cooperative writing of the daily news. Maybe one seems more "usual," more "normal," or more "right" than the other, but that is because the belief systems upon which curriculum and instruction are built seldom appear as peculiar in the here-and-now. That's what dominant systems of ideas do: make things appear "normal" or "natural" or "right." No matter what the time period, the teachers' expectations of students' performances are always placed in accordance with whatever "best" literacy practices of the time are thought to be. Yet what is counted as "best" literacy practices is, of course, not a matter of right and wrong, but a matter of history and power.

Miles Myers (1996) has written a comprehensive history of the educational functions of literacy in the United States. He outlines four shifts in literacy practices: (1) from orality to signature literacy, 1600–1776; (2) from signature to recitation literacy, 1776–1864; (3) from recitation to decoding/analytic literacy, 1864–1916; and (4) from decoding/analytic to critical/translation literacy, 1916–present.

Literacy in the early phases of this country (what Myers calls "oracy" in the 1600s and early 1700s) involved oral/aural memorizing of stories, traditions, transactions, and people's ways. It was an oral culture for the most part; the literacy we're talking about here did not involve much writing or print. Myers summarizes this period by writing, "oral cultures use a conversational logic in which things are connected through a large number of shared inferences, through memory devices like *and* or *then*, through gestures based on the spatial rules of face-to-face events, and through fragments and hesitations which help the speaker avoid looking unnecessarily authoritative and, thus, anti-social" (p. 28). Literacy learning was very localized, taking place at home or in the familiar, and using the rules and grammars of the local communications that make different groups distinctive. This is during a time when "[l]ocal networks bonded people who knew each other and who generally did not move" (p. 56), so commonly shared experiences were important to pass on from neighbor to neighbor, generation to generation. The conventions of an oral form of literacy involve highly tuned linguistic abilities, such as knowing how to use alliterations, sound patterns, rhythm, rhyme, repetition, sequential markers, and formu-laic exchanges as a way to preserve memory (see pp. 23–24).

By the late 1700s, a slightly more mobile population contributed to the need for a form of literacy that Myers calls "signature literacy." The reading and writing abilities of people living during this time varied from the ability to make an X, which was considered completely satisfactory literate behav-ior, to the ability to use invented spellings on postings for central bulletin boards, to focused reading which concentrated on copying small portions of text where writing was an art (see pp. 44–47, pp. 56–57). "In this new society of strangers and signature and recording literacy," writes Myers, "the ability to record simple information and to sign one's name enabled one to borrow money, to post news for distant neighbors, to claim and set-tle land, to record an inventory of moving property … to name only a few essential social functions of recording, remembering, certifying, and informing" (p. 44). Literacy learning during this period involved memoriz-ing, copying, and having good hand-eye coordination. Meaning and com-prehension mattered little (see pp. 49–50): for example, it didn't matter whether you copied from the top-down or from the bottom-up; the mean-ing would be the same in the end, and the text said whatever it said. In schools, students learned how to sign their marks, make and copy lists, read a little bit, but mostly read from memory.

Literacy learning during the "recitation" period, beginning around 1859, involved the oral recitation and memorization of traditional materi-als and (mono)cultural information in the form of national values. The purpose of this type of literacy was to manufacture national cohesion after the Civil War and to erase the language differences found among immi-grants and in fragmented cities. Myers explains that "diverse [school] dis-tricts, which were often organized around specific ethnic communities, mandated that their own values be taught, thereby increasing the ethnic tensions among different groups and providing a continuing rationale for the drive to have schools socialize students into a 'unified' national culture with a unified national language" (p. 66). It was during this time period that students began to be sorted by achievement levels, race, ethnicity, and social class as a "part of a pervasive post-Civil War social response to the fear of disorder" (p. 69). It was also during this time period that the notion of individual closed classrooms as opposed to one-room auditoriums was deliberated, probably as another sorting mechanism, as well as a reaction to all that noisy reciting (see p. 75).

Literacy learning during the United State's "decoding" phase (1916–1983) meant the silent analyzing of unfamiliar texts for the purpose of gain-ing new knowledge. Books were objects to be analyzed, and tasks were bro-ken into sequential elements. Myers points out that a literacy of analyzing and decoding served modern corporations well "through its emphasis on decoding unfamiliar, anonymous texts and its centralization of informa-tion" (p. 98). Basic literacy meant being able to "get" the necessary information. Meanwhile, education became "standardized" and "objective," through means such as Frederick Taylor's "scientific management" principles, 1911; Franklin Bobbit's "social efficiency" model, 1912 (see Kliebard, 1995, p. 84); Ellwood P. Cubberly's school-as-factory model, 1916; Edward L. Thorndike's "essential elements" of reading and writing instruction, 1918; and Management by Behavioral Objectives, 1960–70 (see Myers, pp. 95–97).

Finally, Myers sees a current shift in literacy learning to a "translational" form, which involves reading for multiple perspectives and interpretations. Myers informs us that "the new demands of contemporary economic problems and the workplace, the new demands of pluralism and diversity in our democracy, and the new demands for new supports for personal growth" (p. 117) all are reasons why new standards of literacy are sitting on our school steps now. The growth of information technologies makes the translation and interpretation of a wide variety of texts a priority. Meanings surrounding literacy and language are beginning to undergo changes, as demonstrated by the *Standards for the English Language Arts* (NCTE & IRA, 1996). In it, *text* "refer[s] not only to printed texts, but also to spoken language, graphics, and technological communications"; *language* "encompasses visual communication in addition to spoken and written forms of expression"; and *reading* "refers to listening and viewing in addition to print-oriented reading" (p. 2). Translational literacy, then, would involve the interpretation of many different sign systems as a way to negotiate our differences (see Myers, chapters 9–14). The diversity of the world is on the verge of being recognized.

There are a few additional aspects to highlight in the history of literacy in the United States. First, it's important to note that different forms of literacy have served different types of social cultures over time. For example, Myers points out that "orality ... served the needs of a stable agricultural society in which people lived in the same communities for years, but *signature literacy* served a transient agricultural society in which people moved frequently" (p. 15). This connection between literacy and how it serves cultures is important to keep in mind when considering the types of literacies that have served and continue to serve dominant cultures. People have been completely ignored and/or not served by the type of literacy advocated by the dominant culture; what might it take to envision forms of literacies that might serve multicultures?

Secondly, it's also worth noting the continual pull toward a lack of tolerance and fear of difference despite efforts to the contrary. "For example," writes Myers, "in 1853, the president of the Cincinnati school board argued that teaching German in the public schools was essential" as the diversity of immigrants was valued. "But this tolerance of a variety of languages," Myers continues, "began to disappear after the Civil War, when the country was concerned about the fragmentation created first by the Civil War and second by the increased immigration needed for new factories" (p. 65). As one reads the history of literacy, it becomes striking that the suggestion of the president of the Cincinnati school board is one of the rare times when tolerance and diversity was honored, albeit tolerance and diversity of a Northern European "difference." It becomes clear in the history of this country that concern with plurality only occurs in the context of democracy for the sake of democracy and melting pots for the sake of cultural erasure.

Lastly, and in line with our previous discussion of developmental models of literacy acquisition, it may not actually be a mere coincidence that aspects of the history of literacy in the United States are present in contemporary developmental understandings of literacy learning. Indeed, stages of reading development incorporate aspects of past literacy training practices to the point where they even seem to loosely mimic the same phases that the United States has lived through in its history of literacy instruction: from an "emergent reader" who is typically characterized by natural, environmental, shared, oral, phonemic learning; to a "beginning reader" who has an ability to gain necessary decoding skills for determining the meaning of unfamiliar words; to a reader who is gaining fluency in identifying unfamiliar words and understanding meaning; to a "mature reader" who can reconstruct meanings or shape ideas and who is capable of dealing with a high level of abstraction and interpretation. We are looking at leftovers in the models that speak to developmental learning, traces of history and the influence that dominance provides. Therefore, we have to keep in mind that if readers are presumed to "develop" through these stages, it has less to do with the "nature" of literacy acquisition and more to do with a history of educational thought and knowledge about "the student" in relation to "literate" practices. This cultural history has defined historically specific techniques of "becoming literate," to the point where, in a present moment, students are thought to "develop" as readers by progressing through a continuum of "literate" behaviors. This is not really a matter of progressing from "less literate" to "more literate," but instead it is a matter of progressing through rule-governed conventions determined by a dominant cultural history of what one has to do when one is "becoming literate." The present design and function of literacy, then, is a blend of skills and attitudes from past practices, past beliefs and convictions, which have coalesced into organized and systematic procedures in line with present assumptions about literacy and its acquisition.

We may believe that children learn to read and write naturally along a developmental continuum, but as Myers himself points out, "[c]hildren do not invent their own forms of literacy outside the influence of the cultures in which they live" (p. 2). Despite the glare of history and the influence of culture, the assumption of a developmental (and natural) progression to literacy learning remains. When that assumption is taken for granted and seen as real (as it is today), those students who do not grow naturally along appropriate lines are seen as having a deficit of some sort. The linear progression through a series of developmental levels is considered normal, and those students who do not progress in this way need to be "caught up" or given what they missed. Perhaps they are sent down the hall to catch up one-on-one, "behind the glass" of a Reading Recovery room with its one-way observation window. Perhaps the federal funds of Title I are there for a cure. Maybe the solution is in the regular classroom in the form of a different book or a lower skilldrill. But whatever the cure, it is a deficit model, as if literacy skills are something to give to those who don't have it. The learner who is not learning according to the plan is assumed to have a developmental deficit, and a series of interventions (if you're young) or remediations (if you're older) are created to give the gift, to fill the holes. According to a report put out by Learning First Alliance (1998), *Every Child Reading: An Action Plan*, "[r]eading failure is the overwhelming reason why children are retained, assigned to special education, or given long-term remedial services" (p. 3). Tied to the assumption that deficient students need additional assistance is the assumption that interventions, remediations, retentions, or special education all provide additional chances for success. It follows from this that if the student still doesn't get it, there must be something wrong with the student, or the parent, or poverty in general, but certainly not the system.

Remember, however, that "the system" is built from a history that grounds itself in dominant monocultures and complex systems against which students may (or may not) "measure up." "The system" is built directly upon the assumptions that convince us that those who have "developmental deficits" have been given every opportunity to achieve what is supposed to come naturally. "The system" categorizes and evaluates the very students who are in the midst of its inescapable and tyrannical grasp, even as we suppose "the system" is helping them. As history shows, the varieties, grounds, and validity of the educational knowledge we have available today are influenced by the power of dominant cultures, not by the "natural" development of children.

THE TEACHING: DYSCONSCIOUS RACISM AND EPISTEMOLOGICAL BLINDNESS

Assumptions about teaching literacy are of course closely related to assumptions about learning literacy. Teachers are meant to teach—to help students learn—and if learning does not occur, then teachers are meant to cure, to remediate, to intervene—or to send the kids somewhere where they *can* be educated. We believe we know enough about "the reading process" and "best practice" and how kids learn to truly make a difference. The theories are there, and all educators are trying to do is make use of them.

As shown in the last sections, however, the ways in which we teach literacy are historical and cultural, based on limited and limiting assumptions about how students learn to be literate. One would bank on the hope that thinking human beings (e.g., teachers) would begin to question the practices we think are best in the face of the overwhelming statistics of our educational failure to nonwhite kids. According to 1994 NAEP scores, there is a continuing gap between white students and African-American and Hispanic students: 69% of African-American and 64% of Hispanic fourth grade students scored below the basic proficiency level, as compared to 31% of white fourth grade students. This section considers how it is possible that teacher education and reeducation continually rely on the pedagogies and practices that are considered "normal" in a society where racism and discrimination are the norm.

Theories (about learning, about teaching) are exceptionally powerful in that they form pedagogical belief systems. Information and students are arranged according to educational theories regarding scope and sequence, critical thinking skills, stages of cognitive development, cooperative grouping, guided reading, shared reading, independent reading, paired reading, Bloom's taxonomy, multiple intelligences, all forms of psychometric methods. These are theories and techniques, however, that Cornbleth (1987) would classify as educational myths. They are merely abstractions about how students learn which become the bedrock upon which all future lessons are built. As Cornbleth (1987) points out, "[p]rinciples of learning become *the way people learn* or *learning* itself, and students who do not observe these principles are typically considered deficient or recalcitrant" (p. 188). She goes on to say that such principles are viewed as scientific truths and "can become self-fulfilling as when the presumably deficient or recalcitrant student is treated as such and begins to respond in kind, thus confirming the teacher's expectation and perpetuating the myth and 'non-learning'" (p. 188). A teacher's expectation for a student fixed by a developmental continuum, for example, is confirmed by the expert mediated learning theories. These theories "fix" the student in two ways: first, they produce the belief that children can even be placed on a developmental continuum, fixed somewhere on a spot from "less literate" to "more literate"; and then they create the faith that children with deficits can be helped through interventions, or remediations, or retentions—fixed and repaired using the information from the continuum that got them there. In other words, the information created by the developmental continuum perpetuates the myth of the developmental continuum itself. The "expert" knowledge of teachers, then, actively contributes to the maintenance of the status quo through that "expertise" itself. In effect, long-standing practices prove themselves as appropriate based upon the extent to which they model myths of learning in this expert system. Monaghan and Saul (1987) discuss the weight of tradition in education by saying:

> In determining curricula, one necessarily orders the information to be presented to the child, both in terms of its significance and its assumptions about how children learn. Practices based upon once valid assumptions have a way of perpetuating themselves long after the original raison d'etre has vanished. (p. 86)

As shown in the last section, assumptions about literacy learning are a product of assumptions formed through the historically present need to produce particular kinds of (monoculturally) literate youngsters. Although teachers may always be aware of the functions of education in forming a society, it is secondary in a very daily way to the techniques used to deliver the curriculum, which is already in place and basically unquestioned. The political realities of education remain constrained within an existing framework, oppressive as it is. In many ways, the act of teaching cannot avoid dysconscious racism.

Joyce E. King (1991) defines dysconsciousness as the "uncritical habit of mind (including perceptions, attitudes, assumptions, and beliefs) that justifies inequity and exploitation by accepting the existing order of things as given" (p. 135). She goes on to say that dysconsciousness "is not the *absence* of consciousness (that is, not unconsciousness) but an *impaired* consciousness or distorted way of thinking" (p. 135). Even as teachers think and learn about education for diverse populations, even as scholars write to enlarge teacher perceptions, attitudes, and beliefs, the techniques teachers often come away with are still part of that developmental/deficit model, and are focused, in Zeichner's (1992) words, "on personality factors like motivation" thus ignoring "contextual factors like ethnicity" (p. 4). Zeichner also postulates that "many teacher education students come to their preparation programs viewing student diversity as a problem rather than a resource." While teachers may believe that all students can learn, there is still the ever-present understanding that some may need extra attention to slam them into the mold of a student who is "able" to learn a prescribed, unquestioned, and oppressive content.

Indeed, the tradition of teacher education, including its resulting doctrines, depict merely a fragment of possibilities. While dysconsciously embracing our existing curricular frameworks as if they are given, the monocultural value systems upon which such frameworks are built have been and continue to be overlooked. If we question why racism and discrimination are the norm in this society, the answer is obviously an issue of power, but that power may not be recognized as such when it's hidden in seemingly benign teaching procedures, such as those designed to help children read. We are overlooking the frameworks. We do not recognize the power, so we are blind to the epistemologies that perpetuate racism. We do not think of them as racist, oppressive, problematic power moves; we think we're doing the right thing. Popkewitz (1987) informs us that:

> Power is exercised through the ability to assign categories that provide identity to those whom the categories are to be applied. The techniques of sorting, classifying and evaluating people enable the exercise of sovereignty. (p. ix)

Techniques of sorting, classifying, and evaluating people are embedded in contemporary understandings of literacy acquisition, as demonstrated in our discussions of presumed "developmental progress," but we may not immediately recognize the use of a developmental continuum as an "exercise of sovereignty." We do not readily see that the values which inform our educational decisions are a part of an expert mediated oppression disguised as "best practice." Beyer and Zeichner (1987) examine this phenomenon:

> The 'sacred' knowledge that is communicated overtly and covertly through the rituals and routines of teacher education are in fact *value governed* selections from a much larger universe of possibilities and ... these traditions can be traced both contemporarily and historically to specific economic and social interests. (p. 313, emphasis added)

When we are forced to deal with major inequalities in education, we find ourselves creating "solutions" using the same sorting mechanisms based on existing power structures. The myths of education and learning theories mentioned earlier (stages of development, scope and sequence, thinking skills, etc.) are no more than other ways to define and label people, and sadly, these are the expert mediated tools most often used to deal with serious educational problems.

One only needs to look at the students in remedial tracks as compared to the students of college-bound tracks to realize the extent to which power and sovereignty have operated in very real and very daily ways. Students in the lower tracks do not have the benefit of the type of monocultural capital needed to succeed in today's world. The people who hold and continue to hold positions of power in our society are people who were born into a social epistemology that allowed them to grow up with economic and linguistic capital, as well as a blind side to the inequities. The need for a particular kind of cultural capital is apparent in all aspects of schooling, particularly models of learning and development. Throughout a child's schooling, there are certain ways of being (e.g., speaking with the dominant language), certain behaviors (e.g., knowing how to turn the pages of a book versus knowing how to copy lists), which appear as normal and easy and natural. In Bourdieu's (1974) words, "the culture of the elite is so near to that of the school that children from the lower middle class ... can only acquire with great effort something which is *given* to the children of the cultivated classes" (p. 39).

Cynthia Tyson (1998) takes it one step further: "The racist ideology that drives hegemony moves the oppressed other into a paradigm of survival so that these intersecting cycles of oppression and survival create a particular epistemological view of the world" (p. 22). In other words, the oppressive frameworks of literacy education actually cause us (as teachers and as students) to believe that getting the necessary literacy skills (as defined in an oppressive, regulating continuum of mastery) is the only hope for survival, the only hope to compete in a racist world. The tools for competition in a racist world are basically given to the children for whom race, poverty, and survival are not endless issues. The paradigm of survival, then, is based on the same power structures that created the oppressive pedagogy in the first place. This epistemological view of the world, blind to the racist ideologies which continue to ground the oppression-survival cycle in an ideal that appears valid, places the onus of responsibility on the very people who are overpowered and outmaneuvered by the cycle.

Even as we discuss problems in schools such as low test scores, lack of resources, high dropout rates, tracking, poor teaching, and so forth (see Kozol, 1991), we are dysconsciously furthering the dialogue of the dominant by providing possessively individual excuses (Popkewitz, 1991, pp. 150–152) for educational problems. This means that the explanation for failure or poverty or low social status is assumed to lie within the individuals themselves, as illustrated in the belief that some people have been given all they need to succeed, but they just don't work hard enough or possess the necessary traits to help themselves "get out." Coles (1998) sees these beliefs as including "a national politics that blames the poor for their own problems" (p. 114). He uses political analyst Michael Parenti who demonstrates this frame of mind in contemporary politics by writing:

> In 1995, right-wing Republican leader Newt Gingrich reduced poverty to a matter of personal inclination: "I am prepared to say to the poor, 'You have to learn new habits. The habits of being poor don't work." (Parenti, 1996, p. 18; quoted in Coles, 1998, p. 114)

Basically, the load of change rests upon the individual shoulders of the very people who do not have the necessary power or resources. Individual excuses are techniques of avoidance that cover up the larger social catastrophe. Blaming the victim is a symptom of our epistemological blindness, our epistemological racism.

CONCLUSION: RECONCEPTUALIZING LITERACY IN MULTICULTURAL AND PLURALISTIC TERMS

Contemporary understandings of literacy, then, are built upon a number of assumptions. First, there is the assumption that print literacy is powerful and necessary. While knowing how to read and write appears as a necessity in today's world of print, history shows that this necessity has emerged at the expense of other ways of being, other ways of knowing. It is a history of dominations, control and authority, and the price paid occurs when other ways of finding patterns in life, of making meaning, are not viewed as educationally credible or important, because they are not viewed as "literate" behaviors. The history of "literate" behaviors shows that changes in definitions of literacy are not the effect of the progressive development of mankind, but instead, an effect of historical tensions and cultural dominations in the naming of "the necessary" or "the usual" in regard to reading, writing, and print. Indeed, there have been numerous occasions over the course of history when reading and writing were not societal issues by any means. Whatever is viewed as necessary and powerful, then, is not static, and as educators, we cannot be caught in the trap of teaching only one form of literacy (i.e., the decoding of print) as if it can last for all times and all purposes, simply because it's "usual" today.

The danger of the assumption that literacy is necessary and powerful lies in the automatic equation of particular forms of print literacy with progress. This effectively closes off any serious educational consideration over how meaning might be made and thought might be distributed in nonprint ways, turning potential progress into latent possibilities in the school days filled with "basics." We must remember that the contemporary divide between literacy and illiteracy occurs because we have specific values surrounding print which lead us to believe that other forms of communication are not as productive or efficient, certainly not of educational worth, especially if you're not yet reading. Of course, other forms of distributing thought and making meaning exist beyond decoding a text and "getting" a singular author's message, but they do not yet have educational leverage. There are, for example, many scholarly efforts which problematize contemporary understandings of literacy in an effort to promote "critical literacies" (Lankshear & McLaren, 1993), "new literacies" (Willinsky, 1990), or "translational literacies" (Myers, 1996), to name a few. These "new" forms of literacies speak, in part, to the multiple meanings that can be made through the negotiation and translation of diverse perspectives and the critical interpretation of many types of symbols and graphics (including printed text), but they are not yet meant for "nonreaders." The current educational concern involves the effort to get every child reading by the third grade, which places emphasis on decoding print for the purpose of correctly recounting the author's message (often in multiple choice form). This is not to say that discussions of multiple interpretations do not exist in schools; just that they most often do not coexist with "basic" literacy instruction. They may exist for "gifted" children (e.g., the critical questioning techniques of Junior Great Books) or much later down the developmental continuum *after* the student already knows how to "read" by today's acceptable standards, but the plurality of partial knowledges is trivialized or made extracurricular in favor of the "universal" or canonical forms of knowledge that are at the heart of what it means to "read well" today.

To think outside of this particular assumption means to hold problematic the primacy of print. This does not mean that we need to get rid of books or go "back" to a different standard of literacy. Rather, it means that we need to me more acutely aware of the ways in which twentieth-century understandings of print literacy have marginalized and continue to marginalize the multiple perspectives that exist in every school and every classroom. It means to mediate classroom culture in a way that extends beyond the affirmation of human diversity into the realm of personal voice and empowerment through multiple ways of knowing. It means to help people examine their life experiences, how race has played its role, how central to all meaning all cultures really are. As Lankshear and McLaren (1993) so aptly put it, this form of literacy "sees diversity as a quest for something more than a collection of ethnic 'add-ons' but rather as a politics of *thinking from the margins*, of possessing integral perspectives on the world" (p. 27). It means remembering that "illiteracy" is only automatically a deficit because of the way we have defined "literacy." It means acknowledging the multiplicities of lived experiences and subjugated knowledges.

Secondly, there is the assumption that literacy learning is developmental and progressive. This assumption is harmful when those students who are measured as "behind" on the developmental continuum are thought to have a "deficit" that can be "fixed." To take this assumption at face value and buy into a developmental continuum means to assume that there are particular ways to attack and fix particular reading problems. Yet, as Kohl (1998) points out, "having trouble learning to read is not a generic condition" (p. 170). The intervention and remedial systems currently in place act as if there are specific treatments for specific problems. Kohl goes on to say that these types of remedial programs are:

> based on the assumption that there is one way to not learn how to read, and therefore one fix for the problem. I've found the opposite to be the case: there are as many variants on failure as there are children. In fact, it may be that a version of the first line of *Anna Karenina*—"All happy families are alike, and each unhappy family is unhappy in its own way"—applies to educational misery as well: all readers learn to read in similar ways, and each failed reader fails in his or her own way. (p. 171)

Failed children fail for a number of reasons, but no matter what types of reasons we attach to their failures (lack of concentration, lack of motivation, lack of particular skills, lack of ability), their failures are defined by a system meant to define. While this system appears to mimic natural growth and natural development, in reality, the ways in which we systematize what one has to do in order to become "naturally" literate mimic the regulations of a dominant and seemingly progressive history. As the history of literacy in the United States shows, the current educational understanding of developmental learning is an amalgamation of past literacy practices. The developmental continuum is not a matter of natural growth, but a matter of history and power.

The danger in this assumption of developmental learning is twofold. First, it assumes that a child who is not at the appropriate developmental level can be helped through programmed instruction in the basic skills defined by the continuum. And secondly, it assumes that these basic skills must be acquired (and demonstrated) before one can deal with a higher level of abstraction or multiple interpretations, before one can be a fluent meaning-maker. Certainly teachers may disagree and say that many of their students are fully capable of thinking deep thoughts and engaging in abstractions well before they learn how to read or write. We all have our stories and most make us laugh. Yet, if it is a nonreader/nonwriter thinking deep thoughts, there is not much time even in kindergarten for the "extras" of abstractions because their first priority is to learn a "lower" form of literacy. They can yammer on abstractly during off-hours or for entertainment, but nobody feels satisfied until the dissatisfied child is getting his or her "basic" literacy skills. Maybe there aren't enough hours in the day, maybe there aren't enough teachers in the field, but unfortunately, basic literacy skills (sounds, letters, decoding) are seen as prerequisites to higher order thinking. Educationally, basic literacy skills are even viewed (socially, economically, and politically) as more important than tolerance and diversity of thought.

To think outside of this particular assumption means to hold the developmental continuum itself as problematic: to understand that the developmental continuum is a part of a system that, historically, has been constructed to classify, label and define. When, blindly, achievement outcomes are related to a developmental continuum, the child is at risk of being defined as deficient, as opposed to a child at risk of being a deep thinker, a deep learner. To think outside of this assumption means to hold problematic the arrogance which tells us that deep thinking is a higher order skill, that serious communication must involve the conventions of print, that wise reflection takes practice and is for the privileged few. To think outside of this assumption means to hold problematic the premise that children born in the right place at the right time worked as hard to become literate as children born in the wrong place at the wrong time. It means to hold problematic that the poor are the authors of their own poverty. It means to hold problematic that children with reading deficits have been given every chance to succeed. Gerald Coles (1998) writes:

> Unless assumptions like these and the societal stratification that promotes them are changed, achievement outcomes are likely to remain fairly fixed. Reading instruction might not use formal groups, formal testing might be eliminated, children might not have labels of one kind or another, and there might not be basal readers. Instruction might mix skills and meaning, or might employ whole language and cooperative learning that mix children in many ways. Nonetheless, these modifications will not by themselves eliminate the treatment of children according to what is assumed to be their mental capacity, and predestined educational approaches will continue to fit them to their futures. (pp. 114–115)

In many ways, it seems easy to critique how educational systems are flawed. If, as Coles just stated, "modifications to the system at large will not by themselves eliminate the treatment of children according to what is assumed to be their mental capacity," then what modifications are we to make in order to deal with the problems that exist? As we stand here at the threshold of a new millennium, we have the chance not only to critique how the system is flawed, but also to glimpse how the system might be changed. For starters, we might pay attention to the fact that it is difficult to find a point in history when tolerance and diversity of thought were honored; it is difficult to pinpoint a moment when human beings really tried compassion as a valid form of communication. In education, this might mean that we would take seriously the prior knowledges and particular contexts of all children we encounter, which has nothing to do with a developmental continuum, but more to do with an understanding that human beings interact with each other from within particular points of view. To change the system would mean to get rid of the notion that ways of learning are so established, so fixed, that they can be made permanent on an organized continuum: the organization itself makes us forget that learning is much more fluid and interrelational. What to do on Monday morning? Start by enlisting your students to expand your own horizons: ask them what they think and how they think; critique your attitudes about capacities and achievement levels; quit being the expert. Listen, talk, share, expand. Fall in love with life. No, fall in love with multiple lives.

Third, there is the assumption that contemporary knowledge about teaching literacy is based on scientific truths and knowledges about the ways students learn. This assumption becomes dangerous when we blindly buy into the epistemologies that are based on a kind of dysconscious racism which inadvertently maintains educational inequities through a kind of expert mediated oppression disguised as "best practice." This means that educational techniques that are thought of as "best" may in fact be a part of (or a cause of) the failures that we see before us. When we rationalize what is "good," "better," and "best" practices, we need to remember that it is history and power (not what "really" is better) that name and essentialize that which is "good," "better," and "best." We may forget that turning the pages of a book and knowing how to decode its text is only viewed as a form of literate behavior today. However, history shows that there have been other forms of literate behavior over time. In fact, exhibiting behaviors of past forms of literacy might look vaguely similar to what we would call "illiterate" behaviors today. For example, in today's world, somebody defined as "illiterate" or "not literate enough" might be able to copy a text forwards, backwards, and upside-down, and this child still might be sent down the hall to work on "actual" literacy skills, whereas in earlier years, copying in such a way was viewed as a perfectly legitimate form of "literate" behavior. Instead of buying into the constraints of curricular frameworks and pedagogical expertise, it might be worth a "loosening of the belt," if only for the fresh air. With your belly out and your hair blowing free, the wind outside of dysconscious expertise might inform you that there is still creativity in teaching. You think to yourself, "I never expected to be taken off-guard without being troubled; I never imagined a child this age could do this,

could be so eloquent," and yet, deep in your heart of hearts, you always suspected it might be true.

To think outside of the assumption that teaching is scientific or based
on an expert mediated field of knowledge means to hold problematic any
theories of learning which put kids in boxes. Putting kids in boxes actually
limits creativity in teaching because of the time and effort it takes to meet
with colleagues and other experts to decide on appropriate placements, to
figure out the right interventions. We are all, as teachers, working with our
most heartfelt intentions. There is a programmed way of doing things, yet
there is no time to consider what the child actually knows (and we are not
talking here about whether the child knows his or her sounds; we're talking about what the child knows about life). In addition, there is no time to
consciously (as opposed to dysconsciously) assess our own pedagogical
belief systems about "capacities" and "growth" in relation to the child.
There is no time to critically analyze whether or not our own educational
attitudes, unproblematized and completely unbeknownst to us, are inadvertently forms of oppression. Make the time.

Dysconscious or blind, racist or not, it is oppressive language that informs
our pedagogical belief systems. We need to be critically aware of this. Toni
Morrison (1994) writes: "Oppressive language does more than represent violence; it is violence; does more than represent the limits of knowledge; it limits knowledge" (p. 16). It is oppressive because it confines us to a system that
enables the exercise of power through the enactment of regulatory norms.
We must not buy into this. It is oppressive because it assumes that the here-
and-now is normal or natural, when really, it is a product of a history that has
preferred cultural dominations over multicultural tolerance. We must not
buy into this. It is oppressive because it insulates us from discounted possibilities, multiple perspectives. We must try to overcome this. Perhaps now is the
time to reveal and reject the heedless and mindless representations of dominance firmly established in our local school systems.

These interrelated assumptions about the power of print, the developmentalism of learning, and the expertise of teaching have emerged, as we
have shown, through a history of dominating, monocultural power relations, as they now work through educational programs and pedagogies to
fix children in a system where massive inequalities are already institutionalized. Morrison (1994) writes:

> She has thought about what could have been the intellectual history of any
> discipline if it had not insisted upon, or been forced into, the waste of time
> and life that rationalizations for and representations of dominance
> required—lethal discourses of exclusion blocking access to cognition for
> both the excluder and the excluded. (pp. 18–19)

This chapter has considered how patterns of dominance—regulating,
defining, huge wastes of time and life—have manifested themselves in very

real educational movements and moments. Over time, we have seen how difficult it is to escape the lethal discourses of exclusion; we have glimpsed how oppressive, unyielding language blocks access to understanding and the mutual exchange of ideas. But we have hope that epistemological blindness might be replaced by an acute mindfulness that thoroughly watches and is fascinated with other lives, which might change our attitudes about the child and his or her "capacities" in relation to communication and the sharing of knowledges from numerous vantage points.

REFERENCES

Beyer, L.E., & Zeichner, K.M. (1987). Teacher education in cultural context. In T.S. Popkewitz (Ed.), *Critical studies in teacher education* (pp. 298–334). New York: The Falmer Press.

Bourdieu, P. (1974). The school as a conservative force: Scholastic and cultural inequalities. In J. Eggleston (Ed.), *Contemporary research in the sociology of education*. London: Methuen.

Chall, J.S. (1983). *Stages of reading development*. New York: McGraw-Hill.

Clanchy, M.T. (1979). *From memory to written record: England 1066–1307*. Cambridge: Blackwell.

Coles, G. (1998). *Reading lessons: The debate over literacy*. New York: Hill and Wang.

Cornbleth, C. (1987). The persistence of myth in teacher education and teaching. In T.S. Popkewitz (Ed.), *Critical studies in teacher education* (pp. 186–210). New York: The Falmer Press.

Education Department of Western Australia. (1994). *First steps: Reading developmental continuum*. Portsmouth, NH: Heinemann.

Gee, J. P. (1991). The legacies of literacy: From Plato to Freire through Harvey Graff. In M. Minami & B. P. Kennedy (Eds.), *Language issues in literacy and bilingual/multicultural education, Reprint Series No. 22* (pp. 266–285). Cambridge, MA: Harvard University Press.

Gee, J. P. (1996). *Social linguistics and literacies: Ideology in discourses*. Bristol, PA: Taylor & Francis.

Graff, H. J. (1979). *The literacy myth: Literacy and social structure in the nineteenth-century city*. New York: Academic Press.

Graff, H. J. (Ed.) (1981). *Literacy and social development in the west: A reader*. London: Cambridge University Press.

Graff, H. J. (1987). *The labyrinths of literacy*. New York: The Falmer Press.

Graff, H. J. (Ed.). (1995). *The labyrinths of literacy: Reflections on literacy past and present*. Pittsburgh, PA: University of Pittsburgh Press.

Hoyles, M. (Ed.). (1977). *The politics of literacy*. London: Writers and Readers Publishing Cooperative.

King, J.E. (1991). Dysconscious racism: Ideology, identity, and the miseducation of teachers. *Journal of Negro Education, 60*(2), 133–146.

Kliebard, H.M. (1995). *The struggle for the American curriculum: 1893–1958* (2nd ed.). New York: Routledge.

Kohl, H. (1998). *The discipline of hope: Learning from a lifetime of teaching*. New York: Simon & Schuster.

Kozol, (1991). *Savage inequalities: Children in America's schools.* New York: Crown Publishers.

Langham, D. (1994). The common place MOO: Orality and literacy in virtual reality. *Computer-mediated Communication magazine, 1*(3). [On-Line]. Available: http://sunsite.unc.edu./cmc/mag/ 1994/jul/moo.html

Lankshear, C., & McLaren, P.L. (1993). *Critical literacy: Politics, praxis, and the postmodern.* New York: SUNY Press.

Learning First Alliance. (1998). *Every child reading: An action plan.* [On-Line]. Available: www.learningfirst.org/publications.html

Monaghan, E.J., & Saul, E.W. (1987). A critical look at reading and writing instruction. In T.S. Popkewitz (Ed.), *The formation of the school subjects* (pp. 85–122). New York: The Falmer Press.

Morrison, T. (1994). *The Nobel lecture in literature, 1993.* New York: Alfred A. Knopf.

Myers, M. (1996). *Changing our minds: Negotiating English and literacy.* Urbana, IL: NCTE.

Ong, W.J. (1982). *Orality and literacy: The technologizing of the word.* New York: Methuen.

Parenti, M. (1996). *Dirty truths.* San Francisco: City Lights Books.

Pattanayak, D.P. (1991). Literacy: An instrument of oppression. In D.R. Olson & N. Torrance (Eds.), *Literacy and orality* (pp. 105–108). New York: Cambridge University Press.

Popkewitz, T.S. (1991). *A political sociology of educational reform.* New York: Bantam Books.

Rice, J.M. (1893). *The public-school system of the United States.* New York: Century.

Street, B.V. (1984). *Literacy in theory and practice.* New York: Cambridge University Press.

Thomas, R. (1992). *Literacy and orality in ancient Greece.* New York: Cambridge University Press.

Tyner, K. (1998). *Literacy in a digital world: Teaching and learning in the age of information.* Mahwah, NJ: Lawrence Erlbaum Associates.

Tyson, C.A. (1998). A response to "coloring epistemologies: Are our qualitative research epistemologies racially biased?" *Educational Researcher, 27*(9), 21–22.

Whitaker, R. (1996). Orality and literacy in the poetic traditions of archaic Greece and Southern Africa. In I. Worthington (Ed.), *Voice into text: Orality and literacy in ancient Greece* (pp. 205–220). New York: E. J. Brill.

Willinsky, J. (1990). *The new literacy: Redefining reading and writing in the schools.* New York: Routledge.

Wood, A. (1985). *King Bidgood's in the bathtub.* New York: Harcourt Brace.

Zeichner, K.M. (1992). *Educating teachers for cultural diversity.* (A technical report published by Michigan State University).

CHAPTER 4

LIBERATING LITERACY

**Margaret C. Laughlin, Herbert Martin, Jr., and
Christine E. Sleeter**

Abstract: What counts as literacy, how literacy is defined and how particular
definitions of it are coded into standards for curricula and student testing
has been debated over several decades. In schools, literacy is often operationalized as the ability to decode text. While we do not disagree that children
should learn to read text, in this chapter we liberate literacy from a narrow
definition of reading the word to embrace a more empacipatory approach
that includes thinking critically about and participating in the transformation of our societies. First we consider limits of instrumental approaches to
literacy, and ideology in school curricula. We then present alternative ways of
approaching literacy that critically examine the knowledge in which children
are becoming literate. We discuss a project that connects literacy with community knowledge, drawing on work done in Mexico. We also examine a
"New West" focus for resigning knowledge, arguing that children should
become literate in a pluralistic curriculum.

INTRODUCTION

What counts as literacy, how literacy is defined and how particular definitions of it are coded into standards for curricula and student testing has
been debated for several decades. Resnick and Resnick (1977) traced historical conceptions of what literacy means: "It is only during the present
century that the goal of reading for the purpose of gaining information has
been applied in ordinary elementary schools to the entire population of
students" (p. 383). They argued that policy makers define "real literacy" as
the ability to extract information from common texts, such as newspapers,
and use it in work-related situations. Roth (1984) described this concep-

tion as "literacy as reading," which became reified through the increased use of standardized achievement tests: "Reading ability, then, is fast becoming a thing in itself—a commodity which teachers are to produce and verify through grade-level achievement test scores" (p. 293).

In schools, literacy is often operationalized in the way Roth (1984) defined. For example, in a classroom Heap (1985) studied, reading was conceptualized as literal comprehension of texts. Students were to load information from the text into their memory to retrieve in answer to teacher questions. Teachers sought specific textual information through questioning; students were not to consult their own ideas or knowledge, but only specific passages from the text. Simon and Willinsky (1980) studied how literacy was operationalized in a high school. They found literacy to be defined as consuming and producing "language as a correct form," such as correct word usage, capitalization, and sentence structure (p. 117). They observed, "To have a policy that implies that the essence of language is its correctness reduces it to the level of good grooming" (p. 118). While neither of these case studies can be generalized to classrooms, writ large, they illustrate what we experience as common conceptions of literacy: literacy as correct form, and literacy as the ability to recall and reproduce specific information from texts.

Frank Smith (1989) has argued for a conception of literacy that situates it within social relations. He noted, "Individuals become literate not from the formal instruction they receive, but from what they read and write about and who they read and write with" (p. 355). He argues that literacy cannot be separated from thinking and inquiring, which is a social act. Courts (1991) offers a much broader definition of literacy, "The word literacy, then, suggests a state of being and a set of capabilities through which the literate individual is able to utilize the interior world of self to act upon and interact with the exterior structures of the world around him [or her] in order to make sense of self and other" (p. 4).

In this chapter we would like to liberate literacy from a narrow definition of reading the word to embrace a more emancipatory approach that includes thinking critically about and participating in the transformation of our societies. Freire and Macedo (1987) describe this view of literacy as "...a myriad of discursive forms and cultural competencies that construct and make available the various relations and experiences that exist between learners and the world" (p. 10). As an example, we will describe the connections between critical literacy and participatory research projects undertaken with teachers who are practicing in bilingual classrooms. The final part of our chapter outlines a "New West" conception of multicultural curriculum in which what counts as literacy is drawn from previously excluded "voices" and perspectives. Ultimately, our transformative conception of knowledge leads toward a reconstruction of what we take to be literacy.

THE LIMITS OF INSTRUMENTAL APPROACHES TO LITERACY

Discussion of literacy education in the United States by many reading experts continues to revolve around the differing theoretical orientations that claim to inform what we are now defining as a "balanced" approach to reading instruction. Policymakers continue to rely on a body of knowledge that special reading technicians have created to help us define exactly what is a balanced approach to reading. They are paying particular attention to those who would advocate the systematic instruction of reading skills as a theoretical foundation to the mandated curriculum and standards for the teaching of reading. In this view, "balance" comes to be defined as teaching children to decode text so that they can learn the increasingly standardized curriculum more effectively.

Unfortunately, it is outside the specialized circles of those who are obsessed with the technical aspects of decoding printed language where we find a more purposeful discussion of what it means to be literate. We say "unfortunately" because, as defined by Macedo (1994) and Freire and Macedo (1987), many educational bureaucrats who are telling us what we should think and know about literacy reflect a technical instrumentalist approach. That approach reduces literacy to decoding print and in the process functions to reproduce a Western capitalist cultural hegemony and a level of specialization that reinforces an *illiteracy* in other bodies of knowledge. The specialist, or "learned ignoramus" (Macedo, 1994, p. 21), can read the tiny universe of his/her specialization but cannot read the world.

Spiegel (1998) warns us that, if balanced programs are to have any lasting influence, they need to move away from the dichotomous discourse among researchers around "methods" (such as "whole language versus explicit skill instruction") that may address the current issues but continue to be reactive and mask other issues of balance and equity. She defines several components of balance; most salient are the implications of the role of the classroom teacher, who does not necessarily use the same prescribed program for every child but who "makes thoughtful choices each day about the best way to help each child become a reader and a writer.... . that requires and frees a teacher to be a reflective decision maker and to fine tune and modify what he or she is doing each day in order to meet the needs of each child" (p. 116).

Margaret Moustafa (1997) effectively deconstructs the nature of the literacy crisis in the United States. Based upon data from the National Assessment of Educational Progress (NAEP) in 1993, a "Reading Report Card" (which compared fourth grade reading scores from standardized tests nation wide), she has exposed the misconstruction and exploitation of data by political agendas of conservative, back-to-basic advocates so that it appears that the "whole language movement" is to blame for an apparent failure of children to meet minimal standards in reading. Scores for California, for example, were reported as falling in the lower 20 percentile, while several pertinent factors, such as the number of Limited English Proficient students in this state and the average class size as compared to other states, were ignored. As a reaction to the low scores, research on how to teach phonics was commissioned by "back to basics" conservative policy makers to reinforce public perceptions of needed skills instruction to an illiterate population. In fact, Moustafa reveals other research that compared U.S. children's reading achievement on standardized tests to other countries, in which the United States ranked second to Finland in the fourth grade, and tied among several other countries for second in the ninth grade.[1]

Therefore, even if we accept the narrow and instrumental definition of literacy as the ability of students to perform on standardized assessments which measure word attack, vocabulary, comprehension and grammar, the United States is not faring poorly, as would conservative policy makers have us believe. Where we indeed fail is in our ability to engage students from disenfranchised backgrounds in literate practices that result in their full participation in society. Even in bilingual education program models, Garcia (1998) writes, the bilingual teacher is trained to employ "...a series of mainstream methods, strategies, and approaches reproduced from the standardized knowledge industry in which lock-step, time-on-task, and back-to-basics assumptions are utilized to distribute, implement, and measure the learning abilities of all children regardless of their class, gender, ethnic, racial and physical ability surroundings" (p.81). Although Garcia addresses a current dilemma in bilingual education, he also underscores the realities in schools where teachers are reduced to technocrats whose role is to carry out their educator tasks which are congenitally born from accountability and management schemes and theories.

In order to develop a broader conception of what literacy means, we turn now to consider connections between literacy and ideology.

LITERACY, PLURALISM AND IDEOLOGY

Any conception of literacy must be connected to a conception of language. Courts (1991) argues that "language is the possibility of making meaning of and in the world" (p. 7). Language provides a way of organizing one's consciousness of the world (Freire in Macedo, 1994, p. 117). To make sense of everyday life, we use symbolic systems that draw our attention to some phenomena, filter out others, connect and interpret phenomena. Representations in pictures, words, stories, songs, and text all distort "reality" in order to make sense of it, and to direct us to interpret what we experience in terms of that sense-making.

Ideology is embedded in language in that language provides symbolic systems for the organization of consciousness. Apple (1979) defines ideology as "the formation of the consciousness of the individuals" in a society, particularly their consciousness about how the society works (p. 2). "Ideologies are understood as partial accounts of the world constructed from within particular perspectives, historical contexts, and economic, political, and social interests" (Ellsworth & Whatley, 1990, p. 4). By simplifying the complexity of experience, an ideology provides a way of making sense of it; but in the process, ideologies silence or erase that which seems irrelevant from the vantage point of the ideology.

In classrooms, children acquire literacy to learn the curriculum, which is largely codified in print. In a stratified and multicultural society, however, the concept of curricular literacy is fraught with peril, as E. D. Hirsch's controversial book *Cultural Literacy* (1987) has already demonstrated. His thesis attempts to develop a common core of "cultural" knowledge which he believes everyone must know in order to become "culturally literate." The thousands of names, dates, and so forth, chosen for inclusion reflect a definite Eurocentric and anti-pluralist bias. Underrepresented groups such as Chicanos, Native Americans, Asian Americans, African Americans, women, and others are largely excluded from his compilation of "important" cultural knowledge. Nonetheless, his work positively invites pluralistic scholars to join the discussion with an attempt at balancing his Eurocentric perspective on what it means to be "culturally literate."

The idea of literacy within a conventional curriculum has long been a Eurocentric idea which limits even what is considered important knowledge within the Western European model. Thus, in addition to the conscious or unconscious assumption that Eurocentric patriarchal ideas are "normal," there is also a tacit understanding that never needs to be expressed, that ideas from nonmainstream races, cultures, or other microcultural groups are exotic, strange, unnecessary, or possibly immoral or evil. To the degree that literacy is conceptualized as word recognition and comprehension, then as loading information from texts into memory, any discussion of literacy is also a discussion of texts and the ideology embedded in them. Ideological systems are not announced as ideological systems, however; they come to us as explanations of reality, or as stories or imagery that get our attention, and that have some connection with the reality we experience.

Since schools teach ideas and knowledge about society through the curriculum, we can learn a good deal about the belief systems that children learn by examining what gets taught in school and what doesn't get taught. Apple (1979) points out that school curricula have a tradition of being very selective in patterned ways. For example, in school, most people learn about the development of industry and "free enterprise;" most do not learn much in depth about how workers experienced that development and about organized movements to distribute earnings and decision-making power equitably.

We illustrate how this works through education with a story. When one of us (Sleeter) was in college, she encountered, in an art history textbook, a photo of a stone carving of the ancient Egyptian pharaoh, Akhenaton. The photo conflicted so strongly with a taken-for-granted ideology she had learned about ancient Egypt that she recalls staring at the photo, trying to figure out what was not making sense. She stared and stared, and finally filed the puzzle away in her subconscious and simply moved on. Years later she was sitting in a multicultural curriculum workshop and the facilitator, an African American educator, pointed out that Egypt is located in Africa, not Europe. The picture of Akhenaton flashed into her head and the puzzle that had remained buried in the back of her mind for years was suddenly solved. As soon as she got home, she found the art history book and located Akhenaton's picture. She finally saw what should have appeared obvious but what she had learned not to see: This great pharaoh, as well as untold other ancient Egyptians, was Black African.

Once one sees ancient Egypt as having been shaped and led in part by Black Africans, one must take very seriously the potential of people of African descent to create knowledge and to build civilization that is utterly remarkable. This is precisely why ancient Egypt was reframed through a different, and racist, ideology. Martin Bernal (1987) documented the rewriting of history that shifted an understanding of Greece from its Afro-Asiatic roots, to define Greece as having germinated by itself, and to attribute cultural advances of ancient Egypt to people who were presumably at least part European. During the European colonization of Africa, belief systems were revamped to elevate European culture and render non-Europeans as inferior. The magnificence of ancient Egypt could not be eradicated, but Egypt could be portrayed as essentially Aryan rather than African. Akhenaton has been one of the more admired pharaohs because of his intellect, creativity, and institution of radical cultural and religious changes. Bernal writes: "Egyptologists paid particular attention to giving him and his new religion Aryan, or at least northern, credentials" (p. 383). His physical appearance was explained by crediting him with "foreign" blood.

Through the process of studying the development of "Western Civilization" in school, Sleeter had learned to see ancient Egypt as an extension of Europe. No one ever specifically put it that way, but this was implied by placing the study of ancient Egypt in a story line that began with civilizations in the Middle East, then moved to Greece, then to Rome, then on northward through Europe. What did not fit was that Akhenaton did not look European but rather African. The ideology of Egypt as an outpost of Europe was embedded so strongly in her, however, that she was not able to see what was right in front of her.

This is an example of the "ideological fog" that groups in power produce. Freire (1998) writes, "[E]ven if the ideological fog has not been deliberately constructed and programmed by the dominant class, its power to obfuscate reality undeniably serves the interests of the dominant class.

The dominant ideology veils reality; it makes us myopic and prevents us from seeing reality clearly. The power of the dominant ideology is always domesticating and, when we are touched and deformed by it, we become ambiguous and indecisive" (p. 6).

The damage done by the Eurocentric curriculum to excluded groups is manifested in the high dropout rates for ethnic minorities: 44.5% for American Indian/Alaska natives (1990 census cited by Bennett, 1995), 38.9% for Hispanics, 14.0% for Blacks, and 7.6% for Asian/Pacific Islanders—a group that includes both Japanese Americans (who have a low dropout rate) and Samoans (who have a much higher dropout rate). Compare these figures to a dropout rate of 7.4% for whites (1996 statistics, U.S. Bureau of the Census, 1998). The less of a "match" between the culture of the school and the culture of the student, it appears, the higher the dropout rate. Children of color are also more likely to be suspended, expelled, and placed in special education classes; additionally, people of color are overrepresented in the lowest income groups and underrepresented in decision-making positions. The legacy of misinformation and exclusion is also seen in the suicide and attempted suicide rate among gay and lesbian youth, a rate three times higher than that for heterosexual youth.

Students whose cultures are not valued or even present in the curriculum may, if they do stay in school, come to feel that something is "wrong" with their color, their family, and their culture, and that they must hide or deny this part of themselves and embrace "mainstream" culture to survive or "succeed." This attitude has been reinforced as a goal by school personnel who used soap to wash out the mouths of students or physically beat students who use their home language in school (Nabokov, 1991, p. 220).

It is not only underrepresented groups who suffer from a monocultural ideology, however. As Bennett (1995, p. 17) notes, "the waste of human potential affects us all.... The cumulative loss of talented scientists, artists, writers, doctors, teachers, spiritual leaders, and financial and business experts is staggering." We are all hindered by a curriculum that is rooted in a distorted ideology. A mainstream student who is "educated" with a monocultural curriculum by mainstream teaching methods is ill-prepared to help solve the problems of the planet's future, which include pollution, poverty, hunger, and disease. Global cooperation will be needed in the future, and individuals who have cross-cultural literacy will be vital to the efforts to achieve a clean, safe, and just world.

The dominant curriculum creates ideological fog by acknowledging and describing differences, but interpreting them through dominant groups' experiences and points of view, portraying inequalities as either nonexistent or inevitable, and lauding the accomplishments of dominant groups in a way that suggests that their dominance results from personal virtues that everyone else should emulate (Sleeter & Grant, 1991). As children gain literacy in the dominant curriculum of the school, they also acquire the ideological fog embedded in that curriculum as a conceptual system for organizing their consciousness of the world.

Hegemony refers to the power of dominant groups to maintain existing power relationships and to mystify them. Raymond Williams (1976) describes hegemony as an ideology "which is lived at such a depth, which saturates the society to such an extent, and which ... even constitutes the limit of common sense for most people under its sway" (pp. 204–205). The assumption that civilization emerged directly from Europe is an example of hegemony. Apple (1996) discusses why the idea of hegemony is useful:

> The concept of hegemony refers to a process in which dominant groups in society come together to form a bloc and sustain leadership over subordinate groups. One of the most important elements that such an idea implies is that a power bloc does not have to rely on coercion.... Rather, it relies on winning consent to the prevailing order. (pp. 14–15)

In other words, an unequal society can be sustained through some degree of force and violence (which the U.S. high rate of incarceration represents), as well as convincing most people that society as it exists is fair and the best possible so that they go along with it. As long as an ideology can be fashioned and taught so that most people can see some reflection of their own values and interests, and as long as this ideology is put forth (usually over and over) in a way that makes it seem like commonsense, people tend to adopt it, at least to some extent. Chomsky (1987) writes:

> The process of creating and entrenching highly selective, reshaped, or completely fabricated memories of the past is what we call "indoctrination" or "propaganda" when it is conducted by official enemies, and "education," "moral education," or "character building," when we do it ourselves. It is a valuable mechanism of social control, since it effectively blocks any understanding of what is happening in the world. One crucial goal of successful education is to deflect attention elsewhere—say, to Vietnam, or Central America, or the Middle East, where our problems allegedly lie—and away from our own institutions and their systemic functioning and behavior, the real source of a great deal of violence and suffering in the world. (p. 124).

What all of this suggests is that discussions of literacy should not be separated from discussions of ideas in which children are becoming literate. Whose world views are given greatest value, and whose interests do these world views support?

In research conducted recently by one of us using a participatory research model (Laughlin, 1996), teachers in bilingual/ multicultural classrooms grappled with conflicts between traditional ideologies and hegemonic practices in schools, and the goals these teachers had for their students and for themselves. An interactive, dialogic process involving the sharing of common concerns, and the analysis of emerging themes from the research allowed these teachers to find a deeper and more critical knowledge base around the role of the teacher. The following recommendations came from this project for educators who seek to liberate literacy from the constructs and limitations of the dominant paradigm.

- Critical educators see their roles and potentials as "border crossers," fulfilled through cultural work and by serving as a bridge between the school and the communities in which they teach.
- Critical literacy involves increasing an awareness and sensitivity among those who work in schools of those values and ways of knowing other than the mainstream cultural perspectives.
- Critical literacy means investigating the issues of inequity surrounding language and literacy and challenging the hegemonic structures in schools in which we are implicated as teachers and administrators.
- Liberating literacy is achieved through actions that acknowledge not only the need to master the formal, academic language required to succeed in mainstream society, but that also reinvent a discourse of resistance through the use of the native languages and ways of knowing of people in the communities.
- Liberating literacy means that we allow historically suppressed voices to occupy a space in our curriculum, creating opportunities for oppressed peoples to narrate their stories and experiences as valid within a broader, sociohistorical view of literacy.

INVESTIGATIONS IN LITERACY IN THE COMMUNITY

If I can, when I work with kids in front of whatever objects or dioramas and stuff, really get them to begin to discuss and appreciated these things that they see in *relation to themselves* ... my job becomes to create an environment where kids can begin to explore their own identity and begin to appreciate who they are and what they are. (Heather, a museum educator, Teotitlán del Valle, Mexico, 1997)[2]

The Seminar on Transformative Literacy, a summer seminar in Oaxaca, Mexico, has been an ongoing project developed by a team of educators who have worked together over the last four years. Through the joint efforts of teachers in the United States and Mexico, it has evolved into a collaborative teaching/learning experience that has engaged US participants in rich cultural encounters within the Zapotec community and a much greater understanding of the type of transformative pedagogy that we are discussing here.

During the summer session of 1997, teacher participants worked in teams with local teachers and community members to identify worthwhile investigations of community knowledge. From these investigations, they created original texts, either as picture books or other narratives. The books were presented to the community and donated to the local public library. The teachers then returned to the US with ideas to enrich their curriculum in their own school settings. Some have developed and shared their texts as lessons with students in local schools. The purpose of the research during that particular summer, entitled "Culture and Education, Lessons from the Field" and sponsored by the University of California Research Expeditions Program (UREP) was twofold: (1) to learn from the traditions and practices in a small Zapotec community as potential funds of knowledge for the development of curriculum in the classroom in the United States, and (2) to document the transformation of attitudes, beliefs, and practices of the participant/educators from the United States who are involved in collaborative, cross-cultural experiences. One of the overall goals of the seminar, however, is to promote the ongoing collaboration between Mexican teachers and Zapotec families with U.S. teachers who wish to maintain a relationship of exchange and dialogue around pedagogies for literacy as implemented with children of migrant and immigrant families.

Children who attend schools in Teotitlán del Valle come from homes where Zapoteco is the primary language spoken, and indigenous pre-Columbian traditions are preserved. These traditions are practiced throughout the community in the form of social organizations, religion, agriculture, and the process of weaving rugs, for which the village is known. Upon entering school, children are taught in Spanish by teachers coming from larger cities, and the national curriculum of Mexico is implemented. This presents cultural and linguistic realities that in many ways parallel those that confront educators in the United States. Many Zapotec families have immigrated to the Central Valley of California. Some schools have populations of children whose first language is Zapoteco, whose second language is Spanish, and are expected to learn to read and write in English (Smith, 1995).

In recent anthropological research, teachers have discovered that "funds of knowledge" is a transformative principle in developing literacy and changing their own practices as educators (Moll et al., 1993). Households and communities of their students contain a wealth of cognitive resources and practical knowledge which have been applied in the development of curriculum for the classroom. The profoundness of Zapotec culture provided a context to investigate literacy and to generate life texts that could be applied in math, science, social studies, and other content areas to develop literate practices among students.

The project also reflects a movement toward a critical, transformative pedagogy as an approach to literacy education. It recognizes the knowledge that students bring into the classroom and creates meaningful contexts in which students may actively participate in their own learning. As in the works of Freire (1970, 1994), Ada (1995), Giroux (1988, 1993), McLaren (1989) and others, transformative pedagogy seeks to change the social order maintained by hierarchical structures and equalize the relationships between teachers and learners. In this orientation, the reciprocal relationship between teachers and learners is highlighted by one of the participants from the Oaxaca project,

> We're taking time to sit down and you know, talk to people. Like, come and talk with the woman in my house about the way she makes tortillas. And sometimes in our daily lives we don't even have time to like, feed ourselves. (Heather, 1997)[3]

After the two weeks in which one of us (Laughlin) facilitated this work, the following outcomes have been gathered in this ongoing study. Funds of knowledge that were revealed and identified at first by the participants were those that were expressed by the daily activities in which the people in the community engaged, such as rug weaving, eating customs, the use of Zapotec language, and dress. Later, some were able to gain an understanding of beneath the surface and less obvious funds of knowledge that constitute the complex cultural codes and systems by which people govern their lives.[4]

A few of the participants expressed conflict as they struggled with the projection of their own values into the norms that governed relationships between men and women in the village. Although the structures as perceived through their experience in Mexico were more pronounced, parallels can be found in the roles of men and women in different communities in the many regions of the United States. Many of us tend to evaluate and judge, finding conflict in our own realities, as expressed by one participant:

> ...I guess when we started looking at the role of the woman here, it brought up a lot of issues for me, that are really hard for me to deal with and that I am still trying to deal with in my life in general, ... The issue of judging and the issues of accepting that I don't agree with, culturally. My set of values are confronted with another set of values. How do I take that and live with that? I'm looking at these women, who, in my point of view, are really oppressed by this system. You know, the whole food making process is the most exhausting, elaborated thing that takes forever to do, hours and hours of the day..... And I have to remember to keep being honest with myself and do what I believe. And I also have to learn to respect and to understand choices that other people make. (Susana, bilingual teacher, 1997)[5]

Some of the participants were able to perceive and understand the more subtle and complex cultural codes better than others, but all of them produced narratives and texts that elaborated upon specific themes that were learned through their interactions in the community.

The book titles and projects that were produced over the two weeks in the village and presented on the last day of our stay in Oaxaca were the codifications of common cultural capital manifested in the community and around which people built their lives. The products of their efforts became the literacy framework around which further lessons were developed for instruction in the classroom setting.

Susana and Ruby, a bilingual second grade teacher and a bilingual resource teacher, together wrote and illustrated a picture book entitled, "Zhub: el maiz" (Zhub is the Zapotec word for corn). The process of creating this book involved close collaboration with their family, observation and participation in several family operations using corn, and a study of the "science" of the many uses of corn as an essential sustenance and source of tradition in the community. Some of its illustrations were drawn by their host mother of the family, who also helped to provide the explanations and indigenous names for products made with corn. The book, in its finished form, was a work of art, constructed with colored paper, marking pens and water color, depicting scenes from the village. The entire family came proudly and humbly to present the book to our group of participant teachers. It was the first time that their knowledge was recognized by teachers in a formal school setting, and was a significant event in which they claimed co-authorship in a literate practice, based upon their own ideologies and world view.

Other books that were produced in the project addressed similar themes, such as the one titled *El Alfabeto del Tejer* (The ABC Book of Weaving), written by Holly and Tina, two first grade bilingual teachers. They participated in similar activities with their family, and were able to find a Spanish or Zaptotec word that related to the knowledge, values, and experiences of the community for every letter in the Spanish alphabet. The selected alphabet words were associated with weaving, the main economic enterprise of the community but, more importantly, were reflective of the cultural capital of the community. Each page described and illustrated a word, such as: "hilo" (thread), "guich" (wool), "idolo" (idol, used as symbols in the rugs woven), "jarabe" (a regional dance), "respeto" (respect), and "Xaguia" (Zapotec name for their village). The book represented the literacies of the community using words in their own language, and embedded with the realities of their world. The significance of this work cannot be underestimated when considering the need to make the process of reading relevant to the lives of the reader.

Subsequent titles of the books produced by teachers from this project included: "Plant Use in Teotitlan del Valle," "Goals and Dreams of Mexican Immigrants," "Finding the Meaning of Community in a Community Museum," and "The Process of Making and Dying Wool." What remained to unfold were the lessons, or curricula that were being developed in response to engaging in this process. All of us returned to our local areas, and have been teaching and living with communities of people who represent a wealth of cultural practices and languages. Some, like Holly have been able to appreciate more the complexities of bilingualism that are often overlooked:

I need to ask my students, who I think are Spanish speaking as their first language (and it may be for them but for their parents it wasn't), and ask, and
talk to students, have the students be researchers. What other languages did
your parents learn to speak? Or did your grandparents speak? So that the
study is around self-identity, self-esteem and family. ... At my school we have a
high consciousness about indigenous cultures and indigenous languages.
But I think district wide we need to raise that consciousness, because those
students are all over the district, and all over the state (California). And to
share with people that even though the parents speak Spanish perfectly that
doesn't mean that Spanish is their first language. (Holly, 1997)[6]

The questions that we attempted to answer during our stay in the village
in Oaxaca also have become extremely important when operating within
educational settings that only recognize Spanish as a primary language of
immigrants from Mexico. Through investigations with the children and
their parents, we can learn much around how to instruct and enrich the literacy of our students. The questions that we attempted to answer during
our work in Oaxaca can be applied in any community, upon which we must
continually reflect when considering how to engage students in a critical
literacy program:

1.   What *are* children learning in schools?
2.   What are children learning in their homes and in the community?
3.   What is important for children to learn in order to participate in
     our society? In other words, *why* are we choosing to teach children
     what we teach?
4.   What is the relationship between school and community experiences,
     and how are we bringing the two together in our curriculum? What
     sort of literacy experiences are we constructing for the child that will
     engage him/her in critically addressing his/her own realities?

Most important, however, is the relationship that teachers develop with
their students and their parents in order to know them better. As Susana
reflected after the end of this project:

I learned the value of truly listening and having authentic conversation and
communications with others; that it takes honestly, time and commitment to
do so. (Susana, 1997)[7]

MULTICULTURAL LITERACY: A "NEW WEST" APPROACH CULTURAL LITERACY

What, then, would we consider to be a more balanced and transformative
pluralistic perspective on literacy? Just as Women's History Month is not
enough, celebrating "contributions" during Black History Month or having

a fiesta on Cinco de Mayo does not make knowledge "multicultural" if all the other school days go back to the "normal" monocultural curriculum. What is needed is a curriculum which, every day, includes cross-cultural perspectives and provides the tools for students to develop antiracist behavior. These are the beginnings of "multicultural literacy," which is much broader than the Hirsch model (1987) for cultural literacy.

Often educators follow school district curricula and guidelines with minimal regard for how children from diverse backgrounds are emotionally and culturally impacted by the curriculum. As well, most teachers have not been provided with an alternative language for referencing their teaching, which commonly results in an unproblematized location of their work. In other words, educators remain socially and intellectually unengaged just as most of their training calls for. Monolithic and traditional – it is within this formational context that teachers are denuded of any opportunity to understand their roles more broadly as public intellectuals and cultural workers than just simply as classroom mechanics whose roles are reduced to technicians or clerks (Giroux, 1983).

As confirmed by many of us who view literacy as a cultural practice that is situated in the social and historical realities of humans interacting with the world (Ada, 1995; Freire, 1970; Giroux, 1993; Macedo, 1994), the diverse identities of poor and working class children work against them in the standardized learning school settings. These school settings are socioculturally constructed and positioned for dominant-class children and youth whose gender, ethnicity, race, and everyday life are reflected in the school curricula more closely. It correspondingly attacks the identities of children who are not represented by conservative conceptions of knowing and being.

Discussions of knowledge and literacy need to take seriously the counter-ideologies that arise in marginalized communities. It is here that one is most likely to find an acute sense of how injustices work and play out in everyday life, hope and vision for alternative arrangements, and the cultural and intellectual resources on which to build an alternative. Counter-ideologies situate subordinate groups historically in a manner that articulates a group consciousness, redefines their relationship with the dominant society, and suggests changing that relationship. For oppressed groups, framing teaching as a series of technical decisions made by experts constitutes cultural invasion. The dominant society renders as illegitimate systems of meaning and reality originating in oppressed communities (Freire, 1970). As E. San Juan, Jr. (1992) explained:

> Popular memory, a sense of history inscribed in the collective resistance against, racist, patriarchal, and exploitative forces, is one of the necessary means for oppressed peoples to acquire a knowledge of the larger context of their collective struggles, equipping them to assume transformative roles in shaping history.... The struggle to define and articulate a politics of popular

memory on the face of the populist amnesia which consumerism induces occupies center stage in formulating an agenda for an ethnopoetics sensitive to the racial politics of the twenty-first century." (p. 77)

This does not mean that those of us who are members of the dominant society have no role to play, but rather that we need to listen to those we have learned to ignore, seek out insights and wisdom from people we have learned have little to contribute, and collaborate with those with whom we may never have collaborated before.

The "New West" curriculum approach, a multicultural historical model which is put forth in Patricia Limerick's *The Legacy of Conquest* (1987), calls for a more complete presentation of the many perspectives that exist on the "taming of the West" or the old "frontier" model. She presents a history where it is possible to see the European settler as an "invader" disturbing the homes and lifestyles of countless diverse peoples and animals, not to mention the environment itself. Even though this model, along with others in multicultural education (e.g., Banks, 1999; Bigelow & Peterson 1998; Lee, Menkart & Okazawa-Rey, 1998; Nieto, 1996; Sleeter & Grant, 1999), has been in existence for years, it has yet to be operationalized in the great majority of educational institutions, particularly public schools and teacher preparation programs. In clearing up stereotypes and misinformation, this multicultural curriculum would liberate literacy by allowing students to understand how they are shaped by their own culture, and to get an insider's perspective on the values and world views of other cultures. Multicultural education, says Bennett (1995), "confronts the fact that this is a racist society with a history of White supremacy" (p.17) and, by reducing ignorance, helps us achieve our democratic ideals. Based upon the values of respect for the rights of humans and other life forms, appreciation for cultural diversity, responsibility to a world community, and reverence for the earth (Bennett, 1995), the multicultural curriculum shows students that we can look to other cultures (especially those with a closer relationship to Mother Earth, e.g., the indigenous people of the Americas) for ideas and clues on transforming our world.

New feminist scholars, such as Barbara Mor (Mor & Sjoo, 1987), Riane Eisler (1987), and Vicki Noble (1991) added a powerful gender-equity perspective to the discussion on multicultural literacy. As Vicki Noble (1991) states, "It appears that (partnership societies) had enough food, comfortable and attractive shelters, deeply artistic abilities and the leisure to pursue them, a scientific understanding of the movements of the planets and stars that surpasses our own, and a spiritual sense of being part of something larger. We can see remnants of this consciousness in contemporary Native American culture" (p. 230). The concept of "partnership," as seen by scholars such as Noble (1991) and Eisler (1987), refers to societies in which men and women function in equal partnerships, even in the many cases where women played the central role. These are called "matrifocal" societies and included practically all Native American cultures. The above example not only emphasizes an equal partnership between men and women, but also stresses the idea that this equal partnership extends just as strongly to the natural world.

The truly multiculturally literate person would be knowledgeable then in multiple "ways of seeing," instead of having to depend only on the Eurocentric model. The "New West" curriculum would not only transcend traditional male-centered curricula and teaching materials of present schooling by being gender-balanced throughout, but it would also thoroughly integrate multiculturalism and pluralism throughout this new ground-breaking endeavor. Not only would important knowledge about the history, needs, problems, and aspirations of both genders of humanity be featured, but all of this dramatic story would be painted against the backdrop of cross-cultural understanding through history using appropriate curricular materials and techniques. Some of these techniques include emphasizing multiple ways of seeing the world, using multiple intelligences to plan lessons, using nonlinear sequencing in lesson and unit orders, and always including diverse perspectives on a given problem or event. But what is unique about this new pluralistic curriculum is the integration of the "drama of life" of the animals, plants, the environment, and the very earth we live upon as important and vital parts of our story of cultural transformation that must be considered to engage in a holistic curriculum for literacy.

Ours is a time of both crisis and opportunity for education. There is a sense of dislocation because our old approaches and structures in education have been revealed for the monocultural, homophobic, gender-biased, and environmentally-unconscious systems that they are. There have been attacks on this traditional system from critics of many genres. However, the majority of proposed solutions to this educational myopia have been themselves piecemeal, one-sided, and full of "blind spots." An example of this is the call for a "back-to-the-basics" approach along with "old moral values" by Fundamentalist Christians who have historically and openly discriminated against racial minorities and are now *still* discriminating against human beings who happen to be homosexual.

Another example would be any curriculum that would focus on only one cultural perspective in history. It goes without saying that the environment has, for the most part, been nonexistent as a topic of study to be integrated with any of the above curricula. And, for sure, thinking of the two concepts of *spirituality* and the *environment*, as a team, to be integrated in a multicultural/pluralistic curriculum, has been rare.

This "New West" curriculum would contribute to multicultural literacy by integrating a dramatic "story"-oriented approach to our respective cultural histories; one that would include gender balance, awareness of the "naturalness" of *all* sexual orientations, celebration of the great and rich variety to be found among the diverse peoples and cultures of this planet, and an "earth stewardship" approach for all, to improve our future days on this sacred earth. A sense of the urgency and the mutual global importance of the transformation of our ways of looking at the world and its creatures would be a key integrating emphasis throughout this curriculum.

One of the fundamental problems facing our world today is that most members of the patriarchal macroculture devalue stereotypically feminine attributes and work (for example, child care, keeping a family healthy, and maintaining a clean environment). Ironically, many cultures such as Native American ones and Australian Aboriginal traditions are assumed to be inferior and are likewise devalued and continually exploited because of this very same perception of stereotypically "feminine" attributes and cultural habits which allows the mainstream culture to "marginalize" them in the same manner as women. The irony is that in "high context" cultures, such as Lakota or Cherokee, the very same set of ideals about a healthy family, caring for children and maintaining a clean, healthy environment (in fact, these things have sacred status) are at the heart of the indigenous traditions of North America

Let's look at an example. Most educators are aware that youth violence and alienation are serious problems in U.S. society today. However, most of us are illiterate in thinking about youth through cultural lenses other than that of the dominant society. We can read stories and articles about causes of youth violence and alienation, but as a society, we address the issue poorly. In contrast, indigenous American cultures have knowledge about healthy youth development, in which nonindigenous people are largely illiterate. In contrast to the mainstream culture's lack of positive images for females going through puberty, indigenous cultures such as the Mescalero Apache (Mahdi, Foster & Little, 1987) have a sacred puberty ceremony in which all the men of the tribe pay homage and do a day of celebration with the young women who are celebrating their first menses as part of their initiation rite. In fact, during this rite, the girl is ritually transformed into Changing Woman, the mythological founder of Apache culture (Larrington, 1992, p. 337). This "high context" culture, which centers its tradition on the connection to Mother Earth (The Great Goddess), has an automatic ritual which promotes the self esteem of young women and, simultaneously, builds in the collective esteem of the entire group to promote the empowerment of the young women, who are viewed as the vital life of the people.

Not only do girls need positive images to help them through the rigors of puberty, but boys demonstrate the same need to re-enter the womb of the Great Mother for a sacred initiation. In "Running Wolf: Vision Quest and the Inner Life of the Middle-School Student" (Martin, 1996), such an initiation is described as a vital part of the transformation that should take place during puberty. According to Martin:

> At this crucial stage of their lives, very important questions about their lives are beginning to be asked. This is often a time of great inner turmoil, even

when no outward sign seems to manifest itself, as happens sometimes when poor grades, apathy, or drug abuse point to a possible problem. Sometimes, without any previous warning, parents and teachers find out about a student's inner struggle too late—after he/she has committed suicide. (p. 315)

We need multicultural literacy that teaches as many perspectives as possible on important issues like the above because it has been abundantly clear that patriarchal approaches to critical life passages, like the ones all our children face, have not been effective. The entire monocultural curricular approach should be replaced with the "New West" history approach that incorporates the perspectives of the conqueror and the conquered, as well as attempts to provide an environmentally ethical perspective and a deeply multicultural/pluralistic concern for including all of those who played an important role in creating our history. Gender equity and pluralistic history is vital to this approach and should be considered when thinking of the revision of the very damaging curriculum that has held sway in classrooms into the modern age. It is time for a change. The "New West" curriculum, with its emphasis on multicultural and pluralistic literacy, offers a powerful avenue for this change. Literacy, then, would mean becoming literate in words, and also in knowledges and viewpoints that would enable us to create sustaining and life-supportive social systems.

CONCLUSION

One of the pressing issues of the new millennium is likely to be the very survival of the biosphere. Most of us are aware, for example, of global warming and its possible consequences. There is reason to believe that natural disasters, such as Hurricane Mitch, are wreaking greater havoc than in earlier decades because of human-created changes to the landscape such as logging, removal of natural growth, and alteration of waterways.

The world needs literate citizens who are prepared to address the challenges of creating sustainable and life-supporting systems in a diverse and shrinking society. Literacy must include not only the ability to read words and sentences, but also the ability to make sense of the world through language, and through ideas encoded in language, especially print. For us, liberating literacy does not mean ignoring the technical skills involved in decoding print; indeed, without such skills it is difficult to extract meaning from print. However, literacy should not be held hostage to a narrow definition of what it means to read, and what it means to be literate.

We have argued that young people need to learn not only how to connect print with language, but also how to understand the diverse ideas, perspectives, and funds of knowledge embodied in language as it is used in diverse language and cultural communities.

When children enter school, they come with complex histories as family and community members. And this history is reflected in the used words, the signs, with which they respond to the interactive spaces we as teachers create. And in our response to the children, we help shape their understanding of what it means to be an educated person in our society. If our classrooms are not places of sociocultural breadth and depth, we risk sending messages of alienation, messages that say that educated people are not rooted in their own histories, in strong relationships with people that matter. (Dyson, 1998)

NOTES

1.   Where, in fact, the scores did nothing to correlate to any particular method of reading instruction, Moustafa does offer substantive evidence that Whole Language as an approach to literacy, unlike the systematic instruction phonics and phonemic awareness as in isolated components of instruction, is based upon sound research. Krashen (1998) offers further evidence that, on other measures, reading scores have actually increased in California between 1984 and 1990, when a literature based approach was adopted by the State.

2.   Quotes from "Heather," "Susana," and "Holly" are excerpts of transcripts of recorded dialogue and preliminary data from "Culture and Education: Lessons from the Field," a research project conducted by Laughlin in Teotitlan del Valle, Oaxaca, Mexico, 1997, sponsored by the University of California Research Expeditions Program, Berkeley, California.

3.   See note 2.

4.   Nancy Jean Smith's (1995) work has been significant in its contribution to our understanding of the *tequio* and the *guelaguetza* as social practices that sustain and maintain traditions within the village. *Tequio* can be explained as an elaborate framework in which adults donate their time to an important function, such as serving on committees or as a librarian, policeman, or a dancer in traditional ceremonies for a prescribed time. Dropping out of one's *tequio* has serious consequences. The *guelaguetza* is a practice of borrowing and giving that sustains and guarantees that everyone has the basic needs for everyday life, and also places some in a position of status above others.

5.   See note 2.

6.   See note 2.

7.   See note 2.

REFERENCES

Ada, A.F. (1995). Fostering the home school connection. In J. Fredrickson (Ed.), *Reclaiming our voices: Bilingual education, critical pedagogy and praxis* (pp. 163–178). Ontario: California Association for Bilingual Education.

Apple, M.W. (1979). *Ideology and curriculum*. Boston: Routledge and Kegan Paul.

Apple, M.W. (1996). *Cultural politics and education*. New York: Teachers College Press.

Banks, J.A. (1999). *An introduction to multicultural education* (2nd ed.). Boston: Allyn & Bacon.

Bennett, C.I. (1995). *Comprehensive multicultural education* (2nd ed.). Boston: Allyn & Bacon.

Bernal, M. (1987). *Black Athena: The Afroasiatic roots of classical civilization.* New Brunswick, NJ: Rutgers University Press.

Bigelow, B., & Peterson, B. (1998). *Rethinking Columbus: The next 500 years* (2nd ed.). Milwaukee, WI: Rethinking Schools.

Chomsky, N. (1987). *The Chomsky reader.* [J. Peck, Ed.]. New York: Pantheon Books.

Courts, P.L. (1991). *Literacy and empowerment.* New York: Bergin & Garvey.

Dyson, A.H. (1998). Quoted in Almanzo, M. d. l. A., Habashi, B., and Alcala-Collins, E., Rethinking Literacies, paper presented at the California Association for Bilingual Education Conference, San Jose, CA.

Eisler, R. (1987). *The chalice and the blade.* San Francisco: Harper & Row.

Ellsworth, E., & Whatley, M.H. (1990). *The ideology of images of educational media.* New York: Teachers College Press.

Freire, P. (1970). *Pedagogy of the oppressed.* New York: Continuum.

Freire, P. (1994). *Pedagogy of hope* [Robert R. Barr, Trans.]. New York: Continuum.

Freire, P. (1998). *Teachers as cultural workers.* Boulder, CO: Westview Press.

Freire, P., & Macedo, D. (1987). *Literacy: Reading the word and the world.* South Hadley, MA: Bergin and Garvey Publishers.

García, H.S. (1998). Bilingual education and the politics of teacher preparation. *Cultural Circles, 2,* 75–88.

Giroux, H. (1983). *Theory and resistance in education.* South Hadley, MA: Bergin & Garvey.

Giroux, H. (1988). *Teachers as intellectuals: Towards a critical pedagogy of learning.* South Hadley, MA: Bergin & Garvey Publishers, Inc.

Giroux, H.A. (1993). *Border crossings: Cultural workers and the politics of education.* New York: Routledge.

Heap, J.L. (1985). Discourse in the production of classroom knowledge: Reading lessons. *Curriculum Inquiry, 15,* 245–279.

Hirsch, E.D., Jr. (1987). *Cultural literacy: What every American needs to know.* Boston: Houghton Mifflin.

Larrington, C. (Ed.). (1992). *The feminist companion to mythology.* London: Pandora Press.

Laughlin, P. (1996). *Crossing borders: Transformative experiences of Euro American bilingual teachers in a Spanish speaking context, a participatory study.* Doctoral Dissertation, University of San Francisco.

Limerick, P.N. (1987). *The legacy of conquest.* New York: W. W. Norton & Company.

Macedo, D. (1994). *Literacies of power: What Americans are not allowed to know.* Boulder, CO: Westview Press.

Martin, H.L., Jr. (1996). Running Wolf: Vision quest and the inner life of the middle-school student. In L. Maudi, N.G. Christopher, & M. Meade (Eds.), *Crossroads: The quest for contemporary rites of passage* (pp. 311–319). Chicago/Lasalle, IL: Open Court.

Maudi, L., Foster, S., & Little, M. (Eds.). (1987). *Betwixt & between: Patterns of masculine and feminine initiation.* La Salle, IL: Open Court.

McLaren, P. (1989). *Life in schools: An introduction to critical pedagogy in the foundations of education.* New York: Longman.

Moll, L., Gonzales, N., Floyd-Tenery, M., Rivera, A., Rendon, P., Gonzales, R., & Amanti, C. (1993). *Teacher research on funds of knowledge: Learning from households*

(No. 6). Santa Cruz, CA: National Center for Research on Cultural Diversity and Second Language Learning.

Mor, B., & Sjoo, M.(1987). *The great cosmic mother: Rediscovering the religion of the earth.* San Francisco: Harper Collins.

Moustafa, M. 1997. *Beyond traditional phonics: Research discoveries and reading instruction.* Heinemann.

Nabokov, P. (Ed.). (1991). *Native American testimony,* New York: Penguin Books.

Nieto, S. (1996). *Affirming diversity: The sociopolitical context of multicultural education* (2nd ed.). White Plains, NY: Longman.

Noble, V. (1991) *Shakti woman: Feeling our fire, healing our world—The new female shaminism.* New York: Harper Collins.

Resnick, D.P., & Resnick, L.B. (1977). The nature of literacy: An historical explanation. *Harvard Educational Review, 47,* 370–385.

Roth, R. (1984). Schooling, literacy acquisition and cultural transmission. *Journal of Education, 166,* 291–308.

San Juan, E., Jr. (1992). *Racial formations/Critical transformations.* Atlantic Heights, NJ: Humanities Press International.

Simon, R.I., & Willinsky, J. (1980). Behind a high school literacy policy: The surfacing of a hidden curriculum. *Journal of Education, 162,* 111–121.

Sleeter, C.E., & Grant, C.A. (1991). Textbooks and race, class, gender and disability. In M.W. Apple & L. Christian-Smith (Eds.), *Politics of the Textbook* (pp. 78–110). New York: Routledge, Chapman and Hall.

Smith, F. (1989). Overselling literacy. *Phi Delta Kappan, 70,* 352–359.

Smith, N.J. (1995). *Linguistic genocide and the struggle for cultural and linguistic survival: A participatory research study with a Zapotec community in California.* Doctoral Dissertation, University of San Francisco.

Spiegel, D.L., (1998). Silver bullets, babies, and bath water: Literacy response groups in a balance literacy program. *The Reading Teacher: A Journal of the International Reading Association, 52,* 114–124

U.S. Department of Commerce, Bureau of the Census. (1998). *The condition of education 1998.* http://www.nces.ed.gov/pubs98/condition98/

Williams, R. (1976). Base and superstructure in Marxist cultural theory. In R. Dale et al. (Eds.), *Schooling and capitalism.* London: Routledge and Kegan Paul.

CHAPTER 5

TAKING OWNERSHIP OF LITERACY

Who Has the Power?

Patricia A. Edwards, Jennifer Danridge, Gwendolyn T. McMillon, and Heather M. Pleasants

Abstract: This chapter serves to help teachers redefine their conceptions of literacy for culturally-diverse students. We argue that, within the contexts of school, literacy is sociopolitical in nature and reflects the unequal power structures and relationships in society. Thus, culturally-diverse children and their families can feel disempowered by teachers, which can ultimately alienate them from the process of schooling. Using personal narratives, we present four short stories that illuminate the power struggles that can surface between teachers and African American students and their families. Further, we offer practical instructional strategies for teachers that connect schools to the multiple contexts in which African American children and other children from culturally-diverse backgrounds reside: the community, home, and the church. We invite teachers to listen to our stories and apply their lessons in ways that transform the educational experiences of culturally-diverse children.

INTRODUCTION

A child lives in many worlds. Home, family, school, neighborhood, and society shape the contours of childhood and adolescence. Action in one sphere ripples through the others. In the best of circumstances, these spheres are complimentary and reinforcing, guiding children's development into citizens and adults. The best of circumstances, however, elude large numbers of children, especially poor children and children of color who live in the inner city as well as in rural settings (Edwards & Young, 1992). Often children and their families in these settings encounter people and problems that disempower them academically and socially, causing them to feel powerless. Therefore, when I was invited to write this chapter, I was excited by this prospect and shared some of my thoughts with three of my graduate students. As a group of African American women, we are all very conscious of the issues of power that are deeply embedded within literacy and within the contexts of home, school, and community. Our conversation centers on personal and professional stories that illuminated the struggles that teachers, families, and students face. Each story is different, but the emergent themes and issues are interrelated. I discovered that this was a fascinating way to write a book chapter, and I invited my three graduate students to coauthor this piece.

Our overarching goal is to share four stories about the literacy experiences of African American children in different contexts. In doing so, we draw attention to the ways that adults working with these children can be empowered to understand, use, and build on the knowledge that African American children bring with them to different social environments. In particular, these stories illuminate the many worlds in which these children live: home, family, school, community, and society. Our chapter opens with a narrative about my experiences in Donaldsonville, LA, which focuses upon community involvement as a way to promote home-school relations. Connecting with this theme, Heather and I talk about using parent stories as a strategy for balancing the power between families and teachers by positioning parents as "the more knowledgeable others." Next, we move from focusing on the home to thinking about school contexts, as Jennifer shares her story about the power issues that can surface when teachers and students interact. Finally, Gwen presents contrasting stories of two African American students' experiences in school and church. Because the context of the African American Church offers new insights that schools have not considered in educating African Americans and other culturally-diverse children, we thought it fitting to end our chapter by discussing a story that illustrates the possibilities still to be uncovered in different settings.

Our hope is that these stories will help facilitate the process that teachers must undergo in developing the sensitivity and awareness necessary to effectively teach African American students. By using our experiences as contextual lenses, we offer new lessons from persons who have worked with African American students and their families in positive and productive ways. We want the information presented in this chapter to discourage teachers from making decisions based on quick assessments, stereotypes, or previous negative experiences. Instead, teachers must begin to expand their horizons by considering all of the institutions that greatly influence African American students—the community, the home, school, and the African American church. Although we have chosen to focus on African

American children, we hope that the stories we recount will encourage teachers to look to a variety of contexts in order to successfully teach all students.

MY EXPERIENCES IN DONALDSONVILLE

Students' home lives are both blamed for children's low achievement in school and seen as children's salvation (Richardson & Colfer, 1990). In a growing number of communities, the significant adults and institutions in children's lives pull in opposite directions. Tensions rise, and blame is volleyed back and forth between home and school. An example from a rural southern school illustrates this point.

Donaldsonville Elementary School had been recognized for its "good curriculum," even though teachers were disappointed with the progress of their students. Eighty percent of the student population was African American children, and 20% were White children; most were members of low-income families. Teachers felt that they were doing all they could to help these children at school. Without parental assistance at home, the children at Donaldsonville were going to fail. The teachers' solution was to expect and demand that parents be involved in their children's education by reading to them at home.

To the teachers, this was not an unreasonable request. There is good evidence of positive gains made by "disadvantaged" elementary students when parents and children work together at home on homework and learning packets (Cummins, 1986). What the teachers did not take into account was that 40% of the school's parents were illiterate or semiliterate. When the parents did not seem willing to do as the teachers asked, teachers mistook parents' unfamiliarity with the task being asked of them, coupled with low literacy skills, for lack of interest in their children's education. The continued demand that parents read to their children at home, which had a particular meaning in teachers' minds, sparked hostility and racial tensions between teachers and parents. Each group blamed the other for the children's failures; each felt victimized by the interaction. Children were caught between their two most important teachers—their classroom teacher and their parent.

Moving from Blame to Empowerment

To make productive links between parents and teachers, schools have to think differently about what they want for children and what they expect from families and communities. In Donaldsonville, the missing link was forged by a program created by Edwards (1994, 1995) who never accepted the assumption of parents' lack of interest in their children's success. She solicited community support to attract parents to a reading program, where they would be assisted in learning how to read and how to read with their children. She called on community leaders to recruit parents they knew in contexts outside the school. Church leaders, black and white, agreed to preach from their pulpits about the importance of helping children learn to read. They regularly urged parents to attend the weekly reading sessions to learn to help their children in school, noting the importance of literacy as a tool of faith.

A local bar owner emerged as a strong supporter of the reading program, informing mothers who patronized his establishment that they would no longer be welcome unless they put as much time into learning how to read to their children as they spent enjoying themselves in his bar. He provided transportation to school and back home for participating mothers and secured funds from the city social services department for child care for parents who otherwise could not attend. A grandmother organized a campaign to telephone program participants each week. In sum, the bridge that connected home and school was found in the broader community.

In poor rural communities like Donaldsonville and in inner-city neighborhoods, the social context calls for rethinking the definitions and processes of home/school interactions. Parents, teachers and school administrators, and community leaders all have power, but problems arise when these sources of power act in disconnected ways. When we begin to connect these powers in meaningful ways, everyone becomes empowered and students' educational experiences are transformed.

Creating a Balance of Ownership and Power between Parents and Teachers

The Donaldsonville experience motivated me to continue to encourage teachers and administrators to listen to the voices of parents simply because parents know a great deal about their children. According to Edwards, Pleasants, and Franklin (1999), "parent stories" could be one tool for teachers to draw on when they seek to involve parents in their child's education. It is common practice for professionals like doctors, lawyers, and architects to collect information, which gives them particular insights about their patients/clients. Teachers are often criticized for not living in the neighborhoods in which they teach, but rarely do doctors, lawyers or architects live in the neighborhoods in which they practice their professional craft. Instead these professionals rely on collecting information as a way of developing a professional interaction with their patients/clients.

Similarly, Edwards et al. (1999) approach parent/teacher interaction as a vehicle for exchanging pertinent information, because most teachers, schools, and families admit to a lack of communication. When and how did schools and families diverge? Over the course of time, communities and, thereby, schools have become increasingly fragmented. Parents, schools, and the communities that they serve both have lost sight of each other and the responsibilities each hold. The education system in the United States serves children for 13 years in the public schools, longer if children attend preschool or day care programs. Present communication with parents occurs only a few times per year on an individual basis and probably even less often on a group/social platform. A child's future hangs in this precarious balance. In addition, schools may be very separate from the communities from which some of the children come. Society itself has become less nuclear and communal. Many households are run by single-parents. The extended family may live hundreds of miles apart, weakening support systems for families with young children. The economy dictates that more households operate on two incomes, leaving less time for parents to be involved in a child's general needs. Because of these social, political, and logistical issues, teachers and schools find themselves increasingly disconnected from communities and parents.

Without the support of those two pivotal systems, schools have become overburdened and have lost both the sight and ability to accomplish their original goal, to teach. Indeed, "the diverse and difficult needs of today's youth far exceed the ability of any single institution to meet them. Recognition of this fact has fueled policies that encourage or require strategies such as 'integrated services,' 'interagency collaboration,' 'co-located or school-linked services,' or 'school-community partnerships'" (Heath & McLaughlin, 1996, p. 69).

Realizing that schools and families do not communicate effectively prompts the need to regroup and work together to meet the needs of America's children. How can schools begin to instigate better systems of gathering and sharing information from/with parents? In order to construct the two-way communication necessary to build the groundwork for "parent stories" to evolve, schools, teachers, and parents must enter a partnership not unlike an arranged marriage. Trust must be developed in order to gain maximum information. Through the use of parent stories, Edwards et al. believe that trust will begin to develop between teachers and parents.

USING PARENT STORIES AS A SOURCE OF EMPOWERMENT

Edwards et al. (1999) define parent "stories" as the narratives gained from open-ended conversations and/or interviews. In these interviews, parents respond to questions designed to provide information about traditional and nontraditional early literacy activities and experiences that have happened in the home. They also define parent stories through their ability to construct home literacy environments for teachers, and by their ability to connect home and school. By using stories as a way to express the nature of the home environment, parents can select anecdotes and personal observations from their own individual consciousness to give teachers access to complicated social, emotional, and educational issues that can help to unravel for teachers the mystery around their students' early literacy beginnings.

Many parents have vivid memories of their children's early development; specific interactions they had with their children; observations of their children's beginning learning efforts; ways in which their children learned; perceptions as to whether their occupation determined how they raised their children; descriptions of "teachable moments" they had with their children; and descriptions of things about their children that may not be obvious to the teacher but would help their children's performance if the teacher knew.

Parent stories can provide teachers with the opportunity to gain a deeper understanding of the "human side" of families and children (i.e., why children behave as they do, children's ways of learning and communicating, some of the problems parents have encountered and how these problems may have impacted their children's views about school and the schooling process).

Parent stories allow teachers to identify what it means, specifically, when we use the words "home literacy environment" to talk about students' success or lack of success in school. By using parent stories in this way, teachers are able to look at specific issues, problems and strengths of homes, which influence the literacy development of students. This is the first step toward making connections between parent stories and how they can be used to better educate every child.

Also, parent stories have the potential to alter teachers' own dispositions and practice. The concept of parent stories is supported by work of Taylor and Dorsey-Gaines (1988):

> If we are to teach, we must first examine our own assumptions about families and children and we must be alert to the negative images in the literature … Instead of responding to 'pathologies,' we must recognize that what we see may actually be healthy adaptations to an uncertain and stressful world. As teachers, researchers, and policymakers, we need to think about the children themselves and try to imagine the contextual worlds of their day-to-day lives. (p. 203)

Edwards et al. (1999) believe that parent stories should prompt the investigation and redirection of current "parent-involvement," "parent-teacher communication," and "creation of home-school connections" initiatives. They further assert that parent stories underscore the importance that society must begin to really listen to all parent voices and value their information about their children without prejudice, judgment, or apathy.

They conclude by saying, "If we can do this, we will embrace the multiplicity of experiences that parents have and can bring to the educational adventures of their children."[1]

My experiences in Donaldsonville centered around redefining notions of empowerment via community involvement and home-school connections. The story that Heather and I told shared information about parent stories as strategies for specifically creating collaborative partnerships between families and teachers. We believe that these kinds of connections demonstrate to children that parents and teachers care about them. Caring is essential for effective teaching, and it is the focal point of Jennifer's story.

POWER AND CARING

As I reflect upon my school experiences in Philadelphia, the teachers who made a significant difference in my life were the ones who really cared about me. When I think of Mrs. Johnson, my Advanced Placement English teacher in high school, I remember how all the students said she was "tough but good." Mrs. Johnson showed that she cared by criticizing our work, but not our personhood. She demanded excellence and hated excuses, yet she took time to listen to the problems we had with our families and friends. The fact that Mrs. Johnson cared about me as a student and as a person had a profound impact. I had always loved reading and writing, but Mrs. Johnson showed me that I needed to become more comfortable and competent in using those skills to express myself. In her class, I learned that reading and writing can be full of passion, struggle, and triumph, and should not be limited to the correct answer or to the perspective of the teacher. Reading and writing became deeply personal and meaningful endeavors to me and has been ever since my senior year. I believe that Mrs. Johnson's caring is part of the reason why my graduate work has centered around literacy issues.

Teachers like Mrs. Johnson make as significant difference in children's lives because they care. Although teaching can be a difficult, frustrating job, teachers that care still work hard because they want to see their students succeed. Furthermore, these teachers take time to ensure that students are learning in ways that are personally relevant to their lives. Caring about students means teachers must be concerned about their personal development, not just academically, but socially, psychologically, and emotionally as well.

This is the kind of caring that underlies the work of Nel Noddings (1984), Michelle Foster (1997), and Gloria Ladson-Billings (1994) on teaching and learning. They powerfully portray how "the ethic of caring" transforms students' lives, and they remind educators not to forget and/or underestimate the effects that caring has upon students. Pepper (1999) contends that "when students believe you care about them and how well they do in class, and they trust you to treat them fairly in every situation, you have won half the battle in helping them succeed in school" (p. 7). This statement conveys the profound impact that caring teachers have upon their students and their achievement in school.

Although the ethic of caring is central to effective teaching, it can have negative effects upon students if used in the wrong ways (Noblit, 1993). This is particularly true of teachers dealing with students who are considered "at-risk." Typically, these students are poor and/or culturally-diverse children who live in rural or urban communities and experience difficult family/community situations. Teachers can find it difficult to deal with the overwhelming empathy and sympathy that surface when working with children whose educational potential can be impaired by these multiple risk factors. As a result, teachers desire to "save" their students from these circumstances, and demonstrate their caring in two counterproductive ways: extreme permissiveness or authoritarianism.

Some teachers who are consistently lenient with at-risk students believe that they have low self-esteem or damaged self-images due to social and economic risk factors. Consequently, these kinds of teachers overcompensate by constantly providing positive feedback, reinforcing incorrect answers, and accepting low-level quality of work. Jere Brophy (1998) asserts that teachers who constantly praise their students actually decrease their students' intrinsic motivation to learn because students realize this is disingenuous. Further, this consistent "overpraise" lowers student's expectations and task engagement, because they think that anything they do is acceptable, thus they are less likely to behave appropriately or excel in their schoolwork.

These kinds of behaviors and beliefs might be unimaginable to some, yet they are enacted in many classrooms when teachers believe that they have good intentions, and they care about their students' psychological and emotional well-being. This was the underlying assumption of an urban elementary school teacher who once told me that she sometimes gave her students work that was "too easy" for them as a way of giving them a "feeling of success." She believed that caring about her students, who had been labeled "at-risk," meant protecting their self-esteem. While it is true that teachers should be concerned about how they affect students' psychosocial and emotional development, the way she demonstrated her concern was extremely detrimental for her students. Teachers who really care about at-risk students should not oversimplify academic work because that provides a false impression of competence and achievement, which does students more psychological harm than good in the long run. Caring means setting high expectations and goals for academic work and behavior, and providing appropriate scaffolding to support students' endeavors in achieving those goals.

Although standard-setting and maintaining order is involved, some teachers perceive caring as a strict and inflexible form of discipline. These kinds of teachers control student behavior with rules that are enforced via systematic rewards and punishments and emphasize the outcomes of performance goals (i.e., perfect papers, correct answers) rather than learning and constructing knowledge (Brophy, 1998). Teachers believe that this kind of caring is beneficial for "at-risk" students, particularly when they think that these students aren't getting any guidance, direction, or attention from home. Consequently, these teachers overcompensate for this perceived lack of discipline by demanding that students work and behave in narrowly-prescribed ways. In classrooms such as these, I have heard teachers comment that the students, particularly the African American boys, needed this kind of authoritarian control in order to "learn how to act right" in school. Presumably, these teachers believe that at-risk students have great difficulties controlling themselves, thus caring involves enforcement of law and order.

Educators know that good intentions do not automatically translate into good teaching. What we forget is that good intentions do not always facilitate an ethic of caring that is positive and transformative for students. We believe that our choice to become educators reflects a deep commitment to the "human side" of education; we care about the welfare of our students and we are concerned about their futures. But when we think about caring, we tend to forget about the "power side" of education. Despite the fact that classroom settings maintain unequal power relationships between teachers and students, teachers perceive caring to be a relationship of balanced power between themselves and students. Oftentimes, caring is represented as a reciprocal relationship where both parties benefit. However, there is a significant amount of power in teaching, and teachers must recognize that their relationships and interactions with students cannot be completely equal if they want to teach effectively. So how can teachers use power and care simultaneously?

George Noblit's (1993) work offers this invaluable insight: teachers can use their power and caring effectively if they recognize the ethic of caring within the context of power and distinguish "between power used for its own sake and power used in the moral service of others" (p. 35). When teachers realize that they have power and caring, they discover that their caring mediates the power embedded within their role as teacher. Within this context of caring, power is reconceptualized and views the other as a subject rather than an object (Noddings, 1984). Consequently, this mediated relationship between power and caring enables teachers to courageously help students fight for academic excellence. Rather than using caring in powerless ways that promote permissiveness or authoritarianism, these teachers use the power of teaching to display caring in ways that strengthen, nurture, and support their students' academic and psychosocial development.

Power and Caring: An Urban Educator in Action

Being in a classroom where a teacher is both powerful and caring is literally an inspirational experience. It captures the essence of teaching and learning as a human process, where teachers and students share in co-creating new knowledge about themselves and the world. Teachers who use power and caring create classrooms where academic success is an attainable goal for all students. I had the opportunity to spend one year in this kind of classroom. The teacher's name is Mr. Andrews, and he has been teaching for three years in an urban, Midwestern elementary school. His first grade students come from linguistically and ethnically diverse backgrounds, and include African Americans, European Americans, and Hispanic Americans. Further, a significant number of children in his classroom are eligible for free or reduced lunch. Many of Mr. Andrews' students are considered "at-risk," but he uses his power and caring to develop four critical strategies that support students' academic endeavors.

Power in Self-knowledge

Mr. Andrews is a caring teacher because he has taken time to deeply reflect upon his life experiences and has begun to weave some of the lessons learned into his teaching. In order to use power for the moral service of students, teachers need to know who they are and what they believe. These are the kinds of questions they should ponder: What are my true intentions as a teacher of "at-risk" children? What are my true feelings and beliefs about people who might look, act, and think differently than they do, and how do they deal with those differences? Teachers need to think deeply about these kinds of questions because those who do not know themselves will be more apt to use their caring and power in inappropriate ways.

Mr. Andrews displays a strong sense of caring that comes from the power of cultural self-knowledge. As a Euro American, he has a deep sense of his own cultural identity. He describes himself and his early life experiences as "multicultural" because he has a rich ethnic heritage, and he has interacted with many different kinds of people. He uses his own life experiences to make connections with his students and their experiences. For example, his childhood experiences in the South and his professional/educational experiences in the North give him a deeper appreciation of regional differences in cultures and lifestyles, and he shares those differences with his students as they studied the Fifty States. This openness enables students to freely share some of their families' migratory stories and experiences. Consequently, his notion of diversity expands to include differences in families and their practices, and this becomes a primary focus in Mr. Andrews' classroom. Throughout the year, he encourages his students to share some of their family stories using photographs, talk, and texts.

In this way, Mr. Andrews uses the power of self-knowledge to open himself to learn more about his students and their culture. Teaching is not his personal soapbox because he willingly learns from his students. Since he enjoys learning about cultural diversity, he positions his students as the "more knowledgeable others" as they share their family stories and life experiences. Mr. Andrews demonstrates the power in mutual learning and teaching that occurs when teachers find a balance between sharing their own life experiences and learning from the experiences of their students.

Power in Established Classroom Routines

Mr. Andrews often demonstrates his caring by sharing ownership of the classroom with students. They move freely about the room during work time because he trusts them to complete their tasks and holds them accountable for their own work. He also encourages students to be responsible, not only to him, but to each other. The classroom rules reflect this sense of community: (1) be honest, (2) be responsible, and (3) be a good friend. These rules guide the social and pedagogical practices in Mr. Andrews' classroom. He encourages students to "help their neighbors" if they see a student having difficulty with the seat work or struggling to read a text. This creates a feeling of "we" in his classroom that is symbolic of the shared ownership between Mr. Andrews and his students.

Noblit (1993) views the establishment of classroom routines as "teacher-centered" in the sense that the teacher sets the ground rules and these rules constrain students' behavior. Thus, although Mr. Andrews rules are flexible, they explicitly demonstrate his power. However, the fact that students have some freedom within the constraints of the rules demonstrate his caring. Brophy (1998) suggests that teachers who care provide rules because they help to facilitate a collaborative classroom environment. The rules provide a guide for students as they collaboratively work to support each others learning. Further, classroom rules are very important vehicles for promoting autonomy and self-regulatory behavior because students know what behaviors are acceptable from the onset.

Power in Knowing Students' Families

Mr. Andrews believes in learning about students and their families in proactive ways because he cares. Rather than waiting for parent conferences to meet his students' families, he arranges brief visits to their homes in the beginning of the academic year. These visits give him the opportunity to meet parents in a more relaxed, informal environment. For about 20 minutes, Mr. Andrews and parents discuss their goals and expectations for the year, important dates throughout the year, and some of the child's life experiences. Mr. Andrews believes that meeting parents at their homes makes a significant difference in the amount of parental involvement he receives. He reports that he has 100% at almost every parent conference throughout the year, and has few problems soliciting parent volunteers for special events and field trips.

Mr. Andrews' home visits are significant to his teaching because he gains invaluable information from parents that he incorporates into his curriculum and instruction. For example, Mr. Andrews organized a field trip to the farm after he visited with parents and discovered that many families had not traveled outside of the city. He also purchased class pets with a small grant he received, because many parents could not afford to buy their children pets of their own. In both examples, Mr. Andrews connected these experiences to reading and writing activities. Students wrote in their journals about these experiences, and Mr. Andrews brought in trade books on the theme of animals to share with the class.

Although home visits are a useful idea, teachers must be cognizant of the power issues that can surface during these interactions. Mr. Andrews commented that he has to be very sensitive when he visits parents because, they are not accustomed to having school personnel in their homes. Initially, some parents are wary of the home visit. Because Mr. Andrews is aware of this issue, he does not stay for an extended period of time, and he is very careful about the kinds of questions he asks because he wants to make parents feel as comfortable as possible. It is important for teachers to recognize that power issues can emerge, whether they are interacting with parents during home visits or parent-teacher conferences at school.

Power in Motivated Literacy

Based upon Turner's (1993) work on motivational contexts for literacy instruction, Brophy (1998) defines literacy as activities that are open (student-centered) and authentic rather than closed. These kinds of open activities can range from small group work to whole group discussions, but they typically focus upon tasks that promote higher-order cognitive thinking, collaboration, and pursuit of personal interest. Thus, reading and writing activities connect with students' intrinsic motivation, which can increase student engagement in literacy activities, persistence in reading/writing, and following through to task completion and accomplishment of learning goals.

Mr. Andrews demonstrates that he genuinely cares about his students via motivated literacy activities in the classroom. He uses information gathered from the home visits, such as students' favorite colors, their favorite toys, and their family members, as a way to develop relationships with his students and to create personal and meaningful contexts for their reading and writing activities. The children are always excited about reading and writing because they learn to use these skills to express themselves and to communicate with others. For example, the students are part of Galaxy 2000, a science program that facilitates student pen pals. Mr. Andrews uses letter writing to their pen pals as opportunities to teach writing skills within an authentic context.

Mr. Andrews is also concerned about his students' self-esteem, and his instructional methods reflect this sensitivity. For example, most first grade teachers use ability groups for reading instruction. However, Mr. Andrews is fond of choral readings (he and the children read in unison) and echo readings (the class repeats the text after he reads it). He uses echo and choral reading, particularly with basal stories, to introduce/review vocabulary and to increase sight word recognition. These strategies are very beneficial because they enable all of the children, particularly struggling readers, to hear how fluent reading sounds. Regie Routman (1994) describes this kind of shared reading approach as a "rewarding reading situation in which a learner—or group of learners—sees the text, observes an expert (usually the teacher) reading fluency and expression, and is invited to read along" (p. 33). This kind of apprenticeship signifies caring and power. Mr. Andrews effectively teaches his students to read because he uses his powerful status as expert in a caring way that supports and scaffolds students' reading efforts.

Finally, Mr. Andrews uses a similar style of apprenticeship for shared writing activities. Typically, he explains to the student that he is working with that "they are writing together" and that he will be the scribe. As the student produces the oral text, Mr. Andrews explains what he is writing and why (i.e., "I put a period there because that's where our sentence ends"). Also, as Routman (1994) suggests, he negotiates meaning and word choice with the student throughout the activity. If their oral text is not in "standard" English, then he talks with them about the syntactic differences between conventional and nonconventional English, and writes these differences on paper so the student understands the difference. Then, they settle upon the word choice and continue writing the text. This exemplifies Mr. Andrews' ability to use his power to serve students. He talks with them in a caring, respectful way while he negotiates meanings and word usage that does not co-opt the student's voice. Further, his explanation of the differences between oral text and written text helps to illuminate the conventions of writing. In these teachable moments, the caring must be present in order for teachers to resist taking control of production of texts away from the student.

In closing, power and caring are two essential tools for effective teaching. Teachers like Mr. Andrews recognize and accept that they can use the power of their role as a teacher in caring ways that empower their students in educational and personal ways. Because they care, these teachers are willing to take a proactive approach to establishing partnerships with parents and developing meaningful relationships with students by incorporating their interests, their families, and their cultural experiences into the classroom setting. One significant experience in students' lives that is not drawn upon is their church experiences. In the next story, Gwen uses the voices of two African American boys to uncover some of the vital ways that the African American Church can contribute to teachers' knowledge.

EMPOWERING EXPERIENCES IN THE
AFRICAN AMERICAN CHURCH

I was born the daughter of a Baptist preacher and a primary Sunday School teacher. Some of my fondest memories include participating in classes and activities at church. The church provided a "safe" social outlet for its members, many of whom lived in inner-city neighborhoods. The church also offered classes and educational activities for children. One of the "main events" of the year was the Easter program when all the children would dress up in their fancy dresses with big bows, straw hats with ribbons, patent leather shoes, and three-piece suits with dress shirts and colorful ties, to say their Easter speeches. My mother always expected me to turn my speech into a dramatic presentation. With great articulation and clarity, I had to speak boldly and use hand gestures emphasizing each phrase. Although some of the children were shy, I actually loved the attention. After saying my speech perfectly, I would look at my parents for their approval, curtsy, and wait for the emotional audience to burst into a long applause. Some of them would stand, smiling lovingly, others would shout "Amen!!!" or "Beautiful!!!" My dad would say "That's my baby!!!" Their compliments motivated me to work hard and practice repeatedly whenever I had to speak before an audience. In classes at church, I was one of the children that always wanted to answer questions, pass out paper, or read the scripture. My performances and other experiences in church were transferable to the school setting. I was a very outspoken and enthusiastic learner. I enjoyed reading aloud and always utilized the voice inflections that I heard my mother use when she read to me from her big, red Bible storybook.

During childhood I noticed that all the children in my mother's Sunday School class seemed to enjoy the class. She made sure that everyone participated in classroom discussions and activities, and the students never had behavior problems in her class. However, some of the students complained about their experiences at school. Sometimes during Sunday School the students would share some of the problems that they were having with teachers, administrators and other students in school. My mother would encourage them and try to help them find ways to cope with their situations. I was very unhappy that some of my church friends were not having the types of positive experiences that I was enjoying in school.

My interest in this area was later reestablished while substitute teaching at a high school where I personally knew many of the students. Some of the students and I were members of the same church. I was very surprised to learn that some of them had been placed in Special Education classes, and others were at risk of failing several courses. At church, these students were extremely successful, participating in various activities and classes, and displaying leadership qualities. However, at school they appeared to be disillusioned, uncomfortable and alienated from the school's academic process. I was determined to understand this perplexing phenomenon by trying to find possible sources of the incongruencies between the African American church and America's schools.

From a sociocultural perspective, the African American Church is an institution that must be studied when considering the outside influences that particularly affect African American students (Frazier, 1974; Lincoln & Mayima, 1990). Victoria Purcell-Gates (1995) states: "When we seek to understand learners, we must seek to understand the cultural contexts within which they have developed, learned to interpret who they are in relation to others, and learned how to process, interpret, or decode, their world" (p. 5). Heath (1983) also discusses the importance of studying all the environments within a community: "The ways of living, eating, sleeping, worshiping, using space, and filling time which surrounded these language learners would have to be accounted for as part of the milieu in which the processes of language learning took place" (p. 3). Because the African American church plays an extremely significant role in the black community, it is important for teachers of African American children to become knowledgeable about the literacy experiences that occur within the context of this learning environment. When African American students attend church, they have rich literacy experiences that affect their learning processes, their perceptions about literacy, and ultimately their literacy development at school. I believe that one of the gaps in educational research literature is careful consideration of the major influence that the African American church has in students' lives and the lives of their parents.

In order to gain a student's perspective of the incongruencies between church and school, two African American students were invited to participate in a dialogue addressing this issue. Both students had experienced being considered a failure in school, but a "superstar" in church. Issues of power were prevalent as the participants shared some very compelling stories describing their experiences.

B.J. Retains Power

B.J. grew up in church. He comes from a long line of preachers. God called his father, grandfather, great-grandfather, and great-great-grandfather to preach the "Gospel." Many people are waiting with great anticipation believing that B.J. will preach also. B.J. is a well-mannered, fun-loving teenager who is loved by the young and old at church. He is known for his exceptional oratory skills. From a very young age, he was often chosen to be the Master of Ceremonies for programs at his church and citywide youth programs. His extemporaneous, fervent prayers have touched the hearts of many. As a young teenager, he was asked to do the invocation at the Mayor's Scholarship Ball, and was affectionately known by his schoolmates in middle school as "Preacher Boy." Although he always seems to have a smile, he has had some tough times in his life, outside of the church setting. B.J. reminisced about "the worse year of his life." He was 9 years old, in the 4th grade and his dad decided to put him in a predominantly white, private school. His dad had been told that the school was one of the best elementary schools in the city. B.J. said his life was very distressing at the time. He was living with his father and stepmother. He had to deal with all the issues that come with existing within the complex structure of a blended family, he missed his "real" mom who lived in another city, and he hated his new school. B.J. stated: "Nothing was going right! I hated every day that I had to go to that place. The teachers were prejudice. The kids were prejudice. I was one of three black kids in the school. One was half white, and the other one was black, but thought she was white. I was all alone. Kids would take my ideas for projects. I didn't have any friends. They would hide my papers ... and nobody would believe me. My dad would punish me cause he thought "I wasn't tryin'." The school suggested that B.J.'s dad take him to a learning center where he could be tutored and undergo a series of tests. The learning center recommended that he be put on Ritalin because of some type of brain malfunction.

B.J.'s dad was confused because he did not understand the diagnosis. Although he was a college graduate, the counselor at the learning center did not explain the diagnosis clearly enough for him to understand. If B.J. really had a problem, he wanted to get him the proper help; however, he did not want to give him medicine unnecessarily. After B.J.'s teacher, principal, and tutor at the learning center insisted that he accept their recommendation, he gave B.J. several doses of the medicine but decided to discontinue the medication after discussing the problem with several family and church members. B. J. said:

> When I took that stuff, I felt weird! I knew there was nothing wrong with me. I just needed to be somewhere where I could be me. They were tryin' to make me into something that I wasn't. I set one goal for myself that year—to do whatever it took to get out of that place (the school). There was only one place where I felt good about myself ... that was at church. My Sunday School teacher was Ms. Harris at the time, and she looked out for me big time! She showed me love and let me be me. I would tell her stuff, and she would try to help me out. She taught me how to deal with all the anger that I was feeling. That was the worse time of my life! If it hadn't been for her and some of the other people at church, I don't know what I would've done. It was hard!

At the end of the school year, teachers and administrators at the private school tried to convince B.J.'s dad that he needed to be retained. He did not accept their advice but instead decided to let B.J. go back to his old elementary school, a predominantly black school in his neighborhood. B.J. began to enjoy school again, and his grades changed to all A's and B's without Ritalin.

Marcus Regains Power

Marcus, a well-loved, mannerable, young man who has starred in several dramatic presentations at church, affectionately refers to several women at the church as "mom" and is considered a "son" to many of the older men. Marcus is known for his sincere, heart wrenching prayers and testimonies which he offers extemporaneously. He has often publicly thanked the church people for their prayers, which he believes, have prevented him from becoming a "statistic." At one time, he did not think that he would make it to his 18th birthday because he experienced losing so many of his friends during his mid-teenage years. He has been in church from birth, and his mother (a single mom), has taught him to believe that the people in church love him. When he has had problems, she did not hesitate to request assistance from people at church. She has used the resource people (educators, social workers, informed parents) at the church to help her make educational decisions for her two sons.

Marcus, a gifted drummer (who has never taken drum lessons) was also psychologically tested and prescribed Ritalin. He said that the experience of being tested was overwhelming for him. He began to wonder if something was really wrong. Marcus had been a good student until his 4th grade year. "My teacher was white that year and she tried to make me feel stupid. I couldn't do nothing right. I began to believe her myself. Mrs. C. (an African American church woman) encouraged me and told me to hang in there until I get in her class the next year. She knew that I was upset most of the time in that class." Marcus' mother, similar to B.J.'s dad, wanted to do the right thing. She wanted to help her son if something was wrong. They were both frustrated and confused about giving their sons medication to help them learn, because as parents they had not noticed any problems. She also decided to stop the medication after a while. The following year in Mrs. C's class, Marcus began to flourish again. "Mrs. C. showed me love and told me that I was smart and could do the work. I just needed a teacher who understood where I was coming from."

Power in Teacher-Student Connections and Disconnections

Marcus' and B.J.'s experiences support the belief that students can be at-risk in one classroom or school environment but successful in another. B.J.'s experience in a predominantly white, private school may have occurred because of cultural differences between him, the teachers, and other students, however, Marcus had a similar experience in a predominantly black school with a white teacher. Their experiences compel us to emphasize the need for teachers to become more aware of the power that they have over their student's experiences in and out of their classrooms. Cazden (1988) asserts that it is every teacher's challenge to connect with his/her students each year by adjusting his/her own personal style. She further argues that teachers are responsible for the teacher-student connection. Cazden states: "Teachers, like physicians and social workers, are in the business of helping others. But as a prerequisite to giving help, we have to take in and understand" (p. 26). Unfortunately some teachers do not realize that a major part of their responsibility as teachers is to *understand* their students. Without this understanding, the teacher cannot connect with the student. This disconnection cannot only cause students to be at-risk or possibly fail in their classroom, but the negative learning experience can affect the child's future educational pursuits. Marcus and B.J. were labeled "at-risk" and prescribed medication that was necessary for them to become successful students, according to their teachers and evaluators at the time. If they had continued taking the medication, the mere fact that they were labeled "at-risk" and taking medication could have influenced a counselor's recommendations for their educational careers during middle school and high school. Their future teachers may have assumed that the source of their learning problem was diagnosed carefully and correctly, thereby making certain assumptions about their abilities as students. Teachers must recognize the powerful impact that they have in their students' lives and begin to more carefully utilize their power in positive ways, especially to create connections with their students.

Building a teacher-student connection is a necessary prerequisite for learning. Children are more likely to be receptive to a teacher and value the knowledge that the teacher is sharing in the classroom, if the teacher is receptive to the student and value their knowledge. Marcus' connection with Mrs. C. is a good example of the essential reciprocity that must be found in teacher-student relationships. Their connection was especially unique because she encouraged and motivated him to regain his self-confidence *prior* to him becoming a member of her class. For Marcus, her kind words gave him the power to courageously deal with his current powerless situation by anticipating the excitement of being in her class the following year. In other words, Mrs. C gave Marcus hope. Both years, Marcus fulfilled the prophecy that his teacher projected for him. In his 4th grade classroom, he was almost a failure, which was blamed on his "at-risk" characteristics and his mother's refusal to wholeheartedly accept the recommendations concerning her son. In Mrs. C's class, however, he regained his confidence, his grades improved, and he began to enjoy school again. It is important to note that Mrs. C. was an African-American "church woman." She was familiar with Marcus' background and used the power of familiarity to empower Marcus.

B.J.'s relationship with his Sunday School teacher, Ms. Harris, is also an excellent example of a powerful teacher-student connection. Because B.J. was having problems, Ms. Harris adjusted her personal style of teaching to accommodate him. She spent more time addressing issues that affected her students' day-to-day experiences during Sunday School class time. She provided a forum for her students to discuss their family and school problems and created an opportunity for them to suggest solutions for each other. As a social worker, she used her academic training and work experiences to provide useful coping strategies for her students. These strategies, combined with the Biblical lessons that she taught, empowered her students by helping them understand the relevance of their Christian and cultural beliefs in their daily lives. Her relationship with B.J. included many characteristics that assist in creating teacher-student connections: trust, understanding, time, compassion, knowledge, wisdom, commitment, and willingness.

The African American Church—A Powerful Resource

The relationship between B.J. and Ms. Harris, and Marcus and Mrs. C. represent part of a complex, social network system within the structure of the African American church. Many values and beliefs are taught and internalized in this learning environment. Fordham (1988) describes the relationship orientation of many African Americans as a "fictive kinship system." Within this system, she claims that some values are taught that may clash with values taught within the American educational system. For example, individual accomplishments are highlighted in the school setting. A person is considered "a good student" if they study hard and receive high scores. This element of competition in academic achievement encourages students to "do better than everyone else." The valedictorian and salutatorian are held in high esteem during high school graduation because they have the highest and second highest grades in their class. In the African American community, and especially within the context of the church, individual accomplishments are recognized, but success is measured by one's willingness to utilize their own accomplishments to help others. This cultural value can cause conflict within the conscience of a student who desires to be the "top student" but not at the expense of their friend not being recognized as the "top student." Students must be taught how to successfully negotiate the cultural boundaries of their various worlds within which values may differ. Teachers cannot aid in this process if they are unaware of, or insensitive to, the cultural conflicts that their students may be experiencing. Ms. Harris and Mrs. C were not just aware of the cultural beliefs that B.J. and Marcus had been taught; they shared those beliefs, and were participants of the social network system within the church structure. This social network system is a source of empowerment for all that allow themselves to develop an allegiance through mutual admiration and respect for professional people, as well as people who may not be considered powerful in the outside world, but have acquired wisdom from trials and tribulations in their lives. Ms. Harris and Mrs. C are but two of the many resource people available to students in the African American church. The system includes members of all social classes, neighborhoods, skin tones, and various types of familial structures. The remnants of diversity represented within the African American church are sewn together by a common thread—a great love for a God who is omnipotent and who has continuously used His power to help African Americans in their struggles to achieve liberation and equality in the United States.

Summary

There are many African American students who have had experiences similar to Marcus' and B.J.'s. They find themselves in a classroom with a teacher who does not seem to understand who they are. Unfortunately some of these students do not connect with another teacher/person who empowers them in time to save them from becoming distraught and losing their desire to learn in the school setting. Marcus and B.J. were fortunately reached by teachers who believed in them and who shared many of their beliefs. Their experiences exemplify the idea that the way a person is treated directly affects his probability of success or failure in an environment, which further supports the importance of relationships in learning environments for African American students. From the students' perspective, their decision to learn was based on their connection with the teacher. They learned where they were accepted, valued, motivated, and encouraged. They flourished when they perceived that the teachers believed in their ability. Their success or failure was a self-fulfilling prophecy.

When the teacher's and students' cultures are different, many complications occur. If these conflicts cannot be resolved as a result of teacher awareness and sensitivity, students' educational careers can be ruined. Because our educational successes and failures are so closely tied to our total existence in the United States, teachers have the power to help students create a rung on their ladder to success or knock a student off the ladder completely. Some students are resilient, such as B.J. and Marcus. With the help of church people, family and several devoted teachers they were able to regain their confidence, but many students never come back. They are left powerless and lost forever.

The social network system within the African American church provides numerous resources for its members. People within the context of the church believe it is their personal responsibility to set an example for others by living according to Biblical values, as well as encourage others to do the same. Research conducted in the African American church setting can be especially useful in illuminating various cultural values and informing teachers of African American students. It is essential that teachers become more knowledgeable concerning their students' cultural values. With this knowledge, teachers will gain the power to make the teacher-student connections necessary to ensure a productive learning environment.[2]

CONCLUSION

We have presented four stories as a way to illuminate issues of power and culture that contextualize the literacy development and educational experiences of students who come from ethnically, linguistically, and economically diverse backgrounds. Like Delpit (1995), we recognize that teachers are agents of the "culture of power" because they typically endorse mainstream, middle-class values and norms. The challenge that teachers face is to prepare students from diverse backgrounds to become successful within the culture of power, while respecting and building upon the cultural knowledge and experiences that students bring into the classroom.

The message of our stories is that teachers can use their power in ways that empower students and families from diverse backgrounds. Pat's example from Donaldsonville demonstrates how teachers can reach poor, low-achieving students by building partnerships with parents and communities. Donaldsonville teachers were successful once they recognized that parents' concern about their children's education was greatly mitigated by low literacy. By utilizing powerful community alliances, these teachers supported the literacy development of students and their parents. In doing so, teachers affirmed their commitment to listening to parents from diverse backgrounds. Heather and Pat's example of "parent stories" (Edwards et al., 1999) provides a practical way for teachers to glean pertinent information about children's rich home literacy experiences during their conversations with parents.

Further, it is important for teachers to use their power in ways that are sensitive to and respectful of diversity. Toward this end, Edwards et al. (1999) assert that teachers become more appreciative of cultural diversity when they identify and understand their own cultural heritages. In Jennifer's story, Mr. Andrews was such an effective urban teacher because he understood his European American cultural heritage, and he openly shared his cultural experiences with his students. In doing so, he created a classroom environment that invited students to also share their cultural knowledge. Moreover, Mr. Andrews elicited information about parents' home literacy experiences and cultural practices during home visits. These strategies are integral parts of the "ethic of caring" that Noddings (1984) describes. Caring teachers invest time and energy to learn about their own cultural heritages and those of their students in an effort to craft a pedagogy that is culturally-sensitive and appropriate (Ladson-Billings, 1994).

We believe that when European American teachers understand their own cultural backgrounds, they *can* build strong interpersonal relationships with students from diverse cultures. Without this personal knowledge, teachers can impede student learning through cultural misunderstandings (Cazden, 1988; Heath, 1983). In Gwen's story, Marcus and B.J. were accustomed to building close, trusting relationships with Sunday School teachers and other adults in the African American church environment. When they were unable to make similar connections with their teachers at school, B.J. and Marcus felt frustrated and confused. Although some teachers may feel uncomfortable with the idea of establishing close bonds with their students because of their own cultural values, it is their responsibility to find creative ways to reach beyond their idiosyncrasies to ensure success for their culturally diverse students. As Cazden (1988) asserts, teachers must make "personal adjustments" to reach students in their classrooms each year.

We believe that our stories offer some important suggestions about what teachers can do to work more effectively with students from diverse backgrounds. Ferdman (1990) contends that "in a culturally heterogeneous society, literacy ceases to be a characteristic inherent solely in the individual. It becomes an interactive process that is constantly redefined and renegotiated, as the individual transacts with the socioculturally fluid surroundings" (p. 187). It is important for teachers to listen to the multiple voices in the sociocultural worlds of home, community, school, and church, and to become more aware of the power struggles within these contexts that can potentially mitigate students' academic achievement and literacy development. We believe that our narratives provide opportunities for teachers to encounter "real life" situations that help them understand the lives and experiences of culturally-diverse students and their families. Our hope is that these stories offer new insights that empower teachers and inform instruction for the new millenium.

ACKNOWLEDGMENT

The authors gratefully acknowledge the support of the research reported in this paper from: The Center for the Improvement of Early Reading Achievement (CIERA), under the Educational Research and Development Centers Program, PR/Award Number R305R70004, administered by the Office of Educational Research and Improvement, U.S. Department of Education.

NOTES

1.   For more information on parent stories see Edwards, Pleasants, and Franklin (1999).
2.   A more detailed discussion of the African American Church as a learning environment is forthcoming (McMillon & Edwards, 1999).

REFERENCES

Brophy, J. (1998). *Motivating students to learn.* New York: McGraw-Hill.

Cazden, C.B. (1988). *Classroom discourse.* Portsmouth, NH: Heinemann.

Cummins, J. (1986). Empowering minority students: A framework for intervention. *Harvard Educational Review, 56*(1), 18–36.

Delpit, L. (1995). *Other people's children: Cultural conflict in the classroom.* New York: The New York Press.

Edwards, P.A. (1994). Responses of teachers and African-American mothers to a book reading intervention program. In D. Dickinson (Ed.), *Bridges of literacy: Approaches to supporting child and family literacy* (pp. 175–208). Cambridge, MA: Blackwell.

Edwards, P.A. (1995). Combining parents' and teachers' thoughts about storybook reading at home and school. In L.M. Morrow (Ed.), *Family literacy: Multiple perspectives to enhance literacy development* (pp. 54–60). Newark, DE: International Reading Association.

Edwards, P.A., Pleasants, H.M., & Franklin, S. (1999). *A path to follow: Learning to listen to parents.* Portsmouth, NH: Heinemann.

Edwards, P.A., & Young, L. S. (1992). Beyond parents: Family, community, and school involvement. *Phi Delta Kappan, 74*(1), 72–80.

Ferdman, B. (1990). Literacy and cultural identity. *Harvard Educational Review, 60*(2), 181–204.

Fordham, S. (1988). Racelessness as a factor in black students' school success: Pragmatic strategy or pyrrhic victory? *Harvard Educational Review, 58*(1), 54–84.

Foster, M. (1997). *Black teachers on teaching.* New York: The New Press.

Frazier, E.F. (1974). *The Negro church in America.* New York: Schocken Books.

Heath, S.B. (1983). *Ways with words: Language, life, and work in communities and classrooms.* New York: Cambridge University.

Heath, S.B., & McLaughlin, M.W. (1996). The best of both worlds: Connecting schools and community youth organizations for all-day, all-year learning. In J.G. Cibulka & W.J. Kritek, (Eds.), *Coordination among schools, families, and communities: Prospects for educational reform* (pp. 69–93). Albany: State University of New York Press.

Ladson-Billings, G. (1994). *The dreamkeepers: Successful teachers of African American students.* San Francisco: Jossey-Bass.

Lincoln, C.E., & Mamiya, L.H. (1990). *The Black church in the African American experience.* Durham, NC: Duke University Press.

Mcmillon, G.T., & Edwards, P.A. (1999). *Including the African American church in the conversation concerning the education of African American students: Some are doing badly in school, but doing well in church.* (Unpublished paper)

Noblit, G.W. (1993). Power and caring. *American Educational Research Journal, 30*(1), 23–38.

Noddings, N. (1984). *Caring: A feminine approach to ethics and moral education.* Berkley: University of California Press.

Pepper, K. (1999 Spring). Managing today's classrooms. *New Teacher Advocate, 6*(3), 7.

Purcell-Gates, V. (1995). *Other people's words: The cycle of low literacy.* Cambridge, MA: Harvard University Press.

Richardson, V., & Colfer, P. (1990). Being at-risk in school. In J.I. Goodlad & P. Keating (Eds.), *Access to knowledge: An agenda for our nation's schools* (pp. 107–124). New York: College Entrance Examination Board.

Routman, R. (1994). *Invitations: Changing as teachers and learners K-12* (2nd Ed.). Portsmouth, NH: Heinemann.

Taylor, D., & Dorsey-Gaines, C. (1988). *Growing up literate: Learning from inner-city families.* Portsmouth, NH: Heinemann.

Turner, J. (1993). A motivational perspective on literacy instruction. In D. Leu & C. Kinzer, (Eds.), *Examining central issues in literacy research, theory, and practice: Forty-second Yearbook of the National Reading Conference* (pp. 153–161). Chicago: National Reading Conference, Inc.

PART III

LITERACY AND CULTURE

CHAPTER 6

AN AFRICAN-CENTERED PERSPECTIVE ON LITERACY

Promises and Possibilities

Barbara J. Diamond

Abstract: This chapter reports on case study research that focuses on an African-centered approach to literacy learning. The purpose of the study was to identify how literacy was defined within the context of a first/second grade classroom in an African-centered school, and how it was used to construct meaning in the students' lives. The findings indicate that literacy was *liberating* because students read and wrote about the world they experienced daily and the connection between their lives, their roots and traditions, and the lives of others in the wider world. Literacy was also *implicit* because students were guided daily by a set of principles, rituals, and protocols that encompassed the values of the community and permeated the curriculum throughout the day. These principles, although not directly taught, indirectly influenced how students made meaning of their world and of what they read and wrote. Finally, literacy was *explicit* as the direct teaching of skills and strategies created opportunities for functional uses of reading, writing, speaking, and listening that were embedded in literature and texts that included African and African American characters, traditions and culture. These findings have implications for researchers and educators who seek ways to improve literacy learning and achievement for African American students in urban settings.

INTRODUCTION

Despite efforts to improve the literacy instruction of African American students, they continue to perform at levels significantly below their European American counterparts (Kunjufu, 1984; Pasch et al., 1990; Irvine, 1995; Weiner, 1993). As Edelin (1990) notes, African American students often excel in arenas outside of school, but the talent bank of many of these same students remains untapped within the confines of the classroom. In fact, they often perform at the lower end of the academic achievement spectrum. Sadly, as we move into the millennium, Edelin's concerns continue to hold true.

Confounding the problem are demographic trends which, despite 45 years of desegregation, report that a large number of the African American student population continues to be resegregated and "locked" into our urban schools (Littman, 1998). While the image of the American dream visualizes schools that are multicultural, the reality is that many schools in urban settings will continue to be monocultural, with African American youth comprising 100% of the population. The tragedy is not that they are African American, but that opportunities for academic success remain elusive (Boykin, 1994; Neito, 1996; Weiner, 1993). Moreover, many of these students are disproportionately identified as behavior problems and are placed in special education classes. As educators continue to implement reform efforts and employ new and alternative curricular strategies to lessen the achievement gap, parents and students become increasingly perplexed.

As an African American educator, I have a profound interest in the achievement of all students, but particularly African American students. My work in multicultural literacy has focused on students with diverse backgrounds, including African Americans. In a two-year study (Diamond & Moore, 1991, 1995) my colleague and I investigated the effects of a multicultural literature-based program on the reading achievement and attitudes toward reading, writing, and culture of students in two school districts of diverse populations. The program integrated multicultural literature—including African American literature—into the reading curriculum. Both school districts, one with a small number of African American students, the other with about 50%, reported the vocabulary and total reading achievement (gain scores) between the treatment and comparison conditions were consistently greater for the African American students than for the European American students.

As a result of these findings, and my university work with literacy education and prestudent teachers in urban schools, I wanted to examine more closely literacy programs in which culturally compatible curricular interventions were implemented. Therefore, I looked to urban schools and classrooms with an African American population and a nontraditional approach to curriculum and literacy education. However, it soon became apparent that most urban schools with predominately African American populations continue to use a traditional, European-centered approach to literacy and curriculum instruction (Nieto, 1996; Rossi, 1994), characterized by content, methods, and perspectives that reflect a monocultural, European-oriented America. Thus, I decided to investigate schools and classrooms that adhered to an African-centered approach, classrooms that are purported to emphasize an approach to literacy and curriculum that are inclusive of and driven by African American students' background experiences, histories, and traditions.

To understand the theoretical underpinnings of an African-centered perspective, which has often been misrepresented, misunderstood, and criticized, I begin with a somewhat detailed examination of African-centered education as it is grounded in multicultural theory and research. I then present a case story of one classroom in an African-centered school, focusing on the literacy curriculum and pedagogy within this context. Third, building on insights gained from this case, I discuss implications for literacy-learning of African American students in urban settings, as a beginning of revisioning literacy learning in the twenty-first century.

THEORETICAL PERSPECTIVES

Multicultural Education as Critical Pedagogy

Multicultural education began as an outgrowth of the civil rights movement in the 1960s and 1970s and, as such, has always been connected with critical pedagogy. Because of this history, its conceptualization included an emphasis on the teaching of cultural pluralism as emancipatory (Gay, 1977; Suzuki, 1979), eliminating racism from schools, and being truthful about our history and "the great chasm between the promise of equality and the reality of unequal schooling" (Nieto, 1995, p. 192). This view of multicultural education has been continuously promoted by concerned educators (Asante, 1991; Banks, 1991; Neito, 1996; Sleeter, 1991) even as it has moved through a period of celebrations of diversity rather than its original emphasis on the political struggles for racial equity and, later gender and class equity. This connection between multicultural education and critical pedagogy is at the heart of movements such as African-centered education, feminist pedagogy, and bilingual education, with their constructs of empowerment, problem-posing education, and the social construction of knowledge.

Several studies have focused on African-American student learning and curriculum interventions as a central goal, connecting critical pedagogy with multicultural education. For example, Ladson-Billings (1994) conducted a study of successful strategies of teachers in predominantly Black schools in the United States. She identified strategies rooted in the cultural experiences of the students as well as strategies of sociopolitical activism. These included oratory, and literature as central to students' literacy learning, teachers and students engaged in a collective struggle against the status quo, and students who were taught within a learning community, similar to an extended family.

Similarly, Moses (1989) conducted a study of African American middle school students of varying abilities and their participation in an algebra program. The investigator maintained that math and science instruction for traditionally unsuccessful students must extend beyond simply technical instruction. In this study, Moses used pedagogy based on the civil rights movement—specifically, the Mississippi organizing tradition. As a result of this program, 39% of the graduates of the program achieved placement in honors geometry or algebra courses as they entered high school.

When the experiences that students bring to school are grounded in the students' home, family and community, their learning becomes multicultural by the very nature of the content. Neito (1995) maintains that this focus on students' backgrounds and experiences is also critical pedagogy because it "challenges students to take responsibility for their own learning while at the same time supporting and respecting their cultures, languages, and experiences" (p. 204).

A critical perspective on multicultural education, according to Ogbu (1992), must be guided by knowledge of the nature of learning difficulties of students from specific groups before attempts are made to design interventions and strategies. Consistent with Neito (1995), Ogbu further suggests that there needs to be an emphasis on students' responsibility for their own learning and a focus on active and critical learning on the part of the students. In the section that follows, I examine more specifically, African-centered Education and its historical development.

The Emergence of African-Centered Education

African American scholars such as Carter G. Woodson (1936) and W.E.B. Dubois (1961/1903) challenged the established canon in social science and history in the nineteenth and twentieth centuries. Indeed, Woodson's (1936) classic, *The Mis-education of the Negro*, highlighted the fundamental problems pertaining to the education of the African American in America. Woodson contended that African Americans had been educated in such a way that they adopted and valued European culture to the detriment of their own heritage (p.7). The scholarship of both these men was influential in the African American academic community but largely ignored by the white world (Murtadha, 1995).

It was not until the ethnic studies movement, growing out of the civil rights movement of the 1960s and 1970s, that the Eurocentric canon was again seriously challenged. During this period, a group of Afrocentric scholars (Asante, 1990; Hilliard, 1978; Karenga, 1986; Nobles, 1986) produced information that places African Americans at the center of history. They began by redefining the starting point for African American history beyond slavery to ancient Africa (Murtadha, 1995).

In recent years, building on the impetus created by Afrocentric scholars, hundreds of private and public schools around the country have made efforts to solve the disparity in achievement between African American and European American students by centering the curriculum on African culture (Kantrowitz, Wingert, Rogers, Joseph, & Lewis, 1991) and placing African American students in the center of the educational process (Asante, 1991; Cole, 1989).

Grant and Sleeter (1997) note that, beginning in the late 1980s, African-centered schools and their curricula received extensive publicity in papers like *Education Week*, which reported

...school districts in Atlanta, Indianapolis, Milwaukee, Pittsburgh, Washington and other cities are in various stages of adopting Afrocentric programs inspired by a curriculum pioneered in the predominantly white Portland, Ore. school system. (Viadero, 1990, p. 1)

Asa Hilliard, III (1978) developed the African American Baseline Essays that were used in the Portland Oregon schools. These provided teachers with content in six areas on achievements of African people from the time of Egypt to the present (Sleeter & Grant, 1993).

The movement in the direction of an African-centered curriculum raised scathing criticism from the public and scholars alike. In many instances these were critics who had little understanding or background knowledge of the movement and/or refused to acknowledge a history other than that espoused by European-American scholars.

However, the African-centered approach that is presented here, is acknowledged and legitimized to varying degrees by multicultural scholars in their explanation of approaches to multicultural education. The following section highlights the connection of African-Centered education to multicultural approaches.

African-Centered Education in a Multicultural Framework

According to Grant and Sleeter (1997), there are at least five distinguishable approaches to multicultural education that differ quite significantly. These approaches include the *human relations, teaching the culturally different, single-group studies, multicultural education (or cultural democracy,* and *education that is multicultural and social reconstructionist.* The phrase "single-group studies" refers to a focus on a particular group of people. This approach as one which attempts to raise the social status of the group and explore ways that it has been oppressed. Included in these groups are African Americans, Asian Americans, Native Americans, Latino/a Americans, and Women. In schools, this approach focuses mainly on the curriculum and views school knowledge as political rather than neutral. It presents and examines the status of the group both in the past and currently to further the history of the group. Additionally, this approach advocates that students take action to improve the groups' status in society. Finally, it clearly draws distinct lines of separation between the in-group and the out-groups, and fosters identification and solidarity among members of the specific ethnic or gender target group. Viewing school knowledge as political rather than neutral, this approach offers alternatives to the existing Eurocentric, male-dominant curriculum. Given these characteristics, the African-centered curriculum is closely aligned to the single group studies approach.

While Banks (1997) does not identify a single group approach, he identifies four approaches to the integration of ethnic content into the curriculum. These include the *contributions approach*, characterized by recognition of ethnic heroes/heroines, food, and festivals, which leaves the mainstream curriculum unchanged in its basic structure, goals and other principles. A second approach, the *additive approach*, integrates ethnic content into the curriculum, again, without restructuring it. Banks identifies the third approach, *the transformation approach*, as differing from the first two because, in addition to adding ethnic content to the mainstream core curriculum, the basic assumptions of the curriculum are changed, thus enabling students to view concepts, problems, accomplishments, issues and themes from several perspectives. Banks' final approach, the *social action approach*, includes the elements of the *transformation approach* but motivates students to think critically, become decision makers, and "skilled participants in social change" (Banks, 1997, p. 239). Again, the African-centered curriculum, with its elements of social change and group empowerment is compatible with Banks' transformation approach.

Finally, Neito (1996), while offering cautions about the more nationalistic and ideological models of Afrocentrism, asserts that the reasoning behind Afrocentric schools is understandable and even healthy because of the destruction of large numbers of African American students in traditional school settings. She further argues that

> ...culture-centric responses represent an important challenge to the hegemony and Eurocentrism of the curriculum and pedagogy in most schools (or in the case of schools for females that have a feminist perspective, to the hegemony of patriarchy). They question the promise of equal educational opportunity for all youngsters by demonstrating how this noble ideal has often been betrayed. In addition, because such schools are usually designed by people from the very community that they serve, they provide an important example of self-determination and self-definition. (p. 353)

The work of these multicultural scholars, along with Afrocentric scholars, offers support for the African-centered concept as a legitimate component of the multicultural framework. Importantly, its principles and tenets can provide valuable insight into literacy learning for African American students in urban schools.

LITERACY IN AN AFRICAN-CENTERED CLASSROOM

In this section, I present an insider's view of a classroom in an African-centered School that I visited as a part of a larger research project (Diamond, 1996) conducted in five urban cities. My primary purpose in examining these classrooms was to identify how literacy was defined in the context of African-centered schools and how it was used to construct meaning in the students' lives. I further wanted to understand the role of the teacher and her practices in shaping and implementing literacy curriculum.

Research Context

Although in this chapter I present only one classroom, I used the case study approach within the framework of qualitative research for the larger study. This approach, is defined by Merriam (1988) as "an intensive, holistic description and analysis of a bounded phenomenon such as a program, an institution, a person, a process, or a social unit" (p. 7). I, thus focused on the classroom as the "social unit" and the curriculum and pedagogy as the "program." Ujima Village is a K-12 private African-Centered School in the heart of a large urban city. It is a member the Council of Independent Black Institutions (CIBI),[1] a network of African-centered schools.

Data Collection and Analysis

I collected data from classroom observations, teacher and student interviews, and artifacts (student school work, reading/language arts texts, library books, and school documents, pictures, memos, and goal statements). To meet the case study requirements, the observations were conducted for a full day for 14 days in the month of May. The observations were conducted primarily in the classrooms, with some observations in the library or playground as appropriate.

I reviewed data after each visitation day. This provided an opportunity for initial analysis and refinement of data collection procedures for the next visit. In-depth data analysis began after typing and transcription of audio tapes and field notes were completed. Observations and teacher/student interviews were read and reread for emerging themes (Glaser &

Strauss, 1967). The student work samples, texts and library books, and school documents were examined and evaluated as a means of triangulating the data.

RESULTS

In this section, I present a case story of a 2nd/3rd grade class at Ujima Village, an African-centered school, as a unique example of the African-centered school's literacy program and philosophy. Included is background information about the school itself in order to provide a deeper understanding of the findings.

Ujima Village: A Story of A School, A Classroom, and Its Literacy Program

School Philosophy and Curriculum

The philosophy of the school was outlined by the principal, Nia Henderson, who has been the director since its inception in the 1970s. Henderson, stated, "Our philosophy is that all children are gifted." This means that they have a spark in them that can be developed into something really great. It's left up to us to determine what that is and to help them develop their greatness." She also stated that the school's mission was dedicated to preparing students to take their place in the world. She further emphasized the importance of students' knowledge about their history, and the need to be active in changing society and fighting against racism and injustice.

Henderson described the curriculum as dynamic, with subject content and instruction constantly changing and adapting to the needs of the students and social and political circumstances in the community. As an example of the changing curriculum at Ujima Village, she focused on the instructional materials, emphasizing that the teachers use a variety of materials, including literature, anthologies, artifacts, and textbooks. They (the teachers) are encouraged to be creative in finding and developing instructional materials as concepts are presented. She notes that often reading centers around events in the local newspapers that affect the students' families and communities. Henderson further asserted that:

> We've done it (used a variety of materials from different sources) because we started out that way so it's a matter of ideology and lack of resources. When we started in the 1980s, there were no African-centered materials like there are now. We had to create and hunt around for materials and cast it in age appropriate terms. When we decided we would use textbooks, one of the reasons was because it kind of organized levels of information. We wanted them (the teachers) to learn how to use textbooks. So we went to the textbook. But

last year we kind of slid over into the textbook syndrome. We criticized ourselves and now have a more balanced use of innovative materials and texts.

In the school, broad themes and concepts were identified for each month in the subject areas of math, science, social studies, art, music, grammar, vocabulary, reading, and geography. Principles of the Nguza Saba[2] (see Figure 1) were also incorporated into the curricular plans (see Figure 2) to be stressed during specific months of the school year. For example, the theme for September was I AM SPECIAL/Black Reading Month and the two principles for the month were Umoja (unity) and Kujichaulia (self-determination).

Henderson's description of the school's curriculum and teacher interaction with the curriculum were corroborated by the teachers as I spoke with them both formally and informally.

NGUZO SABA

1. **UMOJA** (Unity): to strive for and maintain unity in the family, community, nation and race.

2. **KUJICHAGULIA** (Self-determination): to define ourselves, name ourselves, create for ourselves and speak for ourselves instead of being defined, named, created for and spoken for by others.

3. **UJIMA** (Collective Work and Responsibility): to build and maintain our community together, and make our sister's and brother's problems our problems and to solve them together.

4. **UJAMAA** (Cooperative Economics): to build and maintain our own stores, shops and other businesses and to profit from them together.

5. **NIA** (Purpose): To make our collective vocation the building and development of our community in order to restore our people to their traditional greatness.

6. **KUUMBA** (Creativity): To do always as much as we can, in the way we can, in order to leave our community more beautiful and beneficial than when we inherited it.

7. **IMANI** (Faith): To believe with all our hearts in our people, our parents, our teachers, our leaders, and the righteousness and victory of our struggle.

Figure 1. The Nguza Saba (The Seven Principles).

I AM SPECIAL/BLACK READING MONTH
Umoja and Kujichagulia

Math:
Chapter 1
Addition/Subtraction to 12

Science:
The Five Senses

Social Studies:
Identity and Race Consciousness

Art:
Books "All About Me"

Music:
Black Reading Month Rap
Traditional Songs of Africa
Spirituals

Vocabulary:
Sense organs,
Self-determination,
unity, race identity

Grammar:
Forms of Be
Nouns
Functional Writing

Reading:
Black Literature for
Children
Caring for books

Vocabulary:
Sense organs, self-determination,
unity, race, identity

Math:
Chapter 1
Addition/Subtraction

Geography:
Identify United States and Africa
on World map and Globe
Midwestern States

Figure 2.   Curricular plans. Overview for September.

Physical Environment

There was a large extended open space as I entered the three elementary and middle elementary level classrooms of Ujima Village. The space was "planned to create an environment of sharing of resources and to build a sense of community," according to the director, who further asserted, "by design we have an open school like this, although sometimes it gets a little harried in here, but most of the time it's pretty peaceful."

The three multiage (ages 6–7 1st grade; 7–9 2nd & 3rd grades; 9–11, 4th & 5th grades) classes in this area were situated on either side of a large aisle and were separated by book cases and storage cabinets. One classroom had a wall that did not extend to the ceiling, but separated the classroom from a multipurpose room with a sink that was sometimes used for science and art classes. The walls and bulletin boards were covered with students' work, African maps, world maps, and colorful kente cloth. There were posters and charts of math facts, and the manuscript and cursive alphabets. A banner with the CIBI pledge (Figure 3) was posted in each classroom.

Mama[3] Aso, a certified teacher of four years, described how the setting first affected her when she came to the school to interview for her teaching job.

> They had a big felt design of Africa that was on the wall ... it took up the whole wall ... they had different countries that were labeled ... the posters of African American leaders, writers, and performers up on the wall ... and the children's work, their poems and pictures of themselves, it gave me a warm feeling ... I said to myself, this is what I'm looking for.

She and her two children have been a part of the "school family" ever since that visit. Mama Aso teaches the students, 6–7 years of age about the Masai Land (named for the Masai Tribe in Africa).

THE CIBI PLEDGE

We are African people struggling for national liberation. We are preparing leaders and workers to bring about positive change for our people. We stress the development of our bodies, minds, souls, and consciousness. Our commitment is to self-determination, self-defense, and self-respect for our race.

For the triumph of Black nationhood,
I pledge to my African nation
To the building of a better people and a better world,
My total devotion, my total resources,
And the total power of my mortal life.

Figure 3.   The Cibi Pledge: The National Pledge of all member schools of the Council of Independent Black Institutions (CIBI).

The Unity Circle: The Day (composite of several) Begins

The typical day in Mama Aso's class was marked by protocols and rituals that were conducted at regular intervals. The opening protocol included a call by a designated teacher or student to come to the unity circle… "Get ready for the unity circle" Mama Aso called. Students from each division (preschool, elementary, high school) formed their circle and stood with arms folded across their chests and recited the national pledge of the CIBI schools. Following this was a time for meditation as students set within the circle. Mama Aso led the meditation on most occasions. On one day, as students closed their eyes to meditate, she discussed with the class the importance of having good thoughts in their hearts about parents, classmates, teachers, and friends and sharing those thoughts by letting them know how they feel. According to Aso, the exercise and discussions are implemented to help students think about their lives and goals for the day, to be quiet and prepare for positive learning experiences. One student in the upper division, suggested,

> …that's our chance to open up personally and just see the other side of ourselves. The lights are off and either a teacher or a student will lead the meditation and we start together, but eventually go off into our own personal inner world … we get a chance to relax for a minute, then we come back from there and we are ready for class.

Engaging in Learning for the Day

Following the unity circle, students go to their classes. Mama Aso's 1st/2nd grade class of 18 children worked at tables and began their daily journal writing activity. The students were allowed to choose their topic, although they typically wrote about something that had happened during meditation. Sarafina disclosed her thoughts about meditation in her journal along with plans for a special birthday event for her great-grandmother (see Figure 4). She also was able to connect home with school as she wrote excitedly about her great-grandmother's birthday. Brandon, on the other hand, shared his imaginary trip to Egypt. His writing demonstrated his retention of knowledge about the African continent that had been introduced in class. Moreover, he was able to use the knowledge to recreate his own story, demonstrating knowledge of both the form and function of language. In this class, Mama Aso encouraged students to write freely and to use invented spelling.

Mama Aso used a combination of whole group and small group configurations in organizing for instruction. Typically, after journal writing the whole group came together on the carpet where she explained the reading/language arts lesson and the primary work at the centers for the day.

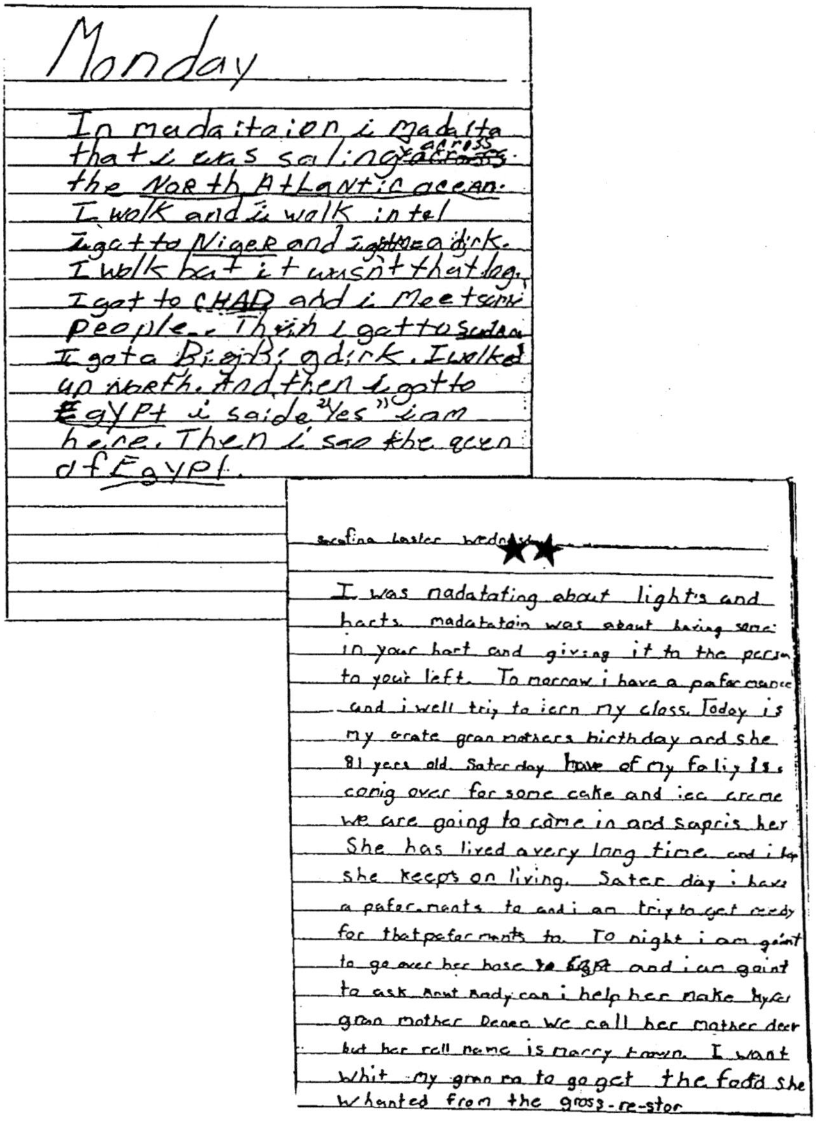

Monday

In madaitaion i madita that i was saling across the North Atlantic ocean. I wolk and i wolk intel i got to Niger and i got a dirk. I wolk but it wasn't that log. I got to CHAD and i meet some people. Then i got to Sudan I got a big big dirk. I wolkd up north. And then i got to EGYPT i saide "Yes" i am here. Then i see the quen of Egypt.

Serafina Lasler wednesday ★★

I was nadatating about lights and harts. madatatoin was about having some in your hart and giving it to the persin to your left. To morrow i have a paformance and i well try to iern my class. Today is my grate gran mothers birthday and she 81 years old. Sater day have of my faliy is conig over for some cake and ice creme we are going to come in and sapris her She has lived a very long time. and i hope she keeps on living. Sater day i have a paformeants to and i am triy to get ready for that paformeants to. To night i am gaint to go over her hase to fight and i am gaint to ask Anut Rady can i help her make hyer gran mother Denea. We call her mother deer but her call name is merry town. I want whit my gran ma to go get the food she whanted from the gross-re-stor

Figure 4.   Students' journal writings.

Five centers were set up and students rotated through them in groups of three to five students. The centers were Reading/Language, Science, Math, Art, and Social Studies.

One lesson was developed from the book *Cornrows* by Yarbrough, which tells the story of braided hair as an African tradition. The students had performed the story as a choral reading after having heard it several times. The following day, Mama Aso brought in information about Queen Nzinga, who had been discussed in *Cornrows*. The students were to read the selection at the center, with partners. However, as she typically did, Mama Aso modeled a vocabulary or comprehension strategy prior to center activity.

Mama Aso: Leslie, please read the first sentence.

Leslie: I will protect you who seek safety and security.

Mama Aso: Good. Now who can tell me what security means, based on how it was used in the sentence?

Students responded with several different comments.

Justin: Like security guards.

Aisha: It means being protected.

Courtney: It means safe … having someone watch over you.

Mama Aso acknowledged the students' responses and explained that the other words in the sentence like *protect* and *safety* could help them figure out the target word. She explained that *security* in this sense meant freedom from someone taking you away and doing harm to you. The students were given one more example before being directed to the centers.

This example of a mini lesson is typical of the direct instruction that occurred in the class. Mama Aso connected and extended students' previous knowledge about cornrows to the new knowledge about Queen Nzinga that they would learn about in the center. In the Reading/Language Arts Center, they were to "partner-read" the selection orally and discuss it with their partner. Finally, they were to look at the words written on the card at the center and write a definition in their folders for each word, using the context clues in the sentence to help them determine the meaning.

Later, Mama Aso explained that the students were accustomed to reading and sharing with partners. Earlier in the school year, she modeled how she identified points in the story that had a personal connection to her life. She gave the students opportunities to practice with partners. "Now they are really good at this. It helps to build their oral language skills as well as comprehension."

The students spend about 40 minutes in a center, working cooperatively, with the teacher and the teacher's aide, who targeted groups and individuals who needed assistance, clarification, or support. In several of the centers, students were engaged in hands-on activities. In the Math Center, for example, they used egg cartons and beads to help them understand the concept of division. In the Art Center, students used the colors of Tanzania, blue, green, and yellow to paint pictures and designs. Students in the Science Center planted seeds, using the organic farming method that they had learned about.

Two girls, Medina and Nataki, were working in the Social Studies Center. They were studying Tanzania and had to copy information about Tanzania from the *Story of Africa and Her Flags to Color* by Bellerophon Books. Mama Aso had explained to the students that they were to read the information and summarize it in their own words. Medina struggled to recast the first sentence into her own words. Nataki, who had written three sentences, helped Medina by pointing out, "You can copy the first sentence because I don't think there's another way to describe 'the surface covers 26,828 square miles.'" Medina, appeared relieved and copied the first sentence. The two girls continued working together. At one point, Medina stopped to help Markule, who walked over from the Paint Center, get out of his paint smock.

This typifies the exchanges that took place and the sense of responsibility that was created in the centers. Students worked well together and were free to assist each other. "There are times when the centers don't work as smoothly as I would like," admitted Mama Aso, "but basically I feel the students are learning and enjoy what they are doing." This statement was confirmed during student interviews when they were asked what they liked most about school. Most of the students responded, "the centers."

The students have sustained silent reading (SSR) immediately after lunch. There are many books of different genre in the classroom, including multicultural books with African American themes. In the afternoons there were often whole group lessons. The day after all the seeds had been planted in the Science Center, students recorded the steps in the process by drawing pictures and writing about the step-by-step procedures used for planting the seeds in their science journals.

Mama Aso then asked all of the students to put their work away while she slipped away. In the meantime she would have a lady come back who planted seeds just as they did. "If it's not ve-e-e-ry quiet, I don't think she'll come." Mama Aso told them. Then she left the classroom and went into the small room across the hall. After a couple of minutes she returned, with a scarf around her head, a hoe in her hand, and an apron around her waist. She began sharing her story of Alethia Browning Tanner, a former slave. She began, "I worked as a hired-out slave and opened a vegetable market in Maryland. I was able to make a lot of money growing vegetables and selling them."

As she continued, she proudly stated that one of her customers was Thomas Jefferson. "I worked very hard and was able to buy the freedom of 17 of my relatives and other slaves. That meant that I had to sell lots and lots of vegetables!" She continued, "But even so, I was active in my church and several other churches. But most of all, boys and girls, I valued my freedom."

She ended by stepping out of her story and becoming Mama Aso again. She spoke very softly, telling her students that many people helped African Americans gain their freedom. Alethia Browning Tanner was one of them. She added, "Freedom boys and girls is something you should always value."

The students were spellbound by the story, which stimulated a great deal of discussion and questions about Tanner's life, freedom and fairness. Students also learned lessons about hard work, perseverance, and pride in their ancestors.

Mama Aso had learned this and other strategies for effectively integrating science with storytelling and making it culturally relevant at a science workshop sponsored by the local university. She frequently used the strategies and found that her students liked the personalized focus that it brought to their study of science.

Ending the Day

The day ended as it began with the unity circle, where students and teachers discussed important academic, social, and cultural events of the day. Specific children are chosen as leaders each day to lead the Seven Harambees. "Harambee" is the Kiswahili word meaning "to pull together." On this day, Mama Aso chose Markele and stated, "We're going to do seven Harambees." With Markele as the leader, the students extended out their right hands and everyone pulled down together seven times as they said Harambee, with a long "Hara-a-a-am-bee!", at the end.

Mama Aso stated why she felt it was important for the children to be in this school. They learn about themselves, they learn that they are gifted. We facilitate their development of the gifts. However, they have to bring it out of themselves. She believed that this facilitation begins with students' learning about their history and their traditions as African people. She shared her experiences as a teacher in the Headstart program prior to coming to Ujima Village, stating:

> Although we always talk about and think about the needs of the children, but in all of the classrooms that I had worked with ... these were all African American children ... it was like ... the whole institution was really mainstream ... and people really didn't see the significance of incorporating our culture and having that as part of the whole curriculum and not just a little short thing here and there.

Curriculum and Teaching Practices: Other Observations

During the time in the classroom, students talked freely among themselves. In fact, there was constant exchange of ideas and thoughts as they worked in the centers. As the children worked in the Math Center, for example, they practiced with flashcards, constantly challenging each other, stating, "I've got a good one for you!"

There were times when students could be heard sharing knowledge of specific skills that they had acquired. For example, as Brandon Foreman wrote his name on his paper, he announced to Myron, as he pointed to the "e" in his last name, "the e is silent." Another example is Barbara's observation and statement to Brandon, I know why division is like subtraction!

Some of the learning was skills-based, rote learning, as students worked in their spelling books, alphabetizing their spelling words. They also used traditional math books and worksheets when they were to practice computations. However, students were again free to talk, even as they completed their work.

Students' knowledge of Africa was expressed naturally in casual conversation. As they worked in the Language Center, Nataki shared with me how the class got its name. She explained, "The Masai tribe comes from Kenya and the Nile runs through Kenya. That's why they say they're in the Nile Valley. We say that our class is the Nile Valley." Other students described the school as the best they had gone to because they learned more about "our African people and how African people got to be in America and how they got to be free." They also connected meditation and pledges with the life experiences of African people, and the importance of meditation in helping them "start off a good day."

DISCUSSION

Shannon (1992) defines literacy as both liberating and dominating. It is liberating when we not only read and write words ... the alphabet in connected passages, but when we read and write the world, constructing meaning in a way that defines who we are and the way we want the world to be.

Literacy is dominating when we read and write only what others prepare for us, and only the printed words on the page or ideas formulated by others. I found Shannon's notion of literacy as liberating, to be particularly applicable to Ujima Village and Mama Aso's classroom as I read and reread, analyzed, pondered and pieced together actions and the subsequent meanings that evolved. It appeared that students in this setting experienced literacy that was liberating, through both implicit experiences and explicit practices.

Literacy as Liberating and Implicit

Literacy was *liberating* as it was crafted by the director, the teachers, and the students. Together they constructed a literacy curriculum that encompassed the values, histories, and social practices that reflected the lives of the students and the community from which the students came. Students, thus, engaged in literacy by reading (and writing) the world from an internal understanding and acceptance of self as African American. Operating from this conception of literacy, the African American students were delivered from practices that created a "double-consciousness," this sense of always looking at one's self through the eyes of others (Dubois, 1961/1903). They further learned to value their own culture, rather than "valuing the European culture to the detriment of their own heritage" (Woodson, 1936, p.7). Literacy was *implicit*, because it was ever-present in the students' classroom and school behaviors as they adhered to a common value system, the Nguzo Saba, and routinely participated in protocols and rituals that reinforced an African-centered value system.

The Nguzo Saba, the set of guiding principles that undergirds the curriculum and pedagogy, such as the Unity Circle, were outlined during the first four months of school, as noted in the Curriculum Overview and were constantly referenced by the teacher and demonstrated in the class through the actions of the teacher and students. The third principle, UJIMA (collective work and responsibility), for example, was exemplified as students worked together cooperatively and responsibly at the centers, helping each other interpret assignments. In fact, there were no instances of competitiveness evident in the classroom during my observations, other than the students' internal desire to achieve their best. The teacher and teacher's aide often encouraged students to use their KUUMBA (creativity) as students were thinking or writing. As they wrote in their journals, they were given a choice of topics about which to write.

The protocols, the step by step routines that were performed at specific times during each day, provided an effective way for students to be cognizant of what they were doing and to develop positive discipline and responsibility.

The rituals, the orally prescribed forms of ceremonial procedures done at regular intervals, the CIBI Pledge, for example, addressed the African struggle, the commitment to self-determination, self-defense, and self-respect. Students who heard and repeated the daily rituals, not only became aware of and internalized African American values, but developed solidarity with each other and became conscious of the need to be active in the struggle for empowerment. Through the rituals, they constructed personal understandings of themselves.

The daily recitation and call-response mode between teacher and student further reflected the African oral tradition. The use of language in this form further builds on this tradition, dating back to the Griot, the oral historian in African Society. The primacy of oral language is important in the child's home, in Church, and in peer groups and is an integral part of knowledge attainment in this classroom. Moreover, the use of the East African language of Kiswahili further promotes African consciousness, pride, and literacy learning. These literacy experiences, which engage students in practices consistent with their history beyond slavery to ancient Africa, are consistent with experiences advocated by Asante (1990), Hilliard (1978), Karenga (1986), Nobles (1986), and other Afrocentric scholars.

Literacy as Explicit

This perspective on literacy is what is taught either directly or indirectly. It is perceived by both students and teachers as facilitating the ability to carry out complex tasks through the use of writing and reading, speaking, viewing and listening both in and out of school.

In Mama Aso's classroom, literacy learning was developed as students were actively involved in constructing meaning. They demonstrated their comprehension by connecting to and drawing on their background and cultural knowledge. In a group they were taught how to use context to determine word meanings. At each of the centers, they were encouraged to share their interpretations of text with others. When literacy occurred in this manner, it created opportunities for the functional uses of listening skills and oral language response modes.

Students further engaged in meaning-making through writing of connected texts, using content that was both personal (journal writing) and related to content areas such as social studies (recording information on Tanzania) and science (recording information about planting). Students were not only expected to read to each other, but again to listen as engaged partners. This type of social engagement and collaboration in learning is often preferred by African American students (Boykin, 1994; Kunjufu, 1984). Further it underscores the functional, meaning-based nature of reading. Significantly, what students read and wrote about was focused on the history and perspectives of Africans and African Americans.

Literacy was also explicitly developed through instruction in decoding… context knowledge, phonic knowledge, and sight word knowledge. There were specific times, for example, when students learned about letter-sound relationships, and phonics generalizations. Most often writing experiences provided important opportunities to help students develop this knowledge. As students considered the spelling of words, they had to consider the relationship between letters and sounds, analyze these relationships, apply generalizations, and develop new insights.

At times students were expected to use "polished" spelling and grammatical form. On the other hand, when writing in their journals, students' grammar and spelling were not a barrier to meaning, and thus were not corrected.

Literacy was further shaped by what students read and what they wrote. In this case the focus was primarily on African and African American stories, informational text, poetry, and magazines. Students were knowledgeable and viewed the information as important and shared it naturally as a normal part of their lives. In addition, traditional basal readers were used as a supplement to literature, in which case the content focused on a range of genre and cultures. It is significant, however, that the African American content was not supplementary, but primary to the students' learning.

Pedagogy

The educational practices that Mama Aso employed can hardly be separated from the literacy curriculum. In fact, it is the manner in which we teach that determines the way students understand and interpret the curriculum. The most significant aspect of her pedagogy was intertwined with whom Mama Aso was as a person. She genuinely cared about and respected her students and the knowledge they brought to the classroom. This feeling was reciprocal, because the students loved Mama Aso. Moreover, students' comments consistently emerged from students, who said "she's like my mama," and "this school is like my family." What they most loved about her was that she "cared." This characteristic was repeatedly cited in the student interviews.

Ladson-Billings (1994) and Irvine and Irvine (1995), in studies of teachers of African American children, found this quality of caring to be pertinant. Collins (as cited in Ladson-Billings) notes that "The ethic of caring suggests that personal expressiveness, emotions, and empathy are central to the knowledge-validation process" (p. 156).

Mama Aso sought to empower her students through allowing them the freedom to be themselves, to work independently, to question, challenge, and explore knowledge. The use of the center concept was her choice. She noted that some parents wanted her to exert more control, have students sit in rows, and employ more direct instruction. She objected because this ran counter to her philosophy. When students could not handle the freedom, she "reined them in," talked with them, and reminded them of aspects of the Nguzo Saba that they pledged to uphold. She further, developed self esteem in students by her constant affirmation of them and by encouraging them to affirm each other.

Finally, her pedagogy was driven by her own passion for learning. Mama Aso constantly sought to update her knowledge by reading, attending workshops, and taking courses. She viewed knowledge as empowering and teaching as serious business, albeit exciting. These beliefs informed her practice.

IMPLICATIONS

In this African-centered school, created in the early 1970s in the heart of the Civil Rights Movement, the curriculum evolved as new knowledge about literacy developed and as the political circumstances changed. However, as we begin the new millennium, this school has survived and even thrived, because it has effectively addressed the needs of the students within the community. It has developed a curriculum that is centered in African American history and culture and a pedagogy that empowers students so that they can achieve. Nia Henderson, the director, reported that more than 85% of the students who completed elementary through high school at Ujima Village, went on to college.

While there are major differences in the context of large urban schools in which most African American students learn and the small setting of the school and targeted classroom at Ujima Village, key aspects of curriculum and pedagogy have implications for classrooms and literacy learning in urban settings.

First, guiding principles, protocols, and rituals can be effective instruments when used to enhance students' sense of self and to foster self-empowerment and social change. Ladson-Billings (1994) notes that many of the efforts aimed toward African American immersion schools, are responses to a call for self-determination. These principles acknowledge that education is serious business, that oppression and racial injustice exists, and that the curriculum must equip students to achieve success in society in order to make it a better place.

Unfortunately, many urban students and their parents and teachers often view their education as disconnected from the world and their futures. For example, one African-centered public school that I observed had the principles of the Nguzo Saba posted within each classroom. However, the teachers and students very seldom recited or addressed these principles as important parts of their school and personal lives.

Simon (1987) argues that "teaching, like language, is not a neutral practice and that teachers, whether consciously or not, help to organize the way students perceive themselves and the world" (p. 160). Urban students, their teachers and parents need a common set of principles and meaningful rituals that are a reinforced daily and throughout the school day, as a way of engaging in reflection, self-affirmation, and greater responsibility for success in learning and in life.

Second, the curriculum should fairly and accurately provide students with insight about the historical, artistic, scientific, and literary aspects of African American culture. Sadly, many African American students in urban settings often learn about other African Americans through the media, primarily television. Many of these images are of drug-ridden neighborhoods, homicides, and police raids. This is a compelling reason to insure that the curriculum reflects the accomplishments of African Americans, and that students learn that they are heirs to a great tradition of science, oratory and storytelling, dance, history, and art. Literature, by and about African Americans, which was virtually absent from the canon in the mid-sixties and early seventies, is much more available today. However, it is still absent from many urban classrooms. This literature not only provides a sense of pride, but can provide challenging information about social issues and conflict, sparking motivation for social action, critical thought, and responsibility for positive social change. Other curricular materials that highlight the experiences of African Americans with which students can connect, such as videos, the internet, magazines, and newspapers often render them genuinely excited about learning.

Although Mama Aso's students were immersed in African American materials, she was instrumental in creating a learning environment in which students were motivated, excited, and even passionate about learning. Once students are "centered" or have a sense of self, their history, and traditions, they acquire confidence, and are better prepared to understand and appreciate the multiple perspectives of students who are different from themselves.

Third, African American students need specific skills and strategies for understanding and using language to communicate in society and to participate in the construction and acquisition of knowledge. Students in Ujima Village took learning seriously, although they did not have a regimented "skill and drill" curriculum. What worked for the students in Mama Aso's class was a balanced approach to literacy. However, many teachers in urban settings find that a more traditional, skills-oriented approach works best for urban students. It would appear that while many reading professionals favor a balanced approach, for African American students, both approaches can be effective, if delivered with consistency, competency, and caring. Delpit (1995) asserts "that those who are most skillful at educating black and poor children ... understand the need for both approaches, the need to help students establish their own voices, and to coach those voices to produce notes that will be heard clearly in the larger society" (p. 46).

Fourth, opportunities for oral language use, group discussion, challenges, and interactions should be incorporated into the curriculum. African American students often excel in the use of open-ended, wide-ranging forms of oral and written language, such as creating and debating alternative plans of action (Heath, 1992), and keen listening and observational skills (Baugh, 1983). Moreover, there is a strong oral tradition and appreciation for group and community among African Americans. In traditional settings and in many urban schools, children are encouraged to read and write as individuals, only, and display their skills and knowledge through worksheets, standardized tests and brief answers to teachers' questions. While these patterns of learning are sometimes necessary, they are in less demand in the workplace as we enter the 21st century. More and more, government and commercial institutions require collaboration and shared knowledge building, as well as an awareness of the power and purpose of written documents. Consequently, students must be encouraged to cultivate and utilize what is at the very heart of being literate: wide ranging uses of language, the sharing of knowledge and skills from multiple sources, and building collaborative activities through reading, writing, speaking, and listening.

Finally, teachers themselves can make a difference. There are many teachers like Mama Aso in urban classrooms who are knowledgeable and committed, and who receive all too few plaudits for their fine teaching. More teachers are needed, however, who know about the African American culture, are sensitive to the different ways that students interact, respect the culture of the home (and community), and *want* to be in the urban classroom. As Aso said, "I knew this was where I wanted to be."

It goes without saying, that these guidelines and suggestions alone, will not solve the deeper institutional and societal needs that plague our urban schools. Change can come only in small pieces, like eating the proverbial elephant, one bite at a time. Urban schools can change, one teacher at a time, one classroom at a time, one school at a time, but as we move toward the millennium, change they must.

NOTES

1. The Council of Independent Black Institutions serves as an umbrella organization to the many black independent schools across the nation. CIBI organizes and implements programming and training institutes for students and teachers.

2. The Nguzo Saba was originally developed by Dr. Maulana Karenga to guide the celebration of Kwanzaa. Today these seven principles are used by many African-centered schools and African Americans as a guide and as an affirmation of their Black heritage.

3. Mama is the Kiswahili word for mother. Baba is the Kishwahili word for father. Both were used to designate the teachers.

REFERENCES

Aronson, E. (1978). *The jigsaw classroom.* Beverly Hills, CA: Sage.

Asante, M. (1990). *Afrocentricity: The theory of social change.* Buffalo, NY: Amulefi.

Asante, M. (1991). The afrocentric idea in education, *Journal of Negro Education, 60,* 170–180.

Banks, J. (1997). Approaches to multicultural curriculum reform. In J. Banks & C. McGee Banks (Eds.), *Multicultural education: Issues and perspectives* (3rd ed.). Boston: Allyn & Bacon.

Baugh, J. (1983). *Black street speech: Its history, structure, and survival.* Austin: University of Texas Press.

Boykin, W.A. (1994). Harvesting talent and culture: African American children and educational reform. In R.J. Rossi (Ed.), *Schools and students at risk: Context and framework for positive change* (pp. 116–138). New York: Teachers College, Columbia University.

Cole, J. (1989). The cultural base in education. In A. Hilliard, L. Payton-Stewart, & L. Williams (Ed.), *Infusion of African and African American content in the school curriculum* (pp. 27–34). Morristown, NJ: Aaron Press.

Delpit, L. (1995). *Other people's children: Cultural conflict in the classroom.* New York: The New Press.

Diamond, B., & Moore, M. (1991). *The effects of a multicultural literature-based reading approach: Year two.* Paper presented at the annual meeting of the National Reading Conference, Palm Springs, CA.

Diamond, B. (1995, December). *Literacy programs in African American Schools: The Promises and possibilities.* Paper presented at the Annual Meeting of the National Reading Conference, New orleans, LA.

Dubois, W.E.B. (1961). *The souls of black folk.* New York: Fawcett. (Original work published 1903).

Edelin, R. (1990). Curriculum and cultural identity. In A. Hilliard, L. Payton-Stewart, & L. Williams (Eds.), *Infusion of African and African American content in the school curriculum* (pp. 37–45). Morristown, NJ: Aaron Press.

Gay, G. (1977). Curriculum design for multicultural education. In C.A. Grant (Ed), *Multicultural education: Commitments, issues, and applications.* Washington, DC: Association for Supervision and Curriculum Development.

Glaser, B., & Strauss, A. (1967). *The discovery of grounded theory: Strategies for qualitative research.* New York: Aldine.

Grant, C.A., & Sleeter, C.E. (1997). Race, class, gender, and disability in the classroom. In J. Banks & C. McGee Banks (Eds.), *Multicultural education: Issues and perspectives* (3rd ed.). Boston: Allyn & Bacon.

Heath, S.B. (1989). Oral and literate traditions among Black Americans living in poverty. *American Psychologist, 44,* 367–73.

Hilliard, A.G., III. (1978). *Anatomy and dynamics of oppression.* Speech delivered at the National Conference on Human Relations. Minneapolis, MN.

Irvine, J., & Irvine, R. (1995). Black youth in school: Individual achievement and institutional/cultural perspectives. In R.L. Taylor (Ed.), *African-American youth: Their social and economic status in the United States.* Westport, CT: Praeger Publishers.

Karenga, M.R. (1986). *Introduction to Black studies.* Los Angeles: University of Sankore Press.

Kunjufu, J. (1984). *Developing positive self-images in Blacks.* Chicago: African American Images.

Ladson-Billings, G. (1994). *The dreamkeepers: Successful teachers of African American children.* San Francisco: Jossey-Bass.

Ladson-Billings, G., & Henry, A. (1990). Blurring the borders: Voices of African liberatory pedagogy in the United States and Canada. *Journal of Education, 172,* 72–88.

Littman, M. (Ed.) (1998). *A statistical portrait of the United States: Social conditions and trends.* Lanham, MD: Bernan Press.

Merriam, S. (1988). *Case study research in education: A qualitative approach.* San Francisco: Jossey-Bass.

Miles, M., & Huberman, M. (1984). *Qualitative data analysis: A sourcebook of new methods.* Beverly Hills, CA: Sage.

Moses, R.P. (1989). The algebra project: Organizing in the spirit of Ella. *Harvard Educational Review, 59,* 27–47.

Murtadha, K. (1995). An African-centered pedagogy in dialog with liberatory multiculturalism. In C. Sleeter & P. McLaren (Eds.), *Multicultural education, critical pedagogy, and the politics of difference.* Albany: State University of New York Press.

Nieto, S. (1995). From brown heroes and holidays to assimilationist agendas: Reconsidering the critiques of multicultural education. In C. Sleeter & P.

McLaren (Eds.), *Multicultural education, critical pedagogy, and the politics of differ-ence.* Albany: State University of New York Press.

Nieto, S. (1996). *Affirming diversity: The sociopolitical context of multicultural education.* White Plains, NY: Longman.

Nobles, W. (1986). *African psychology.* Oakland, CA: Black Family Institute.

Ogbu, J. (1987). Variability in minority school performance: A problem in search of an explanation. *Anthropology and Education Quarterly, 18,* 312–334.

Ogbu, J. (1992. Understanding cultural diversity and learning. *Educational Researcher, 21,* 5–14.

Pasch, M., Karkow M., Johnson, C., Slocum, H. & Stapleton, E. (1990). The disap-pearing minority educator—No illusion: A practical solution. *Urban Education, 25,* 207–218.

Ramirez, B. (1988). Culturally and linguistically diverse children. *Teaching Excep-tional Children, 20,* 45–57.

Rossi, R.J. (Ed.). (1994). *Schools and students at risk: Context and framework for positive change.* New York: Teachers College Press.

Shannon, P. (Ed.). (1991). *Becoming political: Readings and writings in the politics of lit-eracy education.* Portsmouth, NH: Heinemann.

Simon, R.I. (1992). Empowerment as a pedagogy of possibility. In P. Shannon (Ed.) *Becoming political: Readings and writings in the politics of literacy education.* Ports-mouth, NH: Heinemann.

Sleeter, C.E. (Ed.). (1991). *Empowerment through multicultural education.* Albany: State University of New York Press.

Sleeter, C.E. and Grant, C.A. (1993). *Making choices for multicultural education: Five approaches to race, class and gender* (2nd ed.). New York: Merrill.

Spelman, S. (1988). *An imperiled generation: Saving urban schools.* Princeton, NJ: Car-negie Foundation for the Advancement of Teaching.

Spradley, J. (1980). *Participant observation.* New York: Holt Rinehart and Winston.

Suzuki, B. (1979). Multicultural education: What's it all about? *Integrated Education, 17,* 97–98.

Viadero, M. (1990, November). Battle over multicultural education rises in inten-sity. *Education Week,* pp. 10,11.

Weiner, L. (1993). *Preparing teachers for urban schools: Lessons from thirty years of reform.* New York: Teachers College Press.

White, J., & Parham, T. (1990). *The psychology of blacks: An African-American perspec-tive.* Engelwood Cliffs, NJ: Prentice-Hall.

Woodson, C.G. (1936). *The mis-education of the Negro.* Washington, DC: Associated Publishers.

CHAPTER 7

READING, LANGUAGE, CULTURE, AND ETHNIC MINORITY STUDENTS

Jon Reyhner and Ward Cockrum

Abstract. The problem of assessing the impact on students of any reading program is influenced by the personality, cultural background, motivation, and skills of individual teachers and students who can, together or separately, ruin good programs and overcome the weaknesses of poor programs. In this chapter, the authors examine current trends in reading and their impact on the methods, materials, and motivation teachers use to develop students—especially ethnic minority students—into good readers. The chapter closes with a discussion of the goals of reading instruction for ethnic minority students and recommendations as to what to look for in teachers and reading programs.

INTRODUCTION

Approaches to teaching reading can be, at this time, best described as divided. Many politicians and parents are calling for teacher-centered, direct instruction approaches emphasizing phonics. They think the child-centered, whole language approaches popular, but not necessarily practiced, in the last decade have caused standardized test scores to decline. On the other hand, many university professors and teachers rally around more child-centered, literature-based approaches to teaching reading, thinking that the direct instruction approaches turn too many students off of reading.

Phonics is considered a "bottom up" approach where the meaning of any text must be "decoded" by the reader and where students are "reading" when they can "sound out" words on a page. The alternative "top down" approach emphasizes that readers bring meaning to text based on their experiential background and interpret text based on their prior knowledge. The extreme "top down" position, known as "deconstruction," maintains that each reader determines the meaning of any text. As we maintain throughout this chapter, neither extreme makes much sense in an actual classroom.

The phonics/decoding advocates continue the tradition of Rudolf Flesch who wrote the influential and popular book, *Why Johnny Can't Read*, in 1955. On the other end of the spectrum are the whole language advocates who downplay the role of phonics and emphasize exposing children to a rich literate environment. At the extreme, the whole language advocates suggest that students will learn to read on their own by being read to and being exposed to a wide variety of reading material. Stephen Krashen (1993), a well-known researcher on English as a Second Language (ESL) and bilingual education, echoes this idea that students learn to read by reading:

> My conclusions are simple. When children read for pleasure, when they get "hooked on books," they acquire, involuntarily and without conscious effort, nearly all of the so-called 'language skills' many people are so concerned about: They will become adequate readers, acquire a large vocabulary, develop the ability to understand and use complex grammatical instructions, develop a good writing style, and become good (but not necessarily perfect) spellers. Although free voluntary reading alone will not ensure attainment of the highest levels of literacy, it will at least ensure an acceptable level. Without it, I suspect that children simply do not have a chance. (p. 84)

Krashen's thesis, supported by extensive research cited in his 1993 book, *The Power of Reading*, is that the more students practice reading, the better readers they become. According to this argument, if children spent as much time reading as many of them do "shooting hoops," playing video games, or watching television, they would be good readers.

Of course, to get children to spend a lot of time reading, they have to be encouraged to read, have to find reading a rewarding experience, and need easy access to a wide variety of reading material. The encouragement must come from family, friends, and teachers; the rewards depend upon children having access to high interest reading material; and reading material needs to be readily available in homes and in school and community libraries. If children are not encouraged to read, they may well never learn to appreciate the worlds of enjoyment and information that reading can offer. If they find the reading material they do have access to is too difficult, boring, or unrelated to their lives, they will avoid reading and their progress as readers will be stalled. And if reading material is simply not available, efforts to get children to read are doomed.

Despite the great divide, even hostility, between the phonics and whole language camps, a closer look finds some common ground. Flesch and his many followers opposed the "Dick and Jane" whole word approach of many basal reading textbooks in the 1950s. These reading textbooks were collections of specially written stories that carefully controlled and sequenced the number of new words on each page and through repetition of those words, students were expected to learn new vocabulary. This delayed students' introduction to the many children's books, which are not vocabulary controlled, that are found in any well-stocked library. Flesch argued that "The beauty of the written language is usually lost in graded stories which are in look-say or eclectic programs" (1981, p. xxi).

Flesch maintained that by first teaching students the sounds of letters ("phonics-first"), students could sound out new words ("decoding" them) and could start reading quickly—"The child learns the mechanics of reading, and when he's through, he can read" (1981, p. 3). The idea that children who can "sound out" words are reading is based on the assumption that, once they have sounded out the words, they understand them because these words were already in their speaking vocabulary—an assumption that is often not met for students learning to read in a second language or for whom standard English is a second dialect. Lack of reading comprehension was common in schools serving American Indian students in the past. Luther Standing Bear (1928), who became a teacher at the end of the nineteenth century wrote,

> The Indian children should have been taught how to translate the Sioux tongue into English properly; but the English teachers only taught them the English language, like a bunch of parrots. While they could read all the words placed before them, they did not know the proper use of them; their meaning was a puzzle. (p. 239)

In fact, the written versions of American Indian languages are easier to learn to read than English if the students speak those languages, because they tend to have a one-to-one sound symbol relationship, unlike English. Students who learn to read in a non-English language do not have to learn to read all over again in English. Many reading skills are the same in any language (Thonis, 1981).

Students need to know more than a phonics "code" to read. For example, they need to have an oral vocabulary that includes most of the words in any text they are trying to read for successful "decoding" to result in reading comprehension. Successful readers need functional, cultural, and critical literacy to fully understand texts (Garcia & Ahler, 1992). Functional literacy allows the reader to get simple meanings from texts; cultural literacy allows the reader to understand the milieu the writer is coming from (e.g., in an American Indian coyote story is Coyote following accepted cultural practices or is he violating them—this understanding is essential for the reader to fully appreciate the story). Critical literacy allows the reader to get behind the text into the motivation of the author (e.g., what is a particular Coyote story designed to teach the listener about proper behavior). If meanings of texts were simple, there would not be so many Christian denominations, each basing their unique identity on different interpretations of the same biblical passages.

Below we categorize approaches to teaching reading by behaviorist direct-instruction and intervention approaches, constructivist experiential-interactive and whole language approaches, and approaches using computers that can be both behaviorist and constructivist, depending on how they are written.

METHODS

The various methods that have been developed to teach reading are usually promoted as effective with all types of students. However, some methods like direct instruction work better with students who come to school motivated to learn while constructivist approaches are more likely to be adapted to fit a child's cultural background, since they emphasize building on students' prior knowledge, and are more likely to motivate students who come to school with ambivalent feelings about education, as is the case with many minority students.

Direct Instruction Approaches

These approaches to reading are characterized by teachers presenting a lesson with the goal of having the learner master an isolated subskill of reading. A subskill can be as specific as the long sound of the letter a, where the learner is expected to be able to state that "a, says its name," or as general as being able to derive an inference from a given piece of print. Direct instruction is pervasive in American schools and can be found in programs that focus only on phonics instruction to programs that include the additional word identification strategies of structural analysis, using context clues, and dictionary skills, as well as vocabulary and comprehension instruction. When combined with a strong assessment component the approach can identify the strengths and weaknesses of the reader and provide a very clear instructional program for the teacher to follow. This diagnosis-direct instruction model is very well described in *Teaching Reading: Diagnosis, Direct Instruction, and Practice* (Rupley & Blaire, 1988).

The value of a direct instruction approach for ethnic minority students is that the expectations are very clear and growth in reading ability can be clearly documented. In addition, most parents, whether they were educated here, in Mexico, or other countries often identify this approach with what schooling should be because that is the way they were taught in school when they were young. For minority students who come from homes where their family tells them schooling is a positive benefit and a means to achieve greater power and satisfaction in society, direct instruction can be a successful approach. Highly motivated students, such as John Ogbu's (1978, 1983) "autonomous" and "immigrant minorities," can excel in programs that allow them to see their reading growth in terms of success on skill tests given by the teacher. However, Ogbu's "castelike" minorities that include Black Americans, Mexican Americans, American Indians, and others are less likely to profit from direct instruction as they lack the extrinsic motivation they need to keep engaged with their lessons, which often lack any immediate relevance to their lives.

For students from non-English speaking minorities, direct instruction in a structured phonics program can be beneficial. If the phonics program is designed to use consistent sound symbol relationships in English to build the children's oral English vocabulary and a foundation for further instruction, the second language learner might be able to use phonic decoding as a first step to proficient reading in English.

Another advantage for minority children in the direct instruction approach is that clear, precise, measurable learning outcomes can be established at a national level. These outcomes or standards can help insure that children in schools with a large number of low income, minority students are held to the same expectations that children in schools with a large number of high income majority students.

A problem with the direct instruction approach for minority students is that when applied in a diagnosis-direct instruction format it results in students with the lowest levels of achievement in reading having the most diagnosis and related instruction. In our society, students from the lowest income levels tend to be the lowest achievers in school. This group of students has a disproportionately high number of minority students in it. So in the diagnosis-direct instruction approach, minority students appear to be "selected out" as deficient learners in need of fixing. For minority children who do not have a strong motivation to succeed in school, direct instruction can lead to a cycle of failure in school that is reinforced each time a new assessment is given. It is too teacher centered to be used for many minority children who do not see schools as a place to get the skills needed to be successful in society.

Jim Cummins (1992, 1996), a prolific writer on bilingual education, characterizes direct instruction as the transmission approach to teaching and documents its pervasiveness in schools around the world. The word "transmission" is used because the approach focuses on the teacher as a possessor of knowledge who "transmits" that knowledge to children. The Brazilian educator, Paulo Friere (1970/1981) described this as the banking model where the teacher deposits information in the student to be withdrawn at test time. This approach works fairly well with students who come to school highly motivated to learn, but can be a disaster with students, such as Alan Peshkin describes in the motivation section of this paper, who come to school ambivalent about why they are there. Cummins (1992) advocates as an alternative a constructivist "experiential interactive approach."

Constructivist Approaches

Constructivist approaches include literature-based and whole language approaches, focus on student comprehension and are based on research and writing of Vygotsky (1978) and other learning theorists. The idea behind constructivist learning theory is that students learn by actively constructing knowledge from their experiences rather than merely memorizing information transmitted to them by teachers. Constructivist teachers do not advocate the elimination of skills instruction. Rather than teaching isolated skills to every child at the same time, these teachers use their "kid watching skills" (Goodman, 1986) and observation checklists (Cockrum & Castillo, 1991) to develop skill lessons that meet the needs of individual students. These mini lessons are taught as the students need them in the context of reading and writing for a purpose that is more than for instructional reasons. Often this purpose is to find out more about a topic, often chosen by the students, that a thematic unit of instruction has been built around.

Constructivist teachers often build their teaching around themes of high interest to their students. They seek out a large variety of material for students to read that complements the chosen theme and weave in content area instruction in mathematics, science, music, art, and other subjects. They begin the unit and lessons by activating students' background knowledge. Roland Tharp and Ronald Gallimore (1988) emphasize how teachers through what they term "instructional conversation" need to help readers develop their critical thinking skills and their vocabulary by interpreting for themselves the meanings of any text with the assistance of their peers and the teacher. By carefully listening to student comments Tharp and Gallimore maintain that teachers can lead students to an understanding and appreciation of children's literature. Expanding on research done on teaching reading to Native Hawaiian children (Jordan, 1984; Tharp, 1982), Tharp and Gallimore recommend teaching reading in small groups and promoting discussion between students and the teacher on the stories they are reading. To develop students language skills they suggest the teacher ask students open-ended questions such as "Tell me more about _____?" and "What do you mean by _____?" and to rephrase students' responses to check comprehension and establish meaning "In other words, _____." They also recommend that teachers get students to think about the evidence they have for their opinions and conclusions about the story with questions such as "How do you know _____?," "What makes you think that?," "Show us where it says _____?" Teachers are to limit the number of questions they ask that have only one correct, factual answer such as "Who crossed the bridge?," and teachers are asked to be responsive to students' answers in their comments and follow-up questions to provide a connected discourse where the teacher challenges their students in a nonthreatening atmosphere to think deeper about the meaning of the story and how the story relates to their own lives. Students are not asked questions in turn, but are allowed to self-select which questions they will respond to or when they will add their comments to the discussion of the story. Experience with this method indicates that it only works well in an "open classroom" environment where a teacher works with only part of his class while other students are reading silently, working at a learning center, working at computer-assisted instruction, or are otherwise occupied in learning.

Tharp and Gallimore's instructional conversation is in sharp contrast to traditional round robin reading or the scripted questions in many teacher manuals for basal reading textbooks, where there is a whole set of pre-planned questions (with the expected student answers). The problem with the preplanned answers found in textbooks is that they are the right answers based on the experiential background of the author rather than the students. For example, Navajo students at Cameron, Arizona, were asked where you would expect to see a boat, and many answered on the highway. This type of answer would be often judged wrong on the face of it. However, a follow-up question to the students of why they answered that way would elicit the fact that they saw boats passing by their school on the highway all the time, but many had never traveled to Page, Arizona, on Lake Powell to see those same boats put into the water. This problem extends into standardized tests that are used to measure the effectiveness of reading instruction. For example, on test questions Navajo Indian students have associated umbrellas with the sun rather than rain because umbrellas are used by sheep herders for shade, and cows have been associated with ponds of water rather than ducks, because cows on the reservation are often gathered around ponds but ducks are seldom seen at those same ponds.

Another way to handle interaction with students besides small group instruction is through dialogue journals where students write their thoughts about what they are reading and teachers write back to their students. María de la Luz Reyes (1991) researching students learning English as a second language found dialogue journals were more effective than literature logs where students wrote about what they were reading without regular written responses from their teachers. She also found that when a student was discouraged from writing about controversial topics, such as witches, the student lost interest in her schoolwork. The wife of one of this chapter's authors learned English as a second language. She found reading to be very difficult and avoided it. In sixth grade she found a magazine, *True Confessions*, very interesting and was reading it avidly. Her teacher saw her and grabbed the magazine saying "Good girls don't read things like that." A better approach would have been to praise her for reading and then to gently steer her into better reading material.

Literature-based and whole language approaches to teaching reading are based on constructivist learning theory, but they allow for direct instruction. When a teacher observes a child reading from a trade book, having difficulty decoding a specific word, and they give the child a mini lesson related to the decoding of that word, we would say they are engaging in the literature-based or whole language approach to reading instruction. These teachers keep records of the children's performance (and often portfolios of their work) and provide timely instruction related to the observed performance. The structure of this approach has to come from the teacher and should be dictated by the needs of the students. An excellent source of information about teaching reading to ESL students in a whole language approach is *Reading and the ESL Student* (Nurss & Hough, 1992).

The value of a literature-based approach for minority students is that instruction is not based on an assumption that all students come to school with the same language facility. The literature-based teacher attempts to lead each child in developing his/her reading skills by providing books that are of interest to that child or relate to the background of that child. In addition, reading ability is developed with writing ability, so minority children can read their own stories as well as those of their peers which may be a better match to their backgrounds and experiences than trade books provided by the schools.

The problem with the literature-based approach for minority students is that expectations may not be clear to the student and growth is difficult to document. The minority child may feel a sense of security and acceptance in the literature-based classroom but may not grow in his/her reading ability. Keeping performance expectations high for minority students and keeping track of student progress is the challenge for whole language teachers.

While the research is weak on the actual effects of literature-based and whole language instruction on students in the classroom, as is the situation with other approaches to reading instruction, the underlying constructivist learning theory that underlies the whole language approach is strongly supported by research (Ellis & Fouts, 1993).

Intervention Programs

Reading Recovery, Success For All, and Early Intervention Reading are some of the more widely used intervention programs. Intervention programs are designed to give additional help to the struggling reader and are seeing greater and greater use in public schools. These programs are typically designed to provide additional help to the lower achieving students. A common trait of these programs is to provide individual or small group instruction. Classifying the strategies used in the programs as whole language or direct instruction has been somewhat controversial. However, it appears that each is represented in these programs. Teachers criticize programs like Success For All because they are restrictive, scripted, and leave no room for spontaneity, both teachers and students tend to become "robots." These programs, like basal reading textbook programs, can support weak and new teachers because they tell the teachers what to do every minute of reading time. However, they tend to limit strong experienced teachers, who have the knowledge and skills to adapt their instruction to the unique personalities and special needs of their students.

Minority students benefit from the small group/individual instruction of these programs in the same manner as majority students. Nevertheless, the focus on the lower achieving students may also be a benefit to minority children since minority children are often over represented in this group of students. However, the focus on low achieving children may result in an inadvertent spotlighting of minority children. In schools with a high number of majority students this could result in a negative stereotype for all minority students.

Proponents of intervention strategies make great claims of success, but independent documentation usually leads to findings of "no difference" between them and more traditional approaches (Grossen, Coulter, & Ruggles, n.d.; Ruffini et al., n.d.; Viadero, 1999; Walberg & Greenberg, 1998). The proponents counter negative or "no difference" findings, claiming they are based on flawed research or faulty implementation of their program. Besides the shaky research supporting the use of these programs, the cost of these programs in time and money, especially in districts with high teacher turnover as is the case in many schools serving ethnic minority students, can drain resources from other school programs, including the teaching of other subjects such as mathematics and science.

Computers in Reading Instruction

Some reading programs are available on the computer; however, in most schools, the computer is a supplement to reading instruction. Software is available to provide drill and practice on a variety of reading skills. But, when reading instruction turns into reading to learn rather than learning to read, the computer takes an important role in the reading curriculum. Using the computer as an information-gathering tool is a valuable skill for any student wishing to go to college.

The value of the computer for second language minority students is that it can provide repetitive practice and confidential nonstressful error correction for those students without losing patience or giving nonverbal cues of frustration with the students' learning rate. For all minority and majority students, the importance of learning to use computers today and learning their usefulness for gathering information is self-evident. Computers can also aid the teacher by relieving them of the testing and record keeping needed to monitor student progress, which is becoming more important as parents, school boards, and state and federal governments demand more and more accountability. One program being used on the Navajo Indian Reservation that is strongly supported by some teachers is the "Accelerated Reader" program marketed by the Advantage Learning Systems of Wisconsin Rapids, Wisconsin. This program provides computerized quizzes for hundreds of juvenile novels, including Newbery Award winners, that monitor and track student progress.

One issue for minority students and computers is their access to them. If the student comes from a low income home and attends school in a district with a limited tax base, they may not get access to computers. This lack of access to computer literacy could widen the income gap between majority and minority populations in our society because when they graduate they cannot obtain one of the growing number of technology-oriented jobs in society.

MATERIALS

All approaches to teaching reading have implications for the materials to be used with students. Commercial programs designed to teach reading consist of anthologies of stories, poems, and articles, some specially written for the programs and some not that are either bound into textbooks or are in booklet form, some even have the stories on cards. These anthologies usually come with elaborate teaching guides that tell the teachers moment by moment how they are to use the materials.

Literature-based and whole language teachers eschew detailed teaching guides and focus on using books that are not published as part of a particular reading program and are not specifically designed to teach reading. Stephen Krashen (1993, 1999) advocates Free Voluntary Reading (FVR), which requires that a variety of high interest reading material—everything from Fear Street, Goosebumps, Sweet Valley High, Baby-sitters Club, to Newbery Award Winning books—be available to children at home, in libraries, and especially in classrooms for them to select from based on their interests. An Israeli study of interactive reading by first-graders found that series books where the same characters continued from story to story worked better than reading stories by different authors or the same author where the stories did not share the same characters (Rosenhouse, Feitelson, Kita, & Goldstein, 1997). If a teacher finds students like a particular kind of book, whether it is the old Frances, Church Cat, Tarzan, or Nancy Drew books or newer series, they can encourage students to read the rest of the series. This is especially important for reluctant readers.

Programs that advocate time set aside for FVR every day in every classroom such as Sustained Silent Reading (SSR) (McCracken, 1971) and Drop Everything And Read (DEAR) are valuable additions to any school curriculum. Krashen even supports the use of comic books with reluctant and second language readers since comics often contain sophisticated vocabulary and the pictures provide clues for the reader to help them learn what that vocabulary means. Teachers can interest their students in FVR by reading high interest books to their students fifteen minutes or so every day, even in the upper grades. We have seen fourth and fifth grade students who were noisily jumping around in the late afternoon gather around and quiet down when their teacher began reading to them a high interest juvenile novel. Students who might be interested in different types of stories cannot show any interest just because they have no idea of the type of stories that exist. Through reading to their students, teachers can introduce new, slightly more complex material than the students can easily read to pique their interest and expand their horizons.

The representation of diversity in the literature used to teach children to read is also a current trend. A complaint that had been made against the material children had available to read was "that they gave inadequate attention to minority characters and settings and the diversity of modern life" (Graves, Juel, & Graves, 1999, p. 149). This issue appears to become less severe with each year's new book offerings. Books representing a wide variety of cultures are available, and many books are now available in English and a second language. Even "the publishers of today's basals take great pains to choose selections that represent the diversity and multicultural nature of today's society" (Graves et al., 1999, p. 149). In the past, some of the changes in reading textbooks to increase diversity have been superficial to say the least, just changing a character's name and the character's features in the accompanying illustration (McCuchen, Kyle, & Skovina, 1979).

However, increasing the diversity in reading material in basal reading textbooks could aggravate comprehension problems for mainstream students, while not helping students from any particular minority group that much since any single story in a nonmainstream setting will probably relate to the experiential background of only one particular minority group. Constructivist learning theory maintains that students learn new knowledge by relating it to their previous knowledge. If the new knowledge is totally unrelated to the old, then students will not learn it as Luther Standing Bear found with his Sioux students who were forced to learn to read in a language they could not speak by the U.S. Government's English-Only policy of the time. This English-Only policy is still being advocated by many political conservatives in this country who want an amendment to the Constitution making English the official language of the United States.

Literature-based reading advocates avoid the problems of too little or too much diversity in basal readers by allowing students to self-select reading material from a large inventory of books. Polingaysi Qöyawayma, a Hopi teacher, reported in the 1930s the same experiences as Standing Bear. When she became a first grade teacher, she was nervous, but she felt that she at least knew the language her students spoke. However, her supervisors soon reminded her that under the government's English-Only policy she was forbidden to speak Hopi to her students. In her mind she questioned her supervisors' directives and the mainstream English curriculum she was required to teach. In defiance of her supervisors Qöyawayma chose teaching material from the experiential background of her students:

> What do these white-man stories mean to a Hopi child? What is a "choo-choo" to these little ones who have never seen a train? No! I will not begin with the outside world of which they have no knowledge. I shall begin with the familiar. The everyday things. The things of home and family. (p. 125)

She substituted familiar Hopi legends, songs and stories for Little Red Riding Hood and other European tales. This problem of reading material that does not relate to children's experiential background does not necessarily go away as they grow older and widen their horizons. Luis J. Rodriquez (1994), in his autobiography, *Always Running*, describes storming permanently out of a high school literature class because the teachers insisted he read Wordsworth's *Preludes* instead of Beatrice Griffith's *American Me*, which dealt with his Hispanic heritage.

Rather than relying on a set canon of "great" children's literature for the classroom, usually with an American and Western European bias, teachers need to also include stories and books that match the ethnic minority child's background and experience to make reading a meaningful experience. Stephen Krashen (1999), has put forward what he calls the Goodman-Smith hypothesis based on the work of the reading experts Kenneth Goodman (1982) and Frank Smith (1994). This hypothesis states that,

> Before readers encounter a piece of text, they have made predictions about what they are about to read. These predictions come from their knowledge of the world, what they have read so far, and their knowledge of language, which can include knowledge of sound-spelling correspondences. They then look at the text to see if it matches what they have predicted. If the match is "close enough," the text is "understood." (Krashen, 1999, p. 1)

If the content of the text that minority students are reading matches their cultural background, "their knowledge of the world," this will make comprehension easier. The negative side of this issue is that characters in children's stories can be stereotypic of the minority group. Just as many majority group students felt the Scott, Foresman's "Dick and Jane" stories were not representative of their lives, ethnic minority students may not feel comfortable with being perceived as being the same as a storybook character from their ethnic background. By providing a variety of material and supplementing that material with language experience stories written by their students or other students in their school, teachers can compensate for some of the drawbacks of basal reading textbooks.

Teachers need to work to compensate for the fact that many minority communities often lack bookstores and adequate libraries in both their schools and neighborhoods. Community, school, and classroom libraries are being gutted by budget cuts because of the demand for tax relief and because many school boards use what little discretionary money they have to support popular interscholastic athletic programs and to purchase computers and other new technology. It has been argued by some that new media and computers make reading less important, but textbooks remain central to the classrooms today, and one must read webpages, e-mail, and the like on even the newest computers. In fact, the Internet can provide an abundance of varied reading opportunities for students.

Teachers can find help identifying high interest reading material for their students from the abundance of annotated bibliographies of children's literature. For example, Jon C. Stott's (1995) *Native Americans in Children's Literature*, which lists more than 100 books by and about Americans Indians along with short synopses and critiques to help teachers find stories to use in their classrooms, could be used to help build a classroom library for what has been called a heritage reading program for American Indian students (Reyhner, 1992b). Stott's appendix gives examples of how to use traditional American Indian stories in language arts classes and sample lessons. A good source of literature by Native Americans is the non-profit Native American Authors Distribution Project (which can be contacted through the Greenfield Review Press, 2 Middle Grove Road, Greenfield Center, NY 12833; Phone: 518 583 1440; Web Site http:// nativeauthors.com). While less targeted to any specific minority group, there are a number of annotated bibliographies of multicultural children's books. One of the more recent is Beth Beutler Lind's (1996) *Multicultural Children's Literature: An Annotated Bibliography, Grades K-8.*

In communities without bookstores, school administrators should make available children's books for purchase. Teachers through monthly magazine book clubs and librarians through yearly book fairs are often doing this now to a degree. However, book clubs lack a good selection of books on any specific ethnic minority group and other topics of local interests, and today's children want things right now, rather than waiting weeks for the teacher's mail order to come in. It is our experience that most students have money for soft drinks and other junk food and are willing to buy high interest books if they are readily available. In an American Indian school where one of the authors was principal, he used to take a book cart around to every classroom once a week selling paperback books at cost and using the money to buy more books. He sold a lot of books. If there is a student store in your school, we would investigate ways it might sell some books as well as candy and pop. A third possibility is to get your school library to stock some paperback books for sale year around, not just at book fairs one or two times a year.

MOTIVATION

Another reason, besides inappropriate teaching methods and reading material, for poor academic performance of minority students centers around motivation. Alan Peshkin's (1997) *Places of Memory: Whiteman's Schools and Native American Communities* tackles this aspect of the question of why the academic achievement of one minority group is below average, even in minority-controlled schools with minority teachers. Peshkin spent a year observing a New Mexico boarding school serving Pueblo Indians. He found that American Indians planning to attend college have the lowest ACT scores, and once in college they have the highest dropout rate of any New Mexico ethnic group: 75% of Indian students who go to college leave in their first year. At the school Peshkin studied, low academic performance is not a case of Jonathan Kozol's (1991) "savage inequalities" that result from suburban white schools having as much as three times the per student funding as minority schools that enables them to hire better teachers and provide better instructional materials. The school he studied received a combination of Bureau of Indian Affairs (BIA) funding and various federal grants and was staffed with well-educated teachers. The school had the highest percentage of Indian teachers of any high school in New Mexico. In addition, the students' parents valued education, the school met New Mexico accreditation standards, and its goal was to prepare students for college. But success was limited. Students would participate with sustained effort and enthusiasm in basketball, but "regrettably, I saw no academic counterpart to this stellar athletic performance" (p. 5). Peshkin found, .

> In class, students generally were well-behaved and respectful. They were not rude, loud, or disruptive. More often they were indifferent … teachers could not get students to work hard consistently, to turn in assignments, to participate in class, or to take seriously … their classroom performance. (p. 5)

To explain why these students did not enthusiastically embrace education, Peshkin enlarges on the cultural discontinuity (two worlds) theory of academic failure (see, e.g., Henze & Vanett, 1993) and provides evidence from students, parents, and teachers to support that theory. He argues that the "student malaise" originates from an ambivalent attitude of the Pueblo Indians toward schooling. Based on more than 400 years of contact with European colonists, the Pueblos have good reason to be suspicious of anything "white," and schools—even Indian-controlled ones with Indian administrators and Indian teachers—are basically alien "white" institutions.

The New Mexican Pueblos, under cultural attack from all the forces of the majority society, are very concerned with cultural survival. Pueblo culture emphasizes fitting into the group and participating in the life of the village—"standing in" versus "standing out"—in contrast to the individualism found outside the Pueblo. "Schooling is necessary to become competent in the very world that Pueblo people perceive as rejecting them" (p. 107); school is a place of "becoming white" (p. 117). According to Peshkin, "imbued with the ideal of harmony in their community life, Pueblo parents send their children to schools that promote cultural jangle" (p. 117). The sounds in the school are not discordant. The conflict is between what the Pueblo communities teach their young and what the schools teach, and this discordance goes far beyond just the teaching of Pueblo languages in the home and English in schools.

Mick Fedullo (1992), in his book *Light of the Feather: Pathways Through Contemporary Indian America*, illustrates an extreme case of this cultural conflict with a quote from an Apache elder who stated that student's parents had,

> been to school in their day, and what that usually meant was a bad BIA boarding school. And all they remember about school is that there were all these Anglos trying to make them forget they were Apaches; trying to make them turn against their parents, telling them that Indian ways were evil.
>
> Well, a lot of those kids came to believe that their teachers were the evil ones, and so anything that had to do with "education" was also evil—like books. Those kids came back to the reservation, got married, and had their own kids. And now they don't want anything to do with the white man's education. The only reason they send their kids to school is because it's the law. But they tell their kids not to take school seriously. So, to them, printed stuff is white-man stuff. (p. 117)

Cultural conflict and reading may seem far apart, but the selection of the right kind of books can help students work through these cultural conflicts. Teachers cannot hope to be successful on a broad scale with Black, Hispanic, American Indian, or other minority students who see education, school success, and reading as a "selling out" of their ethnic heritage. The juvenile novels of Paul Pitts are excellent examples of the type of books that could help one ethnic minority, American Indian students, find ways of dealing with cultural conflict:

Paul Pitts explores issues that many Native American children face that are not often addressed in children's novels. *Racing the Sun, Shadowman's Way,* and *Crossroads* each portray a young Navajo boy as the main character. The issues these boys face allow the books to be entertaining for both avid and reluctant adolescent readers. The central underlying themes in each of Pitts' books are how young children seek friendship and deal with cultural differences in defining their identity. (Steward, 1996, p. 43)

Pitts' *Shadowman's Way* is a good example of a juvenile novel that could help American Indian children resolve the ambivalence that Peshkin found in the high school he studied. Spencer, a new white kid on the block in a Navajo community, attempts to form friendships but is blocked by racial prejudice. A Navajo boy Nelson, who is open to a new friendship, faces peer pressure and is criticized as a "white man-lover" for his efforts. Spencer is called a "white ape" and "white dog," and Benjamin, a leader of the Navajo boys, declares that Spencer is "just like a white man" because he "pushes his way into some place he doesn't belong and then makes fun of what he finds there" (p. 80). Anglos [white people] "should stay where they belong, with people who understand them" (p. 63). Things come to a head between Nelson and Benjamin over letting the new boy into the Navajo Youth Center. Benjamin declares "the only thing ... I had was the youth center ... it was a tiny place that was mine ... where they couldn't remind me I wasn't good enough" (p. 101). Nelson tries to get Benjamin to look past race, but Benjamin answers that Anglos "won't let you become part of that world" (p. 102). The book brings out how Benjamin's ideas about whites are shaped by his parent's ideas, which were picked up through negative encounters with the "white world." Nelson's mother explains to him,

> Some people decide whether others have any value on the basis of their skin, their clothes, how they talk. You can only hope, if you want those people to accept you, that they will take the time to get to know you as a person. (p. 104)

Few curriculums exist to help minority children resolve the conflicts between home and school that Peshkin documents. One of the few such curriculums available is Edward Tennant's (1994) *"Eye of Awareness": Life Values Across Cultures* curriculum developed for the Bering Strait School District in Alaska.

DISCUSSION

When a goal is set for minority reading instruction today, it all too often sounds like an effort to produce more efficient workers for our country's businesses. This has a certain racist tone to it. We propose that the goal of reading instruction for minority students be the ability to read at a level in which they can have as rich and full life as they desire. They can read for aesthetic purposes as well as pragmatic ones. They can affect their lives through reading as well as be affected.

One should never forget that parents are usually the initial teachers of reading, starting out when they let their kids know that the McDonald's golden arches make the letter "M." There is no school-based program that can compensate for the old fashioned "LAP" method of teaching reading. This method involves putting your preschool child in your lap every evening and reading him or her a bedtime story. It not only teaches pre-reading, reading readiness, and reading skills, it also associates reading in the mind of the child with all the warmth, love, and care that parents ide-ally give their children. Programs, such as Reading Is FUNdamental (RIF), that help get books into homes, and programs that encourage older sib-lings in school to read to their younger siblings still at home are excellent ways to introduce preschool children to reading.

The debate as to which is the superior approach continues to be a major trend in reading instruction. The whole language advocates continue to stress comprehension over pronunciation. However, they have the same ultimate goal as Rudolf Flesch and the phonics advocates. They want to get students into "real" literature as soon as possible, versus the "artificial" con-trolled vocabulary stories found in basal reading textbooks that many stud-ies have described as "boring" at best (Reyhner, 1992a). But there are problems even with "real" literature for minority students. The vast major-ity of books in libraries in this country reflect the European background of many Americans. They are full of European folktales that describe lands and situations, often using archaic words, that are unfamiliar to all Ameri-cans today, let alone for Americans who do not have European ancestry.

The role of the teacher in the reading program will have the greatest influence on how well children achieve in that program. Talented teachers can make a poor reading program work and ineffective teachers can ruin a good reading program. The traits of teachers who will be most likely to have success in teaching ethnic minority children to read are listed below.

Five Things to Look for in Teachers

First, the teacher is knowledgeable about the home cultures of minority students in his/her classroom and is sensitive to the practices of those cul-tures, including what parents expect classrooms and teaching to look like. Through this knowledge teachers can be aware of how their children "learn to learn" at home and avoid mistakes that alienate their students or their parents (Philips, 1993/1983; Swisher & Deyhle, 1992). Implication: Teachers should be recruited from minority cultures, and all teachers should receive pre- and inservice training on the cultural component of education, and they should do home visits to learn more firsthand about their students' lives outside of school.

Second, the teacher is knowledgeable about the language spoken at home by their students and the field of second language acquisition. Ideally, they can speak this language, but even if they cannot, they can be knowledgeable about the differences between the sound system of standard English and the dialect, such as Ebonics (Black English), or native language of the children and adjust their phonics lessons accordingly. For example, some students cannot distinguish between the English sounds of "p" and "b" because their native language does not have this distinction, so the teacher needs to focus on teaching this distinction for these students. Implication: Teachers should learn a second language spoken by their students to realize the difficulty learning a second language involves and to be able to communicate with their students better, and teachers should receive pre- and inservice training in the field of second language acquisition.

Third, the teacher is well trained in the subskills of reading. Implication: Regardless of the approach a teacher uses to teach reading to minority students, they need to be able to diagnose the strengths and weaknesses each child has in reading and have a repertoire of intervention strategies they can call on to help them.

Fourth, the teacher is responsive to the behavior of his or her students. Implication: Teachers need to be careful observers of their students and play an active role in their students reading and writing experiences. They need to be able to develop their own checklists to record the progress their students are making in reading and writing and to adjust their instruction when their students have difficulties.

Fifth, the teacher maintains high standards for all children. Implication: Teachers have to have the same high expectations for minority students as they do for majority students. Being sensitive to the needs of a minority child is not enough. Taking the child to a high level of literacy will do them more good than being a caring teacher who excuses the minority child from hard work in the classroom. All students need to be challenged and need to get a chance to read the great literature from all cultures, including Shakespeare, Cervantes and other European classic authors.

Five Things to Look for in a Reading Program

Language activity. Students, especially ESL students, need lots of opportunity for reading and talking. Students need multiple chances to read and talk in the classroom to develop their language skills. Students should read every day and teachers should read stories to students. By reading to students, teachers can expose students to more advanced material to wet their interest in reading, and the use of strategies such as Sustained Silent Reading provide students the practice they need to become fluent readers. Teachers need to avoid giving students who do not read well painful and stressful experiences such as "Round Robin" reading where their reading difficulties are spotlighted, and teachers need to give opportunities for students to participate in "instructional conversation" where they discuss the meaning of what they read (Saunders & Goldenberg, 1999; Tharp & Gallimore, 1988).

Profitable decoding (phonics). For example, because of the differences between Spanish and English and the fact English that consonants are more regular than English vowels, teaching English consonant sounds and their letter equivalents can help Spanish L1 students read better.

Experientially and culturally appropriate reading material. Students write, with the help of their teacher, language experience stories and/or making their own books that can be used for reading lessons. Teachers should seek out stories from their students' cultures to enrich their reading lessons.

Other quality reading material. High interest reading material readily available in the classroom on a variety of topics at a variety of reading levels, including reading material from a variety of cultures.

Pre- and postreading activities. Teachers doing prereading activities to introduce vocabulary and activate students prior knowledge on the subject of a story before students read and follow-up activities after students read, such as having students retell the story they have read to a reading buddy or writing about the story they read in a literature log.

CONCLUSION

The health of American Indians has suffered greatly because they did not have the immunity to European diseases and the cultural prohibitions about the use of alcohol that immigrants brought with them from Europe. Likewise, the education of American Indian students and immigrant minorities from non-literate cultures have suffered greatly because they do not have cultural teachings about the importance of reading in particular and school in general that many European and Asian immigrants from literate cultures brought with them. Educated European Americans teach the importance and values of reading, as well as prereading skills, to their children before they ever get to school by regularly reading them bedtime stories and having books, magazines, and newspapers scattered around their houses. In fact, some of these students come to school already knowing how to read.

If educators are to turn things around for their minority students, they must not just teach phonics and other skills associated with reading. They must help develop a culture of reading in the communities they teach in by working to get reading materials into the home, building classroom paperback libraries, and maintaining well-run and well-stocked school libraries, and they need to see that students have opportunities to own their own books. However, having a lot of books is not the only criterion; reading materials should be carefully selected as to not be destructive of the student's culture! Educators need to be careful that the reading material they are stocking and promoting does not aggravate the cultural conflicts that Peshkin describes in the Indian school he studied. By working with their students' parents and communities and studying the information on Indian, Hispanic, Black, and other groups, teachers can help their students join what Frank Smith (1988) has called the "literacy club."

We argue that teachers of reading do not have to take sides in the direct instruction versus constructivist and the phonics versus whole language debates. Jean Chall's (1967) "Great Debate" between the phonics-first and the whole language advocates exists more outside the classroom than in it. Baumann, Hoffmann, Moon, and Duffy-Hester (1998) found from a survey of more than 1,000 randomly selected teachers that they are inclined to "provide children a balanced, eclectic program involving both reading skill instruction and immersion in enriched literacy experiences" (pp. 636–637). Based on their research, they conclude that "teachers have long since resolved The Great Debate, instead embracing and implementing a balanced, eclectic philosophy for teaching reading and language arts" (p. 648). This eclecticism is castigated by some whole language proponents (e.g., Edelsky, Altwerger, & Flores, 1991), but if it is based on a thoughtful responsiveness to the needs of students and their families, we support it.

Children who come from homes, whether they are ethnic minority children or not, where they are not read to extensively need early direct instruction in what reading is all about, including phonics. They also need to be immersed in a friendly literacy environment as soon as possible in school that emphasizes how reading can satisfy their curiosity about things they are interested in, whether that is dinosaurs, whales, horses, race cars, motorcycles, basketball, or whatever, and can provide pleasure as well.

However, beyond playing on the immediate interests of children to get them to read, the best books from all cultures—including picture books—help teach children what it means to be a human being in the same manner of traditional stories from oral cultures. Whether these stories are read or heard, they help enculturate children to become productive members of their communities. Children who are denied these oral and written stories are in danger of missing a moral compass that will keep them on course. Educators need to work with parents and communities on a literature-based reading program to provide students with narrative guideposts, both oral and written, that will provide direction for today's youth.

REFERENCES

Baumann, J.F., Hoffmann, J.V., Moon, J., & Duffy-Hester, A.M. (1998). Where are teacher's voices in the phonics/whole language debate? Results from a survey of U.S. elementary classroom teachers. *The Reading Teacher, 51,* 636–650.

Beutler Lind, B. (1996). *Multicultural children's literature: An annotated bibliography, grades K-8.* Jefferson, NC: McFarland.

Chall, J.S. (1967). *Learning to read: The great debate.* New York: McGraw Hill.

Cockrum, W.A., & Castillo, M. (1991). Whole language assessment and evaluation strategies. In B. Harp (Ed.), *Assessment and evaluation in whole language programs* (pp. 73–86). Norwood, MA: Christopher-Gordon.

Cummins, J. (1996). *Negotiating identities: Education for empowerment in a diverse society.* Ontario: California Association for Bilingual Education.

Cummins, J. (1992). The empowerment of Indian students. In J. Reyhner (Ed.), *Teaching American Indian students* (pp. 1–12). Norman: University of Oklahoma Press.

Edelsky, C., Altwerger, B., & Flores, B. (1991). *Whole language: What's the difference.* Portsmouth, NH: Heinemann.

Ellis, A.K., & Fouts, J.T. (1993). *Research on educational innovations.* Princeton Junction, NJ: Eye on Education.

Fedullo, M. (1992). *Light of the feather: Pathways through contemporary Indian America.* New York: William Morrow.

Flesch, R. (1955). *Why Johnny can't read—And what you can do about it.* New York: Harper & Row.

Flesch, R. (1981). *Why Johnny still can't read: A new look at the scandal of our schools.* New York: Harper & Row.

Friere, P. (1970/1981). *Pedagogy of the oppressed.* New York: Continuum.

Garcia, R., & Ahler, J.G. (1992). Indian education, assumptions, ideologies, strategies. In J. Reyhner (Ed.), *Teaching American Indian students* (pp. 13–32). Norman: University of Oklahoma Press.

Goodman, K. (1986). *What's whole in whole language?* Portsmouth, NH: Heinemann.

Goodman, K. (1982). *Language, literacy, and learning.* London: Routledge Kegan Paul.

Graves, M.F., Juel, C., & Graves, B.B. (1998). *Teaching reading in the 21st century.* Boston: Allyn & Bacon.

Grossen, B., Coulter, G., & Ruggles, B. (n.d.). *Reading recovery: An evaluation of benefits and costs.* http://darkwing.uoregon.edu/~bgrossen/rr.htm

Henze, R.C., & Vanett, L. (1993). To walk in two worlds—or more? Challenging a common metaphor of Native education. *Anthropology and Education Quarterly, 24*(2), 116–134.

Jordan, C. (1984). Cultural compatibility and the education of Hawaiian children: Implications for mainland educators. *Educational Research Quarterly, 8*(4), 59–71.

Kozol, J. (1991). *Savage inequalities.* New York: Crown.

Krashen, S. (1999). *Three arguments against whole language & why they are wrong.* Portsmouth, NH: Heinemann.

Krashen, S. (1993). *The power of reading: Insights from the research.* Englewood, CO: Libraries Unlimited.

McCracken, R.A. (1971). Initiating sustained silent reading. *Journal of Reading, 14,* 522–23.

McCutchen, G., Kyle, D., & Skovina, R. (1979). Characters in basal readers: Does "equal" now mean "same"? *The Reading Teacher, 32,* 438–441.

Nurss, J.R., & Hough, R.A. (1992). Reading and the ESL student. In S.J. Samuels & A.E. Farstrup (Eds.), *What research has to say about reading instruction* (2nd ed., pp. 277–313). Newark, DE: International Reading Association.

Ogbu, J. (1983). Minority status and schooling in plural societies. *Comparative Education, 27*(2), 168–190.

Ogbu, J. (1978). *Minority education and caste: The American system in cross-cultural perspective.* New York: Academic Press.

Peshkin, A. (1997). *Places of memory: Whiteman's schools and Native American communities.* Hillsdale, NJ: Lawrence Erlbaum.

Philips, S.U. (1993/1983). *The invisible culture: Communication in classroom and community on the Warm Springs Indian Reservation.* Prospect Heights, IL: Waveland.

Pitts, P. (1988). *Racing the sun.* New York: Avon Camelot.

Pitts, P. (1992). *The Shadowman's way.* New York: Avon Camelot.

Pitts, P. (1994). *Crossroads.* New York: Avon Camelot.

Qöyawayma, Polingaysi (Elizabeth Q. White). 1964). *No turning back: A Hopi Indian woman's struggle to live in two worlds.* Albuquerque: University of New Mexico Press.

Reyes, M. de la Luz. (1991). A Process approach to literacy using dialogue journals. *Research in the Teaching of English, 25*(3), 291–313.

Reyhner, J. (1992a). Adapting curriculum to culture. In J. Reyhner (Ed.), *Teaching American Indian students* (pp. 96–103). Norman: University of Oklahoma Press.

Reyhner, J. (Ed.). (1992b). Teaching reading responsively. In J. Reyhner (Ed.), *Teaching American Indian students* (pp. 157–167). Norman: University of Oklahoma Press.

Rodriquez, L.J. (1994). *Always running—La vida loca: Gang days in L.A.* New York: Touchstone.

Rosenhouse, J., Feitelson, D., Kita, B., & Goldenstein, Z. (1997). Interactive reading aloud to Israeli first graders. Its contribution to literacy development. *Reading Research Quarterly, 32,* 168–183.

Ruffini, S., Feldman, B.I., Edirisooriya, G., Howe, L.F., & Borders, D.G. (n.d.). *Assessment of success for all: School years 1988–1991.* Baltimore City Public Schools, Department of Research and Evaluation.

Rupley, W.H., & Blaire, T.R. (1988). *Teaching reading: Diagnosis, direct instruction, and practice.* Columbus, OH: Merrill College.

Saunders, W.M., & Goldenberg, C. (1999). *The effects of instructional conversations and literature logs on the story comprehension and thematic understanding of English proficient and limited English proficient students.* Santa Cruz, CA: Center for Research on Education, Diversity, and Excellence (CREDE).

Smith, F. (1994). *Understanding reading* (5th ed.). Hillsdale, NJ: Erlbaum.

Smith, F. (1988). *Joining the literacy club: Further essays into education.* Portsmouth, NH: Heinemann.

Standing Bear, L. (1928). *My people the Sioux.* (E.A. Brininstool, Ed.) Boston: Houghton Miflin.

Steward, J. (1996). Review of Paul Pitts' *Racing the sun, The Shadowman's way,* and *Crossroads. Journal of Navajo Education, 13*(3), 43–44.

Stott, J.C. (1995). *Native Americans in children's literature.* Phoenix, AZ: Oryx Press.

Swisher, K., & Deyhle, D. (1992). Adapting instruction to culture. In J. Reyhner (Ed.), *Teaching American Indian students* (pp. 81–95). Norman: University of Oklahoma Press.

Tennant, E. (1994). *"Eye of Awareness": Life values across cultures.* Unalakleet, AK: Bering Strait School District.

Tharp, R.G. (1982). The effective instruction of comprehension: Results and description of the Kamehameha Early Education Program. *Reading Research Quarterly, 17,* 503–27.

Tharp, R.G., & Gallimore, R. (1988). *Rousing minds to life: Teaching, learning, and schooling in social context.* Cambridge: Cambridge University Press.

Thonis, E.W. (1981). Reading instruction for language minority students. In California State Department of Education Division of Bilingual Bicultural Education, *Schooling and language minority students: A theoretical framework* (pp. 147–181). Los Angeles, CA: Evaluation, Dissemination and Assessment Center California state University, Los Angeles.

Viadero, D. (1999, January 27). Miami study critiques "Success for All." *Education Week, 18*(20), 7.

Vygotsky, L.S. (1978). *Mind in society: The development of higher psychological processes* (M. Cole, V. John-Steiner, S. Scribner, & E. Souberman, Eds. & Trans.). Cambridge, MA: Harvard University Press.

Walberg, H.J., & Greenberg, R.C. (1998, April 8). The Diogenes factor. *Education Week, 17*(30).

CHAPTER 8

BEST PRACTICE(S)? THE CULTURAL DISCOURSE OF DEVELOPMENTALISM IN AMERICAN EARLY EDUCATION

A Cross-Cultural Comparison

Diane M. Hoffman

Abstract: Although best practice has become central to early childhood education and literacy learning in recent years, concerns have emerged over the ways in which underlying ideas of developmental appropriateness that are inherent in best practice fail to address issues of cultural diversity and difference. This chapter explores the notion of best practice as contextualized within culturally grounded discourses of developmental appropriateness, child-centeredness, and individualism. Comparing assumptions regarding children's selves and adult-child relations that underlie best practice in the United States with evidence from Japanese early education and Reggio Emilia schools in Italy, the chapter points to alternative views of self, cognition, emotion, and adult-child relations that may serve as a source of critical self-reflection as well as for improvement of practice among U.S. educators.

INTRODUCTION

In recent years, best practice has become a key idea in the area of early literacy education in the United States (Bredekamp, 1987, 1998). Yet, the development of standards and ideas concerning best practice has also generated a large critical literature, much of it concerned with the ways in which the notions of developmental appropriateness that underlie best practice have ignored cultural diversity and are implicitly biased toward a universal model of child development. It has been recognized that the field of child development "remains heavily influenced by the intellectual and social traditions of Western industrialized societies, which include, among other things, individualistic and meritocratic emphasis with Eurocentric interpretations of optimal development" (New & Mallory, 1994, p. 5). Much recent writing has suggested that current formulations of best practice are indeed deeply influenced by the orientations and cultural biases inherent in the field of child development research (Bloch, 1992; Cannella, 1997; Lubeck, 1994, 1996; New, 1993). In this chapter, I suggest that advocates of best practice in early education across the curriculum need to consider the debate about culture, views of children, and child development that has been ongoing in the early childhood education field for some time.

To this end, this chapter explores the notion of best practice as a cultural construct, contextualized within discourses of developmental appropriateness, child-centeredness, and individualism. I draw upon cross-cultural evidence (particularly the literature on Japanese early education and Reggio Emilia schools in Italy) to suggest alternative assumptions about the nature of children's selves and adult-child relations to those that currently ground ideas about best practice in the United States. Rather than abandon the notion of best practice, however, educators ought to reconsider the position of children in adult discourses of literacy and early childhood by attention to the lens through which we view children, as well as by careful attention to the ways best practice is formulated in different cultures and societies around the world.

The Cultural Context of Best Practice

As anthropologists of education have long pointed out, the practices, values, and ideas that shape education in different societal contexts can be partially understood as reflections of particular cultures, shaped by cultural theories of teaching and learning, historical circumstances, and contemporary forces of political, economic, and social change. Most educators would agree that beliefs about what children are like and what is "best" for them are deeply shaped by such cultural values and world-views (and hence will differ from one culture to another).[1] In some sense, then, the formation of guidelines or statements about "best practice" in the United States can also be viewed as a culturally particular enterprise, one that has had an important and growing influence on curriculum development, marketing of educational materials, teacher education, and program evaluation in American education (Raines, 1997).

Despite the pervasive influence of ideas about best practice in contemporary early childhood education, however, many critics have attacked the notion of developmental appropriateness that underlies them. Developmentally appropriate practice is often seen as being incompatible with the cultural backgrounds of children from diverse cultures (Bernhard, 1995; Bloch, 1992; Cannella, 1997; Katz, 1996; Lubeck, 1994, 1996; Mallory & New, 1994). While much of this criticism is justified, it is also fair to say that in the early literacy field best practice has been at least partially responsive to the need for sociocultural contextualization, particularly in (1) efforts to link home and school and to view the home/community environment as an influential factor in literacy acquisition, including efforts to enlist parental behavioral support for children's literacy development (e.g., reading to children, having books in the home); (2) efforts to infuse multicultural content (e.g., multicultural children's literature) into the curriculum; and (3) efforts to connect literacy activities with children's lived experiences and to support more socially situated forms of learning. On the other hand, it can also be argued that in spite of such apparent concerns for sociocultural context, best practice in early literacy instruction has yet to deal in much depth with the complexities of cultural, ethnic, and racial difference—including conflicts between what experts claim as best practice and the strong values or preferences present in some minority communities for literacy experiences and instructional techniques deemed by such experts as outmoded or ineffective.

A case in point concerns round-robin reading—a practice strongly discouraged in contemporary visions of best practice yet one that is, as a colleague remarked one day while discussing her research with me on Native American reservations in the Southwest, a normative one among Native American teachers. In this case, efforts to "individualize" instruction—following the spirit of best practice—were met not with open arms but with resistance on the part of native educators, parents, and students, because the individualization ethos conflicted with certain deeply held and longstanding orientations and expectations concerning classroom process and the "right" way to learn. This point is, of course, not new. As Wolcott observed some time ago, introducing more individualized and creative approaches generated great resistance on the part of his Kwakiutal pupils (Wolcott, 1987). Of course, if done in a culturally sensitive manner, changes in practice can be successful, as ample work by anthropologists of education with other minority groups has illustrated (e.g., McCarty et al., 1991). But in these cases, the formulation of improved practice has not been in terms of a received set of notions defining best practice irrespective of cultural context, but rather in terms of the cultural particularities and needs of the learners and their situation. In this sense, then, successful accounts of change toward improved instructional practice have been "bottom up" rather than "top down." Expertise is not imported from outside the situation in a set of ostensibly culture-free guidelines, but emerges from close attention to the cultural particularities of the learners and their social context.

As this brief illustration suggests, to advance the conceptualization of best practice it is imperative to consider it in the context of its relation to sociocultural context, and to question the extent to which the assumptions guiding best practice may originate in culturally particular notions not shared across diverse cultural contexts. In this part of my analysis, I focus in particular on the links between current formulations of best practice across the curriculum and notions of developmental appropriateness and child-centeredness. At the same time, I also suggest that the cultural diversity critique of best practice (which argues that we simply cannot have a "best practice" because of cultural diversity) fails to recognize that this very claim emphasizes differences over commonalities in children—a notion that, in effect, is itself culturally biased. For when we examine notions of best practice that are, in fact, present in other educational contexts around the world, we find that a different view of children and their "differences" emerges. This suggests that cultural diversity in itself is not the main impediment to development of ideas about best practice, but that the ways in which we view children and position them in the process of constructing knowledge about them may well be.

BEST PRACTICE: CONCEPTUAL ROOTS AND ASSUMPTIONS

Best practice discourse reveals a set of underlying assumptions that revolve around three key ideas: the construct of individual differences (often glossed as abilities and needs); the divided self (having distinct domains of cognition, affect, and social skills); and a particular formulation of the relationship between children and adults that constrains the ways in which we know children. A common thread running across all of these, in turn, is developmentalism, which I am defining here as a general lens through which to view children that emphasizes their position in developmental stages moving progressively from low/deficient performances and capabilities to increasingly higher level competencies and performances.

In a summary/review of recommendations developed by national associations and agencies for best practice across the curriculum, Zemelman et al. (1993) identified a fair degree of commonalilty in the recommended practices across curriculum areas. A list of common ideas or principles about what constitutes best practice across the curriculum includes approaches that are child-centered (as opposed to teacher-centered), experiential, reflective, holistic, social, collaborative, democratic, cognitive, developmental, constructivist, and psycholinguistic. Key terms in the conceptualization of best practice include "progressive," "developmentally appropriate," and "research-based" (Zemelman et al., 1993).

The authors further note that reading and writing are indisputably the most advanced fields in defining and implementing best practice. In the reading area, best practice is characterized by a strong psycholinguistic orientation. Zemelman et al. claim this simply means that "...children learn to read the way they learn to talk, and the school should operate accordingly" (p. 34) which means "surrounding kids with real, natural language" that is holistic—that is, complete, real, and authentic texts. "Children learn to read by playing at reading, making closer and closer approximations of reading behavior" (p. 35). Furthermore, "all this literacy learning is individually developmental—that is, it proceeds through a number of predictable and well-defined stages," while children will inevitably differ in the age and rate at which they progress through these stages (p. 35). Zemelman et al. also remind us that "wise reading teachers are child-centered," which means that children pick the books they want to read (not teachers or parents)—assuming that this exercise of "free choice" is directly connected to motivation, and that children cannot be motivated if they are not given "choice" (p. 36). Best practice also "stresses that reading is a *cognitive* process" (p. 36), which means that readers need to use skills such as predicting and monitoring their own reading processes and strategies—one reason why portfolios, journals and teachers' qualitative observations are "important tools in Best Practice classrooms" (pp. 36–37).

It is fairly clear from this short selection that a number of assumptions are being made about children and their learning that merit closer attention. Since these assumptions become much clearer in the context of a cross-cultural comparison, I use evidence from Japan and Reggio Emilia schools in Italy as a way to foreground the distinctiveness of American ideas and practices.

THE DEVELOPMENTALIST LENS AND THE PARADIGM OF THE INDIVIDUAL

Aside from the historical connections that have existed in the United States between early childhood education and child development research, the very question *why* developmental appropriateness has been so influential as a frame for best practice remains unexplored. It is noteworthy that in Japan, though early education is strongly progressive in character, there is a comparative absence of developmentalist ideas about children. That is, there is little emphasis on determining individual levels of development, behavioral stages, or differences in ability, and few efforts to measure and assess individual "needs" relative to developmental benchmarks. Ideas about the distinctiveness and separation of social, emotional, and cognitive skills associated with developmental domains are comparatively absent, as are views of children as potentially deficient in developmental level. This separation of progressive approaches to education and developmental concepts suggests that perhaps their link is fundamentally cultural, and influenced in the American case by a strong paradigm of "the individual child" defined against all other children and judged principally by criteria of individual difference.

Despite an ostensible emphasis on collaboration and the acknowledgment of the social basis of learning in best practice discourse, the construct of the individual child with a unique set of abilities and needs remains paramount. Collaborative and democratic processes (or activities) never militate against the primacy of the individual child in best practice; even the idea of developmental appropriateness must be contextualized by attention to "individual differences" (as in the quote above concerned with developmental stages). As Bredekamp (1998) notes, "A universal principle of development is that there is a wide range of individual variation on virtually every dimension. Therefore, for practices to be developmentally appropriate, they must also be individually appropriate" (p. 184). Furthermore, as Williams (1994) observes, "The prominence of the individual in the guidelines [for developmentally appropriate practice] is striking. There appears to be an assumption that the highest good in child care and education lies in the perfection of individual capability across domains of development" (p. 159). Thus, there are clear conceptual links between *developmental* and *individual* in the formation of notions of best practice. Developmental appropriateness thus consists of the match between instructional task or activity and individual developmental level; the best instructional environment is one that is matched to the specific needs and developmental level of the individual child. Little is actually said in ideas about best practice about commonalities among children—rather, the emphasis is placed on the individual child and his or her differences.

The Japanese view is that children, on the contrary, are more alike in fundamental ways than they are different; in sum, there is a greater cultural emphasis on the theme of "children's natures" in Japan. Indeed, the highest goal for children in Japan is to fulfill their childlike nature, to be childlike—in contrast to the United States, where the cultural preference is for children to be as "adult-like" in their behavior as early as possible. This does not mean that Japanese teachers do not recognize individual differences: indeed they do, but rather that individual differences are not seen as the starting point for a child's education. In the United States, ideas about individual differences ultimately guide and determine what is offered to children in school, resulting in highly differentiated curricular experiences across assumed levels of ability. In Japan, however, while ability differences are frequently recognized and very much accommodated, particularly in the context of a number of practices such as the *han* [small group], they do not determine the allocation of curricular activities or educational experiences. It is assumed that if the curricular experience or activity is well defined and delivered in the first place, most children will acquire something of value from it, particularly if the child makes enough effort. The Japanese approach strongly discourages assessment of children's abilities (or "levels") as a basis for allocating or differentiating instruction, because to do so is seen as fundamentally inegalitarian.[2] Rather, as numerous observers have remarked, it is assumed that *effort*, not ability, is the salient dimension in children's education (Lewis, 1995; Peak, 1991; Stevenson & Stigler, 1992; Tobin, Wu, & Davidson, 1989).

Moreover, U.S. discourse on individual needs and abilities is strongly linked to developmentalist ideas of children that implicitly convey notions of deficiency. In most cases, as Lubeck (1994), New and Mallory (1994), and Baker (1998) have noted, the developmentalist perspective paints children as lacking in competencies relative to developmental benchmarks, other children, or even adults. Lubeck (1996, p. 152) writes, "Educational discourse has ... become a discourse of deficiency, as we generate new and more finely tuned categories for children." For Bergen, "The development as achievement viewpoint is pervasive in American society and is reflected in such terms as 'developmental milestones,' 'developmental delay,' 'readiness,' and all other concepts that imply that children must strive to achieve developmental and learning goals" (1997, p. 161).

In contrast to the American case, Japanese ideas about child development can be said to almost entirely avoid discussion of children's developmental deficiencies. Indeed, traditional Japanese views of children stressed not their supposed "development" in terms of movement toward a superior state of adulthood but the innate moral and spiritual superiority of childhood over adulthood. Strong value was and still is placed on the "childlike" child—the child who embodies the ideal traits of children: innocence, brightness, energy, cheerfulness, devotion, and sincerity, among others.[3] Thus in at least one sense it is somewhat misleading to speak of child *development* in Japanese education, since the emphasis is on the child remaining true to its childlike nature, rather than throwing off childlike characteristics in favor of attaining adult modes of being and functioning as soon as possible. It is clear that to become an adult is not to achieve a higher or better state of being but a different and perhaps even a lesser one (Azuma, 1986; Boocock, 1992; White & Levine, 1986; Yamamura, 1986). Of course, children eventually need to acquire the habits of social interaction and consciousness of obligations to others that constitute social maturity for the Japanese (and the school is an important means to this end) but the self of the child is not viewed through a developmentalist frame that presupposes the inherent inferiority of children's natures that should be replaced with adult-like behavior as soon as possible. In general, rather than view children through a teleological lens, in which deficiency is always implicit, the Japanese view is much more focused on the child as child, in the present moment, being the way children ought to be. Being a child is not a "stage" through which one passes on the way to adulthood; it is its own world, defined by its own experiences and requiring adults to understand it and in some ways conform to it, rather than the other way around.

The dominance of the paradigm of individual differences in American early education raises a number of troubling issues, especially in the area of assessment and more generally in adult construction of children's abilities and needs (Canella, 1997). Recognizing the frequent horrors of standardized testing, best practice recommends alternative means to assessment of needs and abilities (e.g., portfolios, qualitative observations). However, do such changes really move us beyond the larger cultural frame of assessment practices in general and the assumptions that govern how adults construct knowledge about children? Alternative assessments still do not sufficiently challenge the discourses and practices of assessment of individual "differences" that inform and direct the entire structure of educational practice. While the implementation of "individualized" education in best practice is well intentioned (how could we not want a child's "needs" to go unaddressed?), it unwittingly fails to challenge the larger structural issue of inequality in American schooling and the practices of assessment that support it. As long as assessment remains a primary frame for viewing early education, even in its more benign forms it continues to function to produce inequitable outcomes. Furthermore, "individualized" learning, as Stevenson and Stigler (1992) point out, leads to isolation and loneliness: instead of creating a community of learners united in a process of learning, it creates isolated individuals who, though working "at their own pace," are working toward noncommunal goals, alone.

CHILD-CENTEREDNESS, TEACHER-CENTEREDNESS: A CULTURALLY BASED OPPOSITION?

A second broad area in which to examine the assumptions underlying current formulations of best practice, concerns the notion of child-centeredness and the subtext of choice that underlies this idea in American educational discourse. As Zemelman et al. (1993) note, best practice across the curriculum strongly embraces child-centeredness. Practices deemed child-centered allow children choice, and place children's needs, interests, and experiences ahead of arbitrarily designed and teacher-controlled content. According to Canella (1997), child-centeredness is ostensibly antiauthoritarian and based on ideals of individual choice, democracy, and autonomy.

In best practice discourse, these notions are directly opposed to teacher-centered classrooms in which the dominant mode of teacher-child interaction is whole-group instruction. In whole-group approaches, teachers dictate content and activity, make little provision for children's individual interests and needs, require learner passivity, and exert authoritarian control. Whole-group instruction, while perhaps not totally abandoned in developmentally appropriate classrooms, is typically denigrated as intrinsically opposed to the spirit of child-centeredness. Gestwicki (1995) writes, "large-group activities ... play a lesser role in developmentally appropriate classrooms, [because in the latter] meeting individual needs is a priority.... Teaching strategies of whole-group teacher directed instruction ... are not appropriate methods of teaching young children" (p. 12).

Yet the view of whole-group instruction as being automatically opposed to children's natural interests and learning and damaging to their engagement and motivation is clearly disproved by much evidence to the contrary from Japanese preschools and elementary schools, as well as from Reggio Emilia schools in Italy. In both Japan and Reggio Emilia, whole–group instruction for young children is what Americans would call a highly "child-centered" enterprise in which teachers approach the class enthusiastically, children are intensely engaged and actively involved in the construction of knowledge, and plentiful opportunities for divergent thinking, problem-solving, and multiple approaches to learning are provided (New, 1993; Peak, 1991; Stevenson & Lee, 1997; Stigler & Perry, 1990; White, 1987). Stevenson and Lee (1997) remark,

> [Observers of Japanese approaches to whole-group teaching], expecting to find the teacher as the sole source of information and lone arbiter of what is correct, ... are surprised by the frequency with which the teacher calls upon students for their opinions or explanations of a problem and then seeks the reaction of other students to what has just been suggested.... They often describe the teachers as skilled professionals who approach their classes with enthusiasm and vigor ... The teacher does not assume the role of lecturer but acts as an informed guide who knows that teaching is most effective if students participate in the lesson.... (p. 34)

Children's ideas are taken as the jumping off points for whole-class learning. Teachers typically start a lesson asking children to generate as many different ways as possible to solve a problem, working in small groups, or by engaging children's interest in direct and very child-appealing ways. New (1993) writes that in the case of Reggio Emilia,

> ...Teachers often follow children's leads in pursuing avenues of inquiry, [and] they are willing to take cues from children for curriculum development that would be unwelcome in many U.S. classrooms. Thus, Barbie dolls, video games, and cartoon heroic figures may play prominently in the design and direction of Reggio Emilia projects.... The resulting curriculum might be described as both child-centered *and* (often) teacher-directed. (p. 221)

In Japanese early education, children assume many of the tasks of class-room management and transitions (not teachers), and are invested with far higher levels of responsibility than children are in U.S. classrooms, including taking responsibility for managing their own and others' misbe-havior (Lewis, 1995; Peak, 1991; Tobin, Wu, & Davidson, 1989). This in itself is evidence for far higher degrees of "child-centeredness" in Japan than what is typical in U.S. elementary classrooms. If done well, whole-group instruction is perhaps even more engaging of children's enthusiasm than the individualized American classroom, it can foster a strong sense of shared inquiry, community, and connectedness, instead of an atmosphere in which individuals and groups work alone on separate projects at differ-ent "ability levels." In assigning a minimal role to whole-group activity in American early childhood education, because of the cultural assumption that goals of child-centeredness are inherently opposed to whole-group experience, best practice in effect ignores a primary arena in which teach-ing practice can indeed display impressive amounts of professionalism and be highly engaging to children, as well as being an effective means of teaching/learning. In the long run, a vision of best practice that ignores the value of whole-group activity is a limiting or even self-defeating one, for the genuine refinement of teaching practice becomes even more difficult, if not impossible, in the face of demands for constant juggling of the teacher's attention from one individual and group to another in the indi-vidualized classroom.

A further assumption inherent in best practice ideas concerning child-centeredness is the primacy of choice. While choice is, of course, a central cultural value in the United States, it is not particularly important in many other cultures, nor is it at all a guiding concept in early education. More-over, even where early education does appear by most American criteria to be highly child-centered in its ethos (as in Japan), personal choice is not a particularly strong value. This stands in great contrast to American prac-tices of early socialization, where even two-year-old children will be asked to make many choices throughout the day. In view of the lack of universal-ity of ideas concerning child choice in early education in many diverse cul-tural contexts, choice as a central tenet of child-centered best practice would appear to be more of a culturally particular script than one intrinsi-cally related to best practice in early education.

Moreover, in American classrooms choice is frequently an illusion: for the "choices" are already predetermined or structured by teachers or oth-ers in authority. "Adults actually control the choices that surround children and the capacity for follow-through when choices are made" (Canella, 1997, p. 121). Learning or activity centers—normative parts of the "child-centered" environment of many American preschools and kindergartens—are prime arenas for sustaining the appearance of choice, while undermin-ing it through the imposition of adult prestructuring and regulation ("only three children at each center at any time...").[4] In an analysis of one developmentally appropriate classroom, Goldstein (1997) notes that the teacher, Martha, arranged and directed children's choices to a great degree, and that her pre-selection of choices (particularly in "activity center placements") were grounded on *her* assessments of individual interests and needs: "Martha's students do not have much say in planning or developing activities or units of study" (p. 14). In the context of assigning and allocating activities to individuals based on their supposed needs, it is remarkable that neither the author nor Martha mention issues of inequality—potential or actual—associated with differential assigning or encouragement of children to pursue different levels or types of activity. By its linking up with teachers' judgments about the "needs" of the individual child, choice functions to support dominant American paradigms of individual difference, becoming a key mechanism whereby the cultural ideal of freedom and autonomy can be maintained, alongside the reality of scripts of deficit. Indeed, when children fail to choose, or do not choose the "right" level of activity, immediate attributions of deficit are made:

> When our son Isaac was three we enrolled him in a progressive children's center. The first hour of the day was free choice. Isaac would arrive at school, and the teachers would say, "Choose something you want to do, Isaac." But Isaac did not know how to choose. He did not want to choose. He needed an adult to choose for him, to give him direction. At the time, we and his teachers viewed this inability or unwillingness to choose a play activity as a cognitive or emotional deficit of Isaac's that needed remediation. (Tobin, 1995, pp. 232–233)

There is, in effect, no real choice when one is forced to choose, nor when one's choices are under the surveillance of "professional" judgment, no matter how well intentioned, if the latter is fundamentally allied to paradigms of individual difference/deficit. In this way, discourses of choice ultimately serve to maintain a system of differential access to and success in the American educational system.

WHITHER THE "WHOLE CHILD?"
THE FRAGMENTED SELF IN BEST PRACTICE

According to Zemelman et al. (1993), best practice has a strong cognitive emphasis: "Teachers need to help students develop the specific types of thinking that our civilization values, such as analytical reasoning, interpretation, hypothesizing.... Language, thinking, and conceptual understanding are intertwined as students *construct* [emphasis in original] ideas, systems, and processes for themselves" (p. 12). At the same time, the social context of learning is equally emphasized, especially by encouraging small group activity and collaboration among learners. Yet we need to ask: How rich is this model of collaboration and social interaction, especially in the light of the overarching attention to *the individual child* in best practice? In American classrooms even small group activities are, in New's (1993) words, "designed to foster the child's social competencies in ways that promote the individual rather than the group" (p. 219). Small groups in U.S. classrooms are typically temporary and arranged for specific tasks; in effect, compared to Japanese groups, American groups are focused around individuals' relationships to a task more than they are around individuals' relationships to each other (Hoffman, 1995). Individualistic emphases and outcomes are still more important than experiences of relatedness to others in the group.

A second important consideration concerns how children's selves are constructed in discourse on best practice. While it is recognized that social and affective components are important aspects of the child's total learning, cognitive development is nearly always discussed as a process separate from the development of social skills or affect. Each is essentially a separate analytical domain of the self. This is seen in the extent to which, for many American educators, there is a perceived trade-off between school experience that is geared toward academic (or cognitive) learning and school experience that promotes social skills learning (New, 1993). In their comparative study of beginning American and Japanese teachers, Shimahara and Sakai (1995) noted that not only did American teachers see children's cognitive growth as something separate from their social and moral development, they viewed the cognitive dimension as more important.

The distinctiveness of this discourse on the separateness of cognition, affect, and social skills becomes clearer in comparison to Japanese discourses on the self in early education. Overall, Japanese educators talk in broadly humanistic terms of cultivating the self and place great emphasis in early education on culturally valued qualities of personhood, including *omoiyari* (empathy), perseverance, enthusiasm/energy, *kejime* (ability to shift or adapt the self fluidly to changing social situations), and *hansei* (critical self-reflection). Furthermore, the dichotomization of the self into separate domains of cognition and affect is not present in the Japanese view; instead, there is unity of affect and cognition, heart and mind. The two are in fact conceptually one, as is evident in the term *kokoro*, meaning (approximately) "heart-mind." Teachers of young children place overwhelming emphasis on the having a positive emotional environment in the classroom and cultivating children's positive emotional attachments to each other and to classroom life. From an American perspective they are, in fact, amazingly patient and cheerful, even in the face of extraordinarily trying behavior (Peak, 1991). The single greatest concern of all teachers is that children should *enjoy* coming to school and being a part of the group, and that they should learn emotional empathy (Lewis, 1995; Peak, 1991).

Japanese teachers believe emotions to be intimately involved in children's cognitive learning. Before a math lesson on cubing, for example, students were asked to write a paragraph on how they *felt* about cubing

(White, 1987). Complete, enthusiastic, and energetic participation or commitment to activities is carefully cultivated—even to what Americans would call mundane or trivial ones, for without the necessary positive emotional involvement, learning itself is jeopardized.[5] While American educators certainly want children to understand others' feelings and to acquire social skills such as democratic participation and sharing, there is much less overall emphasis on the cultivation of positive emotion in the classroom environment. Emotion is not seen as intrinsically related to academic achievement.

Further evidence for a fragmented self in American early educational discourse is to be found in the "thinking skills" debate. In the thinking skills discourse, even cognitive activity is subjected to a dichotomization. On the one hand we have so-called "higher-order" thinking (such as problem solving or "critical" thinking), and, on the other, rote, repetition, or "basic skills" approaches. "Real" thinking is opposed to "rote" learning or activity. Best practice recommends that explicit attention be paid to teaching higher order cognition (including "metacognitive" strategies). Yet the opposition between "thinking" and rote/repetitive cognition is fundamentally a cultural one, as a Japanese comparison indicates. In Japan, there is no presumed opposition between "thinking" and "rote." Indeed the best route to higher order thinking is, in effect, through what Americans denigrate as empty ritual, rote, or repetition (Hoffman, 1995, 1998b; Hori, 1994; Rohlen & LeTendre, 1997). The Kumon method of mathematics instruction is another particularly good example of how "rote" activity is intimately tied to higher-order conceptual development (Russell, 1994).

American assumptions concerning the opposition between rote and thinking, or affect and cognition, reflect a culture-bound understanding of children's learning. If best practice is to be truly "best"—especially in the context of cultural diversity—it must be cognizant of its own cultural presuppositions and take cross-cultural evidence into account in the formation of its recommendations.

POSITIONING CHILDREN: THE LENS OF EXPERTISE IN THE FORMULATION OF BEST PRACTICE

Cannella (1997) writes that the field of early childhood education requires a revolutionary reconceptualization that deconstructs adult privilege in the construction of ideas of children. Perhaps the most troubling aspect of American best practice is the particular set of assumptions it brings to teacher-child relationships, both in the ways teachers and other adult experts construct their knowledge about children, and in the ways in which child development expertise, as a critical component of best practice, implicitly contextualizes the adult-child relationship. The lens of child development expertise and child-centeredness insists on the constant need to observe, evaluate, and judge children so as to offer them developmentally appropriate experiences. In sum, it positions children as the objects of adult observation and interpretation. Paradoxically, in this "child-centered" approach to practice, children's own experiences and world-views lose their legitimacy against the constructions and interpretations of them that are made by "professionals." While developmentally appropriate education pays lip-service to the idea of "seeing the world through children's eyes," the practices of surveillance, observation, judgment, and categorization that are implicit in developmentalist approaches belie that ideal. Though the source of knowledge about children has changed (away from the standardized test to the qualitative observation), evaluation and ranking are still going on. The entire tenor of the relationship between teacher and child cannot but be affected by the constant need to determine individual competencies and assign tasks that "match" those competencies—and this needs to be done not for one child, perhaps, but for twenty. Inevitably, the lens used to view "children as individuals" under such circumstances needs to be selective. New (1993) writes, "American early childhood educators employ a highly selective filter through which children's cues are viewed, even as they enthusiastically describe their program as "child-centered" (p. 222).

It is quite instructive to compare Japanese and American beginning teachers on what they see as most important in their relationships with children in the classroom. Americans uniformly say that the children must *not* see the teacher as a friend, and that they need to maintain a certain degree of professional distance from the children so that their authority and position will be respected. Ellen, one of the teachers studied by Shimahara and Sakai (1995), believed that she needed a certain degree of emotional detachment from the children in order to maintain her authority. Her relationship to children was to be grounded in mutual respect that would be threatened by too much emotional closeness. She believed she could be friendly with children only after they had accepted her authority.

Japanese teachers, however, want children to see them first and foremost as a friend. They strive to develop a close personal relationship with each child characterized by *kizuna* or *kakawari*—close emotional bonding. Emotional attachment is seen by the Japanese as the paramount principle behind classroom management (Shimahara & Sakai, 1995). In the Japanese view, emotional closeness is also fundamental to "understanding" children. Understanding does not come from emotionally neutral or distant "observation," nor from research on child development. In contrast to the American case, there is a conspicuous absence of appeal to "knowledge of child development" in Japanese discourses on early childhood education. Rather, the important term is "understanding," and understanding is possible only by cultivating close emotional bonds between teacher and child that are characterized by qualities of sincerety and unpretentiousness. This emotional groundwork allows the teacher to see the world more closely from the child's perspective and to enter more deeply into the child's *kokoro* (heart-mind).

This strong discourse of authentic emotional closeness in Japan stands in stark and troubling contrast to the emotional environment present in child care settings in the United States.[6] Leavitt and Power (1989) and Leavitt (1995) find emotional isolation, depersonalization, and inauthenticity/superficiality in American patterns of care for young children. Empathic emotional closeness—the principal theme in Japanese notions of child care—is almost completely absent, in favor of the kind of detached emotional neutrality associated with "professionalism" in interactions with children (see also Hoffman, 2000; Hoffman, 2001). For Americans, knowledge about children is predicated on presupposition of detached, neutral positioning needed for "observation"—not relation, and least of all close emotional relation.

Hodges (1991) captures well the general spirit of continuous evaluation through observation, informed by child development knowledge, that is found in current ideas of best practice:

> Systematic direct observation, carried out using a variety of checklists and supported by oral and written performance samples, is a useful assessment tool ... It has the advantage of being able to be used almost anytime, which permits teachers to identify their students' levels of development in the classroom... (p. 159)

In American ideas of best practice, the process of evaluation/judgment makes children the objects of adult observation, undermining emotional connection—for emotion would sacrifice the "objectivity" of the developmental assessments teachers are encouraged to perform. Most teachers would no doubt say that their relationships with children are separate from their assessment practices; but in reality, the pervasiveness of the observer's gaze, the need for constant observation to match curriculum with individuals, cannot but have an influence on the tenor of the emotional and interpersonal relationships between teachers and children.

The absence of need to "understand" children in U.S. developmentalist discourse and its replacement with a discourse of objective knowledge about children merits closer consideration. The "need to understand" implies uncertainty and engagement with the unknown, as well as the possibility of discovery. In Japan, this is a very emotional and personal process. But in American views of best practice, it is certitude about "what is known about child development" or "research on young children" that appear as the dominant conceptual tropes. Understanding is predicated on close relationship and empathic identification; observation in the context of child development theory is not. Which approach is more "child-centered" in a genuine sense?

The above analysis suggests an important theoretical as well as practical point in defining best practice: We can never assume isomorphism between perceptions and realities, for often there is a tremendous gap between what educators believe they are doing in their classrooms and what they really do. In her analysis of the teacher Martha, Goldstein (1997) writes: "Martha genuinely believes her classroom is a place where children run the show, even going as far as to tell me: 'I never have the upper hand. Always remember that.' Yet much of what I saw indicated that Martha did have the upper hand much of the time ... This is further evidence of the distance between Martha's words and Martha's practices" (p. 17). This gap between perception and practice is also brought out in Tobin, Wu, and Davidson's (1989) study of preschool in Japan, China, and the United States. As these authors observed, though Americans *believe* they are far less authoritarian than Japanese and Chinese educators in their interactions with children, especially in encouraging children to express themselves verbally, in reality, Americans constrain and limit children's language use to much greater degrees than do Japanese and even Chinese teachers. American teachers (and parents too) monitor children's speech very closely, even when children are talking among themselves, frequently reprimanding children whose words are not "appropriate," for example, "We don't use mean words here," or "You are not allowed to tell someone 'I won't be your friend'" (Tobin, 1995, p. 231).[7] By contrast, great freedom of language has been observed in Reggio Emilia schools in Italy. According to New (1993), the degree of "authorized dissention" that occurs among children in Reggio Emilia schools "...challenges American standards of appropriate social behavior" (p. 219).

Moreover, while American educators believe their classrooms promote autonomy, freedom, and choice, it is in Japanese classrooms that children apparently experience far more freedom, autonomy, and responsibility for themselves as well as for others: "Japanese students had more time, space, and activities that they controlled themselves than the American students did.... [As a result of a large degree of self-initiated and self-directed activity] ... Japanese schools and classrooms are much noisier, more robust, and livelier than their American counterparts. Such characteristics of schools are not just tolerated but expected in Japan" (Shimahara & Sakai, 1995, p. 75). These examples, among many others, illustrate that the gap between what we *say* we do and what we really do in our teaching of young children may be much greater than many Americans are willing to admit (Hoffman, in press).[8]

The mismatch between perceptions and realities in children's education raises the deeper issue of adult construction of children's selves. If it is difficult to be objective about the kinds of educational experiences one creates for children, it may be even more difficult to have accurate perceptions or understandings of children as individuals, despite best intentions to the contrary. Because the discourse of individual differences, needs, and ability levels proceeds largely in the absence of children's voices on such issues, in a sense their very individuality is being constructed *for* them on the basis of an ostensibly benign process of professional but emotionally distant observation. The assumption is that children's individuality is something that can be known from observation—that it is visible and knowable by trained practicioners. Yet in other cultural contexts, no one would presume to understand another's individuality in any deep way, since it is a very private and deeply guarded as well as respected domain of the self that is simply not a part of everyday social life in public settings such as school (see also Hoffman, 1998a). We have not yet come to terms with the ways in which presuming to understand a child's individuality constitutes a potential affront to the child as a person. In the discourse of child development and appropriate practice, there is a need to reflect on the distinction between recognizing a child as an individual, and presuming to understand a child as an individual.[9]

RESURRECTING BEST PRACTICE: BEYOND DIFFERENCES

Critics of developmentally appropriate practice in the United States have been correct in their observation that the determination of what is "appropriate" has been a highly culture-bound enterprise shaped by Eurocentric assumptions parading as universals. As the above comparison with Japanese and Reggio Emilia ways of viewing children illustrates, many of the assumptions regarding child-centeredness, individual differences, and self-other relationships that form the core of best practice are indeed culture-bound, and for this reason, require critical engagement. Delpit (1995) and others have amply illustrated some of the weaknesses of the cultural presumptions underlying some forms of progressive practice in early literacy instruction that conflict with the values and expectations of minority populations. Any effort to create a best practice needs to become cognizant of the ways in which its underlying cultural presuppositions may not be relevant to or compatible with the populations it intends to serve.

It is important to realize, however, that while terminology may differ, notions of best practice are a large part of what early education is concerned about in many parts of the world. Educators in Japan and Reggio Emilia schools are tirelessly engaged in the kind of learning and continuous refinement of practice that all good "best practice" ought to aim for, and children are as "different" from one another in their personalities, talents, interests, and abilities in other countries as they are in the United States, regardless of degree of cultural diversity. The existence of differences (cultural or individual) among children is thus not inherently antithetical to ideals of best practice. The main difficulty with best practice is not that it ignores differences in children, as some critics claim, but that it assumes an overarching paradigm of the individual defined in terms of difference. It is in its assumptions about "the individual child" and "individual difference" that best practice is most culturally insensitive.

Evidence from Japan and Reggio Emilia schools serves as an important conceptual antidote to the reduction to individualism that plagues both best practice and its current critics. In both contexts we have ideas about best practice that paint a much closer match between ideals of child-centeredness and actual practice. Furthermore, in both contexts, while differences among children are recognized, individual differences are not in the driver's seat, so to speak, of practice. Instead, teachers address children as individuals, in the best tradition of child-centeredness, while not assuming that differences are so extreme as to make it impossible for children to benefit from and enjoy whole-group experiences. There is, in sum, virtue in recognizing commonality, as it creates a setting in which children are much freer of adult efforts to construct their individuality and from what may well be the pretense of professionally distant and emotionally neutral observations and assessments. They are freer to be children, to diverge from adult expectations, and to be responsible for others. The need to assess difference imposes its own kind of oppression on the self. And it creates the conditions for inequality to flourish, if such "innate" differences are allowed to determine what kind of education is offered to each child.

What are the conditions under which early educational practice can indeed be refined and honed to levels of "best?" An analogy may be instructive: If every human body were so completely different from another as to make basic surgical procedures impossible, where would we be? Each doctor would have to devise a new form of surgery each time, and there would be no certain guarantee of success. Instead, we have found ways of surgery that have a fair degree of commonality and yet no body is *ever* exactly like another. And it is the presumed commonality—not the differences—that allows us to hone surgical procedure in the first place, and, when the time comes, to have enough expertise to make room for deviations and change.

A second equally important concern relates to the accuracy of educators' own self-perceptions: To what extent is there a gap between what is said or believed about educational practice (the normative ideal) and the realities of the classroom? How can we ever hope to move to "best practice" if we are unwilling to acknowledge just how much our ideals of child-centeredness diverge from our practices? Or how much our ideals about child freedom and equality in education are continuously undermined by our practices? A cross-cultural mirror is invaluable in this regard, for it can show us our own assumptions more clearly and help to hone our self-perceptions. It may be that some cultures provide for an education that encourages more self-awareness and is more supportive of children's selves than others. If so, a concern for best practice means taking a hard look at how our current habits of discourse and perception may obscure a clearer vision of ourselves and of the children around us.

NOTES

1.   At the same time, the history of early childhood education is marked by worldwide cultural diffusion or borrowing of educational ideas and practices, making it difficult to conclude that just because a particular approach to early childhood education emerged in one cultural context, it cannot be applied in another.

2.   It should be noted that my discussion focuses on preschool and elementary education, not secondary education. Furthermore, while Japanese teachers remain strongly egalitarian in the orientation, refusing to offer different educational experiences to "different children" on the grounds that this is inequitable, recent trends are toward more recognition of individual differences, though it is doubtful that the full barrage of assessment and ability grouping practices present in American education will be adopted because of the strong tradition of egalitarianism in Japanese early education.

3.   These qualities are described in detail by Lois Peak (1991) and White and LeVine (1986).

4.   Tobin (1995) writes that the extreme emphasis on choice in American early education reflects the penetration of market economy into early education. Many schools even use an auction system, in which children are required to "bid" for time at the most desirable centers.

5.   One need only spend a few hours in any preschool, kindergarten, or elementary classroom in the United States to note the difference in emotional tenor from Japanese classrooms. Even where developmental appropriateness and child-centeredness are deemed central, one witnesses a constant flow of teacher control-language and activity: reprimand, reminder, suggestion, checks on the board, time-outs. In Japanese classrooms, there is little of this negative emotional subtext because it is the children themselves, not the teacher, who are primarily responsible for managing the classroom.

6.   While daycare in the United States is, in many ways, not comparable with other early childhood environments, Leavitt's (1995) observations on early emotional socialization have strong and suggestive parallels with the notion of "detached concern" that is very much a part of ideal practice in American early childhood education. In Hoffman (2001) analysis of popular discourse on parenting reveals a troubling emphasis on the manipulation and masking of emotions in parent-child relations.

7.   In the literature on Japanese early education there are many examples of children using or shouting out words that would evoke immediate disciplinary action on the part of American teachers but which, on the contrary, are ignored or even—in at least one case—interpreted as occasions to draw the child more closely into the ongoing activity, rather than reprimand or ostracize him.

8.   It may well be that one cultural reason for this difference is the way in which critical self-reflection is taught and encouraged in Japanese and Chinese classrooms. In contrast, prevailing norms in American classrooms encourage feeling good about oneself and boosting self-esteem. While all cultures have gaps between ideals and perceptions and the realities of behavior, these may be greater in the American context because of the American emphasis on having a positive view of oneself. This may lead to avoidance or denial of evidence that one's performances and behavior do not match up to one's ideals.

9.   The anthropologist Dorothy Lee (1976/1986) made this point many years ago. She claimed that while she wanted to be recognized, she never wanted to be understood. To claim to "understand" another person is a presumption upon individual dignity and integrity.

REFERENCES

Azuma, H. (1986). Why study child development in Japan? In H. Stevenson, H. Azuma, & K. Hakuta (Eds.), *Child development and education in Japan* (pp. 3–12). New York: W.H. Freeman and Company.

Baker, B. (1998). Child-centered teaching, redemption, and educational identities: A history of the present. *Educational Theory, 48*(2), 155–174.

Bergen, D. (1997). Perspectives on inclusion in early childhood education. In J.P. Isenberg & M.R. Jalongo (Eds.), *Major trends and issues in early childhood education: Challenges, controversies, and insights* (pp. 151–171). New York: Teachers College Press.

Bernhard, J.K. (1995). Child development, cultural diversity, and the professional training of early childhood educators. *Canadian Journal of Education, 20*(4), 115–436.

Bloch, M.N. (1992). Critical perspectives on the historical relationship between child development and early childhood education research. In S. Kessler & B.B. Swadener (Eds.), *Reconceptualizing the early childhood education curriculum: beginning the dialogue* (pp. 3–20). New York: Teachers College Press.

Boocock, S.S. (1992). The social construction of childhood in contemporary Japan. In G. Levine (Ed.), *Constructions of the self* (pp. 165–190). New Brunswick, NJ: Rutgers University Press.

Bredekamp, S. (1998). Defining standards for practice: the continuing debate. In C. Seefeldt & A. Galper (Eds.), *Continuing issues in early childhood education* (2nd ed., pp. 176–189).

Bredekamp, S. (Ed.). (1987). *Developmentally appropriate practice in early childhood programs serving children from birth through age eight.* Washington, DC: National Association for the Education of Young Children.

Canella, G.S. (1997). *Deconstructing early childhood education: social justice and revolution.* New York: Peter Lang.

Delpit, L. (1995). *Other people's children: Cultural conflict in the classroom.* New York: The Free Press.

Gestwicki, C. (1995). *Developmentally appropriate practice: curriculum and development in early education.* Albany, NY: Delmar Publishers.

Goldstein, L.S. (1997). Between a rock and a hard place in the primary grades: The challenge of providing developmentally appropriate early childhood education in an elementary school setting. *Early Childhood Research Quarterly, 12,* 3–27.

Hodges, C.A. (1991). Instruction and assessment of emergent literacy. In L. Weiss, P. Altbach, G.P. Kelly, & H.G. Petrie (Eds.), *Critical Perspectives on Early Childhood Education* (pp. 153–168). Albany: State University of New York.

Hoffman, D.M. (1995). Models of self and culture in teaching and learning: An anthropological perspective on Japanese and American education. *Educational Foundations, 9*(3), 19–42.

Hoffman, D.M. (1998a). A therapeutic moment? Identity, self and culture in the anthropology of education. *Anthropology and Education Quarterly, 29*(3), 324–346.

Hoffman, D.M. (1998b, December). *Empty ritual, rich ritual: Contrasting approaches to thinking, learning, and the self in Japanese and American education.* Paper presented at the meeting of the American Anthropological Association, Philadelphia, PA.

Hoffman, D.M. (2000). Pedagogies of self in American and Japanese early childhood education: A critical conceptual analysis. *Elementary School Journal.*

Hoffman, D.M. (2001). Enculturating the self: Perspectives on child-rearing in the American middle class. In B. Wong (Ed.), *Readings in family, kin, and community.* Dubuque, IA: Kendall-Hunt.

Hoffman, D.M. (in press). Individualism and individuality in American and Japanese early education: A review and critique. *American Journal of Education.*

Hori, G.V.S. (1994). Teaching and learning in the Rinzai Zen monastery. *Journal of Japanese Studies, 20*(1), 5–35.

Katz, L.G. (1996) Child development knowledge and teacher preparation: Confronting assumptions. *Early Childhood Research Quarterly 11*, 135–146.

Leavitt, R. (1995). The emotional culture of infant-toddler day care. In J.A. Hatch (Ed.), *Qualitative research in early childhood settings* (pp. 3–21). Westport, CT: Praeger.

Leavitt, R., & Power, M. (1989). Emotional socialization in the postmodern era: Children in day care. *Social Psychology Quarterly, 52*(1), 35–43.

Lee, D. (1976/1986). *Valuing the self: What we can learn from other cultures.* Prospect Heights, IL: Waveland.

Lewis, C. (1995). *Educating hearts and minds: reflections on Japanese preschool and elementary education.* Cambridge: Cambridge University Press.

Lubeck, S. (1994). The politics of developmentally appropriate practice: Exploring issues of culture, class, and curriculum. In B.L. Mallory & R.S. New (Eds.), *Diversity and developmentally appropriate practice(s): Challenges for early childhood education* (pp. 17–43). New York: Teachers College Press.

Lubeck, S. (1996). Deconstructing "child development knowledge" and "teacher preparation." *Early Childhood Research Quarterly, 11*, 147–167.

Markus, H.R., Mullally, P.R., & Kitayama, S. (1997). Selfways: Diversity in modes of cultural participation. In U. Neisser & D. Jopling (Eds.), *The conceptual self in context: Culture, experience, understanding* (pp. 13–61). New York: Cambridge University Press.

McCarty, T.L., Wallace, S., Lynch, R.H., & Benally, A. (1991). Classroom inquiry and Navaho learning styles: A call for reassessment. *Anthropology and Education Quarterly, 22*, 42–59.

New, R.S. (1993). Cultural variations on developmentally appropriate practice: challenges to theory and practice. In C. Edwards, L. Gandini, & G. Forman (Eds.), *The hundred languages of children: The Reggio Emilia approach to early childhood education* (pp. 215–232). Norwood, NJ: Ablex.

New, R.S., & Mallory, B.L. (1994). Introduction: The ethic of inclusion. In B.L. Mallory & R.S. New (Eds.), *Diversity and developmentally appropriate practice(s): Challenges for early childhood education* (pp.1–14). New York: Teachers College Press.

Peak, L. (1991). *Learning to go to school in Japan: The transition from home to school life.* Berkeley: University of California.

Raines, S.C. (1997). Developmental appropriateness: Curriculum revisited and challenged. In J.P. Isenberg & M.R. Jalongo (Eds.), *Major trends and issues in early childhood education: Challenges, controversies, and insights* (pp. 75–89). New York: Teachers College Press.

Rohlen, T., & LeTendre, G. K. (1996). (Eds.) *Teaching and Learning in Japan*. New York: Cambridge University Press.

Russell, N.U. (1994). The Kumon approach to teaching and learning. *Journal of Japanese Studies, 20*(1), 87–114.

Shimhara, N.K., & Sakai, A. (1995). *Learning to teach in two cultures: Japan and the United States*. New York: Garland Publishing.

Stevenson, H.W., & Lee, S. (1997). The East Asian version of whole-class teaching. In W.K. Cummings & P.G. Altbach (Eds.), *The challenge of Eastern Asian education: Implications for America* (pp. 33–50). Albany: State University of New York Press.

Stevenson, H.W., & Stigler, J.W. (1992). *The learning gap: How our schools are failing and what we can learn from Japanese and Chinese education*. New York: Touchstone.

Tobin, J. (1994). Japanese preschools and the pedagogy of selfhood. In N. Rosenberger (Ed.) *Japanese sense of self* (pp. 21–39). Cambridge: Cambridge University Press.

Tobin, J. (1995). Poststructural research in early childhood settings. In J.A. Hatch (Ed.), *Qualitative research in early childhood settings* (pp. 222–243). Westport, CT: Praeger.

Tobin, J., Wu, D., & Davidson, D. (1989). *Preschool in three cultures*. New Haven, CT: Yale University Press.

White, M. (1987). *The Japanese educational challenge: A commitment to children*. New York: The Free Press.

White, M., & Levine, R.A. (1986). What is an *ii ko* (good child)? In H. Stevenson, H. Azuma, & K. Hakuta (Eds.), *Child development and education in Japan* (pp. 55–62). New York: W.H. Freeman and Company.

Williams, L.R. (1994). Developmentally appropriate practice and cultural values: a case in point. In B.L. Mallory & R.S. New (Eds.), *Diversity and developmentally appropriate practice(s): Challenges for early childhood education* (pp. 155–165). New York: Teachers College Press.

Wolcott, H. (1987). The teacher as an enemy. In G.D. Spindler (Ed.), *Education and cultural process* (2nd ed., pp. 136–150). Prospect Heights, IL: Waveland.

Yamamura, Y. (1986). The child in Japanese society. In H. Stevenson, H. Azuma, & K. Hakuta (Eds.), *Child development and education in Japan* (pp.28–38). New York: W.H. Freeman.

Zemelman, S. Daniels, H., & Hyde, A. (1993). *Best practice: New standards for teaching and learning in America's schools*. Portsmouth, NH: Heinemann.

CHAPTER 9

AFRICAN AMERICAN YOUNG ADULT SCIENCE FICTION AND FANTASY LITERATURE

Realism for the 21st Century

Randy F. Rush

Abstract: Science fiction and fantasy literature written by and for African Americans lacks attention in the African American literature canon. This same inattention is reflected in young adult literature written for the African American young adult. Although the number of works reflective of these genres are few, in comparison to other genres, there are sufficient quantities to introduce to young adults.

The twenty-first century has been a topic of much speculation in this literature-from racial harmony and disharmony, social and economic catastrophe, and space exploration. Thus, in today's classrooms science fiction and fantasy seem a natural choice for study. These genres provide a means for developing and enhancing critical literacy skills as well as the pure enjoyment of reading.

INTRODUCTION

Revising our concepts of literacy to include multicultural literature has been advocated for many decades. Educators who have adopted a philosophy of inclusion and transforming the school curriculum have not rationalized this position based entirely on a significant diverse student body. Equally incorporated into this philosophy is the introduction of well-written literature, regardless of cultural portrayals, to children and young adults. Providing a curriculum in which multicultural literature is an integral component becomes problematic when we do not reaffirm our philosophies of equally educating all children.

Stanford and Amin (1978) recorded teachers' comments in regards to teaching Black literature that are familiar to many teacher educators and researchers today when discussing multicultural literature, "Black literature? Oh, that was a fad of the sixties. We're into the basics now." Or "We've already done black literature" (p. 4). These barriers still exist in spite of decades of best practice research and teaching.

Thus, I believe that teachers must become familiar with Black literature and its various genres. Toward this goal, I provide insight into a specific genre of Black literature that may be unfamiliar to readers.

Writers of African origins[1] have spent many years (some decades) producing significant works of science fiction and fantasy. These works and their authors are not as well known as contemporary and historical fiction, poetry, and nonfiction writers. Relatively unknown by mainstream readers, these books rarely appear on classroom reading lists. Due to publications such as *The Norton Anthology of African American Literature*, magazines like *Black Issues Book Review*, and *Black Entertainment Television*, audiences beyond the science fiction and fantasy community are discovering these works.

The appeal and, perhaps, lack of appeal of the science fiction and fantasy genres is their speculation or extrapolation to create an image of possible futures and worlds. Much speculation upon the future of American society in the twenty-first century has taken place and now that we are on the brink of experiencing this future, these speculations begin to have a degree of realism.

At a minimum, the relevance for using this literature would be to examine this degree of realism. Furthermore, examining issues within the literature to develop students' critical literacy and cultural literacy skills is vital to the reconceptualization of literacy in this period of increasing social diversity.

Thus, I offer some insights into science fiction and fantasy literature written by Black American and Canadian authors that young adults may find worthy of reading.

THE APPEAL OF THE GENRES

As a school-aged child, I found great pleasure in reading. I read the adventures of Dick, Jane, and their dog Spot more as an affirmation of my reading ability than any consequence of constant pleasure. With no one to recommend books that might have been of interest to me, my library visits consisted of looking at book covers for faces that looked like mine or titles that had some meaning to me (Black Poetry, Black History, etc.).

It was not until graduate study that I understood the theoretical perspectives of my actions as a reader. Sims (1984), in addressing the relevance of multicultural literature, speaks of children's lives being mirrored-their lives, belief systems and values validated in the literature they encounter. This was a stark contrast to those of us who were school children reading and believing Blacks were not in books as depicted in Nancy Larrick's (1965) study.

The first books of fantasy that I read were Dennis McKiernan's Iron Tower Trilogy (*The Dark Tide, Shadows of Doom*, and *The Darkest Day*) and The Silver Call Duology (*The Trek to Kraggen-Kor* and *The Brega Path*). After reading the first book I was hooked on the author and the genre. I searched for more and found David Eddings, Anne McCaffrey, Meredith Ann Pierce, Andre Norton, and Robin McKinley. The appeal of these books for me was the heroism exhibited by the characters and a plot of good overcoming evil.

The negative aspect to my reading experience was that the heroes and heroines were of European descent and the stories were based upon European mythology. An African presence was nonexistent in the worlds created. Yet, heroism and plots of battles between good and evil are appealing to readers regardless of culture, race, ethnicity, or gender. If fantasy does indeed appeal to our need for heroes, for good, and for success against evil (Donelson & Nilsen, 1997), then where there exists too few books that reflect one's culture or gender, one has to ask as Langston Hughes did in 1941:

> But where, in all these books, is that compelling flame of spirit and passion that makes a man say, 'I, too, am a hero, because my race has produced heroes like that!'?…
>
> We have a need for heroes. We have a need for books and plays that will encourage and inspire our youth, set for them examples and patterns of conduct, move and stir them to be forthright, strong, clear-thinking, and unafraid. ("The Crisis," p. 184)

Within the genre of science fiction and fantasy, I find myself still searching the shelves as an adult for works that are reflective of the Black experience. Recently, the search has become somewhat easier. The attention that Black authors of science fiction and fantasy seem to be receiving in print and broadcast media is a welcomed trend that I hope will impact literature recommended for young adults.

WHAT HAS BEEN

Sam Moskowitz, although often criticized as not being an academic or his lack of "being academic" when publishing his findings, is considered to be one of science fiction's leading historians (Clute & Nicholls, 1995). In 1967, he provided a survey of science fiction works that included Blacks. Published as "Negroes in Science Fiction" and later in 1976 as "Civil Rights: Rockets to Green Pastures," approximately 33 works from 1864 to 1970 were recorded.

Moskowitz believed that the works of science fiction from 1879 through 1940 presented, "millions upon millions of white youngsters who read these boys' books were given a very friendly and positive view of the Negro" (1976, p. 57). He further stated that, "It was indeed fortunate that early writers of teen-age science fiction exercised personal responsibility or they could have infected white youths with an even greater virus of color hate" (1976, pp. 68–69). However, it must be noted that Moskowitz did state that during the 1920s science fiction materials approached extremes of preaching genocide.

Clute and Nicholls's (1995) language is not as strong, but they also support Moskowitz's insights on racial portrayals. They state that "...serious speculations being virtually drowned out by anxious speculations and by the kind of unthinking racism and anti-Semitism which were long rife in popular fiction of all kinds" (p. 947).

Although limited, additional scholarship provides insights into the portrayal of Blacks in science fiction. Govan (1984) concluded in a brief survey of the genre that:

> There are a few additional novels and a handful of short stories in which black characters are somehow a part of the plot, but in most of these works, the roles for blacks are minor and/or stereotypic, the underlying assumptions being essentially, though perhaps unconsciously, racist. (p. 44)

In a survey of children's literature, Bishop (1990) acknowledges the underrepresentation of fantasy as a genre in African American literature and in an earlier investigation, I examined African American fantasy literature and found similar results for young adults (Rush, 1996).

HOPE FOR THE FUTURE: BLACK AUTHORS AND CRITICS

As science fiction evolved as an identifiable genre in the 1920s and 1930s, Blacks were primarily nonexistent, or stereotypically portrayed, and race relations were discussed on abstract levels using aliens. An era of thoughtful inclusion and sensitive portrayal began in the 1950s due to the efforts of Black mainstream writers (Clute & Nicholls, 1995).

Today, Blacks, writing exclusively within the genre, provide readers with possible realms in which they are undeniably present and in roles and contexts that reflect the Black experience. Whereas there were only a few recognizable Black authors, more are venturing into the genre, both mainstream writers and those who choose to be identified as writers of science fiction and fantasy.

Charles Saunders, recognized in the 1980s as the only Black fantasist writing black experience heroic fantasy (Bell, 1984; Elliot, 1984; Robinson, 1981), has also served as a critic of the field. Noting the lack of significant literary works of speculative fiction by and about Blacks, he observed that a significant Black readership was not encouraged. Saunders recommended the works being produced by such Black writers as Samuel Delany, Octavia Butler, and Stephen Barnes, and White writers like John Brunner, Robert Silverberg, and Spider Robinson as a means of encouraging a Black audience.

Nalo Hopkinson, a fellow Canadian of Caribbean origin, and recent author of *Brown Girl in the Ring* (1998), similarly speaks of science fiction in North America as traditionally a colonizing literature that doesn't speak to Blacks. She adds that, "It's still very much a literature that does not really include us, except as window dressing. The overall impression you get from book covers is that the humans are the white people, and the aliens are people of color" (p. 77).

UNIQUE WRITING STYLES

Certain characteristics seem to become evident in the works of Black authors publishing in the science fiction genre. Govan (1984) commenting on Samuel Delany's novels, states that memorable Black characters and an affirmation of the diversity and vitality of Black life creates a Black consciousness in his work.

Octavia Butler, the most recognizable Black female consistently writing in the science fiction genre, is praised for her writing style and the themes portrayed in her writing. The genre's highest awards have been bestowed upon Butler for her realistic portrayals of racial and sexual themes in future societies (Clute & Nicholls, 1993; Metzger, 1989). However, it is her portrayal of strong Black women that tends to stand out in critical commentaries.

Butler's novels are about Black women who must face and survive tremendous social constraints (Salvaggio, 1984). Foster's (1982) interview with Butler tells us that Butler writes from her own experience and sensitivities rather than a particular need to champion Black women. This same experiential influence is corroborated by Nalo Hopkinson when she speaks of making use of conventions and languages of science fiction but framing it within a Caribbean context, "it's my default position, like choosing to write black characters" (p. 77).

THE AUTHORS AND THEIR WORKS

In a 1995 interview with *LOCUS*, a science fiction newspaper, Samuel (Chip) Delany stated, "Now whenever anyone asks me how many black science fiction or fantasy writers there are, instead of saying 'four or five,' I can say 'five or six' (p. 83). This response was in reference to the most recent entrant to the field, Nalo Hopkinson. The two individuals mentioned here are representatives of the precursors (Delany) and recent initiates (Hopkinson) of Black writers in the science fiction genre. Identification of the other "four or five" authors are addressed in an autobiographical piece by Octavia Butler that is part of a collection of short stories entitled *Bloodchild* (1996).

Butler discusses in this essay (previously published in 1989) her position as the only Black woman writing science fiction and fantasy and identifies the other Blacks working successfully in the field as Steven Barnes, Charles Saunders, and Samuel Delany.

In addition to the preceding authors, the works of Jewelle Gomez, Tananarive Due, LeVar Burton, Walter Mosley, Virginia Hamilton, and Walter Dean Myers are presented in the following discussion of science fiction and fantasy literature written by and about Blacks. To facilitate this discussion, I focus first upon the authors who are forerunners in the genres and secondly, the authors who are recent writers within the genres.

THE GURUS OF BLACK SCIENCE FICTION AND FANTASY

Charles Saunders, Samuel Delaney, Octavia Butler, and Steven Barnes are acknowledged leaders of and intellectual guides to writers and readers of Black Science Fiction and Fantasy. The works of Octavia Butler and Samuel Delaney are more recognizable, due to their prolific and award-winning publications, but all have written successfully within the field and blazed trails for other writers of African origins entering the field.

Charles Saunders

Charles Saunders wrote Black experience heroic fantasy. An African setting of the past and an African male hero is featured in Charles Saunders *Imaro* trilogy. The books in the trilogy are *Imaro* (1981), *The Quest for Cush* (1984) and *The Trail of Bohu* (1985). These epic novels focus on the growth of five-year-old Imaro, an African tribal youth, into manhood in this African setting and his fight against evil forces that attempt to use him or kill him to thwart his destiny as a hero. An additional plot focuses on Imaro as a member of a tribe that rejects him due to his mixed tribal heritage. His further heroic adventures as an adult are presented in the second and third books.

Unique for the characteristics mentioned above, *Imaro* also counters the Tarzan character of a stereotypical Africa and may be compared to the popular Conan character. Saunders presents authentic insight into Black African mythology and an action-packed adventure that entertains and instructs as good heroic fantasy does.

These books are worthy of introducing young adults to for their rite of passage emphasis and the protagonist's quest for identity. Saunders's works are out of print, but libraries may still carry them. Although born in America, Saunders is a Canadian citizen.

Samuel Delany

Without a doubt Samuel Delany has become one of *the* preeminent science fiction and fantasy authors since his entry in the field in 1962. One desiring to become familiar with science fiction and the role Blacks have had in it must read his work. Delany's work is known for his Black and mixed-race characters, as well as for its exploration of sexuality. The quest motif and use of myth and the inclusion of physically and psychologically damaged characters are often found in his work (Clute & Nicholls, 1995). Also, his insights into society, especially futuristic societies, should be points of departures for discussion.

Ironically, I have not found any references to Delany's fictional works in sources for young adult literature. This may be due to the portrayal of sex in his stories. One reference is made to his nonfiction: *The Jewel-Hinged Jaw: Notes on the Language of Science Fiction* (1977). This is a collection of essays that serve as a critique of the genre. This reference was found in Helen William's *Books by African-American Authors and Illustrators* (1991).

Delany's works are controversial. However, as Masha Rudman reminds us from the introduction to her book *Children's Literature: An Issues Approach* (1995):

> Family relations, divorce, adoption, sibling rivalry, abuse, death, sexuality, old age, war and peace, special needs, gender roles, and different heritages are all potentially volatile and wrenching matters. Books afford the opportunity to explore and confront these issues with children by creating a protected vicarious situation. (p. 2)

Of one of his most recent works, Delany states, "The short novel *Atlantis: Model 1924*, was an attempt to take those old stories you've heard in your family and weave them into something" (*Locus* interview, 1995, p. 5). This novel and several short stories are found in the book *Atlantis: Three Tales*.

Delany is a very prolific writer and many of his works feature young adults. His novels are complex and challenging-well suited for the mature reader. Thus, secondary teachers interested in the genre and multiculturalism may find this author's works of benefit for the young adult reader.

SCIENCE FICTION NOVELS

The Jewels of Aptor (1962) was Delany's first novel. A quest novel featuring a group of friends who journey to Aptor to rescue the kidnapped High Priestess of the Goddess of Argo and restore three jewels of immense power to the control of Argo Incarnate, the reigning High Priestess. Iimmi, a Black university student, who has taken a position as a sailor for the summer is one of the main characters.

The Ballad of Beta-2 (1965) is the story of Joneny Horatio T'wabaga, a university student anthropologist who rediscovers the meaning of a ballad about an old Earth culture that went voyaging in a generations starship, the Beta-2.

Babel-17 (1966) features Rydra Wong, an Asian poet and linguist, and Dr. Markus T'mwarba, an African and also Rydra's psychotherapist. The plot of this story is the cracking of an alien code that is being broadcasted over the radio and suspected to be associated with an invasion. It is a story focused upon language and its ability to shape experiences and perceptions. Rydra breaks the code with the assistance of T'mwarba.

The Einstein Intersection (1967) presents the reader to Lo Lobey, a mythical "Pan" figure, who is described as black. His partner, Friza, is described as a black woman. All of the characters in this story are alien and the plot focus upon these aliens taking on the corporeal form of humans and trying to make sense of this world's cultures and traditions.

In *Nova* (1968) the protagonist is Captain Lorq Von Ray, son of a Senegalese woman and a Norwegian man. This is the story of a galactic quest to obtain a rare element called "Illyrion" which enhances the economic development of the galaxy. Govan also states that among the many themes of power, there is a racial motif of mythic proportions that involves a sexual power struggle—a black man in love with a white woman.

Triton (1976) features Miriamne (a black woman) and Sam (a black man, formally a white woman). A sexual utopia exists in this novel that honors every form of sexual behavior. Sex change operations including refixations to alter sexual preferences are also emphasized. Freedom of choice is a theme that is explored in the plot.

FANTASY NOVELS

Delany has published a series of four books entitled: *Tales of Neveryon* (1979), *Neveryona* (1983), *Flight from Neveryon* (1985), and *The Bridge of Lost Desire* (1987) that are considered sword and sorcery (heroic fantasy) literature. These are tales of Gorgik, a slave who rises to political power and abolishes slavery. Gorgik is described as a Black man and critics have placed the setting as either Asia or Africa in some magical distant past, just as civilization is being created. This is a world of barbarians, Amazons, primitive precocity, prehistoric splendor, and dragons. There is a focus on relationships of power, racial, sexual, and economic.[2]

Octavia Butler

Octavia Butler has published 11 novels. Her latest is *Parable of the Talents* (1998) the sequel to *Parable of the Sower* (1993).

Futuristic Societies

Parable of the Talents is the story of Lauren Olamina and her search for a peaceful community in a futuristic Californian society threatened by gangs and drugs continues. In this sequel, Lauren's daughter Larkin narrates the story.

Lauren has established her community (Acorn) in Northern California. A paramilitary group known as "Christian America" takes Larkin (as an infant) from her mother through a raid on the community. Raised by these individuals, Larkin becomes critical of her mother's Earthseed philosophy that served as the foundation of the Acorn community. In an interview Butler states of Larkin:

> One of the things that she has discovered is that her mother really could have prevented all that happened to them [that pulled them apart]. Not that she could have prevented what happens to Acorn. But Olamina had a way out and it was a comfortable way out. And she didn't take it. (McHenry & Fleming, 1999, p. 18)

Community building, education, and religion in the years 2010–2032 are issues addressed in these novels. Lauren and Larkin are both young adults when introduced in the novels and wrestles with a future of which Butler states:

> In *Parable of the Sower*, when my character is at home in the community she grows up in, things just keep getting worse and worse, until it final goes to hell. In *Parable of the Talents*, Olamina finds a way to rebuild, to make a present and future for herself that doesn't turn out quite the way she expects. Things are getting better for a while, but they are getting better in a way

that's not really helpful to her long-term dream of destiny and all that. (McHenry & Fleming, 1999, p. 16)

Patternmaster and *Mind of Mind* are futuristic books that feature a 4000-year-old immortal that is able to move at will from body to body across time periods. Also central to the story are strong Black female characters who are descendants of the immortal Doro. *Wild Seed* (1980) and *Clay's Ark* (1984) are subsequent books in the series.

Dawn (1987), *Adulthood Rites* (1988), and *Imago* (1989) comprise the Xenogenesis trilogy. The setting of these novels is a post-apocalyptic Earth, which is slowly being restored by extraterrestrials called Oankali. One aspect of this rebirth is the creation of a new human species through inter-breeding of modified genetic material of the humans that survived the war and the aliens.

Historical Societies

Mentioned earlier in this discussion, Willis (1998) identified Butler's work as representative of the genre for young adults written during the period between 1960–1980. In addition to *Patternmaster* (1976) and *Mind of my Mind* (1977) discussed above, *Kindred* (1979) is also highlighted. Willis adds that, "Octavia Butler's creative and unique blend of historical fiction and science fiction offered another means of telling our stories … [these works] are exemplary of her (Butler) creative melding as she addresses historical struggles of race, gender and power" (p. 68).

Kindred is a fantasy that uses time travel to transport Dana, a 26-year-old Black female, from 1976 to America's slave period of 1824. The reader gains insights into the historical realities of the time period and the ethical dilemma slaves faced due to their perception as "nonpersons" by Whites.

SHORT STORIES AND NONFICTION

Bloodchild (1996) is a collection of five previously published short stories describing relationships between humans and aliens. It also contains two essays—one is autobiographical and the other comments on writing science fiction.

Steven Barnes

Steven Barnes' solo works interweave urban environments and African material. They incorporate science in apocalyptic and contemporary societies. His stories are adventurous which many young adults should find appealing.

Gorgon Child (1989) and *Firedance* (1993) continue the story of Aubry Knight, an African American urban hero trained as a street fighter in a twenty-second century post-Great Quake California society that was begun in *Streetlethal* (1983). His most recent works are *Blood Brothers* (1996) and *Iron Shadows* (1998).

Blood Brothers features Derek Waites, an African American male and former outlaw computer hacker trying to support his son and daughter. His life becomes intertwined with Austin Tucker, a White male falsely convicted of killing his family. He is affiliated with white supremacists in prison and now must join Waters in his attempt to save his children and perhaps find out who killed his own family.

The link between the two men is further exacerbated due to their bloodline going back to America's slavery period. It is also a story of human sacrifice and immortality. Set in 1992 Los Angeles, the story's focuses on an evil curse from 200 years in the past invading present day.

A journal format is integrated within the novel to provide historical perspective on the family's genealogy and the origin of the family's curse. The diary is that of Dahlia Childe describing her life as a slave on a plantation called Bloodroot outside of Charleston, South Carolina.

A story of science fantasy, it is foremost a story of family, Black and White linked by blood. Barnes does an excellent job weaving these elements into a believable story.

Iron Shadows is the story of two African-Asian young adults (male and female twins) who have unique healing powers that evolved as a result of their mother's exposure to the atomic bombing of Nagasaki, Japan and an African male who could be deemed an immortal. The twins have developed a cult following that seems to have positive benefits for the members, yet there is something sinister guiding the cult. Jax and Cat are detectives that become entwined in discovering who the twins are and what is behind their powers. The setting is 1995 Los Angeles, California.

Barnes works include a multiethnic cast of characters. The books are distinctively African American through the themes explored within the plots, yet authentic cultural insights are provided into other ethnicities relevant to the story.

THE INITIATES

The writers included in this section have achieved notoriety for their work, and all published within the last decade. I identify them as initiates only because of their recent entries in the genres of science fiction and fantasy.

Jewelle Gomez

Jewelle Gomez describes her book, *The Gilda Stories*, (1991) as:

...Stories ... about Gilda, who escapes from slavery in 1850 and the tales trace her life through the next several centuries [2050]. Gilda, you see, becomes a vampire. My idea was/is to create a super heroic black woman who interprets our lives through a phenomenal perspective. While the premise falls into the fantasy fiction genre, the stories themselves, like all good fantasy or science fiction are really about the human condition: loneliness, love, families, and heroism. (Gomez, 1986, p. 8)

The reader follows "The Girl" through two centuries after she is willingly made into a vampire by her guardian, Gilda, and given her name. The boon and bane of immortality is always present, especially in the friend-ships she develops and eventually has to end whether through constant moves or deaths of these friends. Gilda spends decades of her lifetime as a beautician, writer, and jazz singer. Through these careers, Gomez provides distinct insights into the African-American culture.

Like Octavia Butler, Gomez presents the reader with a strong female protagonist. From the opening of the novel in which the protagonist sur-vives a rape attempt by a White man as a young girl, to her escape from vampire killers at the story's completion, Gilda experiences the horrors of both past and future, yet triumphs. Although Gomez has not been as pro-lific as the previous authors have, her writing should be a study for critics and developing writers.

Tananarive Due

Tananarive Due's second novel *My Soul to Keep* (1997) is a work of fan-tasy and is highlighted in LOCUS's 1997 recommended reading list. Reviewers and critics believe that Due is becoming firmly established in the field of fantasy (Bryant, 1998; Wolfe, 1998).

My Soul to Keep is the story of Jessica and her encounter with Dawitt, an immortal living in present-day America. Due utilizes flashbacks in time, Jazz History, an ancient blood ritual, morality and ethical issues of eternal life, a love story, and a sect of immortals, to create a story of suspense and the supernatural. Although the characters are late 20s and early 30s, the flashbacks take readers back to the character's experiences as younger adults. Her first novel was *The Between* (1995).

Nalo Hopkinson

Nalo Hopkinson's first novel *Brown Girl in the Ring* (1998) won the Warner Aspect New Writer award. Hopkinson, a Canadian citizen born in Jamaica, infuses her Caribbean culture and a futuristic Canadian (Toronto) setting to produce a work of science fiction that brings a new perspective to the genre. It is a story of Ti-Jeanne (a young adult Caribbean female) and her relationships with her grandmother (a herbalist healer, who is also a voodoo worshiper) and her child's father and his life of drugs. It is a story of strong Caribbean women looking out for their children in a society of hardships, yet one of hope. In this futuristic society, organ cultivation and transplants are a reality and the plot of the story surrounds this concept.

LeVar Burton

Another first novelist that young adults may be familiar with is LeVar Burton of *Star Trek* fame. *Aftermath* (1997) is a book that answers the question "What If?" Burton states that his inspiration came from his familiarity with other science fiction writers, namely Heinlein, Asimov, and Clarke. The challenge from their work led to the thought, "What if—like the heroes in their books—I could actually create for myself a future of my own choosing, on my own terms, in *my* [author's emphasis] own image (p. vii)?"

Pursuing this objective, Burton created a story that asks: What if an African American is elected President and then is assassinated by a White extremist? What if a race war develops as a result? What if a "Neuro-Enhancer" that heals the body of disease by maximizing brain functions is created? *Aftermath* is also a story of a nation healing itself.

Walter Mosley

The final first novelist contributing to the genre is Walter Mosley. Mosley is primarily a mystery writer whose stories document the adventures of private detective Easy Rawlins. His new book *Blue Light* (1998) takes readers back to the 1960s when a cosmic shower of blue light falls to earth in the San Francisco Bay area. Individuals who are fully exposed to the blue light find that they have evolved into another stage of humanity resulting in their full potential being realized. The "Blues" experiences increased powers of understanding, communication, and strength. The story is narrated by Chance, a graduate student dropout of biracial heritage. He chronicles the story of the "Blues" in a bible-like format.

Chance and other "Blues" must find one of their own (Gray Man) who was struck by the blue light at his moment of death and has become the embodiment of Death. His objective is to destroy the "Blues." Addy and children Reggie, Alacrity, and Wanita join Chance in this story of survival. As the story develops, so do the children, all except Wanita who does not physically age. This is her gift from the blue light, in addition to her power as a seeress. A very multiethnic cast navigates a world that is either a beginning or end for humans.

RENOWN BLACK YOUNG ADULT AUTHORS

Before concluding this chapter, the works of Walter Dean Myers and Virginia Hamilton are presented due to their readily identifiable and award winning work in young adult literature and ventures into science fiction and fantasy. Unlike the previous authors discussed above, students are more familiar with Hamilton and Myers' works, although they may not be familiar with their works of fantasy and science fiction.

Virginia Hamilton

Virginia Hamilton creates a time travel fantasy into the future that features three African American children (twin brothers and a sister) who possess supersensory powers in *Justice and Her Brothers* (1978). Hamilton continues the adventures of Justice and her brothers in *Dustland* (1980) and *The Gathering* (1981).

In *Dustland* a futuristic Earth is a land of dust and mutant forms of animal and human life. *The Gathering* finds the trio in a battle to save Dustland from a force that threatens to destroy its people.

Two additional works of fantasy were published in the 1980s: *Sweet Whispers Brother Rush* (1982) is a ghost fantasy that features an African American female young adult and the ghost of her uncle who assists her in working out the frustrations she feels from caring for her retarded brother during her mother's long absences.

African American myth and folklore is used to create the story of *The Magical Adventures of Pretty Pearl* (1983). Pearl is an African god whose persona is that of a child. She decides to become a participant in the lives of humans upon witnessing the capture of Africans for importation as slaves. Pearl follows them to America where she renders assistance to them as a young girl/old woman.

Walter Dean Myers

Walter Dean Myers presents an African heroic fantasy in *The Legend of Tarik* (1981). A medieval story set in North Africa that features a young adult African male who desires to avenge his family's murders.

After his village is attacked, Tarik is rescued and healed of wounds by two individuals who would become his mentors as he prepares for his encounter with the killer of his family. Patience, controlling one's anger, and the unexpected outcomes of achieving a desired goal are themes explored in this novel.

Shadow of the Red Moon (1995) is the story of Jon, a 15-year-old Okalian. He is sent on a journey by his parents to search for their ancient homeland. A young girl, her brother, and a black unicorn join him on this journey. Their present home facing annihilation, these searchers attempt to restore their world and race to its former greatness.

SUMMARY

Science fiction and fantasy are genres that have rarely portrayed Blacks as significant participants in their realms of possibilities. However, with the works of the authors discussed above, a Black presence is evolving.

Why is this Important?

These books, with a cast of characters, both young adult and adult; roaming around past, present, and future worlds provide unique insights into the Black experience—whether it has an American, Caribbean, or African flavor. Thus do we dare ask, "What if they were placed in the hands of our students?"

First, science fiction and fantasy abound with heroes and heroines. Yet, until recently these individuals were not Black. Thus, many Black readers were not drawn to the genre. The works produced by the authors discussed in this chapter address this missing dimension and answers Langston Hughes's call for literature that portray the heroes of Black culture. An obvious benefit of this phenomenon is the room for growth for potential writers in these genres.

Second, in creating a culturally appropriate pedagogy, educators cannot overlook or pay brief attention to cultural literature and the various genres of this literature. If cursory attention is given to the more popular genres of realistic fiction, historical fiction, poetry and folktales, then science fiction and fantasy may not be addressed. As presented, a significant quantity of science fiction and fantasy works exists to add to the curriculum. Teachers only need to become familiar with these genres and their representative works.

Science fiction and fantasy literature allows readers to speculate on possible futures based on the known and in doing so requires readers to engage in imaginative and creative thought, make hypotheses, examine moral and ethical issues, and confront realistic problems (Rothlein & Meinbach, 1996).

Additionally, the benefits of reading Black literature to all students still ring true: (1) Developing empathy, (2) understanding Black culture, (3) understanding the effects of racism, and (4) understanding human reactions to racism (Stanford & Amin, 1978).

LeVar Burton's *Aftermath* provides insights into a possible future that experienced a race war. Students may examine the moral and ethical issues of racial discrimination and the events that would precipitate a national conflict. Also, discussions on living peacefully after such a conflict are feasible.

Octavia Butler's *Kindred* places a contemporary Black female back into the past of her ancestors where she becomes a slave. When she returns to the present, she faces the dilemma of her present life as the wife of a white man. Teachers may ask students to respond to Dana's dilemma and ask them to detail their possible experiences if they found themselves in an ancestor's past life.

Jewelle Gomez provides insights into the past, present and possible future of a Black female through *Gilda's* biography. Teachers may ask students to speculate on the concept of immortatlity as well as how Gilda's immortality assisted her in surviving oppressive acts as compared to mortals.

Each of the works discussed in the chapter requires students to engage in imaginative and creative thought and speculate on possible futures. However, contemporary issues faced by students are not omitted. Love, sex, death, survival, drugs, gangs, and other issues are portrayed in the novels. Octavia Butler's *Parable of the Sower* incorporates most of these issues.

Lauren lives in an walled community to protect the residents from gangs. Lauren loses her parents in an ensuing conflict with this gang. She is afraid to love, but finds herself in love with a much older man. In all of these episodes is an encompassing story of survival in a very near future.

Additionally, for Black readers, their history and cultural traditions are affirmed, an opportunity for exploration of survival tactics Blacks used to combat oppression (strong men and women, rather than compliant beings) and an introduction to new ideas and experiences from their culture that may be foreign to them are all part of the stories told in the worlds created by these authors.

Finally, Hale (1994) states that the first step in creating a culturally appropriate literature is the recognition that there is a distinctive African American culture (p. 201). Thus, teachers must reaffirm the teaching of Black literature and recognize that science fiction and fantasy for young adults are a part of that literature.

NOTES

1.   *African-Origin* is a term I use instead of *African American* to make reference to the authors of the literature presented in this chapter. The term refers to a shared ethnic and cultural origin of the authors and the characters they create. Two of the authors are Canadian citizens. Saunders was born in the United States and Hopkinson in Jamaica. Their books were published in the United States and within the publishing parameters; the novels are of the African American literature genre. Thus, for reference purposes, both the authors and the protagonists of their novels are of African origin.

2.   The following sources were very helpful in reviewing the works of Samuel Delany and Octavia Butler:

Beal, F.M. (1986, March/April). Black women and the science fiction genre. [Interview with Octavia Butler]. *The Black Scholar, 17*(2), 14–18.

Govan, S.Y. (1984). The insistent presence of black folk in the novels of Samuel R. Delany. *Black American Literature Forum, 18*(2), 43–48.

Salvaggio, R. (1984, Fall). Octavia Butler and the black science-fiction heroine. *Black American Literature Forum, 18*(2), 78–8.

REFERENCES

Bell, J. (1984). A Charles R. Saunders interview. *Black American Literature Forum, 18* (2), 90–92.

Bishop, R.S. (1990). Walk tall in the world: African American literature for today's children. *Journal of Negro Education, 59*(4), 556–565.

Bryant, E. (1998, February). 1997: The year in review. *LOCUS, 40*(2), 36–38.

Burton, L. (1997). *Aftermath.* New York: Aspect.

Butler, O. (1996). *Bloodchild and other stories.* New York: Seven Stories Press.

Clute, J., & Nicholls, P. (Eds.). (1993). *The encyclopedia of science fiction.* New York: St. Martin's Press.

Clute, J., & Nicholls, P. (Eds.). (1995). *The encyclopedia of science fiction.* New York: St. Martin's Griffin.

Donelson, K.L., & Nilsen, A.P. (1997). *Literature for young adults.* New York: Longman.

Elliot, J.M. (1984). Charles R. Saunders: Kushite in the woodpile. *Fantasy Review,* 7–8.

Gomez, J. (1986). Black women heroes: Here's reality, where's the fiction? *The Black Scholar, 17*(2), 8–13.

Gomez, J. (1991). *The Gilda stories.* Ithaca, NY: Firebrand.

Govan, S.Y. (1984, Summer). The insistent presence of black folk in the novels of Samuel R. Delaney. *Black American Literature Forum, 18*(2), 43–48.

Hale, J.E. (1994). *Unbank the fire: Visions for the education of African American children.* Baltimore, MD: John Hopkins University Press.

Hughes, L. (1941, June). A need for heroes. *The Crisis, 48*(6), 184–185, 206.

McHenry, S., & Fleming, M.M. (1999, January-February). Octavia's mind-trip into the near future. *Black Issues Book Review, 1*(1), 14–18.

Larrick, N. (1965). The all-white world of children's books. *Saturday Review, 48,* 63–65, 84–85.

Metzger, L. (1989). *Black writers.* Detroit, MI: Gale Research Company.

Moskowitz, S. (1967). The negro in science fiction. *Worlds of Tomorrow, 4*(4), 40–54.

Moskowitz, S. (1976). *Strange horizons: The spectrum of science fiction.* New York: Charles Scribner's Sons.

Nalo Hopkinson: Many perspectives. (1999, January). *Locus, 42*(1), 8–9, 76–77.

Robinson, S. (1981). The reference library. *Analog Science Fiction/Science Fact,* 111–119.

Rothlein, L., & Meinbach, A.M. (1996). *Legacies: Using children's literature in the classroom.* New York: HarperCollins.

Rudman, M.K. (1995). *Children's literature: An issues approach.* White Plains, NY: Longman.

Rush, R.F. (1996). *A survey of African American fantasy literature with case study analysis of the responses of four African American adolescents to young adult heroic fantasy literature that features protagonists of African origin.* (Doctoral Dissertation, The Ohio State University, 1996). *Dissertation Abstracts International, 57,* 10A, 4297.

Samuel R. Delany: Teaching and writing. (1995, November). *Locus, 35*(5), 4–5, 82, 84.

Sims, R. (1984, Spring). A question of perspective. *The Advocate, 3,* 145–156.

Stanford, B.D., & Amin, K. (1978). *Black literature for high school students.* Urbana, IL: National Council of Teachers of English.

Williams, H.E. (1991). *Books by African-American authors and illustrators for children and young adults.* Chicago: American Library Association.

Willis, A.I. (1998). Celebrating African American literary achievements. In A.I. Willis (Ed.), *Teaching and using multicultural literature in grades 9–12: Moving beyond the canon* (pp. 37–81). Norwood, MA: Christopher-Gordon Publishers.

Wolfe, G.K. (1998, February). 1997: The year in review. *LOCUS, 40*(2), 29, 32–33.

Reading List

Barnes, S. (1983). *Streetlethal.* New York: Ace Books.

Barnes, S. (1989). *Gorgon child.* New York: Tor Books.

Barnes, S. (1993). *Firedance.* New York: Tor Books.

Barnes, S. (1996). *Blood brothers.* New York: Tom Doherty Associates.

Barnes, S. (1998). *Iron shadows.* New York: Tom Doherty Associates.

Burton, L. (1997). *Aftermath.* New York: Aspect.

Butler, O. (1979). *Kindred.* New York: Doubleday.

Butler, O. (1976). *Patternmaster.* New York: Doubleday.

Butler, O. (1977). *Mind of my mind.* New York: Doubleday.

Butler, O. (1978). *Survivor.* New York: Doubleday.

Butler, O. (1980). *Wild seed.* New York: Doubleday.

Butler, O. (1987). *Clay's ark.* New York: St. Martin's.

Butler, O. (1993). *Parable of the sower.* New York: Four Walls Eight Windows.

Butler, O. (1996). *Bloodchild and other stories.* New York: Seven Stories Press.

Butler, O. (1998). *Parable of the talents.* New York: Seven Stories Press.

Delany, S.R. (1962). *The jewels of aptor.* New York: Ace Books.

Delany, S.R. (1965). *The ballad of beta-2.* New York: Ace Books.

Delany, S.R. (1966). *Babel-17.* New York: Ace Books.

Delany, S.R. (1967). *The Einstein intersection.* New York: Ace Books.

Delany, S.R. (1968). *Nova.* New York: Doubleday.

Delany, S.R. (1976). *Triton.* New York: Bantam.

Delany, S.R. (1977). *Jewel-hinged jaw: Notes on the language of science fiction.* Dragon Publishing Corp.

Delany, S.R. (1979). *Tales of Neveryon.* New York: Bantam.

Delany, S.R. (1983). *Neveryona; or, Tales of signs and cities.* New York: Bantam.

Delany, S.R. (1985). *Flight from Neveryon.* New York: Bantam.

Delany, S.R. (1987). *The bridge of lost desire.* Arbor House.

Delany, S.R. (1995). *Atlantis: Three tales.* Hanover, NH: Wesleyan University Press.

Due, T. (1995). *The between.* New York: Harper Collins.

Due, T. (1997). *My soul to keep.* New York: Harper Collins.

Gates, H.L., & McKay, N. (1997). *The Norton anthology of African American literature.* New York: W. W. Norton and Co.

Gomez, J. (1991). *The Gilda stories.* Ithaca, NY: Firebrand.

Hamilton, V. (1978). *Justice and her brothers.* New York: Greenwillow.

Hamilton, V. (1980). *Dustland.* New York: Greenwillow.

Hamilton, V.(1981). *The gathering.* New York: Greenwillow.

Hamilton, V. (1982). *Sweet whispers, brother rush.* New York: Philomel.

Hamilton, V. (1983). *The magical adventures of pretty Pearl.* New York: Harper.

Hopkinson, N. (1998). *Brown girl in the ring.* New York: Warner Books.

Mosley, W. (1998). *Blue light.* New York: Little Brown and Co.

Myers, W.D. (1981). *The legend of Tarik.* New York: Viking.

Myers, W.D. (1995). *Shadow of the red moon.* New York: Scholastic.

Saunders, C. (1981). *Imaro.* New York: Daw.

Saunders, C. (1984). *The quest for cush.* New York: Daw.

Saunders, C. (1985). *The trail of bohu.* New York: Daw.

CHAPTER 10

ROCKS IN THE BROOK

A Teacher Educator's Reflections

Arlette Ingram Willis

Brooks, without rocks, lose their song

INTRODUCTION

The opportunity to write a narrative about my teaching experiences that occurred during the fall of 1996, provides me with a chance for introspection and a chance to learn more about my teaching and about myself. As Casey (1995) writes "whether implicit or elaborated, every study of narrative is based on a particular understanding of the speaker's self" (p. 213). This text is structured to reflect what I believe were some of the important experiences and events that helped me to learn about my teaching during the combined course (two courses that are taught as one) I taught in the fall of 1996. In this sense, the narrative is manufactured. The story I tell is a part of me, of who I was then and what I believed and understood, and who I am now and what I believe and understand looking backward, inward, and forward. The Popular Memory Group (1982) has argued this point well in their description of narratives as:

> highly constructed text structured around a cultural framework of meaning and shaped by particular patterns of inclusion, omission, and disparity. The principal value of a narrative is that its information comes complete with evaluations, explanations, and theories and with selectivities, silences and slippages that are intrinsic to its representations of reality. (quoted in Casey, 1995, p. 234)

Additionally, the research of Connelly and Clandinin (1990) notes that the role of narrative in the lives of educational researchers is "...the construction and reconstruction of personal and social stories; learners, teachers, and researchers are storytellers and characters in their own and other's stories" (p. 2). The roles and concerns of teachers as researchers are multiple, yet an excellent starting point is the introspection by the teacher educator as researcher who "acknowledges the centrality of the researchers' own experience: their own tellings, livings, relivings, and retellings," Clandinin and Connelly (1994). I support their argument and state now, at the onset, that I am an African American female professor teaching undergraduate courses in language and literacy at a predominately white male institution of higher learning. My declaration is not meant to describe a badge or a knapsack that I wear. It is an affirmation of who I am and where I am teaching. Simply acknowledging who I am and where I teach tells you very little about what I believe is important about teaching and learning and how I go about instructing my students. In the remainder of this chapter, however, I write about how I accommodate the dual roles of teacher and researcher as I reflect on the process of teaching preservice literacy courses that address issues of race, class, gender, and power in English/Language Arts classrooms. Most importantly, in my course I work toward helping students understand that their social responsibilities move beyond the confines of their past, present, and future into a global community.

I am personally committed to embracing the histories, languages, cultures, and literatures of people of color in America. I have taught this course for several years and similar courses which have prepared me to understand that the course and the relationships that follow from it, are a part of the process of understanding myself and critical literacy theory and pedagogy better. I also realize there will be rocky moments when people begin to feel uncomfortable with the content in what otherwise would be a "normal" methods course. My course calls upon students to move outside of their comfort zone—readings, research, strategies—and deal with the affective, emotional, and personal self in a somewhat public format. As much as possible in a university course, I try to help each person personalize their experiences and learning. I also tend not to concentrate on the smooth spaces, preferring to center on the rocky places. I envision the "rocky spaces" as experiences that help to create the special nature of the course and that allow the experience to remain, like a song in my mind and in my heart, long after the course has ended.

My first goal in the course is to achieve a sense of community in which individually students can feel welcomed, affirmed, and safe to share of themselves. My second goal is to empower my students to listen, think, reflect, and teach literacy critically. My third goal is to communicate to students their individual responsibility to create socially just learning/teaching spaces for themselves and their future students. This chapter's focus is on understanding my position as a teacher/researcher and what accounts for change in my course framed on critical literacy theory and pedagogy. I model my understanding of critical theory and practice as I engage in problem posing and problem solving activities with my students, getting to know them individually and collectively as we learn/teach one another about life and literature throughout the semester.

This chapter is not the *entire* story of my fall 1996 class, but it is *my* story as I understood it then, and now. This narrative also includes excerpts, set off in quotations, from videotapes of the classroom conversations (32, three hour sessions). In addition, I audiotaped reflective notes about what I was learning about myself as a teacher/researcher and what I was learning about critical literacy theory and practice as soon after class as possible, usually immediately following the class session. Space does not permit me to restage all the events and every detail of the course. In what follows, I provide some background information about the course and the events of the first few weeks that foreshadowed events that occurred later. I also have interspersed throughout the chapter my reflective thoughts (set off in italics) of four students I identified during the first few weeks as people whose progress I'd like to follow. These reflective notes of my response and interactions with four students provides a framework for a better understanding of the "myself" as teacher educator and the process of adapting a critical literacy pedagogy in a U.S. university literacy methods course.

PRE-CLASS JITTERS

The night before the course begins I am very excited about conducting research in my own classroom. In part, I am wondering of the possibility of endless publications that can be written from the data and see myself presenting at conferences nationwide. Another part of me is always nervous before meeting a new class of students who are strangers to me, even after more than 20 years of teaching. I am nervous because I am preparing to meet 20 individuals with whom I will spend six hours a week with for the next 16 weeks. I also am nervous because there is so much I'd like for them to learn in my course and I am never sure that what I want them to learn is exactly what they learn. *In all my confidence of 20 years of teaching, I take time to pray this will be a successful semester and that my students will learn what they need to know to be effective English teachers. I am not so confident that I think I cannot use God's help.* Awaking from a restless night wondering whether I will remember everything that I believe needs to be said on the first day, I arrive at my office early and type out a "script" of what I need to say and do in the first class session. My goal in this session is to set some guidelines for future classes. For example, I know that I will not be overly engaging as I read through the syllabus with them and explain the long list of assignments. And, though I will remind them that this is not one course but two courses for which they are receiving credit, I anticipate someone suggesting that there is far too much work, too many books to purchase, and too much writing. These are statements that occur every semester that I have taught the course and I can anticipate their recurrence, but they don't worry me. What concerns me most on this first day is setting the climate for the course. I know that in the weeks to come the students as a class will either "gel," or remain in a fluid-like state that moves in and out of class like an amoeba not really growing, just changing shape. I want the class dynamics to be interesting, testy, thoughtful, challenging, and alive. I believe that the climate and tone of the course is set on the first day of class. A lot of effort has already gone into the planning of this day, planning that the students will not learn about until much later in the course and planning they will not be able to appreciate until they have a class of their own. In planning this day and the activities that have become a part of the first day of class, I have drawn from the work of Nanci Atwell, Katherine Au, Paulo Freire, Henry Giroux, and Ira Shor, among others.

THE FIRST WEEK

September 3, 1996

Before leaving my office for my first class, I review the course syllabus checking for errors and misprints. Then, I make a quick check of the roster looking at the names of students to see if there are any names of people I know in the course. This semester the enrollees include two of my graduate advisees and 16 undergraduates (15 seniors and 1 junior). Looking at the names only, I can see that this will be a fairly culturally diverse class of preservice English educators. The first day always begins with the same set of activities, an ice breaker. *This is more for my own comfort level and sense of assurance, than it is for my students. I purposely plan for much of what appears to them as natural.* For example, a few minutes before class begins, I arrive in the classroom and place a list of questions to be answered on the front desk and take a seat. As the students file in and take seats I smile politely. I sit quietly, but observantly, watching their facial expressions, gestures, interactions, mannerism, body language, and eavesdropping on bits and pieces of their conversations. *Part of my response to their arrival is conscious "this is my new class" and a part of my response is subconscious, "she has on expensive shoes."* Many of the students just look at me or past me as they take a seat, unsure of who I am: graduate teaching assistant, instructor, or professor. Some may have taken the time to view the photographs of faculty in the lobby and have an idea of who I am. After five minutes or so, I begin the class by moving to the front of the room. I write my name and the course titles on the board. I ask if everyone is in the right course. *There is usually someone who has misread the schedule and today is no different, one woman leaves.* Then, in my most no-nonsense tone I tell the class that they can only address me as Professor Willis. *I am old fashioned in this sense and see it as sign of respect. As I look around the room I notice in small facial expressions and body language, "Oh, she's the professor! Not what I expected."*

I ask the students to move the furniture to form a circle so that everyone is facing center. I inform the class that I want each person to voluntarily move to the front of the room and follow the directions listed on the piece of paper taped to the front desk. Some of the questions are: What is your hometown? How many years have you taught? and, What is your favorite-color, fruit, vegetable, drink, breakfast? *The questions appear silly and inconsequential to the students, but they are listed to offer me some selective information and they are placed in a definite order. As students voluntarily follow the directions, I take notes on a grid that allows me to chart each person's answers. Later, I use the information to place students in working groups because there is something they share in common based on the answers they have supplied to each question.*

The first person to volunteer is Sharrie, an African-American woman (all names are pseudonyms). She tells us that she is from a wealthy suburb outside a large Midwestern city and likes strawberry margaritas, among other answers. Most students listen politely, and several notice that I am taking notes. *I can sense the climate in the room beginning to change as I look up and there is a sea of eyeballs darting about as if in a tempest.* One student after another volunteers to go to the "head of the class" to share the information requested. As they do, I begin to make mental notes about what I see, hear, and feel—how each person walks, stands, writes, talks, laughs, smiles, looks for approval, etc. *My reactions are both conscious (note taking) and unconscious (mental and visual notes).* I notice that the students are watching me as closely as I am watching them. *They appear to wonder about what I am writing and after the first couple of volunteers the responses grow ever more cautious and conservative. I remember that I am a novelty to some of them and on the first day they are looking for clues and signs from me on what to expect and what is acceptable behavior, style, tone, and interaction in my classroom.* The students also are watching each other. It is obvious that some of them know each other well. *They are communicating with one another in nonverbal signals that agree, dispute, and question what they are hearing, seeing, and feeling about this new class and the responses of their classmates.* I try to ignore what I see and not allow my subconscious opinions to color my first impression of the students in my new class. I try to remain neutral about what I hear and feel and not judge the person in front of me. And, I try to respond to each person in the same monotone manner, thanking them for sharing.

Several more students respond to the questions and the responses begin to sound repetitive. *I think, maybe these 4–5 students are just more conservative, but, I also wonder, is it my notetaking?* For example, when Sharrie said her favorite drink is a strawberry margarita, and some students noticed I was taking notes, everyone's favorite drink became water or coffee. I am not the only who noticed this change, as Sharrie comments aloud after the nth person said their favorite drink is water, "as if I am the only one who drinks, whatever." *I know I need to reconsider this question of your favorite drink, for it does not seem to lend itself to information that is helpful to me and may cause some students to alter the veracity of their responses, especially on the first day of class when they don't know me well.*

The responses by the students to the query, "What is your hometown?" reveal that most of them are from suburbs (some wealthier than others) that surround a major Midwestern city. On this campus, and in this context, a university where a large percentage of students come from the suburbs, it seems important to many people. *The importance of identifying which suburb you are from, always has amazed me. I have purposely asked this question, because it seems to be an important issue for some students: to inform everyone, in a not so subtle manner that they are from a wealthy (and thus, some believe fortunate) background. In reality three quarters of my students are from suburban communities. However, the practice of announcing it for all is like having a calling card, a way of locating oneself on a large campus and a way of informing others about your place in the world. I also use this question because I am from another state and want to reassure all students that suburban locals make little difference to how I see the world.* The response by one European American woman to this question, indicated that she is from XX suburb. Sharrie, shrieks with delight and announces that she is from a rival (high school athletic teams) suburb. They instantly "connect" and carry on a brief conversation about the schools. Several other students noticeably moan aloud in response to the suburban-ness of their excitement, prompting Sharrie to declare, "Well, I am proud to be from RR suburb."

The next volunteer is Martin, a European American male. He moves to the front of the room in what appears to be a stilted manner. *To me it looks as if he would prefer not to participate, but considering he has little choice, he lumbers forward.* With his head bowed, not making eye-contact with anyone, and speaking in a demur manner, he says, "I am from $$ (a very wealthy suburb), and everyone knows everything there is to know about it, but I live in the trailer park." *I am taking notes, but stop briefly with my head still lowered to consider whether or not there are actually trailer parks in this suburb. Something in me kind of doubts it, but I make a mental note to check with a friend who teaches there.* Martin's first response has clearly captured the attention of his classmates, many of whom perk up and face him admiringly. *Is it because his response was a direct "hit" at Sharrie's earlier outburst and comment about being from the suburbs? Or, I wonder, has he taken some kind of rebellious stance for those suburbanites who consider any reference to their home life in the suburbs passé and prefer to downplay and distance themselves from their lives there?* He continues responding to the questions. Then, he looks up, with chin thrust forward and states that his favorite vegetable is collard greens and smiles broadly. No one responds aloud, but some students snicker and others return his smile. *I write his response without making eye-contact with anyone, trying to control my facial expressions and body language as if unaffected. I wonder is he joking, or is*

this his way of suggesting that he's "down with Black folks"? Next, he responds to
the favorite drink question by stating that his favorite drink is Molsen Beer,
again smiling out at his audience. A few students root and chime-in with
sounds of agreement. *I am not the least bit amused. Does he really expect me to
believe that he drinks Molsen Beer and eats collard greens? One or the other I can
handle, but I really don't buy both. I don't drink, but I must admit the people that I
know who eat greens don't drink Molsen Beer. I am unsure if he is trying to be "cute"
or meanspirited. I think he is at least trying to "pull a fast one" over on me. I wonder
is he joking, or is this his way of suggesting that he finds the entire activity a waste of
his time? I determine to keep my eyes and ears ready for this one, who I have already
nicknamed Mr. Collard Greens. If, what he wanted to do was get my attention, he
succeeded. I am suspicious of his responses and his possible motives.*

Once everyone has introduced themselves and participated in this ice-
breaker, I participate by returning to the front of the room and answering
each of the questions. I inform the students that I am from Ohio and that I
think that the suburb name-game is silly. I also inform the students that I
have been teaching for more than 20 years (*which is why I ask the question—
to let them know in a not-so-subtle way that I have lots of classroom experience*).
Finally, I answer the "favorites" question, noting my favorites: yellow, okra,
giraffes, and coffee. I hope that my participation will send a message to the
students by way of demonstration that I am willing to be a part of the class.

Next, I offer a brief explanation of why I have structured the early
moments of the class to be active, that is, announcing that my expectation
is that everyone will participate as learners/teachers in this course. *I want
the students to feel that they are important in our classroom. I expect everyone to
assume the role of learner/teacher and speaker/listener for I see everyone as responsible for helping to make our class a community.* Then, I describe my goals for the
class. First, I want to establish a participatory atmosphere where students
feel welcomed, safe, and free to express themselves. Second, I want to
begin to develop a classroom climate and community that is: active, safe,
welcoming, and open. *Experience has taught me that the issues we will discuss in
the class will make some students uncomfortable as they are called upon to move
away from a purely academic mode and draw upon the affective mode to wrestle with
their understanding and experiences with issues of race, class, gender, and power.* I
also want the course to be student-centered: participatory, emancipatory,
experiential, and multicultural. As a participant in these courses I want students to begin to see themselves in several roles: teacher/learner, listener/
speaker, reader/writer, and thinker/reflector. *I know that it will take weeks to
breakdown the old habits that some of the students have about speaking publically
and honestly in a large group. Moreover, I know that as we begin to address issues of
race, class, gender, and power, some students will become silent observers. I also realize that to begin to develop a working dialog with the group where we can speak safely
and honestly, I need to begin now.* Third, I use the answers supplied by students to place them in cooperative groups. *I realize that I am working at a disadvantage as many of the students know each other from other English courses and*

have developed patterns of response. That is, they know who will speak up on almost any occasion and often do not participate waiting for someone else. I want to believe that these first day activities will provide me with a vehicle for establishing new response patterns through cooperative group and working arrangements among the students. Finally, I state the ground rules for participation and discussion: no personal attacks.

The first day ends, as it began, with me returning to my level of comfort: I assign a 20 minute in-class written response to the following question that I borrowed (with permission) from Hansen-Krening (1992) several years ago, "How does your cultural perspective affect the students you teach?" I ask this question knowing that most students have not taught. Thus, they respond by talking about themselves and their future classrooms. On the first day, given what little they know about the course, most students begin by stating their levels of comfort or discomfort with who they are or how they understand themselves as cultural beings. Here are few examples from their responses to this question: "As an African American," ... "As a white female from an upper class community" ... "I grew up in a homogenous community" ... "I never interacted with other cultures until I came to the U of I," and "My freshman roommate was ___ (person of color) and that was my first experience with someone other than my race." *I have learned from past experience to suspend any judgments about the students individually or collectively until I get to know them better and take their early responses to this question as a starting point to understanding them, individually. Their responses to this question may offer me a window into understanding how they identify with issues of culture and cultural difference. I know that throughout the semester I will get to know them better and when they answer this question on the last day of class, they will recall this first encounter and wonder what they wrote. I hope that by then I will see some growth and change in their response to the question.*

As the title of this chapter implies, I have anticipated that there will be spaces in the course that will run smoothly as a brook and others that will be rocky spaces to move over, around, or through. The responses to this final question and written in-class assignment that ends the first day, usually confirms my suspicions and serves as a mirror into the students' levels of comfort with cultural differences. I know what, and how, I expect the students to respond to my requests, but I also know to expect the unexpected and have a plan ready for reacting to it in a way that will not deter from my larger goals for the students, myself, or the course. *I envision my pedagogical style as similar to James Vasquez's (1998) notion of a "warm demander." A teacher of color, here an African American teacher, "...who provide(s) a tough-minded, no-nonsense, structured, and disciplined classroom environment" (p. 1). I can sense people beginning to realign their geographical and cultural sensibilities in response to the African American female in front of them. My past experiences have taught me that many of my students have never taken a course taught by an African American female professor. This is their first "ethnic" experience with a professor of color and they are not sure what to expect.* After class, several students of color wait until the other students have left and tell me how wonderful they think it is that this course is being taught by a person of color ... they say that they have waited too long to have this experience. *I wonder if it is reaffirming for them to have a person of color teaching this course as I felt affirmed when I enrolled in a course taught by a person of color. Somehow the position, as a professor and a person of color in a university said to me that "all is well." I want my students, all my students, to remember this course as helpful and supportive to their lives and to their careers.*

September 5, 1996

On the second day of class we continue to learn more about one another by sharing artifacts and memories in an effort to begin to build a sense of community. Sharrie and Martin both continue to be very interesting class members. Sharrie, brings a picture of her boyfriend holding her little sister and gives us a brief personal history of her mixed-race (African-European American) parentage. Her ease and straightforward manner in explaining her mixed racial heritage and some incidents that have made her comfortable with being biracial, appears to catch some of the other students off-guard. *I am surprised and impressed. I think she is a beautiful young woman but I would not have guessed she is biracial. It seems odd that her peers did not know this before. I struck by her openness.* Martin shares highlights of his summer in Connecticut working for a Republican candidate for the state senate. *Now, I am more suspicious of his responses from day one!*

Like day one, two students and their responses to the activity and my responses to them, provide me with opportunities to reflect upon myself and my teaching. Emily, a European American woman, volunteers to speak following Mark, a European American male, who has shared a gift of rosary beads he selected from his grandmother's collection. She skips to the front of the room and nervously begins to speak using lots of hand gestures and facial expressions. She declares that she is framing her comments somewhat like Mark and is taking a risk telling others about herself. She states that "people have a tendency to label and assume that people are a certain way and that they have traits like closemindedness ... I am trusting you all **not** to put labels (on me) and to be open-minded." *This comes as a surprise to me since I did not hear Mark say anything about being concerned others would judge him or label him because he chose to share his devotion to Catholicism. There are obviously conversations about this course going on beyond the confines of the classroom.* Next, she opens her Bible and shares a brief story about how she received the Bible as a gift and what she keeps tucked inside (family photos, poems from her boyfriend, spiritual letters, pressed flowers, and trinkets). She offers a brief explanation of why she keeps each of the items and closes by showing a portfolio of poetry she has written, stating that she uses poetry as an outlet for her spirituality. *Perhaps Emily was empowered to speak because of Mark's frankness and devotion to Catholicism, but she is nonetheless fear-*

ful that her religious beliefs may be misunderstood and even possibly be offensive to others. I understand her point as I often do not share, unless I am asked, my own religious beliefs with my classes.

The next student to volunteer is Jerry, a European American male. He is one of six, "not-from-the-suburbs" students in the class, although he is dressed in designer cloths with sandals on his well-scrubbed toes complete with pale mauve nail polish. *I am not sure why he paints his toenails, but it is a "hot topic" among the women in the class as they question him about his changing colors. My first reaction is that he wants to draw attention to himself, but why I wonder?* Jerry shares an "Indian-head" nickel he found while doing service work in the Appalachian mountains that he claims helped him to become more grateful for the many advantages of his life. He explains, "I want to give back to the community ... that is why I want to teach in the inner city (then, through some nonverbal gestures he acknowledges that this is a joke to some)." He follows his nervous laugh by stating that "Sometimes I hate being white, but that's another issue ... another judgment thing here" (in reference to Emily's previous concerns). *Jerry's comment about his whiteness reminds me of other European American males I have had in class who have—in one way or another—informed me that they were committed to "improving society" or "being a role model for inner-city youth." Jerry's comments also seem to have a subtext to me, again like others, he seems to be asking that I do not stereotype him in the pejorative sense as a "white male." I find this idea of white male victimization amusing. I don't have any feelings toward Jerry as a person. I hardly know him and learning to know him will be a process throughout the semester and beyond.*

These first two days offered me ample information about my students, but none that would really help me to know what was informing their responses. I felt in order to better understand each person individually, I needed to learn about their personal histories, experiences, and lives. One of the major assignments of the course is to write an autobiography. From reading each student's autobiography I can learn a great deal more them. In addition, after the first month, when the first journals are due, I will learn more about how each person is making sense of the course. I believe that we are building a community, but the process is almost painfully slow. I really want to move more quickly, but I know from past experiences this snail's pace will pay big benefits later in the semester when we would need smooth spaces and fond memories on which to lean.

THE SECOND WEEK

September 10, 1996

The third day of class begins with students sharing in small groups (selected by some common response on the first day) their autobiographies, or any portion of their autobiography that they are comfortable sharing. I move among the groups listening and learning a little here and there about everyone. The videotape has become indispensable as it captured the small group discussion of autobiographies in which Sharrie, Emily, and Jerry were participants. In their small group, Emily shares in great detail her family lineage of which she is obviously very proud and decides to only mention unpleasant aspects of her heritage without going into detail. Throughout the small group sharing, Sharrie and Jerry remain somewhat aloof, while Emily appears to listen intently to everyone, asking questions for clarification, laughing freely, covering her mouth when embarrassed, and offering unsolicited advice. Next, is Jerry's turn to share, but he states that this isn't his comfort level. He is encouraged by Emily and others to share whatever he'd like. He continues to resist and they continue to encourage him until he finally asks if it would be okay to read his first paragraph. Everyone agrees and he begins, then, suddenly he stops and shares a painful childhood memory. Next, he describes his life in sections: predivorce—(his parents divorced when he was in the 6th grade), postdivorce—precollege, and college years. The group is reminded of the time limit and Sharrie, mindful of the fleeting moments, hurriedly shares her autobiography. She wisely decides to begin with a graph of her family tree indicating her lineage starting with her mother's (German American) side of the family. As she points to different relatives, she offers short stories of interesting aspects of their lives. She concludes with a graph of her father's (African American) side of the family, but offers little detail, perhaps still conscious of the time-limit.

The class reconvenes as a large group to share any portion of their past (or that of their ancestors) that they wish. I begin the process by sharing portions of my autobiography, displaying a family tree I have drawn on the blackboard. I acknowledge all my ancestors (African, English, French, Irish, and Native American) from former slaves to former slave holders. I tell of the tragic–the rape of my maternal great-grandmother by her slave master— and the romantic—how I met my husband. I notice heads bow or shake when the rape story is told and the room grows noticeably quiet and somber. By way of contrasts, the students look upward expectantly and laugh aloud when the romantic story is told. Several students share memories of family traditions that center around Christmas and Easter holidays—some religious and some secular. This leads to one student, a Muslim woman who was raised under strict religious rules, to explain how she has often felt estranged in school during the celebration of Christian religious holidays and how she felt it was important that we, as a class, remember that not all people are Christians, though some non-Christian people, including some Muslims, celebrate these holidays too. *I begin the process with personal disclosure to provide a model as well as to demonstrate autobiographic sharing in this class. In their small groups and journals students declare that doing the assignment brought out stories from their ancestors they had not known before, some humorous, some sad, some romantic, and some tragic. My own religious beliefs, holiday celebrations, and family traditions do cause me to overlook the non-Christian members of my class. I make a mental note to be more sensitive in the future when I discuss "holidays" since I really have reference only Christian holidays. Later, I read all the autobiographies and learn more about each student. I really like reading the students' writing as I get a much better understanding of them individually than when I move among the small groups or when we talked during the large group. The students write well, but most have not done a very good job of proofreading. I scan the papers and decide that it will take hours to correct every error on their papers and write a thoughtful response. I am disappointed because I know they want them back quickly but there is just no way I can correct the many errors on each paper. I fall back on the minimal grading technique, placing check marks in the right-hand margin for each error in the sentence. Even under these circumstances it has taken me hours to correct and respond to 20 3–4-page papers, but I really want to return them as soon as possible. Begrudgingly, I know that this means I will need to spend a weekend correcting essays.*

September 12, 1996

The fourth class meeting brings an end to the first two weeks of class. The class has been warned to only bring the most essential elements of campus life to class because I have a unique activity planned for the class session. Students are asked to individually write definitions for several words that their classmates have used over the last two weeks: culture, diversity, dominant culture, minority culture, multiculturalism, multicultural education, and political correctness. Then, students are placed in teams of four and given worksheets. The directions state that each team will make an unscientific one-hour survey of the definitions people on campus offer for each word (the College of Education is off-limits). Team members should rotate who asks the question, who records the answers, while others look at the nonverbal signs of the respondent. Following their survey students are to return to the College and write a short summary of their findings which will be presented to the class. The groups return, write their summaries and enthusiastically describe their results. After each group has shared their "stories from the field," I ask them to write group definitions for each term, followed by expert definitions I have placed on overheads.

Next, I write the politically correct names for each cultural group in the United States (according the U.S. Bureau of Statistics) on the board and provide statistics detailing the numbers for each group. As a class we briefly discuss the composition of each group and the percentage of the group's population in the United States. Then, I return to my list of politically correct names and offer descriptions of each group from the work of Sonia Neito (1996). The politically correct definitions are followed by my asking for politically incorrect names of each group beginning with the largest group, European Americans. Many students are hesitant to offer a response at first. I work hard at not looking directly at anyone and keep my back to the classroom as I record their response on the board. We move through each of the major ethnic groups, as students call out the politically incorrect names. Then, I inform the class, in my most somber and serious manner, that I do not want to hear any of the politically incorrect terms ever in my classroom. *This day I have fondly nicknamed "the political correct/incorrect day." This first activity is as much a survey of the "person on the street" definition of the terms as it is a bonding activity for the students in an effort to continue to work on community building. The second activity is designed to create for the class a way to communicate in a language with definitions we have developed and understand. The activity briefly informs the students of the history of racism that has given rise to the politically correct (and incorrect) terms and the percentages of each group within the United States. Moreover, the entire day was designed to provide the guidelines for acceptable and unacceptable language in the classroom. I understand the reticence of some students to even offer a politically incorrect term aloud among their classmates and for that reason I spend most of my time with my back to the class—for others fear I will somehow remember what each person says and that I might allow their responses to affect what I think of them, or influence my ability to evaluate their classroom performance.*

THE THIRD WEEK

September 17, 1996

I begin the class session by discussing what my goals have been in terms of community building for the first three weeks of the course. I offer insights drawn from my viewpoint and from observations I have made as a teacher/researcher about how I see the class evolving into a community. I sum up the course to date: the reasons why we have been sharing in small, large, and whole class groupings, information from our personal lives and experiences (introduction's, memories, and autobiographies). I explain that the first few class sessions were designed to help each student to get to know one another better, learn about one another, and teach one another about their life. This is not MY class, it is our class, and we are all here as: learner/teacher, listener/speaker, reader/writer, and thinker/reflector. These behaviors need to become habits of mind for all teacher/learners of literacy. These couplets are important: they begin with what has been assumed to be the more passive role (learner, listener, reader, thinker) while in effect, these roles should also be active. The early days of the course also have been situated within "mainstream" culture and experience. We have spent three weeks expressly working toward what I call, "creating a community of learners." Within this growing community I am trying to establish a respect for the complexity and multiplicity of the lives that we all bring to the class. In addition, I am trying to foster a safe and welcoming classroom climate in which everyone is free to express their ideas and opinions we must learn to respect the expression of ideas by others.

Specifically, I point out how the class seems to be more comfortable publicly addressing issues of difference, in terms of race, class, and gender. I place their definitions of multiculturalism on the board and we review them. Next, I distributed copies of magazines that focus on different ethnic groups in the United States (Irish, Latino/a, African, Vietnamese, and Asian American) and some magazines that focus on gay and lesbian issues. The students peruse the magazines and we discuss the similarities and differences between these magazines and those they purchase for their own pleasure. Then, I revisit the notion of political correctness with the students and read to them several stories from *Politically Correct Bedtime Stories* and *Politically Correct Holiday Stories* (Garner, 1994, 1995).

This discussion reminds several students of a lecture given by a (European American male) professor that they greatly enjoyed and appreciated. For instance, Jerry said that he was very impressed by what he perceived to be the professor's forthright discussion of his own racist baggage. Naturally, there were other students who did not share this opinion, Sharrie being one of them. She supplied a very different and uncomplimentary opposing point of view of the lecture. She told how she was so upset with the lecture that she left the room and scheduled an appointment to speak with the professor privately (along with other African American students in the course who were also offended by his remarks). Other members of the class spoke up and said that she should have stayed for the entire lecture and she would have understood his point of view better. Although I do not generally allow students to discuss my colleagues in class, I could see that this discussion of his lecture was a reference point for some students.

Suddenly, and without warning, Jerry asks if he could pose a hypothetical question. I grant him the floor and he states,

> What would you do when you have a problem with a student? Because if you're actually in the classroom—and many teachers have said this to me—when you're in the classroom and all this stuff you learned at the university kinda goes out the window and you don't deal with issues of theory, but you actually deal with what's going on in the classroom and you have to think on your feet, etc. Well, what would you do if someone comes in and says, "I'm tired of reading all this nigger stuff?"

I am not pleased to have a student so openly disrespect my wishes not to use this language in my classroom after Thursday's very pointed lesson on political correctness. I feel that he is really pushing my limits of patience and testing my authority much like Martin had done on the first day of class. I was unprepared for this query, and in an effort to regroup and pray, I asked him to repeat the question. By the time he has restated the gist of his question all eyes are fixed on me in tense, almost breathless, silence. I begin by suggesting that whenever a student's behavior is inappropriate you, as the teacher, should begin by trying to diffuse the situation. Then, I shared a personal story, with the class. *I did not really know where I was going with the story and I did not know how I was going to tie it into what I really wanted to say, but again I was buying time and working through my own anger.* In a most expressive and dramatic way, I began

> My two female cousins (they are sisters) and I spent many summer days as teenagers watching soap operas during the seventies. The older cousin was very social and outgoing. Her sister was quiet, almost creepy quiet, sitting with you for hours never offering a word of conversation. One day, when my older cousin and I were discussing a comment made by one of the actors and trying to decide—in all our teenage wisdom—what the character really meant, her sister spoke. In reference to the actor's statement she said, "it is a manifestation of a much deeper thought." She really blew us out of the water with that comment and since that time we have quoted her in reference whenever someone says one thing when they mean another.

When I was finished, I understood where I needed to go with the story and the point I wanted to make. I looked directly at Jerry, hoping my point was clear. But, just in case it wasn't clear to him or to anyone else in the class who decides to cross a border I had set, I added "Whenever someone says something like that, then you have to begin to wonder what has prompted the person to speak in a disrespectful manner; there's something else going on in that person's life." *I couldn't stop now that I understood this was an ideal moment to make another important point to the class, half way talking to the students and to myself,*

> You're an adult; you're always supposed to be the person in charge. And even though we are dealing with issues of critical pedagogy, you're still the authority figure within the classroom … any classroom, including the classroom that we're in now. I am the person in charge, if I'm the teacher. And I'm not going to allow anyone to take over my class. I will give people flexibility and allow them to have some room to grow, but its not happening (take over). I'm not going to let someone come in and take charge and ruin my class for me, or my class time.

Now, I was sure that the message was clear. The silence grew, and I grew uncomfortable with my own power, so I asked if there were any more questions. To my surprise, one European American woman, wondered about being in a monocultural setting, being a European American female, and trying to be a voice for many different cultures, knowing what students mean (text and subtext), and how might her students react (to her). Her query created an odd, but welcomed, segue and led to a lengthy whole class discussion with many different people participating; some sharing past experiences and others offering suggestions for how she might approach such a class. The class session had strayed far from my lesson plan, but I considered it an important part of the process and evolution of the course and let it continue longer than was perhaps necessary. I also realized that when critical literacy theory and pedagogy meet the reality of a Western university classroom, some changes in theory must occur to accommodate the reality of the classroom. My reading of critical literacy theory and pedagogy suggests that an authoritative stance does not mean an authoritarian stance. That is, there are times when the teacher needs to be authoritative without becoming an oppressive authoritarian.

Following these discussions we took a much needed break and resumed with a discussion of the books the students have selected to read using the Jigsaw technique (exchange of information in a predetermined pattern). The students moved to their small groups and began discussing their responses to the book as I move among the groups. I offer very little commentary as I listen to individuals in various groups express or argue their opinions among the group members. For example, I moved to a group that selected to read, *The Disuniting of America* (Schlessinger, 1993). This group's discussion had shifted into a debate that is fairly heated and has increased in volume throughout the 30 minute period. *The more conservative members of the group are being challenged to rethink their position. I say nothing but listen to the arguments in support and opposition to Schlessinger's viewpoints. I am making mental notes of who is talking and their point of view. I purposely selected this book to offer balance to a multicultural classroom. Too often the texts in such rooms only reflect supportive viewpoints and I wanted to offer students alternative ways of viewing multiculturalism. On the one hand, the student discussion supplies me with additional bits of insight into their levels of comfort with discussions of difference and their abilities to write and articulate their positions. On the other hand, the choice to include this book may have come at the expense of the supporters of a more conservative viewpoint. One of the students leading the conservative charge, is a quite biracial student, Michelle. I learned she is biracial (Mexican and European American) when I read her autobiography. She is clearly uncomfortable with her biracialness and wrote that she does not identify with her Latino/Latina side. This is not information that she has shared with her classmates and I wonder if her silence is reflective of her conservative viewpoint. After a few minutes of debate, she announces that she will rethink her position, but that she doesn't find anything wrong in having a different opinion. My use of groups based on first day responses may need to be reconsidered. Small group interactions can be hotbeds of discontent, and in this case, painful and hurtful experiences.* We completed the Jigsaw sharing among groups and the day ended with a class discussion following a CSPAN video of Arthur Schlessinger's discussion of his book. This has been an emotional day. It is days like this that make me wonder if the emotional toll is worth the effort. But, I remind myself that some of these very students could be future teachers of my children or children that look like my children, and then I know that it is not only worth it, but necessary if classrooms are ever to become the socially just classrooms we desire for our children.

September 19, 1996

I proudly watch the students come into the room, move the furniture, take their seats and begin conversations among themselves. I hope what I see and what I am beginning to sense is a belongingness among the students—a sense of community. Since our Tuesday class was sidetracked, I begin with Tuesday's lesson: a survey of what my students think children in grades 6–12 know about literacy. This is a survey I created to get students to think about students at these grade levels by listing general characteristics about children in grades 6–12 (divided into sections) and general characteristics about what students in these grades read and write (in and out of school). In small groups the students discuss each issue, record their responses on large pieces of butcher paper, and then tape them on the blackboard for a whole class discussion.

The whole-class discussion began with the general characteristics of children in grades 6–12. Sharrie pointed out that many of the general characteristics listed by groups centered on self-consciousness and self-esteem as well as the budding sense of sexual identity, especially heterosexual and heterosocial identity. She went on to state that "it must be stressful for a child who is homosexual, or at least feel as if they have those preferences, to live in a society that clearly made (heterosexual and heterosocial) an important issue." Another student taking her lead, suggested that what was placed on the board was a reflection of our Western Eurocentric institutionalization of schooling and education. Other students also offered comments, but Martin wanted to return to the issue of homophobia in education and in schools. *Again, I took my lead from the students and allowed the conversation to follow its own course. Although sexual preference is not an issue I address in my class, nor one that I plan for in any specific manner, if it arises in class, I attempt to deal with it.* Martin asked (the class), "Well, what do you do, if someone is homosexual?" I responded first by quoting laws and policies on equal access and harassment. One student recalled an article that had appeared in the local newspaper about the openness of gay and lesbian relationships at a local high school. The article (which I remembered reading) shared the pain and frustration of a young woman to be herself in a heterosexual world and how she had fought and won the right to show signs of affection with her partner in school and to escort her to school social events (homecoming, prom, etc.). Another student reports that she had worked very hard with a group of students from the school in an off-campus group, GALS, gay and lesbian students. Enthusiastically, she shared how the campus group and the high school group were supportive of one another. Students listened, many with heads bowed, but no one made any comments as she continued to share her involvement. *Later, as I read through student journals there were several students however, that revealed that they were not comfortable with the conversation. I acknowledge that I am not sure of how, or what, to say to my students about teaching children who are dealing with sexual preference issues. My personal stance is that the conditions of the classroom, the content, and the assignments should be respectful of every student in the class.*

The class session ended when I returned the autobiographies. I apologized and explained why it had taken me so long to return the papers: their writing is fine, but their grammar needs lots of work. The students read over my comments. I described my grading process (although it was clearly written on a separate page in the class syllabus) and informed the students that they may rewrite the autobiographies (*since I knew they would be horrified by their low scores and I was considering offering an extra point to the original grade if the rewrites—along with the original—were returned by next Thursday*). Several students sit dumbfounded and looked at their papers in disbelief. Others, stuff them into their backpacks and leave the room without saying "good-bye" or "have a nice weekend" (*our unofficial classroom tradition*). Clearly, some students are not pleased with their grades.

Emily stays in the room, as others leave, with her head bowed and her face covered by her hair. She approaches me and begins a conversation about how she enjoys our class, how she is fearful being a white female teaching (student teaching) in a mixed raced setting—particularly an African American setting (*she had applied to student teach in a local high school where the African American population is 23.5 % of the student population, hardly what I'd call predominately African American, but I understood her point*). Then, she leaves the room and I continue to chat with others who want to share one thing or another with me. For instance, Jerry, is asking me to serve as his mentor on a special "honors" project he'd like to do in the community. After nearly everyone has left, Emily, now with tears in her eyes, returns because she is very upset with the grade on her paper. She understood the grade of her life story to be a "B." *I understood the grade to be a mark for the job she had done; one that could easily be improved upon with closer attention to grammar and spelling.* She excused herself for crying and shared that she had a 20 credit course load semester and that she trying really hard. She went on to complain that her courses in the English Department had not prepared her well to deal with grammar. She protested that "...everyone over there only looks at content." (This is an argument that I have heard before and ignore, because I believe that future English teachers should learn the tools of *their* trade). To ease her anxiety, however, I shared with her that I was in no way judging her or her ability to write by the grade on this paper. In addition, I shared with her that more than 50% of the students in the class were also rewriting their autobiographies. She said she loved the class and I told her how much I appreciated her sharing those thoughts with me. Then, she skipped out the door.

THE REST OF THE SEMESTER—WEEKS 4–16

The remainder of the semester was as eventful as the first three weeks. Our community was still "under construction" but it was clear we were growing together. By way of example, one day during the fifth week as the class was taking a break, Jerry danced across the room singing "we are family." At least, for some, the course was changing their ideas about one another and about me.

Several important events, both rocky and smooth spaces, helped me to understand myself better and the experiences of the students in the course. One of the most important of these events is what I call the "Breakpoint" (Willis & Meacham, 1996). This is the turning point in the semester when students, who have politely and civilly participated in all the class work and activities, feel empowered enough to voice, publicly, their concern about the course. I anxiously anticipate this day for it is usually the first break from "teacher expectations" to more passionate interactions and conversations between the students and me, and among the students. Oddly, this moment usually falls around midterm period, and I am unsure if it is the stress of the semester, other obligations, or the literature that we are reading. By this point in the semester we are usually reading Asian American literature. I am not sure why many of my students find it difficult to accept the Asian American point of view of life in America. I think it destroys their idea of the "model minority." Many of my students have become numb to the history and calls of racism from African, Native, and Latino/a Americans, but most have little understanding of experiences with racism endured by Asian Americans.

This year is no different, as a heated discussion occurs in response to Graham Salisbury (1995), *Under the Blood Red Sun*. Although I have been a part of the small group in which the discussion reaches its climax, I have moved to another group before the "breakpoint." One of the members of the group shares with me, openly, that she "couldn't imagine how some of her group members believed that interning the Japanese American citizens was justified." She quoted them as stating, "Well, of course, the Japanese Americans were interred, after all the Japanese had bombed the United States." The students who held this opinion, which they did not share with the entire class, were the same two students who earlier had been supporters of Schlessinger. *She shared her thoughts with me, unsolicited by me, and while I appreciated them for the insight they offered, I made no comment to her.*

When we returned from the break, Jerry asks if he can make a comment. After his last such attempt, I take a deep breath, and agree to let him speak to the class (and me). He states that he is not pleased with the way the class is going and that he believes that some people are clearly not dealing with the issues (my first thought is he is referencing the heated debate from before the group, in which he was a participant). I ask him to "hold his thought" as I want to catch this exchange on the videotape. Then, I ask him to restate his concern. He does, but extends his comments to include the fact that he had lunch with a fellow student and the other student was equally concerned about the course. The "mystery student" speaks up and states that his real concern is that, "in a class that deals with issues of race class, gender, and power ... issues of diversity, it just isn't as abrasive as he thinks it needs to be." Suddenly, many students began to vent, mostly in general statements, about the course and its content. Others, make more specific statements about small group interactions that are left unresolved and how hurtful comments made by their peers have been. Still other students sit quietly by afraid to say anything and afraid the class is falling apart. I allow the conversation to go on for roughly thirty minutes as students talked to one another and argued with one another about the course and the context of the course. Then, I informed them that I had been waiting for this point all semester and thought they would never reach it. Further, I add that I am very pleased with them as a group to have reached this point because I firmly believe it is necessary before we can grow as a class. I tell them that I have been trying to nudge and support them as a class to reach this breakpoint. I offered examples of early tense moments that were unaddressed from classroom interactions in large and small groups and comments that people had made in their journals about the class, the content, the context, and the instruction and instructor. I even shared with them the discussion I had with a member of the group in which there was a heated discussion about the book, *Under the Blood Red Sun.* I went on to say that this kind of break comes in every class and that usually it isn't until after the break that we can move passed the civility and other BS and have more really dynamic conversations. I understand that lots of people brought personal baggage and histories into this classroom and which in one sense impeded the progress of community building. I agreed with the two students who raised the issue that we needed to move forward as a class, stating that until this point, we had approached issues of race, class, gender, power, and sexual preference pretty academically as intellectual exercises, but the time has come to deal with them more openly. I remind the students that this class requires that you bring your emotions, your souls, as well as your mind to class. For some, it is difficult to make public private conversations that they have had in learning to deal with issues but that we are attempting to learn a discourse and a way of expressing ideas that do not offend, but may challenge people's thinking. As the conversation ended, Martin felt compelled to add that he was a very privileged white male and had been privileged all his life, and that every day he hates that privilege. *The class period ended, but I encouraged students to continue the conversations among themselves. Several groups of people stood around in the classroom and talked about the last nine weeks and others took their conversations with them as they left the room and the building. Others, stayed to tell me that they were really upset and scared when the conversation began. They thought I was angry and now they were relieved to know that I had been waiting for this moment all semester.*

By the end of the semester the students were able to see the progress they had made individually and collectively toward becoming a community of learners/teachers. We also became more appreciative, or at least tolerant, of our individual shortcomings and began to flow together as a group. For example, I had invited a couple of local high school English teachers to class, on separate occasions, as guest speakers. Each person spoke to the class about how they teach English in a culturally and linguistically diverse high school. *I felt badly that I had invited them as the students sat silently and politely listened to their lectures they spoke. However, their body language nearly shouted across the room communicating their agreement or disagreement with various points of view.* After one presentation, the students questioned the teacher about how she approached the teaching of Hermann Hesse's, *Siddhartha*, since she had not mentioned how she addressed culture. The teacher replied that culture was not an issue with her when she taught the book. An audible gulp was produced from the class and they looked to me for help. *I had tried desperately to keep my opinions to a minimum and allow them to form their own opinions about authenticity, acceptable text, and teachability (their words) of novels for high school literature.* As several students offered her differing points of view, she clearly was growing tired of the argument and turned to me, as did the students. The teacher asked me for my opinion, at which time I told her (and the class) that I could not imagine teaching the novel without addressing issues of culture, race, class, gender, and power. Another audible sound of agreement rose from the students, but this time there were also smiles and heads nodding in agreement and approval.

I was away from campus one week giving a presentation at national conference, when, in the words of several students, the second "breakpoint" occurred. The night before class a heavy snow had blanketed the area and for 10 minutes many of my students took full advantage of the snow. Like school children during recess, they ran outside rolled down the hill, made snow angles and had one of the "best snowball fights on record."

DISCUSSION

My reflective notes and student writings were helpful in recalling the experiences of the class, but the videotapes were invaluable in capturing the classroom interactions. Although I recorded my reflective notes following each day of the course, I was surprised to read them later and compare them to the videotape. I learned that I was instantly making judgments, the judgments I thought I was working so hard to resist making, about my students and the course. The reflective notes, however, were helpful in revealing to me how I was understanding my experiences as they occurred. Now, several years later and after careful review, I find that the videotapes, my reflective notes, and the student writings together make for a rich source of data about the process. There are many lessons I have learned from this reflection on my teaching. I have listed some of them below.

I consciously know that I am *subconsciously* forming opinions about students from the moment I meet them. Learning to suspend my first impressions, as much as is humanly possible, is beneficial. Working at not allowing early opinions to dominate my thinking allows me time to understand how each person's life is multilayered and complex both inside and outside of my classroom. The students arrive in my course complete with a history and experiences that have helped to form the person I meet. I do not wish to change them into critical pedagogues, but I do want to expose them to, and teach them about different perspectives that people hold. Their experiences in my class also will help to shape who they are and how they see themselves as literacy educators. For example, Martin was quite the intellectual, incredibly knowledgeable about Marxist theory for an undergraduate, and an effective well-prepared classroom presenter; he will carry this knowledge and these skills into his classroom. The students in the course were growing and evolving not just into members of our classroom community, but into members of society.

The students were observing me nearly as closely as I was observing them. They were waiting for "signs" of approval of disapproval whether verbal or nonverbal to clue them in on how to act, respond, interact with each other and with me. The dynamics of the course, from my conception of it to the last day, was a journey of self-discovery.

I think scholar, playwrite, and actress, Anna Deavere Smith (1993) best captures the process and dynamics of our classroom as a community that ". . . lives not in what has been fully articulated, but in what is in the process of being articulated, not in the smooth-sounding words, but in the very moment that the smooth-sounding words fail us. It is alive right now. We might not like what we see, but in order to change it, we have to see it clearly" (Smith, 1993, p. xli).

Learning when and how to respond to students is important. Although I was not always successful, I understood how important it was to be sensitive to non-Christian and sexual preference points of view. These are an area that I need to acquire greater understanding of and strategies for teaching. I also have learned that taking an authoritative voice and stance in a course framed on critical literacy theory and pedagogy is sometimes necessary for the greater good of the course and participants. My personal view of myself as a "warm demander" (Vasquez, 1998), was something very foreign to most of my students. They did not expect me to take an authoritarian stance in my own classroom. Perhaps I will make a more concerted effort in the future to let students know sooner. I believe that classroom control, even in a university classroom, is important.

Another important lesson that I have learned is that monitoring of student groups is essential. It is not acceptable to assume that university students can self-monitor their behavior in small-group sessions. In addition, small group work should vary often, these are adjustments I believe I made during the semester. I formed groups by placing people with strong personalities in one group (i.e., creating couplets that put Martin and Jerry with older women who are graduate students); placing all the people of color (at least those who have identified themselves as such) in one group; and arranging groups by gender. The people of color group worked well, but not as successfully as some of the other groupings. The gender groups were very successful as many of the women commented in their journals how they really appreciated being in a group with all women and not feeling as if they had to compete for airspace (voice) with males.

I also learned that the private conversations I have with students, even sidebar conversations held before, during, or after class, are often understood by students as personal confidences that they are sharing with me. While I may understand their comments differently, I must respect the fact that for some students sharing anything with a professor is risk-taking. In addition, I am learning that students, even college students, use language differently in their worlds. Thus, I must understand how they are using language in their world and attempt to hear the subtext of their speech. My new rule of thumb is to ask permission to share, anonymously, any portion of a private conversation I have with a student. This acknowledgment has led me to better understand that one of my unstated goals has been helping students, through dialog, to build trust with one another.

I have learned a great deal about myself as a teacher and as a researcher in writing this chapter. I have found the words of Grumet (1991) to be quite profound as she observed, "we are, at least partially, constituted by the stories we tell others and to ourselves about experience" (p. 69). The stories of our lives are at best temporal representations (Neumann & Peterson, 1998) of how we view our lives, past and present, and for some, into the future. As we tell, retell, live and relive our stories we are, in part, shaped and reshaped by them. Casey (1995) also writes that "autobiographical reflection is understood not just as an individual exercise but as a process that always takes place within a social context. Both individual and narrative are situated within a network of social relationships" (p. 220). Welcome to my world.

I am still in touch with most of my former students through E-mail, letters, and phone calls. I have been informed of, and invited to, most of their life changing events—graduations, special honor ceremonies, weddings, and the births of their children. The memory of the experience of this class replays like a favorite song in my heart.

NOTES

1. Jacqueline Jordan Irvine and James W. Fraser (1998) cite James Vasquez's notion of a "warm demander" as "African American and other teachers of color . . . who provide a tough-minded, no-nonsense, structured, and disciplined classroom environment for kids whom society has psychologically and physically abandoned. Strongly identifying with their students and determined to give them a future, these teachers believe that culturally diverse children not only can learn but must learn" (p. 1).

2. Just in case you are wondering what has happened to the four students, here's what I know: Sharrie is a graduate student working on her Master's degree and considering enrolling in the doctoral program at a research university; Martin is in Washington, DC, working with a political group; Emily is teaching at an alternative boarding school on the East Coast; and Jerry is teaching in a progressive middle school in the Southwest.

REFERENCES

Casey, K. (1995). The new narrative research in education. In M. Apple (Ed.), *Review of research in education* (Vol. 21, pp. 211–253). Washington, DC: American Educational Research Association.

Clandinin, D.J., & Connelly, M. (1990).

Clandinin, D. J., & Connelly, M. (1994). Personal experience methods. In N. Denzin & Y. Lincoln, (Eds.) *Handbook of qualitative research* (pp. 413–427). Thousand Oaks, CA: Sage Publications.

Garner, J. (1994). *Politically correct bedtime stories.* New York: Simon & Schuster.

Grumet, M. (1991). The politics of personal knowledge. In C. Witherell & N. Noddings (Eds.), *Stories lives tell: Narrative and dialogue in education* (pp. 67–77). New York: Teachers College Press.

Hesse, H. (1982). *Siddhartha.* New York: Bantam Books (original work published in 1953).

Irvine, J., & Fraser, J. (1998). "Warm demanders." *Education Week* (http://www.edweek.org/ew/vol-17/35Irvine).

Neumann, A., & Peterson, P. (Eds.). *Learning from our lives: Women, research, and autobiography in education.* New York: Teachers College Press.

Salisbury, G. (1995). *Under the blood red sun.* Yearling Books.

Schlessinger, A. (1993). *The disuniting of America.* New York: W. W. Norton.

Smith, A. (1993). *Fires in the mirror.* New York: Anchor Books.

The Popular Memory Group. (1982). Popular memory: Theory, politics, method. In R. Johnson, G. McLennan, B. Schwartz, & D. Sutton (Eds.), *Making histories* (pp. 205–252). London: Hutchison.

Willis, A., & Meacham, S. (1996). Complexities and challenges of teacher educators: Teaching preservice multicultural education courses. *Journal for the Assembly on Expanded Perspectives on Learning,* 40–49.

PART IV

STRATEGIES FOR
CONNECTING WITH
MINORITY PERSPECTIVES

CHAPTER 11

ENGLISH LANGUAGE LEARNERS' READING

New Age Issues

Jill Fitzgerald

Abstract: Pivotal and controversial issues are portrayed about U.S. English language learners' English reading and reading instruction. These include: Is a special theory necessary to explain English language learners' reading processes? Are English language learners' reading processes different at different developmental stages? *Must* native language reading precede learning to read in English? *Must* English orality precede English literacy? Are special reading instruction methods *necessary* for English language learners? Research and theory are examined for directions in relation to each of the critical issues.

INTRODUCTION

There is no question about the multicultural and pluralist nature of U.S. society. Moreover, statistics on English language learners in U.S. schools signify that we indeed are living in a new age with a new diversity (Garcia, 1998). Most recent available data indicate that more than three million English language learners were enrolled in schools during the 1994–95 school year (Garcia, 1998). Since 1990–91, increases in the number of English language learners averaged 8% annually (Garcia, 1998). It is also well known that there are pockets of very large numbers of English language learners in U.S. schools. For example, approximately 40% of the nation's English language learners are enrolled in California schools and 15% in Texan schools (Garcia, 1998). However, nearly all states in the nation report increasing proportions of English language learners. In the Midwest, approximately 27% of schools report English language learner presence, whereas 44% do in the South, 72% in the West, and 52% in the Northeast (Garcia, 1998).

Moreover, in general, the educational achievement, including reading achievement, of English language learners has not kept pace with that of native English-speaking Anglos. For example, among Latinos, statistics from a few years ago showed a 40% high school dropout rate, a 35% grade retention rate, and a two- to four-grade-level achievement gap (Garcia, 1992). In some respects, aspects of achievement figures are not surprising given that research suggests that learning English can involve several years and much effort. On average, it may take about two years to learn conversational English at a level comparable to native English speakers (e.g., Cummins, 1981), and up to eight years may be needed for learning more formal or academic language, including learning to read in English (Collier, 1987, 1989; Collier & Thomas, 1989; Cummins, 1981; Krashen & Biber, 1988).

New diversity offers a bountiful array of opportunities for educators and schools to change and grow. Wrapped within these opportunities are crevices of controversy about English language learners' reading and reading instruction. The day-to-day instructional decisions related to these controversial issues are critical to English language learners' reading development. Moreover, because reading is so crucial to students' learning in content areas, as well as to social and general school success, the daily decisions teachers make about reading instruction will ultimately affect many other facets of students' lives.

In this chapter, I portray several pivotal and controversial issues surrounding English language learners' English reading and reading instruction. My focus is on students in the United States, though most, if not all, of the issues I discuss are relevant to second language learners in other parts of the world. I use the term "English language learner" to refer to individuals living in the United States who: (a) were not born in the United States; (b) have native languages other than English; (c) come from environments where English is not dominant, or (d) are Native American or Alaskan natives from environments where languages other than English impact their English proficiency levels (cf. U.S. federal government definition of "limited English proficient" individuals, Public Law 100-297 [1988]). The term "English language learner" is used as a special case of the more general term language minority learner which refers to an individual, from a home "where a language other than English is actively used, who therefore ha[s] had an opportunity to develop some level of proficiency in a language other than English. A language minority student may be of limited English proficiency, bilingual, or essentially monolingual in English" (August & Hakuta, 1997, p. 16). Bilingual learner refers to "an individual with a language background other than English who has developed proficiency in his or her primary language and enough proficiency in English not to be disadvantaged in an English-only school environment" (August & Hakuta, 1997, p. 16).

Though my focus in this chapter is on students who are learning English as a new language, I want to be very clear that I do not in any way advocate an "English only" position. The extent to which English language learners should maintain and develop their native language is in itself a highly politicized issue. I focus on learning English in part because *all* students are developing English proficiencies and in part because in my own career, I have delved more deeply into the English learner reading research than into the broader research on bilingual reading. My efforts to focus on learning English reading should not be construed, however, to mean that I do not advocate bilingualism. To the contrary, research clearly suggests that many benefits may accrue from the development and maintenance of bilingualism, and some long term benefits of bilingual education might outweigh those gained from English only approaches (Hakuta, 1986; Hakuta & Gould, 1987; Snow, 1987; Wong Fillmore & Valadez, 1986).

A contextual frame can illuminate some of the diverse positions on aspects of English language learners' reading. My own background of experience and higher education originate in teaching reading and studying, researching, and learning about reading, all within the mainstream, so to speak. More recently, for about a decade now, I have studied, learned about, and done research on second language reading, focusing on English language learners in particular. I also have recent experience in teaching reading with English language learners. In 1995–1996, I requested and received a reassignment from my university professor position of 18 years to teach as a full time first grade teacher. Over half of the children in my class were Hispanic. (When referring to the children in my class, I use the term Hispanic, rather than Latino, because my children's parents told me they preferred this term.) So my own positions in the following controversies originate deeply within my understanding of reading theory and research done in the mainstream.

There is a myriad of specialized interests in the education arena of second language learning. In general, the teachers' histories hark back, not so much to reading research and theory, but to oral linguistic traditions. Many teachers in the United States have a foreign language interest and are mainly interested in helping native English speakers learn a second language. Other educators who have an English as a second language interest may also study bilingual education, applied linguistics, English for special purposes, and/or university college English. Societies that consider second language learning their primary or secondary focus include the National Association for Bilingual Education, Teachers of English to Speakers of Other Languages, and American Association for Applied Linguistics, to name just three.

U.S. "programs" or "methods" designed specifically for helping English language learners began in university Linguistics departments for college students. Gradually such programs were shared by English departments and, much later, by Education departments and public schools (q.v. Crawford, 1989; Ebel, 1980; Fitzgerald, 1993b; Ramirez, 1994). For many years, this oral linguistic tradition has permeated educators' thinking (Weber, 1991), though in most recent years, gradually, the importance of reading and writing in a second language has achieved more visibility.

CONTROVERSIAL ISSUES

Is a Special Theory Necessary to Explain English Language Learners' Reading Processes?

Whether there is a need for a theory of reading specific to English language learners or second language learners in general is a highly controversial issue. Some scholars have detailed why some pre-existing reading theories are particularly applicable to second language learners (e.g., see Carrell, Devine, & Eskey, 1988, on interactive models of reading for second language learners). Also, some have pointed to the theoretical similarities between second language reading and first language reading. For example, Heath's (1986) notion of transferable generic literacies and Krashen's (1984, 1988) reading hypothesis both assume that second language literacy uses the same basic processes as first language literacy (q.v. Hedgcock & Atkinson, 1993). Others believe that preexisting theories of reading do not sufficiently address specific aspects of second language reading, or that second language reading is actually "a different phenomenon" from first language reading (Bernhardt, 1991, p. 226). Consequently, individuals in the latter group believe that a reading theory specific to second language readers is needed.

One Way to Examine the Question
There are data from research on English language learner reading which can illuminate this issue. Most of the research has been couched in four preexisting theories, models, or views of reading which were originally developed for readers in general and presumably for individuals reading in their native languages: (a) a psycholinguistic view of reading (Goodman, 1970); (b) schema theory (Rumelhart, 1980; (c) an interactive view of reading (Rumelhart, 1985); and (d) views of metacognition in reading (Brown, 1980). In some studies, investigators were specifically "testing" the applicability of aspects of a preexisting theory, model, or view in English language learner situations. Even when researchers were not specifically testing a preexisting view, it is possible, in a broad sense to assess the extent

to which findings from such studies, taken collectively, are good fits to the preexisting outlooks used to frame the investigations.

Weight of Evidence

Findings from a broad array of studies of English language learners' cognitive reading processes (for an in-depth review see Fitzgerald, 1995a) support the contention that the cognitive reading processes of English language learners are *substantively* the same as those of native English speakers, at least with regard to the four categories of reading processes which have mainly been used in the research. Minimally, the processes are more alike than they are different. However, while the same basic processes may be used, a few facets of those processes may be used less or may operate more slowly for English language learners than for native English readers (Fitzgerald, 1995a).

At least two forms of evidence support the contention of essential sameness. First, a comprehensive review of studies done with English language learners in the United States pointed to an image of the cognitive reading processes of English language learners which was highly similar to portraits of the cognitive processes of native English readers found in the more general literature on reading (Fitzgerald, 1995a).

Here is a brief description of a partial image of U.S. English language learners' cognitive reading process that emerges from the research. There was substantial individual variability in vocabulary knowledge and psycholinguistic strategy use. However, on the whole, as readers, English language learners: (a) recognized cognate vocabulary well; (b) monitored comprehension and used metacognitive strategies; (c) used schemata and prior knowledge to assist comprehension and recall, and (d) were affected differently by different types of text structures (Fitzgerald, 1995a).

Further, as compared to less proficient readers, more proficient English language learners: (a) made better use of vocabulary knowledge; (b) used a greater variety of metacognitive strategies and used certain strategies more often; (c) took more action to solve miscomprehension and checked solutions to problems more frequently; (d) used psycholinguistic strategies that were more meaning oriented; (e) used more schema knowledge; and (f) made better and/or more inferences (Fitzgerald, 1995b).

Second, results of studies in which U.S. English language learners were compared as readers to native English readers indicated that the two groups' cognitive processes were substantively more alike than different (Fitzgerald, 1995a). They used similar metacognitive techniques and monitored comprehension during reading, and they identified antecedents in text equally well (Fitzgerald, 1995a). Collectively, these two forms of evidence suggest a reasonably good fit to the preexisting native language reading theories, models, and views in which the studies tended to be grounded.

On the other hand, evidence for the specialness of English language learners' reading processes appears to reside mainly in the amount of use and the amount of time to use selected processes (Fitzgerald, 1995a). Where differences emerged, they tended to suggest that selected facets of cognitive processes may be used less or more slowly by English language learners. On the whole, they used fewer metacognitive strategies and favored some different ones, verbalized metacognitive strategies less, recalled subordinate ideas less well, monitored their comprehension more slowly, and read more slowly (Fitzgerald, 1995a). Also, less proficient English language learners did less acoustic scanning and greater focus on function words than did others, and native language background appeared to be related to preferred text structures (Fitzgerald, 1995a).

So, in all, it appears that, with minor accommodations to account for differences in amount and amount of time to use selected processes, there is a modicum of support for the belief that pre-existing theories, models, and views of reading developed for native English speakers can equally explain the cognitive reading processes of English language learners. We should keep in mind, however, that this conclusion is reached after reviewing reading research done only with individuals in the United States, with a focus on English language learners. It is possible that quite different results could occur for other second language speakers or in other situations. Also, the central features of research interest have been cognitive processes. Consequently, affective and/or social variables and their interplay in English language learners' reading are not addressed in this summary. Research on these constructs might also lead to a need for additional modification of preexisting views, or even to abandonment.

Are English Language Learners' Reading Processes Different at Different Developmental Stages?

I know of no studies that have directly investigated the issue of whether English language learners' reading processes are different at different developmental stages. Consequently, there is no sure response to this issue. Though this is a very important issue for educators to consider, it is one that is often overlooked (q.v. Fitzgerald & Cummins, in press). One way to approach this topic is to consider what is known about the development of reading processes for individuals learning to read in their native language. We can then consider how this body of knowledge might relate to English language learners' reading development (q.v. August & Hakuta, 1997).

Research on native speakers' reading development clearly points to support for a stage model of reading development. Chall's (1983) landmark description of stages of development is an example. In brief, while code breaking and meaning creating are both important at all stages, her descriptions portray the major work of beginning reading as "getting words," while comprehension processes play an increasing role as development continues. Adams' (1990) renowned work on beginning reading further elaborates Chall's description of early reading and emphasizes the critical role of the development of phonological awareness in the very early phases of emergent literacy.

Learning to read is a continually evolving process, with different challenges preeminent at different points. If we assume that a similar developmental model would map onto English language learners' reading, what implications would arise? The main implication is that an already complex process is made more complex because the following variables would likely play mediating roles in the learners' reading development: Age of reader, reading ability in native language, and rhetorical and linguistic comparability between native language and English. In essence, both the focal reading skills and rate of developmental progress might vary according to the specific background of the English language learner. Accounting for the myriad of possible combinations may be impossible. There is some limited research which collectively hints at such developmentally related complexity. Specifically, the relationship between English language learner reading proficiency and English language learner oral proficiency may be stronger at higher grade levels (Carrell, 1991; Lara, 1991; Saville-Troike, 1984; Tragar & Wong, 1984).

For example, a 6-year-old who speaks no English and has not begun to learn to read in his native language might progress through emergent English reading phases in ways akin to native English speakers. There is some limited evidence to support this belief for both phases of learning and rate of learning (Fitzgerald & Noblit, 1999). But a 12-year-old who speaks no English, has never attended school in her native country, and has not begun to learn to read her native language is presented with a more complicated challenge in learning to read English in her fifth grade classroom. To learn alongside her peers, must she travel through each of the developmental stages her peers have already covered? If so, under what conditions might she travel quickly?

In short, we can make some inferences about English language learners' reading development from native English developmental reading theories, and we can acknowledge the complexities involved. Clearly, we know that when we consider an individual's instructional environment, we must think about her developmental reading level in both English and her native language, as well several other factors. However, to my knowledge, there are no existing comprehensive theories of reading development for English language learners. More research on developmental issues would help provide data to inform the need for such a theory. Until very recently, research with preschool through second grade level students has been largely neglected. This is probably due to prior oral primacy beliefs. That is, perhaps researchers have tended to think that young English language learners cannot or should not acquire English literacy, and therefore have not chosen to study children at these ages.

Must Native Language Reading Precede Learning to Read in English?

Many educators believe that English language learners must learn to read in their native language before, or while, they are learning to read in English. Others believe that native language reading is not essential to learning to read in English. The role and timing of native language reading and English reading for English language learners' English reading achievement has been one of the most controversial issues of all. At least two reasons for the highly charged debates stand out. One is that programs that promote either preceding or simultaneous native language reading instruction may be more costly than others. For example, such programs require bilingual teachers and additional reading materials in native languages.

A second reason is that there are underlying sociopolitical attachments to different program configurations. The sociopolitical factors that are associated with language learning are complicated and deep seated. Only a few of these factors will be mentioned here. For instance, many believe that schools should only nurture English. Any form of native language instruction may be considered not only unnecessary, but "un-American." An opposing view is that bilingualism is a national resource and that schools have an abiding responsibility to help individuals to maintain and develop their native languages. Some also consider it important for both national and global citizenship that native English speakers learn another language as well. Further, native language maintenance is often viewed as a means of retaining cultural roots and heritage. My own outlook coincides with these latter positions.

If we focus just on English reading achievement (as opposed to reading achievement in English *and* the native language), there are several avenues of reasoning which lead to the belief that English reading does not necessarily need to be delayed until some optimal level of native language reading proficiency is developed. Note that this line of reasoning does not preclude the possibility that benefits may be accrued from bilingual reading programs or transitional bilingual programs which begin with native language reading. Rather, it addresses the issue of the *necessity* of learning to read in native language first.

First, in general *research* on the role and timing of native language reading and English reading *for English reading achievement* of students learning English in the United States have produced mixed results. That is, findings do not clearly support one form of program over another. A comprehensive review of the research in this area may be found in Fitzgerald (1995b). Three kinds of studies have addressed these issues in the United States.

One was program evaluations. While many program evaluations have been conducted, notably few (only four) of them met criteria for rigor in design in the prior review. A second kind was direct investigations of whether to delay English reading until after some level of native language reading proficiency was achieved. Again, these studies were few in number. Only two were located in the 1995b review. In a third category of four studies, researchers addressed the effects of free reading in Spanish as a supplement or substitute for English reading instruction.

Results of the earlier review suggested that, on the whole, for English reading, primary grade students in submersion or immersion programs (where they received no native language instruction) fared as well as, or better than, students in transitional bilingual education programs, where reading was initially taught in both the native language and English. The effect on English reading achievement of delaying English reading in favor of Spanish reading was not clear either. Finally, neither supplementing nor supplanting English reading instruction with free reading in Spanish helped English reading.

Second, we can examine the data relating to the theoretical assumptions of what Cummins (Fitzgerald & Cummins, in press) calls "linguistic mismatch." Linguistic mismatch refers to the belief that students cannot learn through a language they do not understand. An important prediction arising from the linguistic mismatch hypothesis is that when English language learners are placed in immersion or submersion situations academic retardation will result. However, data do not clearly support this prediction. For example, Canadian research on French immersion programs for majority language students has contradicted this hypothesis for more than 30 years (Fitzgerald & Cummins, in press). In these programs, students from English language home backgrounds are immersed in a completely or predominantly French language during the initial grades. English language arts are introduced usually in second grade. By fourth grade, instruction is equally divided between French and English. The ultimate goal is bilingualism and biliteracy. The important point here, is that, on average, beginning reading in the new language does not adversely affect either learning to read English or academic learning in the new language (Fitzgerald & Cummins, in press).

Third, several theories or models predict that certain cognitive abilities can be developed through learning in either language, and these abilities will transfer to the other language. Three examples of such theories or models are the Common Underlying Proficiency (CUP) model of how two languages are related (Cummins, 1981), the interdependence hypothesis (Cummins, 1979), and transferable generic literacies (Heath, 1986). At a basic level, each theory or model holds that a common set of proficiencies underlies both the first and second languages. What is learned in one language will transfer to another. Also, using a skill or strategy in one language is considered to be pretty much the same process as in another. Ample research supports these theories and models (for example, see Hedgcock & Atkinson, 1993).

Many individuals have interpreted such theories to support the importance of learning to read in one's native language, suggesting that the native language reading skills will then transfer to the new language reading. However, the theories themselves and the supporting data *additionally* suggest that the transferability of skills is *bidirectional.* That is, it is equally possible that certain cognitive abilities learned through reading instruction *in a new language* will transfer to reading in the native language (Fitzgerald & Cummins, in press). The implication for practice is that various sorts of programs, with different configurations of when the new language is used and for how long, might help students to learn English reading.

In sum, for English language learners' English reading achievement, there is ample theory and evidence to suggest that native language reading development is not a *prerequisite* to learning to read in English.

Must English Orality Precede English Literacy?

Some educators have argued that, for English language learners, some optimal level of English orality is a prerequisite to learning to read in English (e.g., Krashen, 1985; Wong Fillmore & Valadez, 1986). Indeed, a recent influential report on preventing reading difficulties (Snow, Burns, & Griffin, 1998) and an International Reading Association resolution (1998) suggest that, if native language reading instruction does not precede or coincide with English reading instruction, then English reading instruction should be delayed until a modicum of oral English proficiency is achieved.

This stance arises largely from two theoretical understandings of the relationship between oral and literate language. In one version, the relationship is directional. Second language reading is dependent upon second language oral proficiency (q.v. Clarke & Silberstein, 1977). In the second, not only is the relationship directional, but a "threshold of linguistic competence" is necessary for successful second language reading (Clarke, 1980; Cummins, 1979).

At the same time, others have argued that English oral proficiency is not a prerequisite to English reading development (e.g., Anderson & Roit, 1996; Fitzgerald, 1993a; Gersten, 1996), even for students with learning disabilities (Klingner & Vaughn, 1996).

Again, there are several lines of reasoning which lead to the belief that English orality does not *necessarily* need to precede English reading development. In fact, it is possible that English reading development can assist English oral development and also that English language learners can perform at more advanced English reading levels than oral English levels.

First, we might ask, what are the correlational relationships between English language learner reading proficiency and English oral proficiency? An in-depth review of such correlational studies done in the United States with kindergartners through adults revealed quite mixed results (Fitzgerald, 1995a). It was not possible to make a simple statement about the relationship between the two variables. The relationship may have varied according to age and/or grade level, being stronger at higher grades, as well as according to native language background. More important, the studies provided virtually no information about the causal direction of the relationship. Consequently, these correlational studies do not provide support either for the position that orality must precede literacy or vice versa. Either position remains viable.

Second, findings from research on emergent literacy done with native English-speaking children overwhelmingly support the notion that orality and literacy develop concomitantly. Formerly, minimal listening and speaking capacities were considered prerequisites to learning to read and write, but considerable research now convincingly points to the interrelated development of orality and literacy (e.g., Teale & Sulzby, 1986). Also, there is evidence that this tenet is supported with English language learners learning in English (Araujo, 1997; Edelsky, 1986; Fitzgerald & Noblit, 1999, in press; Hudelson, 1984; Rigg, 1991; Weber & Longhi, 1996). Additionally, there is evidence that second language learners' oral development can be enhanced through second language reading instruction (e.g., Elley, 1981; Elley & Mangubhai, 1983) and that some children's English reading may outpace their English orality in the beginning stages (Fitzgerald & Noblit, 1999, in press).

Third, another area of research on emergent literacy has important implications for English language learners' reading. Work with native English-speaking children has clearly documented the centrality of phonological awareness in beginning reading (e.g., Adams, 1990; Tumner & Nesdale, 1985). Phonological awareness refers to the ability to hear separate words, chunks within words, and individual phonemes within words. While phonological awareness is critical to learning to read words, research has also shown that it may develop alongside word recognition skills, that is, concomitantly. Therefore, when reading instruction is coupled with instruction that focuses on the development of phonological awareness, success rates for reading development are "dramatic" (Adams, 1990, p. 329).

The notion of concomitant development of phonological awareness and learning about print is extremely important when considering English language learners. Since phonological awareness is a central feature of second language learning, particularly in the early phases of second language learning, we might predict that involving the learner in teacher- and peer-supported reading activities which draw attention to phonological features can support aural/oral development as well.

In short, correlational studies do not support the position that English orality *must* precede English reading. (It should be noted that they also do not support the position that English orality and literacy must develop simultaneously. Rather, findings are mixed, and directionality of relationships has not been investigated.) However, findings from research with young native English speakers clearly document the interrelated development of orality and literacy and that phonological awareness plays a critical role in early reading. These findings lead boldly and clearly to belief that learning to read in English can occur simultaneously with English language learners' oral/aural English development. Some research supports this belief.

Are Special Reading Instruction Methods *Necessary* for English Language Learners?

A comprehensive review of research on English reading instruction for English language learners in the United States revealed very little evidence to support the need for a "special" vision of English language learner reading instruction (Fitzgerald, 1995b). Likewise, as already noted, findings from another review of U.S. research on English language learners' cognitive reading processes suggested a relatively good fit to preexisting reading theories and views widely thought to describe native language readers (Fitzgerald, 1995a).

Especially interesting was a set of findings from direct instruction studies with English language learners which tended to replicate earlier research paradigms done with subjects who were not English language learners—studies on expository text structure, building background knowledge, and metacognitive/strategy training. On the whole, findings from these studies were highly consistent with findings generally reported for native English speakers.

Finally, some very recent instructional studies with emergent English language learners support the contention that, with certain modifications which attend to selected special needs, methods considered sound for native English speaking beginning readers can work equally well with English language learners (Araujo, 1997; Fitzgerald & Noblit, 1999, in press).

The reviews did suggest that teachers should be especially aware of some cognitive processing areas that might deserve extra consideration when teaching English language learners. Some English language learners' slower reading and diminished response in reading situations suggest mainly that teachers might display even more than normal patience with English language learners. They might also take extra care when wording questions and making comments in order to maximize the opportunity for activation of thought processes. Additionally, teachers might even more attention to readers' development of topic knowledge and vocabulary meanings for specific reading selections when working with English language learners.

SUMMARY

New diversity brings with it enormous opportunities for a future filled with multivoiced and multiliterate citizenry. As we stand on the threshold of that multicultural and pluralist future we now argue and debate several pivotal issues related to English language learners' English reading and reading instruction. In this chapter, I have suggested that research and theory provide directions, if not answers, to these critical issues: (a) With minor accommodations for differences in amount and amount of time to use selected cognitive reading process, there is support for the belief that preexisting theories, models, and views of reading developed for native English speakers can explain the cognitive reading processes of U.S. English language learners. (b) Although I know of no research on English language learners' reading development as it occurs across years, it is possible to infer the following from native English developmental reading theories. In particular, for native English speakers, different reading skills and abilities are preeminent at different levels of reading achievement. This is likely to be true for English language learners as well. However, English language learners present additional developmental complexities related to age, reading ability in native language, and rhetorical and linguistic comparability between native language and English. (c) There is ample theory and evidence to suggest that native language reading development is not a *prerequisite* to learning to read in English. (d) English orality is not a *prerequisite* to English reading development. Further, English reading development can assist English oral development, and it is possible that some children's English reading may outpace their oral English development, at least in beginning stages. (e) There is little evidence to support the need for a "special" vision of English reading instruction for English language learners. In general, with attention to minor modifications for certain English language learner needs (such as increased emphasis on vocabulary meanings and developing background knowledge for specific reading material), reading methods considered sound for native English-speaking students can also be helpful with English language learners.

While bilingualism and bilingual education are clearly beneficial, many school situations exist in the United States where students are not afforded the opportunity to learn in their native language. The conclusions reached in this chapter might be especially helpful for educators and students in classrooms where only English is the language of instruction. The conclusions addressed here suggest that, at least for English reading, teachers already hold many keys to the English language learner's success. Much of what they have previously learned about reading theories and processes and about the teaching of reading with native English speakers can also be used with English language learners.

At the same time, educators should modify their instruction to fit the individual needs of their students, and we can all benefit from further learning about many facets of English language learners' lives and schooling. Exemplary programs for success embody multipronged efforts with many goals, including: developing students' English orality and literacy; assisting acculturation by helping various ethnic communities to understand, know, and respect one another; developing students' academic content learning in a wide array of areas; reaching out to parents and families and respecting their knowledge, skills, abilities as well as inviting and appreciating their contributions in children's learning; and genuinely and deeply valuing all students' heritage and culture. In an age of new diversity, educators will learn more and more in all of these areas.

REFERENCES

Adams, M.J. (1990). *Beginning to read: Thinking and learning about print.* Cambridge, MA: MIT Press.

Anderson, V., & Roit, M. (1996). Linking reading comprehension instruction to language development for language minority students. *Elementary School Journal, 96,* 295–310.

Araujo, L. (1997, December). *Making the transition to English literacy.* Paper presented at the annual meeting of the National Reading Conference, Scottsdale, AZ.

August, D., & Hakuta, K. (Eds.). (1997). *Improving schooling for language-minority children: A research agenda.* Washington, DC: National Academy Press.

Bernhardt, E.B. (1991). *Reading development in a second language: Theoretical, empirical, and classroom perspectives.* Norwood, NJ: Ablex.

Brown, A. (1980). Metacognitive development and reading. In R.J. Spiro, B.C. Bruce, & W.F. Brewer (Eds.), *Theoretical issues in reading comprehension: Perspectives from cognitive psychology, linguistics, artificial intelligence, and education* (pp. 453–481). Hillsdale, NJ: Erlbaum.

Carrell, P.L. (1991). Second language reading: Reading ability or language proficiency? *Applied Linguistics, 12,* 159–179.

Carrell, P.L., Devine, J., & Eskey, D. E. (1988). *Interactive approaches to second language reading.* New York: Cambridge University Press.

Chall, J.S. (1983). *Stages of reading development.* New York: McGraw-Hill.

Clarke, M.A. (1980). The short circuit hypothesis of ESL reading—or when language competence interferes with reading performance. *Modern Language Journal, 64,* 203–209.

Clarke, M.A., & Silberstein, S. (1977). Towards a realization of psycholinguistic principles in the ESL classroom. *Language Learning, 27,* 135–154.

Collier, V.P. (1987). Age and rte of acquisition of second language for academic purposes. *TESOL Quarterly, 21,* 617–641.

Collier, V.P. (1989). How long? A synthesis of research on academic achievement in a second language. *TESOL Quarterly, 23,* 509–531.

Collier, V.P., & Thomas, W.P. (1989). How quickly can immigrants become proficient in school English? *Journal of Educational Issues of Language Minority Students, 5,* 26–38.

Crawford, J. (1989). *Bilingual education: History, politics, theory and practice.* Trenton, NJ: Crane.

Cummins, J. (1979). Linguistic interdependence and the educational development of bilingual children. *Review of Educational Research, 49,* 222–251.

Cummins, J. (1981). Four misconceptions about language proficiency in bilingual education. *NABE Journal, 5*(3), 31–45.

Ebel, C. (1980). An update: Teaching reading to students of English as a second language. *Reading Teacher, 33,* 403–407.

Edelsky, C. (1986). *Writing in a bilingual program: Habia una vez.* Norwood, NJ: Ablex.

Elley, W.B. (1981). A comparison of content-interest and structuralist reading programs in Niue primary schools. *New Zealand Journal of Educational Studies, 15,* 39–53.

Elley, W.B., & Mangubhai, F. (1983). The impact of reading on second language learning. *Reading Research Quarterly, 19,* 53–67.

Fitzgerald, J. (1993a). Literacy and students who are learning English as a second language. *The Reading Teacher, 46,* 638–647.

Fitzgerald, J. (1993b). Views on bilingualism in the United States: A selective historical review. *Bilingual Research Journal, 17,* 35–56.

Fitzgerald, J. (1995a). English-as-a-second-language learners' cognitive reading processes: A review of research in the United States. *Review of Educational Research, 65,* 145–190.

Fitzgerald, J. (1995b). English-as-a-second-language reading instruction in the United States: A research review. *Journal of Reading Behavior, 27,* 115–152.

Fitzgerald, J., & Cummins, J. (in press). Bridging disciplines to critique a national research agenda for language-minority children's schooling. *Reading Research Quarterly.*

Fitzgerald, J., & Noblit, G. (1999). About hopes, aspirations, and uncertainty: First-grade English-language learners' emergent reading. *Journal of Literacy Research, 31,* 133–182.

Fitzgerald, J., & Noblit, G. (in press). Balance in the making: Learning to read in an ethnically diverse first-grade classroom. *Journal of Educational Psychology.*

Garcia, E. (1992). Linguistically and culturally diverse children: Effective instructional practices and related policy issues. In H.C. Waxman, J. Walker de Felix, J.W. Anderson, H.P. Baptiste, Jr. (Eds.), *Students at risk in at-risk schools: Improving environments for learning* (pp. 65–86). Newbury Park, CA: Corwin.

Garcia, E.E. (1998, March). *Multilingualism in US schools: From research to practice.* Paper presented at the California Reading and English Language Learner Forum, Sacramento.

Gersten, R. (1996). Literacy instruction for language-minority students: The transition years. *The Elementary School Journal, 96,* 228–244.

Goodman, K.S. (1970). Reading: A psycholinguistic guessing game. In H. Singer & R. Ruddell (Eds.), *Theoretical models and processes of reading* (pp. 259–271). Newark, DE: International Reading Association.

Hakuta, K. (1986). *Mirror of language: The debate on bilingualism.* New York: Basic Books.

Hakuta, K., & Gould, L.J. (1987). Synthesis of research on bilingual education. *Educational Leadership, 44,* 38–45.

Heath, S.B. (1986). Sociocultural contexts of language development. In *Beyond language: Social and cultural factors in schooling language minority students* (pp. 145–186). Los Angeles: California State University, Evaluation, Dissemination and Assessment Center.

Hedgcock, J., & Atkinson, D. (1993). Differing reading-writing relationships in L1 and L2 literacy development? *TESOL Quarterly, 27,* 329–333.

Hudelson, S. (1984). Can yu ret an rayt en ingles: Children become literate in English as a second language. *TESOL Quarterly, 18,* 221–238.

International Reading Association. (1998, May). *Resolution on initial literacy instruction in a first language.* (Available from the International Reading Association, 800 Barksdale Road, Newark, DE)

Klingner, J.K., & Vaughn, S. (1996). Reciprocal teaching of reading comprehension strategies for students with learning disabilities who use English as a second language. *The Elementary School Journal, 96,* 275–294.

Krashen, S.D. (1984). *Writing: Research, theory, and applications.* Oxford: Pergamon.

Krashen, S.D. (1985). *The input hypothesis: Issues and implications.* New York: Longman.

Krashen, S.D. (1988). Do we learn to red by reading? The relationship between free reading and reading ability. In D. Tannen (Ed.), *Linguistics in context: Connecting observation and understanding: Vol. 2. Advances in discourse processes* (pp. 269–298). Norwood, NJ: Ablex.

Krashen, S., & Biber, D. (1988). *On course: Bilingual education's success in California.* Sacramento: California Association for Bilingual Education.

Lara, S.M. (1991) Code switching and reading achievement of first-grade bilingual students. *Dissertation Abstracts International, 52* (01), 99A.

Ramirez, A.G. (1994). Literacy acquisition among second-language learners. In B.M. Ferdman, R.M. Weber, & A.G. Ramirez (Eds.), *Literacy across languages and cultures* (pp. 75–101). Albany: State University of New York Press.

Rigg, P. (1991). Whole language in TESOL. *TESOL Quarterly, 25,* 521–542.

Rumelhart, D.E. (1980). Schemata: The building blocks of cognition. In R.J. Spiro, B.C. Bruce, & W.F. Brewer (Eds.), *Theoretical issues in reading comprehension: Perspectives from cognitive psychology, linguistics, artificial intelligence, and education* (pp. 33–58). Hillsdale, NJ: Erlbaum.

Rumelhart, D.E. (1985). Toward an interactive model of reading. In H. Singer & R.B. Ruddell (Eds.), *Theoretical models and processes of reading* (3rd ed., pp. 722–750). Newark, DE: International Reading Association.

Saville-Troike, M. (1984). What really matters in second language learning for academic achievement? *TESOL Quarterly, 18,* 199–219.

Snow, C.E. (1987). Beyond conversation: Second language learners' acquisition of description and explanation. In J.P. Lantolf & A. Labarca (Eds.), *Research in second language learning: Focus on the classroom* (pp. 3–16). Norwood, NJ: Ablex.

Snow, C.E., Burns, S., & Griffin, P. (Eds.). (1998). *Preventing reading difficulties in young children.* Washington, DC: National Academy Press.

Teale, W., & Sulzby, E. (1986). Emergent literacy as a perspective for examining how young children become readers and writers. In W.H. Teale & E. Sulzby (Eds.), *Emergent literacy: Writing and reading* (pp. vii-xxv). Norwood, NJ: Ablex.

Tragar, B., & Wong, B.K. (184). The relationship between native and second language reading comprehension and second language oral ability. In C. Rivera (Ed.), *Placement procedures in bilingual education: Education and policy issues* (pp. 152–164). Clevedon: Multilingual Matters.

Tumner, W.E., & Nesdale, A.R. (1985). Phonemic segmentation skill and beginning reading. *Journal of Educational Psychology, 77,* 417–427.

Weber, R. (1991). Linguistic diversity and reading in American society. In R. Barr, M.L. Kamil, P.B. Mosenthal, & P.D. Pearson (Eds.), *Handbook of reading research* (Vol. 2, pp. 97–119). New York: Longman.

Weber, R.M., & Longhi, T. (1996, December). *Moving into ESL literacy: Three learning biographies.* Paper presented at the annual meeting of the National Reading Conference, Charleston.

Wong Fillmore, L., & Valadez, C. (1986). Teaching bilingual learners. In M.C. Wittrock (Ed.), *Handbook of research on teaching* (pp. 648–685). New York: Macmillan.

CHAPTER 12

HOME-SCHOOL COLLABORATION

Successful Models in the Hispanic Community

Flora V. Rodríguez-Brown

Abstract: Reports on the condition of education describe Hispanic children as the fastest growing ethnic group in public schools. Still, Hispanics suffer ethnic isolation in school (National Center for Educational Statistics, 1995). They also are more likely to attend schools where the academic environments do not lead to learning (Peng et al., 1995).

Research with Hispanic families indicates that parents are concerned about their children's education and need to find ways to understand and negotiate the American educational system (Delgado-Gaitan, 1992; Delgado-Gaitan & Trueba, 1991; Goldenberg & Gallimore, 1991). From her experience working with Hispanic parents during the last ten years, the author describes Hispanic parents' aspirations for increased parental involvement in their children's education which should become reality in the new millennium. This will help bridge home/school discontinuity problems that currently affect Hispanic children's achievement and their chances for school success.

Two parent involvement models are described as successful practices to involve parents in their children's education. One model is a family literacy program, Project FLAME, that collaborate with parents in learning how to share literacy with their children at home. The other is a "Funds of Knowledge" teacher/educational researcher collaboration in which parents allow teacher researchers to learn about their culture, home life, and knowledge through home visits. These visits serve to inform, and through reflection, transform the way teachers regard their students' home life. The teacher/researchers use their newly acquired knowledge to make the curriculum and their teaching more relevant to the children in the community where they teach.

INTRODUCTION

Findings from a report on the Condition of Education (National Center for Educational Statistics, 1995) reveal that Hispanic children are the fastest growing ethnic group in public schools. The report also shows that Hispanics in school often suffer ethnic isolation. At least 34% of the schools they attend are 90–100 percent minority, an increase of 11% from 1992 (National Center for Educational Statistics, 1995). In addition, Hispanic children are more likely than White children to grow up in poverty and have parents with lower levels of education (National Center for Educational Statistics, 1995, p. 132). They are also more likely to attend schools where the overall academic environment does not lead to learning (Peng et al., 1995). Although dropout rates for Hispanics are declining, their rates are still double those of non-Hispanics, and the trends show that this disparity is not related to recent immigration (Fraser, 1992).

Hispanics remain the most undereducated major segment of the U.S. population. According to the National Council of La Raza (1990), 43% the 19-year-old and older Hispanic population are not in school and do not have a high school diploma. Furthermore, in terms of illiteracy rate (defined as completion of less than five years of schooling), 12.2% of Hispanics 25 years or older were not literate in 1989, in comparison to 2% and 4% for the White and Black population respectively (National Council of La Raza, 1990).

According to Applebee, Langer, and Mullis (1987), "as a group, Hispanic students are well behind Anglo students by grade four, and the difference is not made up for those who attend college" (p. 22). As adults, Hispanics also display lower literacy proficiency as measured by the NALS (Kirch, Jungeblut, Jenkins, & Kilstad, 1993). These disturbing statistics should serve to raise awareness that something has to be done to address the problem. Low academic achievement is a complicated problem which requires broad-based solutions. It is doubtful that efforts either at school or at home would alone be enough to make a significant difference in the learning and school achievement of children who are at risk. According to recent studies, instruction that draws on children's social, cultural and linguistic strengths is successful (Moll & Greenberg, 1990; Serna & Hudelson, 1993). Unfortunately, instruction of low income, linguistic minority students often emphasize decontextualized skills and rote learning (Anyon, 1980; Delgado-Gaitan, 1991; Delgado-Gaitan & Trueba, 1991).

The sociocultural background of families is another factor which should be taken into consideration when addressing the needs of culturally and linguistically different children. Research with Hispanic families indicates that parents are highly concerned about their children's education and their school success. Nevertheless, parents are sometimes uncertain about how to negotiate the American educational system (Delgado-Gaitan, 1992; Delgado-Gaitan & Trueba, 1991; Goldenberg & Gallimore, 1991). According to Heath, 1987, differences in communication style, views of literacy and the difference of literacy interaction between the home and the school can ultimately limit literacy learning. Also, Hispanic parents' lack of fluency in English and low educational levels can result in feelings of inadequacy when they help their children with school work or have to communicate with the school (Rodríguez-Brown, 2001).

ADDRESSING THE NEEDS OF HISPANIC CHILDREN

In addressing the educational needs of Hispanic children it is necessary for the school and the home to work together. Parents should be partners with the schools and involve themselves in their children's learning in order to support higher achievement levels for their children (Epstein, 1990, 1991). Epstein (1991) describes six types of parent involvement: parenting, communicating, volunteering, learning at home, decision making, and collaborating with the community. For the Hispanic community, learning at home seems to be a feasible type of involvement, and family literacy is seen as an especially appropriate approach in seeking to enhance success and achievement among Hispanic children (Ada, 1988; Quintero & Huerta-Macias, 1990). The concept of "familia" is central to cultural descriptions of Hispanic people (Abi-Nader, 1990). Meeting the needs of the family is a great motivation for success in the Hispanic culture. Since literacy learning is a culturally bound activity, it is more likely to be influenced by parental and home factors than are other aspects of school learning (e.g., mathematics). By increasing the opportunities to learn, and using literacy outside the school, particularly at home, the incongruency between home and school literacy can be lessened (Moll et al., 1992; Moll & Greenberg, 1990; Velez-Ibañez & Greenberg, 1992).

Hispanic Parents and Schools Working Together Toward the Common Goal of School Success for Their Children

More than ten years of experience working with Hispanic parents have provided me with some insights on this issue. In the following pages I will describe ways in which schools can show leadership in encouraging parental involvement. For the Hispanic community this is a dream for the new millennium.

A School/home Perspective on Parental Involvement

Schools have to recognize that parents are their children's first and most important teachers. They also need to understand that in the case of the Hispanic community, parents would like to participate more actively in their children's education Delgado-Gaitan (1992), Rodríguez-Brown (2001). However, teachers and schools must find ways to let parents know how to help their children.

There are several issues to be addressed in training parents to work with their children at home. First, parents in households where English is not the home language must understand that they do not need to know English before they can help their children learn at home. They can do so in the language they know best. This is the language they can model best for their children; the language in which they can provide richer interactions. Therefore, Hispanic parents must understand that what they do with their children in Spanish is going to positively affect their children's cognitive development, which underlies learning regardless of language. Second, parents must be aware that not all knowledge comes from schooling and that they have knowledge they can share with their children. The function of a parent program (i.e., family literacy) is to train parents to work with children at their level and to validate their capability as their children's most important teachers. Once the parents feel that their native language and knowledge are validated, they will have a feeling of self-efficacy that will facilitate their role as teachers.

In order for Hispanic parents to better understand that schools want them helping their children to learn, parents need to know how schools in the United States work and what the schools' and teachers' expectations are. Schools need to make parents feel welcome, wanted, and respected if they are to effectively teach their children in collaboration. Unfortunately, for Hispanic parents who may not know English, going to the school their children attend is seldom a positive experience.

As the new millennium begins, it is time for schools to start looking at parents as resources and partners in teaching. We cannot afford to lose parents as resources, particularly in situations where parents can facilitate the home-school connection for children who come from linguistically and culturally different backgrounds. In the following pages, I will describe two program models that have been successful in enhancing parent/school collaborations. Both have enhanced children's learning and increased continuity between the home and the school environment.

Project FLAME—A Family Literacy Program

Family literacy programs are a natural setting to provide parents with information and experiences they can share with their children as they seek to enhance their chances for school success. For Hispanic parents, doing something within the context of "familia" is very relevant and family literacy offers something for everyone (Rodríguez-Brown & Meehan, 1998).

Ten years ago, since Hispanic parents in a community where we work wanted to participate in their children's education, a family literacy program, Project FLAME, was designed and implemented at three schools in Chicago. The program's specific goal was to help parents learn how to support their children's learning at home in order to facilitate the children's transition between home and school (Rodríguez-Brown & Shanahan, 1989).

In designing the program, an effort was made to place school success in the context of "familia." The program is called FLAME—Family Literacy: Aprendiendo, Mejorando, Educando [Learning, Improving, Educating]. There are four basic assumptions underlying the design of the program. First, we believe that a supportive home environment is essential to literacy development. Second, we believe that parents can have a positive effect on their children's learning. Third, we believe that parents who are confident and successful learners themselves will be the most effective teachers of their children. Fourth, we believe that literacy is the school subject most likely to be influenced by the social and cultural contexts of the family. Four objectives support the program design as follows: (1) increase the parents' ability to provide literacy opportunities for their children; (2) increase parents' ability to act as positive literacy models for their children; (3) improve parents' skills so that they can more effectively initiate, encourage, support and extend their children's literacy learning; (4) to increase and improve the relationship between parents and the schools. In support of these objectives, the program design includes four components which are supported by research: literacy opportunity, literacy models, literacy interaction, and school-home relationships.

Literacy Opportunity

A supportive home environment provides children with the opportunity to use literacy. To do well with school literacy learning, children need to be familiar with a culture of literacy. A culture rich in literacy materials includes books, magazines, and writing implements. The availability of materials provides children with the opportunity to see literacy in action and to experiment with literacy. Children with such opportunities do best in school and the provision of such opportunities alone has been found to be a powerful stimulus to literacy learning of young children (Wheeler, 1971). Project FLAME teaches parents to locate and select appropriate books, magazines, and other literacy materials for their children, to increase the amount of library use by the families, and to increase the availability of literacy materials in the home for the children, including appropriate reading and writing materials.

Literacy Models

A literacy model is defined as a significant person in the child's environment who uses literacy in an open and obvious manner. Children who see their mothers and fathers reading and writing have been found to do best in school reading achievement (MetriTech, 1987). Children who have appropriate models attempt to imitate literacy behaviors of those individuals. Efforts to change the mothers' strategies for reading to their children have been successful in improving children's literacy learning with both Hispanic children (Gallimore & Goldenberg, 1989) and other low SES children (Edwards, 1988, 1999). LEP parents often do not share their literacy with their children (Gallimore & Goldenberg, 1989). Sometimes this is because the parents have very limited literacy skills, or at least limited literacy skills in English. Sometimes parents, in their zeal to expose their children to English, do not provide a rich active language environment (Heath, 1987). Studies show that parents are more likely to serve as effective literacy models and to participate in their children's literacy learning when they see themselves as effective learners (National Center for Family Literacy, 1991; Nickse, Speicher, & Buchek, 1988; Van Fossen & Sticht, 1991). Through Project FLAME, we encourage parents to increase their own English literacy and language use and to draw their children's attention to this behavior. Specifically, the program encourages parents to use reading and writing in the company of their children, drawing their children's attention to the more subtle uses of reading and writing. At the same time, they improve their own English proficiency and literacy skills.

Literacy Interaction

Literacy interaction refers to any direct exchange between parent and child that is intended to enhance the child's literacy knowledge. This includes formal direct instruction, but it also includes less formal activities such as reading to children or encouraging them to pretend to read or write. Such interactions have proven to positively influence children's learning (Tobin, 1981).

Research shows that children who are read to often are more successful in school than are those who do not receive such experiences (Feitelson & Goldstein, 1986). It is believed that such reading acquaints children with story structures and literacy conventions (Teale, 1984). Parents in FLAME are shown how to read to their children more effectively and to talk with their children about books. Parents are instructed about how to use songs, games, and other language activities that can increase children's phonemic awareness and other skills (Tobin, 1981). Parents are also shown how to encourage children's invented writing (Henderson & Beers, 1981). Through Project FLAME, parents learn that they should share books with their children often, and in ways that will enhance their children's literacy learning (regardless of their own literacy level), how to create simple language experience activities, how to play simple language games with their children that will enhance literacy learning, and they learn to be more aware of the literacy resources available in their community.

School-Home Relationships

Home-school relations involve all interactions between parents and school. Parents need to understand what their children's teachers are trying to accomplish, and teachers need to know of the parent's concerns and aspirations. Research shows that Hispanic children's literacy knowledge is highest in situations in which teachers and parents maintain frequent contact with each other (Goldenberg, 1987). It has been shown that cultural and social discontinuity between school and home can interfere with literacy learning and that such discontinuities are more likely for the culturally and linguistically different child (Silvern, 1988). Project FLAME is designed to act as an early outreach between school and parents, so as to avoid some of the potential discontinuity.

Project FLAME activities attempt to increase contact between families and schools particularly with regard to improving early communication about literacy learning and home-school cooperation. It also seeks to improve relations by increasing mutual respect between culturally different parents and school personnel, and increase these parents' self-confidence in their ability to communicate with teachers and administrators in their children's schools.

INSTRUCTIONAL PROGRAM

Although FLAME is described in terms of four dimensions, efforts toward the various goals are not separate. The program activities have been designed with the idea that each will contribute to more than a single goal simultaneously, as such, each activity is likely to contribute a greater effect to one or another of the goals. A productive home literacy culture is necessarily complex, and program activities recognize and reflect these subtle intricacies.

As part of the program, Project FLAME parents attend *Parents as Learners* activities twice a week. This includes English as a Second Language (ESL) or GED basic skills classes. During these sessions, parents may develop books for their children, an activity that clearly increases "literacy opportunities." They also participate in *Parents as Teachers* workshops twice a month. These are the primary vehicles for helping parents become models of literacy use for their children. Some of the *Parents as Teachers* sessions require that parents work together with their children. Other sessions emphasize interaction and discussion between parents and the session leaders.

Currently, we work with about 150 families a year in six different settings in Chicago. We meet in schools, libraries or community centers. Nationally, we also provide training support for about 26 projects that have adopted our family literacy model.

PROGRAM "FLAME" EFFECTIVENESS

It is beyond the purpose of this chapter to present data supporting the effectiveness of the program, but data collected between 1992 and 1995 and described elsewhere (Mulhern, 1991; Rodríguez-Brown & Mulhern, 1993; Rodríguez-Brown, Li, Albom, 2000) have provided information about FLAME participants and their attitudes and literacy behaviors, both before and after their participation in Project FLAME. Analyses of parents' pre/post uses of, and attitudes toward, literacy at home show significant changes in the areas of literacy opportunity and literacy interactions. These changes appear to impact children's school performance.

Each year the children of FLAME participants between the ages of three and six are pre-and posttested in order to determine if our work with the parents had an effect on the children's learning and their preparedness for school. For this purpose, children are given a letter recognition test, a test of print awareness, (Clay, 1993) and the Boehm Test of Basic Concepts (The Psychological Corp., 1986). The tests are administered in either Spanish or English, depending on the children's proficiency. Statistical analyses (e.g., t-tests) done with these data show significant gains ($<.001$) from pre-to posttest in all areas tested.

FLAME researchers have also conducted a comparative study. During the third year of the project, one of the FLAME schools agreed to allow us to test a class of preschoolers (three-to five-year-olds). The purpose was to compare their performance to a group of three-to five-year-olds whose parents participated in Project FLAME. Because there were pretest differences between the groups (i.e., the FLAME group scored significantly lower on the test of print awareness (Clay, 1993) [$p < .02$] and lowercase letters [$p < .0001$], ANCOVA was used to control for pretest differences. By the end of the school year, no significant differences were found to exist between the two groups.

These results show that although Project FLAME children lagged behind the comparison children in several areas related to literacy at pretest, they generally caught up during the months their families participated in the program. The children managed to do this despite the fact that many of the FLAME children were not attending preschool or kindergarten. Clearly, the children acquired additional skills while their families were involved with the project. This occurred even though the children experienced no direct intervention. The intervention was aimed at the parents, individuals who typically have very limited literacy skills themselves, limited experience with school, and limited English proficiency.

From working and talking with FLAME parents and also from reading their journals and creative writing, we know that they take seriously their role as their children's first and most important teachers. Through the program they develop a sense of self-efficacy. They know that they can help their children in the language they know best and they realize that not all knowledge comes from school and, as such, they have knowledge they can share with their children. While working with their children at home, parents have also connected with the school and taken more active roles as volunteers in the school. Again, this is an opportunity to reduce the discontinuity between home and school which negatively affects culturally and linguistically different children's achievement and school success.

There are also other ways in which teachers can make school activities and the curriculum more relevant. From our experience in Project FLAME, we know that Hispanic parents are delighted when schools show that they value their knowledge and welcome them as resources in the schools their children attend. This brings up a second model of parent involvement relevant to the Hispanic community and one that allows them to be involved in their children's education in order to fulfill a dream for more home-school collaboration in the new millennium. This collaboration relates to the role of parents and community in supporting teachers' efforts to make the curriculum and their teaching more relevant to *all* children. It involves the idea of using parents as a source of information and as instructional resources that may transform the curriculum and the teaching in the schools attended by their children.

"Funds of Knowledge": Using Community Knowledge as a Teacher Resource

This idea comes from a project taking place in Arizona where a group of school teachers and university researchers have been working on the conceptualization of a model where visits to Hispanic homes become a source of information for teachers. Under the leadership of Luis Moll and his colleagues, teachers and university researchers have learned how to use the community knowledge they collect, through these home visits, to transform the school curriculum and ways of teaching with the goal of enhancing Hispanic children's success in school (Moll, 1992).

This type of collaborative research is a reaction to the type of schooling that low-income, and culturally and linguistically different children receive at school. This schooling can often be characterized as rote learning, drill and practice and with an emphasis on low-level literacy and computational skills (Goldenberg, 1993; Oakes, 1986). Moll describes this type of schooling as reduced in content and limited in application. He correlates it to the "working class identity" which many people attach to the bilingual programs that these children attend. According to Moll (1992), when the context of schooling for Hispanic limited English proficient (LEP) students focus on their "disadvantages," assumptions are made that the children come from "socially and intellectually limited family environments, or that these students lack ability, or there is something wrong with their thinking or their values, especially in comparison to wealthier peers" (p. 20). In contrast to the above described assumptions, Moll (1992) calls for schools to see students' families and the community as resources which can contribute to the enrichment, change, and improvement of the children's education.

Moll's ideas of using community resources to affect school change are based on the work of anthropologists (Velez-Ibañez, 1988; Velez-Ibañez & Greenberg, 1992). These anthropologists have conducted ethnographic research in what is called "funds of knowledge," resources which seem to contribute to socially and culturally authentic educational practices. Teachers can use these practices to make classroom activities socially and academically meaningful for the communities involved (Moll & Greenberg, 1990; Moll et al., 1990).

Based on the principle that communities are resources which should support school change and improvement, Moll and his associates have been studying how "funds of knowledge" can transform teachers and help reduce discontinuities between the home and the school (Gonzalez et al., 1993). "Funds of knowledge" are defined as "those developed and accumulated strategies (e.g., skills, abilities, ideas, practices) or bodies of knowledge that are essential to a household's functioning and well being" (Gonzalez et al., 1993, p. 3).

Using qualitative, mostly ethnographic methodologies, teams of university and teacher researchers have designed procedures for home visits, reflection and practice in order to learn about community resources ("funds of knowledge"). This knowledge is then applied toward the enhancement of teaching and educational practices in the community where they work.

The idea of home visits is not new to teachers. They use home visits to discuss with parents particular problems or difficulties (behavioral and/or subject matter related) which students may have. Other teachers use home visits to introduce themselves to parents. There are also some school programs which require teachers to do home visits to teach parents how to help their children with school work. The home visits done by teacher researchers in the "funds of knowledge" collaboration are different. They are geared to identifying and documenting knowledge which exists in the students' homes. In turn, this information is expected to transform teacher practices and enrich the school curriculum.

The original design of this collaboration called for university researchers to visit the students' homes and identify household knowledge and resources. Information gathered was to be transmitted to teachers who were to apply what they had learned. As the teacher/university household research group evolved, it became apparent that the transmission model, where university researchers passed along the information to teachers about the households, was not as effective as expected. Teachers did not take true ownership of the data (Gonzalez et al., 1993) and felt disconnected from the context of the households. Furthermore, university researchers found that when teachers actually participated in home visits they asked better questions and had easier access to households. They were regarded by parents with respect and honor. Consequently they were not asked as many questions about why the information was being gathered or how it was to be used. Families trusted teachers more than the university researchers. For this reason, the collaborative model changed and the role of teachers became one of teacher-researchers. Currently, teachers are part of a team of researchers. They carry out home-visits which are part of a "systematic, intentional inquiry" as defined by Lytle and Cochran-Smith (1990, p. 84).

Once teachers are trained in ethnographic methods for participant-observations, interviewing and taking field notes, they visit homes. They interview parents, observe in the home and write field notes. They are also advised to keep a personal journal about their experience. It is expected that once the information is collected it will lead to "ethnographic reflection" (Gonzalez et al., 1993, p. 2) and, eventually, transformations which will enrich the children's school experience as well as parent-teacher relations (Gonzalez & Amanti, 1992; Moll et al., 1992).

Design of the "Funds of Knowledge" Teacher/University Researchers Model

In terms of a design of a "funds of knowledge" teachers/university research collaboration, three important components can be described: after-school teacher/researchers "labs," community field work-home visits, and school/teacher component.

After-school Teacher/Researchers "Labs"

These are study groups created to enhance the collaborative nature of the teacher/university researchers. It is in these meeting where teachers learn about methodology issues related to data collection in households. They also serve to inform, assist and support each other's work. Also, teachers talk about their reflections and exchange ideas about the "funds of knowledge" found during their home visits (Moll et al., 1990). These meetings are seen as mediating structures which allow participants to make connections between their household-field work and their classroom practices. Both teachers and university researchers reflect and mentor each other within their areas of expertise. They also discuss issues of methodology, interpretation, and practice.

Community Field Work-Home Visits

This component emphasizes the use of ethnographic methodologies (discussed in the "labs"), which assist researchers in understanding the sociopolitical and economic context of the households (Velez-Ibañez, 1988). The research group places special emphasis on learning about how families develop social networks and how these relationships facilitate their development and exchange of resources (or knowledge).

School/Teacher Component

Through information collected and discussed in the "labs" (after-school meetings), the teachers examine their teaching practices as well as the methods of instruction used and then design innovations where they can use the "funds of knowledge" data to enhance their teaching and/or their curriculum. This could include, for instance, planning integrated units with information gathered in the community and/or bringing parents to share their knowledge with a class.

The teacher researchers in the group play a dual role. Through the "labs" teachers become *learners*. They must internalize the purpose of these home visits as opposed to what they might have done before when they visited homes. They also have to learn about the ethnographic methodologies they will use in the household visits. Through a collaborative and reflective process, teachers learn how to see the home visits as research. This has been challenging for teachers because they tend to view research as based on quantifiable variables (Gonzalez et al., 1993). The second role for the teacher is that of *researcher*. Once teachers are familiar with ethnographic methodologies, they choose two or three children whose home they would like to visit (no attempt is made to find representation in a sample). Then, teachers start their fieldwork in the homes, collecting data through field notes, artifacts, observation, and keeping a personal journal. The data are shared with the rest of the group during "lab" sessions.

This particular model of teacher/university researcher collaboration empowers teachers to share with others what they find relevant in the home visits and to share this knowledge with the rest of the research team. Groups of teacher/university researchers involved in "funds of knowledge" projects such as the one described here become "a community of learners." Everyone in the group has a voice. Teachers and university researchers spend time in theoretical reflection which should lead to positive transformations in their teaching (Gonzalez et al., 1993).

As a byproduct of participation in "funds of knowledge" projects, teachers have reported two areas of transformation. One relates to the definition of culture of households. Culture is seen as a process rather than a normative state. The culture of the household is not defined in terms of such activities as quinceañeras (sweet sixteen parties) or, Día de los Muertos (Day of the Dead) but in terms of the networks and knowledge found there. The second area of transformation is the realization of a need to find alternative models to teach the children beyond the deficit model. This particular type of home/school collaboration benefits both the teacher and the children.

My experience with Hispanic parents through Project FLAME leads me to envision great potential for "funds of knowledge" collaborations. I see this as a form of parental involvement where parents share their knowledge with teachers as researchers, and as such, contribute to changes in school curriculum and ways of teaching. This type of activity will bridge the gap between the home and the school.

CONCLUSION

As we approach a new millennium, there is a great need for parent involvement. Current statistics show that Hispanics are still not doing well in school and that affects their job opportunities as adults. There is also research that shows that Hispanic parents want to get involved in their children's education (Delgado Gaitan, 1992; Goldenberg, 1993; Rodriguez-Brown, 2000). It is time for teachers to recognize parents as resources and use their capabilities and knowledge. This will enhance Hispanic children's chances for school success.

Hispanic parents are greatly interested in their children's education. They would like to get involved, *but* they need to be shown ways to do so. As the new millennium arrives, it is time for schools and teachers to start using parents as resources. This paper describes two models of parent involvement which directly and indirectly involves parents in their children's education. It is my hope and also the dream of many Hispanic parents who currently participate in Project FLAME that schools recognizes parents' knowledge and language as well as their potential as teachers.

REFERENCES

Abi-Nader, J. (1991). *Family values and the motivation of Hispanic youth.* Paper presented at the annual meeting of the American Educational Research Association, Chicago, IL.

Ada, A.F. (1988). The Pajaro Valley Experience: Working with Spanish-speaking parents to develop children's reading and writing skills in the home through the use of children's literature. In T. Skutnabb-Kangas & J. Cummins (Eds.), *Minority Education: From shame to struggle* (pp. 223–238). Clevedon: Multilingual Matters.

Anyon, J. (1980). Social class and hidden curriculum of work. *Journal of Education, 162*(1), 67–92.

Applebee, A.N., Langer, J.A., & Mullis, I. (1987). *Learning to be literate in America.* Princeton, NJ: Educational Testing Service.

Clay, M.M. (1993). *Stones-The concepts about print test.* Auckland: Heinemann Publishers.

Delgado-Gaitan, C. (1992). School matters in the Mexican-American home: Socializing children to education. *American Educational Research Journal, 29,* 495–513.

Delgado-Gaitan, C. (1991). Involving parents in schools; A process of empowerment. *American Journal of Education, 100,* 20–41.

Delgado-Gaitan, & Trueba, H. (1991). *Crossing borders: Education for immigrant families in America.* New York: Farmer Press.

Edwards, P.A. (1988). *Lower SES mothers' learning of book reading strategies.* Paper presented at the annual meeting of the National Reading Conference, Tucson, AZ.

Edwards, P.A. (1999). *A Path to Follow: Learning to listen to parents.* Portsmouth, NH: Heinemann.

Epstein, J. (1991). Effects on student achievement of teachers' practices of parent involvement. In S. Silvern (Ed.), *Advances in reading/language research.* Greenwich, CT: JAI Press.

Epstein, Z.J. (1990). School and family connections: Theory, research, and implications for integrating sociologies of education and family. In D. Unger & M. Sussman (Eds.), *Families in community settings: Interdisciplinary perspectives* (pp. 99–126). New York: Haworth Press.

Feitelson, D., & Goldstein, Z. (1986). Patterns of book ownership and reading to young children in Israeli school-oriented and non-school-oriented families. *Reading Teacher, 39,* 924–930.

Fraser, M. (1992). *Are Hispanics drop out rates related to migration?* Washington, DC: National Center for Educational Statistics.

Gallimore, R., & Goldenberg, C.N. (1989). *School effects on emergent literacy experiences in families of Spanish-speaking children.* Paper presented at the annual meeting of the American Educational Research Association, San Francisco, CA.

Goldenberg, C.N. (1993). The home-school connection in bilingual education. In B. Arias & U. Casanova (Eds.), *Bilingual education: Politics, practice, and research* (pp. 225–250). Chicago: University of Chicago Press.

Goldenberg, C.N. (1987). Low-income Hispanic parents' contributions to their first grade children's word recognition skills. *Anthropology and Education Quarterly, 18,* 149–179.

Goldenberg, C.N., & Gallimore, R. (1991, November). Local knowledge, research knowledge, and educational change: A case study of early Spanish reading improvement. *Educational Researcher, 20,* 2–14.

Gonzalez, N., Moll, L., Floyd-Tenery, M., Rivera, A., Rendon, P., Gonzalez, R., & Amanti, K. (1993). *Teacher research on Funds of Knowledge: Learning from households. Education Practice Report: 6.* Santa Cruz, CA: National Center for Research on Cultural Diversity and Second Language Learning.

Gonzalez, N., & Amanti, C. (1992, November). *Teaching ethnographic methods to teachers: Successes and pitfalls.* Paper presented at the annual meeting of the American Anthropological Association, San Francisco.

Heath, S.B. (1987). Sociocultural context of language development. In *Beyond language: Social and cultural factors in schooling language minority students* (pp. 143–186). Los Angeles: Evaluation Dissemination and Assessment Center.

Henderson, E., & Beers, J. (Eds.) (1981). *Developmental and cognitive aspects of learning to spell.* Newark, DE: International Reading Association.

Kirsch, I.S., Jungeblut, A., Jenkins, L., & Kolstad, A. (1993). *Adult literacy in America: A first look at the results of the national adult literacy survey*. Princeton, NJ: Educational Testing Service.

Lytle, S., & Cochran-Smith, M. (1990). Learning from teacher research: A working typology. *Teachers College Record, 92*(1), 83–103.

MetriTech. (1987). *The Illinois reading assessment project: Literacy Survey*. Champaign, IL: Metritech.

Moll, L.C. (1992). Bilingual classroom studies and community analysis: Some research trends. *Educational Researcher, 21*(2), 20–24.

Moll, L.C., Amanti, C., Neff, D., & Gonzalez, N. (1992). Funds of knowledge for teaching using a qualitative approach to connect homes and classrooms. *Theory Into Practice, 31*(1), 132–141.

Moll, L.C., & Greenberg, J. (1990). Creating zones of possibilities: Combining social contexts for instruction. In L.C. Moll (Ed.), *Vygotsky and education* (pp. 319–348). Cambridge: Cambridge University Press.

Moll, L.C., Velez-Ibañez, C., Greenberg J., Whitmore, K., Saavedra, E., Dworin, J., & Andrade, R. (1990). *Community knowledge and classroom practice: Combining resources for literacy instruction* (OBEMLA Contract No. 300-87-01131). Tucson, AZ: University of Arizona, College of Education and Bureau of Applied Research in Anthropology.

Mulhern, M. (1991, February). *The impact of a family literacy project on three Mexican-immigrant families*. Paper presented at the UIC Literacy Colloquium. Chicago: University of Illinois at Chicago.

National Center for Education Statistics. (1995). *The Educational progress of Hispanic students: Finding from the condition of education 1995*. Washington, DC: US Department of Education.

National Center for Family Literacy. (1991). *The effects of participation in family literacy programs*. Louisville, KY: National Center for Family Literacy.

National Council of La Raza. (1990). *Hispanic Education: A statistical portrait 1990*. Washington, DC: NCLR.

Nickse, R., Speicher, A.M., & Buchek, P.C. (1988). An intergenerational adult literacy project: A family intervention/prevention model. *Journal of Reading, 31*, 634–642.

Oakes, J. (1986). Tracking, inequality, and the rhetoric of school reform. Why schools don't change. *Journal of Education, 168*, 61–80.

Peng, S.S., Wright, D., & Hill, S. (1995). *Understanding racial ethnic differences in secondary schools: Science and Mathematics Achievement*. (NCES 95-710). Washington, DC: National Center for Educational Statistics.

Quintero, F., & Huerta-Macias, A. (1990). Learning together: Issues for language minority parents and their children. *Journal of Educational Issues of Languages, Minority Students, 10*, 41–56.

Rodriguez-Brown, F.V. (2001). Home-School connections in a community where English is the second language. In V. Risko & K. Bromley (Eds.). *Collaboration for diverse learners:* Viewpoints and Practices. Newak, DE: International Reading Association.

Rodriguez-Brown, F.V., Li, R.F., & Albom, J. (2000). Hispanic parents awareness and use of literacy rich environments at home and the community. *Education and Urban Society, 32*(2).

Rodriguez-Brown, F.V., & Meehan, M.A. (1998). Family literacy and adult education: Project FLAME. In C. Smith (Ed.), *Literacy for the Twenty-First Century* (pp. 176–193) Wesport, CT: Praeger.

Rodriguez-Brown, F.V., & Mulhern, M. (1993). Fostering critical literacy through family literacy: A study of families in a Mexican-immigrant community. *Bilingual Research Journal, 17,* 1–16.

Rodríguez-Brown, F.V., & Shanahan, T. (1989). *Literacy for the limited English proficient child: A family approach.* Proposal submitted and funded by OBEMLA/USDE under the Title VII Family Literacy Program.

Serna, I., & Hudelson, S. (1993). Becoming a writer of Spanish and English. *Quarterly of the National Writing Project and the Center for the Study of Writing and Literacy, 15*(1), 1–5.

Shanahan, T., Mulhern, M., & Rodriguez-Brown, F.V. (1995). Project FLAME: Lessons learned from a family literacy program for linguistic minority families. *The Reading Teacher, 48,* 586–593.

Silvern, S. (1988). Continuity/discontinuity between home and early childhood education environments. *Elementary School Journal, 89,* 147–160.

Teale, W. (1984). Reading to young children: Its significance for literacy development. In H. Goelman, A. Oberg, & F. Smith (Eds.) *Awakening to literacy* (pp. 110–121) Portsmouth, NH: Heinemann.

The Psychological Corporation. (1986). *Boehm R-Test of Basic Concepts—Revised.* San Antonio, TX. Harcourt, Brace and Joranovich, Inc.

Tobin, A.W. (1981). *A multiple discriminant cross validation of the factors associated with the development of precocious reading achievement.* Unpublished doctoral dissertation, University of Delaware.

Van Fossen, S., & Sticht, T.G. (1991). *Teach the mother and reach the child: Results of the intergenerational literacy action research project.* Washington, DC: Wider Opportunities for Women.

Velez-Ibañez, C.G. (1988). Networks of exchange among Mexicans in the U.S. and Mexico: Local level mediating responses to national and international transformations. *Urban Anthropology, 17*(1), 27–51.

Velez-Ibañez, C., & Greenberg, J. (1992). Formation and transformation of funds of knowledge among U.S. Mexican households. *Anthropology and Education Quarterly, 23*(4), 313–335.

Wheeler, M.E. (1971). *Untutored acquisition of writing skill.* Unpublished doctoral dissertation, Cornell University.

CHAPTER 13

GETTING THE MOST OUT OF SCHOOL-BASED PROFESSIONAL DEVELOPMENT

William M. Saunders, Gisela O'Brien, David Marcelletti, Kathy Hasenstab, Tina Saldivar, and Claude Goldenberg

Abstract: Schools are being encouraged to establish ongoing, school-based professional development settings within and around the school day. Improving professional development programs for teachers is central to reforming and improving American schools. This is especially true in low-income, urban schools serving large numbers of language and cultural minority children. Such schools often have less experienced staffs and more new teachers with little, if any, preservice training. While there is a growing literature documenting the benefits and challenges of school-based professional development, there remains a need for concrete descriptions of how to make such school settings work. This chapter describes how to design, lead, and sustain four specific school settings that, individually and collectively, can make a substantial contribution to improved teaching and learning: (1) teacher work groups, (2) grade level or department meetings, (3) the academic achievement leadership team, and (4) faculty-wide settings and training workshops. The chapter begins with background information on the projects in which these settings were studied and a set of core principles for effective school-based professional development. Then a section is devoted to each setting, including a general description of what it is, specific guidelines for success, and examples drawn from our experiences.

INTRODUCTION

Improving professional development programs for teachers is central to reforming and improving American schools (Darling-Hammond, 1998; Fullan, 1991; González & Darling-Hammond, 1997; Goodlad, 1984; Tharp & Gallimore, 1988). Schools are being encouraged to establish ongoing, school-based professional development settings within and around the school day for teachers to collaboratively plan and debrief lessons, analyze student work, learn and develop new practices, read and discuss professional literature, and lead and carry out school reform (California Department of Education, 1992).

Professional development is enormously important at schools serving language and cultural minority children, especially in highly concentrated, low-income urban communities. Typically, such schools produce low levels of academic achievement (August & Hakuta, 1997). They also tend to have less experienced staffs and more new teachers with less preservice training (González & Darling-Hammond, 1997). Most of these schools have additional financial resources in the form of Title I funding, but they tend to deploy those resources ineffectively (Fashola & Slavin, 1998). In fact, the additional resources, specialized programs and reform mandates associated with such schools can contribute to greater overload and complexity rather than increased effectiveness and coherence.

Schools that produce high levels of academic achievement in low-income, urban communities are the exception, rather than the norm. They are *unusually* effective. However, the characteristics of unusually effective schools are not a mystery. Three decades of effective schools research (Levine & Lezotte, 1995) and more recent studies of effective schools serving English language learners (August & Hakuta, 1997) have documented several features of high performing schools. They include faculty-wide commitment to improved achievement, high levels of collaboration among staff, highly operationalized expectations, strong and instructionally-oriented leadership, multicultural and language sensitivity, and school-based, practice-oriented professional development. Ultimately, these schools achieve coherence through "insistent, persistent, consistent and resilient" collective efforts to produce high levels of academic achievement for all students (Levine & Lezotte, 1995).

While the features of unusually effective schools are not a mystery, the processes and mechanisms through which they become such are not well understood. For the past decade our research team has been studying school change, assisting staffs to make changes, and documenting processes and outcomes as schools attempt to improve teaching, learning and achievement in culturally and linguistically diverse schools and communities. We have concentrated on improving literacy achievement for two reasons. First, literacy achievement is usually the core issue at schools with large numbers of English language learners. Second, we presume that improved literacy achievement, both basic skills and broader literacy practices, contribute to improved achievement throughout the academic program.

Improving professional development has been at the heart of our work. In particular, we have tried to establish settings for ongoing professional development embedded within a larger school wide improvement effort. While there is a growing literature documenting the benefits and challenges of ongoing, school-based professional development ("Strengthening the Teaching Profession," 1998), there remains a desperate need for nuts and bolts descriptions of how to make such school settings work.

This chapter introduces and describes how to design, lead, and sustain four specific school settings that can, individually and collectively, make a substantial contribution to improved teaching and learning (Goldenberg & Sullivan, 1994). The four settings are:

1. *Teacher Work Groups*—year-long groups organized by interest in which teachers meet for 90–120 minutes at least twice a month to study, develop, implement and evaluate new or refined practices and curriculum.

2. *Grade Level or Department Meetings*—groups of teachers at the same grade level or teaching the same subject who meet monthly for 60 to 90 minutes to identify, assess and discuss how to achieve specific student learning goals relevant to the grade level or department.

3. *Academic Achievement Leadership Team*—a group of teacher representatives and administrators who meet monthly for 90 to 120 minutes to set direction for school improvement efforts, plan and coordinate the other professional development setting meetings, and evaluate school wide improvement efforts and achievement results.

4. *Faculty-Wide Settings and Training Workshops*—60 to 90 minute monthly faculty meetings and training workshops focused on school improvement efforts and specific practices teachers can readily implement.

These settings can be adapted to a wide range of schools serving a wide range of students. The particular content and substance on which the settings—individually and collectively—focus must be determined by the issues and challenges a particular school faces. The examples we use in this chapter all come from our work in linguistically diverse, mostly Latino, elementary schools, where our focus has been improving literacy achievement.

The chapter begins with background information on our projects, followed by a discussion of core principles for effective school-based professional development. A section is then devoted to each setting. Drawing on our experiences over the past 10 years, we provide a general description of the setting and specific guidelines for its success. Within each description we provide examples of specific, literacy-related practices that teachers typically focus on within each setting.

PROJECT BACKGROUND

The first phase of our work involved the development of a model to guide school change and make it possible for increasing numbers of schools to cultivate the same features that characterize unusually effective schools (School Change/Getting Results model, Goldenberg & Sullivan, 1994). The model was developed and initially tested at a single elementary school with a primarily low-income Spanish-speaking student population. While this work was proceeding, we were also working with a group of five other schools to develop, refine, and evaluate a language arts program to help English learners transition from primary language to English instruction (Saunders, in press; Saunders, O'Brien, Lennon, & McLean, 1998). In brief, the program provides students with exposure to quality literature; opportunities to read, write, and discuss this literature; and instructional experiences designed to help students acquire the skills necessary for full English literacy.

The current phase of our research is a large-scale replication study where we are bringing together the results of our work at the previous sites. We are collaborating with administrators and teachers at fifteen elementary schools, six of which are on a multi-track, year-round schedule, within a large urban school district. The goal is to improve language arts teaching and learning for 14,000 elementary students, half of whom are English language learners. We are using both the school change model described in Goldenberg and Sullivan (1994) and the language arts program reported by Saunders (in press; Saunders et al., 1998).

The School Change/Getting Results (SC/GR) model identifies four elements to "leverage" change at school sites: *goals* that are set and shared; *indicators* that measure success; *assistance* by capable others; and *leadership* that supports and pressures. At the site where the model was developed, these four change elements created a dynamic that led to improved teaching and learning (Goldenberg & Sullivan, 1994). Our current work focuses on how these elements can be operationalized and utilized effectively at several school sites simultaneously. We are working to describe what is required at a school to (a) establish concrete academic goals for student learning; (b) develop or adapt, then implement and use, meaningful indicators to gauge student progress; (c) create and sustain assistance and professional development settings that help teachers attain the academic goals; and (d) establish and maintain leadership that provides the necessary support and pressure to sustain school wide improvement efforts.

Our central hypothesis is that schools change by creating new settings and/or restructuring existing settings to be stable, predictable, and focused on the substance and mechanics of improving teaching and learning. "Settings" (Sarason, 1972; Tharp & Gallimore, 1988) is a super-ordinate construct in our conceptualization of school change. As defined by Sarason (1972), a setting is "any instance in which two or more people come together in new relationships over a sustained period of time in order to achieve certain goals" (p. 1). School change takes place not in the abstract, but in specific settings, such as, in our case, teacher work groups, grade level or department meetings, meetings of leadership teams, and faculty-wide settings and workshops.

We are helping the 15 project schools use the School Change/Getting Results model and these four settings to improve literacy instruction and achievement. Teachers and administrators at the school sites are establishing grade level goals for language arts and adapting and developing assessments to regularly evaluate the extent to which students are meeting those goals. Teachers are also receiving assistance from project advisors and each other to implement specific practices from our language arts program: literature units, instructional conversation, literature logs, comprehension strategies, assigned independent reading centers, recreational reading, teacher read-alouds, teaching writing as a process, written language study, and word study (see Saunders et al., 1998, for a full description of the language arts program).

Over the course of our work, we have come to view professional development and school improvement as highly interdependent processes. Each contributes to the other. A school's capacity to improve students' academic achievement increases when teachers are learning and consistently refining and improving their own performance. Similarly, a teacher's willingness and actual participation in professional development settings increase when those opportunities are part of a larger, collective, school wide improvement effort. The settings described in this chapter are the major vehicles through which we try to help schools achieve meaningful professional development and measurable school improvement. We view teacher work groups, grade level and department meetings, the academic leadership team, and faculty wide meetings and workshops as potential settings for teachers' professional development and necessary settings for school improvement.

Some of these settings, at least in name, should be familiar. Most schools, for example, have faculty meetings, grade level or department meetings and some kind of leadership team. The challenge, however, is focusing these settings on teaching and learning and making them productive. Our experience has been that most school settings generally fail, for several reasons, to make meaningful contributions to teachers' professional development and to measurable school improvement.

First, in most cases, the goals of school settings and what participants are expected to take away from them are often unclear. Teachers speak derisively of long, tedious, pointless meetings that do little other than take them away from their classrooms or infringe on their preparation time. Second, the relationship between what goes on in any one setting and what is going on in the rest of the school is also typically unclear. Meetings across the days, weeks, and year often have very little connection among themselves or with what goes on in other school settings. Connections from one school year to the next are virtually unheard of. Finally, the relationship between what goes on in any one setting on the one hand and improving the academic performance of students on the other is usually extremely tenuous. Even in settings nominally devoted to improving teaching or curriculum, such as workshops, inservices, and the like, there is very little evidence that information or material presented has any substantial carryover into the classroom (Fullan, 1991; Goodlad, 1984; Darling-Hammond, 1998; "Strengthening the Teaching Profession," 1998; Tharp & Gallimore, 1988).

In our efforts to analyze and improve this state of affairs, we have identified three core principles for effective, school-based professional development:

- *Connected to a larger purpose.*   School-based professional development should explicitly serve a larger school wide effort to improve teaching, learning and achievement.
- *Coordinated across settings.*   Professional development should be coordinated and supported across multiple school settings.
- *Guided by model elements.*   The elements of the School Change/Getting Results model (goals, indicators, assistance, and leadership) should be used to guide school wide change efforts, but they should *also* be used to guide planning and facilitation of specific settings for professional development.

OVERVIEW OF THE FOUR SETTINGS

In subsequent sections, we describe each setting and discuss guidelines for success. We discuss teacher work groups first because, of all the settings, work groups are most strongly associated with practice-oriented professional development in a conventional sense. In work groups, teachers study and work to implement effectively specific teaching practices. Each of the other three settings contribute toward a coherent school wide focus on improved teaching, learning and achievement and help give purpose to the undertakings of teacher work groups. Grade level meetings focus heavily on establishing specific goals for student achievement at each grade level and conducting regular assessments to evaluate the extent to which students throughout the grade level and school are meeting those goals. The Academic Achievement Leadership Team, comprising grade level representatives, focuses specifically on setting direction for and facilitating activities and undertakings carried out in work groups and grade level meetings. Finally, faculty-wide settings and training workshops focus on school wide coherence and are used to launch, share, and discuss the activities and undertakings of all the other settings and provide, as deemed necessary, common training for everyone.

As a brief example of this coordinated, multisetting system, we describe what transpired at one of our project schools. In their grade level meetings, fourth and fifth grade teachers agreed to work on a specific language arts goal for reading comprehension. They also operationalized the goal by identifying a particular assessment activity: Students should be able to read a portion of an unfamiliar grade appropriate story (with the ending excluded) and demonstrate understanding of plot and character motives in a written summary of the story and a self-generated ending. At the beginning, middle, and end of the year, teachers selected a common story and conducted the assessment activity with their students. In grade level meetings, together with a project advisor, they developed a scoring rubric and then assessed the students' work, tallied up results, and discussed possible strategies they might use to help students improve reading comprehension skills and performance on the assessment activity.

In work groups, teachers studied and worked on successfully teaching specific comprehension strategies (Palinscar & Brown, 1985) and summary writing techniques—proven practices that applied directly to the goal teachers were working on. During work group meetings, teachers read and discussed published articles about the comprehension strategies, received presentations about the summary writing techniques from a project advisor, planned and debriefed specific lessons, reviewed assessments scored in grade level meetings, and continued these collaborative efforts throughout the year, attempting to successfully implement the two practices.

The impetuous for this process came from the Academic Achievement Leadership Team (AALT). The principal, project advisors and grade level representatives (the members of AALT) described and launched the process in a faculty meeting at the beginning of the year. Grade level representatives, with assistance from project advisors, facilitated each of the grade level and work group meetings. During AALT meetings, members planned for and debriefed grade level and work group meetings. During a faculty meeting at the end of the year, grade level representatives and work group members shared the results of their efforts. For the fourth and fifth grade teachers, the results showed actual improvements in students' performance on the assessment activities.

Making this multisetting system work is a matter of maximizing the effectiveness and productivity of each setting and carefully coordinating and building coherence across the different settings. The descriptions and guidelines to follow represent our collective understanding about how to do that. Table 1 provides an overview of the four settings and the ways in which the four elements of the School Change/Getting Results model relate to each of the four settings.

Table 1.   Professional Development Settings by the Change Model Elements

Elements	Teacher Work Groups	Grade Level or Department Meetings	Academic Achievement Leadership Team	Whole Faculty Settings and Training Workshops
Basic Description–>	Groups, typically formed based on related interests, meet twice a month for 90–120 minutes to study and successfully implement, with the help of an assistance-provider, specific methods to achieve specific, selected student learning goals.	Groups meet for approximately 90–120 minutes per month (one meeting or two shorter ones), to develop/refine grade level or course learning goals and assessments, evaluate student performance, identify needs and strategize ways to individually and collectively address student needs.	AALT meets for 90–120 minutes monthly. Group comprises teacher representatives and administrators responsible for directing and coordinating school improvement initiatives, which necessarily will include professional development settings.	Faculty meets for 75–90 minutes each month to receive, review and discuss plans, strategies, data and information that inform the work of all grade levels/departments and receive training in specific areas relevant to the entire faculty, to be followed-up by grade levels, departments, or work groups.
1. Goals that are set and shared	Improved student performance in group's chosen area. Curricular products related to implementing specific methods. Implementation of specific teaching techniques or strategies.	Improved student performance relative to grade level or course goals. Implementation of specific teaching techniques or strategies.	Producing key products (e.g., grade level or course learning goals, assessments to be used in classrooms or at year's end) and whole-faculty buy-in and involvement in improvement efforts.	Shared understandings among the faculty regarding school improvement efforts, and improved teacher knowledge of specific strategies, techniques, and concepts.
2. Indicators that measure success	Ongoing improvement in student work related to the goals in the group's chosen area; also timely completion of curricular products.	Ongoing improvement in student work related to the grade level or department's chosen goals.	Timely completion of key products; increasingly greater degrees of faculty buy-in and involvement over time.	Faculty consensus that workshops, other sessions are clearly related to helping all teachers accomplish school's stated goals for students, as gauged by indicators (developed by AALT)

Table 1. Professional Development Settings by the Change Model Elements

Elements	Teacher Work Groups	Grade Level or Department Meetings	Academic Achievement Leadership Team	Whole Faculty Settings and Training Workshops
3. Assistance by capable others	From an individual with expertise related to the methods the group is trying to implement (demonstrating in the classroom, locating resources, leading discussions).	From all members of the grade level or department. This is an opportunity for pooling knowledge, resources, expertise, etc. to help all colleagues accomplish school's stated goals for students.	Principal, lead-teacher, or outside consultant helps to focus on timely completion of key products; also provides technical help in formulating goals, indicators and securing faculty buy-in.	Teacher, administrator, or outside consultant knowledgeable and skilled in instructional or curricular area deemed important by staff and related to learning goals that have been agreed to.
4. Leadership that supports and pressures	From the expert or other group member(s); involves helping to establish goals, maintaining the meeting schedule, monitoring progress towards goals, making all participants feel accountable for helping group members accomplish the stated goals.	From grade level or department chair; involves establishing goals and schedule for group's work, developing agendas, maintaining the meeting schedule, reminding members of due dates and responsibilities, publishing minutes.	From AALT chair (principal or lead-teacher); involves leading group to develop and carry out a clear plan of coordinated actions with the staff; preparing agendas and reminders, maintaining meeting schedule, and holding people accountable for their assigned responsibilities.	From the principal; involves establishing clear focus during meetings on improving teaching and learning; planning meetings and identifying needed trainings proactively and responsively; and consistently reporting indicators of student progress toward state goals.

SETTING DESCRIPTIONS AND GUIDELINES FOR SUCCESS

Teacher Work Groups

Teacher work groups are regular, ongoing meetings of teachers who share an interest in working on a common aspect of the curriculum (e.g., literature units, reading comprehension strategies, writing process, writing conventions, oral language development). Work groups meet for 90–120 minutes at least twice a month throughout the school year (an annual total of 30–40 hours of professional development). The purpose of the work group is to increase teachers' expertise in an area of interest. The goal is to implement methods that lead to measurable improvement in student learning: More effective teaching should be evident in higher levels of student performance.

The term, "teacher *work* group," is intentional. Teachers use this setting to *work*, to get things done. This includes planning and debriefing lessons, developing needed materials, evaluating student work, reading and discussing articles, and receiving assistance from others (presentations, demonstrations). The assumption underlying teacher work groups is that most teachers need time, assistance, support, and a modest amount of pressure to implement new methods or refine existing ones effectively enough to produce improved student performance.

The work group process is as follows. Work group teachers review student learning goals adopted by the faculty for each grade level or course (see subsequent sections, Grade Level and Department Meetings and Academic Achievement Leadership Team) and identify specific learning goals they would like to see students meet. They locate a colleague or outside consultant with experience and expertise in specific teaching methods that address the goals, and then, as a group, teachers study the methods, attempt to implement them in the classroom, identify and address implementation challenges, and consistently monitor the methods' effects on student performance. The process continues throughout the year as the group moves toward more successful implementation and improved student outcomes.

Guidelines for successful teacher work groups are: (1) identify expertise and assistance for the area of focus; (2) establish a clear focus on student learning goals and methods to achieve the goals; (3) analyze and evaluate related student work regularly; (4) develop concrete products; (5) provide ongoing support, responsiveness and assistance; (6) share and discuss classroom implementation; and (7) record and remind group members about meetings, agenda, and plans.

Identify Expertise and Assistance for the Area of Focus

Expertise and assistance are critical to a work group's success. The group needs an assistance-provider, a capable participant who can guide teachers in studying and implementing selected methods. We have observed, participated in and studied work groups that varied as a function of available expertise (Powell, Goldenberg, & Cano, 1995). In general, teachers report greater satisfaction and classroom progress when the group includes someone with demonstrated expertise and practical experience in the group's area of interest. In some cases, a strong group of teachers can compensate for the lack of assistance from a capable other. They take it upon themselves to study articles, attend relevant conferences or workshops, and together they push themselves through implementation challenges. However, this tends to be the exception rather than the norm. Thus, one of the critical questions to be addressed in forming work groups is: Do we have an individual with demonstrated expertise in the teachers' area of interest?

One might think of "assistance-providers" along a continuum. Their potential is a by-product of two criteria: Does the person have relevant and successful classroom experience in the area? And, does the person have experience assisting teachers in the particular area? When both criteria are met, the potential for teacher learning is high; when both are not met, potential is low; when one or the other criterion is met, potential is somewhere in the middle.

Our project advisors typically meet both criteria. They are highly accomplished classroom teachers with years of experience implementing the specific components of our language arts model: literature studies, reading comprehension strategies, writing process, etc. Additionally, they have several years of experience leading work groups that focus on these specific components. As a result, they know the methods well, and they can anticipate and address the challenges and needs of the teachers. But we have also observed instances where strong work group participants quickly became fairly strong assistance-providers, generally replicating their work group experiences from a prior year for a new group of teachers in a subsequent year.

Establish a Clear Focus on Student Learning Goals and Methods to Achieve the Goals

Often, when a work group begins, teachers define their area of interest broadly (e.g., reading or writing). However, the area of interest needs to be transformed into specific goals for student learning and coupled with specific methods that address the goals. For example, project advisors have led several Instructional Conversation work groups (Saunders, Goldenberg, & Hamann, 1992). Typically, teachers begin with an expressed interest in helping students construct higher-level understandings of stories. Eventually that interest is clarified and transformed into more specific instructional goals, for example, making accurate inferences about characters' motives and feelings, relating relevant personal experiences to those of the characters, identifying and explaining potential story theme(s). Teachers work toward these goals by studying and implementing Instructional Conversation—small-group, teacher-led discussions of story content, themes and students' personal experiences (Goldenberg, 1992/93; Tharp & Gallimore, 1988).

Establishing a clear focus is important in three respects. First, if teachers do not readily perceive that their involvement in the work group is going to have a direct connection to their classroom instruction, they tend to lose interest. Second, the life blood of a work group is the classroom teaching that goes on in between meetings. What make work group meetings relevant are discussing and planning for subsequent instruction and then returning to the group to debrief and analyze how things went. The sooner the work group establishes a clear focus, the sooner teachers can begin trying things in the classroom. Third, the twin focus on student learning goals and specific methods is important. In our experience, it is beneficial to incorporate both means (methods) and ends (goals) in the process of professional development. Without the goals, implementing specific methods becomes the end in-and-of itself. Incorporating goals, and actually assessing student progress toward the goals (the topic of the next subsection), gives teachers something to strive for. It motivates and helps sustain teachers' efforts to continually improve their use of the methods.

Analyze and Evaluate Related Student Work Regularly

Articulating specific learning goals and identifying particular methods incorporates both means and ends. But it is important to help teachers make explicit connections between the two. Regularly analyzing and evaluating student work helps make that connection. For example, in the Instructional Conversation (IC) work group teachers regularly share and discuss writing assignments about story characters and students' related experiences (literature logs). Teachers review the writings to gauge the extent to which students are developing deeper understandings of the story content and themes. In fact, in our most successful IC groups, teachers videotape specific ICs and then watch and discuss them during work group meetings. The tape allows the group to analyze student participation and also discuss IC techniques.

No matter the focus of the work group, teachers should spend some time identifying ways to monitor student progress. Teachers might videotape lessons, assign particular writing tasks, complete checklists, conduct surveys, or administer specific assessments. Some areas are a little more straightforward to evaluate than others, but the evaluation methods do not have to be definitive and exacting. They should simply provide teachers with meaningful information about how students are progressing with respect to the stated goals. They should inform teachers' efforts to implement specific methods and provide direction for what the group might attend to next. For example, one work group was focusing on promoting self-selected pleasure reading. Students kept a simple log of the books, stories and articles they had read on their own. Intermittently, teachers brought these logs to the work group and reviewed them, noting number, length and sophistication of the students' selections. This was a fairly simple procedure, but it helped teachers arrive at important, successive understandings about how to better promote pleasure reading among their students.

Develop Concrete Products

Developing concrete products related to the area of focus also contributes to the success of a work group. The products might be lesson plans, units, assignments, ancillary materials, year-long plans (Year-at-a-Glance), or assessment tools. In most cases, teachers develop these products collaboratively, providing a vehicle for discussing goals and methods and also completing needed preparation. Over the years, we have developed a large inventory of writing projects, literature units, writing conventions lessons, and also oral English language development units. Teachers in work groups that focus on these areas have access to all the existing products, which, in some cases, provides a year-long curriculum. However, we still engage the group in refining existing products and developing new ones. Working on products contributes to teachers' understanding of the methods and provides the group with another concrete goal: producing curriculum.

Provide Ongoing Support, Responsiveness and Assistance

As work group meetings progress, the assistance-provider needs to be attentive to the teachers' comments and questions and responsive to the needs of the group. Work groups should provide teachers with opportunities to experiment, assess their effectiveness and refine their efforts. This can only happen when teachers view the meetings as useful and when they have a say in the content of the sessions. The group has to know that they will be supported in their efforts to implement the methods effectively. Thus, the assistance-provider should be prepared to coach, model, and give explicit feedback to the different members of the group.

Demonstrations and observation are one way to provide support and assistance to work group members. First, demonstrations allow teachers to directly observe the actual teaching behaviors associated with the methods. In some cases (e.g., Instructional Conversation, oral language development lessons), successful implementation depends on teachers improving their interactions with students. Demonstrations (live or via videotape) provide the most effective way to help teachers achieve that. Second, demonstrations provide a common reference for a group of teachers to discuss methods in greater detail. Teachers can identify a specific strategy or event within a demonstration (that all group members have observed) and use that as a springboard to share and discuss both the successes and challenges they encounter in the classroom. Third, demonstrations can help build trust between group members and the assistance-provider, who typically delivers the demonstrations. The assistance-provider models the key elements of the methods and also a constructive approach to reviewing and debriefing the demonstration—what worked and what did not? Trust emanates from teachers' perceptions that the assistance-provider has expertise to share, an appreciation of classroom complexities, and a willingness to subject her own efforts to constructive feedback and review.

Share and Discuss Classroom Implementation

As soon as possible, work group teachers should begin trying specific methods in the classroom and discussing their experiences during meetings. Typically, this should happen by the third or fourth meeting, after goals have been established and teachers have some familiarity with the target methods. Initial implementation efforts can be fairly narrow and preliminary. For example, teachers in an Instructional Conversation work group need not try a whole literature unit involving a series of ICs. Instead, they can start out with single IC with one group of students. Teachers in a writing-as-a-process group need not start out with a full-blown writing project that would entail prewriting, response-groups, revising and editing. Rather, they might begin by incorporating just prewriting activities into an assignment they had already planned to do.

The goal is to quickly make a connection between work group meetings and what teachers are attempting to do in the classroom. In some cases, the decision to begin trying out some methods emerges naturally. Teachers simply feel ready and willing to try an IC or establish a time each day for self-selected silent reading. In other cases, this initial launch has to be pressed a bit by the assistance-provider. We have had experiences where, for a variety of reasons, teachers have been hesitant about trying something out in the classroom. In those instances, we have (in our assistance role) nominated possible first steps and guided the group to a consensus about something everyone felt they could try. By the end of the meeting, there was no ambiguity. Everyone would try a particular thing and be prepared to report back at the subsequent meeting. Although this might involve a little pressure, teachers quickly come to value the idea of focusing meeting activities and discussions on concrete things they are trying to implement in the classroom.

Record and Remind Group Members about Meetings, Agenda, and Plans

A work group needs a leader, an individual who facilitates the overall functioning of the group. The work group leader publishes a list of meeting dates, sends reminders, prepares agendas, insures that needed materials are photocopied, and possibly keeps a brief record of the group's activities at each meeting. Sometimes the role of the leader and the assistance-provider are carried out by the same individual. In other situations, the leader and assistance-provider might be two different individuals. In either case, someone needs to carry out the fairly simply but often overlooked chores involved in making work group meetings happen consistently, as scheduled, and with participants well informed about agenda, location, materials and assignments.

Grade Level or Department Meetings

Grade level or department meetings are fairly common in most schools. Typically, schools use grade levels (elementary) or departments (secondary) as the organizational structure for communication, representation, and carrying out numerous operational duties. Grade levels and departments usually have a designated representative (or chair). The representative leads grade level or department meetings, meets with school administration, shuttles information and concerns across the two settings, and coordinates completion of necessary chores (e.g., ordering materials, arranging field trips, selecting textbooks, coordinating assemblies).

Less common, however, are grade level or department meetings that consistently focus on teaching and learning, provide professional development, and contribute to improved student achievement. Teachers and administrators generally agree that grade level and department meetings *should* focus on teaching and learning, but practically speaking it is not so easy to do. There is always a long queue of seemingly urgent informational and operational topics that gobble up time. The group may intend to plan units and lessons or analyze student work samples, but it is often difficult to preserve and carry out that intent in the face of other competing topics and issues. Nevertheless, grade level and department meetings are an existing setting at most schools and therefore well worth improving.

The guidelines for successful grade level or department meetings are: (1) establish a consistent and regular time for meetings; (2) focus meetings specifically and systematically on goal setting and assessing student work; and (3) provide support and assistance to the grade level or department representatives who lead/facilitate the meetings.

Establish a Consistent and Regular Time for Grade Level or Department Meetings

At project schools, grade levels or departments meet for 90–120 minutes each month, a total of 15–20 hours across the school year. At some schools, this involves one 2 hour meeting per month. At other schools, grade levels or departments convene twice a month, for 45–60 minutes each meeting. These meetings are scheduled into the school's master calendar, and they take place as expected for the full allotted time, without exception. This consistency and regularity is important for two reasons. First, teachers need to view these meetings as a required and a regular part of their work schedule. Second, assuming the intent is to actually focus on teaching and learning, grade levels and departments need to be able to depend on a reasonable allotment of time to do so.

We have observed at schools where grade level or department meetings are held "as needed" and/or scheduling is left to the discretion of each grade level or department (e.g., during lunch). At some schools this might conceivably work, but it does not involve a school wide norm for grade level and department meetings. Typically, without such a norm, teachers do not come to view these meetings as a regular part of their work schedule. A school could establish a policy regarding the frequency and amount of time grade levels and departments should meet and leave the rest up to each group. Unfortunately, that means the dates and times for the meetings have to be determined, possibly on a meeting by meeting basis. This is an example of the kinds of topics that distract from actually getting down to work on teaching and learning.

Even with a regular schedule of meetings, it is important to protect each meeting and the time allotment. If meetings are intermittently cancelled or shortened, teachers' perceptions of the setting degrades: it is not really a regular part of their work schedule, and it is not really an allotted time on which they can depend. The same degradation of perceptions and expectations occurs when planned activities and discussions related to teaching and learning gets displaced by topics and issues unrelated to teaching and learning. Often this happens when the administration needs to disseminate or clarify information about district or school policies, upcoming events or pending decisions. If this happens regularly, however, teachers conclude that this is not really a time and place to focus on teaching and learning; this is where we handle school business.

Focus Grade Level or Department Meetings Specifically on Goals and Indicators

The central issue underlying more effective grade level and department meetings is establishing and sustaining a clear focus on teaching and learning. The most successful way to accomplish this is to make goal setting and assessing students work the central occupation of the meetings. Goal setting and assessment activities provide a concrete and reliable way to initiate, focus and sustain talk about teaching and learning

By goal setting we mean articulating specifically what students should know and be able to do at the end of each grade level or course. The recent proliferation of standards greatly contributes to this process. Grade levels and departments, generally, need not start from scratch in trying to discuss and articulate concrete goals for student learning. In most project schools, the process involves reviewing existing state and district standards, discussing what they mean, and then either adopting them or adapting them in some manner teachers find meaningful (e.g., rewording them, adding to them, organizing them into a pacing schedule for the year). The purpose is twofold: to make student learning a central topic of discussion, and to establish a specific set of goals teachers agree to work toward. Discussions and activities at subsequent meetings then focus directly on efforts to help students achieve the agreed upon goals.

Once specific goals have been set, the most fruitful follow-up activity is assessment. To what extent are students meeting the stated goals? At some project schools, grade levels and departments focus over a prolonged period of time to develop a comprehensive set of grade level or course goals. Assessments begin only after the goal setting process is fully complete. Other schools have pursued these processes simultaneously. As soon as some portion of the goals are established (e.g., written communication and conventions), the grade level or department begins conducting assessment activities by bringing in student work and scoring it with the use of rubrics. As the year unfolds, the group continues to integrate these two major endeavors, assessments of set goals, and ongoing development of goals in additional areas.

Project schools that have completed the goal setting process have, in many cases, established a systematic schedule of assessments that are conducted and scored at the beginning, middle, and end of the year. One or two grade level meetings are devoted at each time in the year to score student work and systematically tally and review the results. Over the course of the year, then, approximately 30–50% of the grade level or department meetings involve assessing student work and interpreting results. The remaining allotment of time is spent sharing and discussing specific strategies teachers are using to help students achieve the learning goals and improve performance on the assessments. The schedule of assessments, at the beginning, middle, and end of the year, provides a structure and purposefulness, a feedback loop, to the discussion and implementation of teaching strategies.

While there are numerous leadership and organizational strategies that support this process (most of which are discussed in the next subsection), goal setting and assessment activities have consistently produced a positive impact on grade level and department meetings at project schools. The goal setting process tends to be more challenging because it often seems abstract to teachers. In contrast, given reasonably good tools, the assessment activities tend to be more straightforward, because they seem more concrete. That is why we typically recommend that schools initiate some assessment activities soon after the goal setting process gets underway. The assessments add energy to the process and introduce an element of purposefulness to the goal setting process. Therefore, we are setting these goals because we are going to genuinely work toward them and systematically evaluate our progress.

Provide Support and Assistance to the Teachers Who Lead/facilitate the Grade Level or Department Meetings

Teachers tend to be skeptical about meetings, as well they should be. If one is in a meeting, for example, one is not grading papers, unless, of course, teachers view it as an *irrelevant* or *inefficient* meeting, in which case they often do grade their papers. Yet, relevancy and efficiency are not particularly hard to achieve. Many, if not most, teachers find goal setting and assessment quite relevant, as long as they are conducted efficiently. The key to efficiency, in our experience, is providing meeting leaders with ongoing assistance and support.

There are any number of generic skills and strategies meeting leaders might need, all of which contribute to meeting efficiency, including developing agendas, facilitating discussions, managing time, taking notes, etc. However, meeting leaders also need and benefit from assistance and support specific to the tasks the grade level or department is to undertake.

For example, at one of the project schools, grade levels engaged in the following as a goal setting task: They reviewed district content standards for reading, discussed and prioritized each goal listed under the reading standards, and then distributed the goals over the four quarters of the school year to arrive at a pacing plan. In preparation for leading this activity, grade level chairs participated in two preparatory meetings in which they read through the district standards, discussed them, and practiced the process of prioritizing and distributing goals across the year for a sample grade level. Based on their own dry-run, they decided to enlarge the district standards for each grade level and cut each of the individual goals into strips. During the actual grade level meetings, teachers read through all the reading standards and goals, then focused on each goal individually, discussed what it meant, and taped it to large butcher paper divided into the four quarters of the school year. These grade level meeting were well received by the staff and productive, yielding a published set of grade level goals for reading.

Part of the success of these meetings is likely attributable to the preparation completed prior to the meeting by the grade level chairs. The two preparatory meetings provided a setting for them to become familiar with the district content standards and develop a process through which they could sustain attention and meaningful discussions among the teachers. It would be easy to overlook the importance of the cutting and taping strategy the chairs developed. Yet, consider for a moment how unpredictable the grade level meetings might have been if the chairs had equipped themselves only with the district standards and the question, What should students know and be able to do when they complete our grade level?

Grade level or department chairs need the same kind of support and assistance when it comes to assessment tasks. At each project school where grade level and department meetings are used to assess student work, the leaders have participated in preparatory meetings where they review scoring rubrics, practice scoring and develop specific protocols for assessing student work with their grade levels or departments (i.e., reviewing example papers, scoring in pairs, tallying up results, etc.)

At project schools, grade level and department chairs are members of the Academic Achievement Leadership Team (the next setting to be described). That team meets on a monthly basis. One of the main purposes of the AALT is to provide support and assistance to the chairs, specifically with regard to leading and facilitating grade level and department meetings.

There are, however, other ways to address efficiency. For example, at some project schools, administrators and coordinators help facilitate grade level or department meetings. If there has not been sufficient time to support and assist the chairs in preparing to lead and facilitate a particular undertaking, one of the administrators or coordinators, who has had sufficient preparation time, leads the meeting.

In some cases, where there is a specific need, an outside consultant might attend meetings and provide direct assistance to the grade level or department. The principal at one school requested the help of our project advisors to assist in planning, organizing and leading the kindergarten grade level meetings at her school. Together, the principal and advisors developed a plan for the whole year of kindergarten meetings, including an analysis of students' beginning of the year assessments, teachers long range planning, and a study of our language arts model. Teachers approved mid- and end-of-year assessments in order to evaluate their students' growth and classroom program. Through classroom visits and demonstrations, the advisors were able to further extend the teachers' understandings and support their implementation of specific language arts practices.

Academic Achievement Leadership Team

The Academic Achievement Leadership Team (AALT) consists of at least one representative from each grade level or department, the principal, and some or all other administrators and coordinators at the school (at some schools parents also serve on the AALT). The AALT meets each month for approximately two hours (a total of 20 hours across the school year). The broad purpose of the AALT is to set direction for and lead school wide efforts to improve student achievement. That involves: (a) leading the process of setting grade level or course goals for student learning; (b) identifying indicators to assess the goals and leading the grade level or department meetings when assessment of student work takes place; (c) identifying and implementing promising curriculum and methods that help students achieve the learning goals; and (d) regularly evaluating school wide achievement and determining next steps (action plans).

School leadership teams are not a new concept. Principals typically meet with grade level or department chairs, if for no other reason than to disseminate information. Moreover, many schools have a curriculum committee, an instructional council or some other duly named group designed to address matters of curriculum and instruction (textbook adoption, report card procedures, topics for professional development). Many contemporary school reform designs (School-based Management, LEARN) explicitly include a leadership group, albeit, one whose charge is typically quite broad. Democratic representation of all stakeholders (students, parents, classified personnel, certificated staff and administration) and shared decision making with regard to budget, hiring, physicial plant, teacher placement, as well as policies regarding curriculum and instruction are considered necessary.

The AALT, as we have designed it, functions differently than the examples described above. First, the AALT is vested with greater responsibility and importance than is usually afforded grade level or department chairs or the typical curriculum committee. The central and unambiguous goal of AALT is improved student achievement. Together, teacher-leaders and administrators develop and carry out with the entire staff several coordinated actions designed to improve teaching, learning, and ultimately achievement. Second, the AALT focuses more narrowly than most reform-based leadership groups. Democratic representation and shared decision-making on budgeting, hiring, teacher placement and broader curricular policies all have a bearing on student achievement. But the relationships are typically complex and indirect. By design, the AALT focuses tightly on mechanisms that most directly relate to student achievement—goals for student learning, assessments and indicators of those goals, and teaching methods that best help students achieve those goals.

In California, schools are required to conduct a Program Quality Review (PQR). The process operates on a four-year cycle. Every four years, the school constitutes a team to conduct a thorough internal evaluation of the academic program, including a review of student work samples, classroom visitations, and an analysis of curriculum and methods. Based on this review, the team then publishes and presents a report of findings and a plan for program improvement for the next four years. At most schools, the PQR team is then disbanded. Another is reconstituted four years later when the process repeats. This review and planning process are analogous to the work of the AALT, except the AALT never disbands. It carries on from one year to the next, guiding the goal setting process, leading assessment activities, identifying promising methods, determining needed professional development, evaluating school wide student achievement levels, and planning next steps.

There are several guidelines for successful Academic Achievement Leadership Teams: (1) strive for a truly representative AALT; (2) set a regular meeting day and time for AALT meetings throughout the year; (3) focus first and foremost on goals and indicators; (4) use AALT meetings to help teachers prepare for meetings they have to lead; (5) anticipate and complete needed work between AALT meetings; (6) strive for constructive and productive discussions; (7) model support and pressure; and (8) anticipate and seek out needed resources and assistance.

Strive for a Truly Representative AALT

The AALT consists of a representative from each grade level or department. It should also provide representation of the different faculty constituencies including skeptics, enthusiasts, veterans, and also younger teachers. Ultimately, the AALT sets direction for and leads the staff in school wide improvement efforts. The more AALT is truly representative, the greater the likelihood that its direction and leadership will resonate with the entire faculty. In some schools, selection of grade level and department chairs is governed by specific contractual regulations. In such cases, the school may want to select AALT representatives separate from "chairs" so that AALT responsibilities are not complicated with the added responsibilities and regulations specified for "chairpersons." Representatives should be selected or recruited, however, with a very clear description of the role of AALT.

Set a Regular Meeting Day and Time for AALT Meetings Throughout the Year

As we discussed with regard to grade level or department meetings, regular meeting days and times and a schedule of meetings for the entire year help establish the perception and reality of AALT as a required part of teachers' work schedule (here specifically for AALT members) and a reliable place and time to work on given tasks. With meeting dates and times scheduled, it is equally important to actually carry out those meetings, avoid cancellations and abbreviations of the designated time, as well as topics and issues not directly related to AALT activities.

Focus First and Foremost on Goals and Indicators

The major responsibilities of the AALT are leading the staff through the process of (a) setting explicit goals for student learning and (b) regularly assessing student work to determine the extent to which students are meeting those goals. These are the two major undertakings AALT should tackle first. These are the two major undertakings AALT should always work to sustain. In any area of the curriculum, reading, writing, oral language, math, social studies, science, physical education, and electives, our basic premise is that improving teaching and learning school wide emanates from a staff genuinely asking and effectively answering two core questions: What are our goals for student learning (i.e., what do we want our students to be able to know and do)? And how are students progressing toward those goals? The job of the AALT is to keep these two questions at the center of the staff's attention.

Use AALT Meetings to Help Teachers to Prepare for Meetings They Have to Lead

AALT members lead and facilitate grade level or department meetings, and in some cases, work group meetings. It is not easy leading and facilitating meetings of your colleagues. The critical enabler, however, is preparation. AALT meetings provide time for AALT members to collectively and individually prepare to lead and facilitate other meetings. The preparation is both conceptual and practical. If, for example, grade levels and departments are going to review state or district standards as part of the goal setting process, AALT members need the opportunity to read and discuss the standards so they can understand them. They need to ask, How are they organized? What do they mean? How might they serve to help teachers set concrete goals for student learning? AALT members also need to have some agenda or process for engaging their grade level or department in reviewing the standards and setting goals. That is, they need to have a practical sense of what they are going to do in their meetings and ask, How can we actually use the standards to set and share goals for student learning and how to prioritize these goals?

Anticipate and Complete Needed Work Between AALT Meetings

In order for the important work of improving academic achievement to be successful, much detail work must be done in between meetings. Agendas for meetings should be made and circulated several days ahead of time. Reminders of meeting dates and specific due dates for tasks stemming from previous meetings should be made on a regular basis. It would be easy to assume that AALT members should be able to autonomously handle the responsibilities of committee work and collateral duties. But teachers' main responsibility is teaching every day. As a result, AALT deadlines can be forgotten, meetings can be missed, and momentum can be lost. Under these circumstances each meeting feels like the first one, where committee members need to be reacquainted with the objectives of the committee and tasks they are responsible for. Published agendas, reminders and meeting summaries can help substantially. The key is to sustain a collective and accessible record, a memory, of the group's activities.

Strive for Constructive and Productive Discussions

One of our central tenets is that improving teaching and learning involves establishing settings in which teachers can learn and work productively together. Such settings necessitate constructive and productive discourse. The group needs talk and interaction that stays on topic, which allows for different points of view, and that ultimately gets things done (e.g., identifies needs, articulates options, formulates plans, addresses questions, makes decisions). The content and character of discourse across all the settings described in this chapter emanate, at least in part, from the discourse of the AALT. *What* is discussed in AALT meetings and *how* it is discussed shapes in important ways *what* is discussed and *how* it is discussed in subsequent grade level and department meetings. We presume the most immediate way to begin fostering more constructive and productive discussions throughout the school is by making them happen within the AALT.

That puts some degree of pressure on the chair or facilitator of the AALT (typically the principal; in some cases, a lead-teacher). However, there are some tried and true principles which, if followed consistently by the group leader/facilitator, do help. They should prepare written agendas with clear articulation of the topics/issues to be addressed and what specifically needs to be accomplished by meeting's end; listen carefully to what people are saying in order to pick up on and/or rearticulate for the whole group the points being made; take brief notes as the discussion unfolds to record key points that need to be preserved or addressed subsequently; as discussions prolong or stray remind the group intermittently of the specific topic/issue at hand and what needs to be accomplished; estimate the amount of time for each agenda item and then manage the available time aggressively, intermittently reminding members of time remaining for a particular item and segue from one item to the next without delay; and finally, evaluate accomplishments at the end of each meeting.

Provide and Model Support and Pressure

If the AALT is functioning effectively, it is consistently getting things done, within the group itself and also with the rest of the staff. It has drafted grade level or course goals, developed or selected specific assessments, conducted assessments and generated tables of results, developed or located curriculum materials, and piloted strategies in the classroom. This kind of work needs support and benefits from an element of pressure. Support usually comes in the form of needed resources such as, typing, xeroxing, binders, release time, compensation for work outside the school day, and outside consultation to fulfill a particular need. These are the kinds of resources the AALT chair must anticipate and relentlessly seek to provide. Pressure typically comes in the form of time tables, deadlines and holding people accountable for doing what they said they would do.

We generally recommend that the school principal serve as the AALT chair, because the principal is usually in the best position to provide the needed support (i.e., make as many of the needed resources happen as possible) and exert the necessary pressure (i.e., hold people accountable). Some may find the element of pressure, particularly holding people accountable, a sensitive or problematic matter. In our experience, however, actually getting things done is an enormous source of satisfaction for most teachers. The kind of pressure and accountability we are talking about here in the context of AALT is generally agreeable, if not welcomed, by teachers. They want to be productive; they want to serve the faculty well. Most AALT members will respond well to deadlines and reminders and will appreciate it when the principal (or anyone else serving as chair) applies heavier pressure to those not fulfilling their responsibilities.

This support and pressure within AALT contributes to AALT's productivity, but it can also provide AALT members with a growing sense of how to get things accomplished within their own grade levels and departments. At some project schools, we have seen AALT members utilize support and pressure mechanisms experienced in AALT with their own grade levels or departments. They learn to marshall resources, set deadlines, and provide reminders, etc.

Anticipate and Seek out Needed Resources and Assistance

All the organization, hard work and good intentions cannot substitute for a lack of expertise in a subject area or a particular undertaking, such as developing a system of assessments for school wide goals. Moving forward on a challenging undertaking without expertise or assistance can undermine the school wide effort. When AALT finds itself in this situation, they should actively seek out the resources and individuals that possess the expert knowledge required to fill the gap.

Faculty-Wide Settings and Training Workshops

The unique characteristic of the faculty-wide setting, whether it is a meeting or training workshop, is that every teacher is present (or, in the case of multi-track, year-round schools at least a majority of teachers are present). Such settings involve enormous challenges and important opportunities. The major challenge is engagement: How do you sustain attention and get things accomplished with a large group of diverse individuals (i.e., from different grade levels, departments and peer groups, and with different levels of interest, experience, and years at the school)? The central opportunity, however, is coherence. Productive faculty meetings and workshops contribute to shared understandings and purposefulness.

Like grade level or department meetings, faculty-wide settings are established school settings that can take on a new role and character. Within the context of the Getting Results/School Change model, faculty-wide settings can be redefined as the context that supports and extends the work of the other settings (i.e., AALT, grade level meetings, teacher work groups). Faculty meetings are pivotal in bringing these groups together to confirm the school wide goals and keep the agenda productively moving forward. This often requires reprioritizing faculty meeting agendas, placing a high priority on school wide improvement efforts and finding other ways to disseminate necessary information regarding school operations (via memos, the weekly bulletin, and more abbreviated reports at faculty meetings). As an example, a 75-minute faculty meeting spends the first 50 minutes on improvement efforts and completes all necessary informational announcements related to school operations in the remaining 25.

Schools, like any other workplace or community, involve substantial ongoing communication—about report card guidelines, district compliance reports, back-to-school nite procedures, campus supervision and security, holiday activities, candy drives, staff parking, are all topics necessary in that communication. Yet most administrators and teachers agree that the delivery of detailed information on such matters at faculty meetings is generally tedious and inefficient. Ultimately, effective communication involves discipline and effort on the part of those delivering information (determining what really needs to be communicated and delivering it orally or in writing succinctly and clearly) and those receiving it (listening attentively to the announcements and reports and reading carefully the memos and bulletins).

Faculty-wide discipline and effort with regard to communication are not easily achieved. They involve substantial and often problematic workplace behaviors. Nevertheless, in our experience, they can be fostered successfully when faculty-wide meetings become increasingly substantive. When faculty meeting time is increasingly and productively devoted to concrete and sustained school improvement efforts, most teachers will pick up the slack by reading their memos and bulletins more carefully and listening to more succinct announcements and reports with greater attention. The key, then, is more substance, focusing more consistently and coherently on school wide improvement efforts related to teaching and learning.

Substance comes in a variety of forms, including reports and discussions on school wide student learning goals, indicators (data), teaching methods and strategies, as well as plans and options for future improvement initiatives. Substance may also come in the form of reports from and feedback to specific groups, such as the AALT, workgroups, grade levels or departments, and other committees. Training workshops also provide substance, if they are carefully selected, planned and targeted to address specific student learning goals set and shared by the faculty.

Guidelines for successful faculty-wide settings and training workshops are: (1) focus faculty-wide settings on student learning goals; (2) use faculty-wide settings to launch grade level or department undertakings; (3) use faculty-wide settings to share grade level, department or workgroup undertakings and connect them to school wide goals; (4) establish and stick to a regular schedule for faculty meetings; (5) develop long-term plans for the content of faculty meetings; (6) select training workshops proactively that lay groundwork for subsequent initiatives; and (7) select training workshops that are responsive to emerging faculty needs.

Focus Faculty-wide Settings on Student Learning Goals

Student learning should be the central focus of the school. One way to establish that focus is by setting and sharing concrete goals for student learning and then continuing to use them as the driving force for school improvement and professional development. For each of the settings previously discussed, we emphasized the importance of focusing on student learning goals. The same holds true for faculty-wide settings.

How does one focus faculty-wide settings on student learning goals? By talking about them and promoting discussion about them, directly, "What do we mean when we say we want our students to read outside of school for at least 100 minutes a week?" In relationship to data and indicators of student performance, what do we know about the number of books our students are reading on their own? In relationship to actions planned and carried out, how might weekly book fairs support students' self-selected reading. In relationship to teaching methods and strategies, does reading aloud to students and letting them share with one another the books they are reading increase interest and motivation to read?

In more specific terms, faculty-wide settings contribute to and benefit from the focus and productivity of the other settings. The faculty-wide setting should be the forum for finalizing and adopting school wide student learning goals. Grade levels and departments, led by AALT members, complete the detailed work of actually developing the goals, but ultimately drafts should be reviewed and then adopted by the entire faculty, together. Similarly, as we described it previously, at different points in the year grade levels and departments should systematically assess how students are progressing with respect to learning goals. The results of those assessments should be shared at faculty meetings. The goals and the indicators are the catalysts for professional development and improvement of student learning.

Use Faculty-wide Settings to Launch Grade Level or Department Undertakings

Any school wide initiative undertaken by staff is best launched in the faculty-wide setting. Whether it is goal setting or assessments or implementing a specific instructional strategy, the faculty-wide setting provides an opportunity to articulate the purpose and process. It establishes a common purpose for the schoolwide effort.

Use Faculty-wide Settings to Share Grade Level, Department or Workgroup Undertakings and Connect Them to Schoolwide Goals

The work of each grade level, department and/or workgroup should be shared in faculty meetings. The faculty should know what all of the different groups are working on and specifically what they are accomplishing. Sharing the activities of each group also provides the opportunity to connect their undertakings back to the schoolwide goals. For example, at one project school, the year begins and culminates with a half-day faculty meeting. At the beginning of the year, the faculty as a whole reviews schoolwide achievement data, grade levels meet to examine their results and determine specific learning goals to target for the year, and then the whole faculty reconvenes to hear from each grade level. At the end of the year, each grade level, work group, and committee present a brief report on the goals targeted, and accomplishments across the year. The settings described in this chapter are designed to provide teachers with regular, ongoing time to articulate with their colleagues, improve their skills and knowledge, and develop and implement improved curriculum and teaching methods. The whole faculty setting provides an opportunity to make things cohere, to consistently articulate and demonstrate the common purpose these settings serve, improving teaching, learning, and ultimately achievement.

Establish and Stick to a Regular Schedule for Faculty Meetings

Schools vary greatly in terms of the frequency with which the entire faculty meets. We have seen schools that hold faculty meetings almost every week (approximately 30 or more per year). We have seen others that have very few (3 or 4 per year). Most project schools hold faculty meetings once a month on a set day and particular week each month (e.g., Tuesday of the first week of each month). The set and regular schedule serves two purposes. First, it provides an established time to debrief and support the other ongoing settings. In one project school, for instance, the AALT determined that procedures for scoring students' work samples in grade level meetings needed to be refined. This was handled effectively and efficiently in the subsequent faculty meeting. AALT members did not have to take time in their subsequent grade level meeting to train the teachers on the new procedure, and a special faculty meeting did not have to be scheduled. The training was simply slotted into the agenda for the next, regularly scheduled faculty meeting.

Second, monthly faculty meetings also provide administrators with a dependable time and place to deliver necessary information. The goal is of course delivering that information efficiently. Recall that we recommended devoting the last 25 minutes of a 75 minute faculty meeting to announcements and preserving the first 50 minutes for school improvement undertakings. But a set time and place to handle such communication helps discipline the communication system. Administrators have to absorb incoming information, filter what truly needs to be passed on to staff, determine what can be delivered in writing and what needs to be addressed orally in a faculty meeting, and then schedule priority topics into upcoming faculty meetings.

Develop Long-term Plans for the Content of Faculty Meetings

The guiding question for faculty meetings is, "What can we do in our faculty meetings that will help move our efforts forward?" The question should be addressed by administrators and the AALT prior to or very early in the year. For example, one of the major undertakings for the coming year is setting and sharing goals for language arts. That work will proceed, under the guidance of AALT members at grade level meetings or within the language arts department. But there will be critical junctures when the work of each grade level or the language arts department needs to be reviewed and discussed by the entire faculty. That would suggest at least 3 faculty meetings where at least some portion of time is devoted to launching the undertaking at a meeting early on, reviewing preliminary drafts sometime later, and then ultimately adopting the final product. It necessitates long-term planning of faculty meetings, coordinated with long-term planning of initiatives to be undertaken across the school year. Such planning, however, has important benefits. With our goal setting example, the three targeted faculty meetings establish a time line for the development of the goals. We're going to launch it at this faculty meeting, review drafts at this one, and finalize them at this one. The faculty meetings serve as deadlines, an appropriate and necessary form of pressure.

As another example, let us say the school, again via grade levels or department meeetings, is going to conduct an assessment of one or more learning goals at the beginning, middle, and end of the year. Much of the work, such as reviewing procedures, scoring student work, and tallying up results, will be completed during grade level or department meetings. But we can anticipate the need to support this effort at faculty-wide meetings around the time of each assessment—to collectively review, interpret, clarify results, and share and discuss next steps.

Select Training Workshops Proactively That Lay Groundwork for Subsequent Initiatives

What can we do in our faculty meetings that will help move our efforts forward? Sometimes the answer to this question is a carefully selected and well-timed training workshop. The staff may need to be trained in how to go about setting goals prior to engaging in the goal setting process in grade level or department meetings. Similarly, the staff may need training in how to evaluate student work samples or conduct particular assessments prior to the grade level or department meetings where the work is going to be completed.

Carefully selected training workshops can also lay the groundwork for a particular instructional initiative. For instance, related to its reading goals, one project school is initiating a school-wide recreational reading campaign. The AALT anticipated that if teachers were going to actively promote recreational reading among their students, they needed to know more about the kinds of books at a variety of difficulty levels student might enjoy. As a result, the AALT planned and conducted at a faculty meeting a 90 minute workshop that introduced teachers to a variety of popular young novels and storybooks. This workshop laid the groundwork for a series of undertakings the faculty pursued across the school year to promote recreational reading.

In each of the examples above the training workshop was purposeful and proactive. The workshops related directly to the school's effort to set, assess, and achieve specific learning goals, and the workshops anticipated the knowledge and skill the staff needed in order to meaningfully and successfully carry out actions designed to address the goals.

Select Training Workshops That Are Responsive to Emerging Faculty Needs

In some cases, the need for training workshops can be identified ahead of time, both prospectively and proactively. In other cases, the need emerges as activities and initiatives get underway. In other words, the guiding question, "What can we do in our faculty meetings that will help move our efforts forward?" has to be entertained and addressed as needed throughout the year as activities and initiatives unfold. In project schools, this kind of "eyes wide open" and "ears to ground" monitoring is conducted by AALT members. When a clear need emerges and there is an available and straightforward way to address the need, a carefully selected and well-timed training workshop can help move things along.

For example, in work groups and grade level meetings at one project school, teachers began teaching and assessing summary writing to gauge students' comprehension of stories. The major thrust was improving students' comprehension, but in the course of their work they also detected problems students were having in another goal area—writing conventions. Together with one of our project advisors, a teacher work group at the school had been studying, implementing and finding positive results with the use of passage dictation to help address particular writing conventions. That information was brought to the AALT, who then decided to schedule a dictation training workshop at an upcoming faculty meeting.

The 90 minute workshop was delivered, teachers responded positively, and supported by follow-up discussions at grade level meetings, most teachers began implementing passage dictation with successful results. Much of the workshop's success likely had to do with the fact that it was purposeful and responsive. It focused on a specific set of learning goals, writing conventions, and it was directly responsive to an emerging need among the staff, how do we best address writing conventions with our students?

DISCUSSION

Educators, researchers, and policymakers around the country are arguing forcefully that school reform requires strengthening the teaching profession through substantive and ongoing opportunities for teachers' professional development. Futrell, Holmes, Christie, and Cushman (1995), for example, write:

> Recently, concerns have been raised across the United States about the slow pace at which reforms are being implemented.... Much of this concern has to do with whether teachers are adequately prepared to work in restructured school environments, and whether traditional staff development methods can overcome factors such as resistance to change, a highly bureaucratized school culture, and educators' isolation from one another and exclusions from the decision-making process. (p. 1)

Our experiences support these observations. School reform without on-site professional development is a hollow promise. Just as we need to take long and hard looks at the contexts in which students learn, we must also take a serious look at the contexts in which teachers are expected to reformulate their teaching. Teachers must learn concepts, activities, and ways of interacting with others that are essential for improving teaching and learning in our schools. They must also learn about what their colleagues are doing, or attempting to do, in their classrooms, otherwise the "egg-crate" ecology of schools will forever doom the collaborative cultures many argue are essential for meaningful school reform (Darling-Hammond, 1997; Fullan, in press).

The settings we have described in this chapter can contribute to creating just such a culture, one in which the learning and development of teachers are accorded a similar priority as the learning and development of students. One teacher who had worked for several years at the school described by Goldenberg and Sullivan (1994) answered the following when asked whether she thought she was a better teacher as a result of the project:

> Definitely. 100% … 200% … Everything, it all comes together. Before, we would just have faculty meetings. Then we started having grade-level meetings. It went from the very general to very specific, and yet, back to the general, because everyone knows what everyone's doing, and you have your meetings, and then you meet with other people and you see what they are doing. *It's like one big classroom instead of one big school.* (Sullivan, 1994, p. 1; emphasis added)

Her comments bring to mind Sarason's often-stated, most recently in 1996, observation that "You cannot create *and* sustain a context of productive learning for others unless that kind of context exists for you" (Sarason, 1996, p. 383). Schools as a whole, not simply individual classrooms, must become settings for productive teaching and learning. If schools do not contain settings to promote teacher learning and development, improvements in student achievement are impossible, and once again we will be staring backward at another failed school reform movement.

Our work has involved almost exclusively schools in low-income, urban communities serving primarily language and cultural minority children. We have no empirical basis for comparing the needs and circumstances of the schools with which we have worked to other schools that serve more affluent or demographically different populations. No doubt, the urgent need to improve professional development programs applies to all schools and educators, regardless of the economic status, culture, language or birthplace of their students. Improving student outcomes depends heavily on improving teachers' knowledge and skills.

Nevertheless, as we have observed it, there are also less tangible but fundamentally important and competing perceptions at play in schools like ours, such as hope and despair, efficacy and futility, commitment and indifference. While we have not fully documented it, our impression is that meaningful and productive school-based professional development coupled with measurable school improvement contributes significantly and positively to teachers' and administrators' perceptions of the value and promise of their work and the potential and capacity of their students. Such perceptions, we believe, are worth striving for at all schools, but they are especially important, in their own right, at schools serving language and cultural minority children in low income, urban communities.

ACKNOWLEDGMENTS

Revised version of a paper presented at the Annual Conference of the American Educational Research Association, Montreal, Canada, April 1999. The Literacy Network, a systemwide Title VII project, is underwritten by the Office of Bilingual Education and Minority Languages Affairs, US Dept. of Education. This work was also supported under the Education Research and Development Program, PR/Award No. R306A60001, the Center for Research on Education, Diversity & Excellence (CREDE), as administered by the Office of Educational Research and Improvement (OERI), National Institute on the Education of At-Risk Students (NIEARS), U.S. Department of Education (USDOE). The opinions expressed here are those of the authors and do not necessarily represent the positions or policies of OBEMLA, OERI, NIEARS, or the USDOE.

REFERENCES

August, D., & Hakuta, K. (Eds.). (1997). *Improving school for language minority children: A research agenda.* Washington, DC: National Academy Press.

California Department of Education. (1992). *It's elementary: The report of the Elementary Grades Task Force.* Sacramento: California Department of Education.

Darling-Hammond, L. (1998). *The right to learn: A blueprint for creating schools that work.* San Francisco: Jossey-Bass.

Fashola, O., & Slavin, R. (1998, January). Schoolwide reform models: What works? *Phi Delta Kappa,* 370–379.

Fullan, M. (1991). *The new meaning of educational change.* New York: Teachers College Press.

Fullan, M. (in press). The three stories of educational reform: Inside; inside/out; outside/in. *Phi Delta Kappan.*

Futrell, M., Holmes, D., Christie, J., & Cushman, E. (1995). *Linking education reform and teachers' professional development: The efforts of nine school districts.* Washington, DC: The George Washington University Graduate School of Education and Human Development.

Goldenberg, C. (1992/93). Instructional conversations: Promoting comprehension through discussion. *The Reading Teacher, 46,* 316–326.

Goldenberg, C., & Sullivan, J. (1994). *Making change happen in a language-minority school: A search for coherence* (Educational Practice Report #13). Santa Cruz: University of California at Santa Cruz, National Center for Research on Cultural Diversity and Second Language Learning.

González, J., & Darling-Hammond, L. (1997). *New concepts for new challenges: Professional development for teachers of immigrant youth.* McHenry, IL: Delta Systems and Center for Applied Linguistics.

Goodlad, J. (1984). *A place called school: Prospects for the future.* New York: McGraw-Hill Book Company.

Levine, D., & Lezotte, L. (1995). Effective schools research. In J. Banks & C. Banks (Eds.), *Handbook on Multicultural Education* (pp. 525–547). New York: Macmillan.

Palinscar, A., & Brown, A. (1985). Reciprocal teaching: A means to a meaningful end. In J. Osborn, P. Wilson, & R. C. Anderson (Eds.), *Reading education: Foundations for a literate America* (pp. 299–310). Lexington, MA: D.C. Heath & Co.

Powell, A., Goldenberg, C., & Cano, L. (1995). *Assisting change: Some settings for professional development work better than others.* Paper presented at the annual meeting of the American Educational Research Association, San Francisco, CA.

Sarason, S. (1972). *The creation of settings and the future societies.* San Francisco: Jossey-Bass.

Sarason, S. (1996). *Revisiting "The culture of the school and the problem of change".* New York: Teachers College Press.

Saunders, W. (in press). Improving literacy achievement for English learners in transitional bilingual programs. *Educational Research and Evaluation.*

Saunders, W., Goldenberg, G., & Hamann, J. (1992). Instructional conversations beget instructional conversations. *Teaching and Teacher Education, 8,* 199–218.

Saunders, W., O'Brien, G., Lennon, D., & McLean, J. (1998). Making the transition to English literacy successful: Effective strategies for studying literature with transition students. In R. Gersten & R. Jimenez (Eds.), *Promoting learning for culturally and linguistically diverse students: Classroom applications from contemporary research* (pp. 99–132). Belmont, CA: Wadsworth.

Strengthening the teaching profession. (1998). [Entire issue]. *Educational Leadership, 55*(5).

Tharp, R., & Gallimore, R. (1988). *Rousing minds to life.* Cambridge: Cambridge University Press.

PART V

TEACHER EDUCATION

CHAPTER 14

PRESERVICE TEACHERS CONNECT MULTICULTURAL KNOWLEDGE AND PERSPECTIVES WITH LITERACY INSTRUCTION FOR MINORITY STUDENTS

Hong Xu

Abstract: Little research has documented how preservice teachers apply a knowledge base gained from a professional course on multicultural education to working with students of diverse cultural and linguistic backgrounds. Adapting Schmidt's (1998a,b, 1999) ABC's Model, this study explores how preservice teachers connect multicultural knowledge and perspectives with literacy instruction for minority students when they are placed in a minority school for field experiences. The field experiences include whole class lesson teaching in reading and language arts and case studies of individual students. The findings of this study indicate that the Model presents preservice teachers with opportunities to learn about themselves and their students, as well as examine and challenge their own belief systems about students of other cultures. Lesson teaching and case studies provide them with a context of reality to translate multicultural knowledge to literacy instruction. This study also suggests an integration of the ABC's Model into teacher education programs to enhance preservice teachers' ability to link multicultural knowledge to literacy instruction for students of diverse backgrounds.

INTRODUCTION

Since 1979, teacher education programs in U.S. universities and colleges have been expected to prepare teachers to teach in various multicultural settings (The National Council for Accreditation of Teacher Education, 1979, 1992, 1994). The current reality is that "schools and classrooms, however, generally are not organized to accommodate diversity in students' background knowledge and experiences" (Zeichner, Grant, Gay, Gillette, Valli, & Villegas, 1998, p. 166). Furthermore, the teaching force still consists of a small number of members from minority groups. Minority students are more likely taught by female teachers who are White and middle class and who have had limited experiences with cultures other than their own (Bennett & LeCompte, 1990). On the other hand, the number of minority students enrolled in school is growing. It is estimated that by the year 2000, one third of school age students will be African, Asian, and Hispanic Americans (Adler, 1993). Therefore, it is critical that teacher educators at the university level continue to prepare White and middle class preservice teachers to work successfully and effectively with students from diverse cultural and linguistic backgrounds.

WHAT WE KNOW

Much research has been conducted to document the effectiveness of preparing preservice teachers for cultural and linguistic diversity (Bollin & Finkel, 1995; Cannella & Reiff, 1994; McDiarmid & Price, 1993; Zeichner et al., 1998). One central theme that has emerged from this area is that professional courses on multicultural education have little impact on preservice teachers' pedagogical practices when they enter schools to work with students of diverse backgrounds. One possible explanation for the lack of the connection between courses on multicultural education and culturally responsive teaching in schools is that preservice teachers may hold the same belief systems before and after the courses (Cannella & Reiff, 1994). Such belief systems have been shaped by their life and school experiences as members of a White middle class and, thus, influence how they respond to needs of students with other cultural backgrounds. It could also be that preservice teachers have had limited field experiences in which to apply what they have learned with diverse students (Hyun & Marshall, 1997; Kleinfeld, 1998) and to challenge their own misconceptions and stereotypes about their students (Cabello & Burstein, 1995).

Another line of research has particularly addressed the impact of field experiences on preservice teachers' abilities to work with students of color (Haberman & Post, 1990; Ladson-Billings, 1991; Larke, Wiseman, & Bradley, 1990; Mahan, 1982). This research has produced inconclusive and mixed results. Some studies have demonstrated modest impact on preservice teachers. For example, Mahan (1982) concluded that preservice teachers at least became comfortable in another culture. Larke, Wiseman, and Bradley's (1990) study indicated a change in preservice teachers' attitudes toward and perceptions of African and Hispanic American students. Other studies, on the other hand, challenged such impact. Ladson-Billings (1991) suggested no significant difference in multicultural attitudes and beliefs between those who took a multicultural course with a component of field experiences and those who did not. Furthermore, Haberman and Post (1990) poignantly pointed out the negative aspect of field experiences. That is, field experiences may negatively reinforce preservice teachers' misconceptions and stereotypes.

WHAT WE DON'T KNOW

The existing research has focused on the effectiveness of multicultural education courses and field experiences, as well as a combination of both. We know little, however, about how preservice teachers use knowledge and concepts learned from a multicultural education course to guide them in providing culturally responsive teaching in content areas, such as literacy instruction. Successful literacy development is deemed the most important indicator of school success (Allington & Walmsley, 1995). Given the fact that minority students continue to experience more school failure than their European American peers (Au, 1998), there is a need for further study to explore how preservice teachers apply their knowledge of multiculturalism in literacy instruction for students of diverse backgrounds. In this chapter, I describe a study that I conducted with preservice teachers to examine how they linked multicultural knowledge and perspectives to literacy instruction for minority students. I was particularly interested in (a) how preservice teachers perceive themselves, students, and teaching within the context of a multicultural school setting, and (b) how they relate multicultural knowledge and perspectives to literacy instruction.

THE ABC'S MODEL

This study was inspired by Schmidt's ABC's Model (1998a,b, 1999). The ABC's Model was developed based on research related to using cultural autobiographies (Banks, 1991; Florio-Ruane, 1994; Florio-Ruane & deTar, 1995), interviews, and cross-cultural analyses (Spindler & Spindler, 1987) to enhance cross-cultural appreciation and understanding. As Schmidt described in the ABC's Model, preservice teachers completed the following tasks:

1. Autobiography was written in detail, including key life events related to education, family, religious tradition, recreation, victories and defeats.
2. Biography of a person culturally different was written from in depth unstructured interviews that include key life events.
3. Cross-cultural analyses of similarities and differences related to the life stories were listed in chart format.
4. Cultural analysis of differences was examined with explanations of personal discomfort and admiration.
5. Communication plans for literacy development and home/school connections were designed with modifications for classroom adaptation. (1998a, p. 28)

In this study, I adapted Schmidt's ABC's Model by incorporating the first three components of the Model into one course requirement—a case study of one minority student. I embedded the last two components in various reflective activities related to field experiences.

METHODS

Participants and Setting

A qualitative case study was the research design for this study (Merriam, 1988). The case study methodology allowed me to investigate preservice teachers' connecting multiculturalism to literacy instruction within the natural context of field experiences in a minority school. The participants in this study were 20 preservice teachers, four of whom identified themselves as minorities. They were Mexican American, Korean and Mexican American, European and Mexican American, and European and Native American. Sixteen out of 20 were from middle-class families; four were from families of lower socioeconomic levels. Five preservice teachers claimed to have had some experiences with minorities.

The preservice teachers were in the second block semester of their professional education courses. In the first block semester, they took a multicultural education course, *School, Society, and Diversity.* During the course, they read the books, *Savage Inequalities* (Kozol, 1991), *The Dreamkeepers: Successful Teachers of African American Children* (Ladson-Billings, 1994), *Valuing Diversity: The Primary Years* (McCracken, 1993), and *Learning Denied* (Taylor, 1991). They also read and discussed articles related to diversity and multicultural issues. Additionally, they spent one hour per week observing either a class or working with individual students. Other course assignments included a research presentation and a multicultural instructional unit.

In the second block semester, the preservice teachers were taking two literacy courses, *Foundations of Reading Instruction* and *Language Literacy Acquisition*, both of which I was teaching. The main textbooks were *Helping Children Learn to Read* (Searfoss & Readence, 1994) and *Language Arts: Content and Teaching Strategies* (Tompkins, 1998). I structured both courses to maximize preservice teachers' opportunities to connect literacy theories with practices and to construct and reconstruct their understandings of literacy instruction for students of diverse backgrounds. Specifically, they participated actively in experiencing and demonstrating, as a student and teacher, instructional strategies, and developed literature units integrating teaching comprehension and skills. Throughout both courses, they also discussed articles and literacy topics in relation to teaching students of diverse backgrounds.

In the sixth week of the semester, the preservice teachers began their field experiences in a school located in a poverty area. The school had predominately Hispanic students as well as some African American and White students. All students were qualified for free or reduced lunches. Twelve cooperating teachers in the school were Hispanic; six were European American. The school was recently rated by the district as a recognized one for students' high academic achievement.

Eighteen out of 20 preservice teachers were placed in sixteen K-6 grade classrooms. Of the remainder, one was in a social adjustment class (Grades 2–5); the other was in an academic adjustment class (Grades 1–6). The preservice teachers were in the assigned classes at least three hours per week for eight weeks.

Data Collection

Lesson Teaching

Each preservice teacher taught at least one whole class lesson in reading and language arts. He or she discussed the lesson content and structure with the cooperating teacher.

Case Study

The cooperating teachers selected the case-study students based on who needed extra assistance in literacy development. The case study consisted of three parts. The first part was related to the first three components of the ABC's Model (Autobiography, Biography, and Cross-cultural Analysis). Before the field experiences, the preservice teachers wrote autobiographies highlighting cultural values, school and home literacy experiences, and how their own cultural backgrounds would affect themselves as teachers. They then interviewed their case-study students regarding their cultural and linguistic backgrounds, and school and home literacy experiences. Later, the preservice teachers gathered additional information from informal chats with the students and cooperating teachers, as well as participatory observations of the students' engagement in literacy events. Finally, they wrote biographies of the students and highlighted similarities and differences between themselves and the students in cross-cultural comparison charts.

The second part of the case study involved informal assessment of the students. The preservice teachers first administered an informal reading inventory (Flynt & Cooter, 1998) and a spelling inventory (Bear, Invernizzi, Templeton, & Johnston, 1996). Then, they wrote anecdotal records about the students and collected samples of the students' writing.

The third part of the case study included the preservice teachers' application of instructional strategies and use of children's literature with the case-study students. They documented, in a strategy or literature sheet, what worked or did not work with the students.

Reflections

During and after their field experiences, the preservice teachers reflected upon their experiences. First, after each lesson, they wrote reflections that included students' reactions to the lesson, strengths and future improvements of the lesson, and applications of theories and course content. Second, after each field experience, the preservice teachers also reflected and composed questions that provided the basis for class discussions. Third, at the end of the field experiences they wrote a summative reflective report in which they briefly described the experiences of whole class teaching and working with the case-study students, and discussed lessons learned about teaching, learning, students, and diversity. Finally, they reflected upon their work with the students in case-study reports. Specifically, they discussed applications of various assessment tools and strategies, children's literature, literacy development of the students, and literacy instruction in relation to the students' linguistic and cultural backgrounds.

Researcher's Role

During the field experiences, I observed preservice teachers' whole class lesson teaching and took notes. Later, I provided them with constructive feedback. I also visited each preservice teacher at least once a week to observe how she or he worked with the case-study student and to respond to questions and concerns. The observations and discussions with each preservice teacher were recorded in field notes. During on-campus discussions of the questions that arose from the field experiences, I acted as a facilitator and a recorder. Key components of the discussions were jotted down in field notes.

Data Sources and Analysis

The data sources for this study were five sets of artifacts and four sets of field notes. The artifacts included: (a) preservice teachers' autobiographies, case-study students' biographies, and cross-cultural comparison charts; (b) reflections on lesson teaching; (c) summative reflective reports of field experiences; (d) case-study reports; and (e) strategy and literature sheets. The field notes contained: (a) observations of preservice teachers' lesson teaching; (b) observations of preservice teachers' working with the case-study students; (c) discussions with the preservice teachers during classroom visits; and (d) class discussions of the questions. The multiple data sources served as triangulation to enhance the validity and reliability of the study (Yin, 1994).

Data were analyzed using inductive coding techniques (Strauss, 1987). Each data set was initially read and reread line by line, and codes were then generated based on emerging patterns. Later, all sets of data were reread together to cross-check the similar and different codes across data sets. To revise the established codes to reflect new emerging patterns, I used the strategies described by Lincoln and Guba (1985) as "filling in, extension, bridging, and surfacing" of codes and subcodes.

FINDINGS

In the following section, I first describe how preservice teachers perceived themselves within the context of field experiences in a minority school. Then, I report how they understood the students and reacted to the differences between themselves and students. Finally, I present how they perceived teaching and how they related multicultural knowledge and perspectives to literacy instruction.

Self

Preservice teachers had a strong sense of self and cultural identity. In the autobiographies, they all acknowledged the importance of their own cultural backgrounds that made them who they were and stressed the importance of being accepted as who they were. Kasey, from a middle-class family background, stated: "My cultural background is important to me in that I believe I am the type of person I am today because of the way I was raised, and I do not want anyone to criticize me or my family for what we believe."

The preservice teachers from minority backgrounds showed their pride in being multicultural. Mary wrote in her autobiography:

> Being from a family that is multicultural, I feel that I have received the best of both worlds, being Korean and Mexican.... My cultural background is very important to me. I have always been proud of the two backgrounds that make me who I am.

While highly valuing their own cultures, the preservice teachers also expressed interests in knowing about other cultures and open-mindedness to accepting people from cultures other than their own. Cindy described her open-mindedness: "I love my culture very much, but I also like to learn about other cultures. Other people's ways and values are very interesting to me.... I think that my interest of other cultures will be very useful to me when I become a teacher."

In addition, six preservice teachers recognized how their cultural experiences shaped the way in which they would relate to the students of other cultures. Maria discussed advantages and disadvantages of being from a Hispanic cultural background:

> I will be able to better understand and relate to students of my cultural background. If I have students of some other background, I may not be able to relate to them or understand things they are talking about or going through.

Four of the six preservice teachers confronted ethnocentric perspectives, biases, and prejudices resulting from their own cultural experiences, which might affect their working with students of other cultures. Anna, a student of European American background, was aware of her limited perspectives as to understanding her students:

> I am very used to friends having the same background and culture as I have grown up with. My culture is the only culture I know well. There might be times that I do not understand the reasoning behind a fellow student or one of my pupils.

Sue described her family as having "two sides." Her mother's side of the family was closely knit and cherished many traditional values while her father's side of family did not "have the same beliefs" and were "Indian, alcoholics, and outspoken." Sue pinpointed biases and prejudices that she might possess: "My mother's side of the family is very prejudiced against certain cultures and ethnic people.... Being part of a family that is prejudiced may affect me as a teacher against some parents."

John, from a family that never had "any fine material possessions," openly confronted his biases toward students from wealthy backgrounds:

> I have to be very careful if I take a job in a wealthy school not to let my poor upbringing influence my ability to teach financially advantaged students.... On the other end of the spectrum, I have to be sure not to glorify my poorer students simply for getting the same education their wealthier classmates are working for.

Students

Through interviews, informal chats, observations, and instructional activities that involved the case-study students, the preservice teachers identified more similarities than differences between themselves and their case-study students. The dominant categories of similarities included cultural values, parental involvement in education, and home and school literacy experiences. The differences lay mostly with ethnicity, native language, socioeconomic status, and family composition. Several preservice teachers, however, observed no differences between themselves and both the case-study and other students. As Alice put it, "in a completely Hispanic classroom including the teacher, I didn't sense or notice much difference from that of my own elementary school."

As to the differences, the preservice teachers exhibited various reactions. The first type of reaction was about discomfort that six of them initially experienced. Carole commented: "I was thrown off a little with lower income all Hispanic classroom." Of the six, three expressed positive effects of their discomfort. Kasey put herself in the position of a minority:

> I at first felt like an outsider, for all of the students but one and the teacher were of different ethnicity to me. But then it occurred to me that in life as in other classrooms, the way I was feeling was just how a minority must feel when placed in a new group.

Anna shared her awareness of the demographic trends: "I was in shock that my classroom was 99% Hispanic with one black student. For once, I was in the minority. It made me realize that minorities are growing at a fast rate." Carole spoke of advantages of such differences between herself and the case-study student: "We did not have much in common but I think that helped both of us. It gave us more to talk about. She would explain her Thanksgiving and we would compare it to mine."

The second type of reaction was related to socioeconomic status. Three preservice teachers expressed shocked responses to some students' social experiences, which, in turn, made them realize their responsibility as teachers. Andrea noticed a huge difference between the community where she grew up and that of the students:

> I could not imagine being told I could not wear a certain brand of jeans because it is associated with gangs and that I could hide drugs or weapons in the pockets.... I know that many students in this neighborhood see a whole lot more of drugs and weapons in their own houses than I can ever imagine. They do live in a different society than I do. The thought of this makes me want to reach out to each of these students and hope that something I teach them will benefit them throughout their lives.

The third type of reaction was about stereotypes. The differences presented four preservice teachers opportunities to challenge their stereotypes about their students. Carole wrote: "I assumed all kindergartners knew the alphabet and it took me a while to adjust my thinking.... Now I realize that something like the language barrier is involved." Similarly, Karla frankly described her changes in thinking:

> Before, I tended to think in the back of my mind that students who were not going to schools in the "nice" part of town were not as smart as students who did. That was awful for me to think and very uneducated. I am glad that I have learned differently.

The fourth type of reaction was related to preservice teachers' admiration for the students. Four out of 20 preservice teachers praised the students' ability to cope with difficult social and home environments and to communicate in two languages. Carole "admired the ability of the students to speak English at school and Spanish at home. I respect them because I couldn't do that when I was at their age." Mary acknowledged the students' efforts to achieve at school:

> Some of their home environments are not stable enough and the burden gets carried over to the schools. I admire the kids who are not as fortunate as the rest of us because it means that they have to work twice as hard to succeed and overcome obstacles to get ahead.

Teaching

When asked to describe how to modify literacy instruction for minority students, the preservice teachers' responses revealed a wide range of understandings. First, five preservice teachers did not see a need to modify literacy instruction. Karla, for example, stated: "It is as if I have become blind to color and only focus on the aspect of teaching and students' learning."

Second, three preservice teachers considered teaching as one way to change students' lives. John commented that "Students are open circuits and what teachers channel through them can have life long ramifications, good or bad." Another three preservice teachers, however, were aware of the limitations as to what they could do to change students' lives. Mary shared what she had witnessed in her classroom about "social difficulties that the students were trying to cope with in addition to attending school," and there was little that a teacher could do for these children. Joan echoed Mary's view:

> It is difficult to teach a group of diverse students because of the differences in all of the students' cultures and ways of doing things. Most teachers will do

their best to be open minded and sensitive to other cultures, but they will never be able to be 100% correct when dealing with their students.

Third, seven preservice teachers described that a teacher should be nurturing and unbiased, as well as make efforts to involve parents and learn about and respect students' cultures. For example, Andrea felt that she needed "to take on the nurturing role for some students who do not receive that at home." Becky asserted: "I used to think that I might be a good teacher, but now I know that I will be because I am able to see and interpret things more clearly without bias." Juliann stressed having "a strong relationship with my students' parents." Joan spoke of the importance of being "knowledgeable in the area of varying cultures," and that she would "adjust to students whose culture and religion do not allow certain things I do in the classroom." Alexis believed it crucial to set up rules in her classroom about mutual respect: "As a teacher, you need to learn where your students are coming from and have a mutual respect with them. You do not disrespect their background. Another rule should be that the students do not disrespect each other either." Furthermore, Becky suggested encouraging students to express their cultures:

> I will provide many opportunities for my students to elaborate and share their cultures that will help them to feel welcome and special. This is important because they will face difficulties all through their life that involve racial differences, and if they have a complete understanding of their own culture, then they will see that racial differences are meaningless when it comes to learning about each other.

Fourth, seven teachers emphasized specific ways to accommodate literacy instruction for minority students. Speaking of the importance of using multicultural literature, Anna wrote: "schools should continue to supply students with literature of different cultures. This makes students think that their culture is just as important to all the other cultures that are mentioned in the school." John agreed, saying, "I believe that all students can identify with some aspect of every book. If they cannot identify with it due to cultural differences, at least they can learn to appreciate it."

Charlene related the supporting collaborative work to the students' cultural learning styles: "Research has suggested that Mexican Americans prefer a more social approach to learning. Perhaps the class would benefit greatly with more types of cooperative activities." Joan suggested organizing literacy instruction in thematic units related to the students' cultures: "I feel that the class should take a week or two and focus on the Hispanic culture. The students could read books on it during their reading time, not only for lessons but for enjoyment. They could make a cultural meal."

Whole Class Lesson Teaching

During the field experiences, the preservice teachers taught whole class lessons. Thirteen out of 20 preservice teachers encouraged the students to participate actively in various literacy events. Some even changed classroom routines (e.g., an abundance of individual seatwork) to enhance cooperative work. As Kasey shared with me during my classroom visit: "I thought these students were always quiet, and I wasn't sure if they understood my lesson or not. Once they got into groups, it seemed everybody knew a lot about contractions, and they enjoyed my lessons." In Anna's classroom in which cooperative work was predominant in the learning environment, Anna observed: "Everybody is taking responsibility in completing Marco Polo's trip to China. I can see the success of my lesson."

Two out of 20 preservice teachers integrated books written in the students' native language (Spanish) in the lessons. Although 98% of the students in the classes were proficient in English, the preservice teachers thought it important to expose the students to their native language. For example, Juliann, who had some knowledge of Spanish, asked the kindergartners to sequence the events of a story written in Spanish. Mary, an English-Spanish bilingual, read aloud the Spanish version of a book after she heard some students suggesting that they could listen to the same story in Spanish. These preservice teachers were supported and encouraged by their cooperating teachers who had a collection of books in Spanish and often integrated books in Spanish in literacy instruction.

Furthermore, three preservice teachers demonstrated in their lesson teaching a respect for students' life experiences and backgrounds. For example, while teaching the concept of compare and contrast, Joan invited the students to work with a buddy and to compare and contrast between themselves. Similarly, Alexis used the students' knowledge of their school and community as an example to illustrate a descriptive text.

During lesson teaching, four preservice teachers followed exactly what and how the cooperating teachers told them to teach. In these classrooms, cooperative learning was absent, and the students engaged busily in seatwork. The students' literacy knowledge was judged by the number of correct and incorrect answers. Interestingly, only two out of four preservice teachers expressed any concerns about such teaching practices conducted by their cooperating teachers. For example, Karen commented: "This environment completely contradicted the philosophy I had begun to form about how students learn. I, too, believe that when the teacher acts less like a dictator and instead leads and facilitates appropriate behavior and learning, the environment for learning is more effective."

Working with Case-study Students

While working with their case-study students on a one-on-one basis, the preservice teachers appeared to be more sensitive to cultural and linguistic backgrounds of the students than teaching whole class lessons. Specifically, the preservice teachers implemented literacy instructional strategies and used children's literature that were appropriate to the case-study students' literacy development, and cultural and linguistic backgrounds. Some preservice teachers became increasingly aware of various social, cultural, and economic factors that contributed to the students' literacy development.

Seventeen out of 20 preservice teachers used with the case-study students the literacy instructional strategies that enhanced the students' active participation. For example, Mary used pattern books to encourage her Hispanic case-study student, Jose, to participate. She noted: "Jose began to repeat the main paragraph of the story after I read a few pages to him. In between illustrations, he made predictions of what was to come next. He was so excited about the book." Similarly, Maria, working with a Hispanic girl, used the strategy of Language Experience Approach (LEA) to write about Jessica's trip back to the South America. At the same time, Maria modeled for Jessica the correct way to spell some words that she often misspelled. Maria commented, "The LEA worked so well. Jessica needs individual help and she doesn't have these opportunities at school because there isn't enough time." Likewise, Becky used word association to help her case-study student, Brad, to construct meanings of an unknown word based on his experiences and knowledge: "I taught Brad a new way to think of meanings. He has never done that before, and later used this strategy to help with other unknown words."

Furthermore, six of 20 preservice teachers used multicultural books or books of interest to the case-study students. Charlene used an English-Spanish book, *In My Family/En Mi Familia* (Garza, 1996), to encourage her case-study student to share his culture and construct meanings while reading together. Charlene learned that "he related to several of the stories, indicating his Mexican cultural was important. Although Spanish was spoken at home, he does not feel comfortable reading or speaking the language." Maria also reported: "I used books interesting to her so that instruction is more enjoyable and meaningful. I also discovered that she enjoyed writing about topics that interested her."

After implementing informal assessment tools, most preservice teachers felt the power of getting to know their case-study students' cultural backgrounds and literacy development. Charlene shared her view about the benefits of informal interviews in relation to her knowledge of her case-study student's outside school experiences:

> Interviewing with her about her cultural and linguistic background gave me very important information. Interviewing every student in a class might be time consuming, but so much valuable information can be learned. Knowing more about the student's cultural background helps tell you why a student may or may not be getting instruction in the home.

Andrea spoke of anecdotal records as a valuable tool to learn about the student's strengths and needs: "Anecdotal records come from actual observation and interaction with a student. These records will help so much in tracking a student's progress and areas of needed instruction."

While all preservice teachers were aware of the cultural and linguistic backgrounds of the case-study students, as shown in cross-cultural comparison charts, only five of them recognized the impact of such backgrounds on literacy development of the students. Sherry praised greater parental involvement in her case-study student: "His parents always helped and pushed him to do his best; his parents were involved in his school and always checked on him." Kasey, on the other hand, expressed her sympathy for her case-study student's home environment:

> Lonny talked fondly of his mother, and mentioned that she read to him when he was young, yet he doesn't live with her since his parents were divorced. He also talked disdainfully about his dad never keeping his promises and being a liar. I feel like this student is at times uneasy about his home life, which could play a role in his literacy development.

Anna discovered the impact of the people around her case-study student:

> I have come to the conclusion that if people, meaning her parents, teachers, and peers, pay more attention to her, she would do so much better in school. This does not mean spending more time teaching her, but making her feel special and wanted. Letting her know that she is worth something.

DISCUSSIONS AND IMPLICATIONS

This study explored preservice teachers' perceptions of themselves, students, and teaching and how they related multicultural knowledge and perspectives to literacy instruction during their literacy course work with a component of field experiences in a minority school. At the level of conceptual understandings, the preservice teachers exhibited a strong sense of self and cultural identity, as well as interests in learning about and accepting other cultures. Importantly enough, a small number of preservice teachers realized a connection between their own cultural experiences and possible biases and prejudices against students of other cultures. Such realization made it possible for them to further examine their own belief systems about other cultures.

Being in a minority school provided the preservice teachers with a context of reality in which they can link their conceptual understandings of multiculturalism to students of other cultures. Such linkage presented them with additional opportunities to test and challenge these understandings. Although the preservice teachers perceived more similarities than differences between themselves and the students, it was important to note that half of them showed positive attitudes toward observed differences. They viewed differences as a challenge to examine their own stereotypes, as a source for admiring their students' unusual abilities, and as a way to enrich their knowledge about other cultures. These positive attitudes may also have helped the preservice teachers reexamine their own belief systems.

One of the most significant findings was that the preservice teachers demonstrated a variety of understandings of literacy instruction in relation to students' cultural and linguistic backgrounds within whole class and individual settings. This study's findings suggested that a majority of the preservice teachers saw a need to modify literacy instruction for minority students. Most of them can verbalize *general* ways to accommodate literacy instruction, such as nurturing, caring, unbiased, and respectful teachers and learning about students' cultures. However, when the preservice teachers were teaching whole class lessons and working with the case-study students, they implemented many *specific* ways to modify instruction to meet the needs of minority students. Additionally, the preservice teachers seemed to be more sensitive to individual students' cultural and linguistic backgrounds during one-on-one literacy instruction than during whole class lesson teaching. Direct and constant interactions with individual students provided the preservice teachers with "tangible" contexts to exercise their multicultural and literacy instruction knowledge.

The findings of this study suggest several practical and research implications. Evidence from the preservice teachers' lesson teaching and working with the case-study students indicated that the preservice teachers encouraged student active participation and cooperative work. Furthermore, it suggested that they viewed the students as knowledgeable and capable enough to contribute information in literacy activities. The combination of whole class lesson teaching and case studies of the individual students offered the preservice teachers a close-up view of the relationship between culture, language, students, and literacy instruction. In particular, whole class lesson teaching presented the breadth of such a view while case studies of the students offered more depth. Similar to Bollin and Finkel's (1995) findings, this study showed that working with individual students was a particularly valuable experience for preservice teachers to learn about students, cultures, and literacy instruction.

This study also illustrated the power of the ABC's Model in fostering preservice teachers' connecting multiculturalism with literacy instruction. Specifically, the Model made it possible for preservice teachers to examine themselves, understand students of other cultures, and challenge their own belief systems through writing autobiographies, biographies of the case-study students, and seeking similarities and differences between themselves and the students. The Model also allowed them to explore their reactions to differences and to make efforts to modify literacy instruction. Used with field experiences, this Model enhanced preservice teachers' abilities to apply multicultural knowledge and perspectives and to observe how culture "functions in education" (Ladson-Billings, 1995, p. 483). The Model thus served as a bridge to help preservice teachers connect multicultural theories and strategies with the reality of teaching minority students in content areas, such as literacy instruction. Such a connection further promoted preservice teachers' abilities to make critical judgments of teaching methods appropriate to students' cultural, linguistic, and academic backgrounds (Kuykendall, 1992). Thus, it is necessary and beneficial to integrate the ABC's Model into field experiences of teacher education programs.

As researchers (e.g., Cabello & Burstein, 1995; Zeichner et al., 1998) have pointed out, cultural sensitivity and awareness of multiculturalism alone do not guarantee that preservice teachers will become effective teachers of children from diverse cultural and linguistic backgrounds. Rather, "intercultural teaching competence" (Zeichner et al., p. 168) enables them to link a multicultural knowledge base to pedagogical practices. Therefore, in order for preservice teachers to develop "intercultural teaching competence," it is essential for them to be involved in field experiences in minority schools where they can witness and experience other cultures and make critical instructional decisions. Since one's belief systems about other cultures cannot be changed as a result of a brief encounter with other cultures, preservice teachers need to be involved in *prolonged* field experiences in minority schools during their teacher education programs. These field experiences would maximize opportunities for preservice teachers to *constantly* and *systematically* examine and reexamine their own belief systems, which can affect and guide their pedagogical practices.

The findings of this study reveal diversity in preservice teachers' abilities to translate multicultural knowledge and perspectives to literacy instruction for minority students. It is not difficult to locate a main source for such diversity, that is, preservice teachers' previous life and cultural experiences. However, this study also implies other sources: Why are some preservice teachers more sensitive to students' backgrounds than others? Why do several preservice teachers perceive differences between themselves and the students in a positive way? Why do some preservice teachers change classroom instructional routines in order to provide better literacy instruction for the students? These questions identify classroom environments, cooperating teachers, and students as other sources that may account for preservice teachers' varied abilities to connect a multicultural knowledge base to literacy instruction. Future research should focus on longitudinal efforts to document the change process of preservice teachers' abilities to apply multicultural knowledge in literacy instruction when they are in minority schools for field experiences. In particular, researchers need to explore various factors (e.g., cooperating teachers, classroom environments, and students), their relationships, and degrees of importance in contributing to preservice teachers' abilities to integrate multicultural knowledge and perspectives in teaching content areas.

REFERENCES

Adler, S. (1993). *Multiculturalism communication skills in the classroom.* Boston, MA: Allyn & Bacon.

Allington, R., & Walmsley, S. (Eds.). (1995). *No quick fix.* New York: Teachers College Press.

Au, K.H. (1998). Social constructivism and the school literacy learning of students of diverse backgrounds. *Journal of Literacy Research, 30,* 297–319.

Banks, J.A. (1991). *Teaching strategies for ethnic studies.* Boston: Allyn & Bacon.

Bear, D.R., Invernizzi, M., Templeton, S., & Johnston, F. (1996). *Words their way.* Upper Saddle River, NJ: Prentice-Hall.

Bennett, K.P., & LeCompte, M.D. (1990). *The way schools work.* New York: Longman.

Bollin, G.G., & Finkel, J. (1995). White racial identity as a barrier to understanding diversity: A study of preservice teachers. *Equity & Excellence in Education, 28*(1), 25–30.

Cabello, B., & Burstein, N.D. (1995). Examining teachers' beliefs about teaching in culturally diverse classrooms. *Journal of Teacher Education, 46,* 285–294.

Cannella, G.S., & Reiff, J.C. (1994). Teacher preparation for diversity. *Equity & Excellence in Education, 27*(3), 28–33.

Florio-Ruane, S. (1994). The future teachers' autobiography club: Preparing educators to support learning in culturally diverse classrooms. *English Education, 26*(1), 52–56.

Florio-Ruane, S., & deTar, J. (1995). Conflict and consensus in teacher candidates' discussion of ethnic autobiography. *English Education, 27*(1), 11–39.

Flynt, E.S., & Cooter, R.B. (1998). *Reading inventory for the classroom* (3rd ed.). Upper Saddle River, NJ: Prentice-Hall.

Garza, C.L. (1996). *In my family/En mi familia.* San Francisco: Children's Book Press.

Haberman, M., & Post, L. (1990). Cooperating teachers' perceptions of the goals of multicultural education. *Action in Teacher Education, 12*(3), 31–35.

Hyun, E., & Marshall, J.D. (1997). Theory of multiple/multiethnic perspective-taking ability for teachers' developmentally and culturally appropriate practice (DCAP). *Journal of Research in Childhood Education, 11,* 188–198.

Kleinfeld, J.S. (1998). The use of case studies in preparing teachers for cultural diversity. *Theory into Practice, 37,* 140–147.

Kozol, J. (1991). *Savage inequalities.* New York: Harper Perennial.

Kuykendall, C. (1992). *From rage to hope: Strategies for reclaiming Black and Hispanic students.* Bloomington, IN: National Education Service.

Ladson-Billings, G. (1991). Beyond multicultural illiteracy. *Journal of Negro Education, 60,* 147–157.

Ladson-Billings, G. (1994). *The dreamkeepers: Successful teachers of African American children.* San Francisco: Jossey-Bass.

Ladson-Billings, G. (1995). Toward a theory of culturally relevant pedagogy. *American Educational Research Journal, 32,* 465–491.

Larke, P.J., Wiseman, D., & Bradley, C. (1990). The minority mentorship project: Changing attitudes of preservice teachers for diverse classrooms. *Action in Teacher Education, 12*(3), 23–30.

Lincoln, Y.S., & Guba, E. (1985). *Naturalistic inquiry.* Beverly Hills, CA: Sage.

Mahan, J.M. (1982). Community involvement components in culturally-oriented teacher preparation. *Education, 103,* 163–172.

McCracken, J. (1993). *Valuing diversity.* Washington, DC: National Association for the Education of Young Children.

McDiarmid, G.W. & Price, J. (1993). Preparing teachers for diversity: A study of student teachers in a multicultural program. In M.J. O'Hair & S.J. Odell (Eds.), *Diversity and teaching: Teacher education yearbook I* (pp. 31–59). Fort Worth, TX: Harcourt Brace Jovanovich.

Merriam, S.B. (1988). *Case study research in education.* San Francisco: Jossey-Bass.

National Council for Accreditation of Teacher Education. (1979). *Approved curriculum guidelines.* Washington, DC: Author.

National Council for Accreditation of Teacher Education. (1992). *Approved curriculum guidelines.* Washington, DC: Author.

National Council for Accreditation of Teacher Education. (1994). *Approved curriculum guidelines.* Washington, DC: Author.

Schmidt, P.R. (1998a). The ABC's of cultural understanding and communication. *Equity & Excellence in Education, 31*(2), 28–38.

Schmidt, P.R. (1998b). The ABC's Model: Teachers connect home and school. In T. Shanahan & F. Rodriguez-Brown (Eds.), *47th Yearbook of the National Reading Conference* (pp. 194–208). Chicago: National Reading Conference.

Schmidt, P.R. (1999). Know thyself and understand others. *Language Arts, 76,* 332–340.

Searfoss, L.W., & Readence, J.E. (1994). *Helping children learn to read* (3rd ed.). Boston, MA: Allyn & Bacon.

Spindler, G., & Spindler, L. (1987). *The interpretive ethnography of education: At home and abroad.* Hillsdale, NJ: Lawrence Erlbaum.

Strauss, A.L. (1987). *Qualitative analysis for social scientists.* New York: Cambridge University Press.

Taylor, D. (1991). *Learning denied.* Portsmouth, NH: Heinemann.

Tompkins, G.E. (1998). *Language arts: Content and teaching strategies* (4th ed.). Upper Saddle River, NJ: Prentice-Hall.

Yin, R.K. (1994). *Case study methodology* (2nd ed.). Newbury Park, CA: Sage.

Zeichner, K.M., Grant, C., Gay, G., Gillette, M., Valli, L., & Villegas, A.M. (1998). A research informed vision of good practice in multicultural education: Design principles. *Theory into Practice, 37,* 163–171.

CHAPTER 15

"RACCOON? WASS DAT?"

Hawaiian Preservice Teachers Reconceptualize Culture, Literacy, and Schooling

Margaret J. Maaka, Kathryn H. Au, Yvonne K. Lefcourt, and L. Pauahi Bogac

Abstract: This research study was designed to examine ways to raise the level of school literacy achievement of Hawaiian[1] children and others from underrepresented groups by improving one area of the educative process—teacher education. We add to the research on effective teacher preparation programs for individuals of diverse backgrounds by examining two preservice teachers' views of their own cultural identity; how their experiences as students shaped their beliefs about culture, literacy, and schooling; and how their views of their cultural identity and their experiences as students informed their development as teachers.

Data were gathered from in-depth life history interviews, and from personal narratives and reaction papers that were prepared as course assignments associated with a literacy class and multicultural issues in education class. The student teachers were asked to express their perceptions of and experiences with a range of issues, such as family histories, celebrations of diversity, and literacy instruction in a Hawaiian setting, including the qualities of an effective teacher. From the data emerged themes of subjugation, conflict, position, power, and voice—themes that suggest connections among colonization, culture, literacy, and schooling.

The student teachers underscored two critical areas of need. First, they called for the development of school curricula that acknowledge and respect the culture and life experiences of Hawaiian children. Second, they called for programmatic efforts that increase the number of well-prepared teachers of Hawaiian ancestry to serve as role models and developers of culturally responsive curricula. The argument was made that, for an education system to be truly meaningful, powerful, and culturally sustaining, Hawaiians must take active roles in the development of educational theories, curricula, and practices.

INTRODUCTION

It is the spring semester, and we are about to observe one of our Ka Lama O Ke Kaiāulu student teachers deliver a mathematics lesson to first grade children in a school on the Wai'anae Coast of O'ahu, Hawai'i. The majority of the children in the classroom are Hawaiian, come from low-income families, and speak Hawai'i Creole English as their first language.

In her mathematics education courses, our student teacher is being encouraged to embrace a teaching approach that emphasizes the importance of children experiencing key mathematical concepts through shared experimentation, practical activities, and real life applications. This approach also encourages and challenges children to talk and write about their mathematical ideas and discoveries. However, for this particular lesson on subtraction, our student teacher has opted to examine an alternative perspective—the school's first grade mathematics curriculum. This involves a basal textbook that requires the children to work through a set of carefully prescribed activities before moving onto independent practice pages. Each page carries a variety of colorful illustrations designed to capture the children's interests. People snow skiing and sledding, reindeer, snowmen, and raccoons drill the notion of subtraction.

Our student teacher begins the lesson by gathering the children at the front of the class. She writes the word "subtraction" on the chalkboard and asks the children to say it. They respond in unison. Next, she introduces the concept of subtraction as directed by the text and follows with the first example: "There are 5 raccoons. Two run away. How many raccoons are left?" A few children answer and a brief discussion ensues. She continues with another example from the text. And then another. On completing the sample problems, she sends the children back to their tables to work independently on the practice pages. With this comes the assumption that they have acquired a rudimentary grasp of the concept of subtraction. As we continue to observe, we notice several children struggling with the assignment. Finally, one child approaches the student teacher. As he presses his unmarked practice pages at her, he complains, "Subtraction? I dunno dis! Raccoon? Wass dat?"

For many children of diverse cultural and linguistic backgrounds, school learning consists of a series of "raccoon-like" experiences. The disparities between teachers' assumptions about what children know and what children *actually* know is one aspect of the mismatch between the culture of the school and culture of the home. A mismatch, many argue, that helps explain the generally poor school literacy achievement levels of children of diverse backgrounds in comparison with their European American counterparts (Au, 1993; Foster, 1991).

Attempts to "reconceptualize literacy in the new age of pluralism and multiculturalism" must take into account an array of contextual considerations. The devastating impact of European and American colonialism on the indigenous peoples of the Pacific is one such consideration. In Hawai'i, the subjugation of the Hawaiian people has resulted in a stripping away of the fundamental markers of their cultural identity—sovereignty, ancestral lands, language, and traditional knowledge. Literacy, in particular, has been used by colonizers as a criterion for assessing the development of Hawaiian society. By defining Hawaiians as primitive and uncivilized, a system of colonial education has dismissed and continues to dismiss their literacy as a record of legitimate knowledge. In the broader context, the dismissal of the identities of indigenous peoples has been the hallmark of European and American colonialism in the Pacific region (see Smith, 1999).

For colonized indigenous peoples, regaining and developing positive identities and strong cultural bases involve constant struggles to recover or "discover" that which has been stripped away (see Giroux & McLaren, 1994; Rosaldo, 1989). Hall (1991) argued that entailed in such a discovery is the

> need to honor the hidden histories from which ... [people] ... come. They need to understand the languages which they have been taught not to speak. They need to understand and revalue the traditions and inheritances of cultural expression and creativity. And in that sense, the past is not only a position from which to speak, but it is also an absolutely necessary resource in what one has to say ... So the relationship of the kind of ethnicity I'm talking about to the past is not a simple, essential one—it is a constructed one. It is constructed in history, it is constructed politically in part. It is part of narrative. We tell ourselves the stories of the parts of our roots in order to come into contact, creatively, with it. So this new kind of ethnicity—the emergent ethnicities—has a relationship to the past, but it is a relationship that is partly through memory, partly through narrative, one that has to be recovered. It is an act of cultural recovery. (pp. 18–19)

A reconceptualization of literacy necessitates a rethinking of the relationship between identity and difference. Hall (1991, p. 18) argued that, in order for people to enter the discourse of identity, they have to "position themselves *somewhere*." For Hawaiians and other colonized indigenous peoples of the Pacific, an understanding of ethnicity in terms of a politics of location, positionality, and enunciation is a critical consideration (Giroux & McLaren, 1994). Attempts to clarify this understanding, however, are hampered by the ever present colonizing influences of more powerful "others."

The present study is part of a line of research examining the themes of cultural identity, experiences with schooling, and literacy development and how these are played out in the life stories of Hawaiian preservice teachers. The research questions central to the present study include:

1. How do Hawaiian preservice teachers view their cultural identity?
2. How have Hawaiian preservice teachers' experiences as students shaped their beliefs about culture, literacy, and schooling?
3. How have Hawaiian preservice teachers' views of their cultural identity and their experiences as students informed their development as teachers?

LITERATURE REVIEW

Cultural Identity

To promote the educational well-being of an individual or a particular group in a culturally-responsive manner, it is necessary to examine the notion of *cultural identity*. For teacher educators, in particular, an examination of the role that cultural identity plays in the preparation of new teachers of diverse backgrounds provides important information for the development of effective teacher preparation programs.

Trask (1999), in her strong denouncement of the colonization of Hawai'i, talked about Hawaiian identity in terms of connectedness to lands, family, and language. For her, bloodlines and birthplace tell of "being Hawaiian." Durie (1998) reiterated Trask's view in his discussion of contemporary Māori values, identities, and aspirations. He described cultural identity as an "amalgam of personal attitudes, cultural knowledge, and participation in Māori society" (p. 57). He drew particular attention to considerations such as self-identification, knowledge of ancestry, involvement with extended family, access to ancestral land, contacts with other Māori, and use of the Māori language.

In short, cultural identity is about time and place. Individual members of any given group are governed by an essential core of self-perception established in the earliest years of life. Elements such as family dynamics, associations with friends, school experiences, and language use shape and mold individual and collective identities (Durie, 1997). For Durie, an essential determinant of the social and economic well-being of any group is its connectedness. When a group is connected, it flourishes. Conversely, when the shared meanings, values, and beliefs that identify group membership break down, so does the group.

A hundred years of colonial rule in Hawai'i has resulted in what Trask (1999) referred to as the degradation and cheapening of the Hawaiian culture. Hawaiians are descendants of the original Polynesian inhabitants of the islands that eventually came to constitute the state of Hawai'i. Since the arrival of the British explorer James Cook in 1778, Hawaiians have experienced a stormy history in their own land. Today Hawaiians, as a group, are in a position of serious social and economic disadvantage in comparison with the two dominant groups in Hawai'i: European and Japanese Americans.

Since 1970, however, there has been a revitalization of the Hawaiian culture, including the revival of the language. As Hawaiians organize themselves for political, economic, and social enhancement, it is contingent upon those in Hawai'i's educational arena to examine ways in which to support this. This support involves the recognition of the right of Hawaiian families and communities to retain shared responsibility for the upbringing, training, education and well-being of their children (Draft United Nations Declaration on the Rights of Indigenous Peoples, August 1994).

By seeking Hawaiian preservice teachers' views about their own cultural identity and their understandings of the significance of a teacher's cultural identity to schooling, this study adds to the research on effective teacher preparation programs for individuals of diverse backgrounds. Few studies have been conducted on the backgrounds and professional preparation of preservice teachers of diverse backgrounds. Some research has been conducted with African American preservice teachers, somewhat less research with Latino preservice teachers, and almost none with Asian American preservice teachers and preservice teachers from indigenous groups (see Gomez, 1994; Gomez & Tabachnick, 1991; Noordhoff & Kleinfeld, 1993).

We are aware of only three studies of Hawaiian preservice teachers. In their study of the recruitment and retention of female preservice teachers of Hawaiian ancestry, Maaka, Au, and Luna (1998) identified the obstacles these women encountered in preparing to become teachers. The study highlighted the need for innovative approaches to increase the participation of Hawaiians and others of diverse cultural and linguistic groups in teacher education programs. To ensure a significant increase in the numbers of candidates from nonmainstream backgrounds who enter the teaching profession, they recommended increasing the availability of financial aid; encouraging systematic support from faculty, family, and peers; providing workshops that give students the skills to meet the language demands of academic institutions; eliminating institutional practices, such as culturally biased admissions tests, that screen out individuals of diverse backgrounds; and teaching students how to persist in the face of discrimination.

Hewett (1998) examined the efforts of six Hawaiian women in a preservice teacher education program to find coherent, functional identities as Hawaiians, as women, and as teachers. The women's stories told of the barriers they encountered throughout their studies and the strategies they employed to overcome these obstacles. The experiences of these women indicated a need for improved teacher preparation programs for Hawaiians. Among her recommendations, Hewett called for the development of curricula that emphasize the important relationship between culture and teaching, and the hiring of university instructors of Hawaiian ancestry to serve as role models and mentors. She concluded her study by asserting the rights of Hawaiians to live and learn as Hawaiians, to reclaim the past, and to secure the present and the future.

Asam (1999) conducted a collective case study of 16 Hawaiian preservice teachers in a teacher preparation initiative designed to improve education in a Hawaiian community. She found that cultural identity played a significant role in the preservice teachers' decisions to become teachers and their views of their roles as teachers. Many were motivated to go into teaching to better the education of Hawaiian children. Many of the preservice teachers reported experiencing discrimination in school, linked to their ethnicity as Hawaiians, and they wanted to spare other Hawaiian students the pain and humiliation they had suffered. Most studies of teacher education have pointed to the limited influence of academic courses on the development of preservice teachers. Counter to this trend, Asam found that both the initiative's courses and field experiences in the classrooms of mentor teachers had significant impacts on the preservice teachers. Asam attributed this influence to the fact that the initiative's curriculum built upon practices known to be effective in classrooms with Hawaiian children; emphasized multicultural education, including field experiences in culturally diverse communities; and provided the support of mentor teachers and university instructors.

Schooling in a Hawaiian Community

As the raccoon anecdote implies, Hawaiian students on the Waiʻanae Coast are no exception to the patterns of low school achievement—especially in literacy—that affect groups of students of diverse backgrounds in the United States and other countries.

The Waiʻanae Coast is a rural area with the lowest housing costs on the island. Most of the residents of the coast are Hawaiian. With a growing population, including many children from low-income families, the seven elementary schools are filled to capacity. Hawaiian students on the Waiʻanae Coast show the patterns of educational disadvantage familiar to educators working in low-income settings. As a group, their scores on standardized tests of reading achievement are in the lowest quartile, and their rates of absenteeism, retention in grade, and referral to special education are far above average.

Several factors contribute to the challenges that many Hawaiian students face in performing at high academic levels in school. One factor is an absence of role models, specifically, Hawaiian teachers from the community. On the Waiʻanae Coast, as in other areas of the state with large proportions of Hawaiian students, relatively few teachers are themselves of Hawaiian ancestry. For example, an evaluation of selected schools with a high number of Hawaiian students showed the following distribution of teachers by ethnicity: 66% Japanese; 17% Chinese; 8.5% White; and 8.5%

Hawaiian (Tikunoff, Ward, & Van Broekhuizen, 1993). Under these conditions, Hawaiian students have relatively little opportunity to be taught by Hawaiian teachers who can serve as role models.

A second factor contributing to low academic achievement and poor motivation to succeed in school is the lack of culturally-responsive curricula. In recent years, there has been a proliferation of research examining the impact of colonial schooling systems on minority indigenous peoples. Much of this research has criticized the assumption that the experiences of the West are sufficiently explanatory for all the peoples of the world (Durie, 1997; Smith, 1999; Trask, 1999). In Hawai'i, Western paradigms dominate school curricula. For example, schools on the Wai'anae Coast, in common with most schools in Hawai'i, tend to rely on textbooks published on the U.S. mainland. Generally, these textbooks are distinguished by an absence of stories by Hawaiian writers and, therefore, an absence of stories about Hawaiian experiences. The raccoon anecdote illustrates this reliance. Exceptional teachers may be successful in making the link between these materials and students' background experiences, but this is a constant struggle. The first grader who lacked the essential mathematics-related knowledge of *raccoon* is typical of many children on the Wai'anae Coast. Had he been asked to subtract humuhumunukunukuāpua'a instead of raccoons, the lesson might have been one of success and motivation rather than confusion and frustration.

What is most often missing in classrooms with large numbers of Hawaiian children is an approach to teaching literacy, as well as the academic content in all other subject areas, through Hawaiian studies and experiences familiar to the students. As discussed earlier, this denial of knowledge valued by Hawaiians denies their legitimacy as a people. It prevents them from gaining that personal and cultural identity necessary for a sense of positioning in time and space. This can contribute to an absence of purpose and the inability to find meaning in school (cf. Hollins, 1996; Roth, 1984). Research supporting the claim that children learn best when they are able to relate new learning to familiar experiences is well established (Au, 1998–99; Hollins & Oliver, 1999). For Hawaiian children, personal and cultural identity and knowledge are the foundation on which knowledge beyond the Hawaiian culture is acquired.

The Hawaiian students of the Wai'anae Coast are in desperate need of improved educational opportunities. We believe that their academic achievement will be greatly enhanced through research and programmatic efforts to increase the number of well-prepared teachers of Hawaiian ancestry, to develop and implement culturally-responsive curricula. A teacher education effort directed at these goals is described below.

Teacher Education for a Hawaiian Community

Ka Lama O Ke Kaiāulu (the Light of the Community, or Ka Lama for short) is one of several preservice elementary teacher education cohorts in the College of Education at the University of Hawai'i. Established in 1995, Ka Lama has the purpose of improving the education of Hawaiian students in public schools on the Wai'anae Coast by recruiting and training teachers with a commitment to the area.

Over a two-year period, the Ka Lama preservice teachers complete their required course work, field experiences, and student teaching requirements together. The course work, which emphasizes literacy learning and teaching, is structured to facilitate connections across content areas and to the field. Literacy is emphasized because effective reading, writing, and critical thinking are regarded as foundational to children's success in all areas of the curriculum. Furthermore, the reading achievement scores of children on the Wai'anae Coast indicate a grave need for effective literacy instruction. Ka Lama's courses also emphasize the importance of culturally-responsive instruction and Hawaiian studies in making connections between the curriculum and children's backgrounds and interests. Issues of multiculturalism, Hawaiian views of education from ancient times to the present, and the views of progressive American educators, such as Dewey, are central components of all courses.

Ka Lama's focus on the educational needs of the Wai'anae Coast has necessitated the establishment of close ties with this community. Because of its community orientation, Ka Lama includes local instructors to teach courses on Hawaiian culture, seeks advice from a community advisory board on how to improve services, and works with principals and teachers in the public schools on curriculum planning, instruction, and evaluation.

Research on Ka Lama seeks to build upon and extend what has been learned in previous studies of literacy instruction for students of diverse backgrounds and from the contributions of teachers who share the culture and ethnicity of their students. Over the past two decades, a body of research conducted at the Kamehameha Elementary Education Program (KEEP), focusing on the learning of young Hawaiian students, has provided insights into their disproportionate and persistent literacy learning problems in school, as well as the attitudes and instructional practices of teachers successful in bringing about high levels of literacy achievement (Au, 1993; Au & Carroll, 1997; Au & Mason, 1983; D'Amato, 1988).

While this research made significant contributions to understandings about Hawaiian children's literacy learning, it did not focus on the knowledge and insights of teachers of Hawaiian ancestry. Yet these insights are critical to the improvement of teacher education programs and the school literacy learning of Hawaiian children. What is needed are Hawaiian voices—those who are the object of the discussion and debate, and who are best able to explain the ways in which the assumptions and practices of others affect the literacy learning of Hawaiian children (cf. Key, 1998; Moss, 1994). Attempts to address sources of disparity and conflict through curricular innovations or teacher preparation programs can be successful only when they have, as their foundation, the essential information about cultural knowledge, experiences, values, and aspirations.

METHOD

Participants

The two participants, Pauahi and Yvonne, were females of Hawaiian ethnicity, aged 23- and 40-years respectively. They were part of a group of 29 students enrolled in the Ka Lama preservice teacher education cohort. About two thirds of the students in Ka Lama identified themselves as Hawaiian, while the others identified themselves as Japanese, Filipino, Chinese, Samoan, and European American. In comparison with other cohorts in the College of Education, the Ka Lama cohort included an unusually high proportion of Hawaiian students. However, it was similar to other cohorts in having only a small number of male students—four, of whom two were Hawaiian.

Pauahi and Yvonne were selected because of their varied life experiences. When asked to describe her ethnicity, Pauahi said she was "chop suey" because of her Hawaiian, Puerto Rican, Filipino, and German ancestries. Pauahi, who was raised by her grandparents, talked about making a conscious decision in the 8th grade to find out more about her Hawaiian culture. After completing her 8th grade year at a private Catholic school, Pauahi chose to continue her studies at a private high school for students of Hawaiian ancestry. Fluent in the Hawaiian language, Pauahi was one of two Ka Lama students preparing to become teachers in the Hawaiian language immersion program. Teachers in this program are pioneers in the effort to revitalize and perpetuate the Hawaiian language. Just over a decade ago, when the immersion program was established, the Hawaiian language was in danger of being lost as a means of everyday communication.

Yvonne, who described herself as "first and foremost" Hawaiian, was of Hawaiian, Japanese, and English ancestries. She graduated from the Hawai'i public school system, was the mother of two grown children, and had an established career in the travel industry before deciding to become a teacher. Yvonne's decision to teach in English language immersion schools was made in response to her concern about the generally poor performance of Hawaiian children in the public school system in Hawai'i. She talked about her deep pride in being Hawaiian and of the importance of being a role model for other Hawaiians.

Procedures

Prior to their immersion in the Ka Lama teacher education courses, life history interviews were conducted with Pauahi and Yvonne. The procedures followed were those for ethnographic interviews, as discussed by Spradley (1979). Questions focused on the themes of cultural identity, schooling, and literacy, and both interviews lasted about 45 minutes. Personal narratives and reaction papers were a second source of data. These were prepared as course assignments associated with a literacy class and a multicultural issues in education class. In the multicultural issues in education class, students developed understandings of their own cultures, as well as understandings of the diverse cultures of others. In encouraging students to formulate their own definitions of multiculturalism and multicultual education, the course required them to examine issues such as inequity in educational opportunities and the origins of minority group status. In the literacy course, students examined the language achievements of children of diverse backgrounds and how literacy is used as a tool of empowerment and disempowerment. In particular, students were encouraged to explore, through literacy, their values and ideas (and the values and ideas of others), and in turn, come to understand similarities and differences among peoples of many cultures.

During the two courses, Pauahi and Yvonne were asked to express their perceptions of and experiences with a range of issues, such as family histories, celebrations of diversity, and literacy instruction in a Hawaiian setting, including the qualities of an effective teacher. Factors affecting the two students' success in education and progress toward becoming teachers were identified following the method of constant comparison (Glaser & Strauss, 1967).

FINDINGS AND DISCUSSION

(Re)conceptualizing Cultural Identity: A Hawaiian Sense of Self

Our examination of Pauahi and Yvonne's views of their cultural identity began with separate life-history interviews that focused on the question: How do Hawaiian preservice teachers view their cultural identity? In her interview, Pauahi was asked to describe the cultural group with which she most closely identified. She replied, "First and foremost, I am Hawaiian." Although, her statement was made with firm self-assurance, Pauahi said that, initially, her cultural identity had been shaped by the Puerto Rican grandparents who raised her. She said it was not until her teenage years that she began thinking about her Hawaiian ethnicity: "Around 8th grade I began thinking..., I live in Hawai'i and I don't understand Hawaiian words. I'm Hawaiian, and I don't know anything about anything. That really started me wanting to find out about things." Later, in a personal narrative, she expanded:

> I never really had a sense of what that (being Hawaiian) meant to me until I entered college. Learning about the plight and history of my people has driven me to do what I feel I need to do in terms of bettering the situation for Hawaiians. I am doing this (going to school, working towards sovereignty, working with the Hawaiian immersion program) for myself, my family, and for my people.

When describing her ethnicity, Yvonne used a reference similar to Pauahi's: "I am a Hawaiian, first and foremost, even though I'm a mixture." She noted, however, that although she was "born and raised as a Hawaiian," it was not until a trip to Aotearoa/New Zealand that she began to think more about the importance of her cultural identity. "The trip was spiritual," she stated. She later explained that her visit with Māori, the indigenous people of Aotearoa/New Zealand, made her aware of the importance of her own Hawaiian cultural knowledge, values, and aspirations: "I started to learn more..., the cosmological point of view, the ocean..., about categorizing the different species, animals, fish. From that trip, I went on with my studies. I took Hawaiian mythology. I began to understand the deeper meaning," she said. It is significant that Yvonne felt more connected with the culture of an indigenous people from another country than she did with the culture of mainstream America. Her obvious pride in being Hawaiian pervaded the interview. In the closing minutes, she added, "...we are a beautiful people..., the heartbeat of the world is here because we have a naturalness about us. This is our Hawaiianness."

Senses of pride and self-affirmation were evident also in poems Pauahi and Yvonne wrote in response to Puanani Burgess' (1998) poem, *Choosing My Name*. In her poem, Burgess talked about her English, Japanese, and Hawaiian ancestries and the identities that came from within herself and from others. She used her names as markers of time and place. In her poem, Yvonne chose to celebrate her Hawaiian middle name, "Kaulukane":

> Kaulukane,
> Inspiration of Man's Life.
> My name I behold.

When asked to talk about her poem, Yvonne replied simply, "...my name is very special to me. I am very proud of this name and my Hawaiian heritage." Previously, in her life-history interview, Yvonne talked about the importance of her name: "My name chant is dear to my heart. This is me, my culture, my language, my lineage. It is my identity..., who I am, where I come from, and why I want to help Hawaiian students appreciate our culture."

Like Yvonne, Pauahi chose to focus on her Hawaiian middle name. The sense of pride in her choice is evident in the last line:

I know you too, friend.
Burden, blessing, amulet:
Pauahi is mine.

By building on the words in the last two lines of Burgess' poem—"burden,"
"blessing," and "amulet," Pauahi alluded to her Hawaiian heritage. However, for her, "Pauahi" embodied a mixture of experiences. In a personal
narrative, Pauahi reiterated the idea of the burdens, blessings, and revitalization of the Hawaiian people. She stated:

> Hawaiians were and continue to be oppressed to the point of being ashamed
> about who they are. We have to fight and struggle to be Hawaiian in this col-
> ony of America. I feel that being Hawaiian is a heavy burden in many ways. I
> also feel I have to do everything in my power to uplift my people.

Pauahi's perception is echoed by Durie (1997) in her commentary on
Māori sense of self and identity: "The implicit messages received by Māori
from society at large are inevitably that, for whatever reasons, Māori children and their families are of lesser status and less deserving than those of
European decent" (p. 156). Pauahi's poem poignantly encapsulates a sense
of growing up in a manner that demanded extra fortitude in the development of a strong personal and social identity.

The act of renaming "new worlds" was central to the process of colonization. Freire (1970, p. 69) noted that "If it is in speaking their word that people, by naming the world, transform it, dialogue imposes itself as the way by
which they achieve significance as human beings. Dialogue is thus an exis-
tential necessity." In her discussion of the colonization of the Māori people,
Smith (1999) argued that the renaming of lands and peoples by colonizers
negated indigenous cultural knowledge. Indigenous names, she instructed,
carried the rich histories (or literacies) of people, places, and events:

> As a result of Christian baptism practices, which introduced Christian names
> and family names, and schooling practices, where teachers shortened names
> or introduced either generic names or nicknames, many indigenous commu-
> nities hid their indigenous names either by using them only in indigenous
> ceremonies or by positioning them as second (middle) names. (p. 157)

Smith's call for the restoration of Māori names has significance for the
Hawaiian people. For example, the naming of children with ancestral
names ensures the perpetuation of cultural histories. By naming their
worlds, the Māori and Hawaiian peoples name their realities. Smith concluded: "For communities there are realities which can only be found in the
indigenous languages; the concepts which are self-evident in the indigenous
language can never be captured by another language" (pp. 157–158).

Issues of Hawaiian identity, autonomy, and self-determination have
important implications for educators in Hawai'i, especially non-Hawaiian

educators. Initiatives for the educational advancement of Hawaiians must include decision making that reflects Hawaiian realities and aspirations. The role of Hawaiians, therefore, is critical. In her personal narrative, Pauahi provided powerful instruction on this issue:

> I have no problem with people (non-Hawaiians) adopting the language/culture, and developing a love of it. But once people start using the phrase "Hawaiian at heart" to describe themselves, my fuse is immediately lit. We have a hard enough time with our identity without foreigners contributing to the problem.

Pauahi's comment reiterates Durie's (1997) assertion that an essential determinant of the social and economic well-being of any group is the shared meanings, values, and beliefs that identify its members and keep them connected. The protection of the inalienable right of Hawaiians to be indigenous, which includes the right to self-determination, is at the heart of Pauahi's comment (see National Organizing Committee of the World Indigenous Peoples' Conference on Education, 1993).

These data allow us to begin to answer the question of how cultural identity may inform the development of Hawaiian preservice teachers, at least in some cases. First, it is clear that Pauahi and Yvonne have strong senses of their cultural identity as Hawaiians. Both found that being of Hawaiian ancestry and, in Yvonne's case, even being raised in a Hawaiian life style did not give them a sufficient understanding of and appreciation for being Hawaiian. Both made conscious decisions at some point in their lives to learn more about their Hawaiian culture. Both saw in their Hawaiian names a connection to the past and a commitment, in the future, to work for the betterment of their people. Both took great pride in their Hawaiian heritage, even as they were aware of what the oppression of modern times had done to Hawaiians.

The significance of the views held by Pauahi and Yvonne are perhaps better understood in contrast to the views typically held by pre- and inservice teachers of mainstream backgrounds. Teachers of mainstream backgrounds often have little awareness of their own cultural identities and may even make statements to the effect that they "have no culture" (Florio-Ruane & Raphael, 1999). Their culture may be invisible to them because it is so pervasive, because they have little experience of other cultures, or because they have never had to reflect on their own cultural identity. The views of cultural identity conveyed by Pauahi and Yvonne are strikingly different from those of many mainstream teachers. Pauahi and Yvonne are aware of the subordinate position of Hawaiians and Hawaiian culture and understand the need deliberately to perpetuate the culture. They have had experiences with other cultures in the family, at school, in the workplace, and during travels, and have chosen to identify themselves as Hawaiians and to become knowledgeable about Hawaiian language and culture. Clearly, an effective teacher education program for Hawaiian preservice teachers must recognize the importance of cultural identity, support its continued exploration through academic courses, foster an understanding of how cultural knowledge can strengthen the teaching of Hawaiian children, and acknowledge the important role of Hawaiians in program development.

In the Ka Lama cohort, literacy is connected to the exploration of cultural identity by having preservice teachers write about their own views and experiences and by having them read literature in which authors of diverse backgrounds address issues of cultural identity. In this way, literacy becomes a tool in the preservice teachers' examination of the meanings, values, and beliefs that they share with members of the same cultural group; the beliefs they have about members of other cultural groups; and the beliefs they have about effective ways to teach children, especially those of diverse backgrounds. Through these experiences, Ka Lama preservice teachers also learn how to use literacy to help children explore their cultural identities. In fact, a number of them have used poetry by Burgess and other writers of Hawaiian ancestry as the basis for literacy lessons taught in elementary classrooms.

Reconceptualizing Schooling: The Impacts of Significant Teachers

Berliner (1986, p. 29) commented that "teachers have no choice but to inquire into each student's unique culture and learning history, to determine what instructional materials might best be used, and to determine when a student's cultural and life experiences are compatible, or potentially incompatible, with instruction." He concluded that "to do less is to build emotional blocks to communication in an already complicated instructional situation." With Berliner's commentary in mind, we focused this section of our study on the question: How have Hawaiian preservice teachers' experiences as students shaped their beliefs about culture, literacy, and schooling?

During a class on multicultural issues in education, Pauahi and Yvonne were asked to write about teachers who had significantly impacted their abilities to learn. We were interested in examining trends in the experiences they deemed compatible and those they deemed incompatible. Rather than ask questions that would prompt recipe-like responses, we asked Pauahi and Yvonne to each write about a typical learning experience with a significantly negative teacher and a typical learning experience with significantly positive teacher.

Pauahi's first narrative was a vivid account of a secondary teacher whose approach created an emotional block to learning. Her classroom, Pauahi clarified, was a hostile place that filled students with self-doubts about their abilities as learners:

She could make me feel embarrassed at any time. She reminded me of one of those women in the opening scene of "Macbeth." She was intimidating, with icy blue eyes. She had a dangerously sharp tongue that could leave me bleeding for weeks on end. She also had an arsenal of red pens that murdered more of my English papers than I care to remember. I hated speaking my thoughts in her class. She always made it a point to embarrass me if my comments were something with which she disagreed. "Shuuurrrly, you muuusst be joooookkkiiinng" still rings in my ears from time to time, as if she were still standing over me.

When asked about how these experiences shaped her beliefs about working in classrooms with large numbers of Hawaiian children, Pauahi wrote in her reaction paper: "The children I teach will not receive such harsh treatment. I must be careful how I treat each child because I do not want to be responsible for any child's dislike of school." She clarified, "I will try to be patient and help every child to learn. Being patient also means I should conduct the class in a calm manner, even when I feel frustrated with the progress of a student or the class."

From her experiences with this teacher, Pauahi said she had come to realize the importance of creating a supportive environment that encouraged children to experiment with a range of literacy learning opportunities. She wrote:

> Literacy is all around us. Whether we realize it or not, literacy is integrated into everything we teach. Student-centered teaching is important. Valuing what the children have to say through oral and written language is crucial for the development of critical and creative thinking. Allowing children free time to read, write, and speak will be an important aspect of my classroom.

In the same paper, Pauahi also emphasized the importance of developing an instructional approach that incorporated each student's unique life experiences:

> It is important to provide an assortment of literature that reflects the different ethnicities found in Hawai'i. Children look for faces similar to theirs in what they read and learn. Being included in the culture of the classroom adds to the positive environment of the classroom. It is important that every student gets the full attention that he or she deserves.

Yvonne's description of her "negative" teacher replicated Pauahi's. She chose to write about the elementary teacher who had referred to her as a "typical lazy Hawaiian who would not amount to much." She began her narrative with a graphic description: "It was as if she were standing ready to lash out at me, the moment I was out of line." Yvonne relied on metaphor in her discussion:

I see my negative teacher as a dragon. Her appearance alone was enough to scare anyone. She never smiled and she looked down on me with her big red beady eyes. Her nostrils were big and she seemed ready to blow steam at me at any minute. Her voice was like a loud roar. While in her presence, I felt terrified. She reminded me of a dragon because she seemed unwilling to change. She was someone out of the past who was set in her ways.

Yvonne went on to recall a hostile classroom environment that filled her with fear and self-doubt:

I was terrified and would never raise my hand to participate in any class activities. It seemed even if I wanted to, she would never call on me anyway. Was I stupid? I would shut down and be turned off by everything about her. She was mean and angry most of the day.

Despite her traumatic experiences, Yvonne wrote in her reaction paper that she considered her experiences with this negative teacher a blessing: "How profound an effect did she have on my life? I now consider her a blessing and a great example of what I will *never* be like in the classroom. She has given me the greatest example of a 'disinviting' teacher." Yvonne's reference to disinviting teaching stems from her interest in Purkey and Novak's (1996) self-concept approach to teaching and learning. Under the coinage, "invitational education," Purkey and Novak proposed an educative approach that centers, in part, on treating children as able, responsible, and valuable, and on developing policies, programs, and processes that invite school success for all children. For Yvonne, invitational education encompassed many of the Hawaiian values that she held dear—'ohana (family), aloha (love), kōkua (helping others), 'ike (knowledge/recognition), ho'oponopono (forgiveness), kuleana (responsibility), laulima (cooperation), and lōkahi (harmony/unity).

Like Pauahi, Yvonne emphasized the importance of developing a culturally responsive instructional approach. In her reaction paper she stated:

It is important for a teacher to have an awareness of the cultural diversity in the classroom. Getting to know the students may provide insights into effective instructional approaches to literacy. It is my belief that all students can become literate given the right environment, opportunities, and support.

For Yvonne, this translated into practices such as the inclusion of a "range of multicultural literature and resources that support the language and literacy learning of students of diverse cultural backgrounds." She continued: "I will encourage Readers' and Writers' Workshops (Au, Carroll, & Scheu, 1997) that promote the sharing of experiences and cultures. I will be sensitive to students' prior knowledge and experiences they bring to the classroom. I will focus on encouraging and not discouraging students."

For her significantly positive teacher, Pauahi looked beyond her formal schooling experiences. She wrote about her grandfather: "Although several people come to mind, my grandfather has influenced me the most." Pauahi began her narrative by describing an upbringing with opportunities to succeed: "It had a lot to do with the safe environment that I was in. I never had to worry about food, or clothes, or anything really…, just school. My world was very different from the worlds of some Hawaiian children."

From her grandfather, whom she described as "pretty well educated," Pauahi learned about the importance of a good education:

> Grampa was my role model. He graduated from high school and then went on to the shipyard. He took different courses including ones at college. He always made sure that I knew how important it was to do well in school. He never yelled at me over it, he just made sure that my homework was completed.

Because her grandfather instilled in her the desire to do well in her studies, Pauahi wrote that she never had problems at school: "I have always been motivated. Because of Grampa, it never occurred to me that I couldn't do anything once I put my mind to it."

As well as encouraging her to value her formal education, Pauahi's grandfather also took on the role of teacher. She described how he would make their day-to-day interactions educational: "Once we went to the Big Island (the island of Hawai'i). I remember going to the black sand beach in Kalapana and listening to Grampa explain why the sand was black instead of white, which was what I was used to seeing." And: "One day, I discovered that Grampa had an extensive vocabulary. As a result, I would spend all day at school thinking up words for him to define, always with the hope that I would stump him. I never could."

Pauahi acknowledged that her grandfather's guidance and teachings were primarily responsible for her success in higher education. With this success came many opportunities: "What I like about being a student is that it has opened up opportunities for me. I would not have experienced many of the things had I not been a (university) student. I have sailed on the Hokule'a, worked in a lo'i (kalo or taro patch), paddled canoes, and gained a lot of knowledge." Pauahi's understanding of the impact of her grandfather's mentoring shaped her development as a teacher. In a personal narrative, she described her role in her future classroom as one of facilitating school success in her students:

> As a teacher I have the power to positively or negatively impact my students' lives. The learning environment that I will provide for them will be stable, safe, and positive. My students will have ownership of their learning and they will be encouraged to value themselves as learners. Through writing, talking, and reading about themselves they will come to value and connect their home lives to the classroom. In a classroom setting that accepts all cultures, my students will learn to value education too.

Yvonne's significantly positive teacher was her kumu (Hawaiian language teacher). He reminded her of a tiger:

> I see him as a tiger because of his masculinity, style, grace, and beauty. There was a certain style and grace to his teaching. Through him, I was able to see how much of my own Hawaiian culture I had missed in my own upbringing. He made learning and speaking Hawaiian lots of fun and interesting. I learned so much about myself and the Hawaiian culture. He was able to express the richness and beauty of the Hawaiian language.

Yvonne explained that with the development of self-knowledge came greater confidence in her herself, especially in her ability to achieve success in higher education: "He was my inspiration to strive for greater heights in my formal education." Just as Pauahi's grandfather had been her role model, so too had Yvonne's kumu been for her. In particular, he taught her how to persevere in the face of discrimination:

> Like a tiger, he stood alert and was always ready to handle any challenges or tasks that came his way. My kumu possessed the persistence and determination necessary to survive in his environment. He did not miss a thing. He challenged me to strive for my greatest potential.

In explaining the importance of role models, especially of Hawaiian ancestry, Yvonne referred to her public school education which was marked by an absence of teachers to whom she felt "connected." In her personal narrative, she wrote: "I don't remember any positive role models. There weren't many Hawaiian teachers." She also noted that, in general, her teachers held low expectations for her and her Hawaiian classmates: "Included in my curriculum were things like cooking and sewing. These were the areas in which we were trained. We weren't trained to become doctors and lawyers." Although Yvonne's schooling took place in the 1960s and 70s, advantages for Hawaiians through education still remain limited. To this day, there are disproportionately high numbers of Hawaiian students in special education or lower ability classes in schools and disproportionately low numbers of Hawaiian students studying at the university level.

The influence of her kumu emerged in Yvonne's discussion of her beliefs about learning and teaching. Like her mentor, she intended to challenge her students to set and achieve the highest goals. In a reaction paper, she called for other teachers to follow her lead:

> Teachers must consciously review their expectations of students and their behaviors toward students of diverse backgrounds to ensure that they are not discriminating. Instructional methods and teaching strategies should accommodate the needs of individual children depending on the environment in which they live. All children should have a quality education and all teachers should make it their primary responsibility to provide this.

Rich literacy instruction was viewed as the key to success. Inspired by Au's (1993) writing on literacy instruction in multicultural settings, Yvonne said she had "developed a greater understanding of and appreciation for the complexities of teaching students of diverse cultural backgrounds to become literate." For her, literacy instruction would be the cornerstone of her classroom curriculum:

> My classroom will have a range of resources and activities that support the learning of all children. I will have learning centers and a library filled with a range of multicultural literature. I will provide opportunities for children to work together, so that they can share their ideas. And, I will encourage my children to make connections between what they know and what they are learning. In short, my children will learn in a safe, nonthreatening classroom environment conducive to learning language and literacy.

The ideas expressed by Pauahi and Yvonne in this section indicate that their own school experiences had profound influences on their beliefs about teaching and the kind of teachers they hoped to become. Both had vivid memories of former teachers. Some teachers were memorable for the dread they instilled, giving Pauahi and Yvonne clear understandings of harmful attitudes and behaviors they would avoid inflicting upon their own students. Other teachers, such as Yvonne's Hawaiian studies teacher, were sources of continuing inspiration. In Pauahi's case, her grandfather had a greater overall influence in fostering her love of learning than any classroom teacher. Because of their schooling experiences, as well as the influences of their university courses, Pauahi and Yvonne believed strongly that the best teachers are those who hold high expectations and communicate these expectations to their students.

Some of the complex connections among cultural identity, literacy, and schooling are clarified in the statements made by Pauahi and Yvonne. Both argued that teachers can better establish positive relationships when they understand students' cultures and can make connections between students' lives at home and at school. In other words, respect for and understanding of students' diverse cultural and linguistic backgrounds serve as the foundation for culturally responsive instruction. The fact that Pauahi and Yvonne seldom experienced culturally responsive instruction during their elementary and high school years appears to have made them all the more determined to provide this kind of instruction for their own students.

Pauahi and Yvonne's understandings about the nature and importance of culturally responsive instruction were made clearer in their descriptions of their approaches to teaching literacy. Both noted the importance of establishing positive relationships with their students in classroom atmospheres free of intimidation. They wanted their students to learn to read and write in accepting atmospheres that encourage risk-taking. They contended that in comfortable classrooms, their students would be more inclined to openly discuss their ideas and feelings with others. Pauahi and Yvonne said that when students of diverse backgrounds feel intimidated or excluded by teachers, they tend to "shut down," refusing to participate and showing passivity during classroom literacy activities (see Key, 1998). Both women reported shutting down in the presence of threatening and overpowering teachers.

Pauahi and Yvonne also emphasized the importance of making a wide range of multicultural literature available to children. They argued that this literature would give validity, in the classroom literacy program, to the culture and life experiences of Hawaiian and other students of diverse cultural backgrounds. Only when teachers foster the important connections between literature and the lives of their students will the students develop an appreciation for and ownership of their literacy learning.

Ka Lama provides course work and related professional development opportunities that emphasize an integrated, culturally responsive approach to literacy learning and teaching. Pauahi, Yvonne and other students in the cohort are encouraged to develop instructional approaches that connect the children's backgrounds and interests to the school curriculum. The successful literacy development of children on the Wai'anae Coast, which includes effective reading, writing, and critical thinking, will best be achieved by teachers who have as their foundation an essential understanding of and respect for the cultural knowledge, experiences, values, and aspirations of their students.

Reconceptualizing Teacher Education: The Educational Well-Being of Hawaiian Children

This section of our research focused on the question: How have Hawaiian preservice teachers' views of their cultural identity and their experiences as students informed their development as teachers? Pauahi, who described herself as politically active (in the Hawaiian sovereignty movement), viewed her responsibility as a teacher in terms of the revitalization of the Hawaiian culture and language. In her life-history interview, she stated, "Culture has a lot to do with being a teacher. As a Hawaiian, it is my responsibility to share my knowledge with the next generation..., especially the language. I hope I can become an immersion (Hawaiian language immersion) teacher." Later, she elaborated in a reaction paper: "I am not getting into immersion for the pay. I'm doing it so my people will have a source of pride and to show the system including the DOE (Hawai'i State Department of Education) that immersion is plausible." For Pauahi, teaching was more than the "3 Rs." It was about reaffirming the rights of Hawaiians. Trask (1999) clarified the important interrelationships among culture and language, politics, and schooling:

In Hawaii and Aotearoa (New Zealand), for example, teaching the Native languages in immersion schools has been at the forefront of a cultural resurgence that also includes reclaiming ancestral lands and moves toward various forms of self-government. In situations such as these, language instruction is understood to be both a cultural and political assertion: *cultural* because it seeks to preserve the core of a way of thinking and being that is uniquely Native, and *political* because this attempt at preservation takes place in a system where the dominant group has employed legal and social means to deny the use and inheritance of the Native language by Natives themselves. (p. 42)

English became the language of instruction in Hawai'i in 1896 after the 1893 overthrow of the Hawaiian monarchy and just before annexation to the United States. The same law prohibited the speaking of Hawaiian in schools. We have heard Hawaiian elders describe being punished for speaking Hawaiian in the classroom, even when they were merely translating the teacher's words for a classmate who did not speak English. The replacement of the Hawaiian language with English had a devastating impact on the Hawaiian culture. The enforced use of English in schools disconnected Hawaiian children from the place where they were born and from the knowledge created by their ancestors (Trask, 1999).

When asked to elaborate further on her understandings about cultural identity and the professional development of teachers, Pauahi wrote in a reaction paper: "Being a teacher is a heavy responsibility. To forget this can lead to serious repercussions for my children. I must always strive to treat them as gifts of life, with limitless potential to achieve whatever goals that they set." In her discussion, Pauahi noted the critical need for the development and implementation of school curricula that accommodate the learning needs and interests of all children, especially those, typically of diverse backgrounds, with poor records of school success.

In her interview, Yvonne talked about the "importance of being a teacher and a positive role model for many children." She noted that her primary goal as a teacher in English language immersion classrooms would be to show children that good educations open many doors of opportunity. She also used her own negative schooling experiences as a point of reference: "As far back as I can remember, Hawaiian girls always received messages of low expectations of academic success." The elementary school teacher who informed Yvonne that she was a "typical lazy Hawaiian who would not amount to much" treated her as one who was incapable of school success: "It was like I was put in a class with other 'typical lazy Hawaiians' and it was assumed that we would not be successful in our academics or otherwise," she said. Clearly, this experience was significant for Yvonne. Several times in her interview, reaction papers, and personal narratives, she mentioned the importance of being a positive role model. In one reaction paper, she wrote: "I believe I am a positive role model for local children. I can demonstrate to them through hard work and a good education that they can attain much in life. I can teach them to persevere despite discrimination."

In a reaction paper, Yvonne wrote that her future classroom would reflect her Hawaiian beliefs:

> My Hawaiian beliefs influence all aspects of my personal and professional lives, from the way I think, to the way I behave, to the way I interact with others. Much of my life is lived by the basic Hawaiian cultural values of 'ohana, aloha, kōkua, 'ike, ho'oponopono, kuleana, laulima, and lōkahi. It is in this environment that my students will learn.

In terms of their development as teachers, Pauahi and Yvonne were very clear about their understandings of the significance of their cultural identity. Each woman said her professional responsibility included bringing about political, social, and economic renewal for Hawaiians through success in schooling—Pauahi in a Hawaiian language immersion classroom and Yvonne in an English language immersion classroom. Addressing the injustices and abuses of the Hawaiian people, who, "over one hundred years ago, had their sense of sovereignty and cultural identity ripped away from them," was significant for Pauahi. The idea that Hawaiian families and communities have the right to retain responsibility for the upbringing, training, education, and well-being of their children, strongly influenced Pauahi and Yvonne's decisions to become teachers. This sentiment was echoed at the 1999 World Indigenous Peoples' Conference on Education in Hawai'i. Many of the Hawaiian educators called for a meaningful, powerful, and culturally-sustaining education system for Hawaiians through the development of educational theories, curricula, and practices by Hawaiians.

As the views of Pauahi and Yvonne suggest, Hawaiian preservice teachers may have definite ideas about the relationships between schooling and cultural identity. We believe that an effective teacher education program must support Hawaiian preservice teachers' moral commitment to teaching while at the same time dealing directly with the tensions and controversies that such a commitment may entail. An obvious tension is seen in the effort to work through a school system that has a long history of failing to meet the educational needs of Hawaiian children. Other Hawaiian preservice teachers, such as Yvonne, may also have been the victims of stereotyping and discrimination during their schooling. How does one work from within such a system to bring about social justice? A teacher education program such as Ka Lama must help preservice teachers learn to function effectively as educators within public schools while at the same time remaining true to the Hawaiian cultural values and commitments that brought them to the teaching profession in the first place.

Another tension is seen in the role of literacy, especially English literacy. During a course on Hawaiian studies, we ask the Ka Lama preservice teachers to consider the historical context for the literacy of Hawaiians. Congregational missionaries from New England first turned Hawaiian into a written language in the 1820s. After Kamehameha III established a system of village schools in 1848, many Hawaiians became literate in their own language, and more than 100 newspapers were published in the Hawaiian language in the late nineteenth century. With the overthrow of the monarchy in 1893, Hawaiians lost control of the public schools. Literacy in English became the goal, and literacy in the Hawaiian language was cast aside. We ask the Ka Lama preservice teachers to consider the ambiguous role of English literacy, which may, from a critical perspective, be seen as an instrument for the subjugation of the Hawaiian people. We believe that preservice teachers must be aware of this history and of the importance of teaching literacy as a means of empowering, not disempowering, Hawaiian students.

CONCLUSION

Today, Hawaiians are faced with the challenge of reconceptualizing their literacy, not only in the new age of pluralism and multiculturalism, but also in the new age of decolonization. The recovery of their language and literacy as their record of legitimate knowledge is inextricably woven with the recovery of two other fundamental markers of their cultural identity—sovereignty and ancestral lands. Hawaiians and other colonized indigenous peoples of the Pacific are demanding the establishment of systems of education that reflect, respect, and embrace those cultural values, philosophies, and ideologies which shaped, nurtured, and sustained them prior to the colonization of their lands.

It is fitting that we conclude by revisiting the story of the small Hawaiian boy from the Wai'anae Coast of O'ahu, Hawai'i and his problematic raccoons. His struggle with a mathematics curriculum that failed to acknowledge his cultural knowledge, experiences, and values is only one of many obstacles that he will probably face throughout his years of schooling. If his experiences are typical of most Hawaiian children in this area, his level of academic achievement will be poor in comparison with children from the two dominant groups in Hawai'i, European and Japanese Americans.

While there is no single or simple solution to raising the level of achievement of Hawaiian children and others from underrepresented groups, this study provides some insights into improving one area of the educative process—teacher education. Our examination of how Pauahi and Yvonne's views of their own cultural identity, how their experiences as students shaped their beliefs about culture, literacy, and schooling, and how their views of their cultural identity and their experiences as students informed their development as teachers add to the research on effective teacher preparation programs for individuals of diverse backgrounds.

In short, Pauahi and Yvonne underscored two critical areas of need. First, they called for the development of school curricula that acknowledge and respect the culture and life experiences of Hawaiian children. In the Ka Lama cohort, we emphasize the importance of helping Hawaiian children develop a sense of meaning and purpose to their schooling through an approach to teaching literacy that integrates Hawaiian studies, other content areas, and students' life experiences. Second, Pauahi and Yvonne called for programmatic efforts that increase the number of well-prepared teachers of Hawaiian ancestry to serve as role models and developers of culturally responsive curricula. As mentioned earlier, for an education system to by truly meaningful, powerful, and culturally sustaining, Hawaiians must take active roles in the development of educational theories, curricula, and practices. The Ka Lama O Ke Kaiāulu teacher education initiative has the purpose of improving the education of Hawaiian students in public schools on the Wai'anae Coast by recruiting and training teachers with commitments to the area.

ACKNOWLEDGMENTS

The authors are members of Mana Wahine, which is a group of educators interested in the recruitment and graduation of people of diverse backgrounds with advanced degrees in education to fill roles in teaching, administration, applied research, and teacher education.

This research is supported by the Spencer Foundation through a grant for the project, *The Successful Education of Hawaiian Children: A Study of Preservice and Mentor Teachers*, and by the Institute for Educational Inquiry through a grant from the W. K. Kellogg Foundation for the project, *Ka Lama O Ke Kaiāulu Diversity in Teacher Education Initiative.*

NOTE

1. *Hawaiian* refers to the indigenous or native people of the islands of Hawai'i.

REFERENCES

Asam, C.L. (1999). *Native Hawaiian perspectives on teacher socialization: The influence of culture and the development of professional identity.* Unpublished doctoral dissertation, University of Hawaii, Honolulu, HI.

Au, K.H. (1993). *Literacy instruction in multicultural settings.* Fort Worth, TX: Harcourt Brace Jovanovich College Publishers.

Au, K.H. (1998–99). Personal narratives, literacy portfolios, and cultural identity. *National Forum of Teacher Education Journal, 8*(1), 14–20.

Au, K.H., & Carroll, J.H. (1997). Improving literacy achievement through a constructivist approach: The KEEP Demonstration Classroom Project. *Elementary School Journal*, 97(3), 203–221.

Au, K.H., Carroll, J.H., & Scheu, J.A. (1997). *Balanced literacy instruction: A teacher's resource book*. Norwood, MA: Christopher-Gordon.

Au, K.H., & Mason, J.M. (1983). Cultural congruence in classroom participation structures: Achieving a balance of rights. *Discourse Processes*, 6(2), 145–167.

Berliner, D. (1986). Does culture affect reading comprehension? *Instructor*, 96(3), 28–29.

Burgess, P. (1998). Choosing my name. [Reprinted in Chock, E. (Ed.), *Growing up local: An anthology of poetry & prose from Hawaii*. Honolulu, HI: Bamboo Ridge Press.]

D'Amato, J. (1988). "Acting": Hawaiian children's resistance to teachers. *Elementary School Journal*, 88(5), 529–544.

Durie, A. (1997). Te Aka Matua: Keeping a Māori identity. In P. Te Whāiti, M. McCarthy, & A. Durie (Eds.), *Mai i Rangiātea: Māori wellbeing and development*. Auckland: Auckland University Press.

Durie, M.H. (1998). *Te Mana, Te Kāwanatanga: The politics of Māori self-determination*. Auckland: Oxford University Press.

Florio-Ruane, S., & Raphael, T.E. (1999). *Culture, autobiography, and the education of literacy teachers*. CIERA Report #3-003. Ann Arbor: Center for the Improvement of Early Reading Achievement, University of Michigan.

Foster, M. (1991). Just got to find a way: Case studies of the lives and practice of exemplary Black high school teachers. In M. Foster (Ed.), *Readings on equal education. Volume 11: Qualitative investigations into schools and schooling* (pp. 273–309). New York: AMS Press.

Freire, P. (1970). *Pedagogy of the oppressed*. New York: Continuum.

Giroux, H.A., & McLaren, P. (Eds.). (1994). *Between borders: Pedagogy and the politics of cultural studies*. New York: Routledge.

Glaser, B.G., & Strauss, A.L. (1967). *The discovery of grounded theory: Strategies for qualitative research*. Chicago: Aldine.

Gomez, M.L. (1994). Teacher education reform and prospective teachers' perspectives on teaching "other people's' children. *Teaching and Teacher Education*, 10(3), 319–334.

Gomez, M.L., & Tabachnick, B.R. (1991). *"We are the answer": Preparing preservice teachers to teach diverse learners*. Paper presented at the annual meeting of the American Educational Research Association, Chicago, Illinois.

Hall, S. (1991). Ethnicity: Identity and difference. *Radical America*, 23(4), 9–20.

Hewett, K.K. (1998). *Ko Makou Mau Mo'olelo: Native Hawaiian Students in a Teacher Education Program*. Unpublished Doctoral Dissertation, University of Hawai'i at Mānoa, Hawaii'i.

Hollins, E.R. (1996). *Culture in school and learning: Revealing the deep meaning*. Mahwah, NJ: Lawrence Erlbaum.

Hollins, E.R., & Oliver, E.I. (Eds.). (1999). *Pathways to success in school: Culturally responsive teaching*. Mahwah, NJ: Lawrence Erlbaum.

Key, D. (1998). *Literacy shutdown: Stories of six American women*. Newark, DE: International Reading Association & Chicago, IL: National Reading Conference.

Maaka, M.J., Au, K.H., & Luna, C.A. (1998). *Starting blocks or stumbling blocks to higher education?: Case studies of Native Hawaiian women.* Paper presented at the annual meeting of the American Educational Research Association, San Diego, CA.

Moss, B.J. (1994). *Literacy across communities.* Cresskill, NJ: Hampton Press.

National Organizing Committee of the World Indigenous Peoples' Conference on Education. (1993). *The Coollongatta statement on Indigenous rights in education.* Coollongatta, Australia: Author.

Noordhoff, K., & Kleinfeld, J. (1993). Preparing teachers for multicultural classrooms. *Teaching and Teacher Education, 9*(1), 27–39.

Purkey, W.W., & Novak, J.M. (1996). *Inviting school success: A self-concept approach to teaching, learning, and democratic practice.* Belmont, CA: Wadsworth.

Rosaldo, R. (1989). *Culture and truth: The remaking of social analysis.* Boston: Beacon.

Roth, R. (1984). Schooling, literacy acquisition and cultural transmission. *Journal of Education, 166*(3), 291–308.

Smith, L.T. (1999). *Decolonizing methodologies: Research and indigenous peoples.* Londan: Zed Books.

Spradley, J.P. (1979). *The ethnographic interview.* New York, NY: Holt, Rinehart & Winston.

Strickland, D. S. (1994). Educating African American learners at risk: Finding a better way. *Language Arts, 71*(5), 328–336.

Tikunoff, W.J., Ward, B.A., & Van Broekhuizen, L.D. (1993). *KEEP evaluation study: Year 3 report.* Los Alamitos, CA: Southwest Regional Laboratory.

Trask, H-K. (1999). *From a native daughter: Colonialism and sovereignty in Hawai'i* (2nd ed.). Honolulu, HI: University of Hawai'i Press.

United Nations Sub-Commission on Prevention of Discrimination and Protection of Minorities. (1994). *Draft United Nations Declaration on the Rights of Indigenous Peoples.* In H- K. Trask. (1999). *From a native daughter: Colonialism and sovereignty in Hawaii'i* (2nd ed.). Honolulu, HI: University of Hawai'i Press.

CHAPTER 16

UNDERSTANDING CULTURE IN OUR LIVES AND WORK

Teachers' Literature Study in the Book Club Program

Taffy E. Raphael, Karen Damphousse, Kathy Highfield, and Susan Florio-Ruane

Abstract: The project we describe in this chapter grew out of our interest in the potential of autobiography and autobiographical fiction to meet the challenge of educating both teachers and students to live and work in a diverse society. In this chapter, we describe the background for Susan Florio- Ruane's and Taffy Raphael's decision to connect their work and the resulting contexts for professional development at Michigan State and Oakland Universities. We then describe the Master's level course that grew out of this collaboration, taught by Taffy at Oakland University, with the assistance of Kathy Highfield. In the second and third sections of this chapter, participants Kathy Highfield and Karen Damphousse describe their experiences in and responses to the adult book club course. We conclude with a discussion of the promises that autobiography book clubs hold for us as teacher educators and teachers, as well as for our students.

Our primary goal was to help teachers come to understand themselves as cultural beings (i.e., as members of one of more cultural groups), to understand literacy as cultural practice, and to extend these understandings to their curriculum development and instructional practices. Our second goal was to create an experience where teachers engaged in conversation-based learning that would parallel the innovative ways of teaching and learning that they were attempting within their classroom literacy instructional practices. Teachers' learning in these book clubs is, as the above examples illustrate, of three kinds: learning about literature and literacy, learning about instruction, and learning about self and others. This learning is situated within and inseparable from the social context of the peer-led book conversations and the nature and content of the autobiographies. Thus, by means of this experience, participants were taught a powerful lesson about literacy and literacy education. Literacy is not merely "reading, writing, speaking, and listening." Nor is it simply a repertoire of skills and strategies for decoding and encoding print. Literacy is situated, meaningful, text-based interaction with others. As such, literacy teaches us about humanity reflected in and seen through the looking glass of our own and others' stories.

INTRODUCTION

"Learning to look through multiple perspectives, young people may be helped to build bridges among themselves; attending to a range of human stories, they may be provoked to heal and transform" (Dewey cited in Greene, 1993, p. 17). In the 1930s, John Dewey foreshadowed the construct of multiculturalism in his emphasis on the importance of building bridges and assuming multiple perspectives. The United States is a pluralistic society, perhaps one of the most diverse in the world. One of our key responsibilities as educators is to help our students learn to live, work, and participate in such a diverse society. Fulfilling this responsibility is one of the greatest challenges we face in our profession, both in the education of our youngsters and in the field of teacher education.

The project we describe in this chapter grew out of our interest in the potential of autobiography and autobiographical fiction to meet the challenge, and their promise for educating both teachers and students to live and work in a diverse society. The project began in 1995 as a collaboration between Susan Florio-Ruane, Ph.D. and Taffy Raphael, Ph.D. Susan and Taffy had worked together on program development and in other roles as colleagues at Michigan State University for several years. Their research collaboration began when they decided to explore how Taffy's research on Book Club (McMahon & Raphael, 1997; Goatley, Brock & Raphael, 1995; Raphael, Brock, & Wallace, 1998) and Susan's research on the Future Teachers' Autobiography Club (Florio-Ruane, 1994; 1997; Florio-Ruane & deTar, 1995) could be combined to address two of the challenges that literacy educators face today—one related to teachers' teaching and development and the other to the diversity of students in today's classrooms.

In this chapter, we describe the background for Susan's and Taffy's decision to connect their work and the resulting contexts for professional development at Michigan State and Oakland Universities. We then describe the Master's level course that grew out of this collaboration, taught by Taffy at Oakland University, with the assistance of Kathy Highfield. In the second and third sections of this chapter, participants Kathy Highfield and Karen Damphousse describe their experiences in and responses to the adult book club course. We conclude with a discussion of the promises that autobiography book clubs hold for us as teacher educators and teachers, to examine issues of diversity and multiculturalism, and draw on our insights as we work with our students.

DEVELOPING THE RESEARCH AGENDA

Susan and Taffy worked together, merging their two lines of research to help support teachers in addressing the challenges they face in teaching today. These challenges relate to (a) diversity among students and between teachers and students and (b) teaching and teacher development. We first detail the challenges, then describe merging the two lines of research.

DIVERSITY WITHIN THE SCHOOL POPULATION

A major challenge facing teachers today stems from the cultural makeup of our teaching force and student population (Au & Raphael, 2000). Today's teaching force can be characterized, on the surface, as extremely homogenous. Despite attempts to increase the racial, ethnic and linguistic diversity of our teaching force, teachers today are primarily European American, monolingual women from working- and middle-class backgrounds. Many of these teachers work with students whose backgrounds are quite similar to their own, and issues of culture and diversity remains largely transparent. This homogeneity does little to prepare students to live in our pluralistic society. At the other end of the spectrum, many other teachers work with groups of students who do not share their racial, linguistic, ethnic, or socioeconomic backgrounds. Teachers in these environments often view culture as something exotic and completely external, associated only with the unnamed "other," and not a part of their own lives, backgrounds, etc. Maxine Greene, citing poet and literary critic, Toni Morrison, has described this perspective as defining ourselves against some "otherness" which we may "thrust away, to master rather than to understand" (1995, pp.161–162). Since literacy and schooling are clearly cultural practices, teachers need to be aware of their own culture and the influence it has had on their own lives if they are to be successful in considering how culture influences the lives and the learning of their students.

By considering how culture influences our students' lives and their literacy development, we, as literacy educators, can make valuable contributions to students' multicultural education. As Banks (1992, p.23) states, "Multicultural education is designed to help unify a deeply divided nation rather than to divide a highly cohesive one." Current practices that emphasize the study of individual cultures may in fact promote stereotyping and division, the very problems that they were designed to erase. Studying cultures as objects tends to frame cultures as static constructs and ignore the reality that there is as much variation within as across cultures.

Thus, our primary goal was to help teachers come to understand themselves as cultural beings (i.e., as members of one of more cultural groups), to understand literacy as cultural practice, and to extend these understandings to their curriculum development and instructional practices. We grounded teachers' learning about culture in a variety of contexts in which, through conversation, they could explore the cultural backgrounds of various authors who have written of their own immigrant experiences, and, in doing so, could make connections between the lives of these authors and their own cultural backgrounds. We embedded these experiences within a model of conversation-based curricula as a way of addressing the second challenge facing teachers today, teaching and teacher development.

Teaching and Teacher Development

Teachers today are expected to teach using conversation-based approaches such as process writing (Calkins, 1986; Dyson, 1992), Literature Circles (Daniels, 1994), and Book Club (McMahon & Raphael, 1997) that are grounded in response-oriented literacy education. Yet, neither teachers' educational history nor their teacher preparation course work have provided the rich experiences needed to teach within such approaches (Burbules, 1993). At best, this creates challenges for today's teachers; worse, it leads to frustration and even disenchantment for teachers, students, administrators, and parents.

These teaching and teacher-development challenges can be traced to innovations in literacy instructional practices in the past decade. First, there have been changes in textual materials, such as moving away from commercially prepared short stories and text excerpts and using original literature as a basis for instruction (Raphael & Au, 1998). Second, there have been changes in curriculum organization, such as moving from isolated instruction in reading, writing, language, and subject matter to intra- and interdisciplinary teaching (Gavelek, Raphael, Biondo, & Wang, 2000). Third, there have been changes in teachers' roles, such as moving from teacher control over topics and turns to teachers assuming multiple roles (direct teaching, modeling and scaffolding, facilitating and participating) with related changes in students' roles, where students are asked to assume more responsibilities for selecting books, initiating discussion topics, and evaluating their progress (Au & Raphael, 1998, 2000).

Thus, our second goal was to create an experience where teachers engaged in conversation-based learning that would parallel the innovative ways of teaching and learning that they were attempting within their instructional practices. In addition to helping prepare teachers to teach using conversation-based approaches, the very nature of the context pro-

motes consideration of alternate positions and points of view as participants make connections between texts, among themselves, and between
the texts and their own lives. McVee (1999) studied the stories that teachers told as they responded to autobiographical literature. Over the course
of a semester, the teachers' stories changed. Teachers positioned and repo-
sitioned themselves with regard to their stance toward race and culture.
Similarly, Raphael and Florio-Ruane (1998) studied the conversations
among teachers during one evening's discussion of Amy Tan's novel, *The
Kitchen God's Wife.* Participants used this fictional account of one woman's
life to consider issues ranging from the secrets within one's own family's
histories to those maintained within culture, gender (specifically among
women), and society. Using the culture of China in the 1950s, 60s, and 70s,
teachers explored racial relationships, class struggles, and gender. In short,
through conversation in response to autobiographical literature, teachers
can examine cultures and multiculturalism, be challenged to face some of
their own biases and stereotypes, and make connections across cultures
and times. All of these experiences support teachers' curriculum development in multicultural education with an eye toward supporting their students' abilities to live in a pluralist society.

Merging the Research Lines

Susan had created a Future Teachers' Autobiography Club in which six
young women preparing to become teachers engaged in six monthly discussions, each one centered on one of six autobiographies Susan had
selected (Florio-Ruane, 1994, 1997, 2001). The autobiographies represented stories of white teachers who chose to work with students from
diverse backgrounds (Paley's [1979] *White Teacher;* Rose's [1989] *Lives on
the Boundary*), of immigrants who left their homelands voluntarily to seek
new educational and financial opportunities (Hoffman's [1989] *Lives in
Translation;* Conway's [1990] *The Road from Coorain*), and of immigrants or
descendants of immigrants who were forced to leave their homeland due
to slavery or economic deprivation (Rodriguez's [1982] *Hunger of Memory;*
Angelou's [1969] *I Know Why the Caged Bird Sings*) (see Florio-Ruane & De
Tar, 1995, and Florio-Ruane, 1996, 2001 for detailed description of this
project).

Autobiography provides an important means by which teachers can
explore the lives of people who are very different from themselves, as well
as explore their own cultural histories (Graham, 1991). As Jill Ker Conway
(1998) suggests in her recent examination of the autobiographical genre:

> Theory can help us read autobiography with more critical awareness. Gender
> studies can help us pay attention to when and where women autobiographers
> seem to have trouble with their narrative. But to answer the question of why

we like to read it, and why individuals sit down at desk or table and begin to tell their story, lies not in theory but in cultural history. It has to do with where we look when we try to understand our own lives, how we read texts and what largely unexamined cultural assumptions we bring to interpreting them (p. 4).

Through their reading, writing, and discussions, the six student teachers heightened their awareness of themselves as cultural beings but struggled to talk about race, culture, and gender. Susan began looking for ways to create a context in which she would have a more clearly defined role as instructor to facilitate discussions about hard-to-talk-about topics while still emphasizing conversation-based learning.

Taffy had collaborated with classroom teachers and university-based colleagues to create the Book Club Program (McMahon &Raphael, 1997; Raphael, Goatley, Woodman, & McMahon, 1994; Raphael, McMahon, Goatley, Bentley, Boyd, Pardo, & Woodman, 1992). The Book Club Program is an instructional context centered on student-led discussion groups. Reading, writing, and discussion strategies are taught to students to enable them to become more comfortable and proficient in reading, writing about, and talking about books (see Raphael, Pardo, Highfield, & McMahon, 1997, for extensive description of the program and specific unit examples).

Book Club emphasized dialogic teaching and learning in whole class and small group settings, and several of the teachers indicated their own discomfort stemming from their own lack of experience in book clubs. Taffy had tried different ways of introducing teachers to book clubs, such as reading and discussing children's literature that they might use in their classrooms. She found that, after a few minutes of talking about the texts, teachers' focus shifted from the books themselves to how they would teach the books. Thus, Taffy was looking for a conceptually strong set of issues that teachers teaching with Book Club could read, write, and discuss in their own book clubs.

Susan and Taffy merged their work, emphasizing the focus on autobiography and its related themes of living in a pluralist society and understanding ourselves as cultural beings, and adapting the Book Club model for use in a Master's level course for practicing teachers. Susan taught the course while Taffy and two research assistants, Susan Wallace and Mary McVee, served as participant observers, audiotaping the classrooms, recording field notes, and interviewing the participants. The structure of the Book Club program, combined with a substantive syllabus of autobiographical texts and selected articles about culture and education, provided the means by which teachers learned about literacy as a cultural practice and themselves as cultural beings (see Florio-Ruane, Raphael, Glazier, McVee, & Wallace, 1997; Florio-Ruane, Raphael & Shellhorn, 1998; Raphael & Florio-Ruane, 1998).

Jerri,[1] one of the teacher participants from the course taught by Susan, stated in an interview in the summer following her participation: "I was one of those people in the beginning who (thought) I had no culture. There's nothing to me. I've had no experiences." Getting culture "on the table" for discussion was an important first step. Jerri described her reading of autobiographies as providing: "experiences, even though I haven't (had them). It's given me a better understanding for some of those things." Further, teachers appreciated the opportunity to experience a model of instruction that they planned to use in their own teaching. Hannah, another teacher in Susan's course, noted in her follow-up interview: "for me it was an excellent, excellent experience because I use book clubs in my classroom. So it was terrific for me to be able to participate in something that I ask my students to participate in."

After the course, the group chose to create the Literary Circle to continue reading, thinking, and talking about autobiography and culture using the Book Club model. Over the next 2 and a half years, the meeting locations changed. Initially, the Literary Circle had met in Susan's home. The second year, we met in a private room at a local coffee shop/book store; members took turns recommending a book to read in advance that fit the theme of literacy and culture. We decided to read a selection of texts that included not only autobiography but also autobiographical fiction such as Amy Tan's (1991) *The Kitchen God's Wife* and Nora Zeale Hurston's (1937) *Their Eyes Were Watching God*, and books such as Peggy Orenstein's (1994) *School Girls* that explore related issues—in this case, gender examined through a series of case studies. These discussions were also researched by Taffy and Susan, along with the aforementioned research assistants (Mcvee and Wallace), as well as Jocelyn Glazier and Bette Shellhorn (for examples, see Florio-Ruane, Raphael, & Shellhorn, 1998; Florio-Ruane, Raphael, Glazier, Mcvee, & Wallace, 1997; Raphael & Florio-Ruane, 1998).

New Course Content and Structure: The Book Club Workshop

When Taffy moved from Michigan State University to Oakland University, she developed a course for practicing teachers—the Book Club Workshop—that extended the original course which Susan had taught. The course introduced practicing teachers to literature-based reading instruction using the Book Club Program as the primary illustration (McMahon & Raphael, 1997; Raphael, Pardo, Highfield, & McMahon, 1997) and promoted teachers' exploration of literacy as a cultural practice and themselves as cultural beings as they read autobiographies written by ethnic minorities who focus on the immigrant experiences (for a detailed course description and syllabus, see Raphael, 2001).

Three activities are core. First, continuing the autobiography book club tradition, participants read four autobiographical texts, each one to be discussed over two class meetings. Though selections vary across semesters, during the course in which Kathy Highfield and Karen Damphousse were participants, the texts used were Conway's (1990) *The Road from Coorain*, Rodriguez's (1982) *Hunger of Memory*, Angelou's (1969) *I Know Why the Caged Bird Sings*, and McBride's (1996) *The Color of Water*. From this experience, teachers reported many of the same responses as did Hannah and Jerri, members of the original course at MSU and the subsequent Literary Circle. Second, drawing on Kathy Au and Jane Hansen's insights on the importance of uncovering our own literacy histories (Au, 1997; Hansen, 1998), each student developed four entries to create a "literacy history portfolio." Each entry detailed how an aspect of literacy had played a role in their own lives. Third, each teacher created a Book Club unit to use in their own teaching. Some participants, not currently teaching, created after-school literature circles for students in their neighborhood. Most, however, created units to implement with students in first-grade through high-school classrooms. Thus, teachers in the course drew on their readings of autobiography and their construction of their own literacy history portfolios as important sources for discovering culture in their own lives as teachers and learners. They drew on their experiences reading, writing, and talking about books as they created Book Club units to implement in their own settings.

In many ways, Kathy Highfield and Karen Damphousse are typical of the students Susan and Taffy taught in both Master's-level autobiography book club courses. Like the majority of the other students in Taffy's class, each was working full time in her respective school site while pursuing a graduate degree part-time through evening courses. When Kathy took the Book Club Workshop course, she had already completed her Master's degree at MSU and had just taken on two new professional challenges—moving from her role as a classroom teacher to working as an Instructional Facilitator (i.e., language arts and technology coordinator) and beginning her doctoral studies at Oakland University. Karen was about to complete her last course in the Oakland University Masters in Reading and Language Arts, while continuing her role as a middle school language arts teacher. Of the students in the class, all spoke English as their first language and Kathy was the only student in the group who spoke a second language fluently. All of the students in the course identified themselves as being from middle- or working-class backgrounds, and most lived in one of the suburban areas surrounding Detroit. Kathy worked in a rural district approximately 75 miles north of the metro area, while Karen worked in a private school quite close to the metro area.

In the next two sections of this chapter, Karen and Kathy describe their experiences in and learning through the Book Club Workshop course. The fact that they have continued to work on the Book Club *Plus* project makes them, in some ways, unique from their peers in the class. However, their experiences within the course appear to be well within the range of experiences described by other participants in similar course(s) we have taught (see Florio-Ruane et al., 1997, 1999).

KATHY'S EXPERIENCES

Taking Taffy's Book Club class was like hiking a familiar wooded trail. The theory, discussions, and readings were familiar. I have been involved in Book Club first-hand since 1991 when, as a graduate student, I joined a teacher research group that focused on implementing the many aspects and interests that are described in *The Book Club Connection: Literacy Learning and Classroom Talk* (McMahon & Raphael, 1997) and *Book Club: A Literature-Based Curriculum* (Raphael et al., 1997). However, as seasons change the landscape on hiking trails, the landscape of Book Club was changing on my professional path in four ways.

First, this was my first experience in an adult book club. My previous Book Club experiences focused on fifth graders reading contemporary realistic fiction, historical fiction, and later a wide variety of genre. Second, autobiography was not a familiar genre for me; yet, there were many similarities to another genre that I enjoy deeply, historical fiction. I have always had a love of the past, an interest in where we have come, for I believe we are a result of our collective and individual pasts. I have also always been interested in culture, being raised in a very open-minded, accepting family where differences were treasured, valued, and respected. Third, my professional role was changing from that of a classroom teacher to becoming an Instructional Facilitator. This job embodies many roles, including curriculum coordination and technology supervision. This meant leaving the classroom and beginning a role that focused on professional and instructional support. Finally, I was making the commitment to begin a course of study toward a doctorate degree at Oakland University where I could continue to work and learn with Taffy.

Adult Book Clubs and My Personal Development

Being involved in my first adult book club affected me personally. There are many stories of my family's collective childhood that continue to be told at family gatherings. I thought we had always openly discussed our shared experiences and memories. What I came to realize through the discussions I had with my peers in the class, however, is that there are many stories in my family where some of the people involved weren't given voice. They stayed hidden underneath the surface of our collective memories. I was convinced that given the size of our family and the diversity between my brothers and sisters, we each had our own view of the events—sometimes our views are similar, while at other times they may vary greatly. In Taffy's class, as we read and discussed autobiographies and began to put together our own personal histories, I realized that two of the primary voices I thought I should have heard were my parents. Ironically, these are the voices missing from my family's stories. This led me to several hours of discussion with my mother about her childhood, her family, and her memories as a child.

I wasn't able to sit down as easily to talk with my father, as he now lives at quite a physical distance from me, in the western part of the United States. However, the physical distance we have today isn't really the reason why communicating with him has been difficult. Even when we lived in the same area, I had always felt that he was a distant man. For example, I remember that whenever I would ask him how he was or what he was feeling, he invariably answered, "Everything is fine." While I might have wished that things really were fine, I often realized that they weren't. With my new interest in family stories, I decided to initiate a conversation with my father through letters and do everything I could to bring the conversations deeper than their typical surface level. The letters that we began writing to each other last year have opened a line of communication that I treasure.

In his letters I heard his voice, as he conveyed his stories of traveling as a teen, his first love, and his memories of childhood. I treasure the new stories because they give me insights into who my father is beyond his role as Dad. I also treasure the stories we both remember from experiences we have shared. In our letter exchanges I write my version—telling him a story from my childhood as I recall the event, people, and feelings. In his letter responding to me, he shares his memory of the same event. It has been fun to read his version, and more important, to see the same event through his eyes. This duality of memory has always fascinated me, the way in which many people can experience the same event and yet recollect a slightly different version where details blend into one another. To be able to enact my own exploration of how this duality worked within my own family, particularly between my father and me, was a very special experience.

Adult Book Clubs and My Professional Development

In addition to the effect of the adult book clubs on me personally, they've also had an effect on me professionally. I have always loved reading and books and I thoroughly enjoyed using Book Club with my fifth-grade students when I was first introduced to the program as a Master's student in 1991. I felt that through Book Club, I could model my love of reading. By modeling my own reading, thinking, and talking about books, and by creating a classroom literacy environment that supported students in their literacy engagement, I hoped to encourage many of my students to begin to love their own reading experiences. My classroom management and the structure of my entire instructional day revolved around the constructivist principles and social interactions that are embodied in Book Club. I enjoyed working within my own classroom, but I also found that I loved sharing what I was doing with other teachers. The adult book club experience actually brought together two other professional events in an important way.

The first event stemmed from the huge growth in the community in which I teach. A new school had just been built and a new principal was hired with a reputation for being dynamic, supportive of teachers' professional development, and interested in classroom innovations. She began to recruit me to assume a position involving curriculum coordination and technology supervision. Initially, I hesitated, since I viewed this as a step away from being directly involved with student book clubs. To return to my metaphor of the hike, I was suddenly faced with a long familiar and much loved trail being changed. A new hiking trail was under construction, transforming the one I both loved and found comfortable. In one sense, I mistakenly feared that my cherished role as a teacher researcher had ended. Without my own classroom, how could I speak of teaching and learning experiences? Without my students, how could I speak of the role of culture in their learning and living? How could I continue my line of teacher research, which focused on the role of discussion in student learning, when I did not have my own class to study?

My hiking trail was leading up a hill and the direction to come was uncertain. I knew the trail would continue but its direction was beyond my field of vision. When I thought about my own life as a story, I had been in one that was relatively predictable. But the offer of a new position happened to come at the same time that I was considering beginning my doctoral studies. I began to move away from my familiar path. At the same time, as I started my role of Instructional Facilitator for my school, I began my advanced course work at Oakland University. As Taffy's graduate assistant, I enrolled in the Book Club Workshop, partly as a teaching assistant and partly to experience the connecting of adult book clubs, curriculum development, and an exploration of my own cultural background. I have always been interested in culture, ever since attending powwows at Indian reservations as a child. The new cultural and autobiographical focus to the Book Club work appealed to me on many levels.

My Instructional Facilitator/doctoral student eyes are still developing and are not yet able to focus clearly on the panoramic view from atop this hill that I'm climbing. My work as Taffy's research assistant involves me directly with the continuation of the work that Susan and Taffy began in 1995, now a part of the Center for the Improvement of Early Reading Achievement (CIERA). We are studying exceptional third-grade teachers who are implementing Book Club *Plus* Autobiography units entitled "Storied Lives." Our focus has extended Book Club to focus on how to help struggling readers. I am involved daily in classroom instruction through observation and discussion with teachers and studying what students learn from participating in these experiences.

Talk of culture and personal histories extend through the elementary students' projects and the professional discussions that take place in our CIERA meetings. I am continuing to learn about autobiographies as I observe and take field notes in classrooms where students are studying authors who tell their stories in children's literature such as Walter Dean Myers, Patricia Polacco, Jamie Lee Curtis, Jean Craighead George, and Gary Paulsen. I am continuing to read autobiographies, many suggested by members of the Literary Circle. I am continuing to exchange letters with my father and to discuss family history with my mother and siblings as I extend my personal history. I am continuing to hike the trail and enjoying the trip along the way.

KAREN'S EXPERIENCES

Finally it was fall term, 1997. I was geared up to take the last class in my masters degree graduate program in Reading and Language Arts at OU. I had done my research in the summer. I knew the professor and the expectations for this final course in my program. I was determined to make this a stress-free experience that would not overly distract me from my own middle school classroom. I already had planned my final project and had even begun the assigned readings. What I didn't know was that a new professor had been hired who was planning to introduce a new elective in the program, Book Club Workshop. And what I really didn't know was that I'd end up in that class stressed to the max, frustrated, challenged, intrigued, and enthralled by the ideas she would present. Like yesterday, I remember how this came to be.

Phew, Friday! I was glad that "week one" of my last Master's course was over, and I was another step closer to the finish line. That morning, however, I received a phone call from my former Oakland University study partner. I hadn't heard from her in months, so naturally I rushed to the workroom to return her call. She was talking so quickly with excitement that I could hardly understand her. Apparently, she had enrolled in a new class that offered tons of professional reading, a demanding, but enthusiastic professor, and a list of adult novels that would be read as part of a book club with the rest of the class. She insisted that this class was "right up my alley." Failing to understand her need to include me in what I thought of as misery (I was nearing the finish line, it was too much reading, and I had my life under control!), I kindly reminded her that I had already completed a week in my "goodbye" class and was quite content to finish the term as planned. I am so glad that my study partner would not give up. She begged me to call the professor before making a final decision, and the rest is history.

After talking with Taffy for a few moments on the phone, I began to feel just what my study partner had felt, that I *needed* to be in her class. The Book Club Workshop combined method training, professional growth and analysis, authentic reading and writing forums, and multicultural awareness—all in one setting. I gave up the safety of my "goodbye" class for what turned out to be one of the most rewarding experiences in my career. It continues to influence both my personal and professional life.

In a career such as education, it can be difficult to distinguish between personal and professional growth. So much of who I am as an individual plays out daily in the classroom. Until the workshop, I had never really thought of this as my "culture" being expressed to the students. One of the major accomplishments of the course was to enlighten me to a new view of culture. I realized that I am a cultural being—me, a white middle-class teacher and fourth generation American. Along with a curriculum, I bring to my students a unique and important set of customs involving family, religion, and education (especially reading and writing habits). This is what brings life into the classroom and passion to the curriculum. My students also bring their important customs to the classroom table each day. They need to recognize how their cultures add life and passion to the learning circle as well. This very ideology suggests that personal and professional growth interweaves. It is the connection of the two that makes for a unique and life long pattern of learning. As a result I cannot neatly categorize my growth, but I can describe how the course began new patterns for my life both in and out of the classroom.

As I mentioned before, the course included several elements. We were required to read the latest articles and textbooks about book clubbing in schools. We were required to read four autobiographical adult novels, keep journal responses about them, and participate in book club discussions using the notes as springboards for conversation. While exploring the history of authors such as Jill Ker Conway, Maya Angelou, James McBride, and Richard Rodriguez through their autobiographies, we were to explore our own pasts especially in terms of our literary development. We needed to find items from our past that identified something unique about our literary history and then write about their significance to our lives. All of this inspired my growth in four key areas. It gave me a reason to read and write about real literature again. It enlightened me to the power of autobiography and taught me that cultural diversity comes in all shapes and sizes, not limited to skin color or birth origin. Finally, it challenged me to remember my own literacy development, both the good and the bad. These are the threads that began the design.

Undeniably, the book club portion of the class had the most dramatic impact on me. Besides providing me a chance to read adult literature for a change, the book club forum promoted authenticity, ownership, excitement, and social awareness in my response to literature. Sharing my ideas about the literature with a group of peers gave me a reason to do my "homework." I felt empowered and compelled to find and share the authors' best and worst techniques. People listened and sympathized when I said that I found the first chapter of *The Road from Coorain* to be painfully slow. I agreed when someone complained that they had to read it twice and didn't like it either time. I read the section again with new vision after another group member suggested that this section was essential to understanding the seclusion and dryness of the outback. I was encouraged to compare my life with the authors' lives. Members were shocked when I described my own experiences of week-long camp meetings at church similar to those that Maya Angelou explains in *I Know Why the Caged Bird Sings* (Angelou,1969), and shared stories of people dancing in the aisles, lifting their hands, and belting out spirituals. No one else in the group had any first hand knowledge of such an emotionally charged atmosphere. I could be their "five senses" for the moment. Later, someone else could be mine. By the time we read the last book, I had begun reading with other group members in mind. I anticipated conversations we would have about a certain section, or planned questions about the text that I knew another group member could answer. All of these interactions improved my motivation and communication skills. They built my confidence and hooked me back into meaningful experiences with literature. Sure, I have a passion for children's literature, but it had been a long time since I'd had such a rewarding experience at my own level.

Another impact of my experience with the book club, a new cultural awareness, developed in part from the content of the novels. Due to the autobiographical and multicultural focus, the book club experience successfully opened my eyes to culture, the life stories within the literature and the stories that they evoked from my life and from the lives of my fellow classmates. The genre encouraged us to look at culture as the experiences and stories that make all of us who we are. The selected texts sprung from a variety of cultures and gave voice to many aspects of the human experience: life on the Australian outback, the African American struggle in the south, interracial conflicts in New York City, and the effect of both displacement and affirmative action on U.S. Mexican minorities are just a few of the experiences and issues embedded in these texts. Yes, these topics do seem typical to the "multicultural" themes that have been added to the curriculum in so many schools this past decade. However, autobiography packs a powerful punch. The real human experience cannot be dismissed as some quaint little story that makes us feel good or some horrifying plot that makes us afraid. Real stories about real people remind us of ourselves. We make connections with the authors as we read about their experiences in the world, and we connect those experiences to our own lives. We try to understand the uniqueness of their experiences and, at the same time, find common ground in human emotions.

So there we were, a class of White American females from middle- and working-class backgrounds reading and discussing how to decipher culture.

We could have thought, "Multiculture is THEM, not us." In fact we did. We all appeared to be so much alike. In other courses about multiculturalism, it was always the "other" races that needed to be explored. But autobiography had the power to undo that stereotype. As it connected each of us to our own struggles and stories, it unraveled our unique "cultures," one for each white face around the table. One woman explained the family conflicts that were developing over the last six months of her pregnancy. Her Greek Orthodox customs conflicted with her husband's Armenian traditions. Another colleague described her recent trip to Lithuania. This was her grandmother's first homecoming after many years of retreat from the wars. Little did we suspect that a classmate on sabbatical from her high school English teaching career to raise her family had been addicted to drugs in high school. Throughout the course, I rediscovered myself as I marveled, sympathized, and connected with the stories of others. This is what I wanted multicultural education to mean in my classroom.

Stimulated by the writing styles of the authors and the open conversation in our book clubs, our own autobiographical sketches about literacy became another important context for cultural awareness. Taffy demonstrated the technique in class. She brought several letters that she had received over the years from various family members. She had one from her father that she received at camp, one from her brother, and a more recent note from her young niece. Of course that one was in picture and scribble form but reflected communication nonetheless. After sharing the letters, she read her vignette about how the family letters continue to influence her views of reading and writing. Other classmates wrote about teachers who had either inspired or discouraged their reading and writing development. Some brought in books they read as children, such as E.B. White's classic *Charlotte's Web,* and discussed the importance of story in their life. I rediscovered a huge stack of stories that I wrote in first grade, pictures and all. Among the many characters whom I'd included, I found my dad, my mother, three animals that seemed exactly like my neighborhood friends, and myself. I also detected the beginnings of poetry: metaphor, simile, onomatopoeia, and alliteration. I read my first vignette to the class:

> "Writing is Life" boldly proclaims itself from a poster on the wall above my desk. It is no coincidence that these words hang in my classroom. Whether from the poster or my students' individual stories, I am continually reminded of the truth behind these words. It was in first grade that I personally realized this truth and made my profession of faith. Mrs. Philips boldly proclaimed the gospel, "All writers are created equal, because each one of you has a story to tell." I took her seriously. Embracing her theology, I wrote more than 300 stories and poems that year. Looking back at these pieces of history, philosophy, poetry, and theology, I understand how truth revealed itself to me and writing became a must, a need, an active voice inside of me. So much a passion in my veins, I never doubted or turned my back on the religious decision

> I made at age six. Now a missionary myself, I continue my journey of faith, offering these pieces as encouragement and proclamation, "Writing is Life!"

I proceeded to share with my Book Club course colleagues a few hand-picked first grade stories that revealed my "culture." Once again this exercise helped me understand others and myself through the context of story. It reinforced my new concept of culture. The time I spent that semester thinking and writing about my own literacy development provided an added benefit for me. It reminded me of my strengths in reading and writing, and it pinpointed some of the reasons why I developed such positive attitudes in these areas. Teachers had confidence in me; they read books out loud and shared their own responses with me. I had plenty of exposure to the arts, especially music. This established a great breeding ground for poetry. Not only did I need to start viewing culture differently in my classroom, I needed to make sure that I was encouraging the same positive attitudes toward reading and writing that had been encouraged in me so many years ago. In other words I needed to share my literary heritage with my students.

Personal and professional growth continues their design. I started to analyze the curriculum and methods in my eighth grade English classes. My students needed the core elements that the Book Club Workshop had provided for me. They needed that sense of ownership and anticipation that comes with authentic conversation about the text. They needed exposure to autobiography, the essential connection between literacy and life. They needed plenty of activities that encouraged the discussion of diversity already present in the classroom and unknown perspectives. In that context, they needed opportunities to contemplate and share their own literacy development. How could I package such demanding elements into the school's core curriculum and keep my sanity in the middle of the school year? Instead of starting from scratch, I built on a mandated book from the next semester's schedule, *Missing May* by Cynthia Rylant (1993).

My job was not as difficult as it could have been. Over the last few years, I had already begun to tweak the mandated curriculum. Now I realize it was my own literary "culture" that had prompted me two years ago to rearrange the school's core literature into thematic units. Thematic units incorporate the kinds of literary exposure that I had been given: good interconnected multigenre literature, writing in response to reading, and connection to the arts. I identified a broad, meaningful, and classic theme: that different cultures vary in their views of life and death. I had a variety of literary genres to represent the theme and a variety of writing opportunities for student response. I knew which mandated literary terms turned up in *Missing May* and had accumulated a large assortment of Rylant's other works to reinforce her style. From the beginning of the school year, I had encouraged class discussions about literature. Although every child did not vocalize his or her opinion, each had a decent understanding of the process of literary discussion. Before the Book Club Workshop, I would have thought this unit was complete. Now I needed a book club book, an autobiography, and classroom activities that encouraged literary and cultural awareness.

Missing May worked perfectly as my first book club attempt. The story was short but the characters and writing were rich. As Summer and Ob moved painfully through the stages of grief, they encouraged students to share loss, to contemplate views of life after death, and to prepare for grief in their own life. Naturally, the issues we raised evoked students' own life stories, their opinions, and their reflections, all of which are so essential to the book club journal and discussion process. Rylant's writing style also stimulated conversation. As she dressed her characterization techniques in simple, humorous metaphors and similes, the enormity and sadness of the situation were buffered. Her words worked through the pain of the experience with a bit of joy and hope just as the characters did. The story and language of this book fostered a smooth transition into student led clubs in my classroom.

Equally perfect for the new approach to the unit, Rylant's (1993) autobiography, *But I'll Be Back Again*, blended the right amount of truth and literary technique to capture my middle school audience. It packed the power to explain Rylant's heritage and to evoke students' stories about their own "culture." Once again the autobiography connected literacy and life.

Meaningful activities that encouraged cultural awareness fell into place as I changed my limited focus. Jokingly, a social studies colleague has always claimed that his subject area should rule all others. Ironically, I looked to social studies and developed large philosophical questions to frame the life and death components. After every reading or activity, I brought the students back to these questions: How can we celebrate the skills, talents, family, and friends we have been given? How do different cultures celebrate life and cope with death? What are common steps in the grieving process? What are your own views about life and life after death? This framework helped me to develop cultural activities and it opened the door for students to share their individual knowledge and opinions. The questions actually improved the students' understanding of theme. So it was true all along, social studies should have power in other subject areas. I had found a new material to enhance the weave.

The Book Club Workshop continues to influence my life. I have taken on new challenges in writing. For example, I am part of a team working on describing how Book Club can be used in middle school classrooms, and my *Missing May* unit has become our model for others. It is part of a web site for teachers and students engaged in book clubs (www.planetbookclub.com). This chapter grew out of my collaboration with colleagues for a presentation at National Council of Teachers of English. I have worked extensively on revising my school curriculum as well. Since that first *Missing May* unit, I have gone on to develop a middle school curriculum (Raphael, Kehus, & Damphousse, 2001). I begin each unit with general but thought-provoking questions. I try to balance the classroom time between all the important elements: literature, writing, clubbing, cultural activities, and the arts. In my private reading I cannot seem to get enough of autobiography. I have an unending appetite for the stories of others. As I investigate others' lives, I understand myself so much more.

Yes, I gave up the safety of my last class and the comfort of my "complete" curriculum, but what I have gained is worth so much more. In the new design, the pattern is never complete and the threads are always changing. I find safety in the journey to the unknown and comfort in the story of others. I only hope that my students will do the same.

CONCLUDING COMMENTS

The story of the Autobiography Book Club line of research, including our curriculum innovations for practicing and preservice teachers and for elementary through middle school students, continues to evolve. Many voices continue to contribute to our understanding of the potential of autobiography and the power of dialogic approaches to teaching and learning.

As we have studied the experiences of teachers in autobiography book clubs, both voluntary clubs and those embedded within courses, we have three initial findings. First, it is clear that teachers find the opportunity to read and talk about autobiographical literature a stimulating form of professional development (Florio-Ruane, Raphael, & Shellhorn, 1998; Raphael & Florio-Ruane, 1998). Second, we have seen how reading, writing, and talking about literature became authentically meaningful activities in participants' lives—and that this gave greater meaning and currency to participants' efforts to help youngsters experience literacy in similarly authentic ways.

Third, to the extent that the autobiographies studied were written by authors of diverse ethnic, linguistic, racial, cultural, and/or socioeconomic backgrounds, participants found them serving as both "mirrors and windows" (Galda, 1998). The stories provided a window into people, places, and events distant from participants' own lives. However, at the same time, the stories also provided a mirror that reflected participants' own lives and experiences, leading to greater self-reflection about cultural backgrounds and their contributions to their own learning and teaching. Experiences like these lie at the heart of multicultural education—a system in which learners of all ages can develop a deep, rich, and complex understanding of culture; can understand how cultures meet, interweave, and give rise to new transformations over time; and can appreciate how, ultimately, our society is enriched by the cultural diversity that characterizes its members. Such understandings are reflected in the curriculum that teachers, such as Kathy and Karen, have created and in the ways they view the texts that their students read and respond to through writing and discussion.

In short, teachers' learning in these book clubs is, as the above examples illustrate, of three kinds: learning about literature and literacy, learning about instruction, and learning about self and others. This learning is situated within and inseparable from the social context of the peer-led book conversations and the nature and content of the autobiographies. Thus, by means of this experience, participants learned a powerful lesson about literacy and literacy education. Literacy is not merely "reading, writing, speaking, and listening." Nor is it simply a repertoire of skills and strategies for decoding and encoding print. Literacy is situated, meaningful, text-based interaction with others. As such, literacy teaches us about humanity reflected in and seen through the looking glass of our own and others' stories.

ACKNOWLEDGMENT

This project was supported, in part, under the Educational Research and Development Centers Program, PR/Award Number R305R70004, as administered by the Office of Educational Research and Improvement, U. S. Department of Education. However, the comments do not necessarily represent the positions or policies of the National Institute of Student Achievement, Curriculum, and Assessment, or the National Institute on Early Childhood Development, or the U. S. Department of Education, and endorsement by the Federal Government should not be assumed.

NOTE

1.   Other than the coauthors of this paper or research assistants, all teachers and students' names are pseudonyms.

REFERENCES

Au, K.H. (1997). Schooling, literacy, and cultural diversity in research and personal experience. In P.L. Peterson & P.A. Neumann (Ed.), *Learning from our lives: Women, research, and autobiography in education* (pp. 71–90). New York: Teachers College Press.

Au, K.H., & Raphael, T.E. (1998). Curriculum and teaching in literature-based programs. In T.E. Raphael & K.H. Au (Eds.), *Literature-based instruction: Reshaping the curriculum* (pp. 123–148). Norwood, MA: Christopher-Gordon Publishers.

Au, K.H., & Raphael, T.E., (2000). Literacy and diversity in the millennium. *Reading Research Quarterly, 35*(1), 170–188.

Banks, J. (1992). Multicultural education: Development, dimensions, and challenges. *Phi Delta Kappan, 75,* 22–28.

Burbules, N. (1993). *Dialogue in teaching: Theory and practice.* New York: Teachers College Press.

Calkins, L.M. (1986). *The art of teaching writing.* Portsmouth, NH: Heinemann.

Daniels, H. (1994). *Literature circles: Voice and choice in the student-centered classroom.* York, ME: Stenhouse Publishers.

Dyson, A.H. (1992). *Social worlds of children learning to write.* New York: Teachers College Press.

Florio-Ruane, S. (1997). To tell a new story: Reinventing narratives of culture, identity, and education. *Anthropology and Education Quarterly, 28,* 162–161.

Florio-Ruane, S. (1994) The Future Teachers' Autobiography Club: Preparing educators to support literacy learning in culturally diverse classrooms. *English Education, 26*(1), 52–66.

Florio-Ruane, S., & deTar, J. (1995). Conflict and consensus in teacher candidates' discussion of ethnic autobiography. *English Education. 27,* 11–39.

Florio-Ruane, S. with deTar, J. (2001). *Teaching and the cultural imagination: Autobiography, conversation, and narrative.* Mahwah, NJ: Erlbaum.

Florio-Ruane, S., Raphael, T. E., Glazier, J., McVee, M., & Wallace, S. (1997). Reading, writing, and talk about autobiography: The education of literacy teachers. In C. Kinzer, D. Leu, & K. Hinchman (Eds.), *Inquiries in literacy theory and practice* (pp. 452–464). Chicago: National Reading Conference.

Florio-Ruane, S., & Raphael, T. E. (with Glazier, J., McVee, M.,Shellhorn, B., & Wallace, S.). (1999). *Culture, autobiography, and the education of literacy teachers* (CIERA Report No. 3-003). Ann Arbor: Center for the Improvement of Early Reading Achievement, University of Michigan.

Florio-Ruane, S., Raphael, T.E., & Shellhorn, B.J. (1998, December). *Immigrant literature and teacher learning about culture.* Paper presented at the annual meeting of the American Anthropological Association, Philadelphia, PA.

Galda, L. (1998). Mirrors and windows: Reading as transformation. In T.E. Raphael & K.H. Au (Eds.), *Literature-based instruction: Reshaping the curriculum* (pp. 1–11). Norwood, MA: Christopher-Gordon.

Gavelek, J.R., Raphael, T.E., Biondo, S.M., & Wang, D. (2001). Integrated literacy instruction. In M. Kamil, P.Mosenthal, P. D. Pearson, & R. Barr (Eds.), *Handbook of reading research* (Vol. 3). pp. 587–607. Mahwah, NJ: Erlbaum.

Goatley, V.J., Brock, C.H., & Raphael, T.E. (1995). Diverse learners participating in regular education "Book Clubs." *Reading Research Quarterly, 30*(3), 352–380.

Graham, R.J. (1991). *Reading and writing the self: Autobiography in education and the curriculum.* New York: Teachers College Press.

Greene, M. (1993). The passions of pluralism, multiculturalism, and the expanding community narrative. *Educational Researcher, 22,* 13–18.

Greene, M. (1995). *Releasing the imagination: Essays on education, the arts and social change.* San Francisco: Jossey-Bass.

Hansen, J. (1998). *When learners evaluate.* Portsmouth, NH: Heinemann.

McMahon, S.I., & Raphael, T.E., with V.J. Goatley & L.S. Pardo (1997). *The Book Club connection: Literacy learning and classroom talk.* New York: Teachers College Press.

McVee, M.B. (1999). *Narrative and the exploration of culture, self, and other in teachers' book club discussion groups.* Unpublished doctoral dissertation, Michigan State University, East Lansing.

Raphael, T.E. (2001). Book Club workshop: Learning about language and literacy through culture. In J. Many (Ed.), *The literacy educators' handbook,* pp. 39–49. Mahwah, NJ: Erlbaum.

Raphael, T.E., & Au, K.H. (Eds.). (1998). *Literature-based instruction: Reshaping the curriculum.* Newton, MA: Christopher Gordon Publications.

Raphael, T.E., Kehus, M., Damphousse, K. (2001). *Book club for middle school.* Lawrence, MA: Small Planet Communications, Inc.

Raphael, T.E., Goatley, V.J., Woodman, D.A., & McMahon, S.I.(1994). Collaboration on the Book Club Project: The multiple roles of researchers, teachers, and students. *Reading Horizons, 34*(5), 381–405.

Raphael, T.E., McMahon, S.I., Goatley, V.J., Bentley, J L., Boyd, F.B., Pardo, L.S., & Woodman, D.A. (1992). Reading instruction reconsidered: Literature and discussion in the reading program. *Language Arts, 69,* 54–61.

Raphael, T.E., Pardo, L.S., Highfield, K., & McMahon, S.I. (1997). *Book Club: A literature-based curriculum.* Littleton, MA: Small Planet Communication, Inc.

Raphael, T.E., Brock, C.H., & Wallace, S. (1998). Encouraging quality peer talk with diverse students in mainstream classrooms: Learning from and with teachers. In J.R. Paratore & R. McCormack (Eds.), *Peer talk in the classroom: Learning from research.* Newark, DE: International Reading Association.

Raphael, T.E., & Florio-Ruane, S. (1998, December). *Questions, insights, and intertextuality: Adult book clubs and cultural patterns.* Paper presented at the annual meeting of the National Reading Conference, Austin, TX.

Autobiographies and Children's Books Cited

Angelou, M.. (1969). *I know why the caged bird sings.* New York: Bantam Books.

Conway, J.K. (1990). *The road from coorain.* New York: Random House.

Hoffman, E.. (1989). *Lost in translation.* New York: Penguin Books.

Hurston, Z.N. (1937). *Their eyes were watching God.* New York: Harper Perennial.

McBride, J. (1996). *The color of water.* New York: Riverhead Books.

Orenstein, P.. (1994). *School girls.* New York: Doubleday.

Paley, V.G. (1979). *White teacher.* Cambridge, MA: Harvard University Press.

Rodriguez, R. (1982). *Hunger of memory.* New York: Bantam Books.

Rose, M. (1989). *Lives on the boundary.* New York: The Free Press.

Rylant, C. (1992). *Missing May.* New York: Orchard Books.

Rylant, C. (1993). *But I'll be back again.* New York: Beech Tree Books.

Tan, A. (1991). *The kitchen God's wife.* New York: Ballantine Books.

CHAPTER 17

THE POWER TO EMPOWER

Creating Home/School Relationships with the ABC's of Cultural Understanding and Communication

Patricia Ruggiano Schmidt

Abstract: Recently, the ABC's of Cultural Understanding and Communication (Schmidt, 1998b) is helping teachers empower students and families. In the process, teachers have gained a better understanding of diversity and have successfully connected home and school for literacy learning (Schmidt, 1998c, 1999). Similar to Greene's (1995) notion of releasing teacher imaginations, teachers created opportunities for dialogue among and between students, families, and teachers. As a result, their classrooms and schools evolved into communities of sharing and learning. This chapter explains the background and literature related to the ABC's Model, reports personal responses to the model, describes adaptations of the model, and discusses implications of the model for teacher education programs.

INTRODUCTION

As we reconceptualize literacy in the new age of pluralism and multiculturalism, it is important to consider the power relations that hinder the literacy development of people from minority groups. First, it is necessary to realize that European American or white culture controls the education system and drives the content of curricula as well as the structure, materials, and methods. Consequently, students and families from minority backgrounds are often ignored in classrooms and schools at all educational levels (Cummins, 1986; Sleeter & Grant, 1991). Furthermore, most educators who are from white, middle class backgrounds have limited knowledge of minority populations, since their information comes from media stereotypes, and few personal experiences (Pattnaik, 1997). Therefore, it is no surprise that students from ethnic and cultural minorities often feel powerless in educational settings that contribute to high dropout rates (Nieto, 1996).

In order to solve this national problem, it has been recommended that teachers take responsibility for making connections between home and school, since they have the power and position to reach out to students and families (Edwards, 1999; Faltis, 1993). Additionally, we know that teachers who practice the sociocultural perspective (Au, 1993; Heath, 1983; Trueba, Jacobs, & Kirton, 1990; Vygotsky, 1978), a promising teaching/learning approach for students from minority as well European American backgrounds, have been effective in connecting home and school cultures to build classroom community for literacy development. However, many teachers are unaware of the sociocultural perspective or do not have the information and experiences necessary for implementation (Kidder, 1989; Paley, 1989; Schmidt, 1998a). As a result, cultural conflict frequently emerges as a key factor in the educational process and minority students and their families feel confusion, frustration, and disempowerment (Cummins, 1986; Schmidt, 1995, 1998; Trueba, Jacobs, & Kirton, 1990).

Recently, a model known as the ABC's of Cultural Understanding and Communication (Schmidt, 1998b), based on the sociocultural perspective and the premise, "Know thyself and understand others," is helping teachers empower students and families. Through intense study of human similarities and differences, multiple perspectives emerge, and teachers begin to use their power to empower. In the process, teachers have gained a better understanding of diversity and have successfully connected home and school for literacy learning (Schmidt, 1998c, 1999). Similar to Greene's (1995) notion of releasing teacher imaginations, they have created opportunities for dialogue among and between students, families, and teachers. As a result, their classrooms and schools have evolved into communities of sharing and learning.

In this chapter, I explain the background and literature related to the ABC's Model, report personal responses to the model, describe adaptations of the model, and discuss the implications of the model for teacher education and home/school connections.

BACKGROUND

Several years ago, I developed the ABC's of Cultural Understanding and Communication while studying a kindergarten program in a suburban school district (Schmidt, 1995, 1998a). I observed teachers from European American backgrounds who did not understand the need to connect home and school for literacy development when working with children from minority backgrounds. Similar to the assimilationist perspective (Cummins, 1986), they believed that ignoring differences was the way to help students fit into the classroom culture, make friends, and develop literacy. The educators were not aware of culturally responsive teaching (Au, 1998) nor culturally relevant pedagogy (Ladson-Billings, 1994, 1995; Osborne, 1996). Consequently, the children, their families, classmates, and teachers experienced cultural conflict and struggles.

Following the kindergarten ethnography, a case study, based on one kindergarten teacher, demonstrated the power relations that exist between teachers and administrators in the same school district (Schmidt, 1996). When that teacher read data from the ethnography, she realized the need to embrace multicultural literacy and the sociocultural perspective. She immediately initiated changes in her classroom and school but was shunned by teacher colleagues and labeled "un-American." Instead of being recognized for her innovative work, she lost her annual school district grant and was told that her emphasis on the "multicultural stuff" in the kindergarten curriculum was not appropriate.

Consistent with the research on teacher education (Cochran-Smith, 1995; Tatum, 1992; Zeichner, 1993), I soon realized that, even when teachers attend workshops, complete course work or become aware of new ideas related to multicultural literacy, they may not have the power, knowledge, or persistence to implement these concepts in their classrooms and schools. They often face the following arguments to prevent change:

"We have to meet the state requirements. We don't have time for multicultural education."

"We are all the same in our school. We don't need to study differences."

"To be economically successful in our country, one must learn how to fit in with the culture."

"In the end, all of the students have to read, write, and speak standard English."

These reasons for maintaining *status quo* reflect the dominant culture's power and lack of minority group recognition and contributions. The problem with this thinking is that, when minority groups are treated as invisible, they experience disillusion and dissatisfaction (Nieto, 1996; Rist, 1978). Similarly, when people from minority groups are recognized for their contributions, the resulting empowerment leads to great accomplishments (Fitchue, 1997).

In the new millennium, ethnic and cultural minority populations will become the majority in our nation's schools (Murdock, 1995). Obviously, it is in everyone's best interests to prepare teachers who will understand, appreciate, and communicate with diverse groups of people and, in turn, prepare our children to do the same. With this information in mind, I decided to create a multicultural literacy course that would help present and future educators begin to understand and appreciate differences, stimulate them to become culturally responsive, and give them the confidence needed to connect home and school for literacy learning in their classrooms and schools. The heart of the course was the "ABC's of Cultural Understanding and Communication."

Multicultural Literacy Course

The ABC's Model, based on findings from previous research (Banks, 1994; Britzman, 1986; Cummins, 1986; Florio-Ruane, 1994; Ladson-Billings, 1994; Noordhoff & Kleinfeld, 1993; Schmidt, 1998b, 1998c; Spindler & Spindler, 1987; Trueba, Jacobs, & Kirton, 1990), provided the major assignments for teachers enrolled in the course. Each teacher completed an autobiography, an interview and biography of a person considered culturally different, cross-cultural analyses, and a home/school connection plan for literacy development. To maintain privacy, I, as the professor, was the only one who read the autobiographies. I assured teachers that anything they decided to share concerning their lives would be confidential. This gave many the confidence to examine their lives and reveal much about their stories. I modeled the writing of my own story and gave them ideas from other teachers for constructing autobiographies and family histories. I also insisted that pseudonyms be used for the protection of interviewees when writing the biographies and performing cross-cultural analyses.

The following part of this chapter explains autobiography, biography, and cross-cultural analyses assignments, includes examples of one teacher's written responses for each assignment, provides supporting research, and presents several teachers' reflections on the ABC's process.

Autobiography

First, teachers wrote autobiographies in the multicultural literacy course. They ranged, in detail, from ten to 100 typed pages and included key life events related to education, family, religious tradition, recreation, victories, and defeats. They began with their own knowledge by thinking and writing about family histories that included memorable events (Schmidt, 1998b). This helped them become aware of personal beliefs and attitudes that form the traditions and values of cultural autobiographies (Banks, 1994).

What follows are excerpts from a typical autobiography, completed by a teacher, as the first assignment for the ABC's of Cultural Understanding and Communication. The teacher readily granted permission to use her work for the purpose of informing others about the process (Iauco, 1997):

JENNIFER'S STORY

I was born at Crouse Irving Memorial Hospital, Syracuse, NY, on April 23, 1970. I was born into a middle class family with two loving parents and a younger sister and grew up in the suburbs of Syracuse where I found that most of my friends' families were similar to my own. My mother is Italian and German descent, while my father is Italian and Polish descent. I am European American. I'm not sure exactly what nationality my physical characteristics came from, but I have blue eyes and blond hair. I grew up with predominately Italian influence. For example, my mother cooked Italian meals and the holiday celebrations always had an Italian entre (compliments of my grandmother). I grew up spending a lot of time with my Italian grandmother.

EARLIEST MEMORIES

A vivid memory, at age two, was the day my maternal Grandfather died of cancer. I remember that my grandmother, father, mother, aunt, uncle, and other family members, including me were at my grandparents' house. All of the adults around me were upset; some were crying. Everyone kept going in and out of my grandparents' bedroom. I remember being curious about this. Nobody would let me into that room to see what was going on. So, I sat in a blue chair in the livingroom, not understanding. Eventually, I managed to get to the bedroom. I remember what seemed to be a lot of people standing around. On the bed was my grandfather. I went over to the bed and clearly remember him reaching out his hand to me. He told me to be a good girl for my mother. Then I was taken out of the bedroom and put into that blue chair.

The next thing I remember was my mother crying hysterically, and the ambulance drivers taking my grandfather out of the house on a stretcher. He had died. When I told my mother about these memories, she confirmed the details. She was unemotional about the incident. I think time has helped her cope with the memory, but I always feel very sad when I recall it. I think that this death, I experienced at such an early age, was traumatic for me. I see signs of this even in my adult life, when dealing with death. I also have some happy and content memories from my childhood.

When I was a child, growing up in the 1970's, I remember playing outside on my swing set, during the summer. My mother would put the radio on, and I would swing all day listening to the music. I remember specific songs such as "Seasons in the Sun," by Terry Jacks, and a lot of Bee Gee's songs. Those times were secure for me. Even now, if I hear those songs, I get a smile on my face. I can remember how the sun felt on my skin and the smells in the air while I played on that swing set. Then I feel a little sad. I wish for that little world of innocence and contentment. I will never again have that feeling of security that my parents are protecting me. I will never know that safe innocent world again. It is impossible to go back to those days, on my swing, in the sun.

MEMORIES OF MY EDUCATION

I went to elementary school, junior high school, and high school in a suburban school district. I have fond memories of elementary school. At this point in my life, school was fairly easy for me. I scored high on standardized tests and did well academically. I was the type of kid who didn't have a problem going home and doing homework. In fact I was considered the "top kid" in the sixth grade. I was a quiet child, but had a lot of friends. I remember "sleepovers" were the thing to do on the weekends. Life was good with no major problems.

The summer before junior high, the guidance counselor called my parents to tell them that I had scored extremely high on the Metropolitan exams and could be in the Honors Program. My parents and I discussed the program and decided to try it. However, when seventh grade began, so did my school difficulties. I couldn't seem to adjust to the new school and the new routines. I was constantly sick. The competition in classes, with other smart kids, frightened me. I had to work extra hard to keep up with classmates, but my determination pulled me through! This was where I developed my academic discipline and drive. Also, the honors students did everything together for two years. We had all of our classes together, except foreign language. We developed some great friendships but were segregated from our peers outside of Honors.

Just as I began to like junior high school, I was transferred to the high school for ninth grade. The difficulty was that half of the ninth grade was at the high school, while the other half was at one of two other junior high schools in the district. Again, it was a big problem for me adjusting to the change. In addition, instead of being in all of my classes with the same group of people, I was thrown in with different people including those who were a grade ahead of me.

For instance, in ninth grade, I was taking biology which was typically a tenth grade science class. Therefore, I was the only ninth grade student put into a group of approximately twenty-five tenth-grade students. This did not go over very well with some of the tenth-grade students. They really did not want anything to do with me. They had their own friends who were their age and had no intention of getting to know me. I had nobody then to work with on experiments and was considered to be the "little brain" in the class. Before the year was over, I retreated into myself. I began to hate school and my grades suffered because of it. I didn't want to be "the brain" anymore; I just wanted to be a normal kid.

By my sophomore year, I decided to drop out of the Honors Program. I was ahead in my course credits, so the following year I tutored kids my own age in biology class, instead of taking another class or study hall.

For my junior year, I was in classes with those my own age. The difficult part about this was that I had been in a self-contained Honors Program for two years and then in classes with kids a year older than me, so it was hard to get to know some of the kids in my graduating class. They had formed their "cliques" and it was hard for me to fit in. Again, I was known as "the brain." However, I tried to make friends from different cliques. This was not always acceptable to group members. For example, I had friends since elementary school in the College Prep English class, but they were now in specific cliques. Several times during the year my English teacher requested that we pick a partner to work with in class. None of the people in the class were my close friends any longer; they knew who they wanted to work with. One day, I lost it and decided not to deal with it. I got up from my seat to ask the teacher if I could go to the nurse. As I went back to my desk to collect my books, one of the popular girls said, "She's just going to the nurse, because nobody wants to be her partner." I will never forget that day and two things always disturbed me. First, I knew that the teacher heard the comment; she was standing next to me and never said a word. Second, the student that made the comment was talking to my friend from elementary school. My old "friend" never defended me.

As I look back on high school, I think I would never want to repeat this period of my life. My self-esteem suffered, and even though I was an intelligent kid, my grades eventually suffered. However, I vowed then that after high school I would become successful and find my self-confidence again.

College

My decision to attend a community college for two years after high school was a wise one. This allowed me to adjust to the idea of college. I didn't have any friends that I wanted to go off to college with, anyway. When I graduated from the community college, I transferred to a small, private school in Upstate New York. I majored in Business Administration and received a wonderful education. I had "fun" like most college students, but I tried to maintain my grades. I fully applied myself the last two semesters and made the Dean's List.

After receiving my B.S. Degree in Business Administration, August 1993, I obtained a job working in an office. I hated the whole atmosphere and began thinking of teaching. By September 1995, I was enrolled in the Masters of Science in Teaching Program, concentrating on Elementary Education, at the same school I had earned a bachelor's degree. That was because of peer pressure. I was a good student and loved some of the teachers and wanted to model myself after those teachers. I wanted to feel worthwhile and make a difference in the lives of children. I realized my dream and am currently working in a fourth grade inclusion classroom. On those days when I can motivate just one student or "get through" to one student, I feel great! I know that I am a good teacher and am helping kids who are our future. I would like the children in my classroom to like school and have fun learning. Also, I want my classroom to be a safe place where kids can feel free to be themselves and concentrate on learning.

Mom and Dad—The Importance of Education

In my family, education is considered very important. My parents are high-school graduates and have additional vocational training. They have done very well for themselves. My mother was an EKG Technician in the medical field for 20 years before she retired. My father has been a professional fire-fighter in the Syracuse Fire Department for 25 years. Although my parents have done well in their lives, they realized that my sister and I would need education beyond high school. My sister became a hairdresser and is currently back in college working toward a degree in computer science. I completed my B.S. in Business Administration and have nearly completed my Masters of Science in Teaching. My father paid for my undergraduate work and my sister's beautician school by working two jobs. I always felt bad that my father had to work two jobs, but he wanted the best for us and is proud of our accomplishments. My mother was always supportive, taking me to the library and trying to help me in any way possible.

FAMILY MATTERS

As I mentioned earlier, when I was growing up, our family was very close. In my house, we always ate together at the dinner table. We talked about what was happening in our lives. Also, every Sunday was dinner at grandma's house (my mother's mother). This was my Italian grandmother who lived alone. She would make any number of pasta dishes and desserts. It was the best! My sister and I would also spend the night at her house on occasion; she would make a breakfast the next morning of eggs, fritatas, toast, etc. Those days were wonderful. I miss my grandmother, who is now in a nursing home with Alzheimer's Disease and Dementia. I have a tough time bringing myself to visit her, because it makes it difficult for me to remember the way she used to be.

My paternal grandfather died when my father was 11 years of age. When my paternal grandmother remarried, my dad and his two brothers never got along with their stepfather, so we rarely saw them. Also, my mother and her sister married my father and his brother. Both women did not get along with their mother-in-law. When I was ten years of age, my paternal grandmother wrote a letter to both of her daughters-in-law stating that she did not want to see any of us again. Basically, she said that her husband was more important to her, and that he didn't want anything to do with us. Well, this "crushed" my father.

Eventually, my father got over his mother's decision and "let it go." However, I know it still bothers him. I get angry because of the way she made him feel and the fact that she discarded all of us. My father wishes that my sister and I could have gotten to know my grandmother better. I don't feel that I missed anything, given the type of person she seems to be. I remind my father that it was her decision. My grandmother made some very unhappy times for my family without going into greater detail. Recently, she is indicating that she wants to take it back. I don't think she can take back the last 17 years, not in my eyes, anyway, and not after what she did to my father.

In spite of my father's mother's harmful influence, we did have some great holidays. Usually, we would go to my Italian grandmother's house for Thanksgiving, Christmas, and Easter. We always had a "ton" of food which usually would include an Italian dish in addition to turkey, ham, salads, mashed potatoes, vegetables, desserts, etc. The holidays included my aunt, uncle, cousin, grandmother, great aunts and uncles, mom, dad, my sister, and me.

MY SISTER

As I write this autobiography, I realize that I haven't said much about my younger sister, Stephanie. We are 2 1/2 years apart and complete opposites. We hardly ever got along when we were growing up, in fact, we had some down right horrible times. Most of the time, my sister and I were literally at each other's throats. We wouldn't just argue; there was punching, scratching, hitting, etc. When we got older and bigger, it was to the point that my mother couldn't get in between us for fear that she would get hurt. I think that we were like this because we were and still are so different.

My sister is very athletic and was not very thrilled with academics, although she is intelligent. Stephanie made a comment once that I was the "smart" one, so she concentrated on athletics while growing up since that is what she did well. I, on the other hand, threw myself into school work, most of the time, and didn't like athletics. Also, my sister has a very strong personality. She is opinionated, aggressive, and doesn't hesitate to speak her mind. I was always quiet, and if I had an opinion, I either kept it to myself or tried not to offend anyone else. I think that people used to really "walk all over me," where this seldom happened to my sister. In school, my sister commanded respect. People wanted her as a friend, rather than an enemy. Stephanie was a varsity soccer player her freshman year of high school and was on a team with the seniors in my graduating class. They all liked her and sometimes this made things a little easier for me in school.

Currently, my sister and I get along fine. I think it helps that we no longer live in the same house and that we are 27 and 25 years of age. I learned from Stephanie not to let people take advantage of me and to speak up. Maybe she even learned from me to be more tactful and tolerant of people. I'm glad that we grew out of that sibling rivalry.

CHURCH

I was raised Roman Catholic. When I was growing up, our family attended church every weekend. My father is a dedicated Catholic and my mother is Protestant but was baptized Catholic. My father demanded that my sister and I attend church regularly. My mother routinely attended church, because my father expected her to, although she never officially converted to Catholicism. I began to resent being "forced" to go to church. At 21 years of age, I sat down and told my dad that I was old enough to make my own decisions. I told him that it wasn't that I didn't believe in the Catholic religion, but I wanted to make my own choices. I also expressed some beliefs that I disagreed with, regarding the church, and made some good points. I thought he was going to be outraged and disappointed. However, my father listened to me and, from that day on, it was my decision whether or not I wanted to attend church. Unfortunately, I don't think that I attend church enough. I make the excuse that I have a busy life and not enough time in the day. This is no excuse; I feel like I need to get back to church.

FRIENDSHIPS

Friendships are something that have been very important to me throughout my life. I think that everybody needs someone other than their family with whom they can confide. I have developed some very "strong" friendships throughout the years, especially during the time I spent in college and have a few "good" friends left from my high school years. I don't think that this is very surprising given my experiences back then. However, college made up for everything.

I met my friend, Kathleen, the first semester I transferred from the community college to the liberal arts, private school that I attended while working on my bachelor's degree. Kathleen is six years older than me and very wise. She is successful in her career, as a human resource corporate manager. I can always count on Kathleen for an objective opinion and intelligent advice.

There is also my friend Laurie. I met Laurie the first semester of my senior year of college. Laurie is always on the go, full of energy and fun. She is very much in her own world, but she is a wonderful friend. Just a year ago I stood up for her wedding.

Another great person that I met through Laurie is my friend Lynn. Lynn is a special education teacher for a suburban school district. She is logical, straight forward, and a down to earth person. When I need advice about teaching, I can always count on Lynn.

ROMANCES

I didn't date until my senior year of high school. Then, I met Jim, who was from a small town approximately a half hour drive from where I lived. I was 18 years of age and he was 20. He was Italian American with brown eyes and brown hair. At the time, I seemed to be attracted to those physical features. I also liked his spontaneous personality characteristics that I associate with the Italian culture. I had a lot of fun with Jim the first year that we knew each other. He was in a band, and I would go to watch him play his bass guitar every week. Also, we did a lot of fun things including parties, spending time with friends, and visiting different places.

After a while, things with Jim weren't so much fun anymore and our relationship started to change. But, about two years into the relationship, Jim's mother got very sick. One day, unexpectedly, she collapsed and was brought to the hospital. Hours later, she and her family were told that cancer was present in her lungs, liver, and brain. Two months later, she died. This was one of the most tragic deaths I have ever seen. Jim had a sister and two brothers. None had seen their father in 12 years because their parents had been divorced. Unfortunately, they had nobody but each other to rely on. At this point, Jim really started to depend on me and life got very serious.

A year after Jim's mother died, his grandfather also suddenly died from a heart attack. To make matters worse, within months, Jim was rushed into surgery and almost died himself. I spent nights and days at the hospital until he was released. I knew at this time that the relationship wasn't going to last, but I felt obligated to see him through his healing process. I couldn't abandon him when he needed me. Yet, I felt like I was too young to be going through all of these tragedies.

When Jim finally healed and could stand on his own, I broke off the relationship. He begged me to stay and said that he wanted to marry me. I tried to convince him that he would never be happy with me. I cared about him, but not enough to spend the rest of my life with him. After almost four years, I ended this part of my life.

A few years later, I met Mark. At the time, I was 23 years of age and he was 29. Initially, Mark was somewhat intimidating. He was a police officer, over six feet tall, with blue eyes and light brown hair, strong, athletic, and very handsome. But, after our first meeting, I knew that there was something special about Mark, and I wanted to spend more time with him. I am still with him today.

Mark has a great personality and a "unique" sense of humor. The first months of our relationship were like a perfect love story. We would go to the gym for a workout, to dinner, the movies, grocery shopping, etc. No matter where we went or what we were doing, we always had fun.

I love the fact that Mark is of Polish descent. I have a Polish background but did not have any influence from this heritage while growing up. By spending time with Mark and his family, I have learned a lot about Polish traditions. For example, Christmas Eve, Mark's family has bread blessed at church for Christmas dinner. After prayer and bread breaking, they have the traditional Polish Catholic meal of fish, coleslaw, potatoes, and pierogies. It is a lot of fun for me to join these celebrations and learn more about a part of my heritage.

I can't imagine my life without Mark. He is a caring and sincere individual, truly one of a kind. Our relationship has matured since we met. I feel that he has become my best friend and confident, as well as my beloved. We have been together through some difficult times in our lives. He has been my inspiration and support throughout the past five years, and I hope that I have done the same for him. I feel that we have a special connection, which leads me to believe that we are destined to be together for eternity. I will now end my life story, so far, with the words of Truman Capote's, *Other Voices, Other Room* (1948),

> their lover's eyes lilacs opening, ship
> lights, school bells, a landscape, remembered
> conversations, friends, a child's Sunday,
> lost voices, one's favorite suit, autumn
> and all seasons, memory, yes, it being the earth
> and water of existence.

Writing an Autobiography

Jennifer revealed many details about her personal life. This is similar to other teachers who have enrolled in the multicultural literacy course. She talked about the profound influence of her grandfather's death, the difficulties with family relationships, the struggles with academic competition, the tension in school friendships, and the problems with being "the brain." She also realized that her European American background had a significant impact on religion, family traditions, and views of the world.

Comparable to other teachers, Jennifer found that the act of writing her autobiography increased self-knowledge and made her think more sensitively about others' lives (Banks, 1994; Schmidt, 1998b). Since it is well documented that writing is linked to the knowledge of self within a social context (Emig, 1971; Yinger, 1985), writing one's life story appears to lessen negative notions about different groups of people and begins to construct connections with universal human tenets (Progoff, 1975). When teachers have written autobiographies, cultural differences can be examined in a positive manner and related to their own personal histories (Banks, 1994; Britzman, 1986; Ladson-Billings, 1994). As a result, teachers acquire an awareness of their own perceptions regarding race, class, gender, and related social issues (Banks, 1994; Sjoberg & Kuhn, 1989).

Additionally, research (Banks, 1994; Florio-Ruane, 1994; Noordhoff & Kleinfeld, 1993; Schmidt, 1998b) suggests that the first step in developing culturally sensitive pedagogy is to discover one's own cultural identity. This seems to be a prerequisite for appreciating the similarities and differences that exist between self and others. Similarly, Jennifer found the process of writing an autobiography a rewarding one that set the stage for learning about another person's life story.

Biography

Next teachers in the multicultural literacy course wrote the biography of a person who is culturally different from themselves, using the in depth unstructured and semi structured interview processes (Spradley, 1979). Studies have demonstrated that, when teachers meet with people who are different from themselves, the personal is accentuated and internalization of information is fostered (Cochran-Smith, 1995; Noordhoff & Kleinfeld, 1993; Tatum, 1992). Similarly, interviewing to write life stories, helps teachers become more culturally sensitive (Schmidt, 1998b, 1998c; Spindler & Spindler, 1987).

With permission from interviewees, the teachers in the course, tape recorded at least three interview sessions, and constructed life stories with reported life events and experiences. They often went beyond the required number of interviews because they discovered that people generally had a need to tell their stories to attentive listeners. Frequently, friendships developed from these associations. The following are excerpts from Jennifer's biography of a woman adopted from Korea composed after numerous interviews (Iauco, 1997).

KIM

Memories of Korea

On February 8, 1972, Kim was born in Seoul, Korea. She had black hair, brown eyes, and an olive skin tone. Kim doesn't remember a lot about Korea, but mostly the hurt and pain she experienced. She has almost no memories of her mother and the memories of her father are but a shadow. When Kim was four years old, her biological father died of a heart attack. In Korea, there was no public assistance and Kim's family was poor, so her mother had no choice but to put Kim and her 5-year-old brother in an orphanage. Kim's mother knew that this was the only chance her children had for a better life. For one devastating year, Kim and her brother lived in an orphanage separated from each other. This was horrific for Kim because her brother was the only one she had left in the world. Kim stated, "In the orphanage, you were not treated like a human being. It was common for the children to experience beatings and whippings. Boys had more value than girls in Korea and were treated somewhat better in the orphanage, but the combination of physical and mental abuse was overwhelming."

MEMORIES OF THE ADOPTION

In 1977, at the time of her adoption, Kim was near death. Her body weight was dangerously low. She was frightened and confused when she first saw her adoptive mother from the United States. But when her new Mother smiled and reached out to her, Kim clung to her. Kim can remember traveling through airports and in taxis as her new mother carried her all the way. She also remembers the teddy bear her new mother brought; Kim still has it today.

Kim's biological brother was also adopted by the same family and believed he was her protector. When they arrived at their new home in the United States, her brother walked into the house and would not let Kim enter, until he made sure it was safe. Kim is very thankful that she and her brother were adopted together.

LEARNING TO SPEAK ENGLISH

Kim remembers that she started learning English as soon as she got into the car with her adoptive mother. Her new family knew almost nothing about the Korean language and culture. Kim and her brother had to learn English quickly if they were going to communicate. In the beginning, her mom got a translator to find out what foods the children liked. Within four months, both children learned English well enough to start school in September.

Being a teacher, their mother planned to keep the children home for a year and prepare them for schools. But, she believed they were ready for school in September and needed to start interacting with other children. So Kim went to kindergarten and her brother to first grade at the urban school where their mother taught.

In school, Kim was sent to ESL for part of the day and the regular classroom for the remainder of the day. This was the first schooling experience. She liked ESL class, but it included nothing about her Korean language or culture. Her mother believed that she needed to become an American and forget her past. There also wasn't a lot of support back then for parents adopting children from other cultures. Today, Kim laments the loss of her Korean language.

Overall, Kim does not have good memories of her school experiences. She felt secure in kindergarten, because she attended the school where her mother worked. However, the following year, in first grade, when she went to school in a suburban school district, she cried. It was scary for her to have to get on a bus and have to deal with children who called her derogatory names relating to her physical appearance. Kim's first grade teacher became aware of this problem and lectured the children about their cruel behaviors.

Kim's life was miserable in the second grade. She felt that the teacher hated her ethnicity. She made Kim feel she could do nothing right. Kim always felt like she was being yelled at for the way she talked. She was continually corrected because of her accent. She also had a very high pitched voice, a tone in which she was taught to speak Korean. The second grade teacher was annoyed and kept telling Kim that she had to change her language, fix her voice, and learn to speak English correctly. Kim recalled the hurt, "Everything I am, wasn't good enough. I had to be like everyone else. She was so harsh." The teacher would also say, "Go in the corner and keep saying that word until you can say it correctly. Don't use that tone!"

Kim felt that second grade was the year that things really started to go down hill for her. Sometimes it was easy for her to keep friends and sometimes it wasn't, because she was different. Kim said, "One day someone liked me and the next day she hated me. I wasn't the blond-haired and blue-eyed girl who always got attention and all the boys liked."

There were only three Asian children in the whole school: Kim, her brother, and another child. The other child had been born in the United States and did not have an accent. Children made fun of Kim's accent with "Chinese talking" and names, etc. She felt that her accent was part of the reason that she had a difficult time keeping friends. It just made her too different. Even when Kim did gain acceptance from the other children, it seemed that their parents did not accept her. They did not want their children playing with Kim because she was Korean. This eventually made the other children even less accepting of her.

Through elementary school, name calling and other prejudicial experiences happened repeatedly. Kim recalls, "I would go into a classroom and someone would call me 'chink' right out loud; the teacher would hear, but do nothing. What I felt inside was anger but, more than the anger, was hurt."

When Kim came home crying, her mom would call the parents of the child or the teacher. Her mother did the best she could to support Kim and "stick up" for her. But sometimes this just wasn't enough. It did not stop the cultural conflicts that Kim would experience the majority of her life.

The year that Kim was to go to middle school, her mother had her transferred out of the suburban school district to the city school district. This was because the teacher that Kim would have been assigned in the suburban school had been abusive to her Korean brother the previous year. So Kim went on to an almost equally bad situation.

The city school that she attended was 90% African American. The children at this school treated her worse than she had been treated before. The name calling was terrible. Kim feels that these children perceived her as weak because of her petite size. Therefore, this gave some of the African American children the opportunity to have power over another person.

Eventually, Kim transferred back to the suburban school district, where her family lived and finished out her high school years. An incident involving her Senior Ball had a big impact on Kim and how she viewed her Asian ethnicity. Kim and her date for the Senior Ball made plans with a group of friends. One of Kim's friends met a new boy and decided that she did not want to go to the dance with Kim and her date. Kim always felt that this incident happened because of her Asian ethnicity. Maybe this friend did not want to have to introduce Kim to a new boyfriend. Kim said, "These types of situations really made me hate being Asian and want to be Caucasian." Sadly, it got to the point in Kim's life where she'd pray every night that she would wake up the next morning and look more like a "white" person.

COLLEGE/DECISIONS TO BECOME A TEACHER

Kim always thought about becoming a teacher but also considered going to college to become a pediatrician. Ultimately, the choice she made was to become a teacher. Kim stated that having both her mother and father involved in the teaching profession was a big reason for her decision. Her mom was the most significant influence, as she always expressed her love for teaching and the rewards it brought. Kim would go into her mother's classroom whenever she had some free time. Kim explained, "A big thing is that I always liked the way my mom taught; I wanted to be just like her."

Kim especially liked the way her mother taught the children to appreciate human differences. If a child offended another in any way, Kim's mom would make sure that the student knew what they did wrong. Kim also praised her mother's teaching when she said, "She has so many great values and she gets the kids excited about learning." Kim saw her mother make a big difference in students' lives and she wanted to have a chance to do the same. Although Kim's personal experiences with her own schooling were negative, her mother made school a more comfortable place in Kim's eyes. She said, "My mom was always there for me and supported me. My dad wasn't thrilled. He wanted me to get into a profession that made more money."

Kim initially chose a state college to begin her education, but almost failed. After a semester, she transferred to a small private college. It made a great difference to her. She enjoyed the personal attention and the great teacher preparation classes. Kim said, "My teacher education classes have triggered memories of what happened to me concerning racial issues in my life. I know exactly how I would handle these situations in my own classroom. Teachers must be proactive and teach children how to appreciate diversity in their classrooms. Children's negative remarks cannot be ignored. They must learn to care about each other."

WHY SO FEW MINORITY TEACHERS IN THE TEACHING PROFESSION?

Kim felt that there are few minorities in the teaching field, because most minorities who seek higher education would rather go into a profession with more status. Asians, known as the "model minority," are stereotyped as highly intelligent people and are expected to become doctors, lawyers, etc. Kim said, "I think that the teaching profession is becoming a lot more respected and in the upcoming years there will probably be more minorities entering the field."

CULTURAL CONFLICT

Kim grew up experiencing stereotypes and racial conflict. She could remember being called various names such as "flat face" and "slant eyes." This happened to her from day one in this country and presently happens from time to time. Kim felt very confused growing up. On the same day, someone might call her, "flat face," and another person might remark about her "pretty face." It seemed she did not know what to believe or how to view herself. She recalled, "I felt as though I had two different identities, a white person, inside, and an Asian, outside."

At the time that Kim was adopted, people from the United States had just begun to adopt Korean children. Therefore, it was not widely accepted by society. Even her adoptive mother's family ostracized her for adopting Asian children. Many times Kim can remember walking into the mall and feeling like people were staring at her. Also, until recent years, there had not been multicultural education in the schools and, therefore, there was not much of an attempt to teach children about cultural differences. Kim felt that children need to learn, early on, about different people and cultures in order to become more accepting of others.

FRIENDS

Kim made friends while growing up despite the racial conflicts that she experienced. She did not have close friends of Asian ethnicity, and admits that this is due to the fact that she did not like being Asian herself. Kim says, "I did not want to be associated with other Asians because I felt like it would mean more trouble for me with racial conflict." In fact, Kim was disgusted with other Asians, feeling that being Asian was "bad" and "ugly."

Kim's only friend from childhood to the present lived around the corner from her. Gina has stayed in touch and plans on being Maid of Honor in Kim's wedding. Kim had many friends from her college years.

FAMILY

Kim's immediate family was a very close one and consisted of her mother, her biological older brother, who is now 26 years of age, and her adopted younger Korean brother and sister, who are now 15 and 13 years of age. Kim's father was not a significant part of her life due to the fact that her parents became divorced. Also, while the children of this family were growing up, their father never did special things with them or spent time with them. Therefore Kim said, "I feel that my father is just an acquaintance." On the other hand, Kim's mother has always been a major support in all of her children's lives. Kim said, "My dad won't be walking me down the aisle when I get married; my mother will."

HOLIDAYS

When Kim was a child, her grandmother, on her mother's side of the family, had all of the holidays at her house. Kim's immediate family, along with aunts and uncles, as well as others, attended. However, when Kim's grandmother died a few years ago, the holiday celebrations began to fade out. Kim's paternal grandmother did not care to see Kim and her siblings, so there was little memory of her.

Currently, holidays are celebrated with only the immediate family; Christmas being the biggest. Another important set of holidays celebrated in Kim's family were the anniversaries of the dates that she, her two brothers, and sister came to the United States from Korea. Their mom wanted to celebrate and remember these dates by doing something special. The parties were comparable to a birthday with gifts and cakes.

RELIGION

Kim was raised as a Roman Catholic. Sunday was a day with church attendance and family dinner but this is no longer the case. Currently, Kim does not attend church every week, but she prays; God is a part of her everyday life. She intends to make Sunday's a special day with her own family, someday.

ROMANCE

Throughout her high school years, Kim rarely dated any boys. She felt that the boys were more interested in girls with blue eyes and blonde hair. Also, she knew that she had to take care of herself and learn to like herself, which took most of her energies. Throughout Kim's college years, she occasionally dated, but it was never serious. One year ago, Kim met a man named Augusto of German descent. He has brown hair and blue eyes, and grew up in Brazil, where his family currently resides. Kim explained that when she told people that Augusto is Brazilian, they automatically assumed that he was "black." She is disgusted with the stereotypes that arise.

Augusto and Kim initially became friends and then their relationship developed into a romantic one. Kim described Augusto as, "...the first person I ever loved and who loved me back the same way."

Kim and Augusto plan on being married in the next few years. He is a professional baseball player who hopes to live in the United States for a while, but will eventually move back to Brazil. As for their interracial marriage, all family members on both sides are accepting. Will society be accepting? Kim said, "I think that Asian interracial marriages are more accepted today because Asians have the stereotype of being very intellectual (the model minority)."

RACIAL ISSUES AND SOME RESOLUTION OF FEELINGS

Kim was a strong-willed child during her elementary school years. However, as she got older, Kim began to hate being an Asian person and as a result, became submissive. She hated the "white mainstream" society, but desperately wanted to become part of it. Kim worked hard to lose her Korean accent and tried to talk like everyone else. She saw other young girls who had blue eyes and blond hair get all the attention from their peers. More and more, the conflict within her grew and consequently, the hate that she felt for herself became unbearable. Kim would pray to God every night that she'd wake up one morning with blue eyes and blond hair. She even rubbed her skin, hoping that it would become white. She even bought special cosmetics to try to make herself look more like a "white person."

At 13 years of age, Kim became so depressed that her mother did not know how to help her. Kim would go to her room and sit in the dark, crying for hours and hating herself. Although her mother was supportive and encouraging, she could not stop or reverse Kim's deep depression. Consequently, Kim went into therapy for eight years. It took a lot of time before Kim began to accept her Asian ethnicity and resolve the conflict within herself which society helped to create. It was the strength of Kim's mother that helped her through these difficult years.

Eventually, Kim resolved the conflict and realized that she was a good person with a lot to offer. Kim is now comfortable with herself and her ethnicity, but does not forget the anger and pain that she felt in the past due to racial conflict. She does not apologize for who she is or try to change herself for anyone. Kim has struggled through the pain with no regrets for what she has endured. She feels that her experiences have made her a stronger person and better able to see people for who they are. She intends to bring to her teaching the knowledge of her experience and the hope that she can educate young children to become more tolerant of others who may be seen as different. Also, Kim hopes that the white mainstream educational system will provide children with more multicultural education and deal more effectively with issues of racial conflict in the classroom. She believes that education professionals can begin by confronting differences/racial issues and realizing that ignoring them will not make them go away. Ignoring them will only let minority children, as well as others, continue to hurt emotionally with little resolved. Kim said, "Children are children no matter how they look or who they are, and teachers should take into consideration feelings along with being aware of the things that are happening in their classrooms."

Finally, Kim has spent the last several years studying her Korean language and culture. She plans to go back to Korea and visit her place of birth. She feels strong enough to face the pain of those early years. Most important, Kim feels comfortable with herself and feels that she has a lot to offer our educational system.

Cross-Cultural Analysis

The interview process and writing Kim's biography was not only a means for Jennifer to learn about Kim's life story, but also, an opportunity to reflect on her own life story. This process helped her become aware of similarities and differences, so necessary for cross-cultural analyses (Spindler & Spindler, 1987).

Jennifer created Table 1, revealing the similarities and differences between her life story and Kim's life story. It was an interesting way for her to compare and contrast and gain an understanding and appreciation of diversity.

Table 1. Jennifer's and Kim's Similarities and Differences

Similarities	Differences
Career choice	Physical appearance
College choice	Family size
Depression	Racial/cultural conflict
Family Celebrations	Intercultural dating
Religion	Racial/cultural conflict
Family celebrations	Adjustment to society
Family support	Adoption
Grandparent relationships	Model minority
Death experiences	Cultural heritage
Motivation to succeed	Abuse
	Siblings
	Divorce
	Parent careers
	Self-perceptions

CULTURAL ANALYSIS OF DIFFERENCES

I think I learned from my past to understand the present and future. After writing my autobiography and Kim's biography, I realized how much I have learned about the two of us as individuals and how we relate to one another. Furthermore, I have learned more about the events in my life which have had an impact on me as a person. It wasn't until I actually wrote the words about my life on paper that I understood how I developed as a person and which specific events of the past had a profound effect on me. For example, I now understand more about my ideas related to family issues. I was raised in a family which is very devoted to one another. My parents have done every-thing humanly possible to make sure that my sister and I have had everything we needed while we were growing up. They have provided us with emotional support, strong values, education, and physical needs. I realized that, because I was supported by my parents throughout my life, I have had oppor-tunities that other people may not have had. For instance, I never worried about having the next meal, I had good clothes, and received a wonderful education. Ultimately, I think that I have a better appreciation for my eco-nomic privileges and my parents hard work throughout the years.

I realized that my drive toward success has come from different places in my life. First, my parents have always reinforced how important it is to have as much education as possible. It was instilled in me that, through education, I could obtain economic and self success. Secondly, my discipline and perse-verance for academic success has come from a desperate struggle for self-esteem. I knew that if I could be successful academically, I would regain the self-confidence that I slowly lost as a child in school. What I found is that my perseverance worked. Now that I have nearly completed my Masters of Sci-ence in Teaching Degree, I feel that I have succeeded in conquering a tre-mendous challenge. Also, I have a better understanding of my fears and my goals for the future.

DISCOMFORTS AND ADMIRATION

Just as importantly, I have learned what makes me uncomfortable, and at the same time, admire a person of another culture. I am somewhat thankful that I never had to experience the racial/cultural conflict that many minorities face every day for I admittedly fear that I would not have been strong enough to overcome it. Also, I really had to ponder those things that make me uncomfortable about the cultural differences between Kim and me. At first, I could only see the similarities and didn't actually feel discomfort with our dif-ferences. After all, Kim has become my friend, and I have never felt uncom-fortable with her. Then I looked further, realizing that I needed to thoroughly investigate the cultural aspects of this situation. I soon found that there were, in fact, discomforts that I have regarding our cultural differences.

I am uncomfortable with the fact that her physical characteristics have brought her pain, while mine make me a member of the dominant white mainstream. I am disturbed, that while growing up, Kim tried not to be Asian because she faced so much racial conflict and "mocking." This resulted in the loss of her cultural identity and the conflict of feeling white inside while looking Asian on the outside. She thought it was necessary to conform to American society. In fact, Kim felt that the ideal physical characteristics to possess would be the blond hair and blue eyes of her oppressors, those accepted by society in the United States. This made me especially uncomfortable because these are my physical characteristics. I think that I fear being unjustly stereotyped as a person who is part of a society that does not accept differences. I may be accused of being one of the oppressors.

Another discomfort arose concerning academics. First, I am bothered by the model minority pressure. Not only do Asian people experience racial conflict, but they also have the added pressure of having to be "smart." Kim admits, that as a young child, she felt pressure to do well in school. She said, "People looked at me and assumed that I am smart, because I am Asian." Kim also revealed, that early in her education, she had difficulties with mathematics. Although, once she worked at it, she excelled. In her adult life, now, Kim feels less pressure from the model minority stereotype. This could be due to the fact that she is now comfortable with herself and who she is as an individual.

The Asian minority in my school proved to be the competition when I was a child. They were the ones who might "beat me" on a test. I did look at the Japanese child in my eighth grade classes and think, "He's smart and I have to keep up with him." Mind you, this thought came before I knew what he was capable of academically. I hesitantly admit my stereotyping. However, I did not truly understand what these thoughts meant at the time. The influence of our society is powerful!

I was extremely uncomfortable when Kim talked about the whippings and other abuse she experienced in the orphanage. They have carried over into her life here. When she saw a movie in school (or elsewhere) that reminded her of Korea or the beatings, she could not watch it. Kim said, "I would go to the bathroom for a while until I thought it was over." I also can't imagine how horrible her life was before she was adopted. She was skin and bones when she arrived in this country and almost died. I don't think I could have survived that treatment. I'm glad she came to this country, but it doesn't seem fair that she had to go through mental abuse in our schools.

I also admire Kim because of her differences. She was able to bring her past experiences with racial conflict to her teaching. I have never had to experience racial prejudices. Therefore, I must work hard to learn how to effectively deal with any situations which may arise in my classroom. I must work hard to provide a classroom that demonstrates acceptance and appreciation of differences. Also, I must work hard to establish efficient communication between myself, minority students and their families.

In addition, I admire Kim's strength. Kim did not let the past destroy her and only became stronger because of it. She has survived abandonment, abuse, and dealing with cultural conflict. She is no longer ashamed or uncomfortable with her Korean ethnicity. Kim has regained her self-esteem and is attempting to regain part of her Korean heritage, while teaching others about it. She appears to be a happy person today, with goals and dreams. It is truly amazing to me that she is completing her teacher education. She will be an invaluable addition to the profession.

Kim is the first minority person that I have really gotten to know. She is a good person who never let her experiences turn her bitter toward those who "look like me." For that I especially admire her. I have learned more from Kim about cultural differences, because we have become friends and shared so much through this interview process. People can learn from one another if they just pay attention, look, and listen.

Jennifer's Analysis

Jennifer's analysis of differences is typical of others who have completed this set of fairly simple assignments in the multicultural literacy course. Teachers who complete the ABC's assignments come to realize the power in the experiences and the effects it may have on their teaching. They also understand that one person does not represent an entire culture, but that learning from one person's perspective in that culture may help in understanding certain aspects of a culture. Moreover, they become aware of the imbalance of power between highly educated teachers and administrators and less educated, often lower-income minority families. They realize that the imbalance of power may prevent the communication necessary for sharing information between home and school (Ogbu, 1983; Kidder, 1989; Edwards, 1997). Furthermore, they understand why educators may fear saying and doing the wrong things with people who are ethnically and culturally different. But since teachers are the ones in power positions, they are the logical ones to reach out to families and connect home and school (Schmidt, 1998a; Edwards, 1999).

And when these same teachers are able to transfer their learning to their students, strong home and school connections necessary for the reconceptualizing of literacy in the new age of multiculturalism and pluralism can take place(Schmidt, 1998b; 1999). Similarly, Jennifer's learning demonstrated that the ABC's process helped her see the need to communicate more effectively with the students in her classroom.

I NEED TO KNOW MY STUDENTS AND CONNECT WITH THEIR FAMILIES

After completing the process of the ABC's Model, I realized the importance of knowing about the students in my classroom. Analyzing the differences and similarities among people gave me a greater understanding and appreciation for celebrating those differences. Also, Kim made me realize that my students may react a certain way in the classroom because of their different backgrounds. For example, when I began working with the Korean boy in my fourth grade class, I noticed that he didn't talk about his family. Whenever I have asked any questions about his family or Korean heritage, he gives me very brief answers. I was somewhat confused about this and mentioned it to Kim. She explained that Korean children may be discouraged from expressing feelings or family information in school, since education is considered serious business. Ultimately, knowing the ethnic and cultural background of the students in my classroom, will allow me to provide an environment where children can feel free to be themselves and concentrate on learning.

Reflections on the ABC's of Cultural Understanding and Communication

Similar to Jennifer's reflections, the following examples of teachers' reflections on the ABC's model support the notion that autobiography, biography, and cross-cultural analyses are a powerful combination for reconceptualizing literacy in the new age of multiculturalism and pluralism. (The following teacher reflections as well as the remaining informants and cases in this chapter are identified with pseudonyms.)

An Italian American teacher announced:

I never would have predicted that I could feel so close to Shandra (all names are pseudonyms), the teacher aide in our building. She knows so much about our children and their families. Her life experiences in the African American community are highlighted by her involvement in church. I didn't think she would want to share. I didn't think I would share my life story with her, but I found myself doing it naturally. She has given me the confidence to begin visiting homes and try new ways of communicating with families.

A German American and Irish American teacher stated:

I never realized how important family is for Juan, our custodian. He came to this country as a teenager, and every year, goes back to Puerto Rico with his wife and children to visit cousins. On his wages, he saves and sends money back home. They live on the bare minimum and do without luxuries. He believes he is teaching his children about what is right. He is so honest that I had to share my life story with him. I now see how important it is to know the families of my children and have them share their home knowledge and experiences.

A teacher from Scotch-Irish, German, and English backgrounds explained:

This experience opened my eyes to my own culture and what I value. I can see that I never gave much thought to other groups of people. I thought we were all alike or should be. When I interviewed Esther, a teacher in our school, I discovered her Jewish background and the importance of her Faith, something we had never shared. It gave me a new view and made me realize how insensitive I've been. We enjoyed the interview and sharing process. Even in my all white classroom, there are differences that my children need to share and appreciate. Opportunities to connect home and school will better prepare my students for the world.

A teacher who called herself "the melting pot" because she claimed to have mixed origins dating back to the Plymouth Rock, talked about her learning:

> Rural poverty is tough. I never actually respected the work of the rural poor. They often have extremely low wages even though they are vital to farming operations. Their lack of education requires all in the family to work and yet they barely have enough for rent, food, and clothing. Many don't have health insurance. Their children come to school and we don't value what they do which is another slap in the face for their hard work. I became aware of this when I interviewed a Native American woman who is a health care aide at the nursing home where my Mother resides. I have also begun to learn about the values that guide her life.

A teacher from Ukrainian and French backgrounds expressed his ideas,

> I thought Mr. Koshi, who teaches Japanese in our high school, liked to stay to himself. I thought it was his culture. After interviewing him, I made a new friend. We have so much in common as human beings. We also have a lot of differences which make the relationship interesting. He has made me aware of stereotypes and the importance of personal contact with people who I think are different. In the past, I only emphasized the Western World in my global studies class. Now I know that we have to study the contributions of peoples around the world. We have a few students from other cultures in our school; they have agreed to visit my class and talk about their families.

These responses from teachers who participated in the ABC's model, as part of a multicultural literacy class, explained the need to use their power as teachers to empower their students by studying similarities and differences. Participation in the ABC's model seemed to bring down the walls of ignorance that separate humans from different cultural and economic backgrounds. They began to realize the importance of strong home and school communication and design plans to connect home and school for literacy development in classrooms and schools based on the first four assignments of the ABC's model. They actually seemed to understand that families are children's first teachers and have much to share in their literacy development. They knew that they must be able to develop collaborative relations with families in an atmosphere of mutual respect, so that students can gain the most from their education (Goldenberg, 1987; Faltis, 1993; McCaleb, 1994). Their learning from the ABC's experience was reinforced with other course assignments.

Other Assignments

Several readings in the Multicultural Literacy course reinforced the ABC's model and stimulated class discussions about self-knowledge and home/school connections for building classroom community with reading, writing, listening, and talking (Vygotsky, 1978; Bloome & Green, 1982; Heath, 1983; Dyson, 1993; Schmidt, 1998a; Edwards, 1999). Other readings emphasized the need for teachers to acquire the cultural and social awareness necessary to help students and their families see the connections between home and school and associate their cultural patterns with the school (Barrera, 1992; Au, 1993; Ladson-Billings, 1994; Nieto, 1996; Schmidt, 1996; Edwards, 1996). Along with relevant readings, invited guests from eight different cultures told their personal stories and responded to questions from the class. The class practiced semi-structured interviews and completed cross-cultural analyses for each visitor. Finally, throughout the course, teachers examined multicultural literature (Diamond & Moore, 1995) and responded to case studies of elementary and secondary students' struggles (Nieto, 1996; Schmidt, 1998a).

Instruction was based on constructivist models (Vygotsky, 1978; Rogoff, 1986). Each time the course was offered, a positive learning community emerged. In an atmosphere of free and respectful expression, all worked in pairs and triads, participated in whole class discussions and role-playing activities. The professor acted as colleague and facilitator in order to create a safe place where conflicts could be openly discussed in relation to knowledge, experience, and reflection (Freire, 1970; Schon, 1987; Palmer, 1995; Willis & Meacham, 1997). Most teachers enthusiastically completed assignments and participated in all class activities. But, there were a few teachers in each of the courses who were particularly interested in systematically applying what they learned to their own classrooms and schools. Their ideas, assignments, and projects are reported in the next section of this chapter.

TEACHERS' PROJECTS

During the last four years, numerous teachers from diverse backgrounds have agreed to share portions of their autobiographies and cultural analyses assignments in published and unpublished papers (Iauco, 1997; Schmidt, 1998b). Twenty teachers from European American backgrounds have also agreed to share their ABC's adaptations as research projects for the Multicultural Literacy course (Schmidt, 1998c, 1999a,b). Urban, rural, and suburban elementary and secondary teachers have opened their classrooms to participant observations, kept journals of their daily reflections, and collected artifacts, field notes, student work, and recordings from family conferences. Data analysis was accomplished through individual coding and categorizing, first. Then comparisons were made between my analysis and each teacher's analysis. Finally, we met in small groups to share patterns. As patterns were discussed, themes took shape in the collaborative sessions for each project (Bogdan & Biklen, 1994; Wasser & Bresler, 1996). It was clear to all that strong connections were successfully made between home and school in elementary, middle and high school classrooms. Teachers used their power to make connections and empower families and students.

In the following portions of this chapter, teachers' adaptations of ABC's home/school communication plans for literacy learning are reported. Suburban, rural, and urban European American teachers reconceptualized literacy to develop the home/school connections and build classroom communities necessary for reading, writing, listening, and speaking in the new age of pluralism and multiculturalism.

Karen's Class and the ABC's

"We have to develop a certain attitude, an open attitude, a multicultural attitude across the curriculum. We can do this in our classes with the ABC's of Cultural Understanding and Communication."

Karen, a teacher for seven years, made this statement three years ago when she first implemented the ABC's plan in her sixth grade. Now teaching in a fifth grade, she believes that suburban schools and their children must become more aware of differences. "The few children from ethnic or cultural minorities in the school are either ignored or glorified giving the school community unrealistic pictures of their cultures."

In Karen's class, there are 11 male and 12 female European American students and one student from Cambodia who is learning English as a second language. Two other students are labeled learning disabled in written language.

Multicultural literature surrounds her classroom as she uses the ABC's model to help students read about, study their own and other cultures and analyze similarities and differences. She also ties these literacy activities to math and science where cultural contributions in all content areas are continuously researched and presented by students and teacher. "Students need to understand that white men were not the only ones making human history."

Karen's students research their family histories and share present home practices. They bring in artifacts, interview as many older family members as possible, and share their findings with partners and small groups. For a final class presentation, they create "something" that represents their family cultures. Students, design mobiles and family crests, compose poetry and music, compile reading materials, write family histories, draw family trees, sew quilts, assemble collages, paint portraits, serve meals, display sports equipment and family tools, post vacation pictures, show religious items and traditional dress, and create salt maps. The reading, writing, listening, speaking, and viewing activities associated with the studies hold everyone's interest and develop strong positive relationships to form classroom community. Last, each student selects a relative or friend to come to class for an hour and share stories related to their lives. These guests are interviewed by the class and each student lists similarities and differences and completes an analysis of differences. "How are we alike? How are we different? What did I admire about this person that is different from my own life story and why?"

Daily, Karen incorporates the study of diverse groups of people in the curriculum. A huge inflatable globe is the center of the classroom and, throughout the school year, students become increasingly aware of the contributions to humanity by diverse groups of people.

Additionally, every student in Karen's class has at least one family member visit the classroom to do one or more of the following: Tell a family story, read a book, explain work, share a hobby, demonstrate a special talent, tutor, chaperone. Families are also encouraged to join teacher workshops and help plan lessons and write curriculum. Karen visits most of her children's homes and usually has perfect family attendance at conferences and special class events.

Karen's Power Empowers

Karen took the initiative three years ago and made the difference. She has used her power as an educator to empower her children and families. She has connected home and school through the study of differences around the world and in her classroom. In the process, her students have celebrated themselves and others. As Karen so aptly states, "Since differences may be helpful or harmful, it is important that they be explored rather than ignored. When we understand differences, then we have the power to make a difference."

Mark's Global Studies Class and the ABC's

Mark was in his fourth year of teaching in a large suburban high school in the Northeast when he chose to initiate the ABC's model in his global studies class, an elective, with 20 juniors. Mark stated, "The syllabus is basically an examination of the accomplishments of great white western males, the focus of the state curriculum." He described his class, "This is an unmotivated group. We have a few eager beavers who act like they're interested, but most students fake attention or interest. One African American student has slept through every class so far."

Mark attempted to create a more positive setting for literacy development as well as a means of helping his students become sensitive to diversity issues. He began with telling the story of his own life, asking the class to take notes for a future quiz. Mark explained, "The students laughed, but actually were involved the entire time. I think I began to empower my students by revealing my life story. They saw me as a teacher who shares himself and models assignments."

Mark then taught the students about appropriate questioning, open-ended unstructured interviews, and allowed them to practice interviewing him from their notes. Following the teacher interview, students wrote their own autobiographies in class. Mark then met with individuals to question and facilitate the writing process and prepare them for oral presentations. They then interviewed in self-selected and teacher-selected pairs and were encouraged to gather artifacts and information from home to share with interviewers. While students listened to classmates' personal stories, Mark showed them how to analyze similarities and differences by designing charts that compare and contrast. Each person also studied differences and talked about the things they admired or were concerned about in another person's life. Finally, Mark invited high school student guests to share stories about their culture and traditions. All, to his surprise, accepted enthusiastically. Students from Southeast Asia, India, Germany, France, Puerto Rico, and Lebanon were thrilled to talk about homes and families, even in an unfamiliar class. Mark's students asked thoughtful questions about the cultures and families and recorded notes. He prepared his students ahead of time for each guest with a map and description of his or her nation of origin. Also Matt's students, on their own initiative, began inviting more guests, such as the language teacher from Japan, soccer coach from Italy, and an aunt from Taiwan. They researched and prepared the class for each guest.

While they were involved in this process, Mark introduced multicultural literature, and actually read aloud stories such as, Yolen's *Encounter* (1992), a Taino Native American child's perspective on Columbus and his men. At first, students said they thought the reading of children's books was childish until they began discussing the concepts portrayed. For example, Eve Bunting's *Terrible Things* (1989), an allegory on the Holocaust, stimulated in-depth discussions concerning slavery, World War II, and global warming.

For the final exam project, students performed a critical analysis of their global studies text. They worked in pairs, in and out of class, and explored chapter information. They attempted to prepare and explain non-Western perspectives on key concepts. Mark encouraged students to use any resource available, such as, internet, interviews, videos, teachers, texts, and television.

Mark's Power Empowers

Mark was extremely pleased with student participation that first semester. Attendance was excellent and the sleepers were awake. The students shared their lives and freely expressed ideas and opinions. The final exam was his first attempt at a cooperative research project. He believed it was a risky move that gave up a lot of teacher power, but students enjoyed the opportunity. Of course, some student work was incomplete, but all students clearly demonstrated, orally and/or in writing, that they understood the problems related to getting only one perspective in a text. Mark also claimed, "I learned more about my students and more from my students than any other year. I also learned about their homes and families from the autobiographies, so that I could better connect with each student. I changed; we all changed."

Jessica, School Reading Specialist, and the ABC's

Jessica, a reading specialist in a rural elementary school in the Northeast, with 99% of the students from European American backgrounds, discovered ways to reconceptualize literacy for the new age of pluralism and multiculturalism on the premise that she was helping teachers prepare students for the new, more rigorous, State English language arts exam given in the fourth grade. Kindergarten through fourth grade teachers felt the pressure of this challenging test that purported to measure reading, writing, listening, and speaking achievement. Jessica's experiences with the ABC's model stimulated ideas for creating a process in collaboration with the teachers and principal. To start, they agreed to coordinate lesson planning before school, after school, and during lunch periods. They established that Jessica would meet with their classes two days a week to introduce lessons. Then, she and the classroom teachers would circulate and support all children during individual, paired and small group activities. In the afternoons, when Jessica met with the children who were pulled out of classes for special literacy needs, she would follow individual remediation plans and reinforce what was taught in language arts classes. The following are descriptions of grade level and school wide literacy activities.

Kindergarten and First Grade ABC's Literacy Activities

First, Jessica read literature related to differences, such as Archambault's *Grandmother's Garden* (1997), and Simon's *Why am I Different* (1976), and *All Kinds of Families* (1983), to give children opportunities to talk about differences, become critical viewers and listeners, and relate their own experiences to stories. When Jessica shared Hamanaka's *All the Colors of the Earth* (1994), the children drew self-portraits using their multicultural crayons to study skin tones of classmates. Shades of pink, peach, and tan, as well as albino, white and Korean coffee skin colors were examined and discussed. Then the whole class shared other characteristics and charted their discoveries. The class chart set the stage for children to create autobiographies that explained their stories through drawings and writing. The following week, children read their stories to each other. This empowering activity helped all become knowledgeable about their classmates and encouraged them to freely discuss unique details in their lives.

Jessica heard the children tell about themselves and their families as they openly described their lives. She expressed her thoughts about children's opportunities to converse in the classroom, "It's amazing how many one word answers I get from the children, but when I probe a little, they tell stories. Getting children with special needs in written and oral language to share verbally enables them to express themselves in writing as well as listening and reading."

Additionally, Jessica introduced the Venn diagram by using a large example on the chalk board. She chose two children as models and drew pictures in the diagrams showing similarities and differences in their hair, eyes, mouths, freckles, moles, and birthmarks. Next, children worked in pairs filling in their own Venn diagrams. Each wrote his or her name over one circle and then drew their similarities in the intersecting portion. Individual differences were placed outside the intersection. From this experience the children collaborated for the creation of class books entitled, *All the Colors of Our Class*, with one page devoted to each child's uniqueness. Furthermore, Venn diagrams became an integral part of future classroom activities as children begged to continue using them to demonstrate similar and different holidays, food portions, guests, distances from school, literature, and weather.

Finally, a study of famous women empowered families, teachers, and children. The teachers decided that children should become aware of the important contributions of women in their lives as well as women in history. Jessica read, Hearne's *Seven Brave Women* (1997), and at the same time introduced the contributions of other brave women in our Nation. Then children told stories about the special women in their lives, wrote/drew about them and, invited them to come to class and explain their work, hobbies, and/or interests. Cousins, aunts, grandmothers, mothers, sisters, and friends were celebrated in a booklet that was sent home to share with families.

Second and Third Grade ABC's Literacy Activities Develop Cultural Awareness

When Jessica began planning lessons with the second and third grade teachers, curriculum objectives stated that students should become aware of cultures and geographic locations around the world. Again, Jessica followed adaptations of the ABC's model and began discussions with student lives and interests. Children practiced jotting notes about themselves on individual charts that included information related to environment, geography, home, family, likes and dislikes, abilities, entertainment, problems, fears, and responsibilities. In small groups and pairs, they read their notes, created Venn diagrams, and recorded information. Additionally, Jessica read folktales from around the world as well as folklore from Northeastern United States. The children learned to compare and contrast the cultures and people of their region with others around the world. Their teachers also read novels such as George's *My Side of the Mountain* (1975), and *Dog Song* (1985), to show children the similarities and differences between their community and differing global communities. Maps and globes became a central focus in classrooms and through charts and Venn diagrams, children began seeing relationships between where one lives and how one lives. The art teacher also introduced examples and activities from cultures, so children might create similar designs and reproductions.

Since the third grade science curriculum emphasized desert and rainforest, Jessica and the teachers chose to focus on the regions and people of the African Continent. Folktales and folklore were read as children investigated people's lives. They compared and contrasted their own lives with the desert and rainforest peoples by listing similarities and differences and writing compare and contrast paragraphs. As a final activity, the children composed letters to imaginary children in the United States from the perspectives of rainforest or desert peoples. The following is an example of a letter written by a typical student from the perspective of a young Bushman from the Kalahari Desert:

Dear Jonathon,
   I am a Bushman who knows how to survive in the Kalahari Desert. I am the oldest in my family. I know how to hunt with my Father and Grandfather. We can read the foot prints in the sand. We can tell how much an animal weighs. We know how old it is. We know where it is going. We know when it has eaten. We even know if it is a girl or boy animal. We can not read books, but we can read the sky in the day and night. We know where to find water. We take care of everybody. We are all family. We help each other all the time. I don't have to go to school. My Father, my Mother and my Grandparents teach me. I don't have to hear or smell cars. Sometimes I see a plane. When I am sick, my Mother gives me special medicine. She can make it herself. When I talk my language, I make a clicking sound in the back of my mouth. I cannot write like you so I told a friend who is not a Bushman to write this letter for me. I like my life.

Sincerely,
Ba(click)

Students in the class shared letters in partners and checked the accuracy of information in their nonfiction and realistic fiction reference centers. Again Jessica modeled the building of classroom community through the study of similarities and differences with global communities. These literacy activities, empowered teachers and students and influenced a school wide program.

School Wide Program

During the spring, *The Soul of Africa*, international art show, came to a nearby urban center. Jessica, the art teacher, librarian, third grade classroom teachers and principal decided that this was an opportunity to not only reinforce third grade studies, but also to inform the entire school. As a result of their collaboration, all classrooms read children and young adult literature from and about the African Continent, learned Bantu and Swahili vocabulary, and explored the artistic elements of African basket-weaving, jewelry-making, painting, and carving.

In what proved to be a successful evening, family program, imitating *Soul of Africa*, children performed song and dance and displayed their renditions of art from African cultures. Model homes of the desert and rainforest, as well as pictures of the many great cities and suburbs appeared in classrooms and hallways. A giant geographical and political map of the African continent, produced by third, fourth and fifth grade children was the focus of the main hallway entrance to the school.

Fourth Grade ABC's Literacy Activities

Similar to the second and third grades, the fourth grades began the year with locating and discussing the origins of folktales and folklore around the world. These activities lead to paragraph writing that compared and contrasted similarities and differences. Following these literacy activities, Jessica, the teachers and children collaborated to bring parents to school for interviews. Students studied interview questions before the guests arrived and practiced appropriate introductions and courtesies. Several Native American parents from Eastern and Western regions in the United States shared Oneida, Otoe, and Ioway languages, dances, artifacts, and philosophies in third through fifth grade classrooms. Also, an Air Force pilot and the principal were interviewed to give the children more perspectives for comparing and contrasting similarities and differences.

As a result of the fourth grade study of the interview process, an assignment with adult family members emerged. First, children asked persons in their families about likes and dislikes as well as what it was like to grow up in their day. The children wrote discoveries and reported them in small groups during class. This evoked questions that lead to more in depth interviews which stimulated return visits with new questions for the interviewees to answer.

Next, the children selected a culture from their own heritage, interviewed other family members, studied family artifacts, searched the internet, and read magazines, maps, biographies, and encyclopedias. Upon sharing information in pairs and small groups, diversity of family heritages became apparent. Children then suggested that family members be invited to tell their stories. Every child had a family visitor.

A mother and father from the Cherokee Nation and mothers from Korea and England were among the interviewed guests. The class members took notes, wrote the interviewees' stories and read them in class. Similarities and differences again were the focus of reports, but differences were accented as positive and interesting realities.

Family Study Group

During the winter months, Jessica created a successful study group with parents and teachers. On Wednesday evenings from 6:30–7:30 pm, they met to find ways for parents to help their children with reading, writing, speaking, and studying. At the meetings, parents of children who had a wide range of ability levels from kindergarten through fifth grade performed literacy activities and talked about their children's possible responses. From these experiences, discussions of home and school connections allowed parents and teachers to ask and answer questions that provided insights into the teaching and learning process. It was clear that Jessica used her power to create a place and time to empower families and herself to strengthen communication between home and school.

Jessica's Power to Empower

Jessica's power as a building reading specialist and adaptations of the ABC's model allowed her to plan with the principal, teachers, families, and children. Her demonstration lessons in classrooms empowered teachers to empower children and their families. Teachers saw how to build classroom community by connecting home and school through reading, writing, listening, and speaking. They gained significant information to help them understand their children's special backgrounds and experiences. The children proudly shared their differences in an open classroom environment where different knowledge and knowledge about differences were valued.

Jessica's school wide efforts, supported by the principal and teachers, empowered everyone to examine similarities and differences and communicate between home and school. In the process they discovered the diversity that existed in the rural school and began to appreciate similarities and differences, locally and globally.

Jessica stated, "The process associated with the ABC's model gave me the confidence to make those connections between home and school that provide the communication necessary for effective literacy development, not only for children from ethnic and cultural minority backgrounds, but for all children and their families."

Mrs. Diamond Uses the ABC's to Communicate With a Parent

Mrs. Diamond taught English math, science, social studies, and Spanish to eight students, aged 12–16. It was her third year of teaching an alternative education program, the last placement before students enter juvenile homes. Six students were from European American backgrounds, two were half European American and half Native American, and all were from lower socioeconomic levels. Mrs. Diamond selected Michael and his Mother as informants for learning how to communicate with families using the ABC's model.

Michael was 13 years of age and had disruptive language and behaviors. His reading comprehension was in the average range, but his written expression was two to three years below grade level. He had negative attitudes toward women and was particularly ashamed of his mother's weight problem. He visited his father once a year at the Reservation, and became hostile toward everyone and everything immediately before and after the meetings. At those times, he would shout obscenities, instigate physical fights, and refuse to do any school work.

After Mrs. Diamond completed her autobiography, she phoned Michael's mother and explained,

> I am taking a class about talking with parents. I would very much like your help. As an assignment, I need to have a discussion with you about the school. If you agree, can we meet in your home or some place of your choosing and talk about the school, Michael, and my teaching?

Michael's Mother agreed to meet at school. For the first session, she arrived at the end of the day after dismissal. Mrs. Diamond started the conference by sharing her autobiography, with family pictures, and then, explaining the ABC's assignments. Within minutes, Michael's Mother began sharing her life story in great detail. She told about early schooling and quickly switched to the frustrations in her life, especially the escape with Michael from the Reservation. She talked of the alcoholism in Michael's Father's family, the mental illness in her own, and the domestic abuse endured on both sides.

Michael's Mother also had many questions for Mrs. Diamond. These allowed Mrs. Diamond to share her own victories and challenges which included the story of how she and her husband received professional help for the abuse he knew as a child. In subsequent conferences, they discussed Michael's education and reasons for his behaviors. After each meeting, Michaels' Mother requested another. She claimed, "These meetings are helping me understand my son, so I can help him."

According to Michael's Mother, Michaels' school years had been mostly negative. One teacher had successfully worked with Michael. That teacher had made an effort to know Michael's Mother and seemed to care about Michaels' learning. None of the other teachers seemed to want to take the time to find out about their lives.

Mrs. Diamond claimed that she was able to connect with Michael's Mother, because her own openness encouraged Michael's Mother to candidly share. Additionally, Mrs. Diamond stated, "I began to work more sensitively with Michael. He learned that I cared. He began to ask questions, ask for help, and spend more time on his written work."

Mrs. Diamond met with Michael's Mother six times in fifteen weeks. They shared educational ideas, supper, and television at Michael's home. These connections encouraged Mrs. Diamond to introduce the ABC's model in her class. She began by sharing her autobiography and family pictures with students. The class then wrote their stories and interviewed each other. Their positive responses lead to an interest in sharing their stories with another class. As a group, they decided to write and read simplified versions of their lives with the third grade down the hall. After the third graders read the life stories of their "big brothers and sisters," it was suggested that together they might create illustrated books. From this experience, they continued to work together to write and illustrate the life stories of the third grade children.

The Power to Empower

Mrs. Diamond described the change in herself and the class because of the ABC's experience.

I gave part of myself to Michael's Mother and saw how positive the response. She, in turn, was empowered to share her life. This allowed me to be empowered with the knowledge necessary to work sensitively with Michael. This also gave me the confidence to try the ABC's with my class who absolutely loved writing their stories and interviewing each other. Working with the third grade was the frosting on the cake. My students were big deals and no one could believe how caring and gentle they were with others.

Mrs. Green Uses the ABC's to Communicate With a Parent

Mrs. Green was in her sixth year of teaching fourth grade in an urban school where 93% of the students received free or reduced breakfasts and lunch. The school population consisted of 60% African American, 37% Latino, and 3% European American. Mrs. Green had reached a point in her career that made her think she should try something drastically new since much of what she had learned in her teacher preparation program was not working with her students.

After completing her autobiography, she decided to interview the parent of a child who demonstrated academic achievement on standardized tests, but almost never paid attention in the classroom. Jarrel, an African American child, was nine years of age, and learned quickly. However, he never completed work and distracted others with strange sounds, physical movements and grimaces. He had been tested for all possible labels, but had received none. His mother came to conferences and explained, "Jarrel's a good boy, but he just don't care about education." Teachers placed him in his desk away from the rest of his classmates and let him do as much as he wanted as long as he didn't disturb anyone. Music and physical education were the only classes he appeared to enjoy. In fact, he had sung a small solo in the annual spring concert and was a team player in physical education and on the playground.

Mrs. Green phoned Jarrel's mother after the first few weeks of school and told her about the home interviews she needed for a college course. Jarrel's mother explained that she couldn't afford a baby sitter, so Mrs. Green would have to come to the house. They set a date for the following week at 4:00 p.m..

The day after the phone call, Jarrel came to school bubbling with questions. "You goin' ta visit us? Why? I'm listenin'. Where do you live? I'm comin' to your place. You bringin' your kids?"

Jarrel appeared anxious and ambivalent about the visit. One minute, he could be heard bragging about the visit to his classmates and the next, he'd be questioning the reasons for the visit and what would happen during and after. He seemed a bit more quiet in class and started several reading and math assignments. However, he continued his distracting noises and grimaces.

When Mrs. Green arrived on the porch of Jarrel's home, he opened the front door in his usual flamboyant manner, before she could knock. He greeted her, took her coat, and offered her a seat on the sofa facing the television, tuned to a children's program. He introduced his two brothers, aged eight and seven and two sisters, aged five and three. The siblings asked questions or giggled. "You teach at school?" "You Jarrel's teacher?" "Why you here?"

Soon after, Jarrel's Mother rushed into the room with Jarrel's baby brother, 4 months of age, and apologized for not greeting her at the door. She sat the baby on her lap with bottle in hand and ordered the children out of the room. The four left together while Jarrel sat next to his mother. She began, "So you want to know about Jarrel?" Mrs. Green replied in the affirmative, but went on to explain that she also wanted to know Jarrel's family. She explained, "I want you to get to know me too so we can think of ways to make this Jarrel's best year."

Mrs. Green started the sharing with her own story of how she grew up on a farm with six brothers and sisters, how her father had died when she was twelve, and how she had struggled financially and academically. Jarrel's mother listened intently, as did Jarrel. He interjected several times with, "Ma, you tell her about us."

Mother told her own story of struggles without a father. She added that Jarrel's Daddy had to work long hours as an electrician to get overtime and so, it was hard on Jarrel.

After about 15 minutes, the siblings meandered back into the room to listen, watch tv, and play with baby brother. The discussion continued for almost an hour with occasional interruptions from the children, but did not disrupt the conversation. Mrs. Green learned about the family's involvement in church and neighborhood. She also saw Jarrel as his Mother's helper. He ran for a bib, found toys, helped little sister find her favorite dolly, and twice, answered the telephone, politely. He also offered and brought Mrs. Green and his Mother a glass of juice with ice. Mrs. Green learned more in an hour than she could have imagined and gained a deeper respect for Jarrel and his family.

The second meeting occurred a week later. Mrs. Green arrived with age appropriate books, alphabet and sight word flash cards, and addition and subtraction games. Jarrel took over when Mrs. Green handed them to him. He ushered his siblings into the next room to show them how to read and play.

Mrs. Green and Jarrel's Mother, with baby in arms, reviewed their life stories and began discussing similarities and differences. They described differences and why they might occur and did the same with similarities. They both listened intently as they asked and answered questions. There were many similarities between the two women; Mrs. Green felt a strong connection with Jarrel's Mother.

At the end of the conference, the children were called to bring books, cards and games back to Mrs. Green. Jarrel carried them in neatly, replaced in their exact order. He explained, "I',m teachin'them, so they be good in school." Jarrel had been reading to his brothers and sisters and playing flash card games with them. At the same time, Jarrel's Mother suggested that the next meeting, be devoted Jarrel's program. She wanted to learn as much as possible about his school day.

For that meeting, Mrs. Green, again, brought books, puzzles, and games. The children squealed with delight as they trotted off with Jarrel. Jarrel's Mother, with baby in arms, immediately, focused on the packet Mrs. Green had brought. They studied Jarrel's schedule and discussed instructional methods and materials. Together they thought of ways to keep Jarrel on task. Finally, they called in Jarrel and asked him questions about home and school. He stated, "I like tv. I like helpin Ma cuz I am the oldes. I like ta put wires together like my Daddy and goin fishin. I like basketball down the street." He also added with a shrug and grimace, "I don know, but I wanna play them big horns."

Mrs. Green and Jarrel's mother spent the next visits discussing the curriculum for the year and ways to involve Jarrel. They considered science units for the year that would help Jarrel stay focused. They were, "Oceans of the World," "Human Body," "Sound," and "Electricity." Mrs. Green asked if Jarrel's father could visit the class, show his tools, and tell about his work. She also explained the music program and the possibility of Jarrel learning the trumpet or some other instrument. Mother then suggested that Mrs. Green keep Jarrel busy with helping others in class. "Can he help you in school? He need a job. He so active." She also suggested that Jarrel could bring in his basketball picture collection for the human body study.

During the few visits to Jarrel's home, Mrs. Green learned enough about him and his family to convince her that the whole class would benefit from adaptations of the ABC's model. Therefore, she introduced the class to human similarities and differences through a paired interview process and explained, "We need to find out information about each other so we can become good friends who help each other during work and recreation." They discussed the kinds of interview questions to ask and what notes to record. After the interviews, they introduced each other to the whole class. Student enjoyment was evident as they asked to continue the process with others in the school.

This was one of the first class assignment that demonstrated Jarrel's abilities to focus and complete work without distracting others. For the next interview, he chose the music teacher and proudly made a copy of his final product to give to him. As the days went by, Mrs. Green placed his desk next to another student. Then she attempted to give him responsibilities. Whenever he finished an assignment, he was allowed to run an errand, help another student, or go to the music room to practice his trumpet. She also found books related to his interests; Louis Armstrong stories were favorites.

By the fifth visit, Jarrel's Mother commented on how much calmer Jarrel seemed at home. He had begun trumpet lessons and practiced 10–15 minutes daily. This delighted his brothers and sisters who laughed and clapped for the sounds. She also shared some family pictures specially ones showing Jarrel fishing with his Daddy and Granddaddy. Additionally, she reported that Jarrel's father would gladly come to school whenever Mrs. Green wanted. He'd cleared it with his boss.

At the end of five weeks, Mrs. Green realized that she needed to continue the ABC's experience with other families. She sent invitations to all parents regarding times in class to share their careers and interests and scheduled visits with the children's families who she needed information for more successful teaching and learning.

The Power to Empower

Mrs. Green was surprised at the extraordinary results from visits to Jarrel's home. She and Jarrel's family were empowered with the information learned and shared. Jarrel's family was empowered with Mrs. Green's positive attention. Mrs. Green was empowered with the experience to change the classroom program to benefit Jarrel as well as his classmates. Jarrel was empowered, because the curriculum was connected to his interests and abilities. Teacher family and student behaviors changed. Finally, the ABC's activities in Mrs. Green's classroom empowered the other children as they studied each other and began to form a community of learners.

DISCUSSION

Reconceptualizing literacy for the new age of pluralism and multiculturalism is necessary if we want a just society that includes all and excludes none. If we want our children to know equal opportunity, explore who they are, learn what they can be, and make national and global contributions, we must design classroom communities based on the sociocultural perspective (Au, 1993; Heath, 1983; Trueba, Jacobs, & Kirton, 1990; Vygotsky, 1978)—ones that connect home and school for literacy learning. Since educators are in positions of power and have the power to empower, they have the responsibility to develop learning communities that connect home and school for reading, writing, listening, and speaking (Edwards, 1999; Faltis, 1993). The ABC's of Cultural Understanding and Communication is a model that appears to empower teachers to do just that.

The ABC's assignments had a profound effect on the teachers presented in this chapter. Writing the autobiography, recording and reporting the interview, and analyzing the cultures allowed them to design plans for connecting home and school for literacy learning. They welcomed and prepared for differences in their classrooms and schools. And in the process, began to reconceptualize literacy for the new age of multiculturalism and pluralism.

Hopefully, the teachers in this chapter will convince teacher educators to attempt the ABC's of Cultural Understanding and Communication in their graduate and undergraduate education programs. However, there are specific aspects of the model that must be considered before implementing it.

ABC's Model for Teacher Education: Commendations and Cautions

Since 1993, I have used the ABC's model in multicultural literacy courses for those in graduate and undergraduate, teacher education programs. On course evaluations, they have added numerous positive statements, such as:

"This should be a required course for all college students. I learned about successful living."

"This course has changed my life. I know who I am and how to think about human differences."

"I look at myself and others in new and positive ways."

"This is the first course I've taken that will really change my classroom."

"I will be connecting with my students' families on a regular basis."

"I have a new way to learn about my students and their families to help them with their reading, writing, listening, and speaking."

These are powerful statements, but there are significant cautionary notes related to the ABC's of Cultural Understanding and Communication. First, the ABC's assignments should be cleared through the Human Subjects Board of the college to prevent any possible abuses related to course work and research. I always assure those in the course that the autobiography is confidential. I explain that the assignment is meant to be rigorous, but should not make one miserable or uncomfortable. I also make clear that life stories, with the greatest detail, are the most helpful for cultural analysis assignments. Additionally, I emphasize that no one's life will be graded and that the autobiographies may actually be the beginnings of family histories. Finally, I share excerpts from my own life story and with permission, autobiographies from previous classes.

Most life stories, from the last seven years, have included intimate details, human tragedies, and traumas. Ninety percent of those enrolled in the teacher education program are white, middle class women, and when I read their stories, I am overwhelmed by the courage and resiliency portrayed.

The biographies are also remarkable in their descriptions. Teachers, after writing their autobiographies, seem to gain the confidence needed to share portions of their own stories with interviewees. This stimulates the interviewees to share in kind. Because pseudonyms are used and the tapes returned to interviewees, they also trust the interviewer. Generally, interviewers meet more than three times with their interviewees; they become fascinated with the people and their stories. As each pair spends time together, much is revealed. Confidences are divulged, and friendships take shape. Interviews occur almost anywhere-homes, restaurants, schools, libraries, taverns, markets, recreation centers, automobiles, synagogues, churches, and mosques. Participants have often described the experience as "wonderful listening and learning."

Similarly, when Jennifer and Kim went through the ABC's process, their friendship developed. Only portions of their stories appear in this chapter, since both decided what they would be comfortable reporting here. They discovered, during the interviews, that they had similar social struggles in school because they were considered different by other students. Discussions around their school memories became the common ground and basis for sharing other different life experiences.

Jennifer's and Kim's Similarities and Differences:
Struggles in School

When Jennifer wrote her autobiography, she realized that specific events and experiences in her life contributed to her struggles in school. Because she was a serious, quiet student, she was considered different enough to be humiliated and ignored by teachers and classmates. Even, a white student, from the mainstream culture, could experience alienation and social devastation because differences were not sensitively appreciated in the school setting.

When Jennifer interviewed Kim, a Korean American woman, and studied her life, she gained knowledge that contributed to an understanding of the dominant mainstream culture. She learned about the difficulties of those who are ethnically and culturally different. School had also alienated Kim, and devastated her socially. Both women struggled in school for being different. Both realized that the teachers did not seem to understand their academic and social struggles. As a result, both Jennifer and Kim expressed the importance of teachers using their power to empower and connecting with students and their families to bring relevancy to learning.

The stories of these two women and other teachers in this chapter support the idea that teacher education programs must prepare teachers for responsive and relevant pedagogy through experiences and assignments similar to the ABC's of Cultural Understanding and Communication.

The Power to Empower Families

When teachers in this chapter wrote their own autobiographies, they became aware of themselves and gained an appreciation for their own struggles and triumphs. They realized that their families had traditions and cultures. They recognized human similarities and differences as they interviewed and analyzed people from different cultures. They learned that one person does not represent an entire culture, but that multiple perspectives can exist within a culture. As a result of this process, they began to create classroom communities that connect home and school in urban, rural, and suburban settings. They made others aware of and sensitive to the human differences in all educational settings.

When teachers shared their lives with families and permitted questions and comments, families returned, in kind, with their stories. Similarly, Edwards (1997), in her parent interviews, found that families have a wealth of knowledge to share that help the teacher motivate and promote the child's reading, writing, listening, and speaking. When a teacher knows the family and/or community values, and also values what the family and /or community knows, the boundaries between home and school become blurred in an atmosphere of learning and collaboration (Schmidt, 1999).

The Power to Empower Students

Since teachers are in positions of power to advocate for their students and reach out to families and communities, they can empower by encouraging all students to make their unique contributions to the classroom and school and be recognized for what they bring to the classroom and school community (Cummins, 1986; Reyhner & Garcia, 1989; Schmidt, 1998c; Trueba, Jacobs, & Kirton, 1990). Students in this chapter were empowered when they had opportunities to share their own lives and families with others in the classroom. Their conversations with classmates encouraged social interactions which promoted their literacy learning. Similar to the sociocultural perspective (Au, 1993; Heath, 1983; Trueba, Jacobs, & Kirton, 1990; Vygotsky, 1978), student learning was based on their families and cultures shared in the classroom and school.

The Power to Imagine

The teachers described in this chapter experienced the ABC's of Cultural Understanding and Communication and successfully adapted the model for their classrooms and schools. They used their power to imagine and create classroom communities for literacy learning that appeared to transform schools and classrooms into setting where pluralism and multiculturalism were valued. These teachers are in the process of developing classroom communities that Maxine Greene (1995) imagines,

> We want our classrooms to be just and caring full of various conceptions of good. We want them to be articulate, with dialogue involving as many persons as possible, opening to one another, opening to the world. And we want our children to be concerned for one another, as we learn to be concerned for them. We want them to achieve friendships among one another, as each one moves to a heightened sense of craft and wide-awakenness, to a renewed consciousness of worth and possibility. (pp. 167–168)

The teachers in this chapter give us hope that our imaginations could become reality.

ACKNOWLEDGMENT

A special thanks to teacher/researchers, Kelly Carpenter, Shana Fogarty, Jennifer Iauco, Elizabeth Olivia, Crystal Ponto, Matt Root, and Johanna Shaw for their contributions toward reconceptualizing literacy in the new age of pluralism and multiculturalism.

REFERENCES

Au, K. (1993). *Literacy instruction in multicultural settings*. New York: Harcourt, Brace Javanovich College Publishers.

Au, K. (1998). Constructivist approaches, phonics, and the literacy learning of students of diverse backgrounds. In T. Shanahan & F.V. Rodriguez-Brown (Eds.), *National reading conference yearbook 47*. National Reading Conference.

Banks, J.A. (1994). *An introduction to multicultural education*. Boston: Allyn & Bacon.

Barrera, R.B. (1992). The culture gap in literature-based literacy instruction. *Education and Urban Society, 24*(2), 227–243.

Bloome, D., & Green, J. (1982). The social contexts of reading: A multidisciplinary perspective. In B.A. Hutson (Ed.), *Advances in reading/language research* (Vol. 1, pp. 309–338). Greenwich, CT: JAI Press.

Bogdan, R.C., & Biklen, S.K. (1994). *Qualitative research for education: An introduction to theory and method* (2nd ed.) Boston: Allyn & Bacon.

Britzman, D. (1986). Cultural myths in the making of a teacher: Biography and social structure in teacher education. *Harvard Educational Review, 56*, 442–456.

Cochran-Smith, M. (1995). Uncertain allies: Understanding the boundaries of race and teaching. *Harvard Educational Review 65*(4), 541–570.

Cummins, J. (1986). Empowering minority students: A framework for intervention. *Harvard Educational Review, 56*(1), 18–36.

Diamond, B., & Moore, M. (1995). *Multicultural literacy: Mirroring the reality of the classroom*. White Plains, NY: Longman Publishing Co.

Derman-Sparks, l. (1992). *Anti-bias curriculum: Tools for empowering young children*. Sacramento, CA: California State Department of Education.

Dyson, A.H. (1993). *Social worlds of children learning to write in an urban primary school*. New York: Teachers College Press.

Edwards, P. (1996). Creating sharing-time conversations: Parents and teachers work together. *Language Arts, 73*, 344–349.

Edwards, P. (1997, May). *Examining dialogues used in facilitating parental understanding of first graders' reading and writing development*. Paper presented at the annual meeting of the International Reading Association, Atlanta, GA.

Edwards, P. (1999). *A path to follow: Learning to listen to parents*. Portsmouth, NH: Heinemann.

Emig, J. (1971). Writing as a mode of learning. *College Composition and Communication, 28*, 122–128.

Faltis, C.J. (1993). Joinfostering: Adapting teaching strategies for the multilingual classroom. New York: Maxwell Macmillan International.

Fitchue, M.A. (1997). Locke and Du Bois: Two major black voiuces muzzled by philanthropic organizations. *The Journal of Blacks in Higher Education, 14*, 111–116.

Florio-Ruane, S. (1994). The future teachers' autobiography club: Preparing educators to support learning in culturally diverse classrooms. *English Education, 26*(1), 52–56.

Freire, P. (1970). *Pedagogy of the oppressed*. New York: Seabury Press.

Goldenberg, C.N. (1987). Low-income Hispanic parents' contributions to their first-grade children's word-recognition skills. *Anthropology and Education Quarterly, 18*, 149–179.

Greene, M. (1995). *Releasing the imagination*. San Francisco: Jossey-Bass.

Heath, S.B. (1983). *Ways with words: Language life and work in communities and class-rooms.* Cambridge: Cambridge University Press.

Iauco, J. (1997). *Between two worlds: A case study using the ABC's Model of Cultural Understanding and Communication.* Unpublished Master's thesis, Le Moyne College, Syracuse NY.

Kidder, T. (1989). *Among schoolchildren.* New York: Avon Books.

Ladson-Billings, G. (1994). *The dreamkeepers: Successful teachers of African American children.* San Francisco: Jossey-Bass.

Ladson-Billings, G. (1995). Culturally relevant teaching. *Research Journal, 32*(3), 465–491.

McCaleb, S.P. (1994). *Building communities of learners.* New York: St. Martin's Press.

Murdock, S.H. (1995). *An America challenged: Population change and the future of the United States.* Boulder, CO: Westview Press.

Nieto, S. (1996). *Affirming diversity: The sociopolitical context of multicultural education.* New York: Longman.

Noordhoff, K., & Kleinfield, J. (1993). Preparing teachers for multicultural class-rooms. *Teaching and Teacher Education, 9*(1), 27–39.

Ogbu, J. (1983). Minority status and schooling in plural societies. *Comparative Educational Review, 27*(2), 168–190.

Osborne, A.B. (1996). Practice into theory into practice: Culturally relevant pedagogy for students we have marginalized and normalized. *Anthropology and Education Quarterly, 27*(3), 285–314.

Paley, V.G. (1989). *White teacher.* Cambridge, MA: Harvard University Press.

Palmer, P. (1995, September/October). Community, conflict, and ways of knowing. *Change,* 20–25.

Pattnaik, J. (1997). Cultural stereotypes and preservice education: Moving beyond our biases. *Equity and Excellence in Education, 30*(3), 40–50.

Progoff, I. (1975). *At a journal workshop: The basic text and guide for using the intensive journal.* New York: Dialogue House Library.

Reyhner, J., & Garcia, R.L. (1989). Helping minorities read better: Problems and promises. *Reading Research and Instruction, 28*(3), 84–91.

Rist, R. (1978). *The invisible children.* Cambridge, MA: Harvard University Press.

Rogoff, B. (1986). Adult assistance of children's learning. In T.E. Raphael (Ed.), *Contexts of school based literacy* (pp.27–40). New York: Random House.

Schmidt, P.R. (1995). Working and playing with others: Cultural conflict in a kindergarten literacy program. *The Reading Teacher, 48*(5), 404–413.

Schmidt, P.R. (1996). One teacher's reflections: Implementing multicultural literacy learning. *Equity and Excellence in Education, 29*(2), 20–29.

Schmidt, P.R. (1998a). *Cultural conflict and struggle: Literacy learning in a kindergarten program.* New York: Peter Lang.

Schmidt, P.R. (1998B). The ABC's of cultural understanding and communication. *Equity and Excellence in Education, 31*(2).

Schmidt, P.R. (1998c). The ABC's Model: Teachers connect home and school. In press. In T. Shanahan & F.V. Rodriguez-Brown (Eds.), *National reading conference yearbook 47.* National Reading Conference.

Schmidt, P.R. (1999a). Focus on research: Know thyself and understand others. *Language Arts, 76*(4), 332–340.

Schmidt, P.R. (1999b, December 1). *Teachers connecting and communicating with families for literacy development.* Symposium paper presented at the 49th meeting of the National Reading Conference, Orlando, FL.

Schon, D. (1987). *Educating the reflective practitioner.* San Francisco: Jossey-Bass.

Sjoberg, G., & Kuhn, K. (1989). Autobiography and organizations: Theoretical and methodological issues. *The Journal of Applied Behavioral Science, 25*(4), 309–326.

Sleeter, C., & Grant, C. (1991). Race, class, gender, and disability in current textbooks. In M.W. Apple & L.K. Christian-Smith (Eds.), *The politics of the textbook.* New York: Routledge & Chapel Hall.

Spindler, G., & Spindler, L. (1987). *The interpretive ethnography of education: At home and abroad.* Hillsdale, NJ: Lawrence Erlbaum Associates.

Spradley, J. (1979). *The ethnographic interview.* New York: Holt, Rinehart & Winston.

Tatum, B. (1992). Talking about race, learning about racism: The application of racial identity development theory in the classroom. *Harvard Educational Review, 62*(1), 1–24.

Trueba, H.T., Jacobs, L., & Kirton, E. (1990). *Cultural conflict and adaptation: The case of the Hmong children in American society.* New York: The Falmer Press.

Vygotsky, L.S. (1978). *Mind in society: The development of higher mental process.* Cambridge, MA: Harvard University Press.

Wasser, J.D., & Bresler, L. (1996). Working in the interpretive zone: Conceptualizing collaboration in qualitative research teams. *Educational Researcher, 25*(5), 5–15.

Willis, A.I., & Meacham, S.J.(1997). Break point: The challenges of teaching multicultural education courses. *Journal of the Assembly for Expanded Perspectives on Learning, 2,* 40–49.

Yinger, R. (1985). Journal writing as a learning tool. *Volga-Review, 87*(5), 21–33.

Zeichner, K. M. (1993). *Educating teachers for cultural diversity.* East Lansing, MI: National Center on Teacher Learning.

Printed in the United States
21457LVS00003B/31-82